MAHOPAC SCHOOL

BOOK # 100   PURCHASE DATE

DATE	NAME	COND.
9/8/94	JARED BRONCO	NEW
9/6/95	Rafat Shibbara	Excellent

FOURTH EDITION

Fundamentals
of
Logic Design

■ FOURTH EDITION

Fundamentals of Logic Design

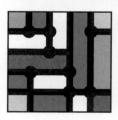

CHARLES H. ROTH, JR.
University of Texas at Austin

WEST PUBLISHING COMPANY
St. Paul ■ New York ■ Los Angeles ■ San Francisco

■ **PRODUCTION CREDITS**

Cover design and art: Christine C. Bentley and Edward M. Rose,
Visual Graphic Systems, Ltd.
Interior design: Geri Davis, Quadrata, Inc.
Copyediting: Gary Phillips
Composition: Syntax International, Pte., Ltd.

99 98 97 96 95 94 93   8 7 6 5 4 3 2 1

Library of Congress Cataloging-in-Publication Data

Roth, Charles H.
    Fundamentals of logic design / Charles H. Roth, Jr.—4th ed.
        p.   cm.
    Includes bibliographical references and index.
    ISBN 0-314-92218-0 (hard)
    1. Logic circuits. 2. Logic design. I. Title.
TK7868.L6R67 1992
621.39′5—dc20   91-30668
                                                    ∞ CIP

Preface

After studying this text, you should be able to apply switching theory to the solution of logic design problems. This means that you will learn both the basic theory of switching networks and how to apply it. After a brief introduction, you will study Boolean algebra, which provides the basic mathematical tool needed to analyze and synthesize an important class of switching networks. Starting from a problem statement, you will learn to design networks of logic gates which have a specified relationship between signals at the input and output terminals. Then you will study the logical properties of flip-flops, which serve as memory devices in sequential switching networks. By combining flip-flops with networks of logic gates, you will learn to design counters, adders, sequence detectors and similar networks.

This text is designed so that it can be used in either a standard lecture course or in a self-paced course. In addition to the standard reading material and problems, study guides and other aids for self-study are included in the text. The content of the text is divided into 27 study units. These units form a logical sequence so that mastery of the material in one unit is generally a prerequisite to the study of succeeding units. Each unit consists of four parts. First, a list of objectives states precisely what you are expected to learn by studying the unit. Next, the study guide contains reading assignments and study questions. As you work through the unit, you should write out the answers to these study questions. The text material and problem set which follow are similar to a conventional textbook.

When you complete a unit, you should review the objectives and make sure that you have met them.

The 27 study units are divided into three main groups. The first 10 units treat Boolean algebra and the design of combinational logic networks. Units 11 through 22 are mainly concerned with the analysis and design of clocked sequential logic networks, including networks for arithmetic operations. Units 23 through 27 cover the special problems encountered in the analysis and design of asynchronous sequential networks. The first 21 units can typically be covered in a one semester course taught at the Sophomore or Junior level. The remaining units can then be used as enrichment material for the better students, or they can be covered in the first part of a second course in digital systems design.

Several of the units include simulation or laboratory exercises. These exercises provide an opportunity to design a logic network and then test its operation. A number of logic simulators, which run on personal computers, may be used to verify the logic designs. The lab equipment required for testing includes a logic patchboard with flip-flops and several types of logic gates. If such equipment is not available, the lab exercises can be simulated or just assigned as design problems. This is especially important for Units 10, 16, and 27 since the comprehensive design problems in these units help to review and tie together the material in several of the preceding units.

This text is written for a first course in the logic design of digital systems. It is written on the premise that the student should understand and learn thoroughly certain fundamental concepts in a first course. Examples of such fundamental concepts are the use of Boolean algebra to describe the signals and interconnections in a logic network, use of systematic techniques for simplification of a logic network, interconnection of simple components to perform a more complex logic function, analysis of a sequential logic network in terms of timing charts or a state graph, and use of a control network to control the sequence of events in a digital system.

The text attempts to achieve a balance between theory and application. For this reason, the text does not overemphasize the mathematics of switching theory; however, it does present the theory which is necessary for understanding the fundamental concepts of logic design. After completing this text, the student should be prepared for a more advanced digital systems design course which stresses more intuitive concepts like the development of algorithms for digital processes, partitioning of digital systems into subsystems, and implementation of digital systems using currently available hardware. Alternatively, the student should be prepared to go on to a more advanced course in switching theory which further develops the theoretical concepts which have been introduced here.

Although the technology used to implement digital systems has changed significantly since the first edition of this text was published, the fundamental principles of logic design have not. Truth tables and state tables are still used to specify the behavior of logic networks, and Boolean algebra is still a basic mathematical tool for logic design. Even though programmable logic devices (PLDs) may be used instead of individual gates and flip-flops, reduction of logic equations is still necessary in order to fit the equations into a small number of PLDs. Making a good state assignment is still required, because without a good assignment, the logic equations may not fit into one of the available PLDs.

This new edition offers a number of improvements over the third edition. Mixed logic and direct polarity notation are introduced and used for analysis and design of logic networks. Greater emphasis is placed on the use of programmable logic devices, and programmable gate arrays are introduced. The role of simulation and computer-aided design is discussed. New exercises and problems have been added to every unit, and several sections have been rewritten to clarify the presentation.

The text is suitable for both computer science and engineering students. All material relating to circuit aspects of logic gates is contained in Appendix A so that this material can conveniently be omitted by computer science students or other students with no background in electronic circuits. The text is organized so that Unit 4 on Algebraic Simplification and Unit 7 on the Quine-McCluskey procedure may be omitted without loss of continuity. Instructors who wish to place less emphasis on logic simplification can omit one or both of these units to allow more time for study of digital design techniques presented in the later units. The following diagram illustrates the unit prerequisite structure for the fourth edition:

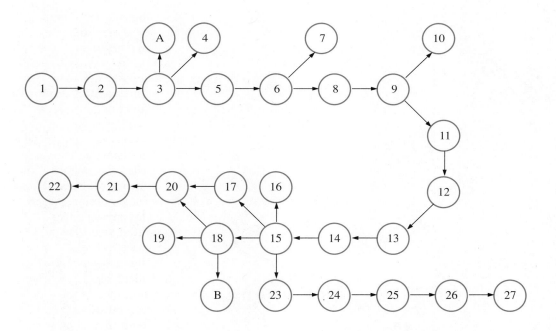

Although many texts are available in the areas of switching theory and logic design, this text was developed specifically to meet the needs of a self-paced course in which students are expected to study the material on their own. Each of the units has undergone extensive class testing in a self-paced environment and has been revised based on student feedback.

Study guides and text material have been expanded as required so that students can learn from the text without the aid of lectures and so that almost all of the students can achieve mastery of all of the objectives. Supplementary materials were developed as the text was being written. An instructor's manual is available which includes suggestions for using the text in a standard or self-paced course, quizzes on each of the units, and suggestions for laboratory equipment and procedures. The instructor's manual also contains solutions to problems, to unit quizzes, and to lab exercises.

Since the computer plays an important role in the logic design process, integration of computer usage into the first logic design course is highly desirable. A computer-aided logic design program, called *LogicAid*™, is suggested for use with this textbook. *LogicAid* allows the student to easily derive simplified logic equations from minterns, truth tables, and state tables. This relieves the student of some of the more tedious computations and permits the solution of more complex design problems in a shorter time. *LogicAid* also provides tutorial help for Karnaugh maps and derivation of state graphs.

How to Use This Book for Self-Study

If you wish to learn all of the material in this text to mastery level, the following study procedures are recommended for each unit:

1. Read the *Objectives* of the unit. These objectives provide a concise summary of what you should be able to do when you complete study of the unit.

2. Work through the *Study Guide*. After reading each section of the text, *write* out the answers to the corresponding study guide questions. In many cases, blank spaces are left in the study guide so that you can write your answers directly in this book. By doing this, you will have the answers conveniently available for later review. The study guide questions will generally help emphasize some of the important points in each section or will guide you to a better understanding of some of the more difficult points. If you cannot answer some of the study guide questions, this indicates that you need to study the corresponding section in the text more before proceeding. The answers to selected study guide questions are given in the back of this book; answers to the remaining questions can generally be found within the text.

3. Several of the units (Units 3, 4, 6, 7, 11, 13, 14, 21, 24, and 25) contain one or more programmed exercises. Each programmed exercise will guide you step-by-step through the solution of one of the more difficult types of problems encountered in this text. When working through a programmed exercise, be sure to write down your answer

for each part in the space provided before looking at the answer and continuing with the next part of the exercise.

4. Work the assigned *Problems* at the end of the unit. Check your answers against those at the end of the book and rework any problems which you missed.

5. Reread the *Objectives* of the unit to make sure that you can meet all of them. If in doubt, review the appropriate sections of the text.

6. If you are using this text in a self-paced course, you will need to pass a readiness test on each unit before proceeding with the next unit. The purpose of the readiness test is to make sure that you have mastered the objectives of one unit before moving on to the next unit. The questions on the test will relate directly to the objectives of the unit, so that if you have worked through the study guide and written out answers to all of the study guide questions and to all of the problems, you should have no difficulty passing the test.

Contents

PREFACE   v

HOW TO USE THIS BOOK FOR SELF-STUDY   ix

1 Introduction
Number Systems and Conversion

	Objectives	1
	Study Guide	2
1.1	Digital Systems and Switching Networks	4
1.2	Number Systems and Conversion	7
1.3	Binary Arithmetic	10
1.4	Binary Codes	12
	Problems	15

2 Boolean Algebra

	Objectives	17
	Study Guide	18
2.1	Introduction	24
2.2	Basic Operations	24
2.3	Boolean Expressions and Truth Tables	27
2.4	Basic Theorems	29

2.5   Commutative, Associative, and Distributive Laws   31
2.6   Simplification Theorems   33
2.7   Multiplying Out and Factoring   34
      Problems   37
      Laws and Theorems of Boolean Algebra   40

3 Boolean Algebra (Continued)

      Objectives   41
      Study Guide   42
3.1   Inversion   47
3.2   Duality   49
3.3   Multiplying Out and Factoring Expressions   50
3.4   Exclusive - OR and Equivalence Operations   51
3.5   Positive and Negative Logic   54
      Programmed Exercises and Problems   57

4 Algebraic Simplification

      Objectives   63
      Study Guide   64
4.1   The Consensus Theorem   66
4.2   Algebraic Simplification of Switching Expressions   68
4.3   Proving Validity of an Equation   70
      Programmed Exercises and Problems   72

5 Applications of Boolean Algebra

      Objectives   79
      Study Guide   80
5.1   Conversion of English Sentences to Boolean Equations   86
5.2   Combinational Network Design Using a Truth Table   88
5.3   Minterm and Maxterm Expansions   89
5.4   General Minterm and Maxterm Expansions   92
5.5   Incompletely Specified Functions   95
5.6   Examples of Truth Table Construction   96
      Problems   99

6 Karnaugh Maps

      Objectives   105
      Study Guide   106
6.1   Minimum Forms of Switching Functions   116
6.2   2- and 3-Variable Karnaugh Maps   118
6.3   4-Variable Karnaugh Maps   123

6.4 Determination of Minimum Expressions Using Essential Prime Implicants   126

6.5 5- and 6-Variable Karnaugh Maps   131

6.6 Other Uses of Karnaugh Maps   135

6.7 Other Forms of Karnaugh Maps   136

Programmed Exercises and Problems   138

7   Quine-McCluskey Method

Objectives   149

Study Guide   150

7.1 Determination of Prime Implicants   155

7.2 The Prime Implicant Chart   158

7.3 Petrick's Method   161

7.4 Simplification of Incompletely Specified Functions   163

7.5 Simplification Using Map-Entered Variables   164

7.6 Conclusion   166

Programmed Exercises and Problems   167

8   Multi-Level Gate Networks NAND and NOR Gates

Objectives   173

Study Guide   174

8.1 Multi-Level Gate Networks   180

8.2 Other Types of Logic Gates   185

8.3 Functionally Complete Sets of Logic Gates   187

8.4 Design of Two-Level NAND- and NOR-Gate Networks   189

8.5 Design of Multi-Level NAND- and NOR-Gate Networks   192

8.6 Network Conversion Using Alternative Gate Symbols   194

8.7 Mixed Logic and Polarity Indication   197

Problems   204

9   Multiple-Output Networks Multiplexers, Decoders, Read-Only Memories, and Programmable Logic Arrays

Objectives   209

Study Guide   210

9.1 Introduction   216

9.2 Design of Two-Level Multiple-Output Networks   217

9.3 Multi-Output NAND and NOR Networks   222

9.4 Multiplexers   223

9.5 Decoders   227

9.6 Read-Only Memories   229

9.7 Programmable Logic Devices   234

Problems   244

10 Combinational Network Design

	Objectives	249
	Study Guide	250
10.1	Review of Combinational Network Design	252
10.2	Design of Networks with Limited Gate Fan-in	253
10.3	Simulation and Testing of Logic Networks	256
	Design Problems	259

11 Flip-Flops

	Objectives	265
	Study Guide	266
11.1	Gate Delays and Timing Diagrams	270
11.2	The Set-Reset Flip-Flop	272
11.3	The Trigger Flip-Flop	276
11.4	The Clocked T Flip-Flop	277
11.5	The J-K Flip-Flop	278
11.6	The Clocked J-K Flip-Flop	279
11.7	The D Flip-Flop	282
11.8	Clocked Flip-Flops with Clear and Preset Inputs	282
11.9	Characteristic Equations	284
	Problems and Programmed Exercises	286

12 Counters and Similar Sequential Networks

	Objectives	293
	Study Guide	294
12.1	Design of a Binary Counter	298
12.2	Counters for Other Sequences	301
12.3	Counter Design Using S-R Flip-Flops	305
12.4	Counter Design Using J-K Flip-Flops	308
12.5	Short-Cut Method for Deriving J-K Flip-Flop Input Equations	311
12.6	Counter Design Using D Flip-Flops	313
12.7	Design of a Code Converter	313
12.8	Shift Registers	315
12.9	Derivation of Flip-Flop Input Equations—Summary	316
	Problems	319

13 Analysis of Clocked Sequential Networks

	Objectives	323
	Study Guide	324
13.1	A Sequential Parity Checker	330
13.2	Analysis by Signal Tracing and Timing Charts	333
13.3	State Tables and Graphs	337

13.4 General Models for Sequential Networks   342
      Programmed Exercises and Problems   345

14   Derivation of State Graphs and Tables

      Objectives   355
      Study Guide   356
14.1 Design of a Sequence Detector   359
14.2 More Complex Design Problems   364
14.3 Guidelines for Construction of State Graphs   368
14.4 Serial Data Code Conversion   371
      Programmed Exercises and Problems   375

15   Reduction of State Tables
State Assignment

      Objectives   385
      Study Guide   386
15.1 Elimination of Redundant States   393
15.2 Equivalent States   396
15.3 Determination of State Equivalence Using an
      Implication Table   397
15.4 Equivalent Sequential Networks   401
15.5 Incompletely Specified State Tables   403
15.6 Derivation of Flip-Flop Input Equations   404
15.7 Equivalent State Assignments   407
15.8 Guidelines for State Assignment   412
      Problems   417

16   Sequential Network Design

      Objectives   425
      Study Guide   426
16.1 Summary of Design Procedure   428
16.2 Design Example—Code Converter   428
16.3 Simulation and Testing of Sequential Networks   433
16.4 Overview of Computer-aided Design   437
      Design Problems   441

17   Iterative Networks

      Objectives   449
      Study Guide   450
17.1 Design of a Parity Checker   453
17.2 Design of a Comparator   455
17.3 Design of a Pattern Detector   458

17.4   Iterative Networks with Outputs from Each Cell   460
       Problems   462

18   **MSI Integrated Circuits in Sequential Network Design**

       Objectives   465
       Study Guide   466
18.1   Integrated Circuit Shift Registers   469
18.2   Integrated Circuit Counters   472
18.3   Design of Sequential Networks Using Counters   477
18.4   Register Transfers and 3-State Logic   480
       Problems   483

19   **Sequential Network Design with Programmable Logic Devices (PLDs)**

       Objectives   487
       Study Guide   488
19.1   Design of Sequential Networks Using ROMs and PLAs   490
19.2   Design of Sequential Networks Using PALs   492
19.3   Other Sequential Programmable Logic Devices (PLDs)   498
19.4   Programmable Gate Arrays (PGAs)   503
       Problems   509

20   **Networks for Addition and Subtraction**

       Objectives   515
       Study Guide   516
20.1   Representation of Negative Numbers   519
20.2   Design of Binary Adders   524
20.3   Binary Subtracters   531
       Problems   533

21   **Networks for Arithmetic Operations**

       Objectives   537
       Study Guide   538
21.1   Serial Adder with Accumulator   540
21.2   Design of a Parallel Multiplier   543
21.3   Design of a Binary Divider   548
       Programmed Exercises and Problems   553

22   **State Machine Design with SM Charts**

       Objectives   565
       Study Guide   566

22.1   State Machine Charts   567
22.2   Derivation of SM Charts   573
22.3   Realization of SM Charts   579
      Problems   583

23   Analysis of Asynchronous Sequential Networks

      Objectives   589
      Study Guide   590
23.1   Introduction   592
23.2   Analysis of an Asynchronous Network with S-R Flip-Flops   594
23.3   Analysis of an Asynchronous Gate Network   598
23.4   Race Conditions and Cycles   601
      Problems   603

24   Derivation and Reduction of Primitive Flow Tables

      Objectives   607
      Study Guide   608
24.1   Derivation of Primitive Flow Tables   609
24.2   Reduction of Primitive Flow Tables   613
      Programmed Exercise and Problems   619

25   State Assignment and Realization of Flow Tables

      Objectives   625
      Study Guide   626
25.1   Introductory Example   629
25.2   State Assignments for 3- and 4-Row Tables   634
25.3   Shared-Row Assignments   637
25.4   Completion of the Output Table   641
25.5   The One-Hot Assignment   643
      Programmed Exercise and Problems   645

26   Hazards

      Objectives   653
      Study Guide   654
26.1   Hazards in Combinational Networks   657
26.2   Detection of Static 0- and 1-Hazards   660
26.3   Dynamic Hazards   663
26.4   Design of Hazard-Free Combinational Networks   664
26.5   Essential Hazards   666
26.6   Hazard-Free Realizations Using S-R Flip-Flops   668
      Problems   673

27 Asynchronous Sequential Network Design

	Objectives	677
	Study Guide	678
27.1	Summary of Design Procedure	679
27.2	Short-Cut Method for Deriving S-R Flip-Flop Input Equations	680
27.3	Design Example	681
27.4	Testing Asynchronous Sequential Networks	689
	Design Problems	690

Appendixes

A Discrete and Integrated Circuit Logic Gates

	Objectives	695
	Study Guide	696
A.1	Diode AND and OR Gates	699
A.2	Transistor Logic Circuits	701
A.3	TTL Integrated Circuit Logic	704
A.4	MOS and CMOS Logic	707
	Problems	711

B IEEE Standard Logic Symbols

| B.1 | Alternative Symbols for Gates and Flip-Flops | 713 |
| B.2 | Representation of MSI Functions | 715 |

C Proofs of Theorems

C.1	Essential Prime Implicants	719
C.2	State Equivalence Theorem	720
C.3	Justification of Short-Cut Method for Deriving S-R Input Equations	720
	REFERENCES	723
	ANSWERS TO SELECTED STUDY GUIDE QUESTIONS AND PROBLEMS	727
	INDEX	765

■ F O U R T H   E D I T I O N

Fundamentals
of
Logic Design

1

Introduction Number Systems and Conversion

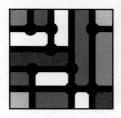

OBJECTIVES

1. Introduction

   The first part of this unit introduces the material to be studied later. In addition to getting an overview of the material in the first part of the course, you should be able to explain:

   a. The difference between analog and digital systems and why digital systems are capable of greater accuracy

   b. The difference between combinational and sequential networks

   c. Why two-valued signals and binary numbers are commonly used in digital systems

2. Number systems and conversion

   When you complete this unit, you should be able to solve the following types of problems:

   a. Given a positive integer, fraction, or mixed number in any base (2 through 16), convert to any other base. Justify the procedure used by using a power series expansion for the number.

   b. Add, subtract, and multiply positive binary numbers. Explain the addition and subtraction process in terms of carries and borrows.

   c. Represent a decimal number in BCD, 6-3-1-1 code, excess-3 code, etc. Given a set of weights, construct a weighted code.

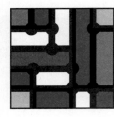

STUDY GUIDE

1. Study Section 1.1, *Digital Systems and Switching Networks,* and answer the following study questions:

   (a) What is the basic difference between analog and digital systems?

   (b) Why are digital systems capable of greater accuracy than analog systems?

   (c) Explain the difference between combinational and sequential switching networks.

   (d) What common characteristic do most switching devices used in digital systems have?

   (e) Why are binary numbers used in digital systems?

2. Study Section 1.2, *Number Systems and Conversion.* Answer the following study questions as you go along:

   (a) Is the first remainder obtained in the division method for base conversion the most or least significant digit?

   (b) Work through all of the examples in the text as you encounter them and make sure that you understand all of the steps.

   (c) An easy method for conversion between binary and octal is illustrated in Equation (1–1). Why should you start forming the groups of three bits at the binary point instead of the left end of the number?

(d) Why is it impossible to convert a decimal number to binary on a digit-by-digit basis as can be done for octal or hexadecimal?

(e) Complete the following conversion table.

Binary (base 2)	Octal (base 8)	Decimal (base 10)	Hexadecimal (base 16)
0	0	0	0
1			
10			
11			
100			
101			
110			
111			
1000			
1001			
1010			
1011			
1100			
1101			
1110			
1111			
10000	20	16	10

(f) Work Problems 1.1(a), (b), (c), (d); 1.2; 1.4(a); and 1.6.

3. Study Section 1.3, *Binary Arithmetic*.

   (a) Make sure that you can follow all of the examples, especially the propagation of borrows in the subtraction process.

   (b) To make sure that you understand the borrowing process, work out a detailed analysis in terms of powers of 2 for the following example:

$$
\begin{array}{r}
1100 \\
-\ 101 \\
\hline
111
\end{array}
$$

4. Work Problems 1.9 and 1.11.

5. Study Section 1.4, *Binary Codes*.

   (a) Represent 187 in BCD code, excess-3 code, 6-3-1-1 code, and 2-out-of-5 code.

(b) Verify that the 6-3-1-1 code is a weighted code. Note that for some decimal digits, two different code combinations could have been used. For example, either 0101 or 0110 could represent 4. In each case the combination with the smaller binary value has been used.

(c) How is the excess-3 code obtained?

(d) How are the ASCII codes for the decimal digits obtained? What is the relation between the ASCII codes for the capital letters and lowercase letters?

(e) Work Problem 1.15.

6. If you are taking this course on a self-paced basis, you will need to pass a readiness test on this unit before going on to the next unit. The purpose of the readiness test is to determine if you have mastered the material in this unit and are ready to go on to the next unit. Before you take the readiness test:

(a) Check your answers to the problems against those provided at the end of this book. If you missed any of the problems, make sure that you understand why your answer is wrong and correct your solution.

(b) Make sure that you can meet all of the objectives listed at the beginning of this unit.

Introduction
Number Systems and Conversion

1.1
Digital Systems and Switching Networks

Digital systems are used extensively in computation and data processing, control systems, communications, and measurement. Because digital systems are capable of greater accuracy and reliability than analog systems, many tasks formerly done by analog systems are now being performed digitally.

In a digital system, the physical quantities or signals can assume only discrete values, while in analog systems the physical quantities or signals may vary continuously over a specified range. For example, the output voltage of a digital system might be constrained to take on only two values such as 0 volts and 5 volts, while the output voltage from an analog system might be allowed to assume any value in the range -10 volts to $+10$ volts.

Because digital systems work with discrete quantities, in many cases they can be designed so that for a given input, the output is exactly correct. For example, if we multiply two 5-digit numbers using a digital multiplier, the 10-digit product will be correct in all 10 digits. On the other hand, the output of an analog multiplier might have an error ranging from a fraction of one percent to a few percent depending on the accuracy of the components used in construction of the multiplier. Furthermore, if we need a product which is correct to 20 digits rather than 10, we can redesign the digital multiplier to process more digits and add more digits to its input. A similar improvement in the accuracy of an analog multiplier would not be possible because of limitations on the accuracy of the components.

The design of digital systems may be divided roughly into three parts—system design, logic design, and circuit design. System design involves breaking the overall system into subsystems and specifying the characteristics of each subsystem. For example, system design of a digital computer could involve specifying the number and type of memory units, arithmetic units, and input-output devices as well as the interconnection and control of these subsystems. Logic design involves determining how to interconnect basic logic building blocks to perform a specific function. An example of logic design is determining the interconnection of logic gates and flip-flops required to perform binary addition. Circuit design involves specifying the interconnection of specific components such as resistors, diodes, and transistors to form a gate, flip-flop, or other logic building block. Most contemporary circuit design is done in integrated circuit form using appropriate computer-aided design tools to lay out and interconnect the components on a chip of silicon. This book is largely devoted to a study of logic design and the theory necessary for understanding the logic design process. Some aspects of system design are treated in Units 20 and 21. Circuit design of logic gates is discussed briefly in Appendix A.

Many of the subsystems of a digital system take the form of a switching network (Fig. 1–1). A switching network has one or more inputs and one or more outputs which take on discrete values. In this text, we will study two types of switching networks—combinational and sequential. In a combinational network, the output values depend only on the present value of the inputs and not on past values. In a sequential network, the outputs depend on both the present and past input values. In other words, in order to determine the output of a sequential network, a sequence of input values must be specified. The sequential network is said to have memory because it must "remember" something about the past sequence of inputs, while a combinational network has no memory. In general, a sequential network is composed of a combinational network with added memory

Figure 1–1
Switching Network

elements. Combinational networks are easier to design than sequential networks and will be studied first.

The basic building blocks used to construct combinational networks are logic gates. The logic designer must determine how to interconnect these gates in order to convert the network input signals into the desired output signals. The relationship between these input and output signals can be described mathematically using Boolean algebra. Units 2 and 3 of this text introduce the basic laws and theorems of Boolean algebra and show how they can be used to describe the behavior of networks of logic gates.

Starting from a given problem statement, the first step in designing a combinational logic network is to derive a table or algebraic logic equations which describe the network outputs as a function of the network inputs (Unit 5). In order to design an economical network to realize these output functions, the logic equations which describe the network outputs generally must be simplified. Algebraic methods for this simplification are described in Unit 4, and other simplification methods (Karnaugh map and Quine-McCluskey procedure) are introduced in Units 6 and 7. Implementation of the simplified logic equations using several types of gates is described in Unit 8, and alternative design procedures using integrated circuits are developed in Unit 9.

The basic memory elements used in the design of sequential networks are called flip-flops (Unit 11). These flip-flops can be interconnected with gates to form counters and registers (Unit 12). Analysis of more general sequential networks using timing diagrams, state tables, and graphs is presented in Unit 13. The first step in designing a sequential switching network is to construct a state table or graph which describes the relationship between the input and output sequences (Unit 14). Methods for going from a state table or graph to a network of gates and flip-flops are developed in Units 15 and 16, and alternative methods of implementing sequential networks are discussed in Units 18 and 19. In Units 20 and 21, combinational and sequential design techniques are applied to the realization of networks for performing binary addition, subtraction, multiplication, and division. The last part of the book (Units 23–27) deals with the design of asynchronous sequential networks. Such networks present special timing problems and are more difficult to design than the synchronous sequential networks described in earlier units.

The switching devices used in digital systems are generally two-state devices; that is, the output can assume only two different discrete values. Examples of switching devices are relays, diodes, and transistors. A relay can assume two states—closed or open—depending on whether power is applied to the coil or not. A diode can be in a conducting state or a nonconducting state. A transistor can be in a cut-off or saturated state, with a corresponding high or low output voltage. Of course, transistors can also be operated as linear amplifiers with a continuous range of output voltages, but in digital applications greater reliability is obtained by operating them as two-state devices. Because the outputs of most switching devices assume only two different values, it is natural to use binary numbers internally in digital systems. For this reason binary numbers will be discussed first before proceeding with the design of switching networks.

1.2
Number Systems and Conversion

When we write decimal (base 10) numbers, we use a positional notation; each digit is multiplied by an appropriate power of 10 depending on its position in the number. For example,

$$953.78_{10} = 9 \times 10^2 + 5 \times 10^1 + 3 \times 10^0 + 7 \times 10^{-1} + 8 \times 10^{-2}$$

Similarly, for binary (base 2) numbers, each binary digit is multiplied by the appropriate power of 2:

$$1011.11_2 = 1 \times 2^3 + 0 \times 2^2 + 1 \times 2^1 + 1 \times 2^0 + 1 \times 2^{-1} + 1 \times 2^{-2}$$

$$= 8 + 0 + 2 + 1 + \frac{1}{2} + \frac{1}{4} = 11\frac{3}{4} = 11.75_{10}$$

Note that the binary point separates the positive and negative powers of 2 just as the decimal point separates the positive and negative powers of 10 for decimal numbers.

Any positive integer R ($R > 1$) can be chosen as the *radix* or *base* of a number system. If the base is R, then R digits $(0, 1, \ldots, R - 1)$ are used. For example, if $R = 8$, then the required digits are 0, 1, 2, 3, 4, 5, 6, and 7. A number written in positional notation can be expanded in a power series in R. For example,

$$N = (a_4 a_3 a_2 a_1 a_0 . a_{-1} a_{-2} a_{-3})_R$$
$$= a_4 \times R^4 + a_3 \times R^3 + a_2 \times R^2 + a_1 \times R^1 + a_0 \times R^0$$
$$+ a_{-1} \times R^{-1} + a_{-2} \times R^{-2} + a_{-3} \times R^{-3}$$

where a_i is the coefficient of R^i and $0 \leq a_i \leq R - 1$. If the arithmetic indicated in the power series expansion is done in base 10, then the result is the decimal equivalent of N. For example,

$$147.3_8 = 1 \times 8^2 + 4 \times 8^1 + 7 \times 8^0 + 3 \times 8^{-1} = 64 + 32 + 7 + \frac{3}{8}$$

$$= 103.375_{10}$$

For bases greater than 10, more than 10 symbols are needed to represent the digits. In this case, letters are usually used to represent digits greater than 9. For example, in hexadecimal (base 16), A represents 10_{10}, B represents 11_{10}, C represents 12_{10}, D represents 13_{10}, E represents 14_{10}, and F represents 15_{10}. Thus,

$$A2F_{16} = 10 \times 16^2 + 2 \times 16^1 + 15 \times 16^0 = 2560 + 32 + 15 = 2607_{10}$$

Next, we will discuss conversion of a decimal *integer* to base R using the division method. The base R equivalent of a decimal integer N can be represented as

$$N = (a_n a_{n-1} \cdots a_2 a_1 a_0)_R = a_n R^n + a_{n-1} R^{n-1} + \cdots + a_2 R^2 + a_1 R^1 + a_0$$

If we divide N by R, the remainder is a_0:

$$\frac{N}{R} = a_n R^{n-1} + a_{n-1} R^{n-2} + \cdots + a_2 R^1 + a_1 = Q_1, \text{ remainder } a_0$$

Then we divide the quotient Q_1 by R:

$$\frac{Q_1}{R} = a_n R^{n-2} + a_{n-1} R^{n-3} + \cdots + a_3 R^1 + a_2 = Q_2, \text{ remainder } a_1$$

Next we divide Q_2 by R:

$$\frac{Q_2}{R} = a_n R^{n-3} + a_{n-1} R^{n-4} + \cdots + a_3 = Q_3, \text{ remainder } a_2$$

This process is continued until we finally obtain a_n. Note that the remainder obtained at each division step is one of the desired digits and the *least* significant digit is obtained first.

EXAMPLE: Convert 53_{10} to binary.

$$
\begin{array}{lll}
2\,\underline{/\,53} & & \\
2\,\underline{/\,26} & \text{rem.} = 1 = a_0 & \\
2\,\underline{/\,13} & \text{rem.} = 0 = a_1 & \\
2\,\underline{/\,\ \ 6} & \text{rem.} = 1 = a_2 & \quad 53_{10} = 110101_2 \\
2\,\underline{/\,\ \ 3} & \text{rem.} = 0 = a_3 & \\
2\,\underline{/\,\ \ 1} & \text{rem.} = 1 = a_4 & \\
\quad\ \ 0 & \text{rem.} = 1 = a_5 &
\end{array}
$$

Conversion of a decimal *fraction* to base R can be done using successive *multiplications* by R. A decimal fraction F can be represented as

$$F = (.a_{-1}a_{-2}a_{-3} \cdots a_{-m})_R = a_{-1}R^{-1} + a_{-2}R^{-2} + a_{-3}R^{-3} + \cdots + a_{-m}R^{-m}$$

Multiplying by R yields

$$FR = a_{-1} + a_{-2}R^{-1} + a_{-3}R^{-2} + \cdots + a_{-m}R^{-m+1} = a_{-1} + F_1$$

where F_1 represents the fractional part of the result and a_{-1} is the integer part. Multiplying F_1 by R yields

$$F_1 R = a_{-2} + a_{-3}R^{-1} + \cdots + a_{-m}R^{-m+2} = a_{-2} + F_2$$

Next, we multiply F_2 by R:

$$F_2 R = a_{-3} + \cdots + a_{-m}R^{-m+3} = a_{-3} + F_3$$

This process is continued until we have obtained a sufficient number of digits. Note that the integer part obtained at each step is one of the desired digits and the *most* significant digit is obtained first.

EXAMPLE: Convert $.625_{10}$ to binary.

$$
\begin{array}{llll}
F = \ \ .625 & F_1 = \ \ .250 & F_2 = \ \ .500 & \\
\underline{\times \quad 2} & \underline{\times \quad 2} & \underline{\times \quad 2} & \quad .625_{10} = .101_2 \\
\ \ \ \ 1.250 & \ \ \ \ 0.500 & \ \ \ \ 1.000 & \\
(a_{-1} = 1) & (a_{-2} = 0) & (a_{-3} = 1) &
\end{array}
$$

This process does not always terminate, but if it does not terminate the result is a repeating fraction.

EXAMPLE: Convert 0.7_{10} to binary.

$$
\begin{array}{l}
.7 \\
\underline{2} \\
(1)\ .4 \\
\underline{2} \\
(0)\ .8 \\
\underline{2} \\
(1)\ .6 \\
\underline{2} \\
(1)\ .2 \\
\underline{2} \\
(0)\ .4 \longleftarrow \text{process starts repeating here since .4 was previously} \\
\underline{2} \qquad\ \ \text{obtained above} \\
(0)\ .8 \qquad 0.7_{10} = 0.1\ \underline{0110}\ \underline{0110}\ \underline{0110} \ldots {}_{2}
\end{array}
$$

Conversion between two bases other than decimal can be done directly by using the procedures given; however, the arithmetic operations would have to be carried out using a base other than 10. It is generally easier to convert to decimal first and then convert the decimal number to the new base.

EXAMPLE: Convert 231.3_{4} to base 7.

$$
231.3_{4} = 2 \times 16 + 3 \times 4 + 1 + \frac{3}{4} = 45.75_{10}
$$

$$
\begin{array}{ll}
7 \underline{\big/ 45} & \qquad .75 \\
7 \underline{\big/\ \ 6} \quad \text{rem. 3} & \qquad \underline{7} \\
\qquad 0 \quad \text{rem. 6} & \quad (5)\ .25 \qquad\qquad 45.75_{10} = 63.5151 \ldots {}_{7} \\
& \qquad \underline{7} \\
& \quad (1)\ .75 \\
& \qquad \underline{7} \\
& \quad (5)\ .25 \\
& \qquad \underline{7} \\
& \quad (1)\ .75
\end{array}
$$

Conversion from binary to octal (and conversely) can be done by inspection since each octal digit corresponds to exactly three binary digits (bits). Starting at the binary point, the bits are divided into groups of three and each group is replaced by an octal digit:

$$
11010111110.0011_{2} = \underbrace{011}_{3}\ \underbrace{010}_{2}\ \underbrace{111}_{7}\ \underbrace{110}_{6} \cdot \underbrace{001}_{1}\ \underbrace{100}_{4} = 3276.14_{8} \quad (1\text{--}1)
$$

Similarly, binary to hexadecimal conversion is accomplished by dividing the binary number into groups of four bits and replacing each group by a hexadecimal digit:

$$1001101.010111_2 = \underset{4}{\underbrace{0100}}\ \underset{D}{\underbrace{1101}} \cdot \underset{5}{\underbrace{0101}}\ \underset{C}{\underbrace{1100}} = 4D.5C_{16} \qquad (1\text{--}2)$$

1.3
Binary Arithmetic

Arithmetic operations in digital systems are usually done in binary because design of logic networks to perform binary arithmetic is much easier than for decimal. Binary arithmetic is carried out in much the same manner as decimal, except the addition and multiplication tables are much simpler.

The addition table for binary numbers is

$$0 + 0 = 0$$
$$0 + 1 = 1$$
$$1 + 0 = 1$$
$$1 + 1 = 0 \qquad \text{and carry 1 to the next column}$$

EXAMPLE: Add 13_{10} and 11_{10} in binary.

$$
\begin{array}{r}
1111 \longleftarrow \text{carries}\\
13_{10} = \quad 1101\\
11_{10} = \quad 1011\\
\hline
11000 = 24_{10}
\end{array}
$$

The subtraction table for binary numbers is

$$0 - 0 = 0$$
$$0 - 1 = 1 \qquad \text{and borrow 1 from the next column}$$
$$1 - 0 = 1$$
$$1 - 1 = 0$$

Borrowing 1 from a column is equivalent to subtracting 1 from that column.

EXAMPLES OF BINARY SUBTRACTION:[1]

(a)
```
      1 ←(indicates
  11101   a borrow
- 10011   from the
   1010   3rd column)
```
(b)
```
  1111 ← borrows
  10000
-    11
   1101
```
(c)
```
   111 ← borrows
  111001
-   1011
  101110
```

---
[1] An alternative to binary subtraction is the use of 2's complement arithmetic, as discussed in Section 20.1.

Note how the borrow propagates from column to column in the second example. In order to borrow 1 from the second column, we must in turn borrow 1 from the third column, etc.

Binary subtraction sometimes causes confusion, perhaps because we are so used to doing decimal subtraction that we forget the significance of the borrowing process. Before doing a detailed analysis of binary subtraction, we will review the borrowing process for decimal subtraction.

If we number the columns (digits) of a decimal integer from right to left (starting with 0), then if we borrow 1 from column n, what we mean is that we subtract 1 from column n and add 10 to column $n - 1$. Since $1 \times 10^n = 10 \times 10^{n-1}$, the value of the decimal number is unchanged, but we can proceed with the subtraction. Consider, for example, the following decimal subtraction problem:

$$\text{column 2} \qquad \qquad \text{column 1}$$

$$\begin{array}{r} 205 \\ -\ 18 \\ \hline 187 \end{array}$$

A detailed analysis of the borrowing process for this example, indicating first a borrow of 1 from column 1 and then a borrow of 1 from column 2, is as follows:

$$
\begin{aligned}
205 - 18 &= [2 \times 10^2 + 0 \times 10^1 + 5 \times 10^0] \\
&- [\qquad\qquad 1 \times 10^1 + 8 \times 10^0]
\end{aligned}
$$

— note borrow from column 1

$$
\begin{aligned}
&= [2 \times 10^2 + (0 - 1) \times 10^1 + (10 + 5) \times 10^0] \\
&- [\qquad\qquad\qquad 1 \times 10^1 + \qquad 8 \times 10^0]
\end{aligned}
$$

— note borrow from column 2

$$
\begin{aligned}
&= [(2 - 1) \times 10^2 + (10 + 0 - 1) \times 10^1 + 15 \times 10^0] \\
&- [\qquad\qquad\qquad\qquad 1 \times 10^1 + 8 \times 10^0] \\
&= [1 \times 10^2 \qquad + \quad 8 \times 10^1 \qquad\qquad + 7 \times 10^0] = 187
\end{aligned}
$$

The analysis of borrowing for binary subtraction is exactly the same, except that we work with powers of 2 instead of powers of 10. Thus for a binary number, borrowing 1 from column n is equivalent to subtracting 1 from column n and adding 2 (10_2) to column $n - 1$. The value of the binary number is unchanged because $1 \times 2^n = 2 \times 2^{n-1}$.

A detailed analysis of binary subtraction example (c) follows. Starting with the rightmost column, $1 - 1 = 0$. In order to subtract in the second column, we must borrow from the third column. Rather than borrow immediately, we place a 1 over the third column to indicate that a borrow is necessary, and we will actually do the borrowing when we get to the third column. (This is similar to the way borrow signals might propagate in a computer.) Now since we have borrowed 1, the second column becomes 10, and $10 - 1 = 1$. In order to borrow 1 from the third column, we must borrow 1 from the fourth column (indicated by placing a 1 over column 4). Column 3 then becomes 10, subtracting off the borrow yields 1, and $1 - 0 = 1$. Now in column 4, we subtract off the borrow leaving 0. In order to complete the subtraction, we must borrow from column 5, which gives 10 in column 4, and $10 - 1 = 1$.

The multiplication table for binary numbers is

$$0 \times 0 = 0$$
$$0 \times 1 = 0$$
$$1 \times 0 = 0$$
$$1 \times 1 = 1$$

The following example illustrates multiplication of 13_{10} by 11_{10} in binary:

$$
\begin{array}{r}
1101 \\
1011 \\
\hline
1101 \\
1101 \\
0000 \\
1101 \\
\hline
10001111 = 143_{10}
\end{array}
$$

Note that each partial product is either the multiplicand (1101) shifted over the appropriate number of places or is zero.

The following example illustrates division of 145_{10} by 11_{10} in binary:

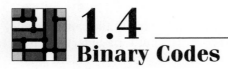

The quotient is 1101 with a remainder of 10.

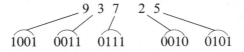

1.4
Binary Codes

Although most large computers work internally with binary numbers, the input-output equipment generally uses decimal numbers. Since most logic circuits only accept two-valued signals, the decimal numbers must be coded in terms of binary signals. In the simplest form of binary code, each decimal digit is replaced by its binary equivalent. For example, 937.25 is represented by

$$
\begin{array}{ccccc}
9 & 3 & 7 & 2 & 5 \\
1001 & 0011 & 0111 & 0010 & 0101
\end{array}
$$

This representation is referred to as binary-coded-decimal (BCD) or more explicitly as 8-4-2-1 BCD. Note that the result is quite different than that obtained by converting the number as a whole into binary.

Table 1–1

Binary Codes for Decimal Digits

Decimal Digit	8-4-2-1 Code (BCD)	6-3-1-1 Code	Excess-3 Code	2-out-of-5 Code	Gray Code
0	0000	0000	0011	00011	0000
1	0001	0001	0100	00101	0001
2	0010	0011	0101	00110	0011
3	0011	0100	0110	01001	0010
4	0100	0101	0111	01010	0110
5	0101	0111	1000	01100	1110
6	0110	1000	1001	10001	1010
7	0111	1001	1010	10010	1011
8	1000	1011	1011	10100	1001
9	1001	1100	1100	11000	1000

Table 1-1 shows several possible sets of binary codes for the 10 decimal digits. Many other possibilities exist since the only requirement for a valid code is that each decimal digit be represented by a distinct combination of binary digits. To translate a decimal number to coded form, each decimal digit is replaced by its corresponding code. Thus 937 expressed in excess-3 code is 1100 0110 1010. The 8-4-2-1 (BCD) code and the 6-3-1-1 code are examples of weighted codes. A 4-bit weighted code has the property that if the weights are w_3, w_2, w_1, and w_0, the code $a_3a_2a_1a_0$ represents a decimal number N, where

$$N = w_3a_3 + w_2a_2 + w_1a_1 + w_0a_0$$

For example, the weights for the 6-3-1-1 code are $w_3 = 6$, $w_2 = 3$, $w_1 = 1$, and $w_0 = 1$. The binary code 1011 thus represents the decimal digit

$$N = 6 \cdot 1 + 3 \cdot 0 + 1 \cdot 1 + 1 \cdot 1 = 8$$

The excess-3 code is obtained from the 8-4-2-1 code by adding 3 (0011) to each of the codes. The 2-out-of-5 code has the property that exactly 2 out of the 5 bits are 1 for every valid code combination. This code has useful error-checking properties since if any one of the bits in a code combination is changed due to a malfunction of the logic circuitry, the number of 1 bits is no longer exactly two. The table shows one example of a Gray code. A Gray code has the property that the codes for successive decimal digits differ in exactly one bit. For example, the codes for 6 and 7 differ only in the fourth bit, and the codes for 9 and 0 differ only in the first bit. A Gray code is often used when translating an analog quantity such as a shaft position into digital form. In this case, a small change in the analog quantity will change only one bit in the code, which gives more reliable operation than if two or more bits changed at a time. The Gray and 2-out-of-5 codes are *not* weighted codes. In general, the decimal value of a coded digit *cannot* be computed by a simple formula when a nonweighted code is used.

Many applications of computers require processing of data which contains numbers, letters, and other symbols such as punctuation marks. In order to transmit such alphanumeric data to or from a computer, or store it internally in a computer, each symbol must be represented by a binary code. One common alphanumeric code is the ASCII code (American Standard Code for Information Interchange). This is a 7-bit code, so 2^7 (128) different code combinations are available to represent letters, numbers, and other symbols. Table 1–2 shows a portion of the ASCII code; the code combinations not listed are used for special control functions like "form feed" or "end of transmission." The word "Start" is represented in ASCII code as follows:

1010011	1110100	1100001	1110010	1110100
S	t	a	r	t

Table 1–2
ASCII Code

Character	A_6	A_5	A_4	A_3	A_2	A_1	A_0	Character	A_6	A_5	A_4	A_3	A_2	A_1	A_0	Character	A_6	A_5	A_4	A_3	A_2	A_1	A_0
space	0	1	0	0	0	0	0	@	1	0	0	0	0	0	0	`	1	1	0	0	0	0	0
!	0	1	0	0	0	0	1	A	1	0	0	0	0	0	1	a	1	1	0	0	0	0	1
"	0	1	0	0	0	1	0	B	1	0	0	0	0	1	0	b	1	1	0	0	0	1	0
#	0	1	0	0	0	1	1	C	1	0	0	0	0	1	1	c	1	1	0	0	0	1	1
$	0	1	0	0	1	0	0	D	1	0	0	0	1	0	0	d	1	1	0	0	1	0	0
%	0	1	0	0	1	0	1	E	1	0	0	0	1	0	1	e	1	1	0	0	1	0	1
&	0	1	0	0	1	1	0	F	1	0	0	0	1	1	0	f	1	1	0	0	1	1	0
'	0	1	0	0	1	1	1	G	1	0	0	0	1	1	1	g	1	1	0	0	1	1	1
(	0	1	0	1	0	0	0	H	1	0	0	1	0	0	0	h	1	1	0	1	0	0	0
)	0	1	0	1	0	0	1	I	1	0	0	1	0	0	1	i	1	1	0	1	0	0	1
*	0	1	0	1	0	1	0	J	1	0	0	1	0	1	0	j	1	1	0	1	0	1	0
+	0	1	0	1	0	1	1	K	1	0	0	1	0	1	1	k	1	1	0	1	0	1	1
,	0	1	0	1	1	0	0	L	1	0	0	1	1	0	0	l	1	1	0	1	1	0	0
–	0	1	0	1	1	0	1	M	1	0	0	1	1	0	1	m	1	1	0	1	1	0	1
.	0	1	0	1	1	1	0	N	1	0	0	1	1	1	0	n	1	1	0	1	1	1	0
/	0	1	0	1	1	1	1	O	1	0	0	1	1	1	1	o	1	1	0	1	1	1	1
0	0	1	1	0	0	0	0	P	1	0	1	0	0	0	0	p	1	1	1	0	0	0	0
1	0	1	1	0	0	0	1	Q	1	0	1	0	0	0	1	q	1	1	1	0	0	0	1
2	0	1	1	0	0	1	0	R	1	0	1	0	0	1	0	r	1	1	1	0	0	1	0
3	0	1	1	0	0	1	1	S	1	0	1	0	0	1	1	s	1	1	1	0	0	1	1
4	0	1	1	0	1	0	0	T	1	0	1	0	1	0	0	t	1	1	1	0	1	0	0
5	0	1	1	0	1	0	1	U	1	0	1	0	1	0	1	u	1	1	1	0	1	0	1
6	0	1	1	0	1	1	0	V	1	0	1	0	1	1	0	v	1	1	1	0	1	1	0
7	0	1	1	0	1	1	1	W	1	0	1	0	1	1	1	w	1	1	1	0	1	1	1
8	0	1	1	1	0	0	0	X	1	0	1	1	0	0	0	x	1	1	1	1	0	0	0
9	0	1	1	1	0	0	1	Y	1	0	1	1	0	0	1	y	1	1	1	1	0	0	1
:	0	1	1	1	0	1	0	Z	1	0	1	1	0	1	0	z	1	1	1	1	0	1	0
;	0	1	1	1	0	1	1	[	1	0	1	1	0	1	1	{	1	1	1	1	0	1	1
<	0	1	1	1	1	0	0	\	1	0	1	1	1	0	0	|	1	1	1	1	1	0	0
=	0	1	1	1	1	0	1	]	1	0	1	1	1	0	1	}	1	1	1	1	1	0	1
>	0	1	1	1	1	1	0	^	1	0	1	1	1	1	0	~	1	1	1	1	1	1	0
?	0	1	1	1	1	1	1	_	1	0	1	1	1	1	1	delete	1	1	1	1	1	1	1

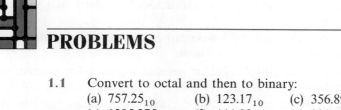

PROBLEMS

1.1 Convert to octal and then to binary:
(a) 757.25_{10} (b) 123.17_{10} (c) 356.89_{10} (d) 1063.5_{10}
(e) 1305.375_{10} (f) 111.33_{10} (g) 301.12_{10} (h) 1644.875_{10}

1.2 Convert to octal and then to decimal:
(a) 10111011.1_2 (b) 1101101.011_2
(c) 10000011.11_2 (d) 11101111.101_2

1.3 Convert to octal and then to decimal:
(a) 11100111.1_2 (b) 110100111.01_2
(c) 1001000.111_2 (d) 101010101.11_2

1.4 (a) Convert to base 5: 165.2_7 (do all of the arithmetic in decimal).
(b) Convert to base 7: 143.21_5 (do all of the arithmetic in decimal).

1.5 (a) Convert to base 3: 375.54_8 (do all of the arithmetic in decimal).
(b) Convert to base 4: 384.74_{10}.

1.6 (a) Convert to hexadecimal: 747.64_{10}. Round to two digits past the hex point.
(b) Devise a scheme for converting hexadecimal directly to base 4 and convert your answer to base 4.
(c) Convert to decimal: $ADE.B_{16}$.

1.7 Devise a scheme for converting base 3 numbers directly to base 9. Use your method to convert the following number to base 9: 220012112021.102_3.

1.8 Convert to hexadecimal and then to binary:
(a) $2983\frac{63}{64}$ (b) 93.70 (c) $1900\frac{31}{32}$ (d) 109.30

1.9 Add, subtract, and multiply in binary:
(a) 1111 and 1011   (b) 1001001 and 111010   (c) 110100 and 11011

1.10 Add, subtract, and multiply in binary:
(a) 1111 and 1001   (b) 1010101 and 111011   (c) 110010 and 11101

1.11 Subtract in binary. Place a 1 over each column from which it was necessary to borrow.
(a) 11011011 − 1101101   (b) 10001100 − 1100101
(c) 110111101 − 11101010

1.12 Subtract in binary. Place a 1 over each column from which it was necessary to borrow.
(a) 11001011 − 1110101   (b) 10010100 − 1001101
(c) 111011011 − 10101101

1.13 Divide in binary:
(a) 1011110 ÷ 1001   (b) 110000001 ÷ 1110   (c) 1110010 ÷ 1001
Check your answers by multiplying out in binary and adding the remainder.

1.14 Divide in binary:
(a) 1011011 ÷ 1010   (b) 110000011 ÷ 1011   (c) 1110100 ÷ 1010

1.15 Construct a table for a 5-3-2-1 weighted code and write 9371 using this code.

1.16 Construct a table for 4-3-2-1 weighted code and write 6472 using this code.

1.17 Is it possible to construct a 5-3-1-1 weighted code? A 6-4-1-1 weighted code? Justify your answers.

1.18 Is it possible to construct a 5-4-1-1 weighted code? A 6-3-2-1 weighted code? Justify your answers.

1.19 Construct a 6-2-2-1 weighted code for decimal digits. What number does 1001 0110 represent in this code?

1.20 Construct a 5-2-2-1 weighted code for decimal digits. What numbers does 1001 0011 represent in this code?

1.21 Convert to hexadecimal, and then give the ASCII code for the resulting hexadecimal number (including the code for the hex point):
(a) 234.71_{10} (b) 196.82_{10}

2

Boolean Algebra

OBJECTIVES

A list of 17 laws and theorems of Boolean algebra is given on page 40 of this unit. When you complete this unit, you should be familiar with and be able to use any of the first 11 of these. Specifically, you should be able to:

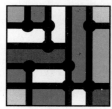

1. Understand the basic operations and laws of Boolean algebra.

2. Relate these operations and laws to networks composed of AND gates, OR gates, and INVERTERS. Also relate these operations and laws to networks composed of switches.

3. Prove any of these laws using a truth table.

4. Apply these laws to the manipulation of algebraic expressions including:

   a. Multiplying out an expression to obtain a sum of products

   b. Factoring an expression to obtain a product of sums

   c. Simplifying an expression by applying one of the laws

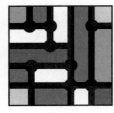

STUDY GUIDE

1. In this unit you will study Boolean algebra, the basic mathematics needed for logic design of digital systems. Just as when you first learned ordinary algebra, you will need a fair amount of practice before you can use Boolean algebra effectively. However, by the end of the course, you should be just as "at home" with Boolean algebra as with ordinary algebra. Fortunately, many of the rules of Boolean algebra are the same as for ordinary algebra, but watch out for some surprises!

2. Study Sections 2.1 and 2.2 of this unit, *Introduction* and *Basic Operations*.

   (a) How does the meaning of the symbols 0 and 1 as used in this unit differ from the meaning as used in Unit 1?

   (b) Two commonly used notations for the inverse or complement of A are $\bar{A}$ and A'. The latter has the advantage that it is much easier for typists, printers, and computers. (Have you ever tried to get a computer to print out a bar over a letter?) We will use A' for the complement of A. You may use either notation in your work, but please don't mix notations in the same equation. Most engineers use $+$ for OR and $\cdot$ (or no symbol) for AND, and we will follow this practice. An alternative notation, often used by mathematicians, is $\vee$ for OR and $\wedge$ for AND.

   (c) Many different symbols are used for AND, OR, and INVERTER logic blocks.[1] We will use

   The shapes of these symbols conform to those commonly used in industrial practice. We have added the $+$ and $\cdot$ for clarity. The above symbols point in the direction of signal flow. This makes it easier to read the network diagrams in comparison with the square or round symbols used in some books.

---

[1] See Section 8.6 and Appendix B.1 for a discussion of alternative gate symbols.

(d) Determine the output of each of the following gates:

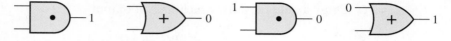

(e) Determine the unspecified inputs to each of the following gates if the outputs are as shown:

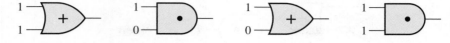

3. Study Section 2.3, *Boolean Expressions and Truth Tables.*

   (a) How many *variables* does the following expression contain?_____

   How many *literals?* _____

   $$A'BC'D + AB + B'CD + D'$$

   (b) For the following network, if $A = B = 0$ and $C = D = E = 1$, indicate the output of each gate (0 or 1) on the network diagram:

   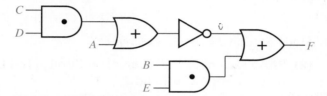

   (c) Derive a Boolean expression for the network output. Then substitute $A = B = 0$ and $C = D = E = 1$ into your expression and verify that the value of F obtained in this way is the same as that obtained on the network diagram in (b).

   (d) Write an expression for the output of the following network and complete the truth table:

   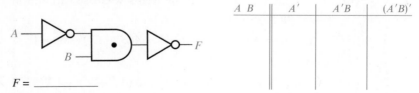

A B	A'	$A'B$	$(A'B)'$

   $F =$ _____

   (e) When filling in the combinations of values for the variables on the left side of a truth table, always list the combinations of 0's and 1's in binary order. For example, for a 3-variable truth table, the first row should be 000, the next row 001, then 010, 011, 100, 101, 110, and 111. Write an expression for the output of the following network and complete the truth table:

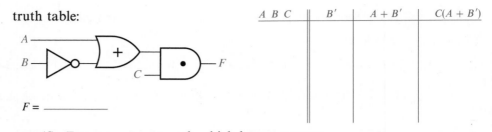

A B C	B′	A + B′	C(A + B′)

F = _____

(f) Draw a gate network which has an output

$$Z = [BC' + F(E + AD')]'$$

(*Hint:* Start with the innermost parentheses and draw the network for AD' first.)

4. Study Section 2.4, *Basic Theorems*.

    (a) Prove each of the theorems (2–4) through (2–8D) by showing that it is valid for both $X = 0$ and $X = 1$.

    (b) Determine the output of each of the following gates:

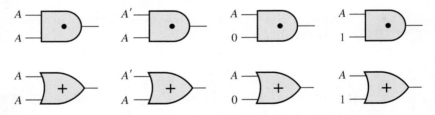

    (c) State which of the basic theorems was used in simplifying each of the following expressions:

$(AB' + C) \cdot 0 = 0$ $A(B + C') + 1 = 1$

$(BC' + A)(BC' + A) = BC' + A$ $X(Y' + Z) + [X(Y' + Z)]' = 1$

$(X' + YZ)(X' + YZ)' = 0$ $D'(E' + F) + D'(E' + F) = D'(E' + F)$

5. Study Section 2.5, *Commutative, Associative, and Distributive Laws.*

   (a) State the associative law for OR.

   (b) State the commutative law for AND.

   (c) Simplify the following network by using the associative laws. Your answer should require only two gates.

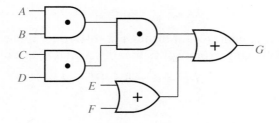

   (d) For each gate determine the value of the unspecified input(s):

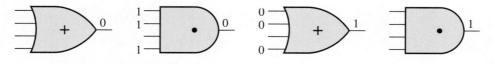

   (e) Using a truth table, verify the distributive law, Equation (2–11).

   (f) Illustrate the distributive laws, Equations (2–11) and (2–11D), using AND and OR gates.

   (g) Verify Equation (2–3) using the second distributive law.

   (h) Show how the second distributive law can be used to factor $RS + T'$.

6. Study Section 2.6, *Simplification Theorems*.

   (a) By completing the truth table, prove that $XY' + Y = X + Y$.

$X\ Y$	XY'	$XY' + Y$	$X + Y$
0 0			
0 1			
1 0			
1 1			

   (b) Which of the theorems (2–12) through (2–14D) was applied to simplify each of the following expressions? Identify X and Y in each case.

   $$(A + B)(DE)' + DE = A + B + DE$$

   $$AB' + AB'C'D = AB'$$

   $$(A' + B)(CD + E') + (A' + B)(CD + E')' = A' + B$$

   $$(A + BC' + D'E)(A + D'E) = A + D'E$$

   (c) Simplify the following network to a single gate:

   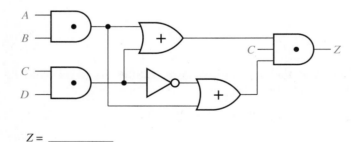

   $Z = $ _____

   (d) Work Problems 2.1, 2.2(a) and (c), 2.3, and 2.14(a) and (b).

7. Study Section 2.7, *Multiplying Out and Factoring*.

   (a) Indicate which of the following expressions are in product-of-sums form, sum-of-products form, or neither:

   $$AB' + D'EF' + G$$
   $$(A + B'C')(A' + BC)$$
   $$AB'(C' + D + E')(F' + G)$$
   $$X'Y + WX(X' + Z) + A'B'C'$$

Your answer to this question should include one product-of-sums, one sum-of-products, and two "neither," not necessarily in that order.

(b) When multiplying out an expression, why should the second distributive law be applied before the ordinary distributive law when possible?

(c) Factor as much as possible using the ordinary distributive law:

$$AD + B'CD + B'DE$$

Now factor your result using the second distributive law to obtain a product of sums.

(d) Work Problems 2.6(a) and (b), 2.9, and 2.12(a) and (b).

8. Probably the most difficult part of the unit is using the second distributive law for factoring or multiplying out an expression. If you have difficulty with Problems 2.6 or 2.9, or you cannot work them *quickly,* study the examples in Section 2.7 again, and then work the following problems.

Multiply out:

(a) $(B' + D + E)(B' + D + A)(AE + C')$

(b) $(A + C')(B' + D)(C' + D')(C + D)E$

As usual, when we say multiply out, we don't mean multiply out by brute force, but rather use the second distributive law whenever you can to cut down on the amount of work required.

Answer to (a) above should be of the following form: $XX + XX + XX$ and (b) of the form: $XXX + XXXXX$, where each X represents a single variable or its complement.

Now factor your answer to (a) to see that you can get back the original expression.

9. Review the first 11 laws and theorems on p. 40. Make sure that you can recognize when to apply them even if an expression has been substituted for a variable.

10. Reread the objectives of this unit. If you are satisfied that you can meet these objectives, take the readiness test.

(*Note:*   You will be provided with a copy of the theorem sheet (p. 40) when you take the readiness test this time. However, by the end of Unit 3, you should know all the theorems by memory.)

Boolean Algebra

2.1
Introduction

The basic mathematics needed for the study of logic design of digital systems is Boolean algebra.[2] Boolean algebra has many other applications including set theory and mathematical logic, but we will restrict ourselves to its application to switching networks in this text. Since all of the switching devices which we will use are essentially two-state devices (such as a transistor with high or low output voltage), we will study the special case of Boolean algebra in which all of the variables assume only one of two values. This two-valued Boolean algebra is often referred to as switching algebra.

We will use a Boolean variable, such as X or Y, to represent the input or output of a switching network. We will assume that each of these variables can take on only two different values. The symbols "0" and "1" are used to represent these two different values. Thus, if X is a Boolean (switching) variable, then either $X = 0$ or $X = 1$.

Although the symbols 0 and 1 used in this chapter *look* like binary numbers, they are not. They have no numeric value, but rather are just two symbols which represent the two values of a switching variable. The symbol 0, for example, might correspond to a low voltage and 1 might correspond to a high voltage. F and T could be used just as well as 0 and 1.

2.2
Basic Operations

The basic operations of Boolean algebra are AND, OR, and complement (or inverse). The complement of 0 is 1, and the complement of 1 is 0. Symbolically, we write

$$0' = 1 \quad \text{and} \quad 1' = 0$$

---

[2] George Boole developed Boolean algebra in 1847 and used it to solve problems in mathematical logic. Claude Shannon first applied Boolean algebra to the design of switching networks in 1939.

where the prime (') denotes complementation. If X is a switching variable,

$$X' = 1 \quad \text{if} \quad X = 0, \quad \text{and} \quad X' = 0 \quad \text{if} \quad X = 1$$

An alternate name for complementation is inversion, and the electronic circuit which forms the inverse of X is referred to as an inverter. Symbolically, we represent an inverter by

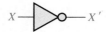

where the circle at the output indicates inversion. If a logic 0 corresponds to a low voltage and a logic 1 corresponds to a high voltage, a low voltage at the inverter input produces a high voltage at the output and vice versa. Complementation is sometimes referred to as the NOT operation since $X = 1$ if X is *not* equal to 0.

The AND operation can be defined as follows:

$$0 \cdot 0 = 0 \quad\quad 0 \cdot 1 = 0 \quad\quad 1 \cdot 0 = 0 \quad\quad 1 \cdot 1 = 1$$

where "·" denotes AND. (Although this looks like binary multiplication, it is not since 0 and 1 here are Boolean constants rather than binary numbers.) If we write the Boolean expression $C = A \cdot B$, then given the values of A and B, we can determine C from the following table:

$A\ B$	$C = A \cdot B$
0 0	0
0 1	0
1 0	0
1 1	1

Note that $C = 1$ iff (if and only if) A *and* B are both 1, hence the name AND operation. A logic gate which performs the AND operation is represented by

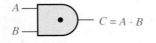

The "·" symbol is frequently omitted in a Boolean expression, and we will usually write AB instead of $A \cdot B$. The AND operation is also referred to as logical (or Boolean) multiplication.

The OR operation can be defined as follows:

$$0 + 0 = 0 \quad\quad 0 + 1 = 1 \quad\quad 1 + 0 = 1 \quad\quad 1 + 1 = 1$$

where "+" denotes OR. If we write $C = A + B$, then given the values of A and B we can determine C from the following table:

$A\ B$	$C = A + B$
0 0	0
0 1	1
1 0	1
1 1	1

Note that $C = 1$ iff A *or* B (or both) is 1, hence the name OR operation. This type of OR operation is sometimes referred to as "inclusive OR". A logic gate which performs the OR operation is represented by

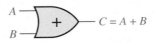

The OR operation is also referred to as logical (or Boolean) addition. Electronic circuits which realize inverters and AND and OR gates are described in Appendix A.

We will next apply switching algebra to describe networks containing switches. We will label each switch with a variable. If switch X is open, then we will define the value of X to be 0; if switch X is closed, then we will define the value of X to be 1.

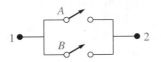

$$X = 0 \rightarrow \text{switch open}$$
$$X = 1 \rightarrow \text{switch closed}$$

Now consider a network composed of two switches in series. We will define the transmission between the terminals as $T = 0$ if there is an open circuit between the terminals and $T = 1$ if there is a closed circuit between the terminals.

$$T = 0 \rightarrow \text{open circuit between terminals 1 and 2}$$
$$T = 1 \rightarrow \text{closed circuit between terminals 1 and 2}$$

Now we have a closed circuit between terminals 1 and 2 ($T = 1$) iff (if and only if) switch A is closed *and* switch B is closed. Stating this algebraically,

$$T = A \cdot B$$

Next consider a network composed of two switches in parallel.

In this case, we have a closed circuit between terminals 1 and 2 iff switch A is closed *or* switch B is closed. Using the same convention for defining variables as above, an equation which describes the behavior of this network is

$$T = A + B$$

Thus, switches in series perform the AND operation and switches in parallel perform the OR operation.

2.3
Boolean Expressions and Truth Tables

Boolean expressions are formed by application of the basic operations to one or more variables or constants. The simplest expressions consist of a single constant or variable, such as 0, X, or Y'. More complicated expressions are formed by combining two or more other expressions using AND or OR, or by complementing another expression. Examples of expressions are

$$AB' + C \tag{2-1}$$

$$[A(C + D)]' + BE \tag{2-2}$$

Parentheses are added as needed to specify the order in which the operations are performed. When parentheses are omitted, complementation is performed first followed by AND and then OR. Thus in (2–1), B' is formed first, then AB' and finally $AB' + C$.

Each expression corresponds directly to a network of logic gates. Figure 2–1 gives the networks for Expressions (2–1) and (2–2) above.

An expression is evaluated by substituting a value of 0 or 1 for each variable. If $A = B = C = 1$ and $D = E = 0$, the value of Expression (2–2) is

$$[A(C + D)]' + BE = [1(1 + 0)]' + 1 \cdot 0 = [1(1)]' + 0 = 0 + 0 = 0$$

Each appearance of a variable or its complement in an expression will be referred to as a *literal*. Thus the following expression, which has 3 variables, has 10 literals:

$$ab'c + a'b + a'bc' + b'c'$$

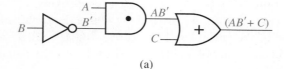

(a)

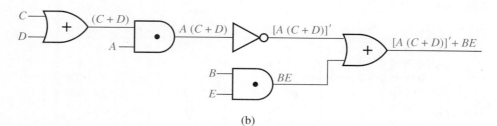

(b)

Figure 2–1
Networks for Expressions (2–1) and (2–2)

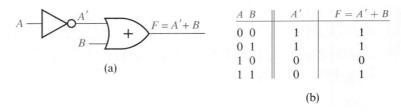

A B	A'	F = A' + B
0 0	1	1
0 1	1	1
1 0	0	0
1 1	0	1

(b)

Figure 2–2
2-input Network and Truth Table

When an expression is realized using logic gates, each literal in the expression corresponds to a gate input.

A *truth table* (also called a table of combinations) specifies the values of a Boolean expression for every possible combination of values of the variables in the expression. The name truth table comes from a similar table which is used in symbolic logic to list the "truth" or "falsity" of a statement under all possible conditions. We can use a truth table to specify the output values for a network of logic gates in terms of the values of the input variables. The output of the network in Fig. 2–2(a) is $F = A' + B$. Figure 2–2(b) shows a truth table which specifies the output of the network for all possible combinations of values of the inputs A and B. The first two columns list the four combinations of values of A and B, and the next column gives the corresponding values of A'. The last column, which gives the values of $A' + B$, is formed by ORing together corresponding values of A' and B in each row.

Next, we will use a truth table to specify the value of Expression (2–1) for all possible combinations of values of the variables A, B, and C. On the left side of Table 2–1, we list the values of the variables A, B, and C. Since each of the three variables can assume the value 0 or 1, there are $2 \times 2 \times 2 = 8$ combinations of values of the variables. These combinations are easily obtained by listing the binary numbers $000, 001, \ldots, 111$. In the next three columns of the truth table, we compute B', AB', and $AB' + C$, respectively.

Two expressions are equal if they have the same value for every possible combination of the variables. The expression $(A + C)(B' + C)$ is evaluated using the last three columns of Table 2–1. Since it has the same value as $AB' + C$ for all

Table 2–1

A B C	B'	AB'	AB' + C	A + C	B' + C	(A + C)(B' + C)
0 0 0	1	0	0	0	1	0
0 0 1	1	0	1	1	1	1
0 1 0	0	0	0	0	0	0
0 1 1	0	0	1	1	1	1
1 0 0	1	1	1	1	1	1
1 0 1	1	1	1	1	1	1
1 1 0	0	0	0	1	0	0
1 1 1	0	0	1	1	1	1

eight combinations of values of the variables A, B, and C, we conclude

$$AB' + C = (A + C)(B' + C) \qquad (2\text{–}3)$$

If an expression has n variables, and each variable can have the value 0 or 1, the number of different combinations of values of the variables is

$$\underbrace{2 \times 2 \times 2 \times \cdots}_{n \text{ times}} = 2^n$$

Therefore, a truth table for an n-variable expression will have 2^n rows.

2.4
Basic Theorems

The following basic theorems of Boolean algebra involve only a single variable:

Operations with 0 and 1:

$X + 0 = X$	(2–4)	$X \cdot 1 = X$	(2–4D)
$X + 1 = 1$	(2–5)	$X \cdot 0 = 0$	(2–5D)

Idempotent laws

$X + X = X$	(2–6)	$X \cdot X = X$	(2–6D)

Involution law

$$(X')' = X \qquad (2\text{–}7)$$

Laws of complementarity:

$X + X' = 1$	(2–8)	$X \cdot X' = 0$	(2–8D)

Each of these theorems is easily proved by showing that it is valid for both of the possible values of X. For example, to prove $X + X' = 1$, we observe that if

$$X = 0, \quad 0 + 0' = 0 + 1 = 1, \quad \text{and if} \quad X = 1, \quad 1 + 1' = 1 + 0 = 1$$

Any expression can be substituted for the variable X in these theorems. Thus, by Theorem (2–5),

$$(AB' + D)E + 1 = 1$$

and by Theorem (2–8D),

$$(AB' + D)(AB' + D)' = 0$$

We will illustrate some of the basic theorems by networks of switches. As before, 0 will represent an open circuit or open switch and 1 will represent a closed circuit or closed switch. If two switches are both labeled with the variable A, this means that both switches are open when $A = 0$ and both are closed when $A = 1$. Thus the network

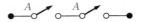

can be replaced with a single switch:

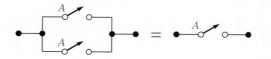

This illustrates the theorem $A \cdot A = A$. Similarly,

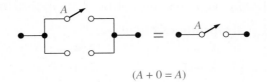

which illustrates the theorem $A + A = A$. A switch in parallel with an open circuit is equivalent to the switch alone

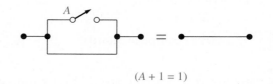

$$(A + 0 = A)$$

while a switch in parallel with a short circuit is equivalent to a short circuit.

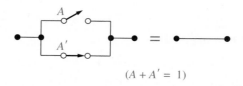

$$(A + 1 = 1)$$

If a switch is labeled A', then it is open when A is closed and conversely. Hence A in parallel with A' can be replaced with a closed circuit since one or the other of the two switches is always closed.

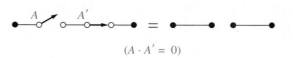

$$(A + A' = 1)$$

Similarly, switch A in series with A' can be replaced with an open circuit (why?).

$$(A \cdot A' = 0)$$

2.5
Commutative, Associative, and Distributive Laws

Many of the laws of ordinary algebra, such as the commutative and associative laws, also apply to Boolean algebra. The commutative laws for AND and OR, which follow directly from the definitions of the AND and OR operations, are

$$XY = YX \qquad (2\text{–}9) \qquad\qquad X + Y = Y + X \qquad (2\text{–}9\text{D})$$

This means that the order in which the variables are written will not affect the result of applying the AND and OR operations.

The associative laws also apply to AND and OR:

$$(XY)Z = X(YZ) = XYZ \qquad\qquad (2\text{–}10)$$

$$(X + Y) + Z = X + (Y + Z) = X + Y + Z \qquad\qquad (2\text{–}10\text{D})$$

When forming the AND (or OR) of three variables, the result is independent of which pair of variables we associate together first, so parentheses can be omitted as indicated in Equations (2–10) and (2–10D).

We will prove the associative law for AND by using a truth table (Table 2–2). On the left side of the table, we list all combinations of values of the variables X, Y, and Z. In the next two columns of the truth table, we compute XY and YZ for each combination of values of X, Y, and Z. Finally, we compute $(XY)Z$ and $X(YZ)$. Since $(XY)Z$ and $X(YZ)$ are equal for all possible combinations of values of the variables, we conclude that Equation (2–10) is valid.

Figure 2–3 illustrates the associative laws using AND and OR gates. In Fig. 2–3(a) two 2-input AND gates are replaced with a single 3-input AND gate. Similarly, in Fig. 2–3(b) two 2-input OR gates are replaced with a single 3-input OR gate.

When two or more variables are ANDed together, the value of the result will be 1 iff all of the variables have the value 1. If any of the variables have the value

Table 2–2

Proof of Associative Law for AND

$X\ Y\ Z$	XY	YZ	$(XY)Z$	$X(YZ)$
0 0 0	0	0	0	0
0 0 1	0	0	0	0
0 1 0	0	0	0	0
0 1 1	0	1	0	0
1 0 0	0	0	0	0
1 0 1	0	0	0	0
1 1 0	1	0	0	0
1 1 1	1	1	1	1

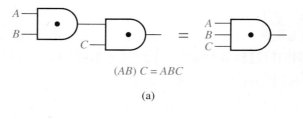

$$(AB)\, C = ABC$$

(a)

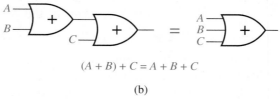

$$(A + B) + C = A + B + C$$

(b)

Figure 2–3
Associative Laws for AND and OR

0, the result of the AND operation will be 0. For example,

$$XYZ = 1 \quad \text{iff} \quad X = Y = Z = 1$$

When two or more variables are ORed together, the value of the result will be 1 if any of the variables have the value 1. The result of the OR operation will be 0 iff all of the variables have the value 0. For example,

$$X + Y + Z = 0 \quad \text{iff} \quad X = Y = Z = 0$$

Using a truth table, it is easy to show that the distributive law is valid:

$$X(Y + Z) = XY + XZ \tag{2–11}$$

In addition to the ordinary distributive law, a second distributive law is valid for Boolean algebra but not for ordinary algebra:

$$X + YZ = (X + Y)(X + Z) \tag{2–11D}$$

Proof of the second distributive law follows:

$$(X + Y)(X + Z) = X(X + Z) + Y(X + Z) = XX + XZ + YX + YZ$$
$$\text{(by (2–11))}$$
$$= X + XZ + XY + YZ = X \cdot 1 + XZ + XY + YZ$$
$$\text{(by (2–6D) and (2–4D))}$$
$$= X(1 + Z + Y) + YZ = X \cdot 1 + YZ = X + YZ$$
$$\text{(by (2–11), (2–5), and (2–4D))}$$

The ordinary distributive law states that the AND operation distributes over OR, while the second distributive law states that OR distributes over AND. This second law is very useful in manipulating Boolean expressions. In particular, an expression like $A + BC$, which cannot be factored in ordinary algebra, is easily factored using the second distributive law:

$$A + BC = (A + B)(A + C)$$

2.6
Simplification Theorems

The following theorems are useful in simplifying Boolean expressions:

$XY + XY' = X$	(2–12)	$(X + Y)(X + Y') = X$	(2–12D)
$X + XY = X$	(2–13)	$X(X + Y) = X$	(2–13D)
$(X + Y')Y = XY$	(2–14)	$XY' + Y = X + Y$	(2–14D)

In each case, one expression can be replaced by a simpler one. Since each expression corresponds to a network of logic gates, simplifying an expression leads to simplifying the corresponding logic network.

Each of the above theorems can be proved by using a truth table, or they can be proved algebraically starting with the basic theorems.

Proof of (2–13): $X + XY = X \cdot 1 + XY = X(1 + Y) = X \cdot 1 = X$

Proof of (2–13D): $X(X + Y) = XX + XY = X + XY = X$
                    (by (2–6D) and (2–13))

Proof of (2–14D): $Y + XY' = (Y + X)(Y + Y') = (Y + X)1 = Y + X$
                    (by (2–11D) and (2–8))

Proof of the remaining theorems is left as an exercise.

We will illustrate Theorem (2–14D) using switches. Consider the following network:

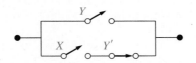

Its transmission is $T = Y + XY'$ since there is a closed circuit between the terminals if switch Y is closed *or* switch X is closed and switch Y' is closed. The following network is equivalent because if Y is closed ($Y = 1$) both networks have a transmission of 1; if Y is open ($Y' = 1$) both networks have a transmission of X.

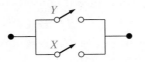

The following example illustrates simplification of a logic gate network using one of the theorems. In Fig. 2–4, the output of network (a) is

$$F = A(A' + B)$$

By Theorem (2–14), the expression for F simplifies to AB. Therefore, network (a) can be replaced with the equivalent network (b).

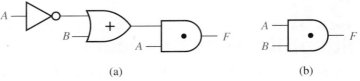

Figure 2–4
Equivalent Gate Networks

Any expressions can be substituted for X and Y in the theorems.

EXAMPLE 1   Simplify $Z = A'BC + A'$

This expression has the same form as (2–13) if we let $X = A'$ and $Y = BC$. Therefore, the expression simplifies to $Z = X + XY = X = A'$.

EXAMPLE 2   Simplify $Z = [\underline{A + B'C} + \underline{D + EF}][\underline{A + B'C} + \underline{(D + EF)'}]$

Substituting: $Z = [\quad X \quad + \quad Y \quad][\quad X \quad + \quad Y' \quad]$

Then, by (2–12D), the expression reduces to

$$Z = X = A + B'C$$

EXAMPLE 3   Simplify $Z = (\underline{AB + C})(\underline{B'D + C'E'}) + \underline{(AB + C)'}$

Substituting: $Z = \quad Y' \quad\quad X \quad + \quad Y$

By (2–14D): $Z = X + Y = B'D + C'E' + (AB + C)'$

Note that in this example we let $Y = (AB + C)'$ rather than $(AB + C)$ in order to match the form of (2–14D).

2.7
Multiplying Out and Factoring

The two distributive laws are used to multiply out an expression to obtain a sum-of-products form. An expression is said to be in *sum-of-products* form when all products are the products of single variables only. This form is the end result when an expression is fully multiplied out. It is usually easy to recognize a sum-of-products expression since it consists of a sum of product terms:

$$AB' + CD'E + AC'E' \tag{2–15}$$

However, in degenerate cases, one or more of the product terms may consist of a single variable. For example,

$$ABC' + DEFG + H \tag{2–16}$$

and

$$A + B' + C + D'E \tag{2–17}$$

are still considered to be in sum-of-products form. The expression

$$(A + B)CD + EF$$

is not in sum-of-products form because the $A + B$ term enters into a product but is not a single variable.

When multiplying out an expression, the second distributive law should be applied first when possible. For example, to multiply out $(A + BC)(A + D + E)$ let

$$X = A, \qquad Y = BC, \qquad Z = D + E$$

Then

$$(X + Y)(X + Z) = X + YZ = A + BC(D + E) = A + BCD + BCE$$

Of course, the same result could be obtained the hard way by multiplying out the original expression completely and then eliminating redundant terms:

$$\begin{aligned}(A + BC)(A + D + E) &= A + AD + AE + ABC + BCD + BCE \\ &= A(1 + D + E + BC) + BCD + BCE \\ &= A + BCD + BCE\end{aligned}$$

You will save yourself much time if you learn to apply the second distributive law as above instead of doing the problem the hard way.

Both distributive laws can be used to factor an expression to obtain a product-of-sums form. An expression is in *product-of-sums* form when all sums are the sums of single variables. It is usually easy to recognize a product-of-sums expression since it consists of a product of sum terms:

$$(A + B')(C + D' + E)(A + C' + E') \qquad (2\text{--}18)$$

However, in degenerate cases, one or more of the sum terms may consist of a single variable. For example,

$$(A + B)(C + D + E)F \qquad (2\text{--}19)$$

and

$$AB'C(D' + E) \qquad (2\text{--}20)$$

are still considered to be in product-of-sums form, but $(A + B)(C + D) + EF$ is not in product-of-sums form. An expression is fully factored iff it is in product-of-sums form. Any expression not in this form can be factored further.

The following examples illustrate how to factor using the second distributive law:

EXAMPLE 1   Factor $A + B'CD$. This is of the form $X + YZ$ where $X = A$, $Y = B'$, and $Z = CD$, so

$$A + B'CD = (X + Y)(X + Z) = (A + B')(A + CD)$$

$A + CD$ can be factored again using the second distributive law, so

$$A + B'CD = (A + B')(A + C)(A + D)$$

EXAMPLE 2   Factor $AB' + C'D$

$AB' + C'D = (AB' + C')(AB' + D)$ ◀—— note how $X + YZ = (X + Y)(X + Z)$ was applied here

$= (A + C')(B' + C')(A + D)(B' + D)$ ◀—— the second distributive law was applied again to each term

EXAMPLE 3   Factor $C'D + C'E' + G'H$

$C'D + C'E' + G'H = C'(D + E') + G'H$ ⟵ first apply the ordinary distributive law, $XY + XZ = X(Y + Z)$

$= (C' + G'H)(D + E' + G'H)$ ⟵ then apply the second distributive law

$= (C' + G')(C' + H)(D + E' + G')(D + E' + H)$ ⟵ now identify X, Y, and Z in each expression and complete the factoring

As in example 3 above, the ordinary distributive law should be applied before the second law when factoring an expression.

A sum-of-products expression can always be realized directly by one or more AND gates feeding a single OR gate at the network output. Figure 2–5 shows the networks for Equations (2–15) and (2–17). Inverters required to generate the complemented variables have been omitted.

A product-of-sums expression can always be realized directly by one or more OR gates feeding a single AND gate at the network output. Figure 2–6 shows the networks for Equations (2–18) and (2–20). Inverters required to generate the complements have been omitted.

The networks shown in Figs. 2–5 and 2–6 are often referred to as two-level networks since they have a maximum of two gates in series between an input and the network output.

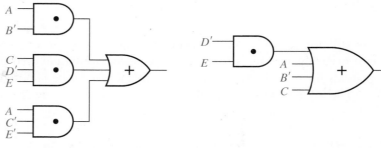

Figure 2–5
Networks for Equations (2–15) and (2–17)

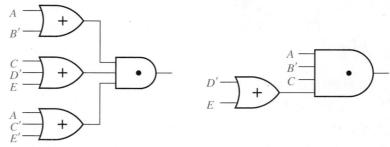

Figure 2–6
Networks for Equations (2–18) and (2–20)

PROBLEMS

2.1   Prove the following theorems algebraically:

(a) $X(X' + Y) = XY$ (b) $(X + Y)(X + Z) = X + YZ$

(c) $XY + XY' = X$ (d) $(A + B)(A + B') = A$

2.2   Illustrate the following theorems using networks of switches:

(a) $X + XY = X$ (b) $XY + XY' = X$

(c) $X + YZ = (X + Y)(X + Z)$ (d) $(X + Y')Y = XY$

In each case, explain why the networks are equivalent.

2.3   Simplify each of the following expressions by applying one of the theorems. State the theorem used (see p. 40).

(a) $ABC' + (ABC')'$ (b) $(AB + CD')(AB + D'E)$

(c) $A + B'C + D'(A + B'C)$ (d) $AB'(C + D) + (C + D)'$

(e) $[(EF)' + AB + C'D'](EF)$ (f) $(AB + C) + (D + EF)(AB + C)'$

2.4   Repeat Problem 2.3 for:

(a) $A'B'C + (A'B'C)'$ (b) $A(B + C'D) + B + C'D$

(c) $A + B + C'D(A + B)'$ (d) $(A'B + CD')(A'B + CE)$

(e) $[AB' + (CD)' + E'F]CD$ (f) $(A' + BC)(D'E + F)' + (D'E + F)$

2.5   Repeat Problem 2.3 for:

(a) $(X + Y'Z)(X + Y'Z)'$ (b) $(W + X' + YZ)(W' + X' + YZ)$

(c) $(V'W + X)'(X + Y + Z + V'W)$ (d) $(V' + W'X)(V' + W'X + Y'Z)$

(e) $(W' + X)YZ' + (W' + X)'YZ'$

(f) $(V' + U + W)(WX + Y + UZ') + (WX + UZ' + Y)$

2.6   Multiply out to obtain a sum of products:

(a) $(A + B)(A + C')(A + D)(BC'D + E)$

(b) $(A + B' + C)(B' + C + D)(A' + C)$

(c) $(A + B'C + D')(B'C + D' + E)(A + E')(AD + E')$

(d) $(A' + BE')(BE' + C + D)(E + C')$

2.7   Multiply out to obtain a sum of products:

(a) $(A' + B)(C' + B'D)(A + E + B'D)$

(b) $(A + B')(A + C + D')(A + B + D')$

(c) $(A + B)(B + C)(B + D')(ACD' + E)$

(d) $(AB + C')(A + C')(A + B' + DE')(B' + C' + DE')$

2.8   Multiply out to obtain a sum of products:

(a) $(A + B')(A + C + D)(A + B' + D)$

(b) $(A' + B)(A' + C)(C + D)(B + D)$

2.9   Factor each of the following expressions to obtain a product of sums:

(a) $DE + F'G'$ (b) $WX' + WY'Z + WYZ$

(c) $A'CD + E'F + BCD$ (d) $ABE + D'E + AC'E$

(e) $AC'D + C'D' + A'D'$ (f) $H + IJ' + K'L$

                                               (answer should be a product of 4 terms, each a sum of 3 variables).

2.10   Factor each of the following expressions to obtain a product of sums:

(a) $H'I' + JK$ (b) $ABC + A'B'C + CD'$

(c) $AB' + ACD + ADE'$ (d) $AB'C + BCD' + EF'$

(e) $WX'Y + W'X' + W'Y'$ (f) $AB' + (CD' + E)$
(answer should be a product of
4 terms, each a sum of 3 variables).

2.11 Factor each of the following expressions to obtain a product of sums:
(a) $W + X'YZ$ (b) $VW + XY' + Z$
(c) $A'B'C + B'CD' + B'E'$ (d) $ABC + ADE' + ABF'$

2.12 Draw a network to realize each of the following functions using only one AND gate and one OR gate:
(a) $(A + B + C + D)(A + B + C + E)(A + B + C + F)$
(b) $WXYZ + VXYZ + UXYZ$
(c) $ABCD + ABCE + ABCF$
(d) $(W + X + Y + Z)(V + X + Y + Z)(U + X + Y + Z)$

2.13 Draw a network to realize the following function using two OR gates and two AND gates:

$$F = (V + W + X)(V + X + Y)(V + Z)$$

2.14 For each of the following networks, find the output and design a simpler network having the same output. (Find the network output by first finding the output of each gate, going from left to right, and simplifying as you go.)

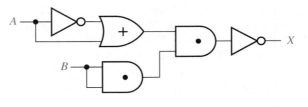

(a)

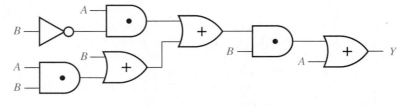

(b)

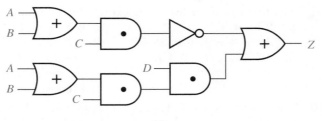

(c)

2.15 Repeat Problem 2.14 for:

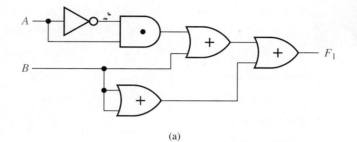

(a)

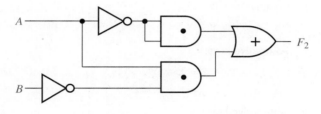

(b)

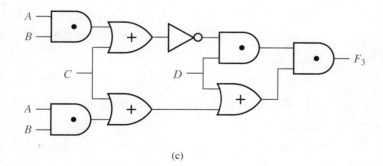

(c)

2.16 Prove the following equations using truth tables:
(a) $W'XY + WZ = (W' + Z)(W + XY)$
(b) $(A + C)(AB + C') = AB + AC'$

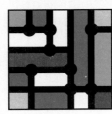

LAWS AND THEOREMS OF BOOLEAN ALGEBRA

Operations with 0 and 1:

1. $X + 0 = X$ 1D. $X \cdot 1 = X$

2. $X + 1 = 1$ 2D. $X \cdot 0 = 0$

Idempotent laws:

3. $X + X = X$ 3D. $X \cdot X = X$

Involution law:

4. $(X')' = X$

Laws of complementarity:

5. $X + X' = 1$ 5D. $X \cdot X' = 0$

Commutative laws:

6. $X + Y = Y + X$ 6D. $XY = YX$

Associative laws:

7. $(X + Y) + Z = X + (Y + Z)$ 7D. $(XY)Z = X(YZ) = XYZ$
$= X + Y + Z$

Distributive laws:

8. $X(Y + Z) = XY + XZ$ 8D. $X + YZ = (X + Y)(X + Z)$

Simplification theorems:

9. $XY + XY' = X$ 9D. $(X + Y)(X + Y') = X$

10. $X + XY = X$ 10D. $X(X + Y) = X$

11. $(X + Y')Y = XY$ 11D. $XY' + Y = X + Y$

DeMorgan's laws:

12. $(X + Y + Z + \cdots)' = X'Y'Z' \cdots$ 12D. $(XYZ \cdots)' = X' + Y' + Z' + \cdots$

13. $[f(X_1, X_2, \ldots, X_n, 0, 1, +, \cdot)]' = f(X_1', X_2', \ldots, X_n', 1, 0, \cdot, +)$

Duality:

14. $(X + Y + Z + \cdots)^D = XYZ \cdots$ 14D. $(XYZ \cdots)^D = X + Y + Z + \cdots$

15. $[f(X_1, X_2, \ldots, X_n, 0, 1, +, \cdot)]^D = f(X_1, X_2, \ldots, X_n, 1, 0, \cdot, +)$

Theorem for multiplying out and factoring:

16. $(X + Y)(X' + Z) = XZ + X'Y$ 16D. $XY + X'Z = (X + Z)(X' + Y)$

Consensus theorem:

17. $XY + YZ + X'Z = XY + X'Z$ 17D. $(X + Y)(Y + Z)(X' + Z)$
$= (X + Y)(X' + Z)$

3

Boolean Algebra (Continued)

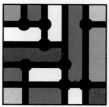

OBJECTIVES

When you complete this unit, you should know from memory and be able to use any of the first 16 laws and theorems of Boolean algebra listed at the end of Unit 2. Specifically, you should be able to:

1. Apply these laws and theorems to manipulation of algebraic expressions including:

   a. Simplifying an expression

   b. Finding the complement or the dual of an expression

   c. Multiplying out and factoring an expression

2. Prove any of the theorems using a truth table or give an algebraic proof if appropriate.

3. Define the exclusive-OR and equivalence operations. State, prove, and use the basic theorems which concern these operations.

4. Define positive and negative logic; apply the negative logic theorem.

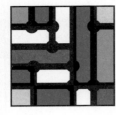

STUDY GUIDE

1. Study Section 3.1, *Inversion*.

2. Find the complement of each of the following expressions as indicated. In your answer, the complement operation should be applied only to single variables.

   (a) $(ab'c')' =$

   (b) $(a' + b + c + d')' =$

   (c) $(a' + bc)' =$

   (d) $(a'b' + cd)' =$

   (e) $[a(b' + c'd)]' =$

3. Since $(X')' = X$, if you complement each of your answers to 2 you should get back the original expression. Verify that this is true.

   (a)

   (b)

   (c)

   (d)

   (e)

4. **(a)** State a single rule which can be used to form the complement of a Boolean expression in one step.

   (b) In the following equation, each AND and OR operation has been given a number for reference:

   $$Z = A \cdot B + C \cdot [D + E \cdot F + G \cdot (H + I \cdot J)]$$
   $$\quad 1 \quad 2 \quad 3 \quad\; 4 \quad 5 \quad 6 \quad 7 \quad 8 \quad 9$$

   When the expression is evaluated, which of the following pairs of operations is performed first?

   8 or 9 ____   6 or 7 ____   4 or 5 ____   2 or 3 ____   1 or 2 ____

By the one-step rule,
$$Z' = A' + B' \cdot C' + D' \cdot E' + F' \cdot G' + H' \cdot I' + J'$$
$$1 \quad 2 \quad 3 \quad 4 \quad 5 \quad 6 \quad 7 \quad 8 \quad 9$$

Fill in the required parentheses in Z' so that each pair of operations is performed in the same order as above. For example, since 9 is performed before 8 in Z, add parentheses so 9 is performed before 8 in Z'. Then add four more pairs of parentheses.

(c) When this rule was applied in Equation (3–8), which parentheses (or brackets) were added in order to preserve the proper hierarchy of operations?

Verify that Equation (3–8) is correct by using Equations (3–1) and (3–2).

5. Given that $F = a'b + b'c$, $F' = $ _____ .
Complete the following truth table and verify that your answer is correct:

$a\ b\ c$	$a'b$	$b'c$	$a'b + b'c$	$(a + b')$	$(b + c')$	F'
0 0 0						
0 0 1						
0 1 0						
0 1 1						
1 0 0						
1 0 1						
1 1 0						
1 1 1						

6. Work Problem 3.3 using the one-step method. Work Problem 3.15.

7. Read Section 3.2, *Duality*. You will find an interesting application of duality when we study positive and negative logic.

(a) How does the dual of an expression differ from the complement?

(b) How are the constants 0 and 1 treated when forming the dual?

When forming the complement?

(c) Observe that the theorems listed at the end of Unit 2 are listed in dual pairs. (Mentally verify that each pair is a dual.) This means that you really have only half as many theorems to learn, since if you know one, you can form its dual by inspection.

(d) Work Problem 3.5.

8. Study Section 3.3, *Multiplying Out and Factoring Expressions.*

    (a) List three laws or theorems which are useful when multiplying out or factoring expressions.

    (b) Use Equation (3–12) to factor each of the following:

$$ab'c + bd =$$
$$abc + (ab)'d =$$

    (c) In the following example, first group the terms so that (3–11) can be applied two times.

$$F_1 = (x + y' + z)(w' + x' + y)(w + x + y')(w' + y + z')$$

    After applying (3–11), apply (3–12) and then finish multiplying out using (3–10).

    If we did not use (3–11) and (3–12) and used only (3–10) on the above expression we would generate many more terms:

$$F = (w'x + w'y' + w'z + \cancel{xx'} + x'y' + x'z + xy + \cancel{yy'} + yz)$$
$$(\cancel{ww'} + w'x + w'y' + wy + xy + \cancel{yy'} + wz' + xz' + y'z')$$
$$= \underbrace{(w'x + w'xy' + w'xz + \cdots + yzy'z')}$$

                        49 terms in all

    This is obviously a *very inefficient* way to proceed! The moral to this story is first group the terms and apply (3–11) and (3–12) where possible.

    (d) Work Programmed Exercise 3.1. Then work Problem 3.9(a) and (b), being careful not to introduce any unnecessary terms in the process.

    (e) In Unit 2 you learned how to factor a Boolean expression using the two distributive laws. In addition, this unit has introduced use of the theorem

$$XY + X'Z = (X + Z)(X' + Y)$$

    in the factoring process. Careful choice of the order in which these laws and theorems are applied may cut down the amount of work required to factor an expression. When factoring, it is best to apply Equation (3–10) first, using as X the variable or variables which appear most frequently. Then Equations (3–11) and (3–12) can be applied in either order depending on circumstances.

    (f) Work Programmed Exercise 3.2. Then work Problem 3.11(a) and (b).

9. Checking your answers:

A good way to partially check your answers for correctness is to substitute in 0's or 1's for some of the variables. For example, if we substitute $A = 1$ in the first and last expression in Equation (3–14), we get

$$1 \cdot C + 0 \cdot BD' + 0 \cdot BE + 0 \cdot C'DE = (1 + B + C')(1 + B + D)$$
$$\cdot (1 + B + E)(1 + D' + E)(0 + C)$$
$$C = 1 \cdot 1 \cdot 1 \cdot 1 \cdot C$$

Similarly substituting $A = 0$, $B = 0$ we get

$$0 + 0 + 0 + C'DE = (0 + C')(0 + D)(0 + E)(D' + E)(1 + C)$$
$$= C'DE \checkmark$$

Verify that the result is also correct when $A = 0$ and $B = 1$.

10. The *method* which you use to get your answer is very important in this unit. If it takes you two pages of algebra and one hour of time to work a problem which can be solved in ten minutes with three lines of work, you have not learned the material in this unit! Even if you get the answer correct, your work is not satisfactory if you worked the problem by an excessively long and time-consuming method. It is important that you learn to solve simple problems in a simple manner—otherwise, when you are asked to solve a complex problem you will get bogged down and never get the answer. When you are given a problem to solve, don't just plunge in, but rather first ask yourself, "What is the easiest way to work this problem?" For example, when you are asked to multiply out an expression, don't just multiply it out term by term by brute force. Instead, ask yourself, "How can I group the terms and which theorems should I apply first so as to reduce the amount of work?" (See Study Guide Question 8.) After you have worked out Problems 3.9 and 3.11, compare your solutions with those in the solution book. If your solution required substantially more work than the one in the solution book, rework the problem and try to get the answer in a more straightforward manner.

11. Study Section 3.4, *Exclusive-OR and Equivalence Operations*.

    (a) Prove Theorems (3–17) through (3–22). You should be able to prove these both algebraically and by using a truth table.

    (b) Show that $(xy' + x'y)' = xy + x'y'$. Memorize this result.

    (c) Prove Theorem (3–24).

(d) Show that $(x \equiv 0) = x'$, $(x \equiv x) = 1$, and $(x \equiv y)' = (x \equiv y')$.

(e) Express $(x \equiv y)'$ in terms of exclusive OR.

(f) Work Problems 3.18 and 3.19.

12. Study Section 3.5, *Positive and Negative Logic.*

   (a) Note the definitions of positive and negative logic.
       If logic $1 = -3$ volts and logic $0 = -6$ volts, is this $+$ or $-$ logic?

       If logic $1 = +3$ volts and logic $0 = +6$ volts, is this $+$ or $-$ logic?

       Does the sign of the voltages have anything to do with whether the logic is $+$ or $-$?

   (b) If a logic gate circuit realizes

   $$Z = [(A + B')C'D + A'BD'](E' + F)$$

   for negative logic, what function does it realize for positive logic?

   (c) Why does an inverter for positive logic also act as an inverter for negative logic?

   (d) Work Problems 3.23 and 3.25.

13. When you take the readiness test, you will be expected to know from memory the first 16 laws and theorems listed at the end of Unit 2. Where appropriate, you should know them "forward and backward"; that is, given either side of the equation you should be able to supply the other. Test yourself to see if you can do this.

14. Reread the objectives stated at the beginning of the lesson. If you are satisfied that you can meet these objectives, take the readiness test.

Boolean Algebra (Continued)

In this unit we continue our study of Boolean algebra to learn additional methods for manipulating Boolean expressions. We introduce methods for finding the complement and dual of Boolean expressions. Then, conversion between product-of-sums expressions and sum-of-products expressions is accomplished by multiplying out and factoring. Such algebraic manipulations permit us to realize a switching function in a variety of forms. The exclusive-OR and equivalence operations are introduced along with examples of their use. Finally, we use the concepts of positive and negative logic to relate high and low voltage levels at gate inputs and outputs to the functions realized by the gates.

3.1
Inversion

The inverse or complement of any Boolean expression can easily be found by successively applying the following theorems, which are frequently referred to as DeMorgan's laws:

$$(X + Y)' = X'Y' \tag{3-1}$$

$$(XY)' = X' + Y' \tag{3-2}$$

We will verify these laws using a truth table:

$X\ Y$	$X'\ Y'$	$X + Y$	$(X + Y)'$	$X'Y'$	XY	$(XY)'$	$X' + Y'$
0 0	1 1	0	1	1	0	1	1
0 1	1 0	1	0	0	0	1	1
1 0	0 1	1	0	0	0	1	1
1 1	0 0	1	0	0	1	0	0

DeMorgan's laws are easily generalized to n variables:

$$(X_1 + X_2 + X_3 + \cdots + X_n)' = X_1'X_2'X_3' \cdots X_n' \tag{3-3}$$

$$(X_1 X_2 X_3 \cdots X_n)' = X_1' + X_2' + X_3' + \cdots + X_n' \tag{3-4}$$

For example, for $n = 3$,

$$(X_1 + X_2 + X_3)' = (X_1 + X_2)'X_3' = X_1'X_2'X_3'$$

Referring to the OR operation as the logical sum and the AND operation as the logical product, DeMorgan's laws can be stated as

The complement of the product is the sum of the complements.

The complement of the sum is the product of the complements.

To form the complement of an expression containing both OR and AND operations, DeMorgan's laws are applied alternately.

EXAMPLE 1   To find the complement of $(A' + B)C'$, first apply (3–2) and then (3–1).

$$[(A' + B)C']' = (A' + B)' + (C')' = AB' + C$$

EXAMPLE 2

$$
\begin{aligned}
[(AB' + C)D' + E]' &= [(AB' + C)D']'E' &&\text{(by (3–1))}\\
&= [(AB' + C)' + D]E' &&\text{(by (3–2))}\\
&= [(AB')'C' + D]E' &&\text{(by (3–1))}\\
&= [(A' + B)C' + D]E' &&\text{(by (3–2))} \qquad (3\text{–}5)
\end{aligned}
$$

Note that in the final expressions, the complement operation is only applied to single variables.

The inverse of $F = A'B + AB'$ is

$$
\begin{aligned}
F' &= (A'B + AB')' = (A'B)'(AB')' = (A + B')(A' + B)\\
&= AA' + AB + B'A' + BB' = A'B' + AB
\end{aligned}
$$

We will verify that this result is correct by constructing a truth table for F and F':

A B	$A'B$	AB'	$F = A'B + AB'$	$A'B'$	AB	$F' = A'B' + AB$
0 0	0	0	0	1	0	1
0 1	1	0	1	0	0	0
1 0	0	1	1	0	0	0
1 1	0	0	0	0	1	1

In the above table, note that for every combination of values of A and B for which $F = 0$, $F' = 1$; and whenever $F = 1$, $F' = 0$.

We can combine the two forms of DeMorgan's law into a single rule which will enable us to complement an entire expression in one step:

> To form the complement of a Boolean expression, replace each variable with its complement, replace 0 with 1, 1 with 0, + with ·, and · with +.

In applying this rule, we must be careful to preserve the proper hierarchy of operations by adding (or deleting) parentheses as required. In a Boolean expression, the normal hierarchy of operations is that AND is performed before OR, unless parentheses indicate otherwise. For the example of Equation (3–5), applying the "one-step" rule for forming the complement gives

$$[(AB' + C)D' + E]' = [(A' + B)C' + D]E' \qquad (3\text{–}6)$$

     └AND is done   add parentheses here so
      before OR   OR is done before AND

On the left side of Equation (3–6), C is ORed with AB'. Thus, parentheses were added on the right side to assure that C' is ANDed with the complement of AB'.

The one-step rule for applying DeMorgan's laws can be written symbolically as

$$[f(X_1, X_2, \ldots, X_n, 0, 1, +, \cdot)]' = f(X_1', X_2', \ldots, X_n', 1, 0, \cdot, +) \qquad (3\text{–}7)$$

This notation simply means that to form the complement of an expression containing variables $X_1, X_2, \ldots, X_n$, constants 0 and 1, and operations $+$ and $\cdot$, replace X_1 with X_1', X_2 with X_2', $\ldots$, X_n with X_n', 0 with 1, 1 with 0, $+$ with $\cdot$, and $\cdot$ with $+$.

In the following example, again note how parentheses are added and deleted so that the proper hierarchy of operations is preserved after applying the one-step rule.

$$[(a'b + c')(d' + ef') + gh + w]' = [(a + b')c + d(e' + f)](g' + h')w' \quad (3\text{--}8)$$

Verify that the above answer is correct by carrying out the complementation one step at a time.

3.2
Duality

Given a Boolean expression, the dual is formed by replacing AND with OR, OR with AND, 0 with 1, and 1 with 0. Variables and complements are left unchanged. This rule for forming the dual can be summarized as follows:

$$[f(X_1, X_2, \ldots, X_n, 0, 1, +, \cdot)]^D = f(X_1, X_2, \ldots, X_n, 1, 0, \cdot, +) \quad (3\text{--}9)$$

EXAMPLE: If $F = ab' + c + 0 \cdot d'(1 + e)$, then the dual expression is $F^D = (a + b')c(1 + d' + 0 \cdot e)$.

Note that the method of forming the dual is similar to the method for forming the complement except that the variables are *not* complemented when forming the dual. An alternate method for forming the dual of an expression is to first form the complement of the expression and then replace each variable by its complement. In the above example,

$$F' = (a' + b)c'(1 + d + 0 \cdot e')$$

from which

$$F^D = (a + b')c(1 + d' + 0 \cdot e)$$

Given that two Boolean expressions which contain the same variables are equal, the duals are also equal. To show that this is true for expressions F and G, first observe that if $F = G$, then $F' = G'$. If we replace each variable in F' and G' by its complement, this will not destroy the equality since this is equivalent to substituting one variable for another on both sides of the equation. Therefore, we can conclude that if $F = G$, then $F^D = G^D$. This means that if a theorem is true, so is its dual. For example, given that $(X + Y')Y = XY$ (Theorem 11), it follows immediately by duality that $XY' + Y = X + Y$ (Theorem 11D).

3.3
Multiplying Out and Factoring Expressions

Given an expression in product-of-sums form, the corresponding sum-of-products expression can be obtained by "multiplying out" using the two distributive laws:

$$X(Y + Z) = XY + XZ \tag{3-10}$$

$$(X + Y)(X + Z) = X + YZ \tag{3-11}$$

In addition, the following theorem is very useful for factoring and multiplying out:

$$(X + Y)(X' + Z) = XZ + X'Y \tag{3-12}$$

Note that the variable that is paired with X on one side of the equation is paired with X' on the other side, and vice versa.

Proof:

If $X = 0$, (3-12) reduces to $Y(1 + Z) = 0 + 1 \cdot Y$ or $Y = Y$.

If $X = 1$, (3-12) reduces to $(1 + Y)Z = Z + 0 \cdot Y$ or $Z = Z$.

Since the equation is valid for both $X = 0$ and $X = 1$, it is always valid.

The following example illustrates the use of Theorem (3-12) for factoring:

$$AB + A'C = (A + C)(A' + B)$$

Note that the theorem can be applied when we have two terms, one which contains a variable and another which contains its complement.

Theorem (3-12) is very useful for multiplying out expressions. In the following example, we can apply (3-12) because one factor contains the variable Q, and the other factor contains Q':

$$(Q + AB')(C'D + Q') = QC'D + Q'AB'$$

If we simply multiplied out by using the distributive law, we would get four terms instead of two:

$$(Q + AB')(C'D + Q') = QC'D + QQ' + AB'C'D + AB'Q'$$

Since the term $AB'C'D$ is difficult to eliminate, it is much better to use (3-12) instead of the distributive law.

In general, when we multiply out an expression, we should use (3-12) along with (3-10) and (3-11). To avoid generating unnecessary terms when multiplying out, (3-11) and (3-12) should generally be applied before (3-10), and terms should be grouped to expedite their application.

EXAMPLE:

$$(A + B + C')(A + B + D)(A + B + E)(A + D' + E)(A' + C)$$

$$= (A + B + C'D)(A + B + E)[AC + A'(D' + E)]$$

$$= (A + B + C'DE)(AC + A'D' + A'E)$$

$$= AC + ABC + A'BD' + A'BE + A'C'DE \qquad (3\text{–}13)$$

(What theorem was used to eliminate ABC? *Hint:* let $X = AC$.)

In this example, if the ordinary distributive law (3–10) had been used to multiply out the expression by "brute force," 162 terms would have been generated and 158 of these terms would then have to be eliminated.

The same theorems that are useful for multiplying out expressions are useful for factoring. By repeatedly applying (3–10), (3–11), and (3–12) any expression can be converted to a product-of-sums form.

EXAMPLE OF FACTORING:

$$AC + A'BD' + A'BE + A'C'DE$$

$$= \underbrace{AC}_{XZ} + \underbrace{A'}_{X'}(\underbrace{BD' + BE + C'DE}_{Y})$$

$$= (A + BD' + BE + C'DE)(A' + C)$$

$$= [\underbrace{A + C'DE}_{X} + \underbrace{B}_{Y}\underbrace{(D' + E)}_{Z}](A' + C)$$

$$= (A + B + C'DE)(A + C'DE + D' + E)(A' + C)$$

$$= (A + B + C')(A + B + D)(A + B + E)(A + D' + E)(A' + C) \quad (3\text{–}14)$$

This is the same expression we started with in (3–13).

3.4
Exclusive-OR and Equivalence Operations

The *exclusive-OR* operation ($\oplus$) is defined as follows:

$$0 \oplus 0 = 0 \qquad 0 \oplus 1 = 1$$
$$1 \oplus 0 = 1 \qquad 1 \oplus 1 = 0$$

The truth table for $X \oplus Y$ is

X Y	$X \oplus Y$
0 0	0
0 1	1
1 0	1
1 1	0

From this table, we can see that $X \oplus Y = 1$ iff $X = 1$ or $Y = 1$, but *not* both. The ordinary OR operation, which we have previously defined, is sometimes called inclusive OR since $X + Y = 1$ iff $X = 1$ or $Y = 1$, or both.

Exclusive OR can be expressed in terms of AND and OR. Since $X \oplus Y = 1$ iff X is 0 and Y is 1 *or* X is 1 and Y is 0, we can write

$$X \oplus Y = X'Y + XY' \tag{3-15}$$

The first term in (3–15) is 1 if $X = 0$ and $Y = 1$; the second term is 1 if $X = 1$ and $Y = 0$. Alternatively, we can derive Equation (3–15) by observing that $X \oplus Y = 1$ iff $X = 1$ or $Y = 1$ *and* X and Y are not both 1. Thus,

$$X \oplus Y = (X + Y)(XY)' = (X + Y)(X' + Y') = X'Y + XY' \tag{3-16}$$

In (3–16), note that $(XY)' = 1$ if X and Y are not both 1.

We will use the following symbol for an exclusive-OR gate:

The following theorems apply to exclusive-OR:

$$X \oplus 0 = X \tag{3-17}$$
$$X \oplus 1 = X' \tag{3-18}$$
$$X \oplus X = 0 \tag{3-19}$$
$$X \oplus X' = 1 \tag{3-20}$$
$$X \oplus Y = Y \oplus X \quad \text{(commutative law)} \tag{3-21}$$
$$(X \oplus Y) \oplus Z = X \oplus (Y \oplus Z) = X \oplus Y \oplus Z \quad \text{(associative law)} \tag{3-22}$$
$$X(Y \oplus Z) = XY \oplus XZ \quad \text{(distributive law)} \tag{3-23}$$
$$(X \oplus Y)' = X \oplus Y' = X' \oplus Y = XY + X'Y' \tag{3-24}$$

Any of these theorems can be proved by using a truth table or by replacing $X \oplus Y$ by one of the equivalent expressions from Equation (3–16). Proof of the distributive law follows:

$$XY \oplus XZ = XY(XZ)' + (XY)'XZ = XY(X' + Z') + (X' + Y')XZ$$
$$= XYZ' + XY'Z$$
$$= X(YZ' + Y'Z) = X(Y \oplus Z)$$

The *equivalence* operation ($\equiv$) is defined by

$$(0 \equiv 0) = 1 \qquad (0 \equiv 1) = 0 \tag{3-25}$$
$$(1 \equiv 0) = 0 \qquad (1 \equiv 1) = 1$$

The truth table for $X \equiv Y$ is

X Y	$X \equiv Y$
0 0	1
0 1	0
1 0	0
1 1	1

From the definition of equivalence, we see that $(X \equiv Y) = 1$ iff $X = Y$. Since $(X \equiv Y) = 1$ iff $X = Y = 1$ or $X = Y = 0$, we can write

$$(X \equiv Y) = XY + X'Y' \qquad (3\text{--}26)$$

Equivalence is the complement of exclusive-OR:

$$(X \oplus Y)' = (X'Y + XY')' = (X + Y')(X' + Y)$$
$$= XY + X'Y' = (X \equiv Y) \qquad (3\text{--}27)$$

Just as for exclusive-OR, the equivalence operation is commutative and associative.

We will use the following symbol for an equivalence gate:

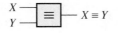

Since equivalence is the complement of exclusive-OR, an alternate symbol for the equivalence gate is an exclusive-OR gate with a complemented output:

$$ X, Y \quad (X \oplus Y)' = (X \equiv Y) $$

The equivalence gate is also called an exclusive-NOR gate.

In order to simplify an expression which contains AND and OR as well as exclusive OR and equivalence, it is usually desirable to first apply (3–15) and (3–26) to eliminate the $\oplus$ and $\equiv$ operations. As an example, we will simplify

$$F = (A'B \equiv C) + (B \oplus AC')$$

By (3–15) and (3–26),

$$F = [(A'B)C + (A'B)'C'] + [B'(AC') + B(AC')']$$
$$= A'BC + (A + B')C' + AB'C' + B(A' + C)$$
$$= B(A'C + A' + C) + C'(A + B' + AB') = B(A' + C) + C'(A + B')$$

When manipulating an expression that contains several exclusive-OR or equivalence operations, it is useful to note that

$$(XY' + X'Y)' = XY + X'Y' \qquad (3\text{--}28)$$

For example,

$$A' \oplus B \oplus C = [A'B' + (A')'B] \oplus C$$
$$= (A'B' + AB)C' + (A'B' + AB)'C \qquad \text{(by (3--15))}$$
$$= (A'B' + AB)C' + (A'B + AB')C \qquad \text{(by (3--28))}$$
$$= A'B'C' + ABC' + A'BC + AB'C$$

3.5
Positive and Negative Logic

Logic gates can be constructed using diodes, transistors, or other switching elements. Several types of logic gate circuits are analyzed in Appendix A. In this section we will discuss the relationship between the voltage levels at the gate inputs and outputs and the logic function performed by the gate.

Under normal operating conditions, the voltage applied to any input terminal of a logic gate is restricted to have one of two nominal values. When the proper input voltages are applied to a logic gate, the voltage at the output terminal will assume one of the two possible nominal values.

Figure 3–1(b)[1] shows the input and output voltages for the logic gate of Fig. 3–1(a). We have assumed that each input and output voltage can have one of two nominal values, 0 volts or $+V$ volts. Since there are three input terminals, eight different combinations of values of input voltages can be applied to the gate. For example, if the input voltages are $e_1 = 0$, $e_2 = +V$ and $e_3 = +V$, the output voltage is $e_o = 0$.

In order to determine the logic function realized by the gate, we must interpret the voltage levels as logic values. Two ways of doing this are:

1. Let $+V$ represent a logic 1 and 0 volts represent a logic 0.
2. Let $+V$ represent a logic 0 and 0 volts represent a logic 1.

These two ways are called positive and negative logic, respectively. In general if we have two voltage levels, positive and negative logic are defined as follows:

Positive logic—the higher of the two voltage levels represents a logic 1 and the lower of the two voltage levels represents a logic 0.

Negative logic—the lower of the two voltage levels represents a logic 1 and the higher of the two voltage levels represents a logic 0.

Both systems are used in practice, so we should be familiar with both.

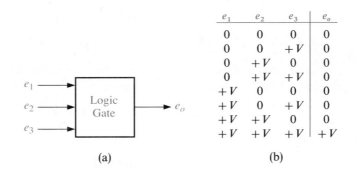

e_1	e_2	e_3	e_o
0	0	0	0
0	0	$+V$	0
0	$+V$	0	0
0	$+V$	$+V$	0
$+V$	0	0	0
$+V$	0	$+V$	0
$+V$	$+V$	0	0
$+V$	$+V$	$+V$	$+V$

Figure 3–1   (a)   (b)

---

[1] See Appendix A.1 for an example of a diode circuit which realizes this table.

If we translate Fig. 3–1(b) according to positive logic (0 volts is a logic 0 and $+V$ volts is a logic 1), we obtain

e_1	e_2	e_3	e_o
0	0	0	0
0	0	1	0
0	1	0	0
0	1	1	0
1	0	0	0
1	0	1	0
1	1	0	0
1	1	1	1

Since e_o is 1 iff e_1, e_2, *and* e_3 are all 1, $e_o = e_1 e_2 e_3$ and the gate performs the AND function for positive logic.

If we translate Fig. 3–1(b) according to negative logic (0 volts is a logic 1 and $+V$ volts is a logic 0), we obtain

e_1	e_2	e_3	e_o
1	1	1	1
1	1	0	1
1	0	1	1
1	0	0	1
0	1	1	1
0	1	0	1
0	0	1	1
0	0	0	0

Since e_o is 1 iff e_1, e_2, *or* e_3 is 1, $e_o = e_1 + e_2 + e_3$, and the gate performs the OR function for negative logic. Note that the function realized for negative logic is the dual of the function for positive logic. Later we will prove that this is true in general for any logic network.

Next, we will consider another type of logic gate which has input and output voltages related as shown in Table 3–1(a).[2]

Table 3–1

(a) voltages				(b) positive logic				(c) negative logic			
e_1	e_2	e_3	e_o	e_1	e_2	e_3	e_o	e_1	e_2	e_3	e_o
0	0	0	0	0	0	0	0	1	1	1	1
0	0	$+V$	$+V$	0	0	1	1	1	1	0	0
0	$+V$	0	$+V$	0	1	0	1	1	0	1	0
0	$+V$	$+V$	$+V$	0	1	1	1	1	0	0	0
$+V$	0	0	$+V$	1	0	0	1	0	1	1	0
$+V$	0	$+V$	$+V$	1	0	1	1	0	1	0	0
$+V$	$+V$	0	$+V$	1	1	0	1	0	0	1	0
$+V$	$+V$	$+V$	$+V$	1	1	1	1	0	0	0	0

[2] See Appendix A.1 for an example of a diode circuit which realizes this table.

Tables 3–1(b) and 3–1(c) show the results when Table 3–1(a) is translated according to positive and negative logic, respectively. For positive logic, e_o is 1 iff e_1, e_2, or e_3 is 1 so $e_o = e_1 + e_2 + e_3$, and Table 3–1(a) represents an OR gate. For negative logic, $e_o = e_1 e_2 e_3$, and Table 3–1(a) represents an AND gate.

If we know the function realized by a switching network for positive logic, we can easily determine the function realized by the same network for negative logic by applying the *negative logic theorem:*

> If a given combinational network realizes a function F when input and output variables are defined according to positive logic, the same network will realize the dual function (F^D) when the input and output variables are defined according to negative logic.

EXAMPLE:

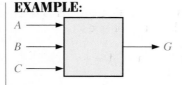

Input and output voltage levels are 0 and $+5$ volts. If for positive logic (logic $0 = 0$ volts, logic $1 = 5$ volts) the network output is

$$G = ABC' + A'B'C$$

then for negative logic (logic $1 = 0$ volts, logic $0 = 5$ volts) the network output is

$$G = (A + B + C')(A' + B' + C)$$

For a given set of input *voltages,* the output *voltage* is the same in both cases. It is just the logical interpretation of these voltages that differs in the two cases.

Proof: Consider the following network where positive logic is used for all variables:

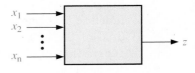

Now relabel the inputs and output using negative logic variables.

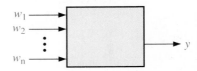

For a given input voltage applied to terminal i, if $x_i = 1$, $w_i = 0$ and if $x_i = 0$, $w_i = 1$. Therefore, $w_i = x_i'$ and similarly, $y = z'$. For the positive logic variables, let $z = f(x_1, x_2, \ldots, x_n)$. Then for the negative logic variables,

$$y' = f(w_1', w_2', \ldots, w_n')$$

Therefore,

$$y = [f(w_1', w_2', \ldots, w_n')]' = f^D(w_1, w_2, \ldots, w_n)$$

since the dual of a function can be formed by complementing a function and then replacing all variables by their complements. If, as was done in the example, we use the same variable names for both positive and negative logic, then for negative logic,

$$z = [f(x_1', x_2', \ldots, x_n')]' = f^D(x_1, x_2, \ldots, x_n)$$

By applying the negative logic theorem, we can see that a logic circuit which realizes an AND gate for positive logic realizes an OR gate for negative logic and vice versa. Since the dual of exclusive OR is

$$(x \oplus y)^D = (x'y + xy')^D = (x' + y)(x + y') = x'y' + xy = (x \equiv y) \quad (3\text{-}29)$$

a gate which realizes exclusive OR for positive logic realizes equivalence for negative logic.

PROGRAMMED EXERCISE 3.1

Cover the answers to this exercise with a sheet of paper and slide it down as you check your answers. *Write* your answer in the space provided before looking at the correct answer.

The following expression is to be multiplied out to form a sum of products:

$$(A + B + C')(A' + B' + D)(A' + C + D')(A + C' + D)$$

First, find a pair of sum terms which have two literals in common and apply the second distributive law. Also apply the same law to the other pair of terms.

Answer: $(A + C' + BD)[A' + (B' + D)(C + D')]$

(*Note:* This answer was obtained by using $(X + Y)(X + Z) = X + YZ$.)

Next, find a pair of sum terms which have a variable in one and its complement in the other. Use the appropriate theorem to multiply these sum terms together without introducing any redundant terms. Apply the same theorem a second time.

Answer: $(A + C' + BD)(A' + B'D' + CD) = A(B'D' + CD) + A'(C' + BD)$
or $A(B' + D)(C + D') + A'(C' + BD) = A(B'D' + CD) + A'(C' + BD)$

(*Note:* This answer was obtained using $(X + Y)(X' + Z) = XZ + X'Y$.)

Complete the problem by multiplying out using the ordinary distributive law.

Final answer: $AB'D' + ACD + A'C' + A'BD$

PROGRAMMED EXERCISE 3.2

Cover the answers to this exercise with a sheet of paper and slide it down as you check your answers. *Write* your answer in the space provided before looking at the correct answer.

The following expression is to be factored to form a product of sums:

$$WXY' + W'X'Z + WY'Z + W'YZ'$$

First, factor as far as you can using the ordinary distributive law.

Answer: $WY'(X + Z) + W'(X'Z + YZ')$

Next, factor further by using a theorem which involves a variable and its complement. Apply this theorem twice.

Answer: $(W + X'Z + YZ')[W' + Y'(X + Z)]$
$$= [W + (X' + Z')(Y + Z)][W' + Y'(X + Z)]$$

or $WY'(X + Z) + W'(X' + Z')(Y + Z)$
$$= [W + (X' + Z')(Y + Z)][W' + Y'(X + Z)]$$

(*Note:*   This answer was obtained by using $AB + A'C = (A + C)(A' + B)$.)

Now, complete the factoring by using the second distributive law.

Final answer: $(W + X' + Z')(W + Y + Z)(W' + Y')(W' + X + Z)$

PROBLEMS

3.3   Find the complement of each of the following expressions (do not simplify the result):

(a) $wx(y'z + yz') + w'x'(y' + z)(y + z')$

(b) $w + (ab + c')(d'e + 1) + g(h' + 0)$

(c) $[ab' + d(e'f' + g'h)][a' + bcd(e' + f'g)]$

3.4   Repeat Problem 3.3 for:
(a) $(a'b + 1)(cd + e') + f(g' + 0) + h$
(b) $a'b'(c + d')(c' + d) + ab(c'd + cd')$
(c) $[abc(d' + e'f) + g][a'g + c(d'e' + f'h)]$

3.5   Find the dual of each of the expressions in Problem 3.3 (do not simplify).

3.6   Find the dual of each of the expressions in Problem 3.4 (do not simplify).

3.7   Find the dual and the complement of the following expressions (do not simplify):
(a) $F = [(AB + C'D + E' + 0)(A' + BC) + 1(D'E + B)](C + E')$
(b) $F = (A' + B \cdot 0 + 1)[1 \cdot (AB' + C)D + E \cdot 0] + A'B \cdot 1$
(c) $F = [AB'(C + DE') \cdot 0] + AC(1 + CD + B'E)$

3.8   Find the dual and the complement of the following expressions (do not simplify):
(a) $F = (1 + AB + C'D)AE + [0 \cdot C'E(A + BD')]$
(b) $F = [A \cdot 0 + B(C + DE') \cdot 1](D' + E \cdot 0 + 1) + D'E \cdot 1$
(c) $F = [1 \cdot (A'B + C) + (D' + CE)(B' + CD + AE' + 0)](B' + E)$

3.9   (a) Multiply out to obtain a sum of four terms:

$$(A' + B + D)(A + C)(A + B' + D)(A' + C' + D')(A' + B)$$

   (*Hint:* Apply $X(X + Y) = X$ to eliminate a term before you start multiplying.)
   (b) Multiply out to obtain a sum of four terms:

$$(B' + C' + D')(A' + B' + C')(A + B + C)(B + C + D)$$

   (c) Multiply out to obtain a sum of three terms:

$$(A' + C' + D)(A' + C)(B + C' + D')(A' + B + C)(C + D)$$

3.10 Repeat Problem 3.9 for:
(a) $(A' + B' + C')(A + C + D')(A + B)(A' + D)(A' + C + D)$
(b) $(A' + B' + C)(A + D')(A' + B + D')(A + B)(A + C + D')$
(c) $(A + B + C)(A' + B' + D')(A' + B' + C')(A + B + D)$

3.11 (a) Factor to obtain a product of four terms: $A'B'C' + A'D' + ABC' + AD$
(b) Factor to obtain a product of four terms: $ACD + A'B'D + A'BC + AC'D'$
(c) Factor to obtain a product of four terms: $A'C'D + AB'D' + A'CD' + BD$

3.12 (a) Factor to obtain a product of four terms: $A'B'C + AC'D + ABC + BC'D'$
(b) Factor to obtain a product of four terms: $AB + A'B' + B'C'D' + BCD'$
(c) Factor to obtain a product of four terms: $AB + A'B'C + B'C'D + BC'D'$

3.13 Simplify each of the following expressions:
(a) $AB' + A'B'D + A'CD'$
(b) $(A' + C' + D)(A + B' + C')(B + C')$
(c) $AB' + AB'CD + ABC'D'$
(d) $CE(A' + B + C' + E')(B + C' + D + E')(A + B + C' + E')$

3.14 Simplify each of the following expressions:
(a) $ABCD' + A'B'CD + CD'$
(b) $AB'C' + CD' + BC'D'$
(c) $(A + B')(A' + B' + D)(B' + C + D')$
(d) $(A' + B + C' + D)(A' + C' + D + E)(A' + C' + D + E')AC$

3.15   Find F and G and simplify:
(a)

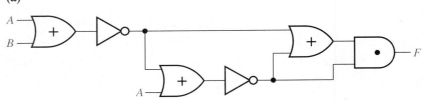

(b)

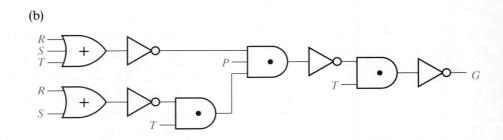

3.16   Convert the following expression to product-of-sums form:
$$WX'Y + WXZ' + Y'Z$$

3.17   Convert the following expression to sum-of-products form:
$$(A' + B)(A' + B' + C)(B + D + E)(A + B' + E')$$

3.18   Write an expression for F and simplify.

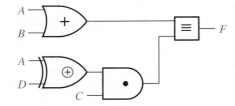

3.19   Answer the following:
(a) Is the following distributive law valid? $A \oplus BC = (A \oplus B)(A \oplus C)$
Prove your answer.
(b) State and prove the associative law for the equivalence operation.

3.20   Simplify to obtain a sum of two terms:
(a) $[A \oplus (B + C')][(A + C) \equiv B'C]$
(b) $(X \oplus Y)(X \oplus Z) + (X \oplus Y)(Y \oplus Z)$

3.21   (a) Show that $x \oplus y = (x \equiv y)'$.
(b) Realize $a'b'c' + a'bc + ab'c + abc'$ using only 2-input equivalence gates.

3.22   Find an expression for F which uses only the exclusive-OR and complement operations.
$$F = a'b'c' + abc' + a'bc + ab'c$$

3.23 The following table shows the input and output voltages for a 2-input logic gate circuit.
(a) Translate this table to a truth table using positive logic. What logic function is realized for positive logic?
(b) Translate this table to a truth table using negative logic. What logic function is realized for negative logic?

e_1	e_2	e_0
−5	−5	+5
−5	+5	−5
+5	−5	−5
+5	+5	+5

3.24 Repeat Problem 3.23 for the following table:

e_1	e_2	e_0
+5	+5	−5
+5	−5	+5
−5	+5	+5
−5	−5	−5

3.25 The following table shows the input and output voltages for a 3-input logic gate circuit.
(a) If +5 volts is a logic 1, and −5 volts is a logic 0, what logic operation does the gate realize?
(b) If −5 volts is a logic 1, and +5 volts is a logic 0, what logic operation does the gate realize?

e_1	e_2	e_3	e_0
+5	+5	+5	+5
+5	+5	−5	+5
+5	−5	+5	+5
+5	−5	−5	+5
−5	+5	+5	+5
−5	+5	−5	+5
−5	−5	+5	+5
−5	−5	−5	−5

4

Algebraic Simplification

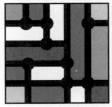

OBJECTIVES

1. Use the consensus theorem to delete terms from and add terms to a switching expression.

2. Simplify a switching expression using the laws and theorems of Boolean algebra.

3. Given an equation, prove algebraically that it is valid or show that it is not valid.

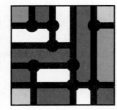

STUDY GUIDE

1. Study Section 4.1, *The Consensus Theorem*. The consensus theorem is an important method for simplifying switching functions.

   (a) In each of the following expressions, find the consensus term and eliminate it:

   $$abc'd + a'be + bc'de$$
   $$(a' + b + c)(a + d)(b + c + d)$$
   $$ab'c + a'bd + bcd' + a'bc$$

   (b) Eliminate two terms from the following expression by applying the consensus theorem:

   $$A'B'C + BC'D' + A'CD + AB'D' + BCD + AC'D'$$

   (*Hint:* First compare the first term with each of the remaining terms to see if a consensus exists, then compare the second term with each of the remaining terms, etc.)

   (c) Study the example given in Equations (4–3) and (4–4) carefully. Now let us start with the four-term form of the expression (Equation 4–3):

   $$A'C'D + A'BD + ABC + ACD'$$

   Can this be reduced directly to three terms by application of the consensus theorem? Before we can reduce the above expression, we must add another term. Which term can be added by applying the consensus theorem?

   Add this term, and then reduce the expression to three terms. After this reduction can the term which was added be removed? Why not?

   (d) Eliminate two terms from the following expression by applying the dual consensus theorem:

   $$(a' + c' + d)(a' + b + c)(a + b + d)(a' + b + d)(b + c' + d)$$

   Use brackets to indicate how you formed the consensus terms. (*Hint:* First find the consensus of the first two terms and eliminate it.)

   (e) Derive Theorem (3–12) by using the consensus theorem.

   (f) Work Programmed Exercise 4.1. Then work Problems 4.4 and 4.11.

2. Study Section 4.2, *Algebraic Simplification of Switching Expressions.*

   (a) What theorems are used for:

   Combining terms?

   Eliminating terms?

   Eliminating literals?

   Adding redundant terms?

   Factoring or multiplying out?

   (b) Note that in the example of Equation (4–8), the redundant term WZ' was added and then was eliminated later after it had been used to eliminate another term. Why was it possible to eliminate WZ' in this example?

   If a term has been added by the consensus theorem, it may not always be possible to eliminate the term later by the consensus theorem. Why?

   (c) You will need considerable practice to develop skill in simplifying switching expressions. Work through Programmed Exercises 4.2 and 4.3.

   (d) Work Problems 4.7, 4.12, and 4.14.

   (e) When simplifying an expression using Boolean algebra, two frequently asked questions are:
   (1) Where do I begin?
   (2) How do I know when I am finished?
   In answer to (1), it is generally best to try simple techniques such as combining terms or eliminating terms and literals before trying more complicated things like using the consensus theorem or adding redundant terms. Question (2) is generally difficult to answer since it may be impossible to simplify some expressions without first adding redundant terms. We will usually tell you how many terms to expect in the minimum solution so that you won't have to waste time trying to simplify an expression which is already minimized. In Units 6 and 7, you will learn systematic techniques which will guarantee finding the minimum solution.

3. Study Section 4.3, *Proving Validity of an Equation.*

   (a) When attempting to prove that an equation is valid, is it permissible to add the same expression to both sides? Explain.

   (b) Work Problem 4.18.

   (c) Show that (4–14) and (4–15) are true by considering both $x = 0$ and $x = 1$.

(d) Given that $a'(b + d') = a'(b + e')$, the following "proof" shows that $d = e$:

$$a'(b + d') = a'(b + e')$$
$$a + b'd = a + b'e$$
$$b'd = b'e$$
$$d = e$$

State two things that are wrong with the "proof." Give a set of values for a, b, d, and e that demonstrates that the result is incorrect.

4. Reread the objectives of this unit. When you are satisfied that you can meet the objectives, take the readiness test.

Algebraic Simplification

4.1
The Consensus Theorem

The consensus theorem is very useful in simplifying Boolean expressions. Given an expression of the form $XY + X'Z + YZ$ the term YZ is redundant and can be eliminated to form the equivalent expression $XY + X'Z$.

The term which was eliminated is referred to as the "consensus term." Given a pair of terms for which a variable appears in one term and the complement of that variable in another, the consensus term is formed by multiplying the two original terms together, leaving out the selected variable and its complement. For example, the consensus of ab and $a'c$ is bc; the consensus of abd and $b'de'$ is $(ad)(de') = ade'$. The consensus of terms $ab'd$ and $a'bd'$ is 0.

The consensus theorem can be stated as follows:

$$XY + X'Z + YZ = XY + X'Z \qquad (4\text{--}1)$$

Proof:

$$XY + X'Z + YZ = XY + X'Z + (X + X')YZ$$
$$= (XY + XYZ) + (X'Z + X'YZ)$$
$$= XY(1 + Z) + X'Z(1 + Y) = XY + X'Z$$

The consensus theorem can be used to eliminate redundant terms from Boolean expressions. For example, in the following expression, $b'c$ is the consensus of $a'b'$ and ac, and ab is the consensus of ac and bc', so both consensus terms can be eliminated:

$$a'b' + ac + bc' + b'c + ab = a'b' + ac + bc'$$

The brackets indicate how the consensus terms are formed.

The dual form of the consensus theorem is

$$(X + Y)(X' + Z)(Y + Z) = (X + Y)(X' + Z) \qquad (4\text{--}2)$$

Note again that the key to recognizing the consensus term is to first find a pair of terms, one of which contains a variable and the other its complement. In this case, the consensus is formed by adding this pair of terms together leaving out the selected variable and its complement. In the following expression, $(a + b + d')$ is a consensus term and can be eliminated by using the dual consensus theorem:

$$(a + b + c')(\overline{a + b + d'})(b + c + d') = (a + b + c')(b + c + d')$$

The final result obtained by application of the consensus theorem may depend on the order in which terms are eliminated.

EXAMPLE:

$$A'C'D + A'BD + BCD + ABC + ACD' \qquad (4\text{--}3)$$

First we eliminate BCD as shown. (Why can it be eliminated?)

Now that BCD has been eliminated, it is no longer there, and it *cannot* be used to eliminate another term. Checking all pairs of terms shows that no additional terms can be eliminated by the consensus theorem.

Now we start over again:

$$A'C'D + A'BD + BCD + ABC + ACD' \qquad (4\text{--}4)$$

This time, we do not eliminate BCD; instead we eliminate *two* other terms by the consensus theorem. After doing this, observe that BCD can no longer be eliminated. Note that the expression reduces to four terms if BCD is eliminated first, but that it can be reduced to three terms if BCD is not eliminated.

Sometimes it is impossible to directly reduce an expression to a minimum number of terms by simply eliminating terms. It may be necessary to first add a term using the consensus theorem and *then* use the added term to eliminate other terms. For example, consider the expression

$$F = ABCD + B'CDE + A'B' + BCE'$$

If we compare every pair of terms to see if a consensus term can be formed, we find that the only consensus terms are $ACDE$ (from $ABCD$ and $B'CDE$) and $A'CE'$ (from $A'B'$ and BCE'). Since neither of these consensus terms appears in the original expression, we cannot directly eliminate any terms using the consensus theorem. However, if we first add the consensus term $ACDE$ to F we get

$$F = ABCD + B'CDE + A'B' + BCE' + ACDE$$

Then we can eliminate $ABCD$ and $B'CDE$ using the consensus theorem, and F

reduces to

$$F = A'B' + BCE' + ACDE$$

The term $ACDE$ is no longer redundant and cannot be eliminated from the final expression.

4.2
Algebraic Simplification of Switching Expressions

In this section we will apply the theorems of Boolean algebra to simplifying switching expressions. This is important because simplifying an expression reduces the cost of realizing the expression using gates. Later we will learn graphical methods for simplifying switching functions, but we will learn algebraic methods first. In addition to multiplying out and factoring, three basic ways of simplifying switching functions are combining terms, eliminating terms, and eliminating literals.

1. *Combining terms.* Use the theorem $XY + XY' = X$ to combine two terms.

    EXAMPLE:

    $$abc'd' + abcd' = abd' \quad [X = abd', Y = c] \qquad (4\text{--}5)$$

    When combining terms by this theorem as above, the two terms to be combined should contain exactly the same variables, and exactly one of the variables should appear complemented in one term and not in the other. Since $X + X = X$, a given term may be duplicated and combined with two or more other terms.

    EXAMPLE:

    $$ab'c + abc + a'bc = ab'c + abc + abc + a'bc = ac + bc$$

    The theorem still can be used, of course, when X and Y are replaced with more complicated expressions.

    EXAMPLE:

    $$(a + bc)(d + e') + a'(b' + c')(d + e') = d + e'$$
    $$[X = d + e', Y = a + bc, Y' = a'(b' + c')]$$

2. *Eliminating terms.* Use the theorem $X + XY = X$ to eliminate redundant terms if possible; then try to apply the consensus theorem ($XY + X'Z + YZ = XY + X'Z$) to eliminate any consensus terms.

    EXAMPLE:

    $$a'b + a'bc = a'b \quad [X = a'b]$$
    $$a'bc' + bcd + a'bd = a'bc' + bcd \quad [X = c, Y = bd, Z = a'b] \quad (4\text{--}6)$$

3. *Eliminating literals.* Use the theorem $X + X'Y = X + Y$ to eliminate redundant literals. Simple factoring may be necessary before the theorem is applied.

EXAMPLE:

$$
\begin{aligned}
A'B + A'B'C'D' + ABCD' &= A'(B + B'C'D') + ABCD' \\
&= A'(B + C'D') + ABCD' \\
&= B(A' + ACD') + A'C'D' \\
&= B(A' + CD') + A'C'D' \\
&= A'B + BCD' + A'C'D' \qquad (4\text{--}7)
\end{aligned}
$$

The expression obtained after applying 1, 2, and 3 above will not necessarily have a minimum number of terms or a minimum number of literals. If it does not, and no further simplification can be made using 1, 2, and 3, deliberate introduction of redundant terms may be necessary before further simplification can be made.

4. *Adding redundant terms.* Redundant terms can be introduced in several ways such as adding xx', multiplying by $(x + x')$, adding yz to $xy + x'z$, or adding xy to x. When possible, the terms added should be chosen so that they will combine with or eliminate other terms.

EXAMPLE:

$$
\begin{aligned}
&WX + XY + X'Z' + WY'Z' \quad \text{(add } WZ' \text{ by consensus theorem)} \\
&= WX + XY + X'Z' + WY'Z' + WZ' \quad \text{(eliminate } WY'Z') \\
&= WX + XY + X'Z' + WZ' \quad \text{(eliminate } WZ') \\
&= WX + XY + X'Z' \qquad (4\text{--}8)
\end{aligned}
$$

The following comprehensive example illustrates the use of all four methods:

$$
\begin{aligned}
&\underbrace{A'B'C'D' + A'BC'D'}_{①\ A'C'D'} + A'BD + \underbrace{A'BC'D}_{②} + ABCD + ACD' + B'CD' \\
&= A'C'D' + \underbrace{BD(A' + AC)}_{③} + ACD' + B'CD' \\
&= A'C'D' + A'BD + \underbrace{BCD + ACD'}_{+ ABC\ ④} + B'CD' \\
&= A'C'D' + A'BD + \underbrace{BCD + ACD' + \overbrace{B'CD' + ABC}^{\text{consensus } ACD'}}_{\text{consensus } BCD} \\
&= A'C'D' + A'BD + B'CD' + ABC \qquad (4\text{--}9)
\end{aligned}
$$

What theorems were used in steps 1, 2, 3, and 4?

If the simplified expression is to be left in a product-of-sums form instead of a sum-of-products form, the duals of the theorems used above should be applied.

EXAMPLE:

$$\underbrace{(A' + B' + C')(A' + B' + C)}_{① (A' + B')}(B' + C)(A + C)\underbrace{(A + B + C)}_{②}$$

$$= (A' + B')\underbrace{(B' + C)(A + C)}_{③} = (A' + B')(A + C) \qquad (4\text{--}10)$$

What theorems were used in steps 1, 2, and 3?

In general, there is no easy way of determining when a Boolean expression has a minimum number of terms or a minimum number of literals. Systematic methods for finding minimum sum-of-products and minimum product-of-sums expressions will be discussed in Units 6 and 7.

4.3
Proving Validity of an Equation

Often we will need to determine if an equation is valid for all combinations of values of the variables. Several methods can be used to determine if an equation is valid:

1. Construct a truth table and evaluate both sides of the equation for all combinations of values of the variables. (This method is rather tedious if the number of variables is large, and it certainly is not very elegant.)
2. Manipulate one side of the equation by applying various theorems until it is identical with the other side.
3. Reduce both sides of the equation independently to the same expression.
4. It is permissible to perform the same operation on both sides of the equation provided that the operation is reversible. For example, it is all right to complement both sides of the equation, but it is *not* permissible to multiply both sides of the equation by the same expression. (Multiplication is not reversible since division is not defined for Boolean algebra.) Similarly, it is not permissible to add the same term to both sides of the equation since subtraction is not defined for Boolean algebra.

To prove that an equation is *not* valid, it is sufficient to show one combination of values of the variables for which the two sides of the equation have different values. When using methods 2 or 3 above to prove that an equation is valid, a useful strategy is to:

1. First reduce both sides to a sum of products (or a product of sums).
2. Compare the two sides of the equation to see how they differ.
3. Then try to add terms to one side of the equation that are present on the other side.

4. Finally, try to eliminate terms from one side that are not present on the other.

Whatever method is used, frequently compare both sides of the equation and let the difference between them serve as a guide as to what steps to take next.

EXAMPLE 1   Show that

$$A'BD' + BCD + ABC' + AB'D = BC'D' + AD + A'BC$$

Starting with the left side, we first add consensus terms, then combine terms and finally eliminate terms by the consensus theorem.

$A'BD' + BCD + ABC' + AB'D$
$= A'BD' + BCD + ABC' + AB'D + BC'D' + A'BC + ABD$

(add consensus of $A'BD'$ and ABC')
  (add consensus of $A'BD'$ and BCD)
    (add consensus of BCD and ABC')

$= AD + A'BD' + BCD + ABC' + BC'D' + A'BC = BC'D' + AD + A'BC$ (4–11)

(eliminate consensus of $BC'D'$ and AD)
(eliminate consensus of AD and $A'BC$)
(eliminate consensus of $BC'D'$ and $A'BC$)

EXAMPLE 2   Show that the following equation is valid:

$$A'BC'D + (A' + BC)(A + C'D') + BC'D + A'BC'$$
$$= ABCD + A'C'D' + ABD + ABCD' + BC'D$$

First, we will reduce the left side:

$A'BC'D + (A' + BC)(A + C'D') + BC'D + A'BC'$

(eliminate $A'BC'D$ using (2–13))

$= (A' + BC)(A + C'D') + BC'D + A'BC'$

(multiply out using (3–12))

$= ABC + A'C'D' + BC'D + A'BC'$

(eliminate $A'BC'$ by consensus)

$= ABC + A'C'D' + BC'D$

Now we will reduce the right side:

(combine $ABCD$ and $ABCD'$) $= ABCD + A'C'D' + ABD + ABCD' + BC'D$
(eliminate ABD by consensus) $= ABC + A'C'D' + ABD + BC'D$
$= ABC + A'C'D' + BC'D$

Since both sides of the original equation were independently reduced to the same expression, the original equation is valid.

As we have previously observed, some of the theorems of Boolean algebra are not true for ordinary algebra. Similarly, some of the theorems of ordinary algebra are not true for Boolean algebra. Consider, for example, the cancellation law for ordinary algebra:

$$\text{If} \quad x + y = x + z, \qquad \text{then} \quad y = z \tag{4–12}$$

The cancellation law is *not* true for Boolean algebra. We will demonstrate this by constructing a counterexample in which $x + y = x + z$ but $y \neq z$. Let $x = 1$, $y = 0$, $z = 1$. Then

$$1 + 0 = 1 + 1 \qquad \text{but} \quad 0 \neq 1$$

In ordinary algebra, the cancellation law for multiplication is

$$\text{if} \quad xy = xz, \qquad \text{then} \quad y = z \tag{4–13}$$

This law is valid provided $x \neq 0$.

In Boolean algebra, the cancellation law for multiplication is also not valid when $x = 0$. (Let $x = 0$, $y = 0$, $z = 1$; then $0 \cdot 0 = 0 \cdot 1$, but $0 \neq 1$). Since $x = 0$ about half of the time in switching algebra, the cancellation law for multiplication cannot be used.

Even though Statements (4–12) and (4–13) are generally false for Boolean algebra, the converses

$$\text{If} \quad y = z, \qquad \text{then} \quad x + y = x + z \tag{4–14}$$

$$\text{If} \quad y = z, \qquad \text{then} \qquad xy = xz \tag{4–15}$$

are true. Thus, we see that although adding the same term to both sides of a Boolean equation leads to a valid equation, the reverse operation of canceling or subtracting a term from both sides generally does not lead to a valid equation. Similarly, multiplying both sides of a Boolean equation by the same term leads to a valid equation, but not conversely. When we are attempting to prove that an equation is valid, it is *not* permissible to add the same expression to both sides of the equation or to multiply both sides by the same expression, because these operations are not reversible.

PROGRAMMED EXERCISE 4.1

Cover the answers to this exercise with a sheet of paper and slide it down as you check your answers. *Write* your answer in the space provided before looking at the correct answer.

The following expression is to be simplified using the consensus theorem:

$$AC' + AB'D + A'B'C + A'CD' + B'C'D'$$

First, find all of the consensus terms by checking all pairs of terms.

Answer: The consensus terms are indicated below.

$$AC' + AB'D + A'B'C + A'CD' + B'C'D'$$

with annotations: $A'B'D'$, $B'CD$, $A'B'D'$, $AB'C'$

Can the original expression be simplified by direct application of the consensus theorem?

Answer: No, since none of the consensus terms appear in the original expression.

Now add the consensus term $B'CD$ to the original expression. Compare the added term with each of the original terms to see if any consensus exists. Eliminate as many of the original terms as you can.

Answer:

$$AC' + \cancel{AB'D} + \cancel{A'B'C} + A'CD' + B'C'D' + B'CD$$

with $(AB'D)$ over $A'CD' + B'C'D' + B'CD$ and $(A'B'C)$ below

Now that we have eliminated two terms, can $B'CD$ also be eliminated? What is the final reduced expression?

Answer: No, since the terms used to form $B'CD$ are gone. Final answer is

$$AC' + A'CD' + B'C'D' + B'CD$$

PROGRAMMED EXERCISE 4.2

Keep the answers to this exercise covered with a sheet of paper and slide it down as you check your answers.

Problem: The following expression is to be simplified

$$ab'cd'e + acd + acf'gh' + abcd'e + acde' + e'h'$$

State a theorem which can be used to combine a pair of terms and apply it to combine two of the terms in the above expression.

Answer: Apply $XY + XY' = X$ to the terms $ab'cd'e$ and $abcd'e$, which reduces the expression to

$$acd'e + acd + acf'gh' + acde' + e'h'$$

Now state a theorem (other than the consensus theorem) which can be used to eliminate terms and apply it to eliminate a term in the above expression.

Answer: Apply $X + XY = X$ to eliminate $acde'$. (What term corresponds to X?) The result is

$$acd'e + acd + acf'gh' + e'h'$$

Now state a theorem that can be used to eliminate literals, and apply it to eliminate a literal from one of the terms in the above expression. (*Hint:* It may be necessary to factor out some common variables from a pair of terms before the theorem can be applied.)

Answer: Use $X + X'Y = X + Y$ to eliminate a literal from $acd'e$. To do this, first factor ac out of the first two terms: $acd'e + acd = ac(d + d'e)$. After eliminating d', the resulting expression is

$$ace + acd + acf'gh' + e'h'$$

(a) Can any term be eliminated from this expression by direct application of the consensus theorem?
(b) If not, add a redundant term using the consensus theorem, and use this redundant term to eliminate one of the other terms.
(c) Finally, reduce your expression to three terms.

Answer:

(a) No
(b) Add the consensus of ace and $e'h'$:

$$ace + acd + acf'gh' + e'h' + ach'$$

Now eliminate $acf'gh'$ (by $X + XY = X$)

$$ace + acd + e'h' + ach'$$

(c) Now eliminate ach' by the consensus theorem. The final answer is

$$ace + acd + e'h'$$

PROGRAMMED EXERCISE 4.3

Keep the answers to this exercise covered with a sheet of paper and slide it down as you check your answers.

$$Z = (A + C' + F' + G)(A + C' + F + G)(A + B + C' + D' + G)$$
$$(A + C + E + G)(A' + B + G)(B + C' + F + G)$$

The above is to be simplified to the form

$$(X + X + X)(X + X + X)(X + X + X)$$

where each X represents a literal.

State a theorem which can be used to combine the first two sum terms of Z and apply it. (*Hint:* The two sum terms differ in only one variable.)

Answer: $(X + Y)(X + Y') = X$
$$Z = (A + C' + G)(A + B + C' + D' + G)(A + C + E + G)(A' + B + G)(B + C' + F + G)$$

Now state a theorem (other than the consensus theorem) which can be used to eliminate a sum term and apply it to the above expression.

Answer: $X(X + Y) = X$
$$Z = (A + C' + G)(A + C + E + G)(A' + B + G)(B + C' + F + G)$$

Next, eliminate one literal from the second term, leaving the expression otherwise unchanged. (*Hint:* This cannot be done by direct application of one theorem; it will be necessary to partially multiply out the first two sum terms before eliminating the literal.)

Answer:

$$(A + C' + G)(A + C + E + G) = A + G + C'(C + E) = A + G + C'E$$

Therefore,

$$Z = (A + C' + G)(A + E + G)(A' + B + G)(B + C' + F + G)$$

(a) Can any term be eliminated from this expression by direct application of the consensus theorem?
(b) If not, add a redundant sum term using the consensus theorem, and use this redundant term to eliminate one of the other terms.
(c) Finally, reduce your expression to a product of three sum terms.

Answer:

(a) No
(b) Add $B + C' + G$ (consensus of $A + C' + G$ and $A' + B + G$).
    Use $X(X + Y) = X$, where $X = B + C' + G$, to eliminate $B + C' + F + G$.
(c) Now eliminate $B + C' + G$ by consensus. The final answer is

$$Z = (A + C' + G)(A + E + G)(A' + B + G)$$

PROBLEMS

4.4   Simplify each of the following expressions using only the consensus theorem (or its dual):
(a) $BC'D' + ABC' + AC'D + AB'D + A'BD'$ (reduce to three terms)
(b) $W'Y' + WYZ + XY'Z + WX'Y$ (reduce to three terms)
(c) $(B + C + D)(A + B + C)(A' + C + D)(B' + C' + D')$

4.5   Repeat Problem 4.4 for:
(a) $W'XY + WXZ + WY'Z + W'Z'$
(b) $A'BC' + BC'D' + A'CD + B'CD + A'BD$
(c) $(A + B + C)(B + C' + D)(A + B + D)(A' + B' + D')$

4.6   Simplify the following expressions using only the consensus theorem or its dual:
(a) $WX'Y' + W'YZ' + W'XZ' + WY'Z'$
(b) $A'B'C + ABD + A'CDE + BCDE + A'BDE$
(c) $(A + B + C)(A + C' + D')(B' + C' + D')(C + D)$
(d) $(W + X')(Y + Z')(W + Y)(X + Y)(W + Z)(X + Z)$

4.7 Simplify each of the following expressions:
(a) $xy + x'yz' + yz$
(b) $(xy' + z)(x + y')z$
(c) $xy' + z + (x' + y)z'$
(d) $a'd(b' + c) + a'd(b + c') + (b' + c)(b + c')$
(e) $w'x' + x'y' + yz + w'z'$
(f) $A'BCD + A'BC'D + B'EF + CDE'G + A'DEF + A'B'EF$ (reduce to a sum of three terms)
(g) $[(a' + d' + b'c)(b + d + ac')]' + b'c'd' + a'c'd$ (reduce to three terms)

4.8 Simplify each of the following expressions:
(a) $a'(b' + c) + a + bc'$
(b) $ab + a'bc' + bc$
(c) $z(x' + y)(x'y + z)$
(d) $w'x'(y' + z) + wx'(y + z') + (y' + z)(y + z')$
(e) $ab + a'c' + b'd' + c'd'$ (reduce to a sum of three terms)
(f) $w'x'y' + w'xz' + [(x + y + w'z)(x' + z' + wy')]'$ (reduce to a sum of three terms)
(g) $ABC' + ABC'D' + ABD'E + A'EFG + CD'EG + CD'EG'$ (reduce to three terms)

4.9 Simplify each of the following expressions:
(a) $F = AB + AC + BC + B'C'$
(b) $F = AB + ABC + BCD' + AB'D + A'CD' + A'BCD$ (reduce to three terms)
(c) $F = AB' + A'BC + AB'C' + A'BD' + A'B'D' + BCD$ (reduce to three terms)

4.10 Simplify to a sum of three terms:
(a) $A'C'D' + AC' + BCD + A'CD' + A'BC + AB'C'$
(b) $A'B'C' + ABD + A'C + A'CD' + AC'D + AB'C'$

4.11 Factor to obtain a product of four terms and then reduce to three terms by applying the consensus theorem: $X'Y'Z' + XYZ$

4.12 Factor $Z = ABC + DE + ACF + AD' + AB'E$ and simplify it to the form $(X + X)(X + X)(X + X + X + X)$ (where each X represents a literal). Now express Z as a minimum sum of products in the form:

$$XX + XX + XX + XX$$

4.13 Repeat Problem 4.12 for $F = A'B + AC + BC'D' + BEF + BDF$.

4.14 Reduce to a minimum sum of products:

$$F = WXY' + (W'Y' \equiv X) + (Y \oplus WZ).$$

4.15 Simplify: $F = a'b \oplus bc \oplus ab \oplus b'c'$.

4.16 Simplify: $F = ab \oplus bc \oplus a'b' \oplus bc'$.

4.17 Prove algebraically that the following equations are valid:
(a) $(A' + B' + D')(A' + B + D')(B + C + D)(A + C')(A + C' + D)$
    $= A'C'D + ACD' + BC'D'$
(b) $(A' + B)(A + C + D)(A' + B + C)(B' + C' + D')(B' + C' + D)$
    $= ABC' + A'C'D + A'B'C$

4.18   Determine which of the following equations are always valid (give an algebraic
       proof):
       (a) $a'b + b'c + c'a = ab' + bc' + ca'$
       (b) $(a + b)(b + c)(c + a) = (a' + b')(b' + c')(c' + a')$
       (c) $abc + ab'c' + b'cd + bc'd + ad = abc + ab'c' + b'cd + bc'd$

4.19   Repeat Problem 4.18 for:
       (a) $xy' + x'z + yz' = x'y + xz' + y'z$
       (b) $(x + y)(y + z)(x + z) = (x' + y')(y' + z')(x' + z')$
       (c) $abc' + ab'c + b'c'd + bcd = ab'c + abc' + ad + bcd + b'c'd$

4.20   Prove algebraically:
       (a) $(A \oplus B)(B + C) + (A \equiv B)(B' + C') = A' + (B \oplus C)$
       (b) $ABC + A'B'C' + ABD + B'C'D = (B + C')(A + B')(A' + C + D)$
       (c) $XZ + Y'Z + WYZ + WX'Y$
           $= (X + W + Y')(X + Y + Z')(X' + Z + Y')$

4.21   Prove algebraically:
       (a) $(X' + Y')(X \equiv Z) + (X + Y)(X \oplus Z) = (X \oplus Y) + Z'$
       (b) $(W' + X + Y')(W + X' + Y)(W + Y' + Z)$
           $= X'Y' + WX + XYZ + W'YZ$
       (c) $ABC + A'C'D' + A'BD' + ACD = (A' + C)(A + D')(B + C' + D)$

4.22   Which of the following statements are always true? Justify your answers.
       (a) If $x(y + a') = x(y + b')$, then $a = b$.
       (b) If $a = b$ then $x(y + a') = x(y + b')$.

4.23   Which of the following statements are always true? Justify your answers.
       (a) If $A + B = C$, then $AD' + BD' = CD$.
       (b) If $A'B + A'C = A'D$, then $B + C = D$.
       (c) If $A + B = C$, then $A + B + D = C + D$.
       (d) If $A + B + C = C + D$, then $A + B = D$.

5

Applications of Boolean Algebra Minterm and Maxterm Expansions

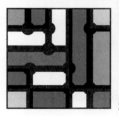

OBJECTIVES

1. Given a word description of the desired behavior of a logic network, write the output of the network as a function of the input variables. Specify this function as an algebraic expression or by means of a truth table as is appropriate.

2. Given a truth table, write the function (or its complement) as both a minterm expansion (standard sum of products) and a maxterm expansion (standard product of sums). Be able to use both alphabetic and decimal notation.

3. Given an algebraic expression for a function, expand it algebraically to obtain the minterm or maxterm form.

4. Given one of the following: minterm expansion for F, minterm expansion for F', maxterm expansion for F, maxterm expansion for F', find any of the other three forms.

5. Write the general form of the minterm and maxterm expansion of a function of n variables.

6. Explain why some functions contain "don't care" terms.

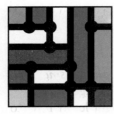

STUDY GUIDE

In the previous units, we placed a "·" inside of the AND-gate symbol, a "+" inside of the OR-gate symbol, and a "⊕" inside the EXCLUSIVE-OR. Since you are now familiar with the relationship between the shape of the gate symbol and the logic function performed, we will omit the ·, +, and ⊕ and use the standard gate symbols for AND, OR, and EXCLUSIVE-OR in the rest of the book.

1. Study Section 5.1, *Conversion of English Sentences to Boolean Equations.*

   (a) Use braces to identify the phrases in each of the following sentences:

   (1) The tape reader should stop if the manual stop button is pressed,

   if an error occurs, or if an end-of-tape signal is present.

   (2) He eats eggs for breakfast if it is not Sunday and

   he has eggs in the refrigerator.

   (3) Addition should occur iff an add instruction is given and

   the signs are the same, or if a subtract instruction is given and

   the signs are not the same.

   (b) Write a Boolean expression which represents each of the sentences in (a). Assign a variable to each phrase, and use a complemented variable to represent a phrase which contains "not".

   (Your answers should be in the *form* $F = S'E$, $F = AB + SB'$, and $F = A + B + C$, not necessarily in that order.)

(c) If X represents the phrase "N is greater than 3", how can you represent the phrase "N is less than or equal to 3"?

(d) Work Problems 5.1 and 5.5.

2. Study Section 5.2, *Combinational Network Design Using a Truth Table.* Previously, you have learned how to go from an algebraic expression for a function to a truth table; in this section you will learn how to go from a truth table to an algebraic expression.

(a) Write a product term which is 1 iff $a = 0$, $b = 0$, and $c = 1$.

(b) Write a sum term which is 0 iff $a = 0$, $b = 0$, and $c = 1$.

(c) Verify that your answers to (a) and (b) are complements.

(d) Write a product term which is 1 iff $a = 1$, $b = 0$, $c = 0$, and $d = 1$.

(e) Write a sum term which is 0 iff $a = 0$, $b = 0$, $c = 1$, and $d = 1$.

(f) For the given truth table, write F as a sum of four product terms which correspond to the four 1's of F.

a b c	F
0 0 0	1
0 0 1	1
0 1 0	0
0 1 1	1
1 0 0	1
1 0 1	0
1 1 0	0
1 1 1	0

(g) From the truth table, write F as a product of four sum terms which correspond to the four 0's of F.

(h) Verify that your answers to both (f) and (g) reduce to $F = b'c' + a'c$.

3. Study Section 5.3, *Minterm and Maxterm Expansions.*

(a) Define the following terms:

minterm (for n variables)

maxterm (for n variables)

(b) Study Table 5–2 and observe the relation between the values of A, B, and C and the corresponding minterms and maxterms.

If $A = 0$, then does A or A' appear in the minterm?

In the maxterm?

If $A = 1$, then does A or A' appear in the minterm?

In the maxterm?

What is the relation between minterm m_i and the corresponding maxterm M_i?

(c) For the table given in Study Guide Question 2(f), write the minterm expansion for F in m-notation and in decimal notation.

For the same table, write the maxterm expansion for F in M-notation and in decimal notation.

Check your answers by converting your answer to 2(f) to m-notation and your answer to 2(g) to M-notation.

(d) Given a sum-of-products expression, how do you expand it to a standard sum of products (minterm expansion)?

(e) Given a product of sums, how do you expand it to a standard product of sums (maxterm expansion)?

(f) In Equation (5–11), what theorems were used to factor f to obtain the maxterm expansion?

(g) Why is the following expression *not* a maxterm expansion?

$$f(A, B, C, D) = (A + B' + C + D)(A' + B + C')(A' + B + C + D')$$

(h) Assuming that there are three variables (A, B, C), identify each of the following as a minterm expansion, maxterm expansion, or neither:

(1) $AB + B'C'$ (2) $(A' + B + C')(A + B' + C)$

(3) $A + B + C$ (4) $(A' + B)(B' + C)(A' + C)$

(5) $A'BC' + AB'C + ABC$ (6) $AB'C'$

Note that it is possible for a minterm or maxterm expansion to have only one term.

4. **(a)** Given a minterm in terms of its variables, the procedure for conversion to decimal notation is
   (1) Replace each complemented variable with a _____ and replace each uncomplemented variable with a _____ .
   (2) Convert the resulting binary number to decimal.

   (b) Convert the minterm $AB'C'DE$ to decimal notation.

   (c) Given that m_{13} is a minterm of the variables A, B, C, D, and E write the minterm in terms of these variables.

   (d) Given a maxterm in terms of its variables, the procedure for conversion to decimal notation is
   (1) Replace each complemented variable with a _____ and replace each uncomplemented variable with a _____ .
   (2) Group these 0's and 1's to form a binary number and convert to decimal.

   (e) Convert the maxterm $A' + B + C + D' + E'$ to decimal notation.

   (f) Given that M_{13} is a maxterm of the variables A, B, C, D, and E write the maxterm in terms of these variables.

   (g) Check your answers to (b), (c), (e), and (f) by using the relation $M_i = m_i'$.

   (h) Given $f(a, b, c, d, e) = \prod M(0, 10, 28)$, express f in terms of a, b, c, d, and e. (Your answer should contain only five complemented variables.)

5. Study Section 5.4, *General Minterm and Maxterm Expansions*. Make sure that you understand the notation here and can follow the algebra in all of the equations. If you have difficulty with this section, ask for help *before* you take the readiness test.

   (a) How many different functions of four variables are possible?

   (b) Explain why there are 2^{2^n} functions of n variables.

(c) Write the function of Table 5–1 in the form of Equation (5–13) and show that it reduces to Equation (5–3).

(d) For Equation (5–19), write out the indicated summations in full for the case $n = 2$.

(e) Study Tables 5–4 and 5–5 carefully and make sure you understand why each table entry is valid. Use the truth table for f and f' (Table 5–1) to verify the entries in Table 5–5. If you understand the relation between Table 5–4 and the truth table for F and F', you should be able to perform the conversions without having to memorize the table.

(f) Given that $f(A, B, C) = \sum m(0, 1, 3, 4, 7)$

The maxterm expansion for f is _____ .
The minterm expansion for f' is _____ .
The maxterm expansion for f' is _____ .

(g) Work Problems 5.16 and 5.17.

6. Study Section 5.5, *Incompletely Specified Functions.*

(a) State two reasons why some functions have "don't care" terms.

(b) Given the following table, write the minterm expansion for Z in decimal form.

(c) Write the maxterm expansion in decimal form.

A	B	C	Z
0	0	0	1
0	0	1	X
0	1	0	0
0	1	1	X
1	0	0	X
1	0	1	1
1	1	0	0
1	1	1	0

(d) Work Problem 5.21 and 5.23(a).

7. Study Section 5.6, *Examples of Truth Table Construction.* Finding the truth table from the problem statement is probably the most difficult part of the process of designing a switching network. Make sure that you understand how to do this.

8. Work Problems 5.7 through 5.10 and 5.15.

9. Read the following and then work Problem 5.19 or 5.20 as assigned:

   When looking at an expression to determine the required number of gates, keep in mind that the number of required gates is generally *not* equal to the number of AND and OR operations which appear in the expression. For example,

   $$AB + CD + EF(G + H)$$

   contains four AND operations and three OR operations, but it only requires three AND gates and two OR gates:

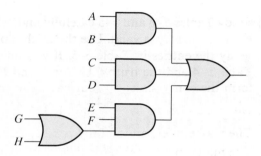

10. *Laboratory Exercise.* (Must be completed before you take the readiness test.) The purpose of this lab exercise is to acquaint you with the laboratory and some of the available lab equipment which you will be using later in a more complex lab design problem.

    (a) Obtain a "Laboratory Information" study unit and follow the instructions in Part I of the study guide attached to the unit.

    (b) Build the network which you designed in Problem 5.19 or 5.20 in the lab. Test the network for all 16 combinations of values for the input variables. Enter the results of your lab testing in a truth table.

11. Reread the objectives of this unit. Make sure that you understand the difference in the procedures for converting maxterms and minterms from decimal to algebraic notation. When you are satisfied that you can meet the objectives, take the readiness test. When you come to take the readiness test, turn in a copy of your solution to Problem 5.19 or 5.20 and the results of lab testing.

Applications of Boolean Algebra Minterm and Maxterm Expansions

In this unit you will learn how to design a combinational switching network starting with a word description of the desired network behavior. The first step is usually to translate the word description into a truth table or into an algebraic expression. Given the truth table for a Boolean function, two standard algebraic forms of the function can be derived—the standard sum of products (minterm expansion) and the standard product of sums (maxterm expansion). Simplification of either of these standard forms leads directly to a realization of the network using AND and OR gates.

5.1

Conversion of English Sentences to Boolean Equations

Logic design problems are often stated in terms of one or more English sentences. The first step in designing a logic network is to translate these sentences into Boolean equations. In order to do this, we must break down each sentence into phrases and associate a Boolean variable with each phrase. If a phrase can have a value of "true" or "false", then we can represent that phrase by a Boolean variable. Phrases like "she goes to the store" or "today is Monday" can be either true or false, but a command like "go to the store" has no truth value. If a sentence has several phrases, we will mark each phrase with a brace. The following sentence has three phrases:

Mary watches TV if it is Monday night and she has finished her homework.

The "if" and "and" are not included in any phrase; they show the relationships among the phrases.

We will define a two-valued variable to indicate the truth or falsity of each phrase:

$F = 1$ if "Mary watches TV" is true; otherwise, $F = 0$.
$A = 1$ if "it is Monday night" is true; otherwise, $A = 0$.
$B = 1$ if "she has finished her homework" is true; otherwise $B = 0$.

Since F is "true" if A and B are both "true", we can represent the sentence by

$$F = A \cdot B$$

The three main steps in designing a single-output combinational switching network are:

1. Find a switching function which specifies the desired behavior of the network.
2. Find a simplified algebraic expression for the function.
3. Realize the simplified function using available logic elements.

For simple problems, it may be possible to go directly from a word description of the desired behavior of the network to an algebraic expression for the output function. In other cases, it is better to first specify the function by means of a truth table and then derive an algebraic expression from the truth table.

The following example illustrates how to go from a word statement of a problem directly to an algebraic expression which represents the desired network behavior. An alarm circuit is to be designed which operates as follows:

The alarm will ring iff the alarm switch is turned on and the door is not closed, or it is after 6 p.m. and the window is not closed.

The first step in writing an algebraic expression which corresponds to the above sentence is to associate a Boolean variable with each phrase in the sentence. This variable will have a value of 1 when the phrase is true and 0 when it is false. We will use the following assignment of variables:

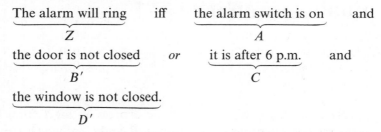

This assignment implies that if $Z = 1$, the alarm will ring. If the alarm switch is turned on, $A = 1$, and if it is after 6 p.m., $C = 1$. If we use the variable B to represent the phrase "the door is closed," then B' represents "the door is *not* closed." Thus $B = 1$ if the door is closed, and $B' = 1$ ($B = 0$) if the door is not closed. Similarly, $D = 1$ if the window is closed and $D' = 1$ if the window is *not* closed. Using this assignment of variables, the above sentence can be translated into the following Boolean equation:

$$Z = AB' + CD'$$

This equation corresponds to the following network:

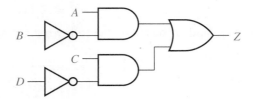

In the above network, A is a signal which is 1 when the alarm switch is on, C is a signal from a time clock which is 1 when it is after 6 p.m., B is a signal from a switch on the door which is 1 when the door is closed, and similarly D is 1 when the window is closed. The output Z is connected to the alarm so that it will ring when $Z = 1$.

5.2
Combinational Network Design Using a Truth Table

The next example illustrates network design using a truth table (Table 5–1). A switching network has three inputs and one output as shown. The inputs A, B, and C represent the first, second, and third bits, respectively, of a binary number N. The output of the network is to be $f = 1$ if $N \geqslant 011_2$ and $f = 0$ if $N < 011_2$. The truth table for f is as follows:

Table 5–1

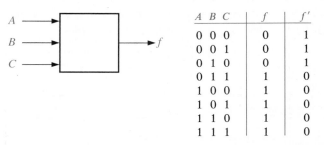

A	B	C	f	f'
0	0	0	0	1
0	0	1	0	1
0	1	0	0	1
0	1	1	1	0
1	0	0	1	0
1	0	1	1	0
1	1	0	1	0
1	1	1	1	0

Next we will derive an algebraic expression for f from the truth table by using the combinations of values of A, B, and C for which $f = 1$. The term $A'BC$ is 1 only if $A = 0$, $B = 1$, and $C = 1$. Similarly, the term $AB'C'$ is 1 only for the combination 100, $AB'C$ is 1 only for 101, ABC' is 1 only for 110, and ABC is 1 only for 111. ORing these terms together yields

$$f = A'BC + AB'C' + AB'C + ABC' + ABC \qquad (5\text{--}1)$$

The above expression equals 1 if A, B, and C take on any of the five combinations of values 011, 100, 101, 110, or 111. If any other combination of values occurs, f is 0 because all five terms are 0.

Equation (5–1) can be simplified by first combining terms and then eliminating A':

$$f = A'BC + AB' + AB = A'BC + A = A + BC \qquad (5\text{--}2)$$

Equation (5–2) leads directly to the following network:

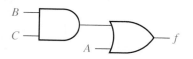

Instead of writing f in terms of the 1's of the function, we may also write f in terms of the 0's of the function. The function defined by Table 5–1 is 0 for three combinations of input values. Observe that the term $A + B + C$ is 0 only if $A = B = C = 0$. Similarly, $A + B + C'$ is 0 only for the input combination 001, and $A + B' + C$ is 0 only for the combination 010. ANDing these terms together yields

$$f = (A + B + C)(A + B + C')(A + B' + C) \qquad (5\text{–}3)$$

The above expression equals 0 if A, B, and C take on any of the combinations of values 000, 001, or 010. For any other combination of values, f is 1 because all three terms are 1. Since Equation (5–3) represents the same function as Equation (5–1) they must both reduce to the same expression. Combining terms and using the second distributive law, Equation (5–3) simplifies to

$$f = (A + B)(A + B' + C) = A + B(B' + C) = A + BC \qquad (5\text{–}4)$$

which is the same as Equation (5–2).

Another way to derive Equation (5–3) is to first write f' as a sum of products, and then complement the result. From Table 5–1, f' is 1 for input combinations $ABC = 000$, 001 and 010, so

$$f' = A'B'C' + A'B'C + A'BC'$$

Taking the complement of f' gives Equation (5–3).

5.3
Minterm and Maxterm Expansions

Each of the terms in Equation (5–1) is referred to as a minterm. In general a *minterm* of n variables is a product of n literals in which each variable appears exactly once in either true or complemented form, but not both. (A *literal* is a variable or its complement.) Table 5–2 lists all of the minterms of the three variables A, B, and C. Each minterm has a value of 1 for exactly one combination of values of the variables A, B, and C. Thus if $A = B = C = 0$, $A'B'C' = 1$; if $A = B = 0$

Table 5–2

Minterms and Maxterms for Three Variables

Row No.	$A\ B\ C$	Minterms	Maxterms
0	0 0 0	$A'B'C' = m_0$	$A + B + C\ \ = M_0$
1	0 0 1	$A'B'C\ \ = m_1$	$A + B + C'\ = M_1$
2	0 1 0	$A'BC'\ \ = m_2$	$A + B' + C\ = M_2$
3	0 1 1	$A'BC\ \ = m_3$	$A + B' + C' = M_3$
4	1 0 0	$AB'C'\ \ = m_4$	$A' + B + C\ = M_4$
5	1 0 1	$AB'C\ \ = m_5$	$A' + B + C' = M_5$
6	1 1 0	$ABC'\ \ = m_6$	$A' + B' + C\ = M_6$
7	1 1 1	$ABC\ \ = m_7$	$A' + B' + C' = M_7$

and $C = 1$, $A'B'C = 1$; etc. Minterms are often written in abbreviated form—$A'B'C'$ is designated m_0, $A'B'C$ is designated m_1, etc. In general, the minterm which corresponds to row i of the truth table is designated m_i (i is usually written in decimal).

When a function f is written as a sum of minterms as in Equation (5–1), this is referred to as a *minterm expansion* or a *standard sum of products*.[1] If $f = 1$ for row i of the truth table, then m_i must be present in the minterm expansion because $m_i = 1$ only for the combination of values of the variables corresponding to row i of the table. Because the minterms present in f are in one-to-one correspondence with the 1's of f in the truth table, the minterm expansion for a function f is unique. Equation (5–1) can be rewritten in terms of m-notation as

$$f(A, B, C) = m_3 + m_4 + m_5 + m_6 + m_7 \qquad (5\text{–}5)$$

This can be further abbreviated by listing only the decimal subscripts in the form

$$f(A, B, C) = \sum m(3, 4, 5, 6, 7) \qquad (5\text{–}5a)$$

Each of the sum terms (or factors) in Equation (5–3) is referred to as a *maxterm*. In general, a maxterm of n variables is a sum of n literals in which each variable appears exactly once in either true or complemented form, but not both. Table 5–2 lists all of the maxterms of the three variables A, B, and C. Each maxterm has a value of 0 for exactly one combination of values for A, B, and C. Thus if $A = B = C = 0$, $A + B + C = 0$; if $A = B = 0$ and $C = 1$, $A + B + C' = 0$; etc. Maxterms are often written in abbreviated form using M-notation. The maxterm which corresponds to row i of the truth table is designated M_i. Note that each maxterm is the complement of the corresponding minterm; that is, $M_i = m_i'$.

When a function f is written as a product of maxterms as in Equation (5–3), this is referred to as a *maxterm expansion* or *standard product of sums*. If $f = 0$ for row i of the truth table, then M_i must be present in the maxterm expansion because $M_i = 0$ only for the combination of values of the variables corresponding to row i of the table. Note that the maxterms are multiplied together so that if any one of them is 0, f will be 0. Because the maxterms are in one-to-one correspondence with the 0's of f in the truth table, the maxterm expansion for a function f is unique. Equation (5–3) can be rewritten in M-notation as

$$f(A, B, C) = M_0 M_1 M_2 \qquad (5\text{–}6)$$

This can be further abbreviated by listing only the decimal subscripts in the form

$$f(A, B, C) = \prod M(0, 1, 2) \qquad (5\text{–}6a)$$

where $\prod$ means a product.

Since if $f \neq 1$, $f = 0$, it follows that if m_i is *not* present in the minterm expansion of f, then M_i is present in the maxterm expansion. Thus, given a minterm expansion of an n-variable function f in decimal notation, the maxterm

---

[1] Other names used in the literature for standard sum of products are *canonical sum of products* and *disjunctive normal form*. Similarly, a standard product of sums may be called a *canonical product of sums* or a *conjunctive normal form*.

expansion is obtained by listing those decimal integers $(0 \leqslant i \leqslant 2^n - 1)$ not in the minterm list. Using this method, Equation (5-6a) can be obtained directly from Equation (5-5a).

Given the minterm or maxterm expansions for f, the minterm or maxterm expansions for the complement of f are easy to obtain. Since f' is 1 when f is 0, the minterm expansion for f' contains those minterms not present in f. Thus, from Equation (5-5),

$$f' = m_0 + m_1 + m_2 = \sum m(0, 1, 2) \qquad (5\text{-}7)$$

Similarly, the maxterm expansion for f' contains those maxterms not present in f. From Equation (5-6),

$$f' = \prod M(3, 4, 5, 6, 7) = M_3 M_4 M_5 M_6 M_7 \qquad (5\text{-}8)$$

Since the complement of a minterm is the corresponding maxterm, Equation (5-8) can be obtained by complementing Equation (5-5):

$$f' = (m_3 + m_4 + m_5 + m_6 + m_7)' = m_3' m_4' m_5' m_6' m_7' = M_3 M_4 M_5 M_6 M_7$$

Similarly, Equation (5-7) can be obtained by complementing Equation (5-6):

$$f' = (M_0 M_1 M_2)' = M_0' + M_1' + M_2' = m_0 + m_1 + m_2$$

A general switching expression can be converted to a minterm or maxterm expansion either using a truth table or algebraically. If a truth table is constructed by evaluating the expression for all different combinations of values of the variables, the minterm and maxterm expansions can be obtained from the truth table by the methods just discussed. Another way to obtain the minterm expansion is to first write the expression as a sum of products and then introduce the missing variables in each term by applying the theorem $X + X' = 1$.

EXAMPLE: Find the minterm expansion of $f(a, b, c, d) = a'(b' + d) + acd'$.

$$\begin{aligned}
f &= a'b' + a'd + acd' \\
&= a'b'(c + c')(d + d') + a'd(b + b')(c + c') + acd'(b + b') \\
&= a'b'c'd' + a'b'c'd + a'b'cd' + a'b'cd + \cancel{a'b'c'd} + \cancel{a'b'cd} \\
&\quad + a'bc'd + a'bcd + abcd' + ab'cd' \qquad (5\text{-}9)
\end{aligned}$$

Duplicate terms have been crossed out, since $X + X = X$. The above expression can then be converted to decimal notation:

$$f = a'b'c'd' + a'b'c'd + a'b'cd' + a'b'cd + a'bc'd + a'bcd + abcd' + ab'cd'$$

  0 0 0 0   0 0 0 1   0 0 1 0   0 0 1 1   0 1 0 1   0 1 1 1   1 1 1 0   1 0 1 0

$$f = \sum m(0, 1, 2, 3, 5, 7, 10, 14) \qquad (5\text{-}10)$$

The maxterm expansion for f can then be obtained by listing the decimal integers (in the range 0 to 15) which do not correspond to minterms of f:

$$f = \prod M(4, 6, 8, 9, 11, 12, 13, 15)$$

An alternate way of finding the maxterm expansion is to factor f to obtain a product of sums, introduce the missing variables in each sum term by using

$XX' = 0$, and then factor again to obtain the maxterms. For the above example,

$$f = (a' + cd')(a + b' + d) = (a' + c)(a' + d')(a + b' + d)$$
$$= (a' + bb' + c + dd')(a' + bb' + cc' + d')(a + b' + cc' + d)$$
$$= (a' + bb' + c + d)(a' + bb' + c + d')(\overline{a' + bb' + c + d'})(a' + bb' + c' + d')$$
$$\quad (a + b' + cc' + d)$$
$$= (a' + b + c + d)(a' + b' + c + d)(a' + b + c + d')(a' + b' + c + d')$$
$$\quad\quad\quad 1000 \quad\quad\quad\quad\quad 1100 \quad\quad\quad\quad\quad 1001 \quad\quad\quad\quad\quad 1101$$
$$\quad (a' + b + c' + d')(a' + b' + c' + d')(a + b' + c + d)(a + b' + c' + d)$$
$$\quad\quad 1011 \quad\quad\quad\quad\quad 1111 \quad\quad\quad\quad\quad 0100 \quad\quad\quad\quad\quad 0110$$
$$= \prod M(4, 6, 8, 9, 11, 12, 13, 15) \quad\quad\quad\quad\quad\quad\quad\quad\quad\quad\quad (5\text{--}11)$$

Note that when translating the maxterms to decimal notation, a primed variable is first replaced with a 1 and an unprimed variable with a 0.

Since the terms in the minterm expansion of a function F correspond one-to-one with the rows of the truth table for which $F = 1$, the minterm expansion of F is unique. Thus, we can prove that an equation is valid by finding the minterm expansion of each side and showing that these expansions are the same.

EXAMPLE: Show that $a'c + b'c' + ab = a'b' + bc + ac'$.

We will find the minterm expansion of each side by supplying the missing variables. For the left side,

$$a'c(b + b') + b'c'(a + a') + ab(c + c')$$
$$= a'bc + a'b'c + ab'c' + a'b'c' + abc + abc'$$
$$= m_3 \;+\; m_1 \;+\; m_4 \;+\; m_0 \;+\; m_7 + m_6$$

For the right side,

$$a'b'(c + c') + bc(a + a') + ac'(b + b')$$
$$= a'b'c + a'b'c' + abc + a'bc + abc' + ab'c'$$
$$= m_1 \;+\; m_0 \;+\; m_7 + m_3 \;+\; m_6 \;+\; m_4$$

Since the two minterm expansions are the same, the equation is valid.

5.4
General Minterm and Maxterm Expansions

Table 5–3 represents a truth table for a general function of three variables. Each a_i is a constant with a value of 0 or 1. To completely specify a function, we must assign values to all of the a_i's. Since each a_i can be specified in two ways, there are 2^8 ways of filling the F column of the truth table; therefore, there are 256 different functions of three variables (this includes the degenerate cases, F identically equal to 0 and F identically equal to 1). For a function of n variables there are 2^n rows in the truth table, and since the value of F can be 0 or 1 for each row, there are $2^{(2^n)}$ possible functions of n variables.

Table 5–3

General Truth Table for Three Variables

A B C	F
0 0 0	a_0
0 0 1	a_1
0 1 0	a_2
0 1 1	a_3
1 0 0	a_4
1 0 1	a_5
1 1 0	a_6
1 1 1	a_7

From Table 5–3, we can write the minterm expansion for a general function of three variables as follows:

$$F = a_0 m_0 + a_1 m_1 + a_2 m_2 + \cdots + a_7 m_7 = \sum_{i=0}^{7} a_i m_i \qquad (5\text{--}12)$$

Note that if $a_i = 1$, minterm m_i is present in the expansion; if $a_i = 0$, the corresponding minterm is not present. The maxterm expansion for a general function of three variables is

$$F = (a_0 + M_0)(a_1 + M_1)(a_2 + M_2) \cdots (a_7 + M_7) = \prod_{i=0}^{7} (a_i + M_i) \quad (5\text{--}13)$$

Note that if $a_i = 1$, $a_i + M_i = 1$, and M_i drops out of the expansion; however, M_i is present if $a_i = 0$.

From Equation (5–13), the minterm expansion of F' is

$$F' = \left[\prod_{i=0}^{7} (a_i + M_i) \right]' = \sum_{i=0}^{7} a_i' M_i' = \sum_{i=0}^{7} a_i' m_i \qquad (5\text{--}14)$$

Note that all the minterms which are not present in F are present in F'. From Equation (5–12), the maxterm expansion of F' is

$$F' = \left[\sum_{i=0}^{7} a_i m_i \right]' = \prod_{i=0}^{7} (a_i' + m_i') = \prod_{i=0}^{7} (a_i' + M_i) \qquad (5\text{--}15)$$

Note that all the maxterms which are not present in F are present in F'. Generalizing Equations (5–12), (5–13), (5–14), and (5–15) to n variables, we have

$$F = \sum_{i=0}^{2^n - 1} a_i m_i = \prod_{i=0}^{2^n - 1} (a_i + M_i) \qquad (5\text{--}16)$$

$$F' = \sum_{i=0}^{2^n - 1} a_i' m_i = \prod_{i=0}^{2^n - 1} (a_i' + M_i) \qquad (5\text{--}17)$$

Given two different minterms of n variables, m_i and m_j, at least one variable appears complemented in one of the minterms and uncomplemented in the other. Therefore, if $i \neq j$, $m_i m_j = 0$. For example, for $n = 3$, $m_1 m_3 = (A'B'C)(A'BC) = 0$. Given minterm expansions for two functions

$$f_1 = \sum_{i=0}^{2^n - 1} a_i m_i \qquad f_2 = \sum_{j=0}^{2^n - 1} b_j m_j \qquad (5\text{--}18)$$

the product is

$$f_1 f_2 = \left(\sum_{i=0}^{2^n-1} a_i m_i \right) \left(\sum_{j=0}^{2^n-1} b_j m_j \right) = \sum_{i=0}^{2^n-1} \sum_{j=0}^{2^n-1} a_i b_j m_i m_j$$

$$= \sum_{i=0}^{2^n-1} a_i b_i m_i \quad (\text{since } m_i m_j = 0 \text{ unless } i = j) \tag{5–19}$$

Note that all of the cross-product terms ($i \neq j$) drop out so that $f_1 f_2$ contains only those minterms which are present in both f_1 and f_2. For example, if

$$f_1 = \sum m(0, 2, 3, 5, 9, 11) \quad \text{and} \quad f_2 = \sum m(0, 3, 9, 11, 13, 14)$$
$$f_1 f_2 = \sum m(0, 3, 9, 11)$$

Table 5–4 summarizes the procedures for conversion between minterm and maxterm expansions of F and F', assuming that all expansions are written as lists of decimal numbers. When using this table, keep in mind that the truth table for an n-variable function has 2^n rows so that the minterm (or maxterm) numbers range from 0 to $2^n - 1$. Table 5–5 illustrates the application of Table 5–4 to the three-variable function given in Table 5–1.

Table 5–4

Conversion of Forms

GIVEN FORM		DESIRED FORM			
		Minterm Expansion of F	Maxterm Expansion of F	Minterm Expansion of F'	Maxterm Expansion of F'
	Minterm Expansion of F	————	maxterm nos. are those nos. not on the minterm list for F	list minterms not present in F	maxterm nos. are the same as minterm nos. of F
	Maxterm Expansion of F	minterm nos. are those nos. not on the maxterm list for F	————	minterm nos. are the same as maxterm nos. of F	list maxterms not present in F

Table 5–5

Application of Table 5–4

GIVEN FORM		DESIRED FORM			
		Minterm Expansion of f	Maxterm Expansion of f	Minterm Expansion of f'	Maxterm Expansion of f'
	$f = \sum m(3, 4, 5, 6, 7)$	————	$\prod M(0, 1, 2)$	$\sum m(0, 1, 2)$	$\prod M(3, 4, 5, 6, 7)$
	$f = \prod M(0, 1, 2)$	$\sum m(3, 4, 5, 6, 7)$	————	$\sum m(0, 1, 2)$	$\prod M(3, 4, 5, 6, 7)$

5.5
Incompletely Specified Functions

A large digital system is usually divided into many subnetworks. Consider the following example in which the output of network N_1 drives the input of network N_2.

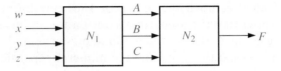

Let us assume that the output of N_1 does not generate all possible combinations of values for A, B, and C. In particular, we will assume that there are no combinations of values for w, x, y, and z which cause A, B, and C to assume values of 001 or 110. Hence, when we design N_2 it is not necessary to specify values of F for $ABC = 001$ or 110, since these combinations of values can never occur as inputs to N_2. For example, F might be specified by Table 5–6.

Table 5–6

$A\ B\ C$	F
0 0 0	1
0 0 1	X
0 1 0	0
0 1 1	1
1 0 0	0
1 0 1	0
1 1 0	X
1 1 1	1

The X's in the table indicate that we don't care whether the value of 0 or 1 is assigned to F for the combinations $ABC = 001$ or 110. In this example, we don't care what the value of F is because these input combinations never occur anyway. The function F is then *incompletely specified*. The minterms $A'B'C$ and ABC' are referred to as "don't care" terms, since we don't care whether they are present in the function or not.

When we realize the function, we must specify values for the don't cares. It is desirable to choose values which will help simplify the function. If we assign the value 0 to both X's, then

$$F = A'B'C' + A'BC + ABC = A'B'C' + BC$$

If we assign 1 to the first X and 0 to the second, then

$$F = A'B'C' + A'B'C + A'BC + ABC = A'B' + BC$$

If we assign 1 to both X's, then

$$F = A'B'C' + A'B'C + A'BC + ABC' + ABC = A'B' + BC + AB$$

The second choice of values leads to the simplest solution.

We have seen one way in which incompletely specified functions can arise, and there are many other ways. In the above example, don't cares were present because certain combinations of network inputs did not occur. In other cases, all input combinations may occur, but the network output is used in such a way that we don't care whether it is 0 or 1 for certain input combinations.

When writing the minterm expansion for an incompletely specified function, we will use "m" to denote the required minterms and "d" to denote the don't care minterms. Using this notation, the minterm expansion for Table 5–6 is

$$F = \sum m(0, 3, 7) + \sum d(1, 6)$$

For each don't care minterm there is a corresponding don't care maxterm. For example, if $F = X$ (don't care) for input combination 001, m_1 is a don't care minterm and M_1 is a don't care maxterm. We will use "D" to represent a don't care maxterm and write the maxterm expansion of the function in Table 5–6 as

$$F = \prod M(2, 4, 5) \cdot \prod D(1, 6)$$

which implies that maxterms M_2, M_4, and M_5 are present in F and don't care maxterms M_1 and M_6 are optional.

5.6
Examples of Truth Table Construction

EXAMPLE 1   We will design a simple binary adder that adds two 1-bit binary numbers, a and b, to give a 2-bit sum. The numeric values for the adder inputs and output are as follows:

a	b	Sum	
0	0	00	$(0 + 0 = 0)$
0	1	01	$(0 + 1 = 1)$
1	0	01	$(1 + 0 = 1)$
1	1	10	$(1 + 1 = 2)$

We will represent inputs to the adder by the logic variables A and B, represent the 2-bit sum by the logic variables X and Y, and construct a truth table:

A	B	X	Y
0	0	0	0
0	1	0	1
1	0	0	1
1	1	1	0

Since a numeric value of 0 is represented by a logic 0 and a numeric value of 1 by a logic 1, the 0's and 1's in the truth table are exactly the same as in the previous table. From the truth table,

$$X = AB \quad \text{and} \quad Y = A'B + AB' = A \oplus B$$

EXAMPLE 2   An adder is to be designed which adds two 2-bit binary numbers to give a 3-bit binary sum. Find the truth table for the network. The network has four inputs and three outputs as shown:

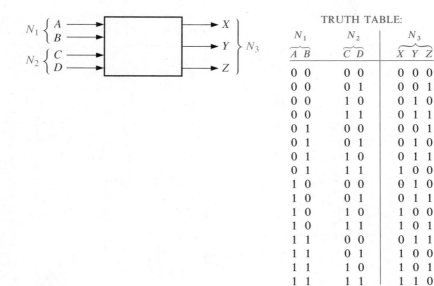

TRUTH TABLE:

N_1		N_2		N_3		
A	B	C	D	X	Y	Z
0	0	0	0	0	0	0
0	0	0	1	0	0	1
0	0	1	0	0	1	0
0	0	1	1	0	1	1
0	1	0	0	0	0	1
0	1	0	1	0	1	0
0	1	1	0	0	1	1
0	1	1	1	1	0	0
1	0	0	0	0	1	0
1	0	0	1	0	1	1
1	0	1	0	1	0	0
1	0	1	1	1	0	1
1	1	0	0	0	1	1
1	1	0	1	1	0	0
1	1	1	0	1	0	1
1	1	1	1	1	1	0

Inputs A and B taken together represent a binary number N_1. Inputs C and D taken together represent a binary number N_2. Outputs X, Y, and Z taken together represent a binary number N_3, where $N_3 = N_1 + N_2$ (+ of course represents ordinary addition here).

In this example we have used A, B, C, and D to represent both numeric values and logic values, but this should not cause any confusion because the numeric and logic values are the same.

In forming the above table, the variables were treated like binary numbers having *numeric* values. Now we wish to derive the switching functions for the output variables. In doing so, we will treat A, B, C, D, X, Y, and Z as switching variables having nonnumeric values 0 and 1. (Remember that in this case the 0 and 1 may represent low and high voltages, open and closed switches, etc.)

From inspection of the table, the output functions are

$$X(A, B, C, D) = \sum m(7, 10, 11, 13, 14, 15)$$
$$Y(A, B, C, D) = \sum m(2, 3, 5, 6, 8, 9, 12, 15)$$
$$Z(A, B, C, D) = \sum m(1, 3, 4, 6, 9, 11, 12, 14)$$

EXAMPLE 3   Design an error detector for 6-3-1-1 binary-coded-decimal digits. The output (F) is to be 1 iff the four inputs (A, B, C, D) represent an invalid code combination.

The valid 6-3-1-1 code combinations are listed in Table 1–1. If any other combination occurs this is not a valid 6-3-1-1 binary-coded-decimal digit and the network output should be $F = 1$ to indicate that an error has occurred. This leads to the following truth table:

A B C D	F
0 0 0 0	0
0 0 0 1	0
0 0 1 0	1
0 0 1 1	0
0 1 0 0	0
0 1 0 1	0
0 1 1 0	1
0 1 1 1	0
1 0 0 0	0
1 0 0 1	0
1 0 1 0	1
1 0 1 1	0
1 1 0 0	0
1 1 0 1	1
1 1 1 0	1
1 1 1 1	1

The corresponding output function is

$$F = \sum m(2, 6, 10, 13, 14, 15)$$
$$= A'B'CD' + A'BCD' + AB'CD' + ABCD' + ABC'D + ABCD$$
$$= A'CD' + ACD' + ABD = CD' + ABD$$

The network realization using AND and OR gates is

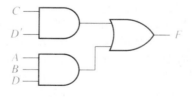

EXAMPLE 4   The four inputs to a network (A, B, C, D) represent an 8-4-2-1 binary-coded decimal digit. Design the network so that the output (Z) is 1 iff the decimal number represented by the inputs is exactly divisible by 3. Assume that only valid BCD digits occur as inputs.

The digits 0, 3, 6, and 9 are exactly divisible by 3, so $Z = 1$ for the input combinations $ABCD = 0000$, 0011, 0110, and 1001. The input combinations 1010, 1011, 1100, 1101, 1110, and 1111 do not represent valid BCD digits and will never occur, so Z is a don't care for these combinations. This leads to the following truth table:

A B C D	Z
0 0 0 0	1
0 0 0 1	0
0 0 1 0	0
0 0 1 1	1
0 1 0 0	0
0 1 0 1	0
0 1 1 0	1
0 1 1 1	0
1 0 0 0	0
1 0 0 1	1
1 0 1 0	X
1 0 1 1	X
1 1 0 0	X
1 1 0 1	X
1 1 1 0	X
1 1 1 1	X

The corresponding output function is

$$Z = \sum m(0, 3, 6, 9) + \sum d(10, 11, 12, 13, 14, 15)$$

In order to find the simplest network which will realize Z, we must choose some of the don't cares (X's) to be 0 and some to be 1. The easiest way to do this is to use a Karnaugh map as described in Unit 6.

PROBLEMS

5.1   Represent each of the following sentences by a Boolean equation:
(a) The air conditioner should be turned on iff the temperature is greater than 75°F, the time is between 8 a.m. and 5 p.m., and it is not a holiday.
(b) The product of A and B is negative iff A is negative and B is positive *or* A is positive and B is negative. (Use only two independent variables.)
(c) The tape drive motor should be running iff
  (1) the tape is properly threaded,
  (2) an end-of-tape signal is not present, and
  (3) the tape drive is in the manual mode and the manual start button has been pressed, *or* it is in the automatic mode and a "tape-on" signal from the computer is present.
(d) The sound system will squeal if the microphone is turned on, *and* the microphone is too close to the speaker or the volume control is set too high.

5.2   Represent each of the following sentences by a Boolean equation:
(a) The answering machine should answer the phone iff the time is not between 8 a.m. and 5 p.m. or it is a weekend or the phone has rung six times.

(b) In a battery-powered computer, the diskette drive motor 1 should be on iff
   (1) there is a diskette in the drive,
   (2) the diskette drive door is closed,
   (3) diskette drive motor 2 is not on,
   (4) the battery low signal is not present, and
   (5) the computer has started a read operation or the computer has started a write operation.
(c) The circuit breaker will trip iff
   (1) the hair drier is turned on and the stereo volume is past 5,
   (2) the microwave oven is used and the toaster is on,
   (3) all the lights in the room are on, or
   (4) there is a short circuit in any appliance.

5.3 Each of the following sentences has two possible interpretations depending on whether the AND or OR is done first. Write an equation for each interpretation.
(a) The buzzer will sound if the key is in the ignition switch and the car door is open or the seat belts are not fastened.
(b) You will gain weight if you eat too much or you do not exercise enough and your metabolism rate is too low.
(c) The loud speaker will be damaged if the volume is set too high and loud music is played or the stereo is too powerful.
(d) The roads will be very slippery if it snows or rains and there is oil on the road.

5.4 A bank vault has three locks with a different key for each lock. Each key is owned by different person. In order to open the door, at least two people must insert their keys into the assigned locks. The signal lines A, B, and C are 1 if there is a key inserted into lock 1, 2, or 3, respectively. Write an equation for the variable Z which is 1 iff the door should open.

5.5 A paper tape reader used as an input device to a computer has five rows of holes as shown below. A hole punched in the tape indicates a logic 1 and no hole indicates a logic 0. As each hole pattern passes under the photocells, the pattern is translated into logic signals on lines A, B, C, D, and E. All patterns of holes indicate a valid character with two exceptions. A pattern consisting of none of the possible holes punched is not used because it is impossible to distinguish between this pattern and the unpunched space between patterns. An incorrect pattern punched on the tape is "erased" by punching all five holes in that position. Therefore, a valid character punched on the tape will have at least one hole, but will not have all five holes punched.
(a) Write an equation for a variable Z which is 1 iff a valid character is being read.
(b) Write an equation for a variable Y which is 1 iff the hole pattern being read has holes punched only in rows C and E.

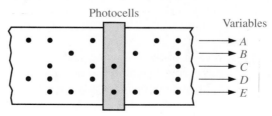

5.6 A computer interface to a line printer has seven data lines that control the movement of the paper and the print head and determine which character to print. The data lines are labeled A, B, C, D, E, F, and G, and each represents a binary 0 or 1. When the data lines are interpreted as a 7-bit binary number with line A being the most significant bit, the data lines can represent the numbers 0 to 127_{10}. The number 13_{10} is the command to return the print head to the beginning of a line, the number 10_{10} means to advance the paper by one line, and the numbers 32_{10} to 127_{10} represent printing characters.

(a) Write an equation for the variable X which is 1 iff the data lines indicate a command to return the print head to the beginning of the line.

(b) Write an equation for the variable Y which is 1 iff there is an advance paper command on the data lines.

(c) Write an equation for the variable Z which is 1 iff the data lines indicate a printable character. (*Hint:* Consider the binary representations of the numbers 0–31 and 32–127 and write the equation for Z with only two terms.)

5.7 A switching network has three inputs and two outputs. The output variables, a and b, represent the first and second bits, respectively, of a binary number, N. N equals the number of inputs which are 0. For example, if $x = 1$, $y = 0$, $z = 1$, then $a = 0$, $b = 1$.

(a) Find the minterm expansion for a and for b.

(b) Find the maxterm expansion for a and for b.

Express each answer in abbreviated notation and also write it out in terms of x, y, and z.

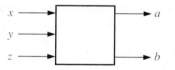

5.8 A switching network has four inputs as shown below. A and B represent the first and second bits of a binary number N_1. C and D represent the first and second bits of a binary number N_2. The output of the network is to be 1 only if the product $N_1 \times N_2$ is less than or equal to 2.

(a) Find the minterm expansion for F.

(b) Find the maxterm expansion for F.

Express your answers in both decimal notation and algebraic form.

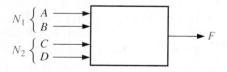

5.9 Given $f(a, b, c) = b + a'c$.

(a) Express f as a minterm expansion (use m notation).

(b) Express f as maxterm expansion (use M notation).

(c) Express f' as a minterm expansion (use m notation).

(d) Express f' as a maxterm expansion (use M notation).

5.10 Work Problem 5.9 using
$f(a, b, c, d) = (b' + d' + a)(c' + a')(b + d + a)(b + c + d' + a)$.

5.11 Work Problem 5.9 using $f(a, b, c) = a'(b + c')$.

5.12 Work Problem 5.9 using $f(a, b, c, d) = ac + bd' + a'c'd + ab'cd + a'b'cd'$.

5.13 Given $F'(A, B, C, D) = \sum m(0, 1, 2, 6, 7, 13, 15)$.
(a) Find the minterm expansion for F (both decimal and algebraic form).
(b) Find the maxterm expansion for F (both decimal and algebraic form).

5.14 Repeat Problem 5.13 for $F'(A, B, C, D) = \sum m(1, 2, 5, 6, 10, 15)$.

5.15 Four chairs are placed in a row:

Each chair may be occupied ("1") or empty ("0"). Write a logic function $F(A, B, C, D)$ which is 1 iff there are no adjacent empty chairs. Express F
(a) as a minterm expansion (standard sum of products) and
(b) as a maxterm expansion (standard product of sums).

5.16 Given $F_1 = \prod M(0, 4, 5, 6)$ and $F_2 = \prod M(0, 3, 4, 6, 7)$, find the maxterm expansion for $F_1 F_2$.
State a general rule for finding the maxterm expansion of $F_1 F_2$ given the maxterm expansions of F_1 and F_2.
Prove your answer by using the general form of the maxterm expansion.

5.17 (a) How many switching functions of two variables (x and y) are there?
(b) Give each function in truth table form and in reduced algebraic form. (Include degenerate cases like $F(x, y) = 0$, $F(x, y) = x$, $F(x, y) = y'$, etc.)

5.18 A combinational switching network has four inputs (A, B, C, and D) and one output Z. The output is 1 iff three or more of the inputs are 1. Design the network using two AND gates and three OR gates. Assume that each gate has a maximum of three inputs so that it will be necessary to partially factor your logic equation before you realize it.

5.19 A combinational switching network has four inputs (A, B, C, and D) and one output Z. The output is 1 iff the Gray coded digit represented by $ABCD$ is less than 5. Design the network using two AND gates and one OR gate. Assume that each gate has a maximum of two inputs so that it will be necessary to partially factor your logic equation before you realize it.

5.20 A combinational switching network has four inputs (A, B, C, and D) and one output Z. The output is to be 0 iff two or more inputs are 1. Design the network using four AND gates and three OR gates. Assume that each gate has a maximum of two inputs so that it will be necessary to partially factor your logic equation before you realize it.

5.21 A combinational network is divided into two subnetworks, N_1 and N_2, as shown below. Network N_1 has the given truth table. Assume that the input combinations of $ABC = 001$ and $ABC = 101$ will never occur. Change as many of the values of D, E, and F to don't cares as you can without changing the output Z. (If either E or F but not both can be a don't care, arbitrarily choose E to be the don't care.)

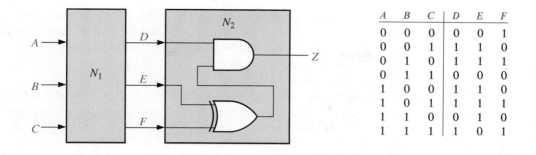

A	B	C	D	E	F
0	0	0	0	0	1
0	0	1	1	1	0
0	1	0	1	1	1
0	1	1	0	0	0
1	0	0	1	1	0
1	0	1	1	1	1
1	1	0	0	1	0
1	1	1	1	0	1

5.22 Work Problem 5.21 using the networks and truth table below. Assume that the input combinations of $ABC = 011$ and $ABC = 110$ will never occur.

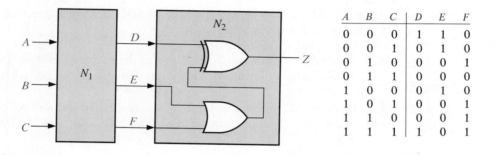

A	B	C	D	E	F
0	0	0	1	1	0
0	0	1	0	1	0
0	1	0	0	0	1
0	1	1	0	0	0
1	0	0	0	1	0
1	0	1	0	0	1
1	1	0	0	0	1
1	1	1	1	0	1

5.23 Work (a) and (b) with the truth table below:

A	B	C	F	G
0	0	0	0	0
0	0	1	1	X
0	1	0	X	0
0	1	1	1	1
1	0	0	0	1
1	0	1	X	0
1	1	0	1	1
1	1	1	0	X

(a) Find the simplest expression for F, and specify the values for the don't cares that lead to this expression.

(b) Repeat (a) for G.

5.24 In each case, determine if $X = Y$:

(a) $X = C(A + B) + AB$, $Y = ABC' + AB'C + BC$

(b) $X = B'C'D' + AB'C + BCD + A'BC'$
$Y = A'C'D' + AB'D' + ACD + A'BD$

(c) $X = A'C' + B + AC$
$Y = A'C' + A'B + AC + AB$

(d) $X = BD(A'C + C') + A'B'(C' + D') + A(BCD' + B'C'D')$
$Y = A'C'(B' + D) + D(BC' + AB) + CD'(A'B' + AB)$
$\quad + AB'(CD + C'D')$

5.25 A combinational network has four inputs (A, B, C, D) and three outputs (X, Y, Z). XYZ represents an binary number whose value equals the number of 1's at the input. For example if $ABCD = 1011$, $XYZ = 011$.
  (a) Find the minterm expansions for X, Y, and Z.
  (b) Find the maxterm expansions for Y and Z.

5.26 A combinational network has four inputs (A, B, C, D) and four outputs (W, X, Y, Z). $WXYZ$ represents an excess-3 coded number whose value equals the number of 1's at the input. For example, if $ABCD = 1101$, $WXYZ = 0110$.
  (a) Find the minterm expansions for X, Y, and Z.
  (b) Find the maxterm expansions for Y and Z.

5.27 A combinational network has four inputs (A, B, C, D), which represent a binary-coded decimal digit. The network has two groups of four outputs—S, T, U, V, and W, X, Y, Z. Each group represents a BCD digit. The output digits represent a decimal number which is 5 times the input number. For example, if $ABCD = 0111$, the outputs are 0011 0101. Assume that invalid BCD digits do not occur as inputs.
  (a) Construct the truth table.
  (b) Write down the minimum expressions for the outputs by inspection of the truth table. (*Hint:* Try to match output columns in the table with input columns.)

5.28 Work Problem 5.27 where the outputs represent a decimal number that is 1 more than 4 times the input number. For example, if $ABCD = 0011$, the outputs are 0001 0011.

6

Karnaugh Maps

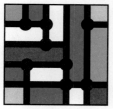

OBJECTIVES

1. Given a function (completely or incompletely specified) of three to six variables, plot it on a Karnaugh map. The function may be given in minterm, maxterm, or algebraic form.

2. Determine the essential (necessary) prime implicants of a function from a map.

3. Obtain the minimum sum-of-products or minimum product-of-sums form of a function from the map.

4. Determine *all* of the prime implicants of a function from a map.

5. Understand the relation between operations performed using the map and the corresponding algebraic operations.

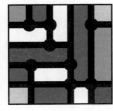

STUDY GUIDE

In this unit we will study the Karnaugh[1] map. Just about any type of algebraic manipulation we have done so far can be facilitated by using the map, provided the number of variables is small.

1. Study Section 6.1, *Minimum Forms of Switching Functions.*

    (a) Define a minimum sum of products.

    (b) Define a minimum product of sums.

    (c) Work Problem 6.3.

2. Study Section 6.2, *2- and 3-Variable Karnaugh Maps.*

    (a) Plot the given truth table on the map. Then loop two pairs of 1's on the map and write the simplified form of F.

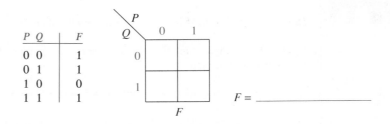

P Q	F
0 0	1
0 1	1
1 0	0
1 1	1

$F = $ _____

Now simplify F algebraically and verify that your answer is correct.

---

[1] Pronounced "*car*-no."

(b) $F(a, b, c)$ is plotted below. Find the truth table for F.

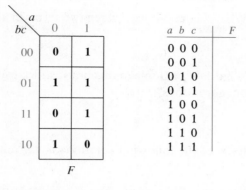

(c) Plot the following functions on the Karnaugh maps given below:

$$F_1(R, S, T) = \sum m(0, 1, 5, 6) \qquad F_2(R, S, T) = \prod M(2, 3, 4, 7)$$

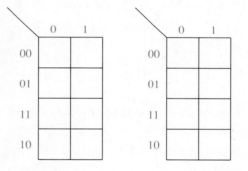

Why are the two maps the same?

(d) Plot the following function on the given map:

$$f(x, y, z) = z' + x'z + yz$$

Do *not* make a minterm expansion or a truth table before plotting.

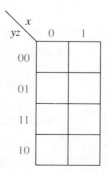

(e) For a 3-variable map, which squares are "adjacent" to square 2?

_____

(f) What theorem is used when two terms in adjacent squares are combined?

(g) What law of Boolean algebra justifies using a given 1 on a map in two or more loops?

(h) Each of the following solutions is *not* minimum.

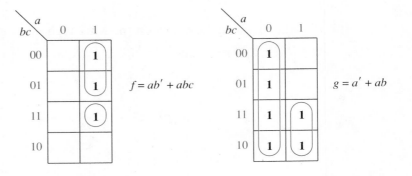

$f = ab' + abc$ $g = a' + ab$

In each case, change the looping on the map so that the minimum solution is obtained.

(i) Work Problem 6.5.

(j) Find two different minimum sum-of-products expressions for the function G which is plotted below.

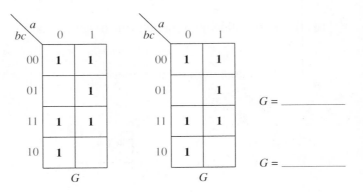

$G = $ _____

$G = $ _____

3. Study Section 6.3, *4-Variable Karnaugh Maps.*

(a) Note the locations of the minterms on 3- and 4-variable maps (Figs. 6–3(b) and 6–10). Memorize this ordering. This will save you much time when you are plotting Karnaugh maps.

The above ordering is valid only for the order of the variables given. If we label the maps as shown below, fill in the locations of the minterms:

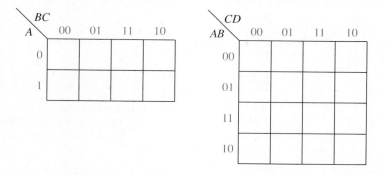

(b) Given the following map, write the minterm and maxterm expansions for F in decimal form:

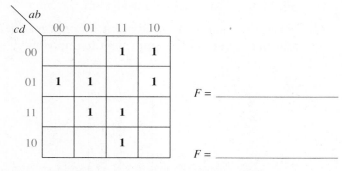

$F =$ _____

$F =$ _____

(c) Plot the following functions on the given maps:
(1) $f(w, x, y, z) = \sum m(0, 1, 2, 5, 7, 8, 9, 10, 13, 14)$
(2) $f(w, x, y, z) = x'z' + y'z + w'xz + wyz'$

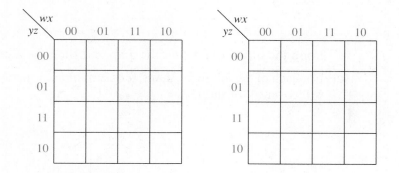

Your answers to (1) and (2) should be the same.

(d) For a 4-variable map, which squares are adjacent to square 14? _____ To square 8? _____

(e) When we combine two adjacent 1's on a map, this corresponds to applying the theorem $xy' + xy = x$ to eliminate the variable in which the two terms differ. Thus, looping the two 1's indicated on the map below is equivalent to combining the corresponding minterms algebraically:

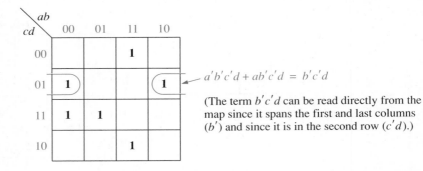

$$a'b'c'd + ab'c'd = b'c'd$$

(The term $b'c'd$ can be read directly from the map since it spans the first and last columns (b') and since it is in the second row ($c'd$).)

Loop two other pairs of adjacent 1's on the map above and state the algebraic equivalent of looping these terms. Now read the loops directly off the map and check your algebra.

(f) When we combine four adjacent 1's on a map (either four in a line or four in a square) this is equivalent to applying $xy + xy' = x$ three times:

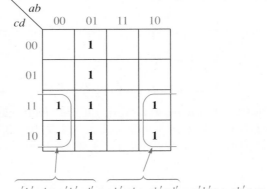

$$a'b'cd + a'b'cd' + ab'cd + ab'cd' = a'b'c + ab'c = b'c$$

Loop the other four 1's on the map and state the algebraic equivalent.

(g) For each of the following maps, loop a minimum number of terms which will cover all of the 1's.

cd \ ab	00	01	11	10
00		1	1	
01		1	1	1
11	1	1		
10		1		

f_1

cd \ ab	00	01	11	10
00				1
01		1		
11	1	1	1	1
10	1			1

f_2

(For each part you should have looped two groups of four 1's and two groups of two 1's).

Write down the minimum sum-of-products expression for f_1 and f_2 from the above maps.

$f_1 =$ _____

$f_2 =$ _____

(h) Why is it not possible to combine 3 or 6 minterms together rather than just 2, 4, 8, etc.?

(i) Note the procedure for deriving the minimum *product of sums* from the map. You will probably make fewer mistakes if you write down f' as a sum of products first and then complement it as illustrated by the example in Fig. 6–14. Work Problems 6.8 and 6.13.

4. Study Section 6.4, *Determination of Minimum Expressions Using Essential Prime Implicants.*

(a) For the map of Fig. 6–15, list three implicants of F other than those which are labeled.

For the same map, is $ac'd'$ a prime implicant of F?

Why or why not?

(b) For the given map, are any of the circled terms prime implicants?

Why or why not?

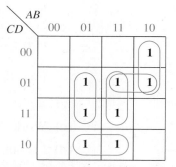

5. Study Fig. 6–18 carefully and then answer the following questions for the map given below:

(a) How many 1's are adjacent to m_0?

(b) Are all these 1's covered by a single prime implicant?

(c) From your answer to (b), can you determine if $B'C'$ is essential?

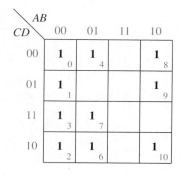

(d) How many 1's are adjacent to m_9?

(e) Are all of these 1's covered by a single prime implicant?

(f) From your answer to (e), is $B'C'$ essential?

(g) How many 1's are adjacent to m_7?

(h) Why is $A'C$ essential?

(i) Find two other essential prime implicants and tell which minterm makes them essential.

6. **(a)** How do you determine if a prime implicant is essential using a Karnaugh map?

(b) For the following map, why is $A'B'$ *not* essential?

Why is BD' essential?

Is $A'D'$ essential? Why?

Is BC' essential? Why?

Is $B'CD$ essential? Why?

Find the minimum sum of products.

CD\AB	00	01	11	10
00	1	1	1	
01	1	1	1	
11	1			1
10	1	1	1	

(c) Work Programmed Exercise 6.1.

(d) List all 1's and X's that are adjacent to 1_0.

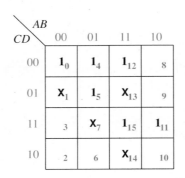

CD\AB	00	01	11	10
00	1_0	1_4	1_{12}	8
01	X_1	1_5	X_{13}	9
11	3	X_7	1_{15}	1_{11}
10	2	6	X_{14}	10

Why is $A'C'$ an essential prime implicant?

List all 1's and X's adjacent to 1_{15}.

Based on this list, why can't you find an essential implicant that covers 1_{15}?

Does this mean that there is no essential prime implicant that covers 1_{15}?

What essential prime implicant covers 1_{11}?

Can you find an *essential* prime implicant that covers 1_{12}? Explain.

Find two prime implicants that cover 1_{12}.

Give two minimum expressions for F.

(e) Work Problem 6.9.

(f) If you have a copy of the *LogicAid*™ program available, use the Karnaugh map tutorial mode to help you learn to find minimum solutions from Karnaugh maps. This program will check your work at each step to make sure that you loop the terms in the correct order. It also will check your final answer. Work Problem 6.10 using the Karnaugh map tutor.

7. (a) In Example 4, p. 98, we derived the following function:

$$Z = \sum m(0, 3, 6, 9) + \sum d(10, 11, 12, 13, 14, 15)$$

Plot Z on the given map using X's to represent don't cares.

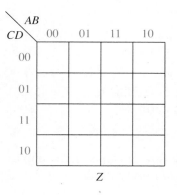

(b) Show that the minimum sum of products is

$$Z = A'B'C'D' + B'CD + AD + BCD'$$

Which *four* don't care minterms were assigned the value 1 when forming your solution?

(c) Show that the minimum product of sums for Z is

$$Z = (B' + C)(B' + D')(A' + D)(A + C + D')(B + C' + D)$$

Which *one* don't care term of Z was assigned the value 1 when forming your solution?

(d) Work Problems 6.14 and 6.15.

8. Study Section 6.5, *5- and 6-Variable Karnaugh Maps.*

(a) The figure below shows a three-dimensional 5-variable map. Plot the 1's and loops on the corresponding two-dimensional map, and give the minimum sum-of-products expression for the function.

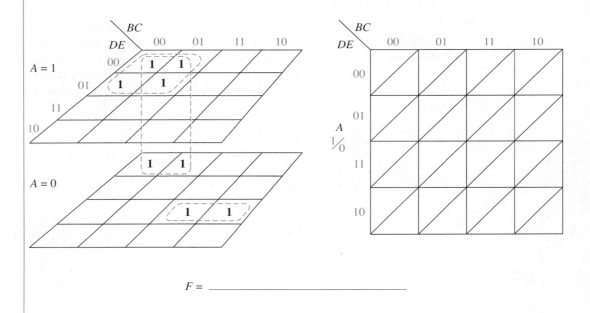

$$F = \underline{\hspace{5cm}}$$

(b) On a 5-variable map (Fig. 6–21), what are the five minterms adjacent to minterm 24?

(c) Work through all of the examples in this section carefully and make sure that you understand all of the steps.

(d) Two minimum solutions are given for Fig. 6–24. There is a third minimum sum-of-products solution. What is it?

(e) Read the material on 6-variable maps to get the basic idea; however, proficiency in deriving minimum solutions from 6-variable maps will not be required in order to pass the readiness test. (*Note:* Proficiency in working with 5-variable maps will be required.)

(f) Work Programmed Exercise 6.2.

(g)

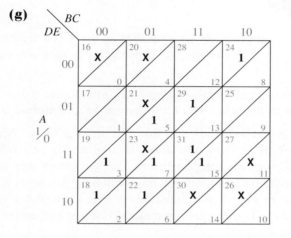

Find the three 1's and X's adjacent to 1_{18}. Can these all be looped with a single loop?

Find the 1's and X's adjacent to 1_{24}. Loop the essential prime implicant that covers 1_{24}.

Find the 1's and X's adjacent to 1_3. Loop the essential prime implicant that covers 1_3.

Can you find an essential prime implicant that covers 1_{22}? Explain.

Find and loop two more essential prime implicants.

Find three ways to cover the remaining 1 on the map and give the corresponding minimum solutions.

(h) If you have the *LogicAid* program available, work Problems 6.28 and 6.36 using the Karnaugh map tutor.

9. Study Section 6.6, *Other Uses of Karnaugh Maps*. Refer back to Fig. 6–8 and note that a consensus term exists if there are two adjacent, but nonoverlapping, prime implicants. Observe how this principle is applied in Fig. 6–27.

10. Work Problems 6.25, 6.27, 6.29, 6.16, and 6.17(a). When deriving the minimum solution from the map, always write down the *essential* prime implicants first. If you don't, it is quite likely that you won't get the minimum solution. In addition, make sure you can find *all* of the prime implicants from the map (see Problem 6.25(b).)

11. Review the objectives and take the readiness test.

Karnaugh Maps

Switching functions can generally be simplified by using the algebraic techniques described in Units 3 and 4. However, two problems arise when algebraic procedures are used:

1. The procedures are difficult to apply in a systematic way.
2. It is difficult to tell when you have arrived at a minimum solution.

The Karnaugh map method studied in this unit and the Quine-McCluskey procedure studied in Unit 7 overcome these difficulties by providing systematic methods for simplifying switching functions. The Karnaugh map is an especially useful tool for simplifying and manipulating switching functions of three or four variables, but it can be extended to functions of five, six, or more variables. Generally, you will find the Karnaugh map method is faster and easier to apply than other simplification methods.

6.1
Minimum Forms of Switching Functions

When a function is realized using AND and OR gates, the cost of realizing the function is directly related to the number of gates and gate inputs used. The Karnaugh map techniques developed in this unit lead directly to minimum cost two-level networks composed of AND and OR gates. An expression consisting of a sum of product terms corresponds directly to a two-level network composed of a group of AND gates feeding a single OR gate (see Fig. 2–5, for example). Similarly, a product-of-sums expression corresponds to a two-level network composed of OR gates feeding a single AND gate (see Fig. 2–6, for example). Therefore, in order to find minimum cost two-level AND-OR gate networks, we must find minimum expressions in sum-of-products or product-of-sums form.

A *minimum sum-of-products* expression for a function is defined as a sum of product terms which (a) has a minimum number of terms, and (b) of all those expressions which have the same minimum number of terms, has a minimum number of literals. The minimum sum of products corresponds directly to a minimum two-level gate network which has (a) a minimum number of gates and (b) a minimum number of gate inputs. Unlike the minterm expansion for a function, the minimum sum of products is not necessarily unique; that is, a given function may have two different minimum sum-of-products forms, each with the same number of terms and the same number of literals. Given a minterm expansion, the minimum sum-of-products form can often be obtained by the following procedure:

1. Combine terms by using $XY' + XY = X$. Do this repeatedly to eliminate as many literals as possible. A given term may be used more than once since $X + X = X$.
2. Eliminate redundant terms by using the consensus theorem or other theorems.

Unfortunately, the result of the above procedure may depend on the order in which terms are combined or eliminated so that the final expression obtained is not necessarily minimum.

EXAMPLE: Find a minimum sum-of-products expression for

$$F(a, b, c) = \sum m(0, 1, 2, 5, 6, 7)$$

$$F = a'b'c' + a'b'c + a'bc' + ab'c + abc' + abc$$

$$= a'b' + b'c + bc' + ab \qquad (6\text{–}1)$$

None of the terms in the above expression can be eliminated by consensus. However, combining terms in a different way leads directly to a minimum sum of products:

$$F = a'b'c' + a'b'c + a'bc' + ab'c + abc' + abc$$

$$= a'b' + bc' + ac \qquad (6\text{–}2)$$

A *minimum product-of-sums* expression for a function is defined as a product of sum terms which (a) has a minimum number of factors, and (b) of all those expressions which have the same number of factors, has a minimum number of literals. Unlike the maxterm expansion, the minimum product-of-sums form of a function is not necessarily unique. Given a maxterm expansion, the minimum product of sums can often be obtained by a procedure similar to that used in the minimum sum-of-products case, except that the theorem $(X + Y)(X + Y') = X$ is used to combine terms.

EXAMPLE:

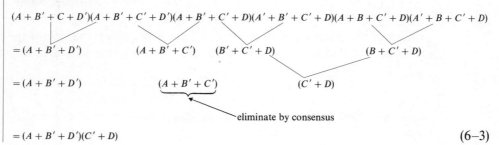

$$(A + B' + C + D')(A + B' + C' + D')(A + B' + C' + D)(A' + B' + C' + D)(A + B + C' + D)(A' + B + C' + D)$$

$$= (A + B' + D') \qquad (A + B' + C') \quad (B' + C' + D) \qquad (B + C' + D)$$

$$= (A + B' + D') \qquad (A + B' + C') \qquad (C' + D)$$

eliminate by consensus

$$= (A + B' + D')(C' + D) \qquad (6\text{–}3)$$

6.2
2- and 3-Variable Karnaugh Maps

Just like a truth table, the Karnaugh map of a function specifies the value of the function for every combination of values of the independent variables. A 2-variable Karnaugh map is shown below. The values of one variable are listed across the top of the map, and the values of the other variable are listed on the left side. Each square of the map corresponds to a pair of values for A and B as indicated.

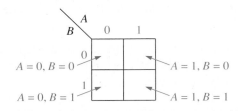

Figure 6–1 shows the truth table for a function F and the corresponding Karnaugh map. Note that the value of F for $A = B = 0$ is plotted in the upper left square and the other map entries are plotted in a similar way in Fig. 6–1(b). Each 1 on the map corresponds to a minterm of F. We can read the minterms from the map just like we can read them from the truth table. A 1 in square 00 of Fig. 6–1(c) indicates that $A'B'$ is a minterm of F. Similarly, a 1 in square 01 indicates that $A'B$ is a minterm. Minterms in adjacent squares of the map can be combined since they differ in only one variable. Thus, $A'B'$ and $A'B$ combine to form A', and this is indicated by looping the corresponding 1's on the map in Fig. 6–1(d).

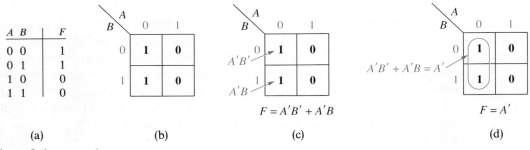

A B	F
0 0	1
0 1	1
1 0	0
1 1	0

(a)

(b)

$F = A'B' + A'B$

(c)

$F = A'$

(d)

Figure 6–1

Figure 6–2 shows a 3-variable truth table and the corresponding Karnaugh map.[2] The value of one variable (A) is listed across the top of the map, and the values of the other two variables (B, C) are listed along the side of the map. The rows are labeled in the sequence 00, 01, 11, 10 so that values in adjacent rows

---

[2] See Fig. 6–28 for an alternative way of labeling maps.

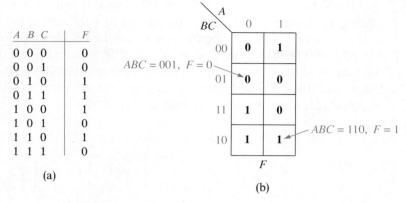

A B C	F
0 0 0	0
0 0 1	0
0 1 0	1
0 1 1	1
1 0 0	1
1 0 1	0
1 1 0	1
1 1 1	0

(a)

(b)

Figure 6–2
Truth Table and Karnaugh Map for
3-Variable Function

differ in only one variable. For each combination of values of the variables, the value of F is read from the truth table and plotted in the appropriate map square. For example, for the input combination $ABC = 001$, the value $F = 0$ is plotted in the square for which $A = 0$ and $BC = 01$. For the combination $ABC = 110$, $F = 1$ is plotted in the $A = 1$, $BC = 10$ square.

Figure 6–3 shows the location of the minterms on a 3-variable map. Minterms in adjacent squares of the map differ in only one variable and therefore can be combined using the theorem $XY' + XY = X$. For example, minterm 011 ($a'bc$) is adjacent to the three minterms with which it can be combined— 001 ($a'b'c$), 010 ($a'bc'$), and 111 (abc). In addition to squares which are physically adjacent, the top and bottom rows of the map are defined to be adjacent since corresponding minterms in these rows differ in only one variable. Thus 000 and 010 are adjacent, and so are 100 and 110.

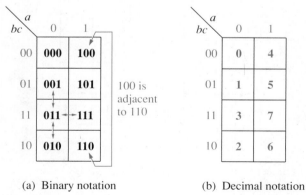

(a) Binary notation

(b) Decimal notation

Figure 6–3
Location of Minterms on a 3-Variable
Karnaugh Map

Given the minterm expansion of a function, it can be plotted on a map by placing 1's in the squares which correspond to minterms of the function and 0's in the remaining squares (the 0's may be omitted if desired). Figure 6–4 shows the plot of $F(a, b, c) = m_1 + m_3 + m_5$. If F is given as a maxterm expansion, the map is plotted by placing 0's in the squares which correspond to the maxterms and then filling in the remaining squares with 1's. Thus $F(a, b, c) = M_0M_2M_4M_6M_7$ gives the same map as Fig. 6–4.

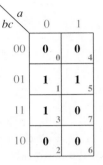

Figure 6–4
Karnaugh Map of
$F(a, b, c) = \sum m(1, 3, 5) = \prod M(0, 2, 4, 6, 7)$

Figure 6–5 illustrates how product terms can be plotted on Karnaugh maps. To plot the term b, 1's are entered in the four squares of the map where $b = 1$. The term bc' is 1 when $b = 1$ and $c = 0$, so 1's are entered in the two squares in the $bc = 10$ row. The term ac' is 1 when $a = 1$ and $c = 0$, so 1's are entered in the $a = 1$ column in the rows where $c = 0$.

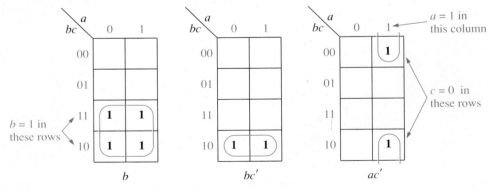

Figure 6–5
Karnaugh Maps for Product Terms

If a function is given in algebraic form, it is unnecessary to expand it to min-term form before plotting it on a map. If the algebraic expression is converted to sum-of-products form, then each product term can be plotted directly as a group of 1's on the map. For example, given that

$$f(a, b, c) = abc' + b'c + a'$$

we would plot the map as follows:

1. The term abc' is 1 when $a = 1$ and $bc = 10$, so we place a 1 in the square which corresponds to the $a = 1$ column and the $bc = 10$ row of the map.
2. The term $b'c$ is 1 when $bc = 01$, so we place 1's in both squares of the $bc = 01$ row of the map.
3. The term a' is 1 when $a = 0$, so we place 1's in all the squares of the $a = 0$ column of the map. (*Note:* since there already is a 1 in the $abc = 001$ square, we do not have to place a second 1 there because $x + x = x$.)

Figure 6–6 illustrates how a simplified expression for a function can be derived using a Karnaugh map. The function to be simplified is first plotted on a Karnaugh map in Fig. 6–6(a). Terms in adjacent squares on the map differ in only one variable and can be combined using the theorem $XY' + XY = X$. Thus $a'b'c$ and $a'bc$ combine to form $a'c$, and $a'b'c$ and $ab'c$ combine to form $b'c$ as shown in Fig. 6–6(b). A loop around a group of minterms indicates that these terms have been combined. The looped terms can be read directly off the map. Thus, for Fig. 6–6(b), term T_1 is in the $a = 0$ (a') column and it spans the rows where $c = 1$, so $T_1 = a'c$. Note that b has been eliminated since the two minterms in T_1 differ in the variable b. Similarly, term T_2 is in the $bc = 01$ row so $T_2 = b'c$, and a has been eliminated since T_2 spans the $a = 0$ and $a = 1$ columns. Thus the minimum sum-of-products form for F is $a'c + b'c$.

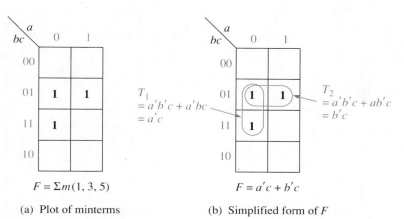

(a) Plot of minterms   (b) Simplified form of F

Figure 6–6
Simplification of a 3-Variable Function

The map for the complement of F (Fig. 6–7) is formed by replacing 0's with 1's and 1's with 0's on the map of F. To simplify F', note that the terms in the top row combine to form $b'c'$ and the terms in the bottom row combine to form bc'. Since $b'c'$ and bc' differ in only one variable, the top and bottom rows can then be combined to form a group of four 1's, thus eliminating two variables and leaving $T_1 = c'$. The remaining 1 combines as shown to form $T_2 = ab$, so the minimum sum-of-products form for F' is $c' + ab$.

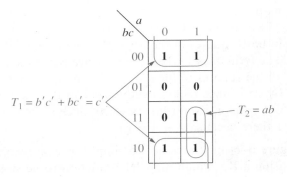

Figure 6–7
Complement of Map in Fig. 6–6(a)

The Karnaugh map can also illustrate the basic theorems of Boolean algebra. Figure 6–8 illustrates the consensus theorem, $XY + X'Z + YZ = XY + X'Z$. Note that the consensus term (YZ) is redundant because its 1's are covered by the other two terms.

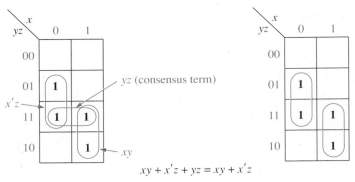

Figure 6–8
Karnaugh Maps Which Illustrate the
Consensus Theorem

If a function has two or more minimum sum-of-products forms, all of these forms can be determined from a map. Figure 6–9 shows the two minimum solutions for $F = \sum m(0, 1, 2, 5, 6, 7)$.

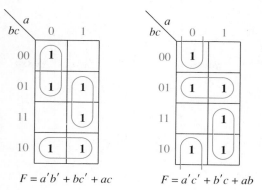

$$F = a'b' + bc' + ac \qquad F = a'c' + b'c + ab$$

Figure 6–9
Function with Two Minimum Forms

6.3
4-Variable Karnaugh Maps

Figure 6–10 shows the location of minterms on a 4-variable map. Each minterm is located adjacent to the four terms with which it can combine. For example, m_5 (0101) could combine with m_1 (0001), m_4 (0100), m_7 (0111), or m_{13} (1101) because it differs in only one variable from each of the other minterms. The definition of adjacent squares must be extended so that not only are top and bottom rows adjacent as in the 3-variable map, but also the first and last columns are adjacent. This requires numbering the columns in the sequence 00, 01, 11, 10 so that minterms 0 and 8, 1 and 9, etc., are in adjacent squares.

CD \ AB	00	01	11	10
00	0	4	12	8
01	1	5	13	9
11	3	7	15	11
10	2	6	14	10

Figure 6–10
Location of Minterms on 4-Variable
Karnaugh Map

We will now plot the following 4-variable expression on a Karnaugh map (Fig. 6–11):

$$f(a, b, c, d) = acd + a'b + d'$$

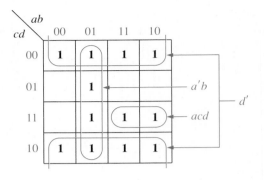

Figure 6–11
Plot of $acd + a'b + d'$

The first term is 1 when $a = c = d = 1$, so we place 1's in the two squares which are in the $a = 1$ column and $cd = 11$ row. The term $a'b$ is 1 when $ab = 01$, so we place four 1's in the $ab = 01$ column. Finally, d' is 1 when $d = 0$, so we place eight 1's in the two rows for which $d = 0$. (Duplicate 1's are not plotted since $1 + 1 = 1$.)

Next we will simplify the functions f_1 and f_2 given in Fig. 6–12. Since the functions are specified in minterm form, we can determine the locations of the 1's on the map by referring to Fig. 6–10. After plotting the maps, we can then combine adjacent groups of 1's. Minterms can be combined in groups of 2, 4, or 8 to eliminate 1, 2, or 3 variables, respectively. In Fig. 6–12(a), the pair of 1's in the $ab = 00$ column and also in the $d = 1$ rows represents $a'b'd$. The group of four 1's in the $b = 1$ columns and $c = 0$ rows represents bc'.

In Fig. 6–12(b), note that the four corner 1's span the $b = 0$ columns and $d = 0$ rows, and therefore can be combined to form the term $b'd'$. The group of eight 1's covers both rows where $c = 1$, and therefore represents the term c. The pair of 1's which is looped on the map represents the term $a'bd$ since it is in the $ab = 01$ column and spans the $d = 1$ rows.

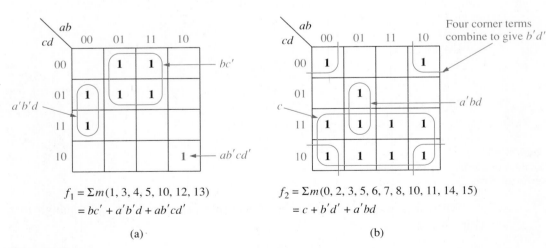

$f_1 = \Sigma m(1, 3, 4, 5, 10, 12, 13)$
$= bc' + a'b'd + ab'cd'$

(a)

$f_2 = \Sigma m(0, 2, 3, 5, 6, 7, 8, 10, 11, 14, 15)$
$= c + b'd' + a'bd$

(b)

Figure 6–12
Simplification of 4-Variable Functions

The Karnaugh map method is easily extended to functions with don't cares. The required minterms are indicated by 1's on the map, and the don't care minterms are indicated by X's. When choosing terms to form the minimum sum of products, all the 1's must be covered, but the X's are only used if they will simplify the resulting expression. In Fig. 6–13, the only don't-care term used in forming the simplified expression is 13.

ab
cd
00
01
11
10
00
01
11
10
X
1
1
X
1
1
1
X

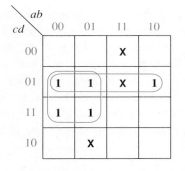

$$f = \Sigma m(1, 3, 5, 7, 9) + \Sigma d(6, 12, 13)$$
$$= a'd + c'd$$

Figure 6–13
Simplification of an Incompletely Specified Function

Use of Karnaugh maps to find a minimum sum-of-products form for a function has been illustrated in Figs. 6–1, 6–6, and 6–12. A minimum product of sums can also be obtained from the map. Since the 0's of f are 1's of f', the minimum sum of products for f' can be determined by looping the 0's on a map of f. The complement of the minimum sum of products for f' is then the minimum product of sums for f. The following example illustrates this procedure for

$$f = x'z' + wyz + w'y'z' + x'y$$

First, the 1's of f are plotted in Fig. 6–14. Then, from the 0's,

$$f' = y'z + wxz' + w'xy$$

and the minimum product of sums for f is

$$f = (y + z')(w' + x' + z)(w + x' + y')$$

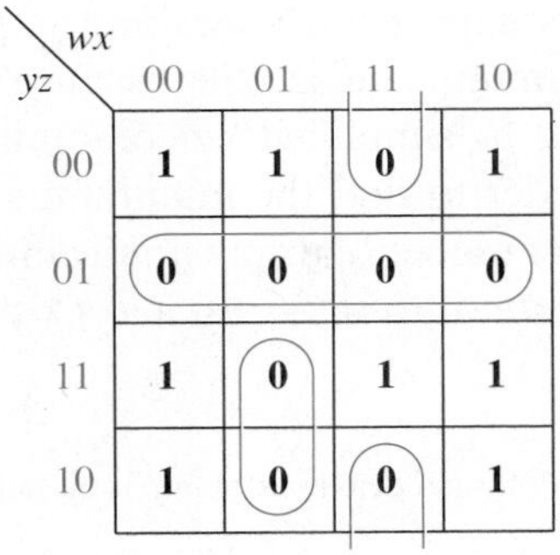

wx
yz
00
01
11
10
00
01
11
10
1
1
0
1
0
0
0
0
1
0
1
1
1
0
0
1

Figure 6–14

6.4
Determination of Minimum Expressions Using Essential Prime Implicants

Any single 1 or any group of 1's which can be combined together on a map of the function F represents a product term which is called an *implicant* of F.[3] Several implicants of F are indicated in Fig. 6–15. A product term implicant is called a *prime implicant* if it cannot be combined with another term to eliminate a variable. In Fig. 6–15, $a'b'c$, $a'cd'$, and ac' are prime implicants because they cannot be combined with other terms to eliminate a variable. On the other hand, $a'b'c'd'$ is not a prime implicant because it can be combined with $a'b'cd'$. Neither abc' nor $ab'c'$ is a prime implicant since these terms combine together to form ac'.

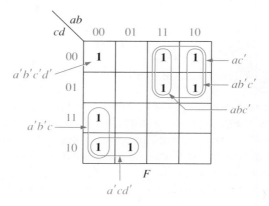

Figure 6–15

All of the prime implicants of a function can be obtained from a Karnaugh map. A single 1 on a map represents a prime implicant if it is not adjacent to any other 1's. Two adjacent 1's on a map form a prime implicant if they are not contained in a group of four 1's, four adjacent 1's form a prime implicant if they are not contained in a group of eight 1's, etc.

The minimum sum-of-products expression for a function consists of some (but not necessarily all) of the prime implicants of a function. In other words, a sum-of-products expression containing a term which is not a prime implicant cannot be minimum. This is true because if a nonprime term were present, the expression could be simplified by combining the nonprime term with additional minterms. In order to find the minimum sum of products from a map, we must find a minimum number of prime implicants which cover all of the 1's on the map. The function plotted in Fig. 6–16 has six prime implicants. Three of these prime

---

[3] See Section 7.1 for a formal definition of implicant and prime implicant.

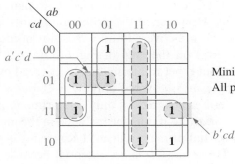

Minimum solution: $F = a'b'd + bc' + ac$

All prime implicants: $a'b'd, bc', ac, a'c'd, ab, b'cd$

Figure 6–16
Determination of all Prime Implicants

implicants cover all of the 1's on the map, and the minimum solution is the sum of these three prime implicants. The shaded loops represent prime implicants which are not part of the minimum solution.

When writing down a list of *all* of the prime implicants from the map, note that there are often prime implicants which are not included in the minimum sum of products. Even though all of the 1's in a term have already been covered by prime implicants, that term may still be a prime implicant provided that it is not included in a larger group of 1's. For example, in Fig. 6–16, $a'c'd$ is a prime implicant because it cannot be combined with other 1's to eliminate another variable. However, abd is not a prime implicant because it can be combined with two other 1's to form ab. The term $b'cd$ is also a prime implicant even though both of its 1's are already covered by other prime implicants. In the process of finding prime implicants, don't cares are treated just like 1's. However, a prime implicant composed entirely of don't cares can never be part of the minimum solution.

Since all of the prime implicants of a function are generally not needed in forming the minimum sum of products, a systematic procedure for selecting prime implicants is needed. If prime implicants are selected from the map in the wrong order, a nonminimum solution may result. For example, in Fig. 6–17, if CD is

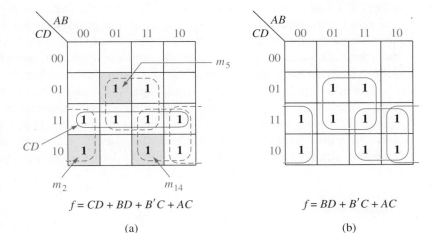

$$f = CD + BD + B'C + AC$$

$$f = BD + B'C + AC$$

Figure 6–17
(a)
(b)

chosen first, then BD, $B'C$, and AC are needed to cover the remaining 1's, and the solution contains four terms. However, if the prime implicants indicated in Fig. 6–17(b) are chosen first, all 1's are covered and CD is not needed.

Note that some of the minterms on the map of Fig. 6–17(a) can be covered by only a single prime implicant, but other minterms can be covered by two different prime implicants. For example, m_2 is covered only by $B'C$, but m_3 is covered by both $B'C$ and CD. If a minterm is covered by only one prime implicant, that prime implicant is said to be *essential* and it must be included in the minimum sum of products. Thus, $B'C$ is an essential prime implicant because m_2 is not covered by any other prime implicant. However, CD is *not* essential because each of the 1's in CD can be covered by another prime implicant. The only prime implicant which covers m_5 is BD, so BD is essential. Similarly, AC is essential because no other prime implicant covers m_{14}. In this example, if we choose all of the essential prime implicants, all of the 1's on the map are covered and the nonessential prime implicant CD is not needed.

In general, in order to find a minimum sum of products from a map, we should first loop all of the essential prime implicants. One way of finding essential prime implicants on a map is simply to look at each 1 on the map that has not already been covered, and check to see how many prime implicants cover that 1. If there is only one prime implicant which covers the 1, that prime implicant is essential. If there are two or more prime implicants which cover the 1, we cannot say whether these prime implicants are essential or not without further checking. For simple problems, we can locate the essential prime implicants in this way "by inspection" of each 1 on the map. For example, in Fig. 6–16, m_4 is covered only by the prime implicant bc', and m_{10} is covered only by the prime implicant ac. All other 1's on the map are covered by two prime implicants; therefore, the only essential prime implicants are bc' and ac.

For more complicated maps, and especially for maps with five or more variables, we need a more systematic approach for finding the essential prime implicants. When checking a minterm to see if it is covered by only one prime implicant, we must look at all squares adjacent to that minterm. If the given minterm and all of the 1's adjacent to it are covered by a single term, then that term is an *essential* prime implicant.[4] If all of the 1's adjacent to a given minterm are *not* covered by a single term, then there are two or more prime implicants which cover that minterm and we cannot say whether these prime implicants are essential or not without further checking. Figure 6–18 illustrates this principle.

The adjacent 1's for minterm m_0 (1_0) are 1_1, 1_2, and 1_4. Since no single term covers these four 1's, no essential prime implicant is yet apparent. The adjacent 1's for 1_1 are 1_0 and 1_5, so the term which covers these three 1's ($A'C'$) is an essential prime implicant. Since the only 1 adjacent to 1_2 is 1_0, $A'B'D'$ is also essential. Since the 1's adjacent to 1_7 (1_5 and 1_{15}) are not covered by a single term,

---

[4] This statement is proved in Appendix C.1.

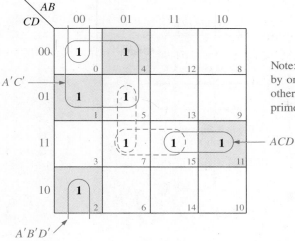

Figure 6–18

Note: 1's shaded in blue are covered by only one prime implicant. All other 1's are covered by at least two prime implicants.

neither $A'BD$ nor BCD is essential at this point. However, since the only 1 adjacent to 1_{11} is 1_{15}, ACD is essential. To complete the minimum solution, one of the nonessential prime implicants is needed. Either $A'BD$ or BCD may be selected. The final solution is

$$A'C' + A'B'D' + ACD + \left\{ \begin{matrix} A'BD \\ \text{or} \\ BCD \end{matrix} \right\}$$

If a don't care minterm is present on the map, we do not have to check it to see if it is covered by one or more prime implicants. However, when checking a 1 for adjacent 1's, we treat the adjacent don't cares as if they were 1's since don't cares may be combined with 1's in the process of forming prime implicants. The following procedure can then be used to obtain a minimum sum of products from a Karnaugh map:

1. Choose a minterm (a 1) which has not yet been covered.
2. Find all 1's and X's adjacent to that minterm. (Check the n adjacent squares on an n-variable map.)
3. If a single term covers the minterm and all of the adjacent 1's and X's, then that term is an essential prime implicant, so select that term. (Note that don't cares are treated like 1's in steps 2 and 3 but not in step 1.)
4. Repeat steps 1, 2, and 3 until all essential prime implicants have been chosen.
5. Find a minimum set of prime implicants which cover the remaining 1's on the map. (If there is more than one such set, choose a set with a minimum number of literals.)

Figure 6–19 gives a flowchart for this procedure.

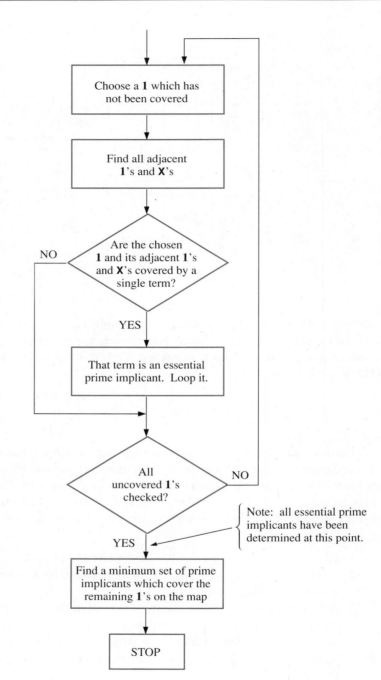

Figure 6–19
Flowchart for Determining the Minimum
Sum-of-Products Using a Karnaugh Map

The following example (Fig. 6–20) illustrates the above procedure. Starting with 1_4, we see that the adjacent 1's and X's (X_0, 1_5, and 1_6) are *not* covered by a single term, so no essential prime implicant is apparent. However, 1_6 and its adjacent 1's and X's (1_4 and X_7) are covered by $A'B$, so $A'B$ is an essential prime implicant. Next, looking at 1_{13}, we see that its adjacent 1's and X's (1_5, 1_9, and X_{15}) are *not* covered by a single term, so no essential prime implicant is apparent. Similarly, examination of the terms adjacent to 1_8 and 1_9 reveals no essential prime implicants. However, 1_{10} has only 1_8 adjacent to it, so $AB'D'$ is an essential prime implicant since it covers both 1_{10} and 1_8. Having first selected the essential prime implicants, we now choose $AC'D$ since it covers both of the remaining 1's on the map.

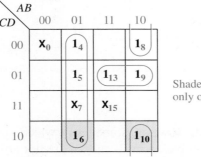

Shaded 1's are covered by only one prime implicant

Figure 6–20

Judicious selection of the order in which the minterms are selected (step 1) reduces the amount of work required in applying the above procedure. As will be seen in the next section, this procedure is especially helpful in obtaining minimum solutions for 5- and 6-variable problems.

6.5
5- and 6-Variable Karnaugh Maps

A 5-variable map can be constructed in three dimensions by placing one 4-variable map on top of a second one. Terms in the bottom layer are numbered 0 through 15 and corresponding terms in the top layer are numbered 16 through 31, so that terms in the bottom layer contain A' and those in the top layer contain A. To represent the map in two dimensions, we will divide each square in a 4-variable map by a diagonal line and place terms in the bottom layer below the line and terms in the top layer above the line (Fig. 6–21).[5] Terms in the top or bottom layer combine just like terms on a 4-variable map. In addition, two terms in the same square which are separated by a diagonal line differ in only one variable

---

[5] An alternate representation is to draw the two layers side by side as in Fig. 6–29, but most individuals find adjacencies more difficult to see when this form is used.

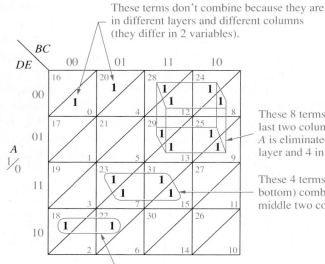

These terms don't combine because they are in different layers and different columns (they differ in 2 variables).

These 8 terms combine to give BD' (B from last two columns and D' from top two rows; A is eliminated since 4 terms are in the top layer and 4 in the bottom).

These 4 terms (2 from top layer and 2 from bottom) combine to give CDE (C from the middle two columns and DE from the row).

These 2 terms in the top layer combine to give $AB'DE'$.

Figure 6–21
A 5-Variable Karnaugh Map

and can be combined. However, some terms which appear to be physically adjacent are not. For example, terms 0 and 20 are not adjacent because they appear in a different column and a different layer. Each term can be adjacent to exactly five other terms, four in the same layer and one in the other layer (Fig. 6–22). When checking for adjacencies, each term should be checked against the five possible adjacent squares.

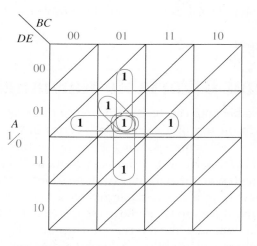

Figure 6–22

Two examples of 5-variable minimization using maps follow. Figure 6–23 is a map of

$$F(A, B, C, D, E) = \sum m(0, 1, 4, 5, 13, 15, 20, 21, 22, 23, 24, 26, 28, 30, 31)$$

Prime implicant P_1 is chosen first since all of the 1's adjacent to minterm 0 are

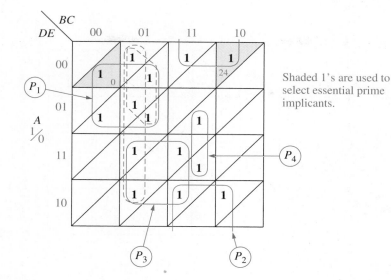

Figure 6–23

covered by P_1. Prime implicant P_2 is chosen next since all of the 1's adjacent to minterm 24 are covered by P_2. All of the remaining 1's on the map can be covered by at least two different prime implicants, so we proceed by trial and error. After a few tries, it becomes apparent that the remaining 1's can be covered by three prime implicants. If we choose prime implicants P_3 and P_4 next, the remaining two 1's can be covered by two different groups of four. The resulting minimum solution is

$$F = \underset{P_1}{A'B'D'} + \underset{P_2}{ABE'} + \underset{P_3}{ACD} + \underset{P_4}{A'BCE} + \begin{Bmatrix} AB'C \\ \text{or} \\ B'CD' \end{Bmatrix}$$

Figure 6–24 is a map of

$$F(A, B, C, D, E) = \sum m(0, 1, 3, 8, 9, 14, 15, 16, 17, 19, 25, 27, 31)$$

All 1's adjacent to m_{16} are covered by P_1, so choose P_1 first. All 1's adjacent to m_3 are covered by P_2, so P_2 is chosen next. All 1's adjacent to m_8 are covered by P_3, so P_3 is chosen. Since m_{14} is only adjacent to m_{15}, P_4 is also essential. There are no more essential prime implicants, and the remaining 1's can be covered by two terms, P_5 and (1-9-17-25) or (17-19-25-27). The final solution is

$$F = \underset{P_1}{B'C'D'} + \underset{P_2}{B'C'E} + \underset{P_3}{A'C'D'} + \underset{P_4}{A'BCD} + \underset{P_5}{ABDE} + \begin{Bmatrix} C'D'E \\ \text{or} \\ AC'E \end{Bmatrix}$$

A 6-variable map can be constructed in three dimensions by stacking up four 4-variable maps. Plot values of AB on the layers and values of CD and EF on the rows and columns in each layer. Assign $AB = 00$ to the bottom layer, $AB = 01$ to the second layer, $AB = 11$ to the third layer, and $AB = 10$ to the top layer. Then terms in adjacent layers differ in only one of these variables. (In this sense the top and bottom layers are adjacent.) A 6-variable map can be drawn in two

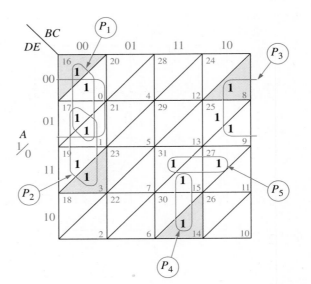

Figure 6–24

dimensions by dividing each square of a 4-variable map into four parts as shown below. Minterms 0–15 are plotted in the bottom (00 layer), 16–31 in the next (01) layer, 32–47 in the top (10) layer, and 48–63 in the third (11) layer.

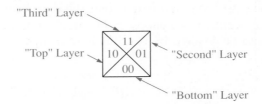

Figure 6–25 shows a 6-variable example. Note that terms in adjacent columns (or rows) are adjacent only if they are in the same layer. Term 1 in the second

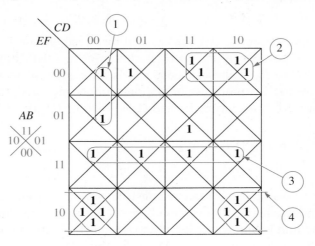

Figure 6–25
A 6-Variable Map

layer is $A'BC'D'E$. Term 2 spans the second and third layers and is $BCE'F'$. Term 3 in the third layer is $ABEF$. Term 4 spans all four layers, eliminating both A and B. Term 4 is $D'EF'$. The remaining two 1's on the map do *not* combine with another term. They are not adjacent to the nearest terms because these terms are in different layers.

6.6
Other Uses of Karnaugh Maps

Many operations that can be performed using a truth table or algebraically can be done using a Karnaugh map. If we plot an expression for F on a map, we can read off the minterm and maxterm expansions for F and for F'. From the map of Fig. 6–14, the minterm expansion of f is

$$f = \sum m(0, 2, 3, 4, 8, 10, 11, 15)$$

and since each 0 corresponds to a maxterm, the maxterm expansion of f is

$$f = \prod M(1, 5, 6, 7, 9, 12, 13, 14)$$

We can prove that two functions are equal by plotting them on maps and showing that they have the same Karnaugh map. We can perform the AND operation (or the OR operation) on two functions by ANDing (or ORing) the 1's and 0's which appear in corresponding positions on their maps. This procedure is valid because it is equivalent to doing the same operations on the truth tables for the functions.

A Karnaugh map can facilitate factoring an expression. Inspection of the map reveals terms which have one or more variables in common. For the following map, the two terms in the first column have $A'B'$ in common; the two terms in the lower right corner have AC in common.

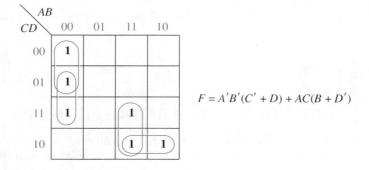

$$F = A'B'(C' + D) + AC(B + D')$$

Figure 6–26

When simplifying a function algebraically, the Karnaugh map can be used as a guide in determining what steps to take. For example, consider the function

$$F = ABCD + B'CDE + A'B' + BCE'$$

From the map (Fig. 6–27), we see that in order to get the minimum solution, we must add the term $ACDE$. We can do this using the consensus theorem:

$$F = ABCD + B'CDE + A'B' + BCE' + ACDE$$

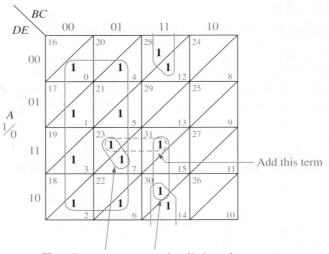

Figure 6–27

Then these two terms can be eliminated

Add this term

As can be seen from the map, the above expression now contains two redundant terms, $ABCD$ and $B'CDE$. These can be eliminated using the consensus theorem, which gives the minimum solution

$$F = A'B' + BCE' + ACDE$$

6.7
Other Forms of Karnaugh Maps

Instead of labeling the sides of a Karnaugh map with 0's and 1's, some people prefer to use the labeling shown in Fig. 6–28. For the half of the map labeled A, $A = 1$; and for the other half, $A = 0$. The other variables have a similar interpretation. A map labeled this way is sometimes referred to as a Veitch diagram. It is particularly useful for plotting functions given in algebraic form rather than in minterm or maxterm form. However, when using Karnaugh maps to solve

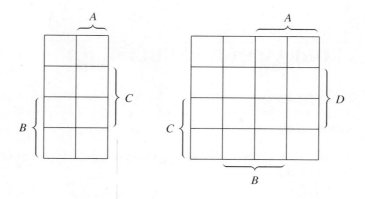

Figure 6–28
Veitch Diagrams

sequential network problems (Units 12 through 17), the use of 0's and 1's to label the maps is more convenient.

Two alternative forms for 5-variable maps are used. One form simply consists of two 4-variable maps side by side as in Fig. 6–29(a). A modification of this uses a "mirror image" map as in Fig. 6–29(b). In this map, first and eighth columns are "adjacent," as are second and seventh columns, third and sixth columns, and fourth and fifth columns. The same function is plotted on both these maps. Similarly, a 6-variable map may be represented as four 4-variable maps arranged in a square.

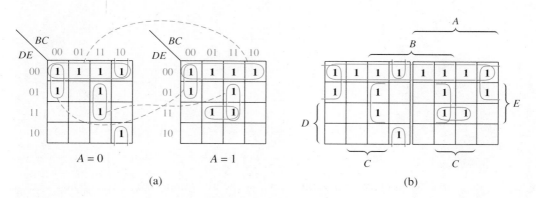

$$F = D'E' + B'C'D' + BCE + A'BC'E' + ACDE$$

Figure 6–29
Other Forms of 5-Variable Karnaugh Maps

PROGRAMMED EXERCISE 6.1

Cover the answers to this exercise with a sheet of paper and slide it down as you check your answers. *Write* your answers in the space provided before looking at the correct answer.

Problem: Determine the minimum sum of products and minimum product of sums for

$$f = b'c'd' + bcd + acd' + a'b'c + a'bc'd$$

First, plot the map for f.

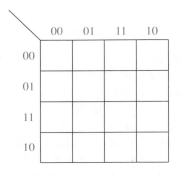

Answer:

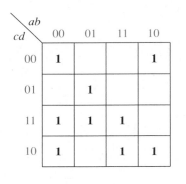

(a) The minterms adjacent to m_0 on the above map are _____ and _____.

(b) Find an essential prime implicant containing m_0 and loop it.

(c) The minterms adjacent to m_3 are _____ and _____.

(d) Is there an essential prime implicant which contains m_3?

(e) Find the remaining essential prime implicant(s) and loop it (them).

Answers:

(a) m_2 and m_8 (b)
(c) m_2 and m_7 (e)
(d) No

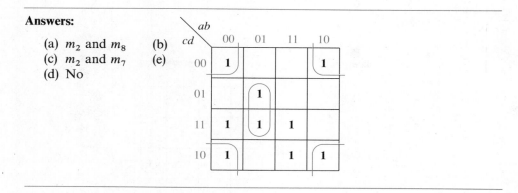

Loop the remaining 1's using a minimum number of loops.

The two possible minimum sum-of-products forms for f are

$f =$ _____ and

$f =$ _____

Answer:

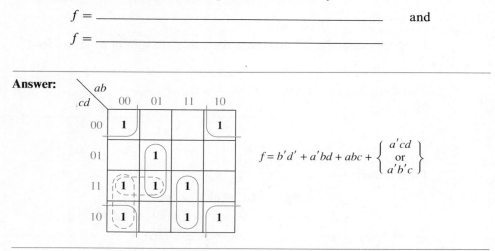

$$f = b'd' + a'bd + abc + \begin{cases} a'cd \\ \text{or} \\ a'b'c \end{cases}$$

Next, we will find the minimum product of sums for f. Start by plotting the map for f'.

Loop all essential prime implicants of f' and indicate which minterm makes each one essential.

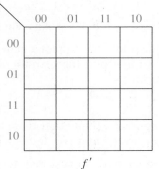

f'

Answer:

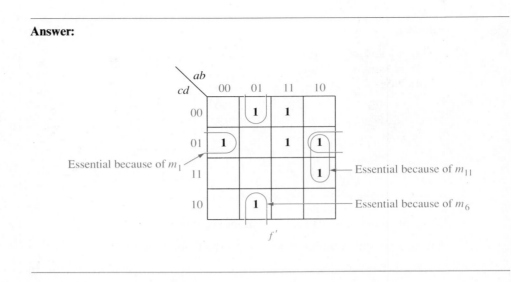

Loop the remaining 1's and write the minimum sum of products for f'.

$f' =$ _____

The minimum product of sums for f is therefore

$f =$ _____

Final answer:

$$f' = b'c'd + a'bd' + ab'd + abc'$$
$$f = (b + c + d')(a + b' + d)(a' + b + d')(a' + b' + c)$$

PROGRAMMED EXERCISE 6.2

Problem: Determine a minimum sum-of-products expression for

$$f(a, b, c, d, e) = (a' + c + d)(a' + b + e)(a + c' + e')(c + d + e')$$
$$(b + c + d' + e)(a' + b' + c + e')$$

The first step in the solution is to plot a map for f. Since f is given in product-of-sums form, it is easier to first plot the map for f' and then complement the map. Write f' as a sum of products:

$f' =$ _____

Now plot the map for f'. (Note that there are three terms in the "upper layer," one term in the "lower layer," and two terms which span the two layers.)

Next convert your map for f' to a map for f.

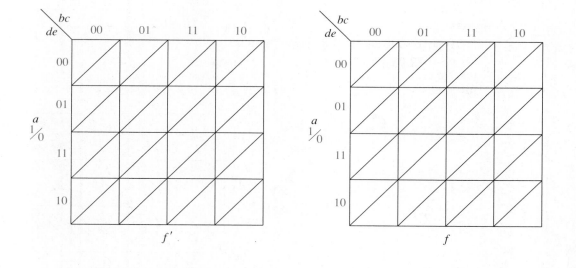

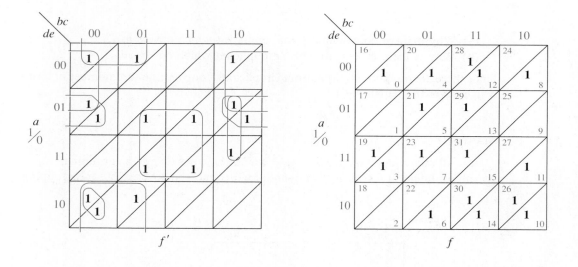

The next step is to determine the essential prime implicants of f.

(a) Why is $a'd'e'$ an essential prime implicant?

(b) Which minterms are adjacent to m_3? _____ to m_{19}? _____

(c) Is there an essential prime implicant which covers m_3 and m_{19}? _____

(d) Is there an essential prime implicant which covers m_{21}? _____

(e) Loop the essential prime implicants which you have found. Then find two more essential prime implicants and loop them.

Answers:

   (a) It covers m_0 and both adjacent minterms.

   (b) m_{19} and m_{11}; m_3 and m_{23}

   (c) No

   (d) Yes

   (e)

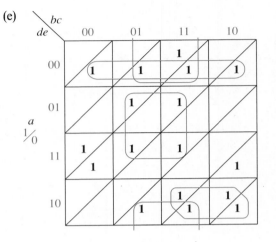

   (a) Why is there no essential prime implicant which covers m_{11}?

   (b) Why is there no essential prime implicant which covers m_{28}?

Since there are no more essential prime implicants, loop a minimum number of terms which cover the remaining 1's.

Answers:

   (a) All adjacent 1's of m_{11} (m_3, m_{10}) cannot be covered by one grouping.

   (b) All adjacent 1's of m_{28} (m_{12}, m_{30}, m_{29}) cannot be covered by one grouping.

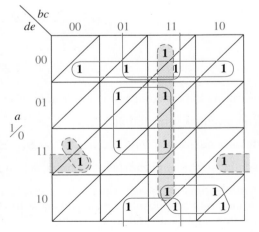

Note: There are five other possible ways to loop the four remaining 1's.

Write down two different minimum sum-of-products expressions for f.

$f =$ _____

$f =$ _____

Answer:

$$f = a'd'e' + ace + a'ce' + bde' + \begin{Bmatrix} abc \\ \text{or} \\ bce' \end{Bmatrix} + \begin{Bmatrix} b'c'de + a'c'de \\ b'c'de + a'bc'd \\ ab'de + a'c'de \end{Bmatrix}$$

PROBLEMS

6.3 A small corporation has 100 shares of stock, and each share entitles its owner to one vote at a stockholders' meeting. Mr. Akins owns 10 shares, Ms. Barnes owns 20 shares, Mr. Clay owns 30 shares, and Ms. Drake owns 40 shares. A two-thirds majority is required in order to pass a measure at a stockholders' meeting. Each of the four stockholders has a switch which he or she closes to vote yes for all of his or her shares and opens to vote no. A switching circuit is to be designed to turn on a light if the measure passes.

(a) Derive a truth table for the output function (Z).

(b) Write the minterm expansion for Z and simplify algebraically to a minimum sum-of-products form.

(c) Write the maxterm expansion for Z and simplify algebraically to a minimum product-of-sums form.

(d) Check to see that your answer to (c) is equivalent to the answer to (b).

(e) Design a minimum network of switches and a minimum AND-OR gate network to realize Z.

6.4 A spacecraft uses two ground-based computers and one on-board computer to control the thrusters used to make course corrections. There is also a manual override control that will switch control of the thrusters directly to the on-board computer in case the spacecraft is unable to contact the ground station. If the manual override is off (logic 0), then the thrusters will fire iff at least two of the three computers output a logic 1. If the manual override is on (logic 1), then the thrusters will fire iff the on-board computer outputs a logic 1. Let A represent the manual override switch, B represent the output of the on-board computer, and C and D represent the outputs of the two ground computers.

(a) Derive a truth table for the output function Z which is 1 iff the thrusters fire.

(b) Write the minterm expansion for Z and simplify algebraically to a minimum sum-of-products form.

(c) Write the maxterm expansion for Z and simplify algebraically to a minimum product-of-sums form.

(d) Check to see that your answer to (c) is equivalent to the answer for (b).

(e) Design a minimum AND-OR gate network to realize Z.

6.5 Find the minimum sum-of-products for each function using a Karnaugh map.

(a) $f_1(a, b, c) = m_1 + m_3 + m_4 + m_6$ (b) $f_2(d, e, f) = \sum m(1, 4, 5, 7)$

(c) $f_3(r, s, t) = r't' + rs' + rs$ (d) $f_4(x, y, z) = M_1 \cdot M_7$

6.6 Work Problem 6.5 for the following:

(a) $f_1(a, b, c) = m_1 + m_4 + m_5 + m_6$ (b) $f_2(d, e, f) = \prod M(0, 2, 4, 7)$

(c) $f_3(r, s, t) = r's't + rt + st + rst'$

6.7 (a) Plot the following function on a Karnaugh map. (Do *not* expand to minterm form before plotting.)

$$F(A, B, C, D) = A'B' + CD' + ABC + A'B'CD' + ABC'D$$

(b) Find the minimum sum of products.

(c) Find the minimum product of sums.

6.8 Work Problem 6.7 for $F(A, B, C, D) = B'C' + A'BD + ABCD' + B'C$.

6.9 Find the minimum sum-of-products expression for each function.

(a) $f(a, b, c, d) = \sum m(0, 1, 2, 4, 6, 7, 8, 9, 13, 15)$

(b) $f(a, b, c, d) = \prod M(1, 2, 4, 9, 11)$

(c) $f(a, b, c, d) = \sum m(0, 1, 5, 8, 12, 14, 15) + \sum d(2, 7, 11)$

(d) $f(a, b, c, d) = \prod M(0, 1, 4, 5, 10, 11, 12) \cdot \prod D(3, 8, 14)$

6.10 Find the minimum sum-of-products expression for each function.

(a) $f(a, b, c, d) = \sum m(0, 2, 3, 4, 7, 8, 14)$

(b) $f(a, b, c, d) = \sum m(1, 2, 4, 15) + \sum d(0, 3, 14)$

(c) $f(a, b, c, d) = \prod M(1, 2, 3, 4, 9, 15)$

(d) $f(a, b, c, d) = \prod M(0, 2, 4, 6, 8) \cdot \prod D(1, 12, 9, 15)$

6.11 Find the minimum sum-of-products expression for:

(a) $\sum m(0, 2, 3, 5, 6, 7, 11, 12, 13)$ (b) $\sum m(2, 4, 8) + \sum d(0, 3, 7)$

(c) $\sum m(1, 5, 6, 7, 13) + \sum d(8, 4)$

6.12 A logic network realizes the function $F(a, b, c, d) = a'b' + a'cd + ac'd + ab'd'$. Assuming that $a = c$ never occurs when $b = d = 1$, find a simplified expression for F.

6.13 A switching network has two control inputs (C_1, C_2), two data inputs (X_1, X_2), and one output (Z). The network performs one of the logic operations AND, OR, EQU (equivalence), or XOR (exclusive-OR) on the two data inputs. The function performed depends on the control inputs:

C_1	C_2	Function Performed by Network
0	0	AND
0	1	OR
1	0	EQU
1	1	XOR

(a) Derive a truth table for Z.

(b) Use a Karnaugh map to find a minimum AND-OR gate network to realize Z.

6.14   For the maps given below:
       (a) Find the minimum sum of products for f_1.
       (b) Find the minimum *product of sums* for f_2.

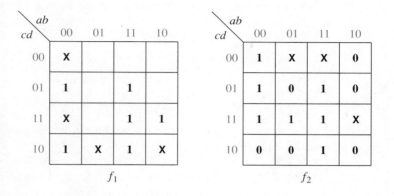

$$f_1 \qquad\qquad\qquad f_2$$

6.15   Find the minimum sum of products for F. Underline the essential prime implicants in your answer.

6.16   Given $F = AB'D' + A'B + A'C + CD$.
       (a) Use a Karnaugh map to find the maxterm expression for F (express your answer in both decimal and alphabetic notation).
       (b) Use a Karnaugh map to find the minimum sum-of-products form for F'.
       (c) Find the minimum product of sums for F.
       (d) Given the map for F, we can find a map for the dual for F by complementing all of the 0's and 1's on the map and also complementing all the 0's and 1's in the column and row headings. Use this method to find the minimum sum-of-products form for F^D. (Be careful when reading the F^D map since the column and row headings will not be in the usual order.) Verify algebraically that your expression for F^D is correct.

6.17   Find the minimum sum-of-products for the expressions below. Then make the specified minterm a don't care and verify that the minimum sum-of-products is unchanged. Now start again with the original expression and find each

single minterm which could be made a don't care without changing the minimum sum-of-products.
(a) $F(A, B, C, D) = A'C' + B'C + ACD' + BC'D$, minterm 5
(b) $F(A, B, C, D) = A'BD + AC'D + AB' + BCD + A'C'D'$, minterm 7

6.18   Find all possible minimum sum-of-products expressions for each function:
(a) $f(a, b, c) = \prod M(2, 3, 4)$
(b) $f(d, e, f) = \sum m(1, 6) + \sum d(0, 3, 5)$
(c) $f(p, q, r) = (p + q' + r)(p' + q + r')$
(d) $f(s, t, u) = \sum m(1, 2, 3) + \sum d(0, 5, 7)$
(e) $f(a, b, c) = \prod M(3, 4)$
(f) $f(d, e, f) = \sum m(1, 4, 6) + \sum d(0, 2, 7)$

6.19   Find a minimum sum-of-products and a minimum product-of-sums expression for each function:
(a) $f(A, B, C, D) = A'B' + A'B'C' + A'BD' + AC'D + A'BD + AB'CD'$
(b) $f(A, B, C, D) = \prod M(0, 2, 10, 11, 12, 14, 15) \cdot \prod D(5, 7)$

6.20   Assuming that the inputs $ABCD = 0101$, $ABCD = 1001$, $ABCD = 1011$ never occur, find a simplified expression for

$$F = A'BC'D + A'B'D + A'CD + ABD + ABC$$

6.21   For each of the following functions, find the essential prime implicants and then find all of the minimum sum-of-products expressions:
(a) $f(a, b, c, d) = \sum m(1, 5, 6, 7, 11, 13, 15)$
(b) $f(w, x, y, z) = \sum m(0, 3, 5, 7, 8, 9, 10, 12, 13) + \sum d(1, 6, 11, 14)$

6.22   Given $F = \sum m(0, 1, 3, 7, 8, 9, 13, 15) + \sum d(2, 11)$.
(a) Find all of the prime implicants.
(b) Find all of the essential prime implicants and tell why each one is essential.
(c) Find a minimum sum-of-products expression for F.

6.23   Find all of the prime implicants for each of the functions plotted on p. 141.

6.24   Find all of the prime implicants for each of the functions plotted below:

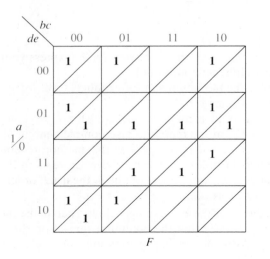

F

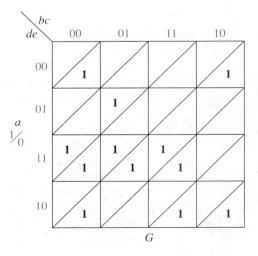

G

6.25 $F(a, b, c, d, e) = \sum m(0, 3, 4, 5, 6, 7, 8, 12, 13, 14, 16, 21, 23, 24, 29, 31)$
(a) Find the essential prime implicants using a Karnaugh map, and indicate why each one of the chosen prime implicants is essential (there are 4 essential prime implicants).
(b) Find all of the prime implicants by using the Karnaugh map (there are 9 in all).

6.26 $F(a, b, c, d, e) = \sum m(0, 1, 4, 5, 9, 10, 11, 12, 14, 18, 20, 21, 22, 25, 26, 28)$
(a) Find the essential prime implicants using a Karnaugh map, and indicate why each one of the chosen prime implicants is essential (there are 4 essential prime implicants).
(b) Find all of the prime implicants by using the Karnaugh map (there are 13 in all).

6.27 $F(A, B, C, D, E) = \sum m(0, 2, 6, 7, 8, 10, 11, 12, 13, 14, 16, 18, 19, 29, 30)$
$\qquad + \sum d(4, 9, 21)$

Find the minimum sum-of-products expression for F. Underline the essential prime implicants in this expression.

6.28   Work Problem 6.27 with

$$F(A, B, C, D, E) = \sum m(0, 1, 2, 6, 7, 9, 10, 15, 16, 18, 20, 21, 27, 30)$$
$$+ \sum d(3, 4, 11, 12, 19)$$

6.29 $F(A, B, C, D, E) = \prod M(3, 6, 7, 8, 9, 10, 18, 20, 21, 22, 23, 25, 26, 28, 29, 30)$
Find the minimum sum-of-products expression for F. Underline the essential prime implicants in this expression.

6.30   Work Problem 6.29 with

$$F(A, B, C, D, E) = \prod M(2, 3, 4, 8, 9, 10, 14, 15, 16, 18, 19, 20, 23, 24, 30, 31)$$

6.31   Find the minimum product of sums for:
(a) $F(a, b, c, d, e) = \sum m(1, 2, 3, 4, 5, 6, 25, 26, 27, 28, 29, 30, 31)$
(b) $F(a, b, c, d, e) = \sum m(1, 5, 12, 13, 14, 16, 17, 21, 23, 24, 30, 31)$
$\qquad + \sum d(0, 2, 3, 4)$

6.32   Using 6-variable Karnaugh maps, find the minimum sum-of-products expressions for the following functions.
(a) $G = C'E'F + DEF + AD'E'F' + BC'E'F + AD'EF'$
(b) $H = A'B'CDF' + A'CD + A'B'CD'E + BCDF'$

6.33   Find a minimum sum-of-products expression for each of the following functions. Underline the essential prime implicants in your answers.
(a) $f(a, b, c, d, e) = \sum m(0, 1, 3, 4, 6, 7, 8, 10, 11, 15, 16, 18, 19, 24, 25, 28, 29, 31)$
$\qquad + \sum d(5, 9, 30)$
(b) $f(a, b, c, d, e) = \sum m(1, 3, 5, 8, 9, 15, 16, 20, 21, 23, 27, 28, 31)$

6.34   Find a minimum product-of-sums expression for each of the following functions.
(a) $F(v, w, x, y, z) = \sum m(4, 5, 8, 9, 12, 13, 18, 20, 21, 22, 25, 28, 30, 31)$
(b) $F(a, b, c, d, e) = \prod M(2, 4, 5, 6, 8, 10, 12, 13, 16, 17, 18, 22, 23, 24)$
$\qquad \cdot \prod D(0, 11, 30, 31)$

6.35   Simplify the following expression first by using a Karnaugh map and then by using Boolean algebra. Use the map as a guide to determine which theorems to apply to which terms for the algebraic simplification.

$$F = a'b'c' + a'c'd + bcd + abc + ab'$$

6.36 $F(V, W, X, Y, Z) = \prod M(0, 3, 6, 9, 11, 19, 20, 24, 25, 26, 27, 28, 29, 30)$
$$\cdot \prod D(1, 2, 12, 13)$$

(a) Find two minimum sum-of-products expressions for F.

(b) Underline the essential prime implicants in your answer and tell why each one is essential.

7

Quine-McCluskey Method

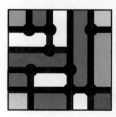

OBJECTIVES

1. Find the prime implicants of a function by using the Quine-McCluskey method. Explain the reasons for the procedures used.

2. Define "prime implicant" and "*essential* prime implicant."

3. Given the prime implicants, find the essential (necessary) prime implicants and a minimum sum-of-products expression for a function using a prime implicant chart and using Petrick's method.

4. Minimize an incompletely specified function using the Quine-McCluskey method.

5. Find a minimum sum-of-products expression for a function using the method of map-entered variables.

STUDY GUIDE

1. Review Section 6.1, *Minimum Forms of Switching Functions.*

2. Read the introduction to this unit and then study Section 7.1, *Determination of Prime Implicants.*

   (a) Using variables *A*, *B*, *C*, *D*, and *E*, give the algebraic equivalent of

$$10110 + 10010 = 10\text{--}10$$

$$10\text{--}10 + 10\text{--}11 = 10\text{--}1\text{--}$$

   (b) Why won't the following pairs of terms combine?

$$01101 + 00111$$
$$10\text{--}10 + 001\text{--}0$$

   (c) When using the Quine-McCluskey procedure for finding prime implicants, why is it only necessary to compare terms from adjacent groups?

   (d) How can you determine if two minterms from adjacent groups will combine by looking at their decimal representations?

   (e) When combining terms, why is it permissible to use a term which has already been checked off?

   (f) In forming Column II of Table 7–1, note that terms 10 and 14 were combined to form 10, 14 even though both 10 and 14 had already been checked off. If this had not been done, which term in Column II could not be eliminated (checked off)?

   (g) In forming Column III of Table 7–1, note that minterms 0, 1, 8, and 9 were combined in two different ways to form –00–. This is equivalent to looping the minterms in two different ways on the Karnaugh map, as shown below.

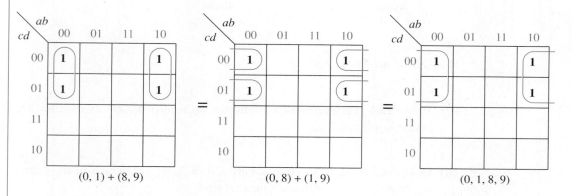

(0, 1) + (8, 9)   (0, 8) + (1, 9)   (0, 1, 8, 9)

(h) Using a map, find *all* the prime implicants of Equation (7–2) and compare your answer with Equation (7–3).

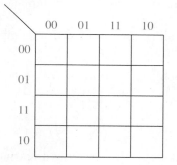

(i) The prime implicants of $f(a, b, c, d) = \sum m(4, 5, 6, 7, 12, 13, 14, 15)$ are to be found using the Quine-McCluskey procedure. Column III is given below; find Column IV and check off the appropriate terms in Column III.

	Column III	Column IV
(4, 5, 6, 7)	01––	
(4, 5, 12, 13)	–10–	
(4, 6, 12, 14)	–1–0	
(5, 7, 13, 15)	–1–1	
(6, 7, 14, 15)	–11–	
(12, 13, 14, 15)	11––	

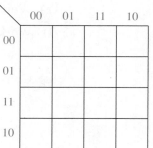

Check your answer using a Karnaugh map.

3. (a) List all seven product term implicants of

$$F(a, b, c) = \sum m(0, 1, 5, 7)$$

Which of these implicants are prime?

Why is $a'c$ not an implicant?

(b) Define a prime implicant.

(c) Why must every term in a minimum sum-of-products expression be a prime implicant?

(d) Given that $F(A, B, C, D) = \sum m(0, 1, 4, 5, 7, 10, 15)$, which of the following terms are *not* prime implicants and why?

$$A'B'C' \qquad A'C' \qquad BCD \qquad ABC \qquad AB'CD'$$

4. Study Section 7.2, *The Prime Implicant Chart.*

(a) Define an *essential* prime implicant.

(b) Find all of the essential prime implicants from the following chart.

	a b c d	0	4	5	10	11	12	13	15
(0, 4)	0 – 0 0	X	X						
(4, 5, 12, 13)	– 1 0 –		X	X			X	X	
(13, 15)	1 1 – 1							X	X
(11, 15)	1 – 1 1					X			X
(10, 11)	1 0 1 –				X	X			

Check your answer using a Karnaugh map.

(c) Why must all essential prime implicants of a function be included in the minimum sum of products?

(d) Complete the solution of Table 7–5.

(e) Work Programmed Exercise 7.1.

(f) Work Problems 7.2(a) and (b), and 7.3(a) and (b).

5. Study Section 7.3, *Petrick's Method* (optional).

(a) Consider the following reduced prime implicant chart for a function F:

		m_4	m_5	m_7	m_{13}
P_1	bd		X	X	X
P_2	bc'	X	X		X
P_3	a'b	X	X	X	
P_4	c'd		X		X

We will find all minimum solutions using Petrick's method. Let $P_i = 1$ mean the prime implicant in row P_i is included in the solution. Which minterm is covered iff $(P_1 + P_3) = 1$? _____ Write a sum term which is 1 iff m_4 is covered. _____. Write a product of sum terms which is 1 iff all m_4, m_5, m_7, and m_{13} are all covered:

$P =$ _____

(b) Reduce P to a minimum sum of products. (Your answer should have four terms, each one of the form $P_i P_j$.)

$P =$ _____

If $P_1 P_2 = 1$, which prime implicants are included in the solution? _____

How many minimum solutions are there? _____

Write out each solution in terms of a, b, c, and d.
(1) $F =$ _____   (2) $F =$ _____
(3) $F =$ _____   (4) $F =$ _____

6. Study Section 7.4, *Simplification of Incompletely Specified Functions.*

   (a) Why are don't care terms treated like required minterms when finding the prime implicants?

   (b) Why aren't the don't care terms listed at the top of the prime implicant chart when finding the minimum solution?

   (c) Work Problem 7.4(a).

   (d) Work Problem 7.12(a) and check your solution using a Karnaugh map.

7. If you have *LogicAid* or a similar computer program available, use it to check your answers to some of the problems in this unit. *LogicAid* accepts Boolean functions in the form of equations, minterms or maxterms, and truth tables. It finds simplified sum-of-products and product-of-sums expressions for the functions using a modified version of the Quine-McCluskey method. It can also find one or all of the minimum solutions using Petrick's method.

8. Study Section 7.5, *Simplification Using Map-Entered Variables.*

   (a) For the following map, find MS_0, MS_1, and F. Verify that your solution for F is minimum by using a 4-variable map.

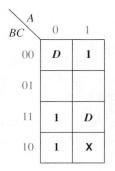

(b) Use the method of map-entered variables to find an expression for F from the following map. Treat C and C' as if they were independent variables. Is the result a correct representation of F? Is it minimum?

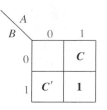

(c) Work Problem 7.13(a) and (b).

9. In this unit you have learned a "turn-the-crank" type procedure for finding minimum sum-of-products forms for switching functions. In addition to learning how to "turn the crank" and grind out minimum solutions, you should have learned several very important concepts in this unit. In particular, make sure you know:

(a) What a *prime implicant* is

(b) What an *essential* prime implicant is

(c) Why the minimum sum-of-products form is a sum of prime implicants

(d) How don't cares are handled when using the Quine-McCluskey procedure and the prime implicant chart

10. Reread the objectives of the unit. If you are satisfied you can meet the objectives, take the readiness test.

Quine-McCluskey Method

The Karnaugh map method described in Unit 6 is an effective way to simplify switching functions which have a small number of variables. When the number of variables is large or if several functions must be simplified, use of a digital computer is desirable. The Quine-McCluskey method presented in this unit provides a systematic simplification procedure which can be readily programmed for a digital computer.

The Quine-McCluskey procedure reduces the minterm expansion (standard sum-of-products form) of a function to obtain a minimum sum of products. The procedure consists of two main steps:

1. Eliminate as many literals as possible from each term by systematically applying the theorem $XY + XY' = X$. The resulting terms are called prime implicants.

2. Use a prime implicant chart to select a minimum set of prime implicants which, when ORed together, are equal to the function being simplified and which contain a minimum number of literals.

7.1
Determination of Prime Implicants

In order to apply the Quine-McCluskey procedure to determine a minimum sum-of-products expression for a function, the function must be given as a sum of minterms. (If the function is not in minterm form, the minterm expansion can be found by using one of the techniques given in Section 5.3.) In the first part of the Quine-McCluskey procedure, all of the prime implicants of a function are systematically formed by combining minterms. The minterms are represented in binary notation and combined using

$$XY + XY' = X \qquad (7\text{–}1)$$

where X represents a product of literals and Y is a single variable. Two minterms will combine if they differ in exactly one variable. The examples given below show both the binary notation and its algebraic equivalent.

$AB'CD' + AB'CD = AB'C$

$\underbrace{1\ 0\ 1}_{X}\ \underbrace{0}_{Y} + \underbrace{1\ 0\ 1}_{X}\ \underbrace{1}_{Y'} = \underbrace{1\ 0\ 1}_{X}\ \text{–}$ (the dash indicates a missing variable)

$A'BC'D + A'BCD'$ (won't combine)

$0\ 1\ 0\ 1 + 0\ 1\ 1\ 0$ (won't combine)

In order to find all of the prime implicants, all possible pairs of minterms should be compared and combined whenever possible. To reduce the required number of comparisons, the binary minterms are sorted into groups according to the number of 1's in each term. Thus,

$$f(a, b, c, d) = \sum m(0, 1, 2, 5, 6, 7, 8, 9, 10, 14) \qquad (7\text{–}2)$$

is represented by the following list of minterms:

group 0	0	0000
group 1	1	0001
	2	0010
	8	1000
group 2	5	0101
	6	0110
	9	1001
	10	1010
group 3	7	0111
	14	1110

In the above list, the term in group 0 has zero 1's, the terms in group 1 have one 1, those in group 2 have two 1's, and those in group 3 have three 1's.

Two terms can be combined if they differ in exactly one variable. Comparison of terms in nonadjacent groups is unnecessary since such terms will always differ in at least two variables and cannot be combined using $XY + XY' = X$. Similarly, comparison of terms within a group is unnecessary since two terms with the same number of 1's must differ in at least two variables. Thus, only terms in adjacent groups must be compared.

First we will compare the term in group 0 with all of the terms in group 1. Terms 0000 and 0001 can be combined to eliminate the fourth variable, which yields 000−. Similarly, 0 and 2 combine to form 00−0 ($a'b'd'$) and 0, 8 combine to form −000 ($b'c'd'$). The resulting terms are listed in Column II of Table 7–1.

Whenever two terms combine, the corresponding decimal numbers differ by a power of 2 (1, 2, 4, 8, etc.). This is true because when the binary representations differ in exactly one column, if we subtract these binary representations, we get a 1 only in the column in which the difference exists, and a binary number with a 1 in exactly one column is a power of 2.

Since comparison of group 0 with groups 2 and 3 is unnecessary, we proceed to compare terms in groups 1 and 2. Comparing term 1 with all terms in group. 2, we find that it combines with 5 and 9 but not with 6 or 10. Similarly, term 2 combines only with 6 and 10, and term 8 only with 9 and 10. The resulting terms are listed in Column II. Each time a term is combined with another term, it is checked off. A term may be used more than once since $X + X = X$. Even though two terms have already been combined with other terms, they still must be compared and combined if possible. This is necessary since the resultant term may be needed to form the minimum sum solution. At this stage, we may generate redundant terms, but these redundant terms will be eliminated later.

We finish with Column I by comparing terms in groups 2 and 3. New terms are formed by combining terms 5 and 7, 6 and 7, 6 and 14, and 10 and 14.

Table 7–1

Determination of Prime Implicants

		Column I			Column II			Column III
group 0	0	0000 ✓		0, 1	000− ✓		0, 1, 8, 9	−00−
	1	0001 ✓		0, 2	00−0 ✓		0, 2, 8, 10	−0−0
group 1	2	0010 ✓		0, 8	−000 ✓		0, 8, 1, 9	−00−
	8	1000 ✓		1, 5	0−01		0, 8, 2, 10	−0−0
	5	0101 ✓		1, 9	−001 ✓		2, 6, 10, 14	−−10
	6	0110 ✓		2, 6	0−10 ✓		2, 10, 6, 14	−−10
group 2	9	1001 ✓		2, 10	−010 ✓			
	10	1010 ✓		8, 9	100− ✓			
group 3	7	0111 ✓		8, 10	10−0 ✓			
	14	1110 ✓		5, 7	01−1			
				6, 7	011−			
				6, 14	−110 ✓			
				10, 14	1−10 ✓			

Note that the terms in Column II have been divided into groups according to the number of 1's in each term. Again, we apply $XY + XY' = X$ to combine pairs of terms in Column II. In order to combine two terms, the terms must have the same variables, and the terms must differ in exactly one of these variables. Thus, it is only necessary to compare terms which have dashes (missing variables) in corresponding places and which differ by exactly one in the number of 1's.

Terms in the first group in Column II need only be compared with terms in the second group which have dashes in the same places. Term 000– (0, 1) combines only with term 100– (8, 9) to yield –00–. This is algebraically equivalent to $a'b'c' + ab'c' = b'c'$. The resulting term is listed in Column III along with the designation 0, 1, 8, 9 to indicate that it was formed by combining minterms 0, 1, 8, and 9. Term (0, 2) combines only with (8, 10), and term (0, 8) combines with both (1, 9) and (2, 10). Again, the terms which have been combined are checked off. Comparing terms from the second and third groups in Column II, we find that (2, 6) combines with (10, 14) and (2, 10) combines with (6, 14).

Note that there are three pairs of duplicate terms in Column III. These duplicate terms were formed in each case by combining the same set of four minterms in a different order. After deleting the duplicate terms, we compare terms from the two groups in Column III. Since no further combination is possible, the process terminates. In general, we would keep comparing terms and forming new groups of terms and new columns until no further terms could be combined.

The terms which have not been checked off because they cannot be combined with other terms are called prime implicants. Since every minterm has been included in at least one of the prime implicants, the function is equal to the sum of its prime implicants. In this example we have

$$f = a'c'd + a'bd + a'bc + \quad b'c' \quad + \quad b'd' \quad + \quad cd' \qquad (7\text{--}3)$$
$$(1, 5) \quad (5, 7) \quad (6, 7) \quad (0, 1, 8, 9) \quad (0, 2, 8, 10) \quad (2, 6, 10, 14)$$

In the above expression, each term has a minimum number of literals, but the number of terms is not minimum. Using the consensus theorem to eliminate redundant terms yields

$$f = a'bd + b'c' + cd' \qquad (7\text{--}4)$$

which is the minimum sum-of-products expression for f. Section 7.2 discusses a better method of eliminating redundant prime implicants using a prime implicant chart.

Next, we will define implicant and prime implicant and relate these terms to the Quine-McCluskey procedure described above.

Definition: Given a function F of n variables, a product term P is an *implicant* of F iff for every combination of values of the n variables for which $P = 1$, F is also equal to 1.

In other words, if for some combination of values of the variables, $P = 1$ and $F = 0$, then P is *not* an implicant of F. For example, consider the function

$$F(a, b, c) = a'b'c' + ab'c' + ab'c + abc = b'c' + ac \qquad (7\text{--}5)$$

If $a'b'c' = 1$, then $F = 1$; if $ac = 1$, then $F = 1$; etc. Hence the terms $a'b'c'$, ac, etc., are implicants of F. In this example, bc is *not* an implicant of F because when $a = 0$ and $b = c = 1$, $bc = 1$ and $F = 0$. In general, if F is written in sum-of-products form, every product term is an implicant. Every minterm of F is also an implicant of F, and so is any term formed by combining two or more minterms. For example, in Table 7–1, all of the terms listed in any of the columns are implicants of the function given in Equation (7–2).

Definition: A *prime implicant* of a function F is a product term implicant which is no longer an implicant if any literal is deleted from it.

In Equation (7–5), the implicant $a'b'c'$ is *not* a *prime* implicant because a' can be eliminated, and the resulting term $(b'c')$ is still an implicant of F. The implicants $b'c'$ and ac are *prime* implicants because if we delete a literal from either term, the term will no longer be an implicant of F. Each prime implicant of a function has a minimum number of literals in the sense that no more literals can be eliminated from it by combining it with other terms.

The Quine-McCluskey procedure illustrated above finds all of the product term implicants of a function. The implicants which are nonprime are checked off in the process of combining terms, so that the remaining terms are prime implicants.

A minimum sum-of-products expression for a function consists of a sum of some (but not necessarily all) of the prime implicants of that function. In other words, a sum-of-products expression which contains a term which is not a prime implicant cannot be minimum. This is true because the nonprime term does not contain a minimum number of literals—it can be combined with additional minterms to form a prime implicant which has fewer literals than the nonprime term. Any nonprime term in a sum-of-products expression can thus be replaced with a prime implicant, which reduces the number of literals and simplifies the expression.

7.2
The Prime Implicant Chart

The second part of the Quine-McCluskey procedure employs a prime implicant chart to select a minimum set of prime implicants. The minterms of the function are listed across the top of the chart and the prime implicants are listed down the side. A prime implicant is equal to a sum of minterms, and the prime implicant is said to *cover* these minterms. If a prime implicant covers a given minterm, an X is placed at the intersection of the corresponding row and column. Table 7–2 shows the prime implicant chart derived from Table 7–1. All of the prime implicants (terms which have not been checked off in Table 7–1) are listed on the left.

Table 7–2
Prime Implicant Chart

		0	1	2	5	6	7	8	9	10	14
(0, 1, 8, 9)	$b'c'$	X	X					X	Ⓧ		
(0, 2, 8, 10)	$b'd'$	X		X				X		X	
(2, 6, 10, 14)	cd'			X		X				X	Ⓧ
(1, 5)	$a'c'd$		X		X						
(5, 7)	$a'bd$				X		X				
(6, 7)	$a'bc$					X	X				

In the first row, X's are placed in columns 0, 1, 8, and 9, since prime implicant $b'c'$ was formed from the sum of minterms 0, 1, 8, and 9. Similarly, X's are placed in columns 0, 2, 8, and 10 opposite the prime implicant $b'd'$, and so forth.

If a minterm is covered by only one prime implicant, then that prime implicant is called an *essential* prime implicant and must be included in the minimum sum of products. Essential prime implicants are easy to find using the prime implicant chart. If a given column contains only one X, then the corresponding row is an essential prime implicant. In Table 7–2, columns 9 and 14 each contain one X, so prime implicants $b'c'$ and cd' are essential.

Each time a prime implicant is selected for inclusion in the minimum sum, the corresponding row should be crossed out. After doing this, the columns which correspond to all minterms covered by that prime implicant should also be crossed out. Table 7–3 shows the resulting chart when the essential prime implicants and the corresponding rows and columns of Table 7–2 are crossed out. A minimum set of prime implicants must now be chosen to cover the remaining columns. In this example, $a'bd$ covers the remaining two columns, so it is chosen. The resulting minimum sum of products is

$$f = b'c' + cd' + a'bd$$

which is the same as Equation (7–4). Note that even though the term $a'bd$ is included in the minimum sum of products, $a'bd$ is *not* an *essential* prime implicant. It is the sum of minterms m_5 and m_7; m_5 is also covered by $a'c'd$ and m_7 is also covered by $a'bc$.

When the prime implicant chart is constructed, some minterms may be covered by only a single prime implicant, while other minterms may be covered by two

Table 7–3

		0	1	2	5	6	7	8	9	10	14
(0, 1, 8, 9)	$b'c'$	X̶	X̶					X̶	X̶		
(0, 2, 8, 10)	$b'd'$	X̶		X̶				X̶		X̶	
(2, 6, 10, 14)	cd'			X̶		X̶				X̶	X̶
(1, 5)	$a'c'd$		X̶		X						
(5, 7)	$a'bd$				X		X				
(6, 7)	$a'bc$					X̶	X				

or more prime implicants. A prime implicant is *essential* (or necessary) to a function f iff the prime implicant contains a minterm which is not covered by any other prime implicant of f. The essential prime implicants are chosen first since all essential prime implicants must be included in every minimum sum. After the essential prime implicants have been chosen, the minterms which they cover can be eliminated from the prime implicant chart by crossing out the corresponding columns. If the essential prime implicants do not cover all of the minterms, then additional nonessential prime implicants are needed. In simple cases, the non-essential prime implicants needed to form the minimum solution may be selected by trial and error. For larger prime implicant charts, additional procedures for chart reduction can be employed.[1] Some functions have two or more minimum sum-of-products expressions, each having the same number of terms and literals. The next example shows such a function.

EXAMPLE WITH A CYCLIC PRIME IMPLICANT CHART: A prime implicant chart which has two or more X's in every column is referred to as "cyclic." The following function has such a chart:

$$F = \sum m(0, 1, 2, 5, 6, 7) \tag{7-6}$$

Derivation of prime implicants:

0	000 ✓		0, 1	00–	
1	001 ✓		0, 2	0–0	
2	010 ✓		1, 5	–01	
5	101 ✓		2, 6	–10	
6	110 ✓		5, 7	1–1	
7	111 ✓		6, 7	11–	

Table 7–4 shows the resulting prime implicant chart. All columns have two X's, so we will proceed by trial and error. Both (0, 1) and (0, 2) cover column 0, so we will try (0, 1). After crossing out row (0, 1) and columns 0 and 1, we examine column 2, which is covered by (0, 2) and (2, 6). The best choice is (2, 6) because it covers two of the remaining columns while (0, 2) covers only one of the remaining columns. After crossing out row (2, 6) and columns 2 and 6, we see that (5, 7)

Table 7–4

---

[1] For a discussion of such procedures, see E. J. McCluskey, *Introduction to the Theory of Switching Circuits.* McGraw-Hill, 1965.

covers the remaining columns and completes the solution. Therefore, one solution is $F = a'b' + bc' + ac$. However, we are not guaranteed that this solution is minimum. We must go back and solve the problem over again starting with the other prime implicant that covers column 0. The resulting table (Table 7–5) is

Table 7–5

			0	1	2	5	6	7
P_1	(0, 1)	$a'b'$	X	X				
P_2	(0, 2)	$a'c'$	X		X			
P_3	(1, 5)	$b'c$		X		X		
P_4	(2, 6)	bc'			X		X	
P_5	(5, 7)	ac				X		X
P_6	(6, 7)	ab					X	X

Finish the solution and show that $F = a'c' + b'c + ab$. Since this has the same number of terms and same number of literals as the expression for F derived in Table 7–4, there are two minimum sum-of-products solutions to this problem. Compare these two minimum solutions for Equation (7–6) with the solutions obtained in Fig. 6–9 using Karnaugh maps. Note that each minterm on the map can be covered by two different loops. Similarly, each column of the prime implicant chart (Table 7–4) has two X's, indicating that each minterm can be covered by two different prime implicants.

7.3
Petrick's Method

Petrick's method is a technique for determining all minimum sum-of-products solutions from a prime implicant chart. The example shown in Tables 7–4 and 7–5 has two minimum solutions. As the number of variables increases, the number of prime implicants and the complexity of the prime implicant chart may increase significantly. In such cases, a large amount of trial and error may be required to find the minimum solution(s). Petrick's method is a more systematic way of finding all minimum solutions from a prime implicant chart than the method used above. Before applying Petrick's method, all essential prime implicants and the minterms they cover should be removed from the chart.

We will illustrate Petrick's method using Table 7–5. First we will label the rows of the table P_1, P_2, P_3, etc. We will form a logic function, P, which is true when all of the minterms in the chart have been covered. Let P_1 be a logic variable which is true when the prime implicant in row P_1 is included in the solution, P_2 be a logic variable which is true when the prime implicant in row P_2 is included in the solution, etc. Since column 0 has X's in rows P_1 and P_2, we must choose row P_1 or P_2 in order to cover minterm 0. Therefore, the expression $(P_1 + P_2)$ must be true. In order to cover minterm 1, we must choose row P_1 or P_3; therefore, $(P_1 + P_3)$ must be true. In order to cover minterm 2, $(P_2 + P_4)$

must be true. Similarly, in order to cover minterms 5, 6, and 7, the expressions $(P_3 + P_5)$, $(P_4 + P_6)$ and $(P_5 + P_6)$ must be true. Since we must cover all of the minterms, the following function must be true:

$$P = (P_1 + P_2)(P_1 + P_3)(P_2 + P_4)(P_3 + P_5)(P_4 + P_6)(P_5 + P_6) = 1$$

The expression for P in effect means that we must choose row P_1 or P_2, *and* row P_1 or P_3, *and* row P_2 or P_4, etc.

The next step is to reduce P to a minimum sum of products. This is easy since there are no complements. First, we multiply out using $(X + Y)(X + Z) = X + YZ$ and the ordinary distributive law:

$$\begin{aligned}
P &= (P_1 + P_2P_3)(P_4 + P_2P_6)(P_5 + P_3P_6) \\
&= (P_1P_4 + P_1P_2P_6 + P_2P_3P_4 + P_2P_3P_6)(P_5 + P_3P_6) \\
&= P_1P_4P_5 + P_1P_2P_5P_6 + P_2P_3P_4P_5 + P_2P_3P_5P_6 + P_1P_3P_4P_6 \\
&\quad + P_1P_2P_3P_6 + P_2P_3P_4P_6 + P_2P_3P_6
\end{aligned}$$

Next, we use $X + XY = X$ to eliminate redundant terms from P, which yields

$$P = P_1P_4P_5 + P_1P_2P_5P_6 + P_2P_3P_4P_5 + P_1P_3P_4P_6 + P_2P_3P_6$$

Since P must be true ($P = 1$) in order to cover all of the minterms, we can translate the equation back into words as follows. In order to cover all of the minterms, we must choose rows P_1 and P_4 and P_5, or rows P_1 and P_2 and P_5 and P_6, or . . . , or rows P_2 and P_3 and P_6. Although there are five possible solutions, only two of these have the minimum number of rows. Thus, the two solutions with the minimum number of prime implicants are: choose rows P_1, P_4, and P_5 or rows P_2, P_3, and P_6. The first choice leads to $F = a'b' + bc' + ac$, and the second choice to $F = a'c' + b'c + ab$, which are the two minimum solutions derived in Section 7.2.

In summary, Petrick's method is as follows:

1. Reduce the prime implicant chart by eliminating the essential prime implicant rows and the corresponding columns.
2. Label the rows of the reduced prime implicant chart P_1, P_2, P_3, etc.
3. Form a logic function P which is true when all columns are covered. P consists of a product of sum terms, each sum term having the form $(P_{i0} + P_{i1} + \ldots)$, where P_{i0}, P_{i1}, . . . represent the rows which cover column i.
4. Reduce P to a minimum sum-of-products by multiplying out and applying $X + XY = X$.
5. Each term in the result represents a solution, that is, a set of rows which covers all of the minterms in the table. To determine the minimum[2] solutions, find those terms which contain a minimum number of variables. Each of these terms represents a solution with a minimum number of prime implicants.
6. For each of the terms found in step 5, count the number of literals in each prime implicant and find the total number of literals. Choose the term or

---

[2] See Section 6.1 for a definition of minimum.

terms which correspond to the minimum total number of literals, and write out the corresponding sums of prime implicants.

Application of Petrick's method is very tedious for large charts, but it is easy to implement on a computer.

7.4
Simplification of Incompletely Specified Functions

Given an incompletely specified function, proper assignment of values to the don't care terms is necessary in order to obtain a minimum form for the function. In this section, we will show how to modify the Quine-McCluskey procedure in order to obtain a minimum solution when don't care terms are present. In the process of finding the prime implicants, we will treat the don't care terms as if they were required minterms. In this way, they can be combined with other minterms to eliminate as many literals as possible. If extra prime implicants are generated because of the don't cares, this is all right since the extra prime implicants will be eliminated in the next step anyway. When forming the prime implicant chart, the don't cares are *not* listed at the top. In this way, when the prime implicant chart is solved, all of the required minterms will be covered by one of the selected prime implicants. However, the don't care terms are not included in the final solution unless they have been in the process of forming one of the selected prime implicants. The following example should clarify the procedure.

EXAMPLE OF SIMPLIFICATION OF AN INCOMPLETELY SPECIFIED FUNCTION:

$$F(A, B, C, D) = \sum m(2, 3, 7, 9, 11, 13) + \sum d(1, 10, 15)$$
(the terms following d are don't cares)

The don't cares are treated like required minterms when finding the prime implicants:

1	0001 ✓	(1, 3)	00−1 ✓	(1, 3, 9, 11)	−0−1
2	0010 ✓	(1, 9)	−001 ✓	(2, 3, 10, 11)	−01−
3	0011 ✓	(2, 3)	001− ✓	(3, 7, 11, 15)	−−11
9	1001 ✓	(2, 10)	−010 ✓	(9, 11, 13, 15)	1−−1
10	1010 ✓	(3, 7)	0−11 ✓		
7	0111 ✓	(3, 11)	−011 ✓		
11	1011 ✓	(9, 11)	10−1 ✓		
13	1101 ✓	(9, 13)	1−01 ✓		
15	1111 ✓	(10, 11)	101− ✓		
		(7, 15)	−111 ✓		
		(11, 15)	1−11 ✓		
		(13, 15)	11−1 ✓		

The don't care columns are omitted when forming the prime implicant chart:

	2	3	7	9	11	13
(1, 3, 9, 11)		✗		✗	✗	
*(2, 3, 10, 11)	✗	✗			✗	
*(3, 7, 11, 15)		✗	✗		✗	
*(9, 11, 13, 15)				✗	✗	✗

$$F = B'C + CD + AD$$

* indicates an essential prime implicant.

Note that although the original function was incompletely specified, the final simplified expression for F is defined for all combinations of values for A, B, C, and D and is therefore completely specified. In the process of simplification we have automatically assigned values to the don't cares in the original truth table for F. If we replace each term in the final expression for F by its corresponding sum of minterms, the result is

$$F = (m_2 + m_3 + m_{10} + m_{11}) + (m_3 + m_7 + m_{11} + m_{15}) + (m_9 + m_{11} + m_{13} + m_{15})$$

Since m_{10} and m_{15} appear in this expression and m_1 does not, this implies that the don't cares in the original truth table for F have been assigned as follows:

for $ABCD = 0001$, $F = 0$;   for 1010, $F = 1$;   for 1111, $F = 1$

7.5
Simplification Using Map-Entered Variables

Although the Quine-McCluskey method can be used with functions with a fairly large number of variables, it is not very efficient for functions that have many variables and relatively few terms. Some of these functions can be simplified by using a modification of the Karnaugh map method. By using map-entered variables, Karnaugh map techniques can be extended to simplify functions with more than four or five variables. Figure 7–1(a) shows a 4-variable map with two addi-

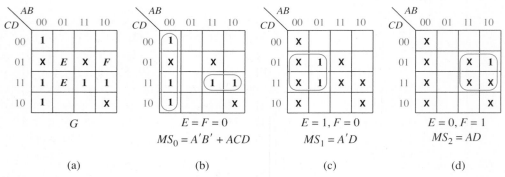

Figure 7–1
Use of Map-Entered Variables

tional variables entered in the squares in the map. When E appears in a square, this means that if $E = 1$, the corresponding minterm is present in the function G, and if $E = 0$, the minterm is absent. Thus, the map represents the 6-variable function

$$G(A, B, C, D, E, F) = m_0 + m_2 + m_3 + Em_5 + Em_7 + Fm_9$$
$$+ m_{11} + m_{15} (+\text{don't care terms})$$

where the minterms are minterms of the variables A, B, C, and D. Note that m_9 is present in G only when $F = 1$.

We will now use a 3-variable map to simplify the function

$$F(A, B, C, D) = A'B'C + A'BC + A'BC'D + ABCD + (AB'C)$$

where the $AB'C$ is a don't care. Since D appears in only two terms, we will choose it as a map-entered variable, which leads to Fig. 7–2(a). We will simplify F by first considering $D = 0$ and then $D = 1$. First set $D = 0$ on the map, and F reduces to $A'C$. Setting $D = 1$ leads to the map of Fig. 7–2(b). The two 1's on the original map have already been covered by the term $A'C$, so they are changed to X's since we don't care whether they are covered again or not. From Fig. 7–2(b), $F = C + A'B$ when $D = 1$. Thus the expression

$$F = A'C + D(C + A'B) = A'C + CD + A'BD$$

gives the correct value of F both when $D = 0$ and when $D = 1$. This is a minimum expression for F, as can be verified by plotting the original function on a 4-variable map; see Fig. 7–2(c).

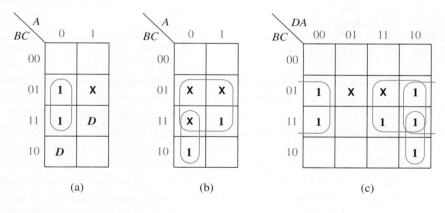

(a)   (b)   (c)

Figure 7–2
Simplification Using a Map-Entered Variable

Next we will discuss a general method of simplifying functions using map-entered variables. In general, if a variable P_i is placed in square m_j of a map of function F, this means that $F = 1$ when $P_i = 1$ and the variables are chosen so that $m_j = 1$. Given a map with variables P_1, P_2, . . . entered into some of the squares, the minimum sum-of-products form of F can be found as follows:

Find a sum-of-products expression for F of the form

$$F = MS_0 + P_1MS_1 + P_2MS_2 + \cdots$$

where

MS_0 is the minimum sum obtained by setting $P_1 = P_2 = \cdots = 0$.

MS_1 is the minimum sum obtained by setting $P_1 = 1$, $P_j = 0$ $(j \neq 1)$, and replacing all 1's on the map with don't cares.

MS_2 is the minimum sum obtained by setting $P_2 = 1$, $P_j = 0$ $(j \neq 2)$ and replacing all 1's on the map with don't cares.

(Corresponding minimum sums can be found in a similar way for any remaining map-entered variables.)

The resulting expression for F will always be a correct representation of F. This expression will be minimum provided that the values of the map-entered variables can be assigned independently. On the other hand, the expression will not generally be minimum if the variables are not independent (for example, if $P_1 = P_2'$).

For the example of Fig. 7–1(a), maps for finding MS_0, MS_1, and MS_2 are shown in Figs. 7–1(b), (c), and (d), where E corresponds to P_1 and F corresponds to P_2. The resulting expression is a minimum sum of products for G:

$$G = A'B' + ACD + EA'D + FAD$$

After some practice, it should be possible to write the minimum expression directly from the original map without first plotting individual maps for each of the minimum sums.

7.6
Conclusion

We have discussed four methods for reducing a switching expression to a minimum sum-of-products or a minimum product-of-sums form: algebraic simplification, Karnaugh maps, Quine-McCluskey, and Petrick's method. Many other methods of simplification are discussed in the literature, but most of these methods are based on variations or extensions of the Karnaugh map or Quine-McCluskey techniques. Karnaugh maps are most useful for functions with 3 to 5 variables. The Quine-McCluskey technique can be used with a high-speed digital computer to simplify functions with up to 15 or more variables. Such computer programs are of most value when used as part of a computer-aided design (CAD) package that assists with deriving the equations as well as implementing them. Algebraic simplification is still valuable in many cases, especially when different forms of the expressions are required. For problems with a large number of variables and a small number of terms, it may be impossible to use the Karnaugh map, and the Quine-McCluskey method may be very cumbersome. In such cases, algebraic simplification may be the easiest method to use. In situations where a minimum solution is not required or where obtaining a minimum solution requires too much computation to be practical, heuristic procedures may be used to simplify switching functions. One of the more popular heuristic procedures is the

Espresso-II method,[3] which can produce near minimum solutions for a large class of problems.

The minimum sum-of-products and minimum product-of-sums expressions we have derived lead directly to two-level networks that use a minimum number of AND and OR gates and have a minimum number of gate inputs. As discussed in Unit 8, these networks are easily transformed into networks that contain NAND or NOR gates. Such minimum expressions may also be useful when designing with some types of array logic as discussed in Unit 9. However, many situations exist where minimum expressions do not lead to the best design. For practical designs, many other factors must be considered, such as: What is the maximum number of inputs a gate can have? What is the maximum number of outputs a gate can drive? Is the speed with which signals propagate through the network fast enough? How can the number of interconnections in the network be reduced? Does the design lead to a satisfactory circuit layout on a printed circuit board or on a silicon chip? Up to now we have considered realizing only one switching function at a time. Unit 9 describes design techniques and components that can be used when several functions must be realized by a single network.

PROGRAMMED EXERCISE 7.1

Cover the answers to this exercise with a sheet of paper and slide it down as you check your answers.

Find a minimum sum-of-products expression for the following function:

$$f(A, B, C, D, E) = \sum(0, 2, 3, 5, 7, 9, 11, 13, 14, 16, 18, 24, 26, 28, 30)$$

Translate each decimal minterm into binary and sort the binary terms into groups according to the number of 1's in each term.

[3] This method is described in R. K. Brayton et al., *Logic Minimization Algorithms for VLSI Synthesis.* Kluwer Academic Publishers, 1984.

Answer:

0	00000 ✓		0, 2	000−0
2	00010 ✓			
16	10000			
3	00011			
5	00101			
9	01001			
18	10010			
24	11000			
7	00111			
11	01011			
13	01101			
14	01110			
26	11010			
28	11100			
30	11110			

Compare pairs of terms in adjacent groups and combine terms where possible. (Check off terms which have been combined.)

Answer:

0	00000 ✓	0, 2	000−0 ✓	0, 2, 16, 18	−00−0
2	00010 ✓	0, 16	−0000		
16	10000 ✓	2, 3	0001−		
3	00011 ✓	2, 18	−0010		
5	00101 ✓	16, 18	100−0 ✓		
9	01001 ✓	16, 24	1−000		
18	10010 ✓	3, 7	00−11		
24	11000 ✓	3, 11	0−011		
7	00111 ✓	5, 7	001−1		
11	01011 ✓	5, 13	0−101		
13	01101 ✓	9, 11	010−1		
14	01110 ✓	9, 13	01−01		
26	11010 ✓	18, 26	1−010		
28	11100 ✓	24, 26	110−0		
30	11110 ✓	24, 28	11−00		
		14, 30	−1110		
		26, 30	11−10		
		28, 30	111−0		

Now compare pairs of terms in adjacent groups in the second column and combine terms where possible. (Check off terms which have been combined.) Check your work by noting that each new term can be formed in two ways. (Cross out duplicate terms.)

Answer: (third column)

0, 2, 16, 18	$-00-0$	(check off (0, 2), (16, 18), (0, 16) and (2, 18))
16, 18, 24, 26	$1-0-0$	(check off (16, 18), (24, 26), (16, 24) and (18, 26))
24, 26, 28, 30	$11--0$	(check off (24, 26), (28, 30), (24, 28) and (26, 30))

Can any pair of terms in the third column be combined? Complete the given prime implicant chart.

	0 2
(0, 2, 16, 18)	

Answer: No terms in the third column combine.

	0	2	3	5	7	9	11	13	14	16	18	24	26	28	30
(0, 2, 16, 18)	X	X								X	X				
(16, 18, 24, 26)										X	X	X	X		
(24, 26, 28, 30)												X	X	X	X
(2, 3)	X	X													
(3, 7)		X		X											
(3, 11)		X			X										
(5, 7)			X	X											
(5, 13)			X			X									
(9, 11)					X	X									
(9, 13)					X		X								
(14, 30)									X						X

Determine the essential prime implicants, and cross out the corresponding rows and columns.

Answer:

	0	2	3	5	7	9	11	13	14	16	18	24	26	28	30
*(0, 2, 16, 18)	Ⓧ	X								X	X				
(16, 18, 24, 26)										X	X	X	X		
*(24, 26, 28, 30)												X	X	Ⓧ	X
(2, 3)		X	X												
(3, 7)			X	X											
(3, 11)			X				X								
(5, 7)				X	X										
(5, 13)				X				X							
(9, 11)						X	X								
(9, 13)						X		X							
*(14, 30)									Ⓧ						X

* Indicates an essential prime implicant.

Note that all remaining columns contain two or more X's. Choose the first column which has two X's and then select the prime implicant which covers the first X in that column. Then choose a minimum number of prime implicants which cover the remaining columns in the chart.

Answer:

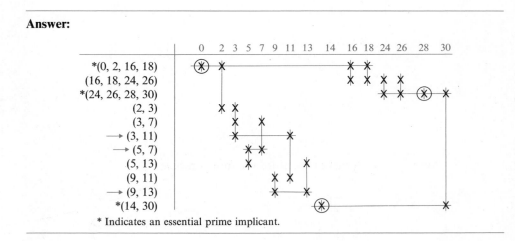

* Indicates an essential prime implicant.

From the above chart, write down the chosen prime implicants in 0, 1, – notation.

Then write the minimum sum of products in algebraic form.

Answer: $-00-0$, $11--0$, $0-011$, $001-1$, $01-01$, and -1110

$$f = B'C'E' + ABE' + A'C'DE + A'B'CE + A'BD'E + BCDE'$$

The prime implicant chart with the essential prime implicants crossed out is repeated below. Find a second minimum sum-of-products solution.

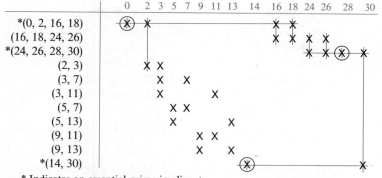

* Indicates an essential prime implicant.

Answer: Start by choosing prime implicant (5, 13).

$$f = BCDE' + B'C'E' + ABE' + A'B'DE + A'CD'E + A'BC'E$$

PROBLEMS

7.2   For each of the following functions, find all of the prime implicants using the Quine-McCluskey procedure.
   (a) $f(a, b, c, d) = \sum m(1,5,7,9,11,12,14,15)$
   (b) $f(a, b, c, d) = \sum m(0, 1, 3, 5, 6, 7, 8, 10, 14, 15)$
   (c) $f(a, b, c, d) = \sum m(0, 3, 4, 5, 7, 9, 11, 13)$
   (d) $f(a, b, c, d) = \sum m(2, 4, 5, 6, 9, 10, 11, 12, 13, 15)$

7.3   Using a prime implicant chart, find *all* minimum sum-of-products solutions for each of the functions given in Problem 7.2.

7.4   For each function, find a minimum sum-of-products solution using the Quine-McCluskey procedure.
   (a) $f(a, b, c, d) = \sum m(1, 3, 4, 5, 6, 7, 10, 12, 13) + \sum d(2, 9, 15)$
   (b) $f(a, b, c, d) = \sum m(2, 3, 4, 7, 9, 11, 12, 13, 14) + \sum d(1, 10, 15)$
   (c) $f(a, b, c, d) = \sum m(0, 1, 5, 6, 8, 9, 11, 13) + \sum d(7, 10, 12)$
   (d) $f(a, b, c, d) = \sum m(3, 4, 6, 7, 8, 9, 11, 13, 14) + \sum d(2, 5, 15)$

7.5   Work Problem 6.19 using the Quine-McCluskey method.

7.6   Work Problem 6.27 by the Quine-McCluskey method.

7.7   Using the Quine-McCluskey procedure, find all minimum sum-of-products expressions for
   (a) $f(A, B, C, D, E) = \sum m(0, 1, 2, 3, 6, 8, 9, 10, 11, 17, 20, 21, 23, 25, 28, 30, 31)$
   (b) $f(A, B, C, D, E) = \sum m(0, 4, 5, 6, 9, 10, 11, 14, 15, 16, 17, 21, 22, 26, 27, 30, 31)$

7.8   Work Problem 6.15 using the Quine-McCluskey method.

7.9   Work Problem 6.25 by the Quine-McCluskey method.

7.10 $G(A, B, C, D, E, F) = \sum m(1, 2, 3, 16, 17, 18, 19, 26, 32, 39, 48, 63)$
$$+ \sum d(15, 28, 29, 30)$$

(a) Find all minimum sum-of-products expressions for G.

(b) Circle the *essential* prime implicants in your answer.

(c) If there were no don't cares present in the original function, how would your answer to (a) be changed? (Do this by inspection of the prime implicant chart; do *not* rework the problem.)

7.11 Work Problem 7.10 for
$$G(A, B, C, D, E, F) = \sum m(17, 23, 27, 28, 31, 43, 44, 49, 51, 59, 63)$$
$$+ \sum d(14, 34, 38, 42)$$

7.12 Find all prime implicants of the following function; then find all minimum solutions using Petrick's method:

(a) $F(A, B, C, D) = \sum m(9, 12, 13, 15) + \sum d(1, 4, 5, 7, 8, 11, 14)$

(b) $F(A, B, C, D) = \sum m(7, 12, 14, 15) + \sum d(1, 3, 5, 8, 10, 11, 13)$

7.13 Using the method of map-entered variables, use 4-variable maps to find a minimum sum-of-products expression for

(a) $F(A, B, C, D, E) = \sum m(0, 4, 5, 7, 9) + \sum d(6, 11) + E(m_1 + m_{15})$, where the m's represent minterms of the variables A, B, C, D.

(b) $Z(A, B, C, D, E, F, G) = \sum m(0, 3, 13, 15) + \sum d(1, 2, 7, 9, 14)$
$$+ E(m_6 + m_8) + Fm_{12} + Gm_5$$

(c) $F(A, B, C, D, E) = \sum m(0, 4, 6, 13, 14) + \sum d(2, 9) + E(m_1 + m_{12})$

(d) $Z(A, B, C, D, E, F, G) = \sum m(2, 5, 6, 9) + \sum d(1, 3, 4, 13, 14)$
$$+ E(m_{11} + m_{12}) + F(m_{10}) + G(m_0)$$

7.14 (a) Rework Problem 7.13(a) using a 5-variable map.

(b) Rework Problem 7.13(a) using the Quine-McCluskey procedure. Note that you must express F in terms of minterms of all five variables; the original 4-variable minterms cannot be used.

7.15 Work Problem 6.32 using a 4-variable map with map-entered variables.

8

Multi-Level Gate Networks NAND and NOR Gates

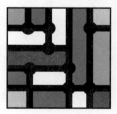

OBJECTIVES

1. Design a minimal two-level or multi-level network of AND and OR gates to realize a given function. (Consider *both* networks with an OR gate at the output and networks with an AND gate at the output.)

2. Define a functionally complete set of logic gates and determine if a given set of gates is functionally complete.

3. Design or analyze a two-level gate network using any one of the eight basic forms (AND-OR, NAND-NAND, OR-NAND, NOR-OR, OR-AND, NOR-NOR, AND-NOR, and NAND-AND).

4. Design or analyze a multi-level NAND-gate or NOR-gate network.

5. Explain mixed logic and direct polarity indication. Apply these concepts to the analysis and design of gate networks.

6. Convert networks of AND and OR gates to networks of NAND gates or NOR gates, and conversely, (a) by adding or deleting inversion bubbles and (b) by using mixed logic with direct polarity indication.

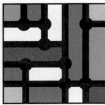

STUDY GUIDE

1. Study Section 8.1, *Multi-Level Gate Networks*.

   (a) What are two ways of changing the number of levels in a gate network?

   (b) By constructing a tree diagram, determine the number of gates, gate inputs, and levels of gates required to realize Z_1 and Z_2:

   $$Z_1 = [(A + B)C + DE(F + G)]H \qquad Z_2 = A + B[C + DE(F + G)]$$

   Check your answers by drawing the corresponding gate networks.

   (c) In order to find a minimum two-level solution, why is it necessary to consider both a sum-of-products form and a product-of-sums form for the function?

(d) One realization of $Z = ABC(D + E) + FG$ is

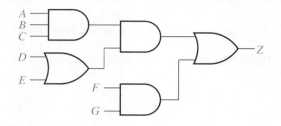

Redraw the network so that it uses one less gate and so that the output of an AND gate never goes directly to the input of another AND gate.

(e) Work Problems 8.1 and 8.3(a) and (b). Unless otherwise specified, you may always assume that both the variables and their complements are available as network inputs.

2. Study Section 8.2, *Other Types of Logic Gates.*

(a) For each gate, specify the missing inputs:

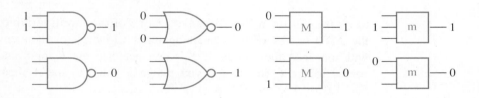

(b) Review the definitions of positive and negative logic, and also review the negative logic theorem (Section 3.5). Make sure that you know the difference between the dual and the inverse. Work Problem 8.7.

(c) Write a logic equation for F.

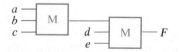

3. Study Section 8.3, *Functionally Complete Sets of Logic Gates.*

   (a) What is meant by a functionally complete set of logic gates?

   (b) How can you show that a set of logic gates is functionally complete?

   (c) Show that the network given below is functionally complete.

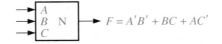

$$F = A'B' + BC + AC'$$

First, we must find a way to realize the complement of a variable. To do this, we will try to assign constant values to two of the network inputs in such a way that the complement of the third input will appear at the output. If we set A equal to X in the equation for F, find values of B and C such that $F = X'$.

   $B =$ _____ $C =$ _____

Next, we will try to find a value for one of the input variables such that the AND or OR of the remaining input variables (or their complements) will appear at the output. If Y is connected to the B input and Z is connected to the C input, can you assign a value to the A input such that $F = YZ$ or $Y'Z$ or YZ' or $Y'Z'$? _____

Still keeping $B = X$ and $C = Y$, assign a value to A such that F reduces to an expression that contains two literals ORed together.

   $A =$ _____   and F reduces to _____

Now draw a diagram showing how two N networks can be connected to realize $Y + Z$ (with appropriate values assigned to the A inputs).

Show how to realize YZ using three N networks.

Explain why N is functionally complete.

   (d) Work Problems 8.9 and 8.11.

4. Study Section 8.4, *Design of Two-Level NAND- and NOR-Gate Networks.*

   (a) Draw the network corresponding to Equation (8–18).

   (b) Derive Equation (8–19).

   (c) Make sure that you understand the relation between Equations (8–14) through (8–22) and the diagrams of Fig. 8–14.

   (d) Why is the NOR-NAND form degenerate?

   (e) What assumption is made about the types of inputs available when the procedures for designing two-level NAND-NAND and NOR-NOR networks are used?

   (f) For these procedures the literal inputs to the output gate are complemented but not the literal inputs to the other gates. Explain why. Use an equation to illustrate.

   (g) A general OR-AND network is shown below. Transform this to a NOR-NOR network and prove that your transformation is valid.

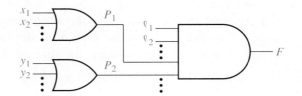

   (h) Work Problem 8.12(a).

5. Study Section 8.5, *Design of Multi-Level NAND- and NOR-Gate Networks.*

   (a) Verify that the NAND network of Fig. 8–16 is correct by dividing the corresponding network of AND and OR gates into two-level subnetworks and transforming each subnetwork.

   (b) If you wish to design a two-level network using only NOR gates, should you start with a minimum sum of products or a minimum product of sums?

(c) Note that direct conversion of a network of AND and OR gates to a NAND-gate network requires starting with an OR gate at the output, but direct conversion to a NOR-gate network requires starting with an AND gate at the output. This is easy to remember since a NAND is equivalent to an OR with the inputs inverted:

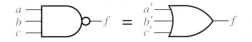

and a NOR is equivalent to an AND with the inputs inverted:

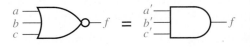

(d) Convert the network of Fig. 8–1(b) to all NAND gates.

(e) Work Problems 8.13, 8.15(a), 8.16(a), and 8.17(a).

6. Study Section 8.6, *Network Conversion Using Alternative Gate Symbols*.

(a) Determine the logic function realized by each of the following networks:

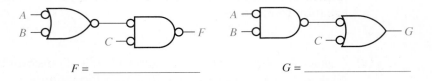

$F =$ _____ $G =$ _____

(b) Convert the network of Fig. 8–16(a) to NAND gates by adding bubbles and complementing input variables when necessary. (You should have added 12 bubbles. Your result should be similar to Fig. 8–16(b), except some of the NAND gates will use the alternative symbol.)

(c) Draw a network of AND and OR gates for the following equation:

$$Z = A[BC + D + E(F + GH)]$$

Then convert to NOR gates by adding bubbles and complementing inputs when necessary. (You should have added 10 bubbles and complemented 6 input variables.)

(d) Work Problem 8.24.

7. Study Section 8.7, *Mixed Logic and Polarity Indication.*

   (a) For each gate, show the internal logic values for the inputs and output.

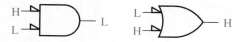

   For each gate, show the external logic levels for the inputs and output.

   (b) What function is realized by each of the following gates?

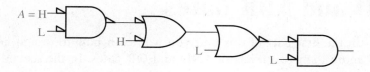

   $F =$ _____ $F =$ _____

   Note that when the signal polarities match the gate polarities, no inversion occurs.

   (c) Indicate on the logic diagram whether each gate output is H or L. Then indicate the changes which will occur if input A is changed to L.

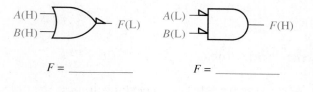

   (d) Determine the function realized by the following NOR-gate network:

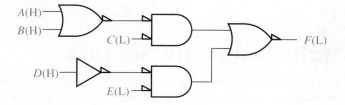

(e) Determine the function realized by each gate:

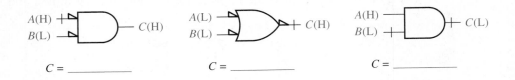

$C = $ _____ $C = $ _____ $C = $ _____

(f) Realize $F = A'B + C$ using two NAND gates with polarity indication. (Assume that input signals with the necessary polarity are available and F is active high.)

(g) Realize $F = A'B + C$ using two NOR gates with polarity indication. (Assume that input signals with the necessary polarity are available and F is active low.)

(h) Work Problems 8.25 and 8.26.

8. When you are satisfied that you can meet the objectives of this unit, take the readiness test. The techniques learned in this unit will be applied to a design problem in Unit 10.

Multi-Level Gate Networks
NAND and NOR Gates

In the first part of this unit you will learn how to design networks which have more than two levels of AND and OR gates. In the second part you will learn techniques for designing with NAND and NOR gates. These techniques generally consist of first designing a network of AND and OR gates and then converting it to the desired type of gates. These techniques are easy to apply *provided* that you start with the proper form of network.

8.1
Multi-Level Gate Networks

The maximum number of gates cascaded in series between a network input and the output is referred to as the number of *levels* of gates (not to be confused with voltage levels). Thus, a function written in sum-of-products form or in product-of-sums form corresponds directly to a two-level gate network. As is usually the case in digital networks where the gates are driven from flip-flop[1] outputs, we will assume that all variables and their complements are available as network inputs. For this reason, we will not normally count inverters which are connected directly to input variables when determining the number of levels in a network. In this unit we will use the following terminology:

1. *AND-OR network* means a two-level network composed of a level of AND gates followed by an OR gate at the output.
2. *OR-AND network* means a two-level network composed of a level of OR gates followed by an AND gate at the output.
3. *OR-AND-OR network* means a three-level network composed of a level of OR gates followed by a level of AND gates followed by an OR gate at the output.
4. *Network of AND and OR gates* implies no particular ordering of the gates; the output gate may be either AND or OR.

The number of levels in an AND-OR network can usually be increased by factoring the sum-of-products expression from which it was derived. Similarly, the number of levels in an OR-AND network can usually be increased by multi-plying out some of the terms in the product-of-sums expression from which it was derived. Logic designers are concerned with the number of levels in a network for several reasons. Sometimes factoring (or multiplying out) to increase the num-ber of levels of gates will reduce the required number of gates and gate inputs and thus reduce the cost of building the network, but in other cases increasing the number of levels will increase the cost. In some applications, the number of gates which can be cascaded is limited by gate delays. When the input of a gate is switched, there is a finite time before the output changes. When several gates are cascaded, the time between an input change and the corresponding change in the network output may become excessive and slow down the operation of the digital system.

The number of gates, gate inputs, and levels in a network can be determined by inspection of the corresponding expression. In the example of Fig. 8–1(a), the tree diagram drawn below the expression for Z indicates that the corresponding network will have 4 levels, 6 gates, and 13 gate inputs, as verified in Fig. 8–1(b). Each node on the tree diagram represents a gate, and the number of gate inputs is written beside each node. We can change the expression for Z to 3 levels by partially multiplying it out:

$$Z = (AB + C)[(D + E) + FG] + H$$
$$= AB(D + E) + C(D + E) + ABFG + CFG + H$$

As shown in Fig. 8–2, the resulting network requires 3 levels, 6 gates, and 19 gate inputs.

---

[1] Flip-flops are discussed in Unit 11.

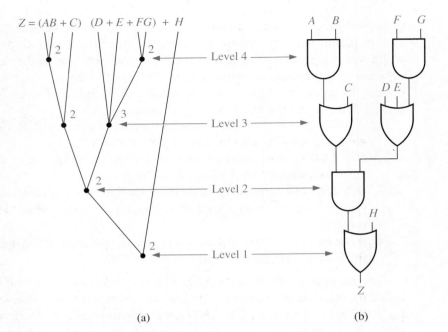

$Z = (AB + C) \ (D + E + FG) \ + H$

Level 4

Level 3

Level 2

Level 1

(a)   (b)

Figure 8–1
Four-Level Realization of Z

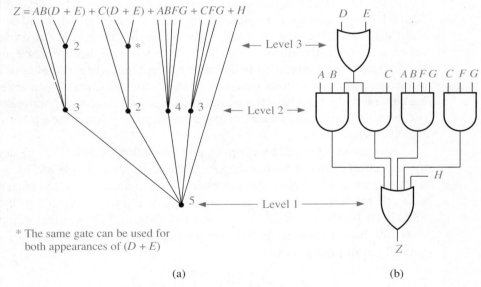

$Z = AB(D + E) + C(D + E) + ABFG + CFG + H$

Level 3

Level 2

Level 1

* The same gate can be used for
  both appearances of $(D + E)$

(a)   (b)

Figure 8–2
Three-Level Realization of Z

EXAMPLE OF MULTI-LEVEL DESIGN USING AND AND OR GATES

Problem: Find a network of AND and OR gates to realize

$$f(a, b, c, d) = \sum m(1, 5, 6, 10, 13, 14)$$

Consider solutions with two levels of gates and three levels of gates. Try to minimize the number of gates and the total number of gate inputs. Assume that all variables and their complements are available as inputs.

Solution: First simplify f by using a Karnaugh map (Fig. 8–3):

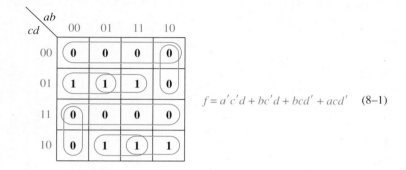

$$f = a'c'd + bc'd + bcd' + acd' \quad (8\text{–}1)$$

Figure 8–3

This leads directly to a two-level **AND-OR** gate network (Fig. 8–4):

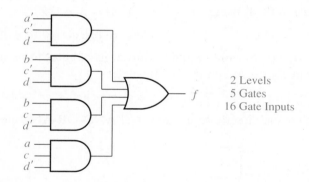

2 Levels
5 Gates
16 Gate Inputs

Figure 8–4

Factoring Equation (8–1) yields

$$f = c'd(a' + b) + cd'(a + b) \quad (8\text{–}2)$$

which leads to the following three-level **OR-AND-OR** gate network (Fig. 8–5):

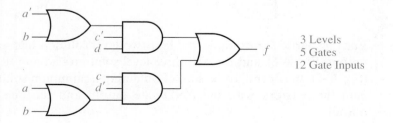

3 Levels
5 Gates
12 Gate Inputs

Figure 8–5

Both of these solutions have an OR gate at the output. A solution with an AND gate at the output might have fewer gates or gate inputs. A two-level OR-AND network corresponds to a product-of-sums expression for the function. This can be obtained from the 0's on the Karnaugh map as follows:

$$f' = c'd' + ab'c' + cd + a'b'c \tag{8-3}$$

$$f = (c + d)(a' + b + c)(c' + d')(a + b + c') \tag{8-4}$$

Equation (8–4) leads directly to a two-level OR-AND network (Fig. 8–6):

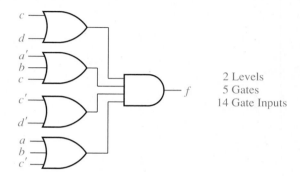

2 Levels
5 Gates
14 Gate Inputs

Figure 8–6

To get a three-level network with an AND gate output, we partially multiply out Equation (8–4) using $(X + Y)(X + Z) = X + YZ$:

$$f = [c + d(a' + b)][c' + d'(a + b)] \tag{8-5}$$

Equation (8–5) would require four levels of gates to realize; however, if we multiply out $d'(a + b)$ and $d(a' + b)$ we get

$$f = (c + a'd + bd)(c' + ad' + bd') \tag{8-6}$$

which leads directly to a three-level AND-OR-AND network (Fig. 8–7):

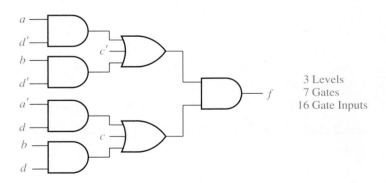

3 Levels
7 Gates
16 Gate Inputs

Figure 8–7

For this particular example, the best two-level solution had an AND gate at the output (Fig. 8–6), and the best three-level solution had an OR gate at the output (Fig. 8–5). In general, to be sure of obtaining a minimum solution, one must find *both* the network with the AND-gate output and the one with the OR-gate output.

If an expression for f' has n levels, the complement of that expression is an n-level expression for f. Therefore, to realize f as an n-level network with an AND-gate output, one procedure is first to find an n-level expression for f' with an OR operation at the output level, and then complement the expression for f'. In the above example, factoring Equation (8–3) gives a three-level expression for f':

$$f' = c'(d' + ab') + c(d + a'b')$$
$$= c'(d' + a)(d' + b') + c(d + a')(d + b') \qquad (8–7)$$

Complementing Equation (8–7) gives Equation (8–6), which corresponds to the three-level AND-OR-AND network of Fig. 8–7.

8.2
Other Types of Logic Gates

Up to this point we have designed logic networks using AND gates, OR gates, and inverters. Exclusive-OR and equivalence gates have also been introduced in Unit 3. In this section we will define NAND and NOR gates. These gates can be constructed using transistor logic (Appendix A.2), and they are commonly available in integrated-circuit form (Appendix A.3). Logic designers frequently use NAND and NOR gates because they are generally faster and use fewer components than AND or OR gates. As will be shown in Section 8.3, any logic function can be implemented using only NAND gates or only NOR gates.

Figure 8–8(a) shows a 3-input NAND[2] gate. The small circle (or "bubble") at the gate output indicates inversion, so the NAND gate is equivalent to an AND gate followed by an inverter as shown in Fig. 8–8(b). The gate output is

$$F = (ABC)' = A' + B' + C'$$

The output of the n-input NAND gate in Fig. 8–8(c) is

$$F = (X_1 X_2 \cdots X_n)' = X_1' + X_2' + \cdots + X_n' \qquad (8–8)$$

The output of this gate is 1 iff one or more of its inputs are 0.

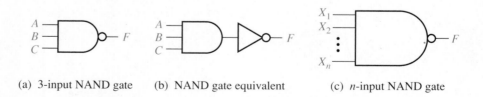

(a) 3-input NAND gate   (b) NAND gate equivalent   (c) n-input NAND gate

Figure 8–8
NAND Gates

---

[2] A more appropriate name would be an AND-NOT gate, but we will follow common usage and call it a NAND gate.

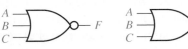 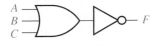 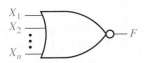

(a) 3-input NOR gate   (b) NOR gate equivalent   (c) *n*-input NOR gate

Figure 8–9
NOR Gates

Figure 8–9(a) shows a 3-input NOR gate.[3] The small circle at the gate output indicates inversion, so the NOR gate is equivalent to an OR gate followed by an inverter. The gate output is

$$F = (A + B + C)' = A'B'C'$$

The output of an *n*-input NOR gate, shown in Fig. 8–9(c), is

$$F = (X_1 + X_2 + \cdots + X_n)' = X_1'X_2' \cdots X_n' \qquad (8\text{--}9)$$

The output of this gate is 1 iff all inputs are 0.

From Equations (8–8) and (8–9), note that the NAND and NOR functions are duals. Thus, by applying the negative logic theorem (Section 3.5), if a given circuit realizes the NAND function for positive logic, it realizes the NOR function for negative logic.

A *majority* gate has an odd number of inputs, and its output is 1 iff a majority of its inputs are 1. Thus, a 3-input majority gate (Fig. 8–10(a)) has an output of 1 if two or three of its inputs are 1. A *minority* gate has an odd number of inputs, and its output is 1 iff a minority of its inputs are 1. Thus, a 3-input minority gate has an output of 1 if none or one of its inputs is 1.

From the truth table, the function realized by a 3-input majority gate is

$$F_M = a'bc + ab'c + abc' + abc = bc + ac + ab \qquad (8\text{--}10)$$

By inspection of the table, $F_m = F_M'$, so the 3-input minority gate realizes

$$F_m = (bc + ac + ab)' = (b' + c')(a' + c')(a' + b') \qquad (8\text{--}11)$$

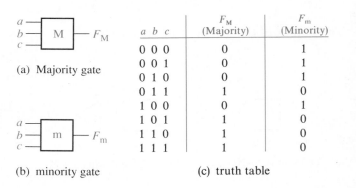

(a) Majority gate

(b) minority gate

a b c	F_M (Majority)	F_m (Minority)
0 0 0	0	1
0 0 1	0	1
0 1 0	0	1
0 1 1	1	0
1 0 0	0	1
1 0 1	1	0
1 1 0	1	0
1 1 1	1	0

(c) truth table

Figure 8–10
Majority and Minority Gates

---

[3] A more appropriate name would be an OR-NOT gate, but we will follow common usage and call it a NOR gate.

8.3
Functionally Complete Sets of Logic Gates

A set of logic operations is said to be *functionally complete* if any Boolean function can be expressed in terms of this set of operations. The set AND, OR, and NOT is obviously functionally complete since any function can be expressed in sum-of-products form, and a sum-of-products expression uses only the AND, OR, and NOT operations. Similarly, a set of logic gates is functionally complete if all switching functions can be realized using this set of gates. Since the set of operations AND, OR, and NOT is functionally complete, any set of logic gates which can realize AND, OR, and NOT is also functionally complete. AND and NOT are a functionally complete set of gates since OR can also be realized using AND and NOT:

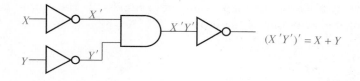

If a single gate forms a functionally complete set by itself, then any switching function can be realized using only gates of that type. The NAND gate is an example of such a gate. Since the NAND gate performs the AND operation followed by an inversion, NOT, AND, and OR can be realized using only NAND gates as shown in Fig. 8–11.

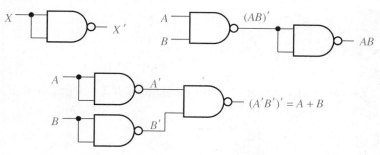

Figure 8–11
NAND Gate Realization of NOT, AND, and OR

Thus, any switching function can be realized using only NAND gates. An easy method for converting an AND-OR network to a NAND network is discussed in the next section.

The following procedure can be used to determine if a given set of gates is functionally complete. First, write out a minimum sum-of-products expression for the function realized by each gate. If no complement appears in any of these expressions, then NOT cannot be realized and the set is not functionally complete. If a complement appears in one of the expressions, then NOT can generally be realized by an appropriate choice of inputs to the corresponding gate. (We will always assume that 0 and 1 are available as gate inputs). Next, attempt to realize AND or OR, keeping in mind that NOT is now available. Once AND or OR has been realized, the other one can always be realized using DeMorgan's laws if no more direct procedure is apparent. For example, if OR and NOT are available, AND can be realized by

$$XY = (X' + Y')'$$

EXAMPLE: Show that all switching functions can be realized using only 3-input minority gates.

Solution: First we will derive the function realized by a 3-input minority gate using a Karnaugh map as shown in Fig. 8–12. The output is 1 if no inputs are 1 or if exactly one of the inputs is 1.

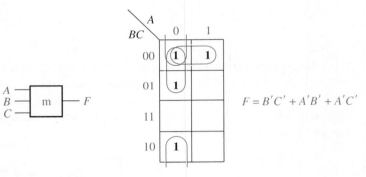

$$F = B'C' + A'B' + A'C'$$

Figure 8–12
Derivation of Minority Gate Output Function

We can easily realize the complement of X by letting $A = B = C = X$.

$$F = X'X' + X'X' + X'X' = X'$$

Next, we will try to realize AND using minority gates. To be specific, we will determine inputs to a minority gate such that the gate output will be XY. Looking at the expression for the gate output, we see that if we set $A = 1$, F reduces to $B'C'$. Then, in order to get $F = XY$, we must set $B = X'$ and $C = Y'$. Since we already know how to realize X' and Y', the AND operation can be realized as shown in Fig. 8–13(a). Figure 8–13(b) shows a way to realize XY with only two minority gates. Since the output gate is connected as an inverter, its input must be $X' + Y'$. If we set $C = 0$, F reduces to $B' + A'B' + A' = A' + B'$, so the inputs to the first gate must be $A = X$, $B = Y$, and $C = 0$ in order to get $X' + Y'$ at its output.

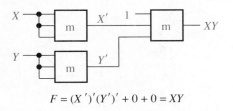 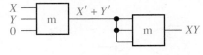

$$F = (X')'(Y')' + 0 + 0 = XY$$

(a) 3-gate realization for AND

$$F = (X' + Y' + X'Y')' = (X' + Y')' = XY$$

(b) Alternate form for AND

Figure 8–13
Realization of AND Using Minority Gates

OR can then be realized by using $(X + Y) = (X'Y')'$.

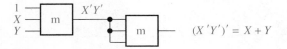

$$(X'Y')' = X + Y$$

Since AND, OR, and NOT can all be realized using only minority gates, any switching function can be realized using only minority gates.

8.4
Design of Two-Level NAND- and NOR-Gate Networks

A two-level network composed of AND and OR gates is easily converted to a network composed of NAND gates or of NOR gates. This conversion is carried out by using $F = (F')'$ and then applying DeMorgan's laws:

$$(X_1 + X_2 + \cdots + X_n)' = X_1'X_2' \cdots X_n' \tag{8–12}$$

$$(X_1X_2 \cdots X_n)' = X_1' + X_2' + \cdots + X_n' \tag{8–13}$$

The following example illustrates conversion of a minimum sum-of-products form to several other two-level forms:

$$F = A + BC' + B'CD = [(A + BC' + B'CD)']' \tag{8–14}$$

$$= [A' \cdot (BC')' \cdot (B'CD)']' \qquad \text{(by 8–12)} \tag{8–15}$$

$$= [A' \cdot (B' + C) \cdot (B + C' + D')]' \qquad \text{(by 8–13)} \tag{8–16}$$

$$= A + (B' + C)' + (B + C' + D')' \qquad \text{(by 8–13)} \tag{8–17}$$

Equations (8–14), (8–15), (8–16), and (8–17) represent the AND-OR, NAND-NAND, OR-NAND, and NOR-OR forms, respectively, as shown in Fig. 8–14.

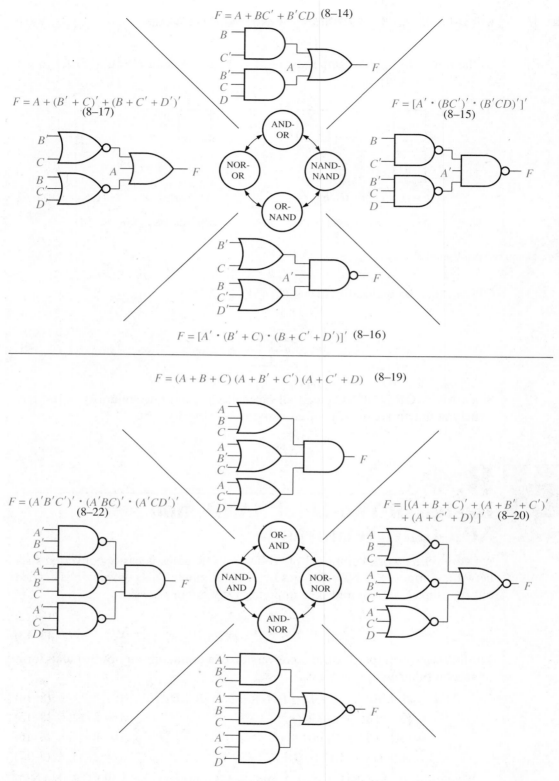

Figure 8–14
Eight Basic Forms for Two-Level Networks

Rewriting Equation (8–17) in the form

$$F = \{[A + (B' + C)' + (B + C' + D')']'\}' \qquad (8\text{–}18)$$

leads to a three-level NOR-NOR-INVERT network. However, if we want a two-level network containing only NOR gates, we should start with the minimum product-of-sums form for F instead of the minimum sum of products. After obtaining the minimum product of sums from a Karnaugh map, F can be written in the following two-level forms:

$$
\begin{aligned}
F &= (A + B + C)(A + B' + C')(A + C' + D) & & (8\text{–}19)\\
&= \{[(A + B + C)(A + B' + C')(A + C' + D)]'\}'\\
&= [(A + B + C)' + (A + B' + C')' + (A + C' + D)']' & \text{(by 8–13)} & (8\text{–}20)\\
&= (A'B'C' + A'BC + A'CD')' & \text{(by 8–12)} & (8\text{–}21)\\
&= (A'B'C')' \cdot (A'BC)' \cdot (A'CD')' & \text{(by 8–12)} & (8\text{–}22)
\end{aligned}
$$

Equations (8–19), (8–20), (8–21), and (8–22) represent the OR-AND, NOR-NOR, AND-NOR,[4] and NAND-AND forms, respectively, as shown in Fig. 8–14.

The other eight possible two-level forms (AND-AND, OR-OR, OR-NOR, AND-NAND, NAND-NOR, NOR-NAND, etc.) are degenerate in the sense that they cannot realize all switching functions. Consider, for example, the following NAND-NOR network:

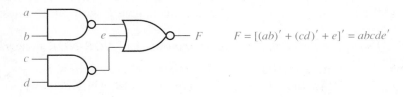

$$F = [(ab)' + (cd)' + e]' = abcde'$$

From the above example, it is clear that the NAND-NOR form can realize only a product of literals and not a sum of products.

Since NAND and NOR gates are readily available in integrated-circuit form, two of the most commonly used network forms are the NAND-NAND and the NOR-NOR. Assuming that all variables and their complements are available as inputs, the following method can be used to realize F with NAND gates:

Procedure for designing a minimum two-level NAND-NAND network

1. Find a minimum *sum-of-products* expression for F.
2. Draw the corresponding two-level AND-OR network.
3. Replace all gates with NAND gates leaving the gate interconnections unchanged. If the output gate has any single literals as inputs, complement these literals.

---

[4] Two-level AND-NOR (AND-OR-INVERT) networks are available in integrated-circuit form. Some types of NAND gates can also realize AND-NOR networks when the so-called "wired OR" connection is used.

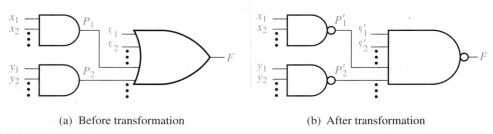

(a) Before transformation   (b) After transformation

Figure 8–15
AND-OR to NAND-NAND Transformation

Figure 8–15 illustrates the transformation of step 3. Verification that this transformation leaves the network output unchanged follows. In general, F is a sum of literals $(\ell_1, \ell_2, \ldots)$ and product terms $(P_1, P_2, \ldots)$:

$$F = \ell_1 + \ell_2 + \cdots + P_1 + P_2 + \cdots$$

After applying DeMorgan's law,

$$F = (\ell_1' \ell_2' \cdots P_1' P_2' \cdots)'$$

So the output OR gate is replaced with a NAND gate with inputs $\ell_1', \ell_2', \ldots, P_1', P_2', \ldots$. Since product terms $P_1, P_2, \ldots$ are each realized with an AND gate, $P_1', P_2', \ldots$ are each realized with a NAND gate in the transformed network.

Assuming that all variables and their complements are available as inputs, the following method can be used to realize F with NOR gates:

Procedure for designing a minimum two-level NOR-NOR network

1. Find a minimum *product-of-sums* expression for F.
2. Draw the corresponding two-level OR-AND network.
3. Replace all gates with NOR gates leaving the gate interconnections unchanged. If the output gate has any single literals as inputs, complement these literals.

The above procedure is similar to that used for designing NAND-NAND networks. Note, however, that for the NOR-NOR network, the starting point is a minimum *product of sums* rather than a sum of products.

8.5
Design of Multi-Level NAND- and NOR-Gate Networks

The following procedure may be used to design multi-level NAND-gate networks:

1. Simplify the switching function to be realized.
2. Design a multi-level network of AND and OR gates. The output gate must be OR. AND-gate outputs cannot be used as AND-gate inputs; OR-gate outputs cannot be used as OR-gate inputs.

3. Number the levels starting with the output gate as level 1. Replace all gates with NAND gates, leaving all interconnections between gates unchanged. Leave the inputs to levels 2, 4, 6, . . . unchanged. Invert any literals which appear as inputs to levels 1, 3, 5, ...

The validity of the above procedure is easily proved by dividing the multi-level network into two-level subnetworks and applying the previous results for two-level networks to each of the two-level subnetworks. The example of Fig. 8–16 illustrates the above procedure. Note that if step 2 is performed correctly, each level of the network will contain only AND gates or only OR gates.

The procedure for design of multi-level NOR-gate networks is exactly the same as for NAND-gate networks except the output gate of the network of AND and OR gates must be an AND gate, and all gates are replaced with NOR gates.

EXAMPLE:

$$F_1 = a'[b' + c(d + e') + f'g'] + hi'j + k$$

Figure 8–16 shows how the AND-OR network for F_1 is converted to the corresponding NAND network.

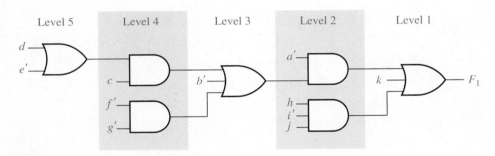

(a) AND-OR network

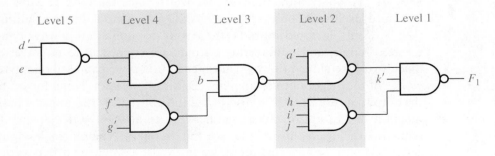

(b) NAND network

Figure 8–16
Multi-Level Network Conversion to NAND Gates

8.6
Network Conversion Using Alternative Gate Symbols

Logic designers who design complex digital systems often find it convenient to use more than one representation for a given type of gate. For example an inverter can be represented by

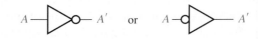

In the second case, the inversion "bubble" is at the input instead of the output. Figure 8–17 shows some alternative representations for AND, OR, NAND, and NOR gates. These equivalent gate symbols are based on the identities

$$AB = (A' + B')', \quad A + B = (A'B')', \quad (AB)' = A' + B', \quad (A + B)' = A'B'$$

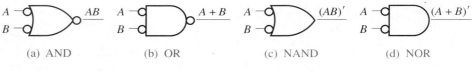

(a) AND   (b) OR   (c) NAND   (d) NOR

Figure 8–17
Alternative Gate Symbols

The above alternative symbols can be used to facilitate the analysis and design of NAND and NOR gate networks. Figure 8–18(a) shows a simple NAND-gate network. To analyze the network, we will replace the NAND gates at the first and third levels with the alternative NAND gate symbol. In the resulting network (Fig. 8–18(b)), inverted outputs (those with a bubble) are always connected to inverted inputs, and noninverted outputs are connected to noninverted inputs. Since two inversions in a row cancel each other, we can easily analyze the network without algebraically applying DeMorgan's laws. Note, for example, that the output of gate 2 is $[(A' + B)C]'$, but the term $(A' + B)C$ appears in the output function. We can also convert the network to an AND-OR network by simply removing the double inversions (see Fig. 8–18(c)). When a single input variable is connected to an inverted input, we must also complement that variable when we remove the inversion from the gate input. For example, A in Fig. 8–18(b) becomes A' in Fig. 8–18(c).

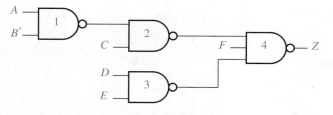

(a) NAND-gate network

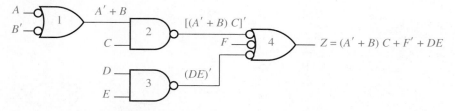

(b) Alternate form for NAND-gate network

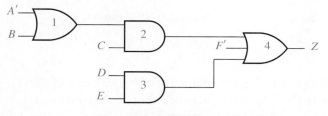

(c) Equivalent AND-OR network

Figure 8–18
NAND-Gate Network Conversion

The network of AND and OR gates shown in Fig. 8–19(a) can easily be converted to a NOR-gate network since the output gate is an AND gate, and AND and OR gates alternate throughout the network. That is, AND gate outputs connect only to OR gate inputs, and OR gate outputs connect only to AND gate inputs. To carry out conversion to NOR gates, we first replace all of the OR and AND gates with NOR gates as shown in Fig. 8–19(b). Since each inverted gate output drives an inverted gate input, the pairs of inversions cancel. However, when an input variable drives an inverted input, we have added a single inversion, so we must complement the variable to compensate. Therefore, we have complemented C and G. The resulting NOR-gate network is equivalent to the original AND-OR network.

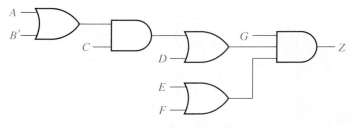

(a) AND-OR network

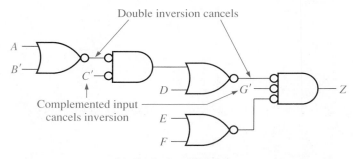

(b) Equivalent NOR-gate network

Figure 8–19
Conversion to NOR Gates

Even if AND and OR gates do not alternate, we can still convert an AND-OR network to a NAND or NOR network, but it may be necessary to add extra inverters so that each added inversion is cancelled by another inversion. The following procedure may be used to convert to a NAND (or NOR) network:

1. Convert all AND gates to NAND gates by adding an inversion bubble at the output. Convert all OR gates to NAND gates by adding inversion bubbles at the inputs. (To convert to NOR, add inversion bubbles at all OR gate outputs and all AND gate inputs.)
2. Whenever an inverted output drives an inverted input, no further action is needed since the two inversions cancel.
3. Whenever a noninverted gate output drives an inverted gate input or vice versa, insert an inverter so that the bubbles will cancel. (Choose an inverter with the bubble at the input or output as required.)
4. Whenever a variable drives an inverted input, complement the variable (or add an inverter) so the complementation cancels the inversion at the input.

In other words, if we always add bubbles (or inversions) in pairs, the function realized by the network will be unchanged. To illustrate the procedure we will convert Fig. 8–20(a) to NANDs. First, we add bubbles to change all gates to NAND gates (Fig. 8–20(b)). In four places (highlighted in blue), we have added only a single inversion. This is corrected in Fig. 8–20(c) by adding two inverters and complementing two variables.

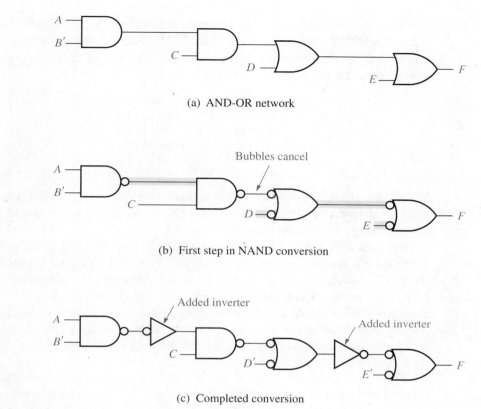

(a) AND-OR network

(b) First step in NAND conversion

(c) Completed conversion

Figure 8–20
Conversion of AND-OR Network to NAND Gates

8.7
Mixed Logic and Polarity Indication

In Section 3.5 we discussed positive and negative logic. For positive logic, a "true" condition (logic 1) is represented by a high voltage and a "false" condition (logic 0) is represented by a low voltage. For negative logic, a "true" condition (logic 1) is represented by a low voltage and a "false" condition (logic 0) is represented by a high voltage. Up to this point, we have assumed that all logic variables are defined according to positive logic. Some logic designers use mixed logic, in which some logic variables are defined using positive logic and other variables are defined using negative logic. The term *active high* is often used to describe a positive logic variable since the active or true state of this variable corresponds to a high voltage. Similarly *active low* is used for a negative logic variable since the active or true state corresponds to a low voltage. For example, consider a variable "ENABLE" which is used to enable the operation of a logic circuit. If ENABLE is active high, this implies that a high voltage will enable the logic circuit, and if ENABLE is active low, a low voltage will enable the circuit.

When mixed logic is used, it is important to have some method to distinguish active high and active low logic variables. Unfortunately, there is no well-established standard for this. Here are some examples of different naming conventions for the variable ENABLE:

Active High	Active Low
ENABLE(H)	ENABLE(L)
ENABLE.H	ENABLE.L
ENABLE+	ENABLE−
ENABLE	~ENABLE
ENABLE	/ENABLE

We will use (L) to indicate active low (negative logic) variables and (H) to indicate active high (positive logic) variables since this is recommended by the *IEEE Standard for Logic Circuit Diagrams.*[5]

Up until now, we have been using a small circle (or "bubble") at a gate output to indicate a complement (logic negation). When the "bubble" symbol is used, the *IEEE Standard for Logic Circuit Diagrams* "requires the adoption of a single logic convention, either positive or negative, for the whole diagram." We will conform to this standard and continue to use positive logic throughout when we use the bubble notation. When both active high and active low logic variables are used on the same diagram, the *IEEE Standard* requires the use of direct polarity notation as explained below.

The *IEEE Standard Graphic Symbols for Logic Functions* provides for two types of inversion symbols as illustrated in Fig. 8–21. The area between each pair of dashed lines represents the inside of some logic device. Only 0 and 1 logic values may be used inside a logic device. A small circle at an input indicates logic negation, which means that an external logic 0 produces an internal logic 1, and a 1 produces a 0 (Fig. 8–21(a)). The half-arrow symbol at an input indicates an active-low input, which means that a low level (L) at the input produces an internal logic 1 and a high level (H) produces a 0 (Fig. 8–21(b)). Similarly, an output circle indicates that an internal logic 1 produces an external logic 0, and a 0 produces a 1 (Fig. 8–21(c)). A half-arrow at the output indicates an active-low output. This means that an internal logic 1 produces an external L, and a 0 produces an H (Fig. 8–21(d)). The half-arrow is referred to as a ''polarity'' symbol. The polarity symbol is intended for use when circuit functions are described in terms of H and L levels rather than in terms of logic 1's and 0's. When polarity symbols are used, the relation between an internal logic value and the corresponding external voltage level is directly indicated on the logic diagram; hence the name direct polarity notation. If "bubbles" are used, an external logic 1 could correspond to either an H or L level depending on whether the positive or negative logic convention is used.

---

[5] *Logic Symbols and Diagrams,* published by the IEEE in 1987, contains both the *ANSI/IEEE Std 91–1984, IEEE Standard Graphic Symbols for Logic Functions* and *ANSI/IEEE Std 991–1986, IEEE Standard for Logic Circuit Diagrams.*

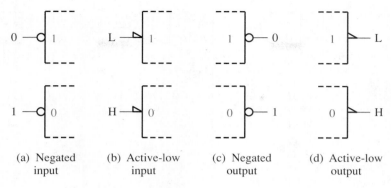

Figure 8–21
Standard Inversion Symbols

(a) Negated input   (b) Active-low input   (c) Negated output   (d) Active-low output

The inverters shown in Fig. 8–22 use direct polarity indication. When positive logic is used, an inverter forms the complement of its input. When mixed logic is used, the same inverter can simply convert an active high variable to an active low variable. In both cases, the inverter output is L (low) when the input is H (high), and vice versa (Fig. 8–22(a)). Using the positive logic convention for both input and output, we get the truth table shown in Fig. 8–22(b) from which $B = A'$.

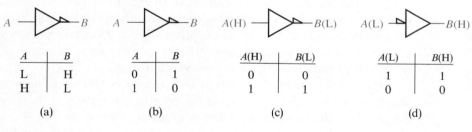

A	B
L	H
H	L

(a)

A	B
0	1
1	0

(b)

$A(H)$	$B(L)$
0	0
1	1

(c)

$A(L)$	$B(H)$
1	1
0	0

(d)

Figure 8–22
Inverters with Polarity Indication

However, if we use positive logic for the input and negative logic for the output, we get the table in Fig. 8–22(c), from which $B(L) = A(H)$. Figure 8–22(d) shows an alternate symbol for the inverter. If we use negative logic for the input and positive logic for the output, the resulting truth table shows that $B(H) = A(L)$. Note that in the last two cases, the inverter changes the logic polarity instead of complementing the input.

When A is low, A' is high and vice versa, therefore $A'(L) = A(H)$ and $A'(H) = A(L)$. When using mixed logic notation, it is generally simpler to use $A(H)$ and $A(L)$ rather than $A'(L)$ and $A'(H)$, and we will usually follow this practice.

Next, consider the NAND gate in Fig. 8–23(a), which has an L output only if both inputs are H. Translating the table according to positive logic yields Fig. 8–23(b) and the gate output is $C = (AB)'$. However, if we assume active high inputs and an active low output, the truth table in Fig. 8–23(c) shows that the

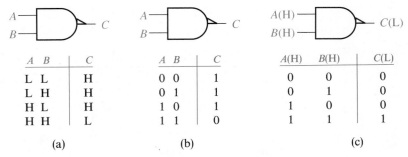

Figure 8–23
NAND Gates with Polarity Indication

output is $C(L) = A(H)B(H)$. In this case, we can think of the polarity symbol as converting the output to negative logic rather than complementing the output as in Fig. 8–23(b).

Figure 8–24(a) shows an alternate symbol for the NAND gate of Fig. 8–23(a). Note that the H-L tables are the same. Translating the table according to positive logic yields Fig. 8–24(b) from which we can write the gate output as $C = A' + B' = (AB)'$. However, if we assume active low inputs and an active high output, the truth table in Fig. 8–24(c) shows that the output is $C(H) = A(L) + B(L)$. In this case, we can think of the input polarity symbols as converting the inputs from negative logic to positive logic rather than complementing the inputs as in Fig. 8–24(b). Comparing Figs. 8–23(c) and 8–24(c) we see that, for mixed logic, the same physical NAND gate can serve as either an AND gate or an OR gate depending on the conventions used.

Figure 8–25 shows the analysis of a simple NAND-gate network using (a) "bubbles" with positive logic and (b) polarity indication with mixed logic. In Fig. 8–25(a), the complementation is explicitly shown. In Fig. 8–25(b), we can think of the polarity symbol as converting a positive logic (active high) variable to a negative logic (active low) variable, or vice versa. Inside of the gate symbols, we will always use positive logic so that the shape of the symbol determines whether the AND or OR function is realized internally.

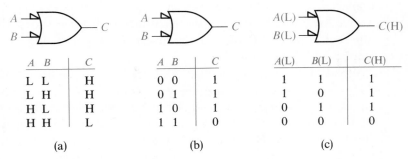

Figure 8–24
Alternate NAND Gate Symbol with
Polarity Indication

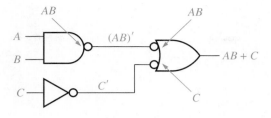

(a) Positive logic

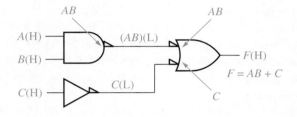

Figure 8–25

(b) Mixed logic

We will use the following rules for diagrams with direct polarity indication:
(1) Associate active high logic variables with inputs and outputs which have no
polarity symbol. (2) Associate active low logic variables with inputs and outputs
which have a polarity symbol. (3) Connect outputs with a polarity symbol to inputs with a polarity symbol, and connect outputs with no polarity symbol to
inputs with no polarity symbol. When these rules are used consistently, it is easy
to read logic functions directly off the logic diagram as illustrated by the NOR
gate network of Fig. 8–26. Note that each gate performs either an AND or an
OR function, and no complementation is required. We must be careful when we
interpret the equation for Z since $Z = 1$ is represented by a high voltage, but
$C = 1$ is represented by a low voltage, etc.

Everything works fine as long as we follow the rules given above. However,
we may have to violate one of the rules if the variables with the correct polarity
are not available. If any of the rules are violated, then extra complements must

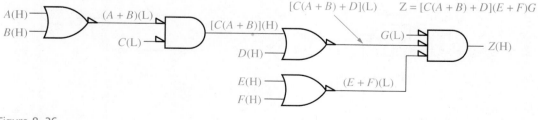

Figure 8–26
NOR-Gate Network with Polarity Indication

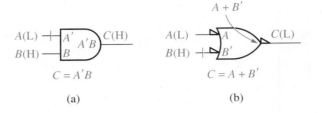

Figure 8–27
Input Mismatches

be introduced. Figure 8–27 shows two cases where the polarity of the input signal does not match the input polarity indicated on the gate symbol. We will place a vertical bar across the connecting line to call attention to the mismatch, a practice which is suggested in the *IEEE Standard for Logic Circuit Diagrams*. Note that in Fig. 8–27(a), A(L) applied to an active high input produces A' inside the gate, and in Fig. 8–27(b), B(H) applied to an active low input produces B' inside the gate.

Figure 8–28 shows two cases where the polarity of the output signal does not match the polarity of the gate output. In Fig. 8–28(a), an active low output is labeled C(H), so AB inside the gate produces $(AB)'$ externally. In Fig. 8–28(b), an active high output is labeled C(L), so $(A + B)$ inside the gate produces $(A + B)'$ externally. Again, we use vertical bars to call attention to polarity mismatches.

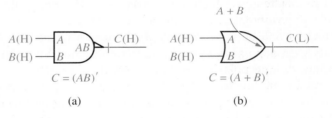

Figure 8–28
Output Mismatches

Figure 8–29 shows the analysis of a mixed logic network which has three mismatches. For gate 2, the polarity of B matches the gate input polarity, but the

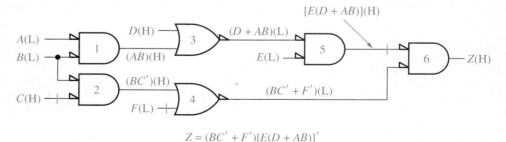

Figure 8–29
Mixed Logic Network with Mismatched
Gate Inputs

polarity of C does not, so the gate output is BC'. Similarly, the BC' input of gate 4 matches, but the F input does not, so the output is $BC' + F'$.

Synthesis of NAND (or NOR) gate networks using mixed logic can be carried out using the following steps:

1. Design a network of AND and OR gates to realize the desired function. (At this stage, ignore the polarity of the available logic signals.)
2. Convert all AND gates to NAND gates by adding a polarity symbol at the output. Convert all OR gates to NAND gates by adding polarity symbols at the inputs. (To convert to NOR, add polarity symbols at all OR gate outputs and all AND gate inputs.)
3. Whenever an active low output drives an active low input, or an active high output drives an active high input, no further action is needed since the polarities match.
4. Whenever an active low gate output drives an active high gate input or vice versa, insert an inverter (level changer) so that the polarities will match.
5. Whenever an uncomplemented variable drives a gate input, choose the polarity of the input signal to match the gate input polarity. Whenever a complemented variable drives a gate input, choose the polarity of the input signal opposite to the gate input polarity. (Also add a vertical bar across the signal line to call attention to the mismatched input.)
6. Compare the polarity of the available signals with the required input polarities. If an input signal of the correct polarity is not available, add an inverter. (Choose the proper inverter symbol so that its output polarity matches the next gate input.)

The following example illustrates the procedure:

Realize $G = AB'C + DE + F'$ using 2-input NAND gates (and inverters).

Assume that the following signals are available as inputs: A(H), B(H), B(L), C(H), D(H), E(L), and F(H). The first step is to draw the AND-OR network of Fig. 8–30(a). Next we convert to NAND gates by adding polarity symbols as shown in Fig. 8–30(b). Note that we added two inverters to correct polarity mismatches between gate outputs and inputs. The input signal polarities have been assigned to match the polarities of the corresponding gate inputs except for B and F, since B' and F' are required. Finally, since E(H) is not available, we must add an inverter to change the polarity of E(L).

In this section we have introduced the concept of direct polarity indication, which shows for each gate input and output whether an L or H voltage level corresponds to a logic 1. We have also introduced the use of mixed logic, where both positive and negative logic variables (active high and active low variables) are used on the same logic diagram. We use the suffixes (H) and (L) to distinguish between active high and active low variables. When mixed logic variables are used in a consistent manner with direct polarity indication, then the function realized by a gate network can be read directly from the logic diagram without using complementation. However, when mismatches occur between gate polarity

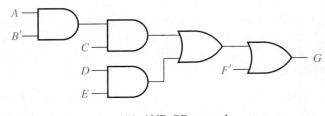

(a) AND-OR network

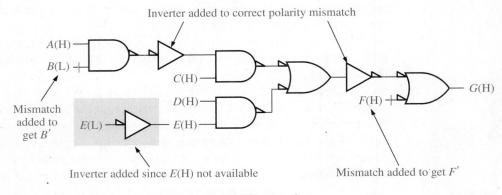

(b) NAND network

Figure 8–30
Realization of a NAND-Gate Network Using
Mixed Logic

and signal polarity, complementation does occur. Some logic designers use mixed logic together with the bubble notation, but this may lead to confusion since the same bubble symbol is used both for inversion and for polarity indication.

PROBLEMS

8.1   Using AND and OR gates, find a minimum network to realize

$$f(a, b, c, d) = M_1 M_2 M_5 M_9 M_{10} M_{14}$$

(a) using two-level logic
(b) using three-level logic   (12 gate inputs minimum)

8.2   Using AND and OR gates, find a minimum network to realize

$$f(a, b, c, d) = M_0 M_1 M_3 M_{13} M_{14} M_{15}$$

(a) using two-level logic
(b) using three-level logic   (12 gate inputs minimum)

8.3   Realize the following functions using AND and OR gates. Assume that there are no restrictions on the number of gates which can be cascaded and minimize the number of gate inputs.
(a) $ACD' + B'CD' + B'E + AC'D + AE$
(b) $ABDF + ABEF + ABG + CDF + CEF + CG$
(c) $ABC' + ACD + A'BC + A'C'D$
(d) $ABCE + ABEF + ACD' + ABEG + ACDE$

8.4   Using AND and OR gates, find a minimum two-level network to realize
(a) $F = a'c + bc'd + ac'd$
(b) $F = (b' + c)(a + b' + d)(a + b + c' + d)$

8.5   Using AND and OR gates, find a minimum two-level network to realize
(a) $F = a'cd' + a'bc + ad$
(b) $F = a'b + ac + bc + bd'$

8.6   A combinational switching network has 4 inputs (A, B, C, D) and one output (F). $F = 0$ iff 3 or 4 of the inputs are 0.
(a) Write the maxterm expansion for F.
(b) Using AND and OR gates, find a minimum three-level network to realize F (5 gates, 12 inputs).

8.7   The input and output voltages for a given 3-input gate are tabulated below. If the voltages are interpreted according to the positive logic convention, what type of gate is it? What type of gate is it for negative logic?

A	B	C	F
0	0	0	+V
0	0	+V	0
0	+V	0	0
0	+V	+V	0
+V	0	0	0
+V	0	+V	0
+V	+V	0	0
+V	+V	+V	0

8.8   In the following table, H represents a high level voltage and L represents a low level voltage.
(a) What logic function is realized for positive logic?
(b) For negative logic?

E_1	E_2	E_3	E_4
H	H	H	H
H	H	L	L
H	L	H	H
H	L	L	L
L	H	H	L
L	H	L	L
L	L	H	H
L	L	L	H

8.9   Which of the following sets of operations are functionally complete? (You may assume that 0 and 1 are available as gate inputs.) Justify your answers.
(a) OR and NOT   (b) AND and OR
(c) Exclusive-OR and OR   (d) Equivalence and OR

8.10   A 3-input network has the truth table shown below.

A	B	C	Z
0	0	0	1
0	0	1	1
0	1	0	0
0	1	1	1
1	0	0	1
1	0	1	0
1	1	0	1
1	1	1	1

(a) Write an equation for Z.
(b) Show how to realize NOT with this network (0 and 1 may be used as inputs).
(c) Is it possible to realize AND using one or two of these networks (0 and 1 may be used as inputs)?
(d) Is it possible to realize OR using one or two of these networks?
(e) Is this network functionally complete?

8.11   An IMPLICATION gate has two inputs (X and Y); the output is 1 except when $X = 1$ and $Y = 0$.

(a) Show that the implication gate by itself is functionally complete.
(b) Realize $F = A'B + AC'$ using only implication gates. (Only A, B, C, 0, and 1 may be used as gate inputs.) Four gates are sufficient.

8.12   Find eight different minimum two-level gate networks to realize
(a) $F(w, x, y, z) = xy'z + x'yz + w$
(b) $F(w, x, y, z) = (x + y' + z)(x' + y + z)w$
(c) $F(a, b, c, d) = \sum m(4, 5, 8, 9, 13)$

8.13 $f(a, b, c, d, e) = \sum m(0, 2, 5, 8, 10, 11, 13, 15, 18, 21, 26, 27, 28, 29, 30, 31)$
(a) Find a minimum two-level NOR-gate network to realize f.
(b) Find a minimum three-level NOR-gate network to realize f.

8.14   Work Problem 8.13 for
$$f(a, b, c, d, e) = \sum m(2, 3, 6, 12, 13, 16, 17, 18, 19, 22, 24, 25, 27, 28, 29, 31)$$

8.15   Design a minimum three-level NOR-gate network to realize:
(a) $f = a'b + ad' + ab'c'$ (b) $f = a'b' + abd + acd$

8.16   Realize the following functions using only 2-input NAND gates. Minimize the number of gates required.
(a) $F = A'[B' + C'D' + DE]$ (b) $F = A + BCD' + BCE' + BDE'$

8.17   Find a minimum network to realize the following functions using only 2-input NOR gates. Only A, B, C, and D are available and not their complements. (Four gates are sufficient.) (*Hint:* Find a network of 2-input OR and AND gates and convert to NORs.)
(a) $F = A'B'D' + B'C'D'$ (b) $F = (A + C)B'D'$

8.18 Find a minimum four level NAND- or NOR-gate network to realize
(a) $Z = abe'f + c'e'f + d'e'f + gh$
(b) $Z = (a' + b + e + f)(c' + a' + b)(d' + a' + b)(g + h)$

8.19 Design a logic network that has a 4-bit binary number as an input and one output. The output should be 1 iff the input is a prime number (greater than 1) or zero.
(a) Use a two-level NAND-gate network.
(b) Use a two-level NOR-gate network.
(c) Use only 2-input NAND gates.

8.20 Work Problem 8.19 for a network that has an output 1 iff the input is evenly divisible by 3 (0 is divisible by 3).

8.21 Realize each of the functions given in Problem 6.21 using a minimum two-level NAND-gate network and also using a minimum two-level NOR-gate network.

8.22 Realize each of the functions given in Problem 6.19 using a minimum two-level AND-NOR network and also using a minimum two-level OR-NAND network.

8.23 Realize the following functions using only 2-input NAND gates. Repeat using only 2-input NOR gates.
(a) $F = A'BC' + BD + AC + B'CD'$
(b) $F = A'CD + AB'C'D + ABD' + BC$

8.24 (a) Convert the following network to all NAND gates, by adding bubbles and inverters where necessary.
(b) Convert to all NOR gates.

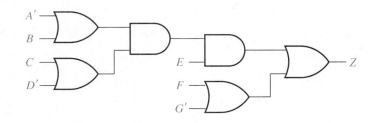

8.25 Realize $Z = A[BC' + D + E(F' + GH)]$ using NOR gates with direct polarity indication. Assume that only the following signals are available as inputs to the network: $A(H)$, $B(L)$, $C(H)$, $D(H)$, $E(H)$, $F(L)$, $G(L)$, and $H(L)$; the output should be $Z(H)$. Follow the three rules given in Section 8.7, but add vertical bars to indicate any input mismatches and add inverters if necessary.

8.26 Repeat Problem 8.24 except use direct polarity indication. Assume that all variables are available in both active high and active low form.

8.27 Realize $Z = A + (B + C')D[E + F'(G + J')]$ using NAND gates with direct polarity indication. Assume that only the following signals are available as inputs to the network: $A(H)$, $B(L)$, $C(H)$, $D(H)$, $E(L)$, $F(H)$, $G(L)$, and $J(H)$; the output should be $Z(H)$. Follow the rules for logic diagrams with direct polarity indication. Add vertical bars to indicate any input mismatches and add inverters if necessary.

8.28 (a) Find a minimum network of 2-input AND and 2-input OR gates to realize

$$F(A, B, C, D) = \sum m(0, 1, 2, 3, 4, 5, 7, 9, 11, 13, 14, 15)$$

(b) Convert your network to 2-input NAND gates using direct polarity notation. Add inverters where necessary. Assume that only $A(L)$, $B(H)$, $C(L)$,
and $D(H)$ are available as inputs, and the output should be $F(H)$. Use
vertical bars to indicate any polarity mismatches which occur at gate
inputs.

(c) Repeat (b), except convert to 2-input NOR gates.

9

Multiple-Output Networks Multiplexers, Decoders, Read-Only Memories, and Programmable Logic Arrays

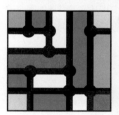

OBJECTIVES

1. Design a minimal two-level multiple-output AND-OR, OR-AND, NAND-NAND, or NOR-NOR network using Karnaugh maps.

2. Explain the function of a multiplexer. Use a multiplexer to implement a logic function.

3. Explain the operation of a decoder. Use a decoder with added gates to implement a set of logic functions.

4. Explain the operation of a read-only memory (ROM). Use a ROM to implement a set of logic functions.

5. Explain the operation of a programmable logic array (PLA). Use a PLA to implement a set of logic functions. Given a PLA table or an internal connection diagram for a PLA, determine the logic functions realized.

6. Explain the operation of a PAL. Determine the fuse pattern required to realize a set of logic functions with a PAL.

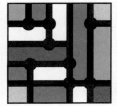

STUDY GUIDE

1. Read Section 9.1, *Introduction.*

2. Study Section 9.2, *Design of Two-Level Multiple-Output Networks.*

   (a) In which of the following cases would you replace a term xy' with $xy'z + xy'z'$?
   (1) Neither $xy'z$ or $xy'z'$ is used in another function.
   (2) Both $xy'z$ and $xy'z'$ are used in other functions.
   (3) Term $xy'z$ is used in another function, but $xy'z'$ is not.

   (b) In the second example (Fig. 9–4), in f_2, c could have been replaced by $bc + b'c$ since bc and $b'c$ were available "free" from f_1 and f_3. Why wasn't this replacement made?

   (c) In the following example, compute the cost of realizing f_1 and f_2 separately; then compute the cost using the term $a'b'c$ in common between the two functions. Use a two-level AND-OR network in both cases.

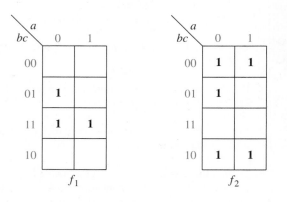

   (d) Find expressions which correspond to a two-level, minimum multiple-output, AND-OR realization of F_1, F_2, and F_3. Why should the term cd not be included in F_1?

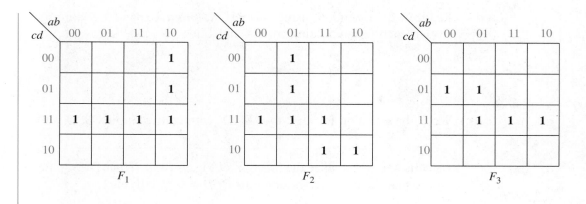

$$F_1 =$$
$$F_2 =$$
$$F_3 =$$

(e) Work Problems 9.1(a), 9.2(a), 9.3, and 9.6.

(f) Work Problem 9.8. (*Hint:* Work with the 0's on the maps and first find a minimum solution for f_1', f_2', and f_3'.)

3. Study Section 9.3, *Multi-Output NAND and NOR Networks.*

(a) Derive expressions for the F_1 and F_2 outputs of the NOR networks of Fig. 9–9(b) by finding the equation for each gate output, and show that these expressions reduce to the original expressions for F_1 and F_2.

(b) Work Problem 9.9.

4. Study Section 9.4, *Multiplexers.*

(a) Write the logic equation and draw the internal logic diagrams for a 2-to-1 MUX.

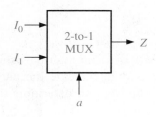

(b) Write the equation for a 4-to-1 MUX with control inputs A and C.

$$Z = \underline{\hspace{5cm}}$$

Realize Equation (9–5) using this MUX. (*Hint:* Expand Equation (9–5) so that each term contains both *A* and *C*.)

(c) Write the equation for an 8-to-1 MUX with control inputs *B*, *C*, and *D*.

$$Z = \text{_____}$$

Use this MUX to realize the function of Fig. 9–14(a). (*Hint:* Draw patches on the map below corresponding to *BCD* = 000, 001, etc.)

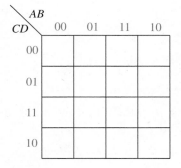

(d) Realize the same function using a 4-to-1 MUX with control inputs *A* and *C* and two added gates. (*Hint:* The map should be divided into four square patches.)

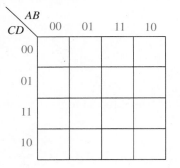

(e) The 5-variable function shown below is to be realized using a 16-to-1 MUX with control inputs *B*, *C*, *D*, and *E*. Indicate the patches on the map which correspond to I_0, I_1, I_2, and I_8 and determine the values of these *I*'s from the map.

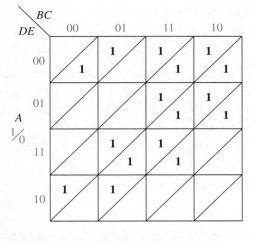

(f) Work Problems 9.14 and 9.15.

5. Study Section 9.5, *Decoders.*

(a) The 7442 4-to-10 line decoder (Fig. 9–18) can be used as a 3-to-8 line decoder. To do this, which three lines should be used as inputs? _____

The remaining input line should be set equal to _____.

(b) Work Problem 9.19.

6. Study Section 9.6, *Read-Only Memories.*

(a) The following diagram shows the pattern of 0's and 1's stored in a ROM with 8 words and 4 bits per word. What will be the values of

$$F_1, F_2, F_3 \text{ and } F_4 \text{ if } A = 0, B = C = 1?$$

Give the minterm expansions for F_1 and F_2:

$F_1 =$
$F_2 =$

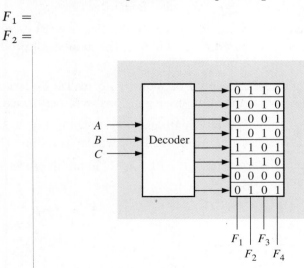

(b) When asked to specify the size of a ROM, give the number of words and the number of bits per word.

What size ROM is required to realize 4 functions of 5 variables?

What size ROM is required to realize 8 functions of 10 variables?

(c) When specifying the size of a ROM, assume that you are specifying a standard size ROM with 2^n words.

What size ROM is required to convert 8-4-2-1 BCD code to 2-out-of-5 code? (See Table 1–1, p. 13.)

What size ROM would be required to realize the decoder given in Fig. 9–18?

(d) Draw an internal connection diagram for a ROM which would perform the same function as the network of Fig. 9–3. (Indicate the presence of switching elements by dots at the intersection of the word lines and output lines.)

(e) Explain the difference between a mask-programmable ROM, a PROM and an EPROM. Which would you use for a new design which had not yet been debugged?

7. Study Section 9.7, *Programmable Logic Devices.*

(a) When you are asked to specify the size of a PLA (programmable logic array), give the number of inputs, the number of product terms, and the number of outputs.

What size PLA would be required to realize Equations (9–1) if no simplification of the minterm expansions were performed?

(b) If the realization of Equations (9–1) shown in Fig. 9–3 were converted to a PLA realization, what size PLA would be required?

(c) Specify the contents of the PLA of (b) in tabular form. (Your table should have four rows.)

(d) Draw an internal connection diagram for the PLA of (b). (Use dots to indicate the presence of switching elements in the AND and OR arrays.)

(e) Given the following PLA table, plot maps for Z_1, Z_2, and Z_3.

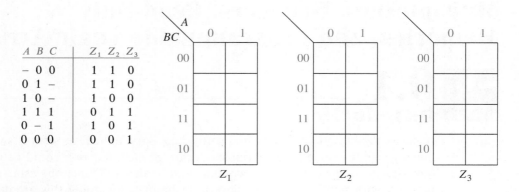

A B C	Z_1 Z_2 Z_3
– 0 0	1 1 0
0 1 –	1 1 0
1 0 –	1 0 0
1 1 1	0 1 1
0 – 1	1 0 1
0 0 0	0 0 1

(The Z_1 map should have 6 1's, Z_2 should have 5, and Z_3 should have 4.)

(f) For a truth table, any combination of input values will select exactly one row. Is this statement true for a PLA table?

For any combination of input values, the output values from a PLA can be determined by inspection of the PLA table. Consider Table 9–1, which represents a PLA with 3 inputs and 4 outputs. If the inputs are ABC = 110, which 3 rows in the table are selected?

In a given output column, what is the output if some of the selected rows are 1's and some are 0's? (Remember that the output bits for the selected rows are ORed together.)

When ABC = 110, what are the values of $F_0 F_1 F_2 F_3$ at the PLA output?

When ABC = 010, which rows are selected and what are the values of $F_0 F_1 F_2 F_3$ at the PLA output?

(g) Work Problems 9.20 and 9.22.

8. Study the section on *Programmable Array Logic (PALs)*.

(a) Which fusible links in Fig. 9–30(a) must be blown in order to realize the function shown in Fig. 9–30(b)?

(b) Referring to Table 9–2, which type of PAL could be used to realize the 8-to-1 MUX of Fig. 9–11? The quad MUX of Fig. 9–12?

    (c) Verify that the A_2 output function (Equation (9–10)) is correctly realized in Fig. 9–32 by tracing all of the signals from the PAL inputs to the A_2 output.

    (d) Work Problem 9.27.

9. When you are satisfied that you can meet all of the objectives, take the readiness test.

Multiple-Output Networks Multiplexers, Decoders, Read-Only Memories, and Programmable Logic Arrays

9.1
Introduction

In large digital systems, it is frequently necessary to realize several switching functions of the same input variables. Although each function could be realized separately, it is generally more economical to realize the functions using a single network with multiple outputs. Several techniques for doing this are discussed in this unit. First, methods for designing multiple-output gate networks are described. Later in the unit, design techniques using decoders, read-only memories, and programmable logic devices are developed.

    Up to this point we have mainly been concerned with basic principles of logic design. We have illustrated these principles using gates as our basic building blocks. In this unit we introduce the use of more complex integrated circuits (ICs) in logic design. Integrated circuits may be classified as small-scale integration (SSI), medium-scale integration (MSI), large-scale integration (LSI), or very-large-scale integration (VLSI) depending on the number of gates per integrated circuit package and the type of function performed. SSI functions include NAND, NOR, AND, and OR gates, inverters, and flip-flops.[1] SSI integrated circuit packages typically contain 1 to 4 gates, 6 inverters, or 1 or 2 flip-flops. MSI integrated circuits, such as adders, multiplexers, decoders, registers, and counters, perform more complex functions. Such integrated circuits typically contain the equivalent of 12 to 100 gates in one package. More complex functions such as memories and microprocessors are classified as LSI or VLSI integrated circuits. An LSI integrated circuit generally contains 100 to a few thousand gates in a single package, and a VLSI integrated circuit contains several thousand gates.

---

[1] Flip-flops, registers, and counters are introduced in Units 11 and 12.

It is generally uneconomical to design digital systems using only SSI integrated circuits. By using MSI, LSI, and VLSI functions, the required number of integrated circuit packages is greatly reduced. The cost of mounting and wiring the integrated circuits as well as the cost of designing and maintaining the digital system may be significantly lower when MSI, LSI, and VLSI functions are used.

After a discussion of multiple output gate networks, this unit introduces the use of MSI multiplexers and decoders in logic design. Then read-only memories (ROMs) are described and used to implement multiple-output combinational logic networks. Finally, other types of programmable logic devices (PLDs), including programmable logic arrays (PLAs) and programmable array logic devices (PALs), are introduced and used in combinational logic design.

9.2
Design of Two-Level Multiple-Output Networks

Solution of digital design problems often requires realization of several functions of the same variables. Although each function could be realized separately, use of some gates in common between two or more functions sometimes leads to a more economical realization. The following example illustrates this:

Design a network with four inputs and three outputs which realizes the functions

$$F_1(A, B, C, D) = \sum m(11, 12, 13, 14, 15)$$
$$F_2(A, B, C, D) = \sum m(3, 7, 11, 12, 13, 15)$$
$$F_3(A, B, C, D) = \sum m(3, 7, 12, 13, 14, 15) \qquad (9\text{--}1)$$

First, each function will be realized individually. The Karnaugh maps, functions, and resulting network are given in Figs. 9–1 and 9–2. The cost of this network is 9 gates and 21 gate inputs.

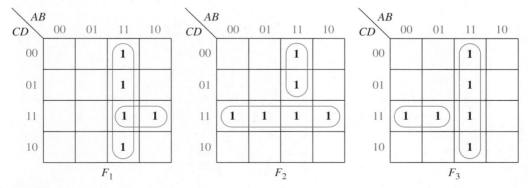

Figure 9–1
Karnaugh Maps for Equations (9–1)

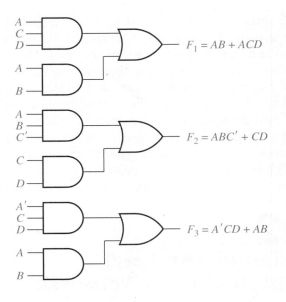

Figure 9–2
Realization of Equations (9–1)

An obvious simplification is to use the same gate for AB in both F_1 and F_3. This reduces the cost to 8 gates and 19 gate inputs. A further, but less obvious, simplification is possible. Observing that the term ACD is necessary for the realization of F_1 and $A'CD$ is necessary for F_3, if we replace CD in F_2 by $A'CD + ACD$, realization of CD is unnecessary and one gate is saved. Figure 9–3 shows the reduced network, which requires 7 gates and 18 gate inputs. Note that F_2 is realized by the expression $ABC' + A'CD + ACD$ which is *not* a minimum sum of products, and two of the terms are *not* prime implicants of F_2. Thus in realizing multiple-output networks, use of a minimum sum of prime implicants for each function does not necessarily lead to a minimum cost solution for the network as a whole.

When designing multiple-output networks, you should try to minimize the total number of gates required. If several solutions require the same number of

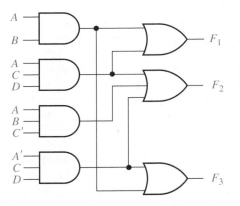

Figure 9–3
Multiple-Output Realization of Equations (9–1)

gates, the one with the minimum number of gate inputs should be chosen. The next example further illustrates the use of common terms to save gates. A 4-input, 3-output network is to be designed to realize

$$f_1 = \sum m(2, 3, 5, 7, 8, 9, 10, 11, 13, 15)$$
$$f_2 = \sum m(2, 3, 5, 6, 7, 10, 11, 14, 15)$$
$$f_3 = \sum m(6, 7, 8, 9, 13, 14, 15) \qquad (9\text{–}2)$$

First, we plot maps for f_1, f_2, and f_3 (Fig. 9–4).

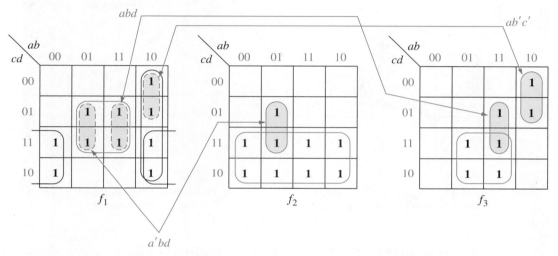

Figure 9–4

If each function is minimized separately, the result is

$$f_1 = bd + b'c + ab'$$
$$f_2 = c + a'bd \qquad (9\text{–}2a)$$
$$f_3 = bc + ab'c' + \begin{cases} abd \\ \text{or} \\ ac'd \end{cases} \quad \begin{array}{l} 10 \text{ gates,} \\ 25 \text{ gate inputs} \end{array}$$

By inspection of the maps, we can see that terms $a'bd$ (from f_2), abd (from f_3), and $ab'c'$ (from f_3) can be used in f_1. If bd is replaced with $a'bd + abd$, then the gate needed to realize bd can be eliminated. Since m_{10} and m_{11} in f_1 are already covered by $b'c$, $ab'c'$ (from f_3) can be used to cover m_8 and m_9, and the gate needed to realize ab' can be eliminated. The minimal solution is therefore

$$f_1 = \underline{a'bd} + \underline{abd} + \underline{ab'c'} + b'c$$
$$f_2 = c + \underline{a'bd} \qquad \begin{array}{l} 8 \text{ gates,} \\ 22 \text{ gate inputs} \end{array} \qquad (9\text{–}2b)$$
$$f_3 = bc + \underline{ab'c'} + \underline{abd}$$

(Terms which are used in common between two functions are underlined.)

When designing multiple-output networks, it is sometimes best not to combine a 1 with its adjacent 1's, as illustrated in the example of Fig. 9–5.

The solution with the maximum number of common terms is not necessarily best, as illustrated in the example of Fig. 9–6.

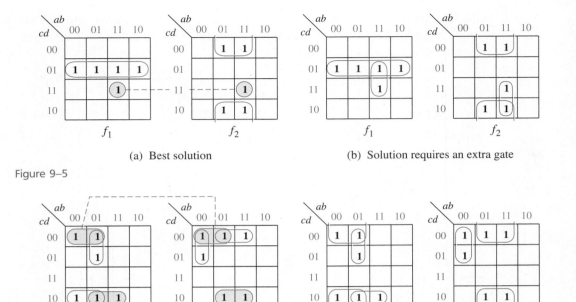

(a) Best solution   (b) Solution requires an extra gate

Figure 9–5

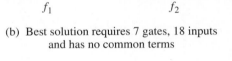

(a) Solution with maximum number of
common terms requires 8 gates, 26 inputs

(b) Best solution requires 7 gates, 18 inputs
and has no common terms

Figure 9–6

Determination of Essential Prime Implicants for Multiple-Output Realization

As a first step in determining a minimum two-level multiple-output realization, it is often desirable to determine essential prime implicants. However, we must be careful because some of the prime implicants essential to an individual function may not be essential to the multiple-output realization. For example, in Fig. 9–4, bd is an essential prime implicant of f_1 (only prime implicant which covers m_5), but it is not essential to the multiple-output realization. The reason that bd is not essential is that m_5 also appears on the f_2 map and hence might be covered by a term which is shared by f_1 and f_2.

We can find prime implicants which are essential to one of the functions *and* to the multiple-output realization by a modification of the procedure used for the single-output case. In particular, when we check each 1 on the map to see if it is covered by only one prime implicant, we will only check for adjacencies to those 1's which do not appear on the other function maps. Thus in Fig. 9–5 we find that $c'd$ is essential to f_1 for the multiple-output realization (because of m_1), but abd is not essential because m_{15} also appears on the f_2 map. In Fig. 9–6, the only minterms of f_1 which do not appear on the f_2 map are m_2 and m_5. The only *prime* implicant which covers m_2 is $a'd'$; hence $a'd'$ is essential to f_1 in the multiple-output realization. Similarly, the only prime implicant which covers m_5 is $a'bc'$, and $a'bc'$ is essential. On the f_2 map, bd' is essential (why?). Once the essential prime implicants for f_1 and f_2 have been looped, selection of the remaining terms to form the minimum solution is obvious in this example.

The techniques for finding essential prime implicants outlined above cannot be applied in a problem like Fig. 9–4 where every minterm of f_1 also appears on the f_2 or f_3 map. More sophisticated techniques are available for finding essential multiple-output terms for such problems, but such techniques are beyond the scope of this text.

Design of a Code Conversion Network

Conversion of decimal digits from one code to another is frequently necessary. The following example illustrates design of a network to convert from 8-4-2-1 BCD code to excess-3 code. The network has four inputs and four outputs. The inputs $abcd$ represent one of the ten decimal digits in BCD code, and the outputs $wxyz$ represent one of the ten decimal digits in excess-3 code. The table in Fig. 9–7 specifies the four functions to be realized by the network. It will be assumed that the input combinations which do not correspond to decimal digits will never occur as inputs; therefore w, x, y, and z are don't cares for these input combinations. The Karnaugh maps are plotted in Fig. 9–8. The minimum solution for z is obviously d'. Checking for common terms between the w, x, and y maps reveals that use of common terms will not help simplify the network. Therefore, the minimum two-level AND-OR solution (10 gates) is

$$w = a + bc + bd$$
$$x = bc'd' + b'd + b'c$$
$$y = c'd' + cd$$
$$z = d'$$

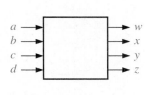

a b c d	w x y z
0 0 0 0	0 0 1 1
0 0 0 1	0 1 0 0
0 0 1 0	0 1 0 1
0 0 1 1	0 1 1 0
0 1 0 0	0 1 1 1
0 1 0 1	1 0 0 0
0 1 1 0	1 0 0 1
0 1 1 1	1 0 1 0
1 0 0 0	1 0 1 1
1 0 0 1	1 1 0 0

Figure 9–7
Code Conversion Network

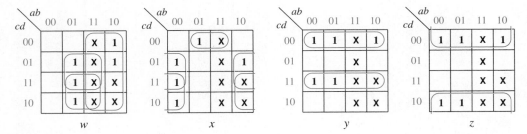

Figure 9–8

A three-level solution with 9 gates is possible if w and x are factored to get the common term $c + d$ as follows:

$$w = a + b(c + d)$$
$$x = bc'd' + b'(c + d)$$

9.3
Multi-Output NAND and NOR Networks

The procedure given in Section 8.5 for design of single-output multi-level NAND- and NOR-gate networks also applies to multiple output networks. If all of the output gates are OR gates, direct conversion to a NAND-gate network is possible. If all of the output gates are AND, direct conversion to a NOR-gate network is possible. Figure 9–9 gives an example of converting a 2-output network to NOR gates. Note that the inputs to the first and third levels of NOR gates are inverted.

$$F_1 = [(a + b')c + d](e' + f) \qquad F_2 = [(a + b')c + g'](e' + f)h$$

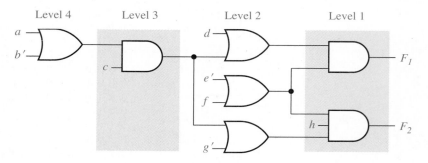

(a) Network of AND and OR gates

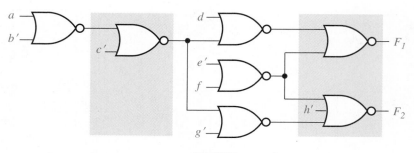

(b) NOR network

Figure 9–9
Multi-Level Network Conversion to NOR

9.4
Multiplexers

A multiplexer (or data selector) has a group of data inputs and a group of control inputs. The control inputs are used to select one of the data inputs and connect it to the output terminal. Figure 9–10 shows diagrams for a 4-to-1 multiplexer, 8-to-1 multiplexer, and 2^n-to-1 multiplexer.[2]

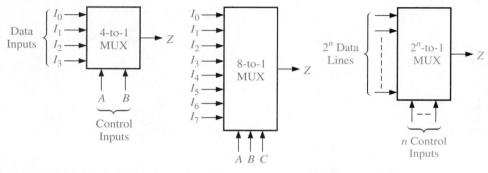

Figure 9–10
Multiplexers

The 4-to-1 multiplexer (abbreviated as MUX) is described by the equation

$$Z = A'B'I_0 + A'BI_1 + AB'I_2 + ABI_3 \qquad (9\text{–}3)$$

If the control inputs are $AB = 00$, the output is I_0; similarly, the control inputs 01, 10, and 11 give outputs of I_1, I_2, and I_3, respectively. The 8-to-1 MUX is described by the equation

$$Z = A'B'C'I_0 + A'B'CI_1 + A'BC'I_2 + A'BCI_3$$
$$+ AB'C'I_4 + AB'CI_5 + ABC'I_6 + ABCI_7 \qquad (9\text{–}4)$$

When the control inputs are $ABC = 011$, the output is I_3, and other outputs are selected in a similar manner. Figure 9–11 shows an internal logic diagram for the 8-to-1 MUX. In general, a multiplexer with n control inputs can be used to select any one of 2^n data inputs. The general equation for the output of a MUX with n control inputs and 2^n data inputs is

$$Z = \sum_{k=0}^{2^n-1} m_k I_k$$

where m_k is a minterm of the n control variables and I_k is the corresponding data input.

---

[2] IEEE standard symbols for multiplexers, decoders, and other MSI devices are discussed in Appendix B.2.

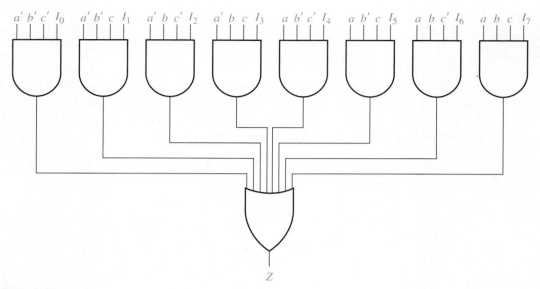

Figure 9–11
Logic Diagram for 8-to-1 MUX

Multiplexers are frequently used in digital system design to select the data which is to be processed or stored. Figure 9–12 shows how a quadruple 2-to-1 MUX is used to select one of two 4-bit data words. If the control is $A = 0$, the values of x_0, x_1, x_2, and x_3 will appear at the Z_0, Z_1, Z_2, and Z_3 outputs; if $A = 1$, the values of y_0, y_1, y_2, and y_3 will appear at the outputs.

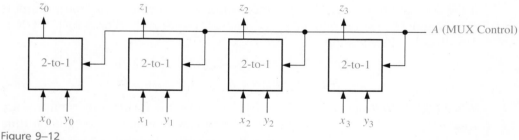

Figure 9–12
Quad Multiplexer Used to Select Data

Multiplexers can also be used to realize combinational logic functions. A 4-to-1 MUX can realize any 3-variable function with no added logic gates. As an example, we will realize

$$F(A, B, C) = A'B' + AC \qquad (9\text{–}5)$$

Expanding F so that all terms include both control inputs, A and B, yields

$$F = A'B' + AC(B + B') = A'B' \cdot 1 + AB' \cdot C + AB \cdot C \qquad (9\text{–}6)$$

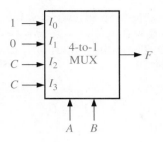

Figure 9–13
Realization of Equation 9-5

Comparing Equations (9–3) and (9–6), we see that the two equations will be identical if $I_0 = 1$, $I_1 = 0$, $I_2 = C$, and $I_3 = C$. Therefore, Equation (9–5) can be realized as shown in Fig. 9–13.

An 8-to-1 MUX can be used to realize any 4-variable function with no added gates. Three of the variables are used as control inputs to the MUX and the remaining variable is used as required on the data inputs. As an example, consider the 4-variable function (Z) plotted on the Karnaugh map of Fig. 9–14(a). We will select A, B, and C as control inputs and then determine the I_k's in Equation (9–4). Setting $ABC = 000$ in Equation (9–4) gives $Z = I_0$, setting $ABC = 001$ gives $Z = I_1$, etc. Performing the corresponding operation on the Karnaugh map identifies "patches" on the map which correspond to I_0, I_1, etc. Thus when the values of ABC are fixed at 000, the 4-variable map reduces down to the 1-variable map labeled I_0 in Fig. 9–14. Similarly, setting $ABC = 001$ means that we have selected the $AB = 00$ column of the map and the $C = 1$ rows, which gives us the 1-variable map labeled I_1. Since we have fixed the values of A, B, and C in each

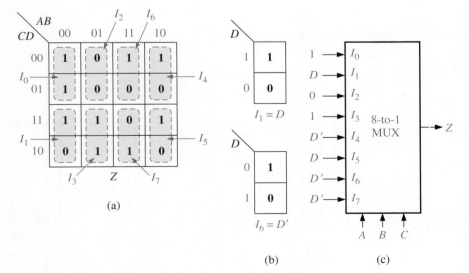

Figure 9–14
MUX Realization of a 4-Variable Function

case, each 1-variable map gives the value of I_k in terms of D. For the I_0 map, $I_0 = 1$ for both $D = 0$ and $D = 1$, so $I_0 = 1$; for the I_1 map, $I_1 = 1$ only when $D = 1$, so $I_1 = D$. The other values of I_k are read off the map in a similar manner as shown below:

$ABC = 000$	$Z = I_0 = 1$	$ABC = 100$	$Z = I_4 = D'$
$ABC = 001$	$Z = I_1 = D$	$ABC = 101$	$Z = I_5 = D$
$ABC = 010$	$Z = I_2 = 0$	$ABC = 110$	$Z = I_6 = D'$
$ABC = 011$	$Z = I_3 = 1$	$ABC = 111$	$Z = I_7 = D'$

Figure 9–14(c) shows the final realization of Z using an 8-to-1 MUX.

If different control inputs are chosen for the multiplexer, the position of the patches on the map will change accordingly. Figure 9–15 shows the patches and multiplexer inputs for control inputs A, B, and D. For $ABD = 000$, we see that $I_0 = 1$ when $C = 0$, so $I_0 = C'$.

The function plotted in Fig. 9–14(a) can also be realized using a 4-to-1 MUX with added gates as shown in Fig. 9–16. If we select AB as the control inputs,

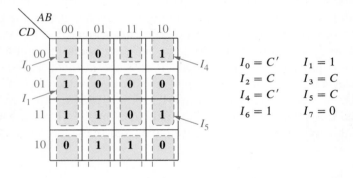

Figure 9–15
MUX Realization with Control Inputs A, B, and D

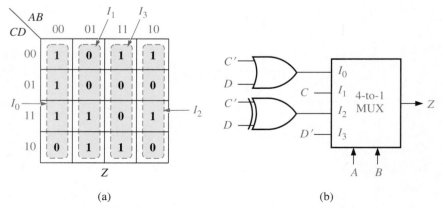

(a)   (b)

Figure 9–16
Realization Using a MUX with Added Gates

then Equation (9–3) applies. Setting $AB = 00, 01, 10$, and 11 yields $Z = I_0, I_1, I_2$, and I_3, respectively. The corresponding operation on the map of Fig. 9–16 yields the patches labeled I_0, I_1, I_2, and I_3. Each patch represents a 2-variable map expressing I_k in terms of C and D. Thus, $I_0 = C' + D$, $I_1 = C$, $I_2 = C'D' + CD = C' \oplus D$ and $I_3 = D'$, which gives the realization of Fig. 9–16(b).

In addition to the primary application of data selection in digital systems, we have seen how multiplexers can be used to realize combinational switching functions. Multiplexers are commonly available in integrated circuit packages in the following configurations: quadruple 2-to-1, dual 4-to-1, 8-to-1, and 16-to-1. As we have seen, the 4-to-1 and 8-to-1 multiplexers can be used to realize 3- and 4-variable functions, respectively. Similarly, a 16-to-1 MUX, which has four control inputs, can be used to realize any 5-variable function without added gates.

9.5
Decoders

The decoder is another commonly used type of integrated circuit. Figure 9–17 shows the diagram and truth table for a 3-to-8 line decoder. This decoder generates all of the minterms of the three input variables. Exactly one of the output lines will be 1 for each combination of values of the input variables.

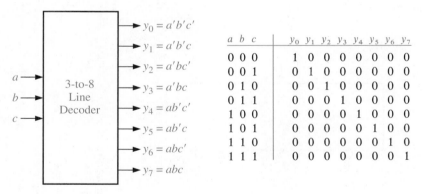

$a\ b\ c$	$y_0\ y_1\ y_2\ y_3\ y_4\ y_5\ y_6\ y_7$
0 0 0	1 0 0 0 0 0 0 0
0 0 1	0 1 0 0 0 0 0 0
0 1 0	0 0 1 0 0 0 0 0
0 1 1	0 0 0 1 0 0 0 0
1 0 0	0 0 0 0 1 0 0 0
1 0 1	0 0 0 0 0 1 0 0
1 1 0	0 0 0 0 0 0 1 0
1 1 1	0 0 0 0 0 0 0 1

Figure 9–17
3-to-8 Line Decoder

Figure 9–18 illustrates a 4-to-10 decoder. This decoder has inverted outputs[3] (indicated by the small circles). For each combination of values of the inputs, exactly one of the output lines will be 0. When a binary-coded-decimal digit is used as an input to this decoder, one of the output lines will go low to indicate which of the 10 decimal digits is present.

---

[3] Most standard integrated circuit decoders, including the type 7442 illustrated in Fig. 9–18, have inverted outputs.

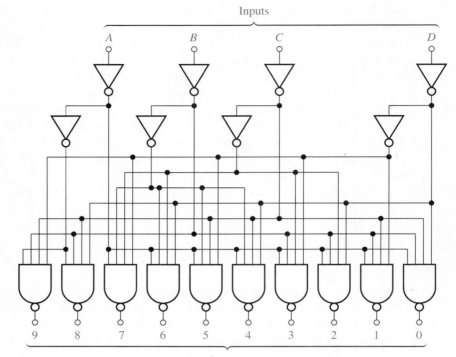

Inputs

(a) Logic diagram

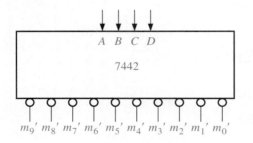

(b) Block diagram

BCD Input	Decimal Output									
A B C D	0	1	2	3	4	5	6	7	8	9
0 0 0 0	0	1	1	1	1	1	1	1	1	1
0 0 0 1	1	0	1	1	1	1	1	1	1	1
0 0 1 0	1	1	0	1	1	1	1	1	1	1
0 0 1 1	1	1	1	0	1	1	1	1	1	1
0 1 0 0	1	1	1	1	0	1	1	1	1	1
0 1 0 1	1	1	1	1	1	0	1	1	1	1
0 1 1 0	1	1	1	1	1	1	0	1	1	1
0 1 1 1	1	1	1	1	1	1	1	0	1	1
1 0 0 0	1	1	1	1	1	1	1	1	0	1
1 0 0 1	1	1	1	1	1	1	1	1	1	0
1 0 1 0	1	1	1	1	1	1	1	1	1	1
1 0 1 1	1	1	1	1	1	1	1	1	1	1
1 1 0 0	1	1	1	1	1	1	1	1	1	1
1 1 0 1	1	1	1	1	1	1	1	1	1	1
1 1 1 0	1	1	1	1	1	1	1	1	1	1
1 1 1 1	1	1	1	1	1	1	1	1	1	1

(c) Truth table

Figure 9–18
A 4-to-10 Line Decoder

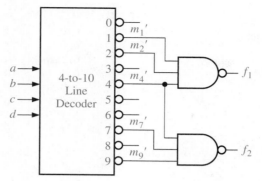

Figure 9–19
Realization of a Multiple-Output Network Using
a Decoder

In general, an n-to-2^n line decoder generates all 2^n minterms (or maxterms) of the n input variables. The outputs are defined by the equations

$$y_i = m_i, \quad i = 0 \text{ to } 2^n - 1 \qquad \text{(noninverted outputs)} \qquad (9\text{–}7)$$

or

$$y_i = m_i' = M_i, \quad i = 0 \text{ to } 2^n - 1 \qquad \text{(inverted outputs)} \qquad (9\text{–}8)$$

where m_i is a minterm of the n input variables and M_i is a maxterm.

Since an n-input decoder generates all of the minterms of n variables, n-variable functions can be realized by ORing together selected minterm outputs from a decoder. If the decoder outputs are inverted, then NAND gates can be used to generate the functions as illustrated in the following example. Realize

$$f_1(a, b, c, d) = m_1 + m_2 + m_4 \text{ and } f_2(a, b, c, d) = m_4 + m_7 + m_9$$

using the decoder of Fig. 9–18. Rewriting f_1 and f_2, we have

$$f_1 = (m_1' m_2' m_4')' \qquad f_2 = (m_4' m_7' m_9')'$$

Then f_1 and f_2 can be generated using NAND gates as shown in Fig. 9–19.

9.6
Read-Only Memories

A read-only memory (ROM) is an LSI circuit which consists of an array of semiconductor devices (diodes, bipolar transistors or field-effect transistors) which are interconnected to store an array of binary data. Once binary data is stored in the ROM, it can be read out whenever desired, but the data which is stored cannot be changed under normal operating conditions. Figure 9–20(a) shows a ROM which has 3 input lines and 4 output lines. Figure 9–20(b) shows a typical truth table which relates the ROM inputs and outputs. For each combination of input values on the 3 input lines, the corresponding pattern of 0's and 1's appears

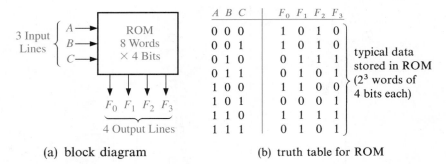

A B C	F_0 F_1 F_2 F_3
0 0 0	1 0 1 0
0 0 1	1 0 1 0
0 1 0	0 1 1 1
0 1 1	0 1 0 1
1 0 0	1 1 0 0
1 0 1	0 0 0 1
1 1 0	1 1 1 1
1 1 1	0 1 0 1

typical data stored in ROM (2^3 words of 4 bits each)

(a) block diagram   (b) truth table for ROM

Figure 9–20
An 8-Word × 4-Bit ROM

on the ROM output lines. For example, if the combination $ABC = 010$ is applied to the input lines, the pattern $F_0 F_1 F_2 F_3 = 0111$ appears on the output lines. Each of the output patterns which is stored in the ROM is called a *word*. Since the ROM has 3 input lines, we have $2^3 = 8$ different combinations of input values. Each input combination serves as an *address* which can select one of the 8 words stored in the memory. Since there are 4 output lines, each word is 4 bits long, and the size of this ROM is 8 words × 4 bits.

A ROM which has n input lines and m output lines (Fig. 9–21) contains an array of 2^n words, and each word is m bits long. The input lines serve as an address to select one of the 2^n words. When an input combination is applied to the ROM, the pattern of 0's and 1's which is stored in the corresponding word in the memory appears at the output lines. For the example in Fig. 9–21, if $00 \cdots 11$ is applied to the input (address lines) of the ROM, the word $110 \cdots 010$ will be selected and transferred to the output lines. A $2^n \times m$ ROM can realize m functions of n variables since it can store a truth table with 2^n rows and m columns. Typical sizes for commercially available ROMs range from 32 words × 4 bits to 8192×8 bits.

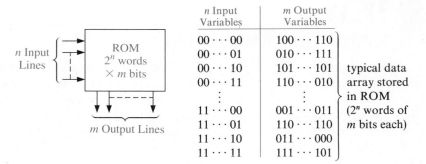

n Input Variables	m Output Variables
$00 \cdots 00$	$100 \cdots 110$
$00 \cdots 01$	$010 \cdots 111$
$00 \cdots 10$	$101 \cdots 101$
$00 \cdots 11$	$110 \cdots 010$
$\vdots$	$\vdots$
$11 \cdots 00$	$001 \cdots 011$
$11 \cdots 01$	$110 \cdots 110$
$11 \cdots 10$	$011 \cdots 000$
$11 \cdots 11$	$111 \cdots 101$

typical data array stored in ROM (2^n words of m bits each)

Figure 9–21
Read-only memory with n inputs and m outputs

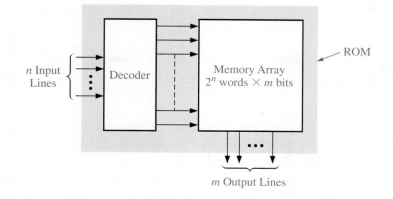

Figure 9–22
Basic ROM structure

A ROM basically consists of a decoder and a memory array as shown in Fig. 9–22. When a pattern of n 0's and 1's is applied to the decoder inputs, exactly one of the 2^n decoder outputs is 1. This decoder output line selects one of the words in the memory array, and the bit pattern stored in this word is transferred to the memory output lines.

Figure 9–23 illustrates the internal structure of the 8-word × 4-bit ROM shown in Fig. 9–20. The decoder generates the 8 minterms of the 3 input variables.

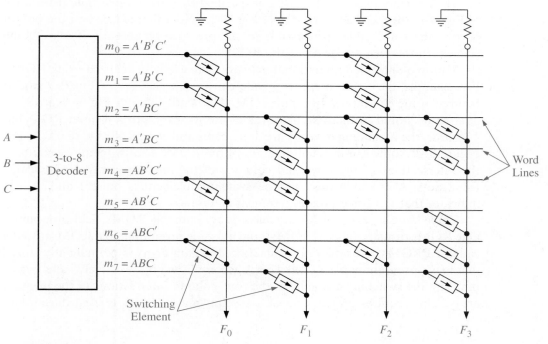

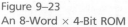

Figure 9–23
An 8-Word × 4-Bit ROM

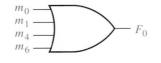

Figure 9–24
Equivalent OR Gates for F_0

The memory array forms the 4 output functions by ORing together selected minterms. A switching element[4] is placed at the intersection of a "word line" and an "output line" if the corresponding minterm is to be included in the output function; otherwise, the switching element is omitted. The switching elements which are connected in this way in the memory array effectively form an OR gate for each of the output functions. For example, m_0, m_1, m_4, and m_6 are ORed together to form F_0. Figure 9–24 shows the equivalent OR gate. In general, those minterms which are connected to output line F_i by switching elements are ORed together to form the output F_i. Thus, the ROM in Fig. 9–23 generates the following functions:

$$F_0 = \sum m(0, 1, 4, 6) = A'B' + AC'$$
$$F_1 = \sum m(2, 3, 4, 6, 7) = B + AC'$$
$$F_2 = \sum m(0, 1, 2, 6) = A'B' + BC'$$
$$F_3 = \sum m(2, 3, 5, 6, 7) = AC + B$$

(9–9)

The contents of a ROM is usually specified by a truth table. The truth table of Fig. 9–20(b) specifies the ROM in Fig. 9–23. Note that a 1 or 0 in the output part of the truth table corresponds to the presence or absence of a switching element in the memory array of the ROM.

Multiple-output combinational networks can easily be realized using ROMs. For example, the BCD to excess-3 code conversion network of Fig. 9–7 can be realized using a 4-input, 4-output ROM. The truth table of Fig. 9–7 gives the data to be stored in the first 10 words of the ROM. Since a 4-input ROM has 16 words, the remaining 6 words are don't cares and can be filled with 0's (or 1's). Figure 9–25 shows an internal diagram of the ROM. The switching elements at the intersections of the rows and columns of the memory array are indicated using dots. A dot indicates that the switching element is present and no dot indicates that the corresponding element is absent.

Three basic types of ROMs are mask-programmable ROMs, field-programmable ROMs (usually called PROMs), and erasable programmable ROMs (usually called EPROMs). At time of manufacture, the data array is permanently stored in a mask-programmable ROM. This is accomplished by selectively including or omitting the switching elements at the row–column intersections of the memory array. This requires preparation of a special "mask" which is used during fab-

---

[4] Diodes, bipolar transistors, or field-effect transistors may be used as switching elements. See Appendix A.

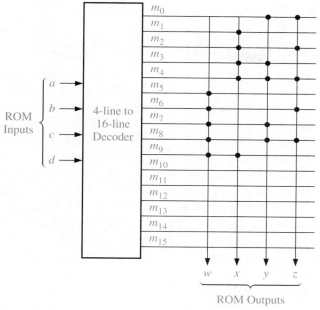

Figure 9–25
ROM Realization of Code Converter

rication of the integrated circuit. Preparation of this mask is expensive, so use of mask-programmable ROMs is economically feasible only if a large quantity (typically 1000 or more) are required with the same data array.

If only a small quantity of ROMs are required with a given data array, PROMs can be used. PROMs are typically manufactured with all switching elements present in the memory array, but the connection at each row–column intersection is made by means of a fusible link. In order to store data in the PROM, these fusible links are selectively "blown" using appropriate voltage pulses supplied by special equipment called a PROM programmer. Once the links are blown, the data is permanently stored in the memory array.

During developmental phases of a digital system, it is often necessary to modify the data stored in a ROM. To avoid the expense of using a new PROM each time the data must be changed, EPROMs may be used. Instead of fusible links, EPROMs use a special charge-storage mechanism to enable or disable the switching elements in the memory array. In this case, the PROM programmer provides appropriate voltage pulses to store electronic charges in the memory array locations. The data stored in this manner is generally permanent until it is erased using an ultraviolet light. After erasure, a new set of data can be stored in the EPROM. The electrically erasable PROM (or EEPROM) is a more recent development. It is similar to the EPROM, except that erasure is accomplished using electrical pulses instead of ultraviolet light.

9.7
Programmable Logic Devices

A programmable logic device (or PLD) is a general name for a digital integrated circuit capable of being programmed to provide a variety of different logic functions. In this section we will discuss several types of combinational PLDs, and in Section 19.3 we will discuss sequential PLDs. Typical combinational PLDs are capable of realizing from 2 to 10 functions of 4 to 16 variables with a single integrated circuit. Thus a single PLD can replace a number of SSI and MSI integrated circuits, and this leads to lower cost designs. When a digital system is designed using a PLD, changes in the design can easily be made by changing the programming of the PLD without having to change the wiring in the system. Available types of PLDs include PLAs (programmable logic arrays), PALs (programmable array logic), EPLDs (erasable PLDs), PEELs (programmable electrically erasable logic), and GALs (generic array logic).

Programmable Logic Arrays

A programmable logic array (PLA) performs the same basic function as a ROM. A PLA with n inputs and m outputs (Fig. 9–26) can realize m functions of n variables. The internal organization of the PLA is different from that of the ROM. The decoder is replaced with an AND array which realizes selected product terms of the input variables. The OR-array ORs together the product terms needed to form the output functions.

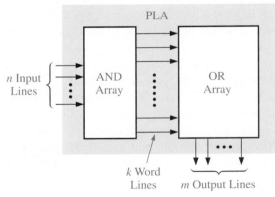

Figure 9–26
Programmable Logic Array Structure

Figure 9–27 shows a PLA which realizes the same functions as the ROM of Fig. 9–23. Product terms are formed in the AND array by connecting switching elements[5] at appropriate points in the array. For example, to form $A'B'$, switch-

---

[5] Either the AND function or OR function may be realized by the switching elements depending on the manner in which they are connected. For example, see the discussion of diode gates in Appendix A.1.

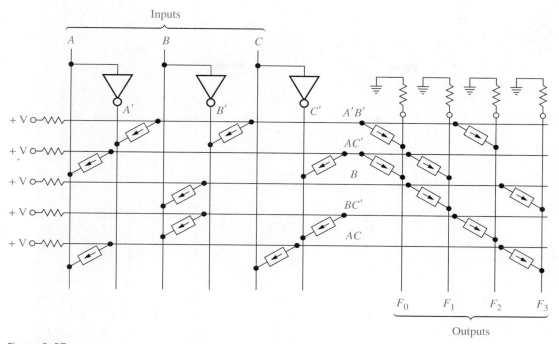

Figure 9–27
PLA with 3 Inputs, 5 Product Terms,
and 4 Outputs

ing elements are used to connect the first word line with the A' and B' lines. Switching elements are connected in the OR array to select the product terms needed for the output functions. For example, since $F_0 = A'B' + AC'$, switching elements are used to connect the $A'B'$ and AC' lines to the F_0 line. The connections in the AND and OR arrays of this PLA make it equivalent to the AND-OR array of Fig. 9–28.

The contents of a PLA can be specified by a modified truth table. Table 9–1 specifies the PLA in Fig. 9–27. The input side of the table specifies the product terms. The symbols 0, 1, and – indicate whether a variable is complemented, not complemented, or not present in the corresponding product term. The output side of the table specifies which product terms appear in each output function.

Table 9–1
PLA Table for Fig. 9–27

Product Term	Inputs A B C	Outputs F_0 F_1 F_2 F_3
$A'B'$	0 0 –	1 0 1 0
AC'	1 – 0	1 1 0 0
B	– 1 –	0 1 0 1
BC'	– 1 0	0 0 1 0
AC	1 – 1	0 0 0 1

$$F_0 = A'B' + AC'$$
$$F_1 = AC' + B$$
$$F_2 = A'B' + BC'$$
$$F_3 = B + AC$$

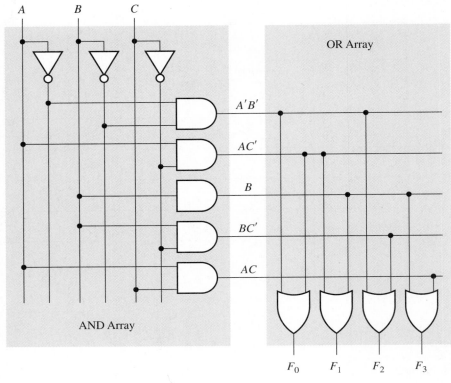

Figure 9–28
AND-OR Array Equivalent to Fig. 9–27

A 1 or 0 indicates whether a given product term is present or not present in the corresponding output function. Thus, the first row of Table 9–1 indicates that the term $A'B'$ is present in output functions F_0 and F_2, and the second row indicates that AC' is present in F_0 and F_1.

Next we will realize Equations (9–2) using a PLA. Using the minimum multiple-output solution given in Equations (9–2b), we can construct a PLA table, Fig. 9–29(a), with one row for each distinct product term. Figure 9–29(b) shows the corresponding PLA structure, which has 4 inputs, 6 product terms, and 3 outputs. A dot at the intersection of a word line and an input or output line indicates the presence of a switching element in the array.

A PLA table is significantly different than a truth table for a ROM. In a truth table each row represents a minterm; therefore, exactly one row will be selected by each combination of input values. The 0's and 1's of the output portion of the selected row determine the corresponding output values. On the other hand, each row in a PLA table represents a general product term. Therefore, zero, one, or more rows may be selected by each combination of input values. To determine the value of f_i for a given input combination, the values of f_i in the selected rows of the PLA table must be ORed together. The following examples refer to the

a b c d	f_1 f_2 f_3
0 1 – 1	1 1 0
1 1 – 1	1 0 1
1 0 0 –	1 0 1
– 0 1 –	1 0 0
– – 1 –	0 1 0
– 1 1 –	0 0 1

(a) PLA table

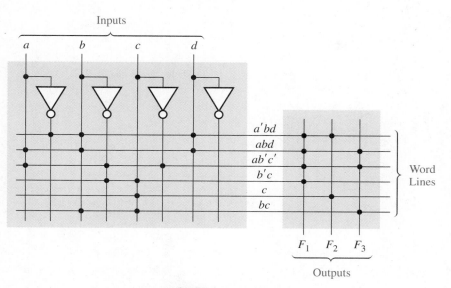

(b) PLA structure

Figure 9–29
PLA Realization of Equations (9–2b)

PLA table of Fig. 9–29(a). If $abcd = 0001$, no rows are selected, and all f_i's are 0. If $abcd = 1001$, only the third row is selected, and $f_1 f_2 f_3 = 101$. If $abcd = 0111$, the first, fifth, and sixth rows are selected. Therefore, $f_1 = 1 + 0 + 0 = 1$, $f_2 = 1 + 1 + 0 = 1$, and $f_3 = 0 + 0 + 1 = 1$.

Both mask-programmable and field-programmable PLAs are available. The mask-programmable type is programmed at the time of manufacture in a manner similar to mask-programmable ROMs. The field-programmable logic array (FPLA) has fusible links which can be blown to store a pattern in the AND and OR arrays. A typical FPLA has 16 inputs, 48 product terms, and 8 outputs.

When the number of input variables is small, a PROM is generally more economical to use than a PLA. However, when the number of input variables is large, PLAs often provide a more economical solution than PROMs. For example, to realize 8 functions of 16 variables would require a PROM with 65,536 8-bit words. Since PROMs of this size are not readily available, the functions would have to

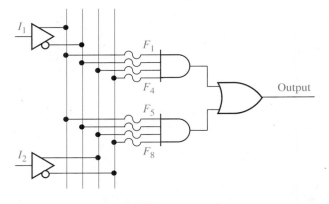

(a) Unprogrammed

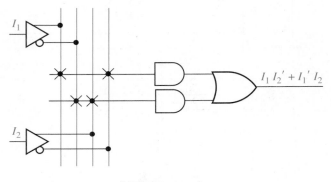

(b) Programmed

Figure 9–30
PAL Segment

be decomposed so that they could be realized using a number of smaller PROMs. The same 8 functions of 16 variables could easily be realized using a single PLA provided that the total number of product terms is small. If more terms are required, the outputs of several PLAs can be ORed together.

Programmable Array Logic (PALs)

The PAL (programmable array logic) is a special case of the programmable logic array in which the AND array is programmable and the OR array is fixed. The basic structure of the PAL is the same as the PLA shown in Fig. 9–26. Because only the AND array is programmable, the PAL is less expensive than the more general PLA, and the PAL is easier to program. For this reason, logic designers frequently use PALs to replace individual logic gates when several logic functions must be realized.

Figure 9–30(a) represents a segment of an unprogrammed PAL. The symbol

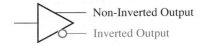

represents an input buffer which is logically equivalent to

A buffer is used since each PAL input must drive many AND gate inputs. When the PAL is programmed, the fusible links $(F_1, F_2, \ldots, F_8)$ are selectively blown to leave the desired connections to the AND gate inputs. Connections to the AND gate inputs in a PAL are represented by X's as shown below:

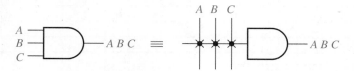

As example, we will use the PAL segment of Fig. 9–30(a) to realize the function $I_1 I_2' + I_1' I_2$. The X's indicate that the I_1 and I_2' lines are connected to the first AND gate, and the I_1' and I_2 lines are connected to the other gate (see Fig. 9–30(b)).

Table 9–2 gives the characteristics of some of the available types of combinational PALs. Figure 9–31 shows the internal logic diagram for a PAL 14L4, which has 14 inputs and 4 outputs. Each of the 4 output NOR gates is driven from 4

Table 9–2

Characteristics of Combinational PALs

Type No.*	No. of Inputs	No. of Outputs	Gate Configuration	No. of Inputs per OR GATE
10H8	10	8	AND-OR	2
12H6	12	6	AND-OR	4, 2, 2, 2, 2, 4
14H4	14	4	AND-OR	4
16H2	16	2	AND-OR	8
16C1	16	1	AND-OR/NOR	16
20C1	20	1	AND-OR/NOR	16
10L8	10	8	AND-NOR	2
12L6	12	6	AND-NOR	4, 2, 2, 2, 2, 4
14L4	14	4	AND-NOR	4
16L2	16	2	AND-NOR	8
12L10	12	10	AND-NOR	2
14L8	14	8	AND-NOR	4, 2, 2, 2, 2, 2, 2, 4
16L6	16	6	AND-NOR	4, 4, 2, 2, 4, 4
18L4	18	4	AND-NOR	4
20L2	20	2	AND-NOR	8
16L8	16	8	AND-NOR	8
20L8	20	8	AND-NOR	8
20L10	20	10	AND-NOR	4

* The type number contains two numbers separated by H, L, or C. The first number is the number of inputs, and the last number is the number of outputs. H indicates active high outputs, L active low, and C both active high and low.

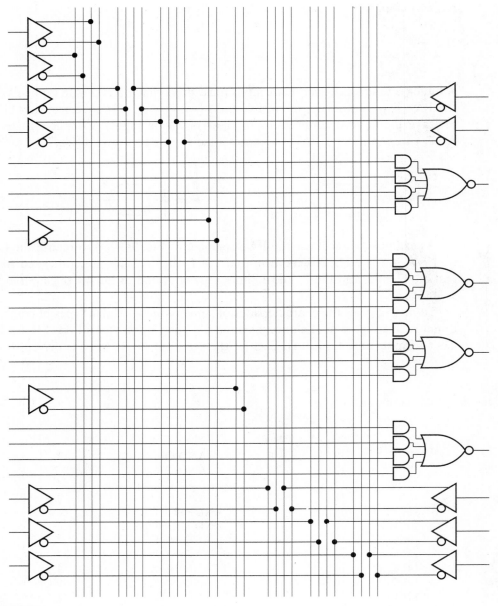

Figure 9–31
Logic Diagram for PAL14L4 (Courtesy of
Monolithic Memories)

AND gates. The 14H4 is identical to the 14L4, except the NOR gates are replaced with OR gates. The 12H6 (Fig. 9–32) has 12 inputs and 6 outputs. Two of the output OR gates are each driven from 4 AND gates, and four of the OR gates are each driven from 2 AND gates. The X's indicate connections to the AND gates which will be explained in the next example.

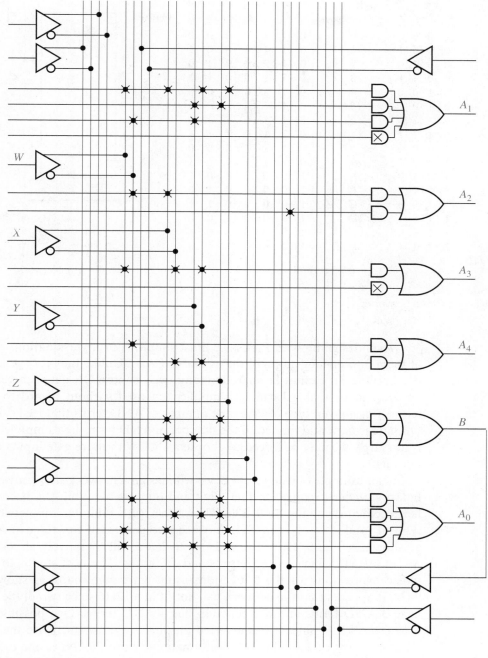

Figure 9–32
Logic Diagram for PAL12H6 (Courtesy of
Monolithic Memories)

Input	Hex	ASCII Code for Hex Digit						
W X Y Z	Digit	A_6	A_5	A_4	A_3	A_2	A_1	A_0
0 0 0 0	0	0	1	1	0	0	0	0
0 0 0 1	1	0	1	1	0	0	0	1
0 0 1 0	2	0	1	1	0	0	1	0
0 0 1 1	3	0	1	1	0	0	1	1
0 1 0 0	4	0	1	1	0	1	0	0
0 1 0 1	5	0	1	1	0	1	0	1
0 1 1 0	6	0	1	1	0	1	1	0
0 1 1 1	7	0	1	1	0	1	1	1
1 0 0 0	8	0	1	1	1	0	0	0
1 0 0 1	9	0	1	1	1	0	0	1
1 0 1 0	A	1	0	0	0	0	0	1
1 0 1 1	B	1	0	0	0	0	1	0
1 1 0 0	C	1	0	0	0	0	1	1
1 1 0 1	D	1	0	0	0	1	0	0
1 1 1 0	E	1	0	0	0	1	0	1
1 1 1 1	F	1	0	0	0	1	1	0

(a) Truth table   (b) Network

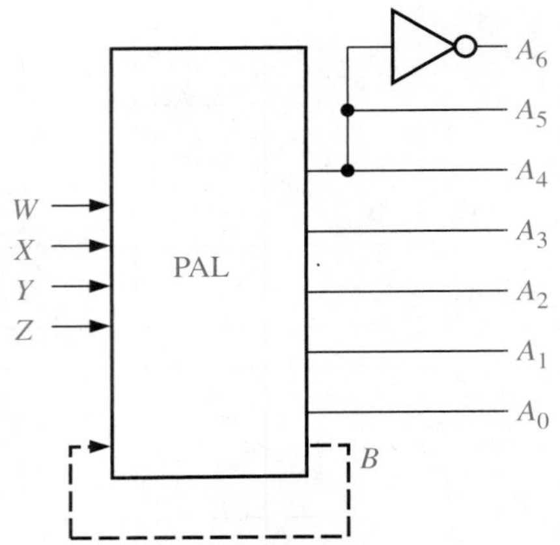

Figure 9–33
Binary to ASCII Converter

When designing with PALs, we must simplify our logic equations and try to fit them into one (or more) of the available PALs. Unlike the more general PLA, the AND terms cannot be shared among two or more OR gates; therefore, each function to be realized can be simplified by itself without regard to common terms. For a given type of PAL, the number of AND terms that feed each output OR gate is fixed and limited. If the number of AND terms in a simplified function is too large, we may be forced to choose a PAL with more gate inputs and fewer outputs.

As an example of using a PAL, we will design a network that converts a 4-bit binary number to a hexadecimal digit and outputs the 7-bit ASCII code for the hexadecimal digit. Figure 9–33(a) shows the truth table for the network. Since $A_5 = A_4$ and $A_6 = A_4'$, the PAL only needs to generate 5 functions of 4 variables as shown in Fig. 9–33(b). From Table 9–2, we will tentatively choose a 12H6 or 12L6 PAL, which has 6 outputs and 12 inputs. The next step is to find simplified expressions for the 5 functions using Karnaugh maps, as shown in Fig. 9–34. It appears that the network will not fit in a 12H6 since two of the functions have 3 AND terms and one function has 4 AND terms. One possible solution is to use a 12L6. Since it has inverted outputs, we must start with the functions A_4', A_3', A_2', A_1', and A_0'. Two of these functions require 4 ANDs, and one requires 3 single-input ANDs so it appears that we cannot use a 12L6 either. Going back to the 12H6, observe that there is one unused output. We can rewrite the equation for A_2 as

$$A_2 = W'X + (XZ + XY) = W'X + B, \text{ where } B = XZ + XY \quad (9\text{--}10)$$

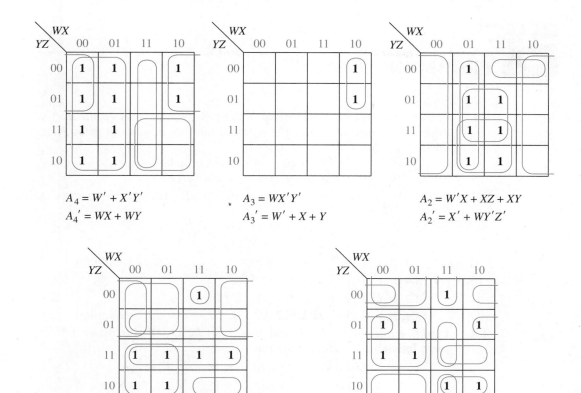

$$A_4 = W' + X'Y'$$
$$A_4' = WX + WY$$

$$A_3 = WX'Y'$$
$$A_3' = W' + X + Y$$

$$A_2 = W'X + XZ + XY$$
$$A_2' = X' + WY'Z'$$

$$A_1 = WXY'Z' + YZ + W'Y$$
$$A_1' = W'Y' + Y'Z + X'Y' + WYZ'$$

$$A_0 = W'Z + X'Y'Z + WXZ' + WYZ'$$
$$A_0' = W'Z' + WYZ + WXZ + X'Y'Z'$$

Figure 9–34
Karnaugh Maps for Binary to ASCII Converter

We can then use the extra PAL output to generate B and connect B to one of the PAL inputs as shown in Fig. 9–33(b). In this way, we can generate all five functions with a single PAL and no external logic. The X's on the diagram (Fig. 9–32) indicate the variables which are connected to the AND-gate inputs in the PAL. An X inside an AND gate indicates that the gate is not used.

Computer-aided design programs for PALs are widely available. Such programs will accept logic equations or truth tables as inputs and automatically generate the required fuse patterns. These patterns can then be downloaded into a PLD programmer which will blow the required fuses and verify the operation of the PAL. Some of the newer types of PLDs are erasable and reprogrammable in a manner similar to EPROMs and EEPROMs. Additional types of PLDs, which contain both gates and flip-flops, are discussed in Unit 19.

PROBLEMS

9.1 Find a two-level multiple-output AND-OR gate network to realize the following functions. Minimize the required number of gates (6 gates minimum for each part).
(a) $f_1 = a'c + a'd' + b'c$ and $f_2 = c'd' + ab' + ac'$
(b) $f_1 = ac + ad + b'd$ and $f_2 = a'b' + a'd' + cd'$

9.2 Find minimum two-level multiple-output AND-OR gate networks to realize these functions.
(a) $f_1(A, B, C, D) = \sum m(4, 5, 10, 11, 12)$,
$f_2(A, B, C, D) = \sum m(0, 1, 3, 4, 8, 11)$,
$f_3(A, B, C, D) = \sum m(0, 4, 10, 12, 14)$ (11 gates minimum)
(b) $f_1(A, B, C, D) = \sum m(3, 4, 6, 9, 11)$
$f_2(A, B, C, D) = \sum m(2, 4, 8, 10, 11, 12)$
$f_3(A, B, C, D) = \sum m(3, 6, 7, 10, 11)$ (11 gates minimum)

9.3 Find a minimum two-level multiple-output AND-OR gate network to realize these functions (8 gates minimum).
$$f_1(a, b, c, d) = \sum m(0, 2, 9, 10) + \sum d(1, 8, 13)$$
$$f_2(a, b, c, d) = \sum m(1, 3, 5, 13) + \sum d(0, 7, 9)$$
$$f_3(a, b, c, d) = \sum m(2, 8, 10, 11, 13) + \sum d(3, 9, 15)$$

9.4 Find a minimum two-level multiple-output AND-OR gate network to realize these functions (8 gates minimum).
$$f_1(a, b, c, d) = \sum m(10, 11, 12, 15) + \sum d(4, 8, 14)$$
$$f_2(a, b, c, d) = \sum m(0, 4, 8, 9) + \sum d(1, 10, 12)$$
$$f_3(a, b, c, d) = \sum m(4, 11, 13, 14, 15) + \sum d(5, 9, 12)$$

9.5 Draw a multiple-output, multiple-level network equivalent to Fig. 9–9(a) using:
(a) NAND and AND gates
(b) NAND gates only (a direct conversion is *not* possible)

9.6 Design a network of AND and OR gates to convert from excess-3 code to 8-4-2-1 BCD code.

9.7 Design a network of AND and OR gates to convert from 8-4-2-1 BCD code to 6-3-1-1 code.

9.8 Find a minimum two-level OR-AND network to realize the functions given in Equations (9–2) on p. 219 (9 gates minimum).

9.9 (a) Find a minimum two-level NAND-NAND network to realize the functions given in Equations (9–2) on p. 219.
(b) Find a minimum two-level NOR-NOR network to realize the functions given in Equations (9–2).

9.10 (a) Find a minimum multiple-output two-level OR-AND network to realize $f_1 = b'd + a'b' + c'd$ and $f_2 = a'd' + bc' + bd'$.

(b) Realize the same functions with a minimum two-level NAND-NAND network.

9.11 Repeat Problem 9.10 for $f_1 = ac' + b'd + c'd$ and $f_2 = b'c + a'd + cd'$.

9.12 (a) Find a minimum multiple-output two-level NAND-NAND network to realize $f_1 = \sum m(3, 6, 7, 11, 13, 14, 15)$ and $f_2 = \sum m(3, 4, 6, 11, 12, 13, 14)$.
(b) Repeat for a minimum two-level NOR-NOR network.

9.13 (a) Find a minimum multiple-output two-level NAND-NAND network to realize $f_1 = \sum m(0, 2, 4, 6, 7, 10, 14)$ and $f_2 = \sum m(0, 1, 4, 5, 7, 10, 14)$.
(b) Repeat for a minimum multiple-output two-level NOR-NOR network.

9.14 (a) Show how two 2-to-1 multiplexers (with no added gates) could be connected to form a 3-to-1 MUX. Input selection should be as follows:

If $AB = 00$, select I_0

If $AB = 01$, select I_1

If $AB = 1-$ (B is don't care), select I_2

(b) Show how two 16-to-1 and one 2-to-1 multiplexers could be connected to form a 32-to-1 MUX with five control inputs.

9.15 (a) Realize the function in Fig. 6–18 using an 8-to-1 MUX with control inputs A, C, and D.
(b) Repeat part a using a 4-to-1 MUX. Select the control inputs to minimize the number of added gates.

9.16 Repeat Problem 9.15 for $F(a, b, c, d) = \sum m(1, 2, 3, 6, 8, 9, 11, 14)$.

9.17 Realize the function of Problem 6.27
(a) using a 16-to-1 MUX with control inputs A, B, C, and D
(b) using an 8-to-1 MUX with control inputs A, B, and C and added gates

9.18 Repeat Problem 9.17 for the function of Problem 6.28.

9.19 Realize a BCD to excess-3 code converter (Fig. 9–7) using a 4-to-10 line decoder (Fig. 9–18) and four NAND gates.

9.20 The internal connection diagram for a PLA is given below.
(a) Write the equations realized by the PLA.

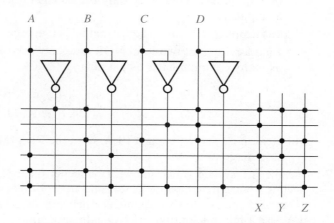

(b) Specify the truth table for a ROM which would realize the same functions as the PLA.

9.21 The PLA below will be used to implement the following equations:

$$X = ABD + A'C' + BC + C'D'$$
$$Y = A'C' + AD + C'D'$$
$$Z = CD + A'C' + AB'D$$

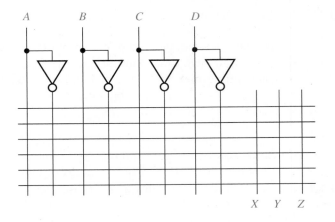

(a) Indicate the connections that will be made to program the PLA to implement these equations.

(b) Specify the truth table for a ROM which realizes these same equations.

9.22 (a) An adder for Gray-coded decimal digits (see Table 1–1) is to be designed using a ROM. The adder should add two Gray-coded digits and give the Gray-coded sum and a carry. For example, $1011 + 1010 = 0010$ with a carry of 1 ($7 + 6 = 13$). Draw a block diagram showing the required ROM inputs and outputs. What size ROM is required? Indicate how the truth table for the ROM would be specified by giving some typical rows.

(b) If the same adder were implemented using a PLA, what size PLA would be required? (Assume that only the 10 legal gray-coded digits can occur as inputs.)

9.23 Repeat Problem 9.22 for an adder that adds two excess-3 coded decimal digits.

9.24 (a) Find a minimum two-level NOR gate network to realize F_1 and F_2. Use as many common gates as possible.

$$F_1(a, b, c, d) = \sum m(1, 2, 4, 5, 6, 8, 10, 12, 14)$$
$$F_2(a, b, c, d) = \sum m(2, 4, 6, 8, 10, 11, 12, 14, 15)$$

(b) Realize F_1 and F_2 using a PLA. Give the PLA table and internal connection diagram for the PLA.

9.25 Braille is a system which allows a blind person to "read" alphanumerics by feeling a pattern of raised dots. Design a network that converts BCD to Braille. The table shows the correspondence between BCD and Braille.

(a) Use a multiple-output NAND-gate network.

(b) Use a PLA. Give the PLA table.

(c) Use a PAL. Specify the PAL type and fuse pattern.

A	B	C	D	W $\vert$ X
				Z $\vert$ Y
0	0	0	0	• $\vert$ •
0	0	0	1	• $\vert$
0	0	1	0	• $\vert$ •
0	0	1	1	• $\vert$ •
0	1	0	0	• $\vert$ •
0	1	0	1	• $\vert$
0	1	1	0	• $\vert$ •
0	1	1	1	• $\vert$ •
1	0	0	0	• $\vert$ •
1	0	0	1	• $\vert$ •

9.26 (a) Implement your solution to Problem 9.2(a) using a PLA. Specify the PLA table and draw the internal connection diagram for the PLA using dots to indicate the presence of switching elements.

(b) Repeat (a) for Problem 9.2(b).

9.27 Using a PAL14L4, design a code converter that accepts as input the last five bits of the ASCII code for a hexadecimal number and outputs the corresponding 4-bit binary code. For example, if the input is 00101, the output is 1110 (E in hex). Assume that the ASCII codes that do not represent hex digits will never occur as inputs. Note that the PAL14L4 uses AND-NOR logic. Mark X's on a copy of the PAL logic diagram to indicate the required fuse pattern.

9.28 A network has four inputs $RSTU$ and four outputs $VWYZ$. $RSTU$ represents a binary-coded decimal digit. VW represents the quotient and YZ the remainder when $RSTU$ is divided by 3 (VW and YZ represent 2-bit binary numbers). Assume that invalid inputs do not occur. Realize the network using
(a) a minimum two-level NAND-gate network
(b) a PLA (specify the PLA table)

9.29 Repeat Problem 9.28 if the inputs $RSTU$ represent a decimal digit in the Gray code (see Table 1–1).

9.30 Show how a quadruple 3-to-1 multiplexer could be implemented using a PAL14L4. Each MUX has three separate inputs and two control inputs, which are common to the four multiplexers. Each MUX works as follows: When the control inputs are $AB = 01$, input 1 is selected; when $AB = 10$, input 2 is selected; when $AB = 11$, input 3 is selected. The complement of the selected input appears at the MUX output. Show the PAL fuse pattern on a copy of the PAL logic diagram.

9.31 Show how a 10L8 PAL can be used to implement two 3-8 decoders. The inputs to the decoders are $A_1B_1C_1$ and $A_2B_2C_2$ and S. If $S = 0$, $A_1B_1C_1$ is decoded to the outputs $D_0, D_1, D_2, D_3, D_4, D_5, D_6$, and D_7. If $S = 1$, $A_2B_2C_2$ is decoded to the outputs $D_0 \cdots D_7$. The outputs should be high unless selected. Show the PAL fuse pattern on a copy of the PAL logic diagram.

9.32 Design a network which converts 12-hour time to 24-hour time. The inputs and outputs should represent the hours in BCD form. The network has 6 inputs: $BA_3A_2A_1A_0P$, where B represents the first digit of the 12-hour time, $A_3A_2A_1A_0$ represents the second digit, and $P = 1$ indicates P.M. The network has 6 outputs: $D_1D_0C_3C_2C_1C_0$, where D_1D_0 represents the first digit of the

24-hour time and $C_3C_2C_1C_0$ the second digit. Derive the output equations (use a computer-aided logic design program such as LogicAid) and specify which type(s) of PALs listed in Table 9–2 could be used to realize the network.

9.33   Repeat Problem 9.32, except convert 24-hour time to 12-hour time.

9.34   Using a 14H4 PAL, design a parity generator network which has 7 inputs and 1 output. The output should be 1 iff the total number of input bits which are 1 is odd. *Hint:* First write the output equation in terms of exclusive-OR. Group the terms into three parts, and feed back two of the PAL outputs into PAL inputs.

9.35   Design a network which multiplies a BCD digit by a second digit which is 0, 1, 2, or 3. The network has 6 inputs (4 bits for a BCD digit and 2 bits for the multiplier), and 6 outputs (2 bits for the first BCD digit and 4 bits for the second BCD digit). Derive the output equations (use a CAD program) and specify which type(s) of PALs listed in Table 9–2 could be used to realize the network.

9.36   A binary-coded-decimal priority encoder has nine inputs $(X_1, X_2, \ldots, X_9)$ and four outputs (A, B, C, D). If only the X_i input is 1, the outputs $ABCD$ represent a binary number equal to i. For example, if $X_1 = 1$, then $ABCD = 0001$, and if $X_9 = 1$, $ABCD = 1001$. If two or more of the X_i's are 1, then the largest value of i takes priority. For example, if $X_1 = X_2 = X_5 = X_8 = 1$ (and the other inputs are 0), then $ABCD = 1000$. If all inputs are 0, then $ABCD = 0000$.

(a) Derive a PLA table for the priority encoder (10 rows).

(b) By inspection of the table, find product-of-sums expressions for A, B, C, and D.

(c) What types of PALs could be used to implement the encoder? (Assume that either active high or active low outputs are acceptable.)

·UNIT·

10

Combinational Network Design

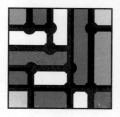

OBJECTIVES

1. Design a multiple-output NAND or NOR network.

2. Test your design using a logic simulator or by building it in lab.

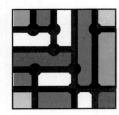

STUDY GUIDE

1. Obtain your design problem assignment from your instructor.

2. Study Section 10.1, *Review of Combinational Network Design.*

3. Generally, it is possible to redesign a network which has two AND gates cascaded or two OR gates cascaded so that AND and OR gates alternate. If this is not practical, the conversion to a NAND or NOR network by the techniques of Section 8.5 is still possible by introducing a dummy 1-input OR (AND) gate between the two AND (OR) gates. When the conversion is carried out, the dummy gate becomes an inverter. Try this technique and convert the following network to all NAND gates. Alternatively, you may use the procedures given in Sections 8.6 and 8.7 to do the conversion.

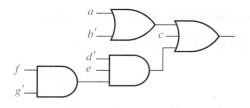

4. Study Section 10.2, *Design of Networks with Limited Gate Fan-in.*

   (a) If a realization of a switching expression requires too many inputs on one or more gates, what should be done?

   (b) Assuming that all variables and their complements are available as inputs and that both AND and OR gates are available, does realizing the complement of an expression take the same number of gates and gate inputs as realizing the original expression?

   (c) When designing multiple-output networks with limited gate fan-in, why is the procedure of Section 9.2 of little help?

5. Study Section 10.3, *Simulation and Testing of Logic Networks*.

   Verify that Table 10.1 is correct. Consider both the case where the unknown value, X, is 0 and the case where it is 1.

6. The following network was designed to realize the function

$$F = [A' + B + C'D][A + B' + (C' + D')(C + D)]$$

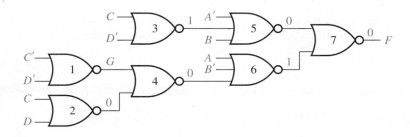

   When a student builds the network in lab, he finds that when $A = C = 0$ and $B = D = 1$ the output F has the wrong value and that the gate outputs are as shown above. Determine some possible causes of the incorrect output if $G = 0$ and if $G = 1$.

7. Study your assigned design problem and prepare a design which meets specifications. Note that only 2- and 3-input NAND gates (or NOR gates as specified) and inverters are available for this project; therefore, factoring some of the equations will be necessary. Try to make an economical design by using common terms; however, do not waste time trying to get an absolute minimum solution. When counting gates, count both NAND (or NOR) gates and inverters, but do not count the inverters needed for the input variables.

8. Check your design carefully before simulating it. Test it "on paper" by applying some input combinations of 0's and 1's and tracing the signals through to make sure that the outputs are correct.

   If you have a CAD program such as *LogicAid* available, enter the truth table for your design into the computer, derive the minimum two-level equations, and compare them with your solution.

9. In designing multi-level, multiple-output circuits of the type used in the design problems in this unit, it is very difficult and time-consuming to find a minimum solution. You are *not* expected to find the best possible solution to these problems. The total number of gates and inverters (not counting input inverters) for the best known solutions to the design problems in this unit are:

   10.1–17, 10.2–14, 10.3–13, 10.4–13, 10.5–17, 10.6–18, 10.7–12, 10.8–18, 10.9–18, 10.10–18, 10.11–19, 10.12–18, 10.13–18, 10.14–18.

All of these solutions involve some "tricks," and it is unlikely that you could find them without trying a large number of different ways of factoring your equations. Therefore, if you already have an acceptable solution, do *not* waste time trying to find the minimum solution. Since integrated circuit gates are quite inexpensive, it is not good engineering practice to spend a large amount of time finding the absolute minimum solution unless a very large number of units of the same type are to be manufactured.

10. Obtain a Unit 10 supplement from your instructor and follow the instructions therein regarding simulating and testing your design.

Combinational Network Design

10.1
Review of Combinational Network Design

The first step in the design of a combinational switching network is usually to set up a truth table which specifies the output(s) as a function of the input variables. For n input variables this table will have 2^n rows. If a given combination of values for the input variables can never occur at the network inputs, the corresponding output values are don't cares. The next step is to derive simplified algebraic expressions for the output functions using Karnaugh maps, the Quine-McCluskey procedure, or a similar method. In some cases, particularly if the number of variables is large and the number of terms is small, it may be desirable to go directly from the problem statement to algebraic equations, without writing down a truth table. The resulting equations can then be simplified algebraically. The simplified algebraic expressions are then manipulated into the proper form, depending on the type of gates to be used in realizing the network.

The number of levels in a gate network is equal to the maximum number of gates through which a signal must pass going between the input and output terminals. The minimum sum of products (or product of sums) leads directly to a minimum two-level gate network. However, in some applications it is desirable to increase the number of levels by factoring (or multiplying out) because this may lead to a reduction in the number of gates or gate inputs.

When a network has two or more outputs, common terms in the output functions can often be used to reduce the total number of gates or gate inputs. If each function is minimized separately, this does not always lead to a minimum multiple-output network. For a two-level network, Karnaugh maps of the output functions can be used to find common terms. All of the terms in the minimum multiple-output network will not necessarily be prime implicants of the individual functions. When designing networks with three or more levels, looking for common terms on the Karnaugh maps may be of little value. In this case, the designer will often minimize the functions separately and then use ingenuity to factor the expressions in such a way to create common terms.

A set of gates which is capable of realizing all switching functions is said to be *functionally complete*. A set of gates is functionally complete if it can realize AND, OR, and NOT. Examples of functionally complete sets are AND and NOT, EXCLUSIVE-OR and AND, NAND, and NOR.

Minimum two-level AND-OR, NAND-NAND, OR-NAND, and NOR-OR networks can be realized using the minimum sum of products as a starting point. Minimum two-level OR-AND, NOR-NOR, AND-NOR, and NAND-AND networks can be realized using the minimum product of sums as a starting point.

Design of multi-level, multi-output NAND-gate networks is most easily accomplished by first designing a network of AND and OR gates. Usually, the best starting point is the minimum sum-of-products expressions for the output functions. These expressions are then factored in various ways until an economical network of the desired form can be found. If this network has an OR gate at each output and is arranged so that an AND (OR) gate output is never connected directly to an AND (OR) gate input, direct conversion to a NAND-gate network is possible. Conversion is accomplished by replacing all of the AND and OR gates with NAND gates and then inverting any literals which appear as inputs to the 1st, 3rd, 5th, ... levels (output gates are the 1st level).

If the AND-OR network has an AND gate (or OR gate) output connected to the same type of gate, then extra inverters must be added in the conversion process (see Section 8.6, *Network Conversion Using Alternative Gate Symbols*).

Similarly, design of multi-level, multi-output NOR-gate networks is most easily accomplished by first designing a network of AND and OR gates. In this case the best starting point is usually the minimum sum-of-products expressions for the *complements* of the output functions. *After* factoring these expressions to the desired form, they are then complemented to get expressions for the output functions, and the corresponding network of AND and OR gates is drawn. If this network has an AND gate at each output, and AND (OR) gate outputs are not connected to AND (OR) gate inputs, direct conversion to a NOR-gate network is possible. Otherwise, extra inverters must be added in the conversion process.

10.2
Design of Networks with Limited Gate Fan-in

In practical logic design problems, the maximum number of inputs on each gate (or the fan-in) is limited. Depending on the type of gates used, this limit may be 2, 3, 4, 8, or some other number. If a two-level realization of a network requires more gate inputs than allowed, factoring the logic expression to obtain a multi-level realization is necessary.

EXAMPLE: Realize $f(a, b, c, d) = \sum m(0, 3, 4, 5, 8, 9, 10, 14, 15)$ using 3-input NOR gates.

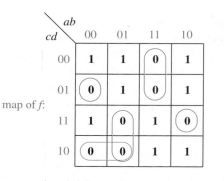

map of f:

$$f' = a'b'c'd + ab'cd + abc' + a'bc + a'cd'$$

As can be seen from the above expression, a two-level realization requires two 4-input gates and one 5-input gate. The expression for f' is factored to reduce the maximum number of gate inputs to three and then it is complemented:

$$f' = b'd(a'c' + ac) + a'c(b + d') + abc'$$
$$f = [b + d' + (a + c)(a' + c')][a + c' + b'd][a' + b' + c]$$

The resulting NOR-gate network is shown in Fig. 10–1.

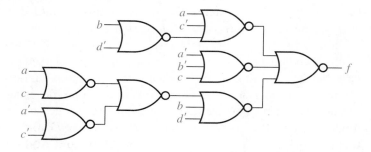

Figure 10–1

The techniques for designing two-level multiple-output networks given in Section 9.2 are not very effective for designing multiple-output networks with more than two levels. Even if the two-level expressions had common terms, most of these common terms would be lost when the expressions were factored. Therefore, when designing multiple-output networks with more than two levels, it is usually best to minimize each function separately. The resulting two-level expressions must then be factored to increase the number of levels. This factoring should be done in such a way as to introduce common terms wherever possible.

EXAMPLE: Realize the functions given in Fig. 10–2 using only 2-input NAND gates and inverters.

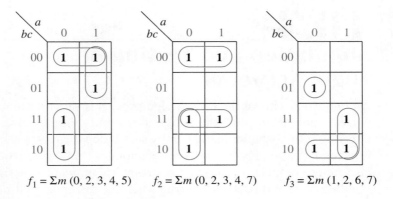

Figure 10–2 $f_1 = \Sigma m\,(0, 2, 3, 4, 5)$ $f_2 = \Sigma m\,(0, 2, 3, 4, 7)$ $f_3 = \Sigma m\,(1, 2, 6, 7)$

If we minimize each function separately, the result is

$$f_1 = b'c' + ab' + a'b$$
$$f_2 = b'c' + bc + a'b$$
$$f_3 = a'b'c + ab + bc'$$

Each function requires a 3-input OR-gate, so we will factor to reduce the number of gate inputs:

$$f_1 = b'(a + c') + \underline{a'b}$$
$$f_2 = b(a' + c) + b'c' \quad \text{or} \quad f_2 = (b' + c)(b + c') + \underline{a'b}$$
$$f_3 = a'b'c + b(a + c')$$

The second expression for f_2 has a term common to f_1, so we will choose the second expression. We can eliminate the remaining 3-input gate from f_3 by noting that

$$a'b'c = a'(b'c) = a'(b + c')'$$

Figure 10–3(a) shows the resulting network using common terms $a'b$ and $a + c'$. Since each output gate is an OR, conversion to NAND gates, shown in Fig. 10–3(b), is straightforward.

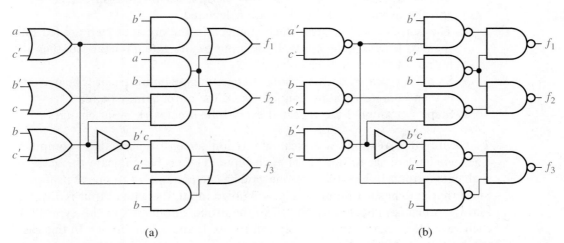

(a)   (b)

Figure 10–3
Realization of Fig. 10-2

10.3
Simulation and Testing of Logic Networks

An important part of the logic design process is verifying that the final design is correct and "debugging" the design if necessary. Logic networks may be tested either by actually building them or by simulating them on a computer. Simulation is generally easier, faster, and more economical. As logic networks become more and more complex, it is very important to simulate a design before actually building it. This is particularly true when the design is built in integrated circuit form, since fabricating an integrated circuit may take a long time and correcting errors may be very expensive. Simulation is done for several reasons, including: (1) verification that the design is logically correct, (2) verification that the timing of the logic signals is correct, and (3) simulation of faulty components in the circuit as an aid to finding tests for the circuit.

To use a computer program for simulating logic networks, you must first specify the network components and connections, then specify the network inputs, and finally observe the network outputs. The network description may be input to a simulator in the form of a list of connections between the gates and other logic elements in the network, or the description may be in the form of a logic diagram drawn on a computer screen. Most modern logic simulators use the latter approach. A typical simulator which runs on a personal computer uses switches or input boxes to specify the inputs, and probes to read the logic outputs. Alternatively, the inputs and outputs may be specified as sequences of 0's and 1's or in the form of timing diagrams (see Chapter 11 for examples of timing diagrams).

A simple simulator for combinational logic works as follows:

1. The network inputs are applied to the first set of gates in the network, and the outputs of those gates are calculated.
2. The outputs of the gates which changed in the previous step are fed into the next level of gate inputs. If the input to any gate has changed, then the output of that gate is calculated.
3. Step 2 is repeated until no more changes in gate inputs occur. The network is then in a steady-state condition and the outputs may be read.
4. Steps 1 through 3 are repeated every time a network input changes.

Figure 10–4(a) shows a typical simulation screen on a personal computer. The switches are set to 0 or 1 for each input. The probes indicate the value of each gate output. In Fig. 10–4(b), one gate has no connection to one of its inputs. Since that gate has a 1 input and an unknown input, the gate output is also unknown, which is indicated by an "X" in the probe. Simulators of this type allow each variable to have three possible values—0, 1, and X (unknown). In this case, the AND and OR functions are computed using Table 10–1.

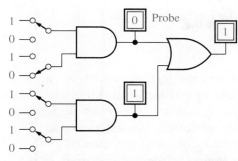   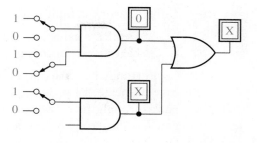

Figure 10–4   (a) Simulation screen showing switches and   (b) Simulation screen with missing gate input
probes

Table 10–1

AND and OR Functions for Three-Valued Simulation

·	0	1	X		+	0	1	X
0	0	0	0		0	0	1	X
1	0	1	X		1	1	1	1
X	0	X	X		X	X	1	X

The table shows the results of applying the AND and OR operators to the nine possible pairs of input values. For example, if one OR gate input is 0 and the other input is unknown (X), the output will be X. For gates with more than two inputs, the operations may be applied several times. For an AND gate, if one of the inputs is 0, the output is always 0, regardless of the other input value. For an OR gate, if one of the inputs is 1, the output is always 1, regardless of the other input value.

A combinational logic network with a small number of inputs may easily be tested with a simulator or in lab by checking the network outputs for all possible combinations of input values. When the number of inputs is large, it is usually possible to find a relatively small set of input test patterns which will test for all possible faulty gates in the network.[1]

If a network output is wrong for some set of input values, this may be due to several possible causes:

1. Incorrect design
2. Gates connected wrong
3. Wrong input signals to the network

---

[1] Methods for test pattern generation are described in Miczo, Alexander, *Digital Logic Testing and Simulation.* Harper and Row, 1986.

If the network is built in lab, other possible causes include:

4. Defective gates
5. Defective connecting wires

Fortunately, if the output of a combinational logic network is wrong, it is very easy to locate the problem systematically by starting at the output and working back through the network until the trouble is located. For example, if the output gate has the wrong output and its inputs are correct, this indicates that the gate is defective. On the other hand, if one of the inputs is wrong, then either the gate is connected wrong, the gate driving this input has the wrong output, or the input lead is defective.

EXAMPLE: The function $F = AB(C'D + CD') + A'B'(C + D)$ is realized by the following network:

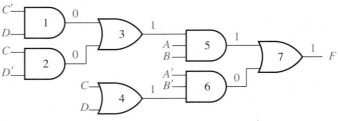

Figure 10–5
Logic Network with Incorrect Output

When a student builds the network in lab, he finds that when $A = B = C = D = 1$, the output F has the wrong value, and that the gate outputs are as shown in Fig. 10–5. The reason for the incorrect value of F can be determined as follows:

1. The output of gate 7 (F) is wrong, but this wrong output is consistent with the inputs to gate 7, that is, $1 + 0 = 1$. Therefore, one of the inputs to gate 7 must be wrong.
2. In order for gate 7 to have the correct output ($F = 0$), both inputs must be 0. Therefore, the output of gate 5 is wrong. However, the output of gate 5 is consistent with its inputs since $1 \cdot 1 \cdot 1 = 1$. Therefore, one of the inputs to gate 5 must be wrong.
3. Either the output of gate 3 is wrong, or the A or B input to gate 5 is wrong. Since $C'D + CD' = 0$, the output of gate 3 is wrong.
4. The output of gate 3 is *not* consistent with the outputs of gates 1 and 2 since $0 + 0 \neq 1$. Therefore, either one of the inputs to gate 3 is connected wrong, gate 3 is defective, or one of the input leads to gate 3 is defective.

The above example illustrates how to find the trouble in a logic network by starting at the output gate and working back until the wrong connection or defective gate is located.

DESIGN PROBLEMS

Seven-Segment Indicator

Several of the problems involve the design of a network to drive a seven-segment indicator (See Fig. 10–6). The seven-segment indicator can be used to display any one of the decimal digits 0 through 9. For example, "1" is displayed by lighting segments 2 and 3, "2" by lighting segments 1, 2, 7, 5, and 4, and "8" by lighting all seven segments. A segment is lighted when a logic 1 is applied to the corresponding input on the display module.

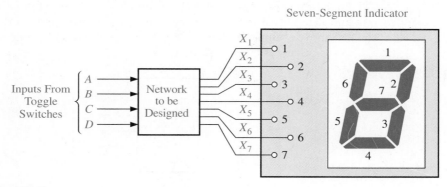

Figure 10–6
Network Driving Seven-Segment Display Module

10.1 Design an 8-4-2-1 BCD code converter to drive a seven-segment indicator. The four inputs to the converter network (A, B, C, D in Fig. 10–6) represent an 8-4-2-1 binary-coded decimal digit. Assume that only input combinations representing the digits 0 through 9 can occur as inputs, so that the combinations 1010 through 1111 are don't cares. Design your network using only 2- and 3-input NAND gates and inverters. Try to minimize the number of gates required. The variables A, B, C, and D will be available from toggle switches.

Use ┗ (not ┗) for 6.   Use ⁹ (not ⁹) for 9.

Any solution that uses 21 or fewer gates and inverters (not counting the 4 inverters for the inputs) is acceptable.

10.2 Design an excess-3 code converter to drive a seven-segment indicator. The four inputs to the converter network (A, B, C, D in Fig. 10–6) represent an excess-3 coded decimal digit. Assume that only input combinations representing the digits 0 through 9 can occur as inputs, so that the six unused combinations are don't cares. Design your network using only 2- and 3-input

NAND gates and inverters. Try to minimize the number of gates and inverters required. The variables A, B, C, and D will be available from toggle switches.

Use ⎍ (not ⎍) for 6.   Use ⎍ (not ⎍) for 9.

Any solution with 20 or fewer gates and inverters (not counting the 4 inverters for the inputs) is acceptable.

10.3   Design a circuit which will yield the product of two binary numbers n_2 and m_2, where $00_2 \leqslant n_2 \leqslant 11_2$ and $000_2 \leqslant m_2 \leqslant 101_2$. For example, if $n_2 = 10_2$ and $m_2 = 001_2$, then the product is $n_2 \times m_2 = 10_2 \times 001_2 = 0010_2$.

Let the variables A and B represent the first and second digits of n_2, respectively (i.e., in the above example $A = 1$ and $B = 0$). Let the variables C, D, and E represent the first, second, and third digits of m_2, respectively (in the above example $C = 0, D = 0$, and $E = 1$). Also let the variables W, X, Y, and Z represent the first, second, third, and fourth digits of the product. (In the above example $W = 0$, $X = 0$, $Y = 1$, and $Z = 0$.) Assume that $m_2 > 101_2$ never occurs as a network input.

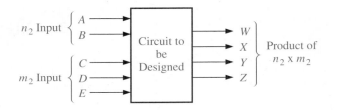

Design the network using only 2- and 3-input NOR gates and inverters. Try to minimize the total number of gates and inverters required. The variables A, B, C, D, and E will be available from toggle switches. Any solution that uses 16 or fewer gates and inverters (not counting the 5 inverters for the inputs) is acceptable.

10.4   Work Design Problem 10.3 using 2- and 3-input NAND gates and inverters instead of NOR gates and inverters. Any solution that uses 16 gates and inverters or less (not counting the 5 inverters for the inputs) is acceptable.

10.5   Design a network which multiplies two 2-bit binary numbers and displays the answer in decimal on a seven-segment indicator. In Fig. 10–6, A and B are two bits of a binary number N_1, and C and D are two bits of a binary number N_2. The product ($N_1 \times N_2$) is to be displayed in decimal by lighting appropriate segments of the seven-segment indicator. For example, if $A = 1$, $B = 0$, $C = 1$, and $D = 0$, the number "4" is displayed by lighting segments 2, 3, 6, and 7.

Use ⎍ (not ⎍) for 6.   Use ⎍ (not ⎍) for 9.

Design your network using only 2- and 3-input NAND gates and inverters. Try to minimize the number of gates required. The variables A, B, C, and D will be available from toggle switches. Any solution that uses 23 or fewer gates and inverters (not counting the 4 inverters for the inputs) is acceptable.

10.6   Design a Gray code converter to drive a seven-segment indicator. The four inputs to the converter network (A, B, C, D in Fig. 10–6) represent a decimal digit coded using the Gray code of Table 1–1. Assume that only input combinations representing the digits 0 through 9 can occur as inputs, so that the six unused combinations are don't cares. Design your network using only 2- and 3-input NAND gates and inverters. Try to minimize the numbers of gates and inverters required. The variables $A, B, C,$ and D will be available from toggle switches.

Use ⌐ (not ⌐) for 6.   Use ⌐ (not ⌐) for 9.

Any solution with 23 or fewer gates and inverters (not counting the 4 inverters for the inputs) is acceptable.

10.7   Design a network that will add either 1 or 2 to a 4-bit binary number N. Let the inputs N_3, N_2, N_1, N_0 represent N. The input K is a control signal. The network should have outputs M_3, M_2, M_1, M_0, which represent the 4-bit binary number M. When $K = 0, M = N + 1$. When $K = 1, M = N + 2$. Assume that the inputs for which $M > 1111_2$ will never occur.

Design the network using only 2- and 3-input NAND gates and inverters. Try to minimize the total number of gates and inverters required. The input variables $K, N_3, N_2, N_1,$ and N_0 will be available from toggle switches. Any solution that uses 15 or fewer gates and inverters (not counting the 5 inverters for the inputs) is acceptable.

10.8   Work Problem 10.1, except use 4-2-1-8 code instead of 8-4-2-1 code. For example, in 4-2-1-8 code, 9 is represented by 0011. Also change the representations of digits 6 and 9 to the opposite form given in Problem 10.1. Any solution with 24 or fewer gates and inverters is acceptable (not counting the 4 inverters for the inputs).

10.9   Work Problem 10.2, except use excess-2 code instead of excess-3 code. (In excess-2 code, 0 is represented by 0010, 1 by 0011, 2 by 0100, etc.).

10.10   Design a network which will multiply a 3-bit binary number CDE by 2, 3, or 5, depending on the value of a 2-bit code AB, to produce a 4-bit result $WXYZ$. If the result has a value greater than or equal to 15, $WXYZ$ should be 1111 to indicate an overflow. Assume that the code $AB = 11$ will never occur. Design your network using only 2- and 3-input NOR gates and inverters. Try to minimize the number of gates required. The inputs $A, B, C, D,$ and E will be available from toggle switches. Any solution which uses 23 or fewer gates and inverters (not counting the 5 inverters for the inputs) is acceptable.

10.11   Design a network which will divide a 5-bit binary number by 3 to produce a 4-bit binary quotient. Assume that the input number is in the range 0 through 27 and that numbers in the range 28 through 31 will never occur as inputs. Design your network using only 2- and 3-input NAND gates and inverters. Try to minimize the number of gates required. The inputs $A, B, C, D,$ and E will be available from toggle switches. Any solution which uses 23 or fewer gates and inverters (not counting the 5 inverters for the inputs) is acceptable.

10.12 Design an excess-3 code converter to drive a seven-segment indicator. The 4 inputs (A, B, C, D) to the converter network represent an excess-3 digit. Input combinations representing the numbers 0 through 9 should be displayed as decimal digits. The input combinations 0000, 0001, and 0010 should be interpreted as an "error", and an "E" should be displayed. Assume that the input combinations 1101, 1110, and 1111 will never occur. Design your network using only 2- and 3-input NOR gates and inverters. Any solution with 25 or fewer gates and inverters is acceptable (not counting the 4 inverters for the inputs).

Use (not ⎍) for 6.   Use 9 (not ⎍) for 9.

10.13 Design a network which displays the letters A through J on a seven-segment indicator. The network has 4 inputs W, X, Y, Z which represent the last four bits of the ASCII code for the letter to be displayed. For example, if $WXYZ = 0001$, "A" will be displayed. The letters should be displayed in the following form:

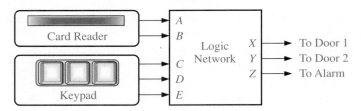

Design your network using only 2- and 3-input NOR gates and inverters. Any solution with 24 or fewer gates and inverters is acceptable (not counting the 4 inverters for the inputs).

10.14 A simple security system for two doors consists of a card reader and a keypad.

Card Reader → A B

Keypad → C D E

Logic Network → X To Door 1, Y To Door 2, Z To Alarm

A person may open a particular door if he or she has a card containing the corresponding code, and enters an authorized keypad code for that card. The outputs from the card reader are as follows:

	A	B
No card inserted	0	0
Valid code for door 1	0	1
Valid code for door 2	1	1
Invalid card code	1	0

To unlock a door, a person must hold down the proper keys on the keypad and then insert the card in the reader. The authorized keypad codes for door 1 are 101 and 110, and the authorized keypad codes for door 2 are 101 and 011. If the card has an invalid code or if the wrong keypad code is entered, the alarm will ring when the card is inserted. If the correct keypad code is entered, the corresponding door will be unlocked when the card is inserted.

Design the logic network for this simple security system. Your network's inputs will consist of a card code AB, and a keypad code CDE. The network will have three outputs XYZ (if X or $Y = 1$, door 1 or 2 will be opened; if $Z = 1$, the alarm will sound). Design your network using only 2- and 3-input NOR gates and inverters. Any solution with 20 or fewer gates and inverters is acceptable (not counting the 5 inverters for the inputs). Use toggle switches for inputs A, B, C, D, and E when you test your network.

11

Flip-Flops

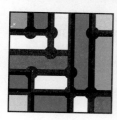

OBJECTIVES

In this unit you will study one of the basic building blocks used in sequential
networks—the flip-flop. Some of the basic analysis techniques used for sequential
networks are introduced here. In particular, you will learn how to construct timing
diagrams which show how each signal in the network varies as a function of time.
Specific objectives are:

1. Explain the operation of S-R, T, clocked T, J-K, clocked J-K, and clocked D
   flip-flops.

2. Make a table and derive the characteristic (next-state) equation for such
   flip-flops. State any necessary restrictions on the input signals.

3. Draw a timing diagram relating the input and output of such flip-flops.

4. Show how simple flip-flops can be constructed using gates.

5. Explain the advantages of a clocked flip-flop over an unclocked flip-flop.

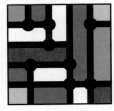

STUDY GUIDE

1. **(a)** Study Section 11.1, *Gate Delays and Timing Diagrams*. Complete the timing diagram for the network given below. Assume that the AND gate has a 30-ns propagation delay and the inverter has a 20-ns delay.

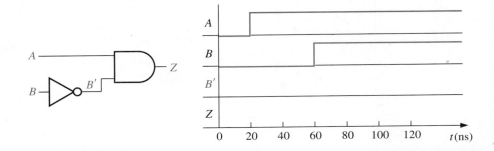

(b) In the network shown below, suppose that at some instant of time the inputs to both inverters are zero. Is this a stable condition of the network?

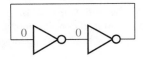

Assuming that the output of the left inverter changes before the output of the right inverter, what stable state will the network reach? (Indicate 0's and 1's on the inverter inputs and outputs.)

(c) Work Problem 11.1.

2. Study Section 11.2, *The Set-Reset Flip-Flop*.

(a) Describe in words the behavior of the S-R flip-flop.

(b) For Fig. 11–6(d), what values would P and Q assume if $S = R = 1$?

(c) What restriction is necessary on S and R so that the two outputs of the S-R flip-flop are complements?

(d) State in words the meaning of the equation $Q^+ = S + R'Q$.

(e) Work Problems 11.4 and 11.5.

3. Study Section 11.3, *The Trigger Flip-Flop.*

   (a) Describe in words the behavior of the T flip-flop.

   (b) Truth tables, such as Table 11–2, Fig. 11–15(a), and Fig. 11–18 are used in this unit to describe flip-flop behavior. When interpreting these tables, keep in mind that Q^+ and Q both represent the output (state) of the flip-flop; however, Q^+ is measured at a later time than Q. Thus, these tables imply that there is a delay between the time the flip-flop input changes and the time the output changes.

   (c) Trace out the operation of the T flip-flop of Fig. 11–11(b) using the timing diagram of Fig. 11–12(a).

   (d) Work Problem 11.6.

4. Read Section 11.4, *The Clocked T Flip-Flop.*

   (a) Compare the timing diagrams in Figs. 11–12(a) and 11–14. Note that in the first case, the flip-flop changes state after the T pulse, and in the second case, the change occurs after the clock pulse.

   (b) Complete the following timing diagram (assume that $Q = 0$ initially):

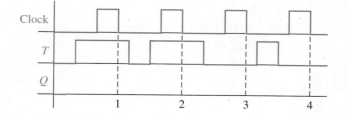

5. Study Section 11.5, *The J-K Flip-Flop.*

   (a) Describe in words the behavior of the J-K flip-flop.

(b) Derive the next-state equation for the J-K flip-flop.

(c) Trace out signals in the network of Fig. 11–15(c) and verify the table of 11–15(a). What timing restriction should be made when *J* and *K* are pulsed simultaneously assuming that the S-R flip-flop is the type shown in Fig. 11–12(b)?

6. Study Section 11.6, *The Clocked J-K Flip-Flop.*

   (a) Trace signals through the network of Fig. 11–17(a) and verify the timing diagram of Fig. 11–17(b).

   (b) The unclocked J-K flip-flop and the clocked J-K flip-flop have the same next state equation. Explain the difference in interpretation of the equation for the two flip-flops.

   (c) Is there any restriction on the maximum clock pulse width for a master-slave J-K flip-flop? Explain. Compare with the answer to 5(c).

   (d) Work Problem 11.8.

7. Study Section 11.7, *The D Flip-Flop.*

   (a) Describe in words the behavior of the clocked D flip-flop.

   (b) Given a clocked D flip-flop with the following inputs, sketch the waveform for *Q*.

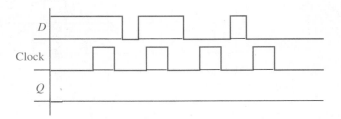

   (c) Work Programmed Exercise 11.17.

8. Study Section 11.8, *Clocked Flip-Flops with Clear and Preset Inputs.*

   (a) To set the flip-flop of Fig. 11–20 to $Q = 1$ without using the clock, the clear input should be set to _____ and the preset input to

_____. To reset the flip-flop of Fig. 11–21(a) to $Q = 0$ without using the clock, the _____ input should be set to _____.

(b) Work Problem 11.13.

9. Study Section 11.9, *Characteristic Equations*.

(a) Given one of the flip-flops in this chapter, or a similar flip-flop, you should be able to derive the characteristic equation which gives the next state of the flip-flop in terms of the present state and inputs. You should understand the meaning of each of the characteristic equations given in Section 11.9.

(b) An S-R flip-flop can be converted to a T flip-flop by adding gates at the S and R inputs. The S and R inputs must be chosen so that the flip-flop will change state whenever T is pulsed. In order to determine the S and R inputs, ask yourself the question, "Under what conditions must the flip-flop be set to 1, and under what conditions must it be reset?" The flip-flop must be set to 1 if $Q = 0$ and $T = 1$.
Therefore, $S = $ _____. In a similar manner, determine the equation for R and draw the network which converts an S-R flip-flop to a T flip-flop. Compare your answer with Fig. 11–11(b).

(c) Work Problems 11.10, 11.11, and 11.12.

10. Optional lab exercise:

(a) Construct an S-R flip-flop using two NOR gates and verify its operation.

(b) Construct the master-slave J-K flip-flop shown in Fig. 11–17(a), using two NOR gates for each S-R flip-flop. Verify the timing diagram of Fig. 11–17(b) by putting in the given sequence of T, J, and K signals and observing the P and Q outputs. (Use a toggle switch for T as well as J and K.)

11. When you are satisfied that you can meet the objectives of this unit, take the readiness test.

Flip-Flops

Sequential switching networks have the property that the output depends not only on the present input but also on the past sequence of inputs. In effect, these networks must be able to "remember" something about the past history of the inputs in order to produce the present output. Flip-flops are the most commonly used memory devices in sequential networks. Basically, a flip-flop is a memory device which can assume one of two stable output states, which has a pair of complementary outputs, and which has one or more inputs that can cause the output state to change. Several common types of flip-flops are described in this unit.

11.1
Gate Delays and Timing Diagrams

When the input to a logic gate is changed, the output will not change instantaneously. The transistors or other switching elements within the gate take a finite time to react to a change in input, so that the change in the gate output is delayed with respect to the input change. Figure 11–1 shows possible input and output waveforms for an inverter. If the change in output is delayed by time ϵ with respect to the input, we say that this gate has a propagation delay of ϵ. In practice, the propagation delay for a 0 to 1 output change may be different than the delay for a 1 to 0 change. Propagation delays for integrated circuit gates may be as short as a few nanoseconds (1 nanosecond $= 10^{-9}$ second), and in many cases these delays can be neglected. However, in the analysis of some types of sequential networks, even short delays may be important.

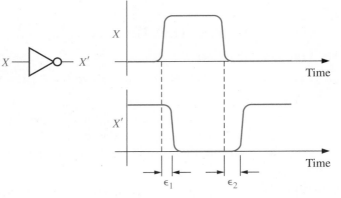

Figure 11–1
Propagation Delay in an Inverter

Timing diagrams are frequently used in the analysis of sequential networks. These diagrams show various signals in the network as a function of time. Several variables are usually plotted with the same time scale so that the times at which these variables change with respect to each other can easily be observed.

Figure 11–2 shows the timing diagram for a network with 2 gates. We will assume that each gate has a propagation delay of 20 ns (nanoseconds). This timing diagram indicates what happens when gate inputs B and C are held at constant

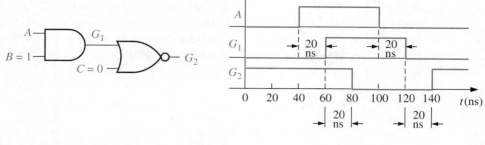

Figure 11–2
Timing Diagram for AND-NOR Network

values 1 and 0, respectively, and input A is changed to 1 at $t = 40$ ns and then changed back to 0 at $t = 100$ ns. The output of gate G_1 changes 20 ns after A changes, and the output of gate G_2 changes 20 ns after G_1 changes.

Figure 11–3 shows a timing diagram for a network with an added delay element. The input X consists of two pulses, the first of which is two microseconds $(2 \times 10^{-6}$ second) wide and the second is three microseconds wide. The delay element has an output Y which is the same as the input except that it is delayed by one microsecond. That is, Y changes to a 1 value one microsecond after the rising edge of the X pulse and returns to 0 one microsecond after the falling edge of the X pulse. The output of the AND gate (Z) should be 1 during the time interval in which both X and Y are 1. If we assume a small propagation delay in the AND gate (ϵ), then Z will be as shown in the diagram.

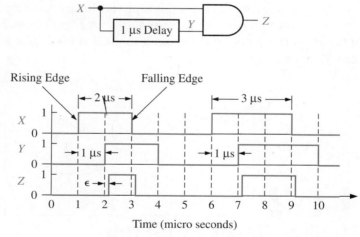

Figure 11–3
Timing Diagram for Network with Delay

The switching networks we have studied so far have not had feedback connections. In order to construct a switching network that has memory, such as a flip-flop, we must introduce feedback into the network. By feedback we mean that the output of one of the gates is connected back into the input of another gate in the network so as to form a closed loop. For example, in the NOR-gate network of Fig. 11–6(a), the output of the second NOR gate is fed back into the input of the first NOR gate. In simple cases, we can analyze networks with feedback by tracing signals through the network. For example, consider the network in Fig. 11–4(a).

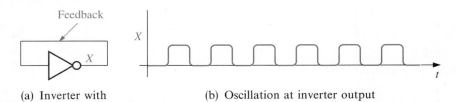

Figure 11–4   (a) Inverter with feedback   (b) Oscillation at inverter output

If, at some instant of time, the inverter input is 0, this 0 will propagate through the inverter and cause the output to become 1. This 1 is fed back into the input, so after the propagation delay, the inverter output will become 0. When this 0 feeds back into the input, the output will again switch to 1, and so forth. The inverter output will continue to oscillate back and forth between 0 and 1 as shown in Fig. 11–4(b), and it will never reach a stable condition. The rate at which the network oscillates is determined by the propagation delay in the inverter.

Next, consider a feedback loop which has two inverters in it, shown in Fig. 11–5(a). In this case, the network has two stable conditions, often referred to as stable states. If the input to the first inverter is 0, its output will be 1. Then the input to the second inverter will be 1, and its output will be 0. This 0 will feed back into the first inverter, but since this input is already 0, no changes will occur. The network is then in a stable state. As shown in Fig. 11–5(b), a second stable state of the network occurs when the input to the first inverter is 1 and the input to the second inverter is 0.

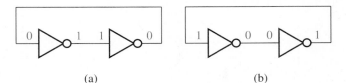

Figure 11–5   (a)   (b)

11.2
The Set-Reset Flip-Flop

We can construct a simple flip-flop by introducing feedback into a NOR-gate network, as seen in Fig. 11–6(a). As indicated, if the inputs are $S = R = 0$, the network can assume a stable state with $Q = 0$ and $P = 1$. Note that this is a stable condition of the network because $P = 1$ fed into the second gate forces the output to be $Q = 0$, and $Q = 0$ fed into the first gate allows its output to be 1. Now if we change S to 1, P will become 0. This is an unstable condition or state of the network since both the inputs and output of the second gate are 0; therefore Q will change to 1, leading to the stable state shown in Fig. 11–6(b).

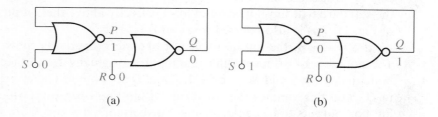

Figure 11–6   (a)   (b)

If S is changed back to 0, the network will remain in the above state since $Q = 1$ fed back into the first gate will cause P to remain 0, shown in Fig. 11–6(c). Note that the inputs are again $S = R = 0$, but outputs are different than we started with. Thus the network has two different stable states for a given set of inputs. If we now change R to 1, Q will become 0 and P will then change back to 1, as seen in Fig. 11–6(d). If we then change R back to 0, the network remains in this state and we are back where we started.

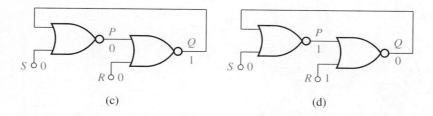

Figure 11–6   (c)   (d)

This network is said to have "memory" because its output depends not only on the present inputs but also on the past sequence of inputs. If we restrict the inputs so that $R = S = 1$ is not allowed, the stable states of the outputs P and Q are always complements, that is, $P = Q'$. To emphasize the symmetry between the operation of the two gates, the network is often drawn in "cross-coupled" form (see Fig. 11–7(a)). As shown in Figs. 11–6(b) and (d), an input $S = 1$ "sets" the

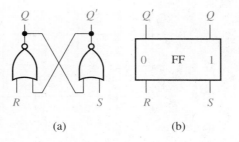

(a)   (b)

Figure 11–7
S-R Flip-Flop

output to $Q = 1$, and an input $R = 1$ "resets" the output to $Q = 0$. When used with the restriction that R and S cannot be 1 simultaneously, the network is commonly referred to as a set-reset (S-R) flip-flop and given the symbol shown in Fig. 11–7(b). Note that although Q comes out of the NOR gate with the R input, the standard S-R flip-flop symbol has Q directly above the S input. The network of Fig. 11–7(a) is also referred to as an S-R latch.

   If $S = R = 1$, the flip-flop will not operate properly as shown in Fig. 11–8. The notation $1 \rightarrow 0$ means that the input is originally 1 and then changes to 0. Note that when S and R are both 1, P and Q are both 0. Therefore, P is not equal to Q', and this violates the basic rule of flip-flop operation, which requires the flip-flop outputs to be complements. Furthermore, if S and R are simultaneously changed back to 0, P and Q may both change to 1. If $S = R = 0$ and $P = Q = 1$, then after the 1's propagate through the gates, P and Q will become 0 again, and the flip-flop may continue to oscillate if the gate delays are exactly equal.

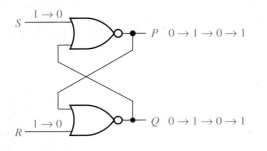

Figure 11–8
Improper S-R Flip-Flop Operation

   Figure 11–9 shows a timing diagram for the S-R flip-flop. Note that when S changes to 1 at time t_1, Q changes to 1 a short time (ϵ) later. (ϵ represents the response time or delay time of the flip-flop.) At time t_2, when S changes back to 0, Q does not change. At time t_3, R changes to 1, and Q changes back to 0 a short time (ϵ) later. The duration of the S (or R) input pulse must normally be at least as great as ϵ in order for a change in the state of Q to occur. If $S = 1$ for a time less than ϵ, the gate output will not change and the flip-flop will not change state.

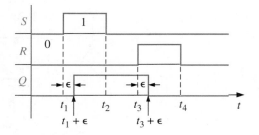

Figure 11–9
Timing Diagram for S-R Flip-Flop

Table 11–1

S-R Flip-Flop Operation

$S(t)$	$R(t)$	$Q(t)$	$Q(t+\epsilon)$
0	0	0	0
0	0	1	1
0	1	0	0
0	1	1	0
1	0	0	1
1	0	1	1
1	1	0	$-\rbrace$ inputs not allowed
1	1	1	$-$

The behavior of the S-R flip-flop is summarized by Table 11–1. The fifth row of this table means that if at some time the inputs are $S = 1$ and $R = 0$ and the output of the flip-flop is $Q = 0$, then at a time ϵ later, the flip-flop output will be $Q = 1$. Other rows are interpreted in a similar manner.

When discussing flip-flops, we will use the term *present state* to mean the state of the Q output of the flip-flop at the time the input signals are applied (or changed), and the term *next state* to mean the state of the Q output after the flip-flop has reacted to these input signals. In the above table, $Q(t)$ represents the "present state" of the flip-flop, ϵ is the time required for a change of state to occur, and $Q(t + \epsilon)$ is the "next state" of the flip-flop. For example, if $S = 0$ and $R = 1$ at time t, the next state of the flip-flop will be $Q = 0$, regardless of its present state. Normally, we will be concerned only with the state of the flip-flop when the outputs are stable. Therefore, we will not discuss the flip-flop behavior during the interval t to $t + \epsilon$, during which the outputs may be changing.

By using a Karnaugh map for $Q(t + \epsilon)$, we can derive an equation which describes the behavior of the flip-flop (Fig. 11–10). The inputs which are not allowed are treated as don't cares.

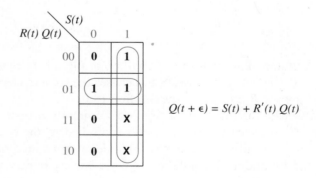

$$Q(t + \epsilon) = S(t) + R'(t)\,Q(t)$$

Figure 11–10
Map for $Q(t + \epsilon)$

Normally, we will write this equation without including time explicitly, using Q to represent the present state of the flip-flop and Q^+ to represent the next state:

$$Q^+ = S + R'Q \qquad (SR = 0)$$

In words, this equation tells us that the next state of the flip-flop will be 1 either if it is set to 1 with an S input, or if the present state is 1 and it is not reset. The condition $SR = 0$ implies that S and R cannot both be 1 at the same time. An equation which expresses the next state of a flip-flop in terms of its present state and inputs will be referred to as a "next-state equation" or "characteristic equation".

11.3
The Trigger Flip-Flop

The trigger or T flip-flop in Fig. 11–11(a) has a single input. Applying a pulse to this input causes it to change state. For example, if $Q = 1$ and the T input is pulsed, Q changes to 0. If T is pulsed again, Q changes back to 1. A simple T flip-flop can be constructed using an S-R flip-flop and two AND gates, shown in Fig. 11–11(b).

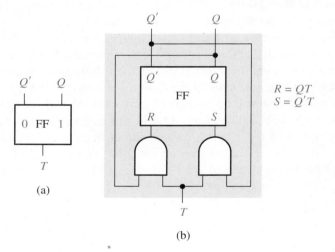

Figure 11–11   (b)

A timing diagram for the T flip-flop of Fig. 11–11(b) is shown in Fig. 11–12(a). If Q is 0, a pulse on T pulses S and causes the state to change to 1. If Q is 1, a pulse on T pulses R and resets the flip-flop to 0.

In order for this type of flip-flop to operate properly, there must be a finite delay (δ) between the time a pulse is applied to the S or R input and the time the flip-flop output Q changes. This delay in change of state could be accomplished by adding capacitance or extra logic circuitry within the S-R flip-flop. Figure 11–12(b) indicates symbolically how the basic S-R flip-flop of Fig. 11–6(a) could be modified to delay the change of state. In Fig. 11–12(a), note that the T pulse must be terminated before the change of state is completed. Then no further state change can occur until another pulse is applied to T. If T is too long or the delay in the S-R flip-flop (δ) is too short, the change in Q will propagate back to the AND gate inputs in Fig. 11–11(b) while T is still 1 causing another

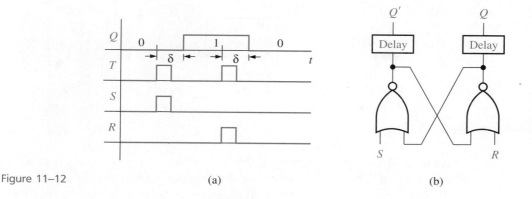

Figure 11–12   (a)   (b)

change of state. If T remains 1, then the flip-flop will change state again and it will continue to oscillate until T becomes 0. Other types of T flip-flops change state in response to the rising or falling edge of the input pulses, in which case the pulse width is not critical.

The next-state table and characteristic equation for the T flip-flop are given in Table 11–2.

Table 11–2

T Flip-Flop Operation

T Q	Q^+
0 0	0
0 1	1
1 0	1
1 1	0

$$Q(t + \epsilon) = T'(t)Q(t) + T(t)Q'(t)$$
$$\text{or}$$
$$Q^+ = T'Q + TQ' = T \oplus Q$$

The above equation states that the next state of the flip-flop (Q^+) will be 1 iff the present state (Q) is 1 and no T pulse occurs or the present state is 0 and a T pulse occurs.

11.4
The Clocked T Flip-Flop

In Units 12 through 16, we will discuss the analysis and design of synchronous sequential networks. In such sequential networks, it is common practice to synchronize the operation of all flip-flops by a common clock or pulse generator. The clock pulse may be fed into each flip-flop through external gates, or internal gating may be used as is the case with most integrated circuit flip-flops. Use of the clock to synchronize the operation of several flip-flops is illustrated in Units 12 and 13. When a clock is used, all flip-flops which change state do so in response to the clock pulse rather than in response to some other input signal.

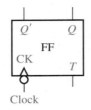

Figure 11-13
Clocked T Flip-Flop

Figure 11–13 shows a clocked T flip-flop, which has a clock input (CK) as well as a T input. The arrowhead on the flip-flop input identifies the clock input, and the small circle (inversion symbol) indicates that the flip-flop changes state on the falling edge of the clock pulse. Figure 11–14 shows a timing diagram for the clocked T flip-flop. At times t_2 and t_4 the T input is 1 and the flip-flop state (Q) changes a short time (ϵ) after the falling edge of the clock pulse. At times t_1 and t_3 the T input is 0, and the clock pulse does not cause a change of state. The next state table and characteristic equation for the clocked T flip-flop are the same as those for the unclocked T flip-flop. However, for the clocked T flip-flop, we must interpret Q as the state of the flip-flop before the clock and Q^+ as the state after the clock.

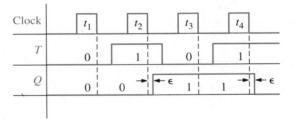

Figure 11-14
Timing Diagram for Clocked T Flip-Flop

Proper operation of the T flip-flop described in Section 11.3 requires careful control of the input pulse width and the delays in the circuit. By careful design of the clocked T flip-flop, these timing problems can be eliminated, and the flip-flop will operate properly for a wide range of clock pulse widths. Proper internal design of the clocked T flip-flop requires asynchronous design techniques (see Section 24.1 and Fig. 24–2).

11.5
The J-K Flip-Flop

The J-K flip-flop (Fig. 11–15) combines the features of the S-R and T flip-flops. A 1 input applied to J or K alone acts exactly like an S or R input, respectively. That is, if $J = 1$, the flip-flop output is set to $Q = 1$; and if $K = 1$, the flip-flop output is reset to $Q = 0$. Unlike the S-R flip-flop, it is permissible to apply a 1

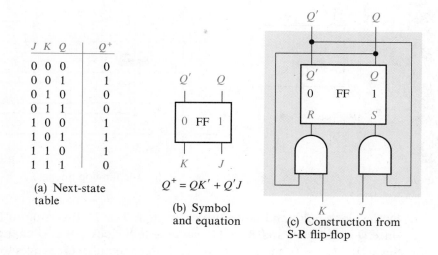

J K Q	Q^+
0 0 0	0
0 0 1	1
0 1 0	0
0 1 1	0
1 0 0	1
1 0 1	1
1 1 0	1
1 1 1	0

(a) Next-state table

$$Q^+ = QK' + Q'J$$

(b) Symbol and equation

(c) Construction from S-R flip-flop

Figure 11–15
J-K Flip-Flop

input simultaneously to J and K, in which case the flip-flop changes state just like a T flip-flop. For example, if $Q = 0$ and we momentarily apply a 1 input to both J and K, the flip-flop state will change to $Q = 1$. The next-state table and characteristic equation for the J-K flip-flop are given in Fig. 11–15.

Figure 11–15(c) shows one way of constructing a J-K flip-flop using an S-R flip-flop with added gates. If $Q = 0$, an input of $J = 1$ will set the flip-flop to $Q = 1$. If $Q = 1$, an input of $K = 1$ will reset the flip-flop to $Q = 0$. If the J and K inputs are pulsed simultaneously ($J = K = 1$), then the flip-flop acts just like the T flip-flop of Fig. 11–11(b), and a state change occurs. Again, the change of state of the S-R flip-flop must be delayed, as shown in Fig. 11–12(b), to assure proper operation. When J and K are pulsed at the same time, timing problems may arise if the pulses are too long or if they do not arrive at exactly the same time. To overcome such timing problems, a clocked J-K flip-flop of the type discussed in the next section can be used.

11.6
The Clocked J-K Flip-Flop

Figure 11–16(a) shows a clocked J-K flip-flop. This flip-flop has three inputs— J, K, and the clock input, which is usually labeled CK. As illustrated in Fig. 11–16(b), this flip-flop changes state a short time (ϵ) after the falling edge of the clock pulse provided that J and K have appropriate values. If $J = 1$ during the clock pulse, Q will be set to 1 immediately following the clock pulse. If $K = 1$ during the clock pulse, Q will be set to 0 after the clock pulse. Similarly, if $J = K = 1$, Q will change state after the clock pulse. The change in state is initiated

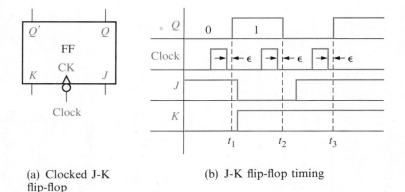

(a) Clocked J-K	(b) J-K flip-flop timing

Figure 11–16   flip-flop

by the clock pulse and never by a change in J or K. Referring to Fig. 11–16(b), since $Q = 0$, $J = 1$, and $K = 0$ during the first clock pulse, Q changes to 1 at t_1. Since $Q = 1$, $J = 0$, and $K = 1$ during the second pulse, Q changes to 0 at t_2. Since $Q = 0$, $J = 1$, and $K = 1$ during the third pulse, Q changes to 1 at t_3. The arrowhead on the flip-flop symbol identifies the clock input, and the small circle (inversion symbol) indicates that the state changes occur on a high to low transition, that is, after the falling (rather than the rising) edge of the clock pulse.

The next state table and characteristic equation previously given for the unclocked J-K flip-flop also apply to the clocked J-K flip-flop, if Q is interpreted as the state of the flip-flop before the clock pulse and Q^+ as the state after the clock pulse. Thus, the presence of a clock signal is implied and does not appear explicitly in the equation.

One way of realizing the clocked J-K flip-flop is with two S-R flip-flops connected in a master-slave arrangement as shown in Fig. 11–17(a). Master-slave clocked J-K flip-flops are commonly constructed in integrated circuit form.

Figure 11–17(b) shows a detailed timing diagram for the master-slave clocked J-K flip-flop. The slopes of the rising and falling edges of the clock pulse have been exaggerated in order to better illustrate the internal operation. Gates 3 and 4 in Fig. 11–17(a) are designed to operate at a different time during the clock pulse than gates 1 and 2. On the rising edge of the clock pulse, gates 3 and 4 open to isolate the slave flip-flop inputs from the master at point a. In other words, following point a the inputs x_3 and x_4 act like 0's, so the P and P' signals cannot pass through the gates and the slave flip-flop cannot change state. Next, at point b on the rising edge of the clock pulse, gates 1 and 2 close to allow the master flip-flop to be set to the proper state. That is, the inputs x_1 and x_2 will act like 1's so that the J or K signals can pass through the gates if Q has the proper value. On the falling edge of the clock pulse, gates 1 and 2 open to isolate the inputs from the master at point c, and gates 3 and 4 close at point d so that the output of the master is transferred to the slave.

In Fig. 11–17(b), note that since $J = 1$ during the first clock pulse, P is set to 1 at time t_b and Q is set to 1 at time t_d. The state change of the master takes place on the rising edge of the clock pulse, and the state change of the slave follows on the falling edge. In order to assure that the flip-flop works properly, that is, obeys

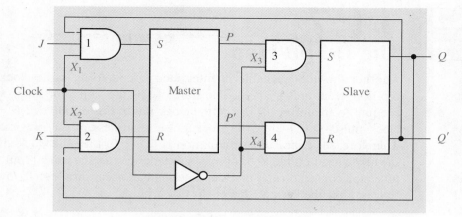

(a) Master-slave J-K flip-flop

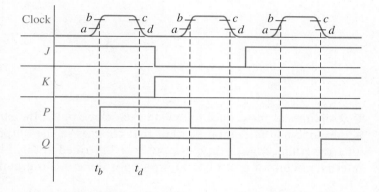

Figure 11–17

(b) Internal timing diagram for master-slave J-K flip-flop

the equation $Q^+ = JQ' + K'Q$, any changes in the J and K inputs must occur between clock pulses as illustrated in Fig. 11–17(b). The change of flip-flop state always occurs on the falling edge of the clock pulse regardless of pulse width. Therefore, as long as the clock pulse width exceeds a certain minimum value, proper operation of the flip-flop does not depend on pulse width.

Another type of clocked flip-flop is the "edge-triggered" flip-flop. Like the master-slave flip-flop, an edge-triggered flip-flop will change state in response to a change on the clock input. However, unlike the master-slave flip-flop, the other inputs may change during the clock pulse without causing improper operation. The same symbol is sometimes used for the J-K master-slave flip-flop and the J-K edge-triggered flip-flop,[1] and their external behavior is the same as long as J and K do not change during the clock pulse.

---

[1] For example, the 7473 and 74LS73 have the same symbol and external connections; however, the 7473 is master-slave and the 74LS73 is edge-triggered.

11.7
The D Flip-Flop

Another flip-flop available in integrated circuit form is the clocked D (delay) flip-flop, seen in Fig. 11–18. The state of this flip-flop after the clock pulse (Q^+) is equal to the input (D) before the clock pulse. For example, if $D = 1$ before the clock pulse, $Q = 1$ after the clock pulse regardless of the previous value of Q. Therefore, the characteristic equation is $Q^+ = D$. Like the clocked J-K flip-flop, the arrowhead on the D flip-flop symbol designates the clock input and the small inversion circle indicates that the state changes occur on a high to low transition—that is, after the falling edge of the clock pulse.

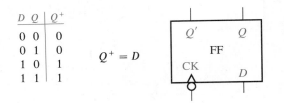

D	Q	Q^+
0	0	0
0	1	0
1	0	1
1	1	1

$Q^+ = D$

Figure 11–18
Clocked D Flip-Flop

If D changes at most once following each clock pulse, the output of the flip-flop is the same as the D input, except that changes in the output are delayed until after the falling edge of the clock pulse as illustrated in Fig. 11–19. Analysis of the internal circuit for a clocked D flip-flop is done in Programmed Exercise 11.17.

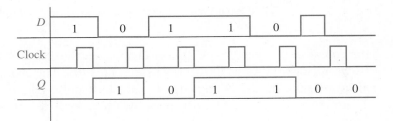

Figure 11–19
Timing for Clocked D Flip-Flop

11.8
Clocked Flip-Flops with Clear and Preset Inputs

Clocked integrated circuit flip-flops often have additional inputs which can be used to set the flip-flop to an initial state independent of the clock. Figure 11–20 shows a clocked J-K flip-flop with clear (CLR) and preset (PRE) inputs. The small

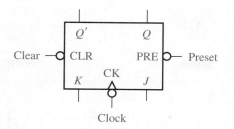

Figure 11–20
Clocked J-K Flip-Flop with Clear and
Preset Inputs

circles (inversion symbols) on these inputs indicate that a logic 0 (rather than a 1) is required to clear or set the flip-flop. Thus, a 0 applied to the clear input will reset the flip-flop to $Q = 0$, and a 0 applied to the preset input will set the flip-flop to $Q = 1$. These inputs override the clock and J-K inputs. That is, a 0 applied to the clear input will reset the flip-flop regardless of the values of J, K, and the clock. Under normal operating conditions, a 0 should not be applied simultaneously to clear and preset. When the clear and preset inputs are both held at logic 1, the J, K, and clock inputs operate in the normal manner.

Figure 11–21 shows two types of clocked D flip-flops with clear (CLR) inputs. The small inversion circle on the clear input indicates that a 0 (rather than a 1) will reset the flip-flop to $Q = 0$. The clear input overrides the clock and D inputs. When the clear input is held at 1, the D and clock inputs operate in the normal manner. In Fig. 11–21(a), the inversion symbol on the clock indicates that the flip-flop responds to a high-to-low transition—that is, to the falling edge of the clock pulse—whereas in Fig. 11–21(b), the lack of an inversion symbol indicates that the state changes will occur on a low-to-high transition—that is, on the rising edge of the clock. Unless otherwise specified, we will use the former type of D flip-flop throughout the remainder of this text.

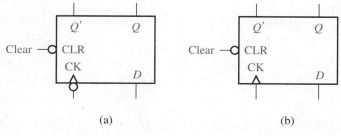

(a)   (b)

Figure 11–21
Clocked D Flip-Flops with Clear

Several D flip-flops may be grouped together with a common clock to form a register (Fig. 11–22). The register may also have a common clear input as shown. Since each flip-flop can store one bit of information, this register can store four bits of information. The clear input is normally 1. If it is changed momentarily

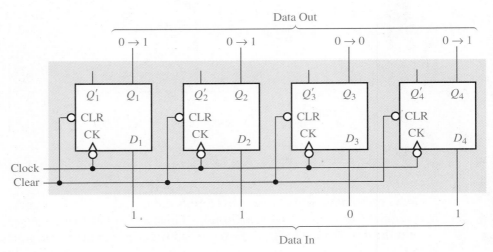

Figure 11–22
D Flip-Flop Register

to 0, the Q output of all four flip-flops will become 0. When the clock is pulsed, the data applied to the D inputs will be loaded into the flip-flops. For example, if the data inputs are $D_1 = 1$, $D_2 = 1$, $D_3 = 0$ and $D_4 = 1$, after the clock pulse the flip-flop outputs will be $Q_1 = 1$, $Q_2 = 1$, $Q_3 = 0$, and $Q_4 = 1$.

11.9
Characteristic Equations

The characteristic (next-state) equation for a flip-flop can be derived as follows: First, make a truth table which gives the next state (Q^+) as a function of the present state (Q) and the inputs. Any illegal input combinations should be treated as don't cares. Then plot a map for Q^+ and read the characteristic equation from the map.

The characteristic equations for the flip-flops discussed in this chapter are:

$$Q^+ = S + R'Q \quad (SR = 0) \qquad \text{(S-R flip-flop)} \qquad (11–1)$$
$$Q^+ = T \oplus Q = TQ' + T'Q \qquad \text{(T flip-flop)} \qquad (11–2)$$
$$Q^+ = JQ' + K'Q \qquad \text{(J-K flip-flop)} \qquad (11–3)$$
$$Q^+ = D \qquad \text{(D flip-flop)} \qquad (11–4)$$

In each case, Q represents an initial or present state of the flip-flop, and Q^+ represents the final or next state. These equations are valid only when the appropriate restrictions on the flip-flop inputs are observed. For the S-R flip-flop, $S = R = 1$ is forbidden. If the T flip-flop is of the type shown in Fig. 11–11(b), the T pulse must be of appropriate duration. For the master-slave clocked J-K flip-flop, J and K should not change during the clock pulse.

The characteristic equations given above apply to both clocked and unclocked flip-flops, but their interpretation is different for the two cases. For example, for the unclocked J-K flip-flop (Fig. 11–15), Q^+ represents the state of the flip-flop a short time after one of the inputs changes. However, for the clocked J-K flip-flop (Fig. 11–16), Q^+ represents the state of the flip-flop a short time after the clock pulse.

It is usually possible to convert one type of flip-flop to another by adding external gates. Figures 11–11(b) and 11–15(c) show how an S-R flip-flop can be converted to a T flip-flop or a J-K flip-flop. Next we will convert a clocked J-K flip-flop to a clocked T flip-flop. When $T = 1$, we want the flip-flop to change state, so we must have $J = K = 1$. Similarly, when $T = 0$, we want no state change, so $J = K = 0$. Therefore, we must have $J = K = T$, as shown in Fig. 11–23(a).

In many cases, the necessary flip-flop input equations can be found by determining the conditions under which the flip-flop must be set or reset (in the case of an S-R flip-flop), or the conditions under which the flip-flop must change state (in the case of a T flip-flop).

EXAMPLE: Convert an S-R flip-flop to a clocked D flip-flop. Figure 11–18 shows the desired behavior of the flip-flop after conversion. The flip-flop must be set to 1 if $D = 1$ and a clock pulse occurs. Therefore, $S = D(CK)$. Similarly, the flip-flop must be set to 0 if $D = 0$ and a clock pulse occurs. Therefore, $R = D'(CK)$. Figure 11–23(b) shows the result of the conversion.

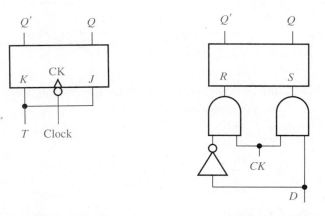

Figure 11–23

(a) Conversion of J-K
flip-flop to T flip-flop

(b) Conversion of S-R flip-flop
to clocked D flip-flop

In the above example, an intuitive approach to conversion of one type of flip-flop to another type has been presented. In the next unit, systematic methods for deriving flip-flop input equations are described. These systematic methods can also be applied to convert one flip-flop type to another.

The most commonly used types of clocked flip-flops are the J-K and D flip-flops. Both of these types are readily available in integrated circuit form. When a T flip-flop is needed, a J-K flip-flop with J and K connected together can be used. The S-R flip-flop is more commonly used in asynchronous sequential network design (see Section 24.1) than in synchronous design (see Section 12.3).

PROBLEMS

11.1   Complete the timing diagram for the given network. Assume that both gates have a propagation delay of 5 ns.

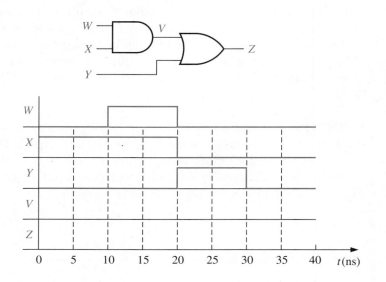

11.2   Complete the timing diagram for the given network. Assume that both gates have a propagation delay of 5 ns.

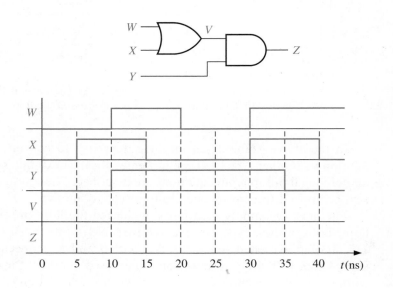

11.3 Assume that the inverter in the network below has a propagation delay of 5 ns and the AND gate has a propagation delay of 10 ns. Draw a timing diagram for the network showing X, Y, and Z. Assume that X is initially 0, Y is initially 1, X becomes 1 for 80 ns, and then X is 0 again.

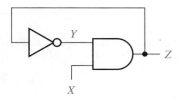

11.4 A flip-flop can be constructed from two NAND gates connected as follows:

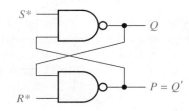

(a) What restriction must be placed on S^* and R^* so that P will always equal Q' (under steady-state conditions)?

(b) Construct a next-state table and derive the characteristic (next-state) equation for the flip-flop.

(c) Complete the following timing diagram for the flip-flop.

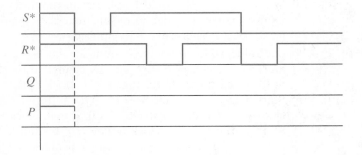

(d) What is the relation between S^* and R^* in this problem and the S and R inputs for the NOR-gate flip-flop of Fig. 11–7(a)?

11.5 This problem illustrates the improper operation that can occur if both inputs to an S-R flip-flop are 1 and are then changed back to 0. For Fig. 11–8 complete the following timing chart, assuming that each gate has a propagation delay of exactly 10 ns. Assume that initially $P = 1$ and $Q = 0$. Note that when $t = 100$ ns, S and R are both changed to 0. Then 10 ns later, both P and Q will change to 1. Since these 1's are fed back to the gate inputs, what will happen after another 10 ns?

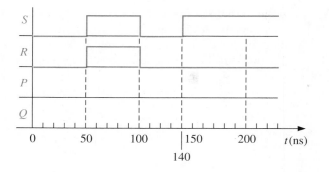

11.6   For the T flip-flop of Fig. 11–11(b), draw a timing diagram similar to Fig. 11–12(a), which shows what happens when T remains 1 for a time equal to 2.5δ.

11.7   Work Problem 11.6 for T remaining 1 for a time equal to 1.5δ.

11.8   (a) Using Fig. 11–17(a), trace the signals through the master-slave J-K flip-flop when the following input sequence is applied starting with $J = K = P = Q = 0$: JK change to 11, clock pulse, JK change to 01, clock pulse, JK change to 10, clock pulse. Draw a timing diagram which includes P, Q, J, K, and the clock.

   (b) Improper operation may occur if J or K is changed while the clock is high. Starting with $J = K = $ clock $= P = Q = 0$, the inputs are changed in the following order: $J = 1$, clock $= 1$, $J = 0$, $K = 1$, clock $= 0$. What is the final value of Q?

   (c) Repeat (b) when the inputs are changed in the order clock $= 1$, $J = 1$, clock $= 0$. Note that the final value of Q is determined by the values of J and K before the clock pulse in (b) but not in (c).

   (d) What restrictions should be placed on the times at which the J and K inputs change in order to ensure that the equation $Q^+ = QK' + Q'J$ holds for a master-slave J-K flip-flop?

11.9   Work Problem 11.8(a) for these input sequences:

   (a) Start with $J = K = P = Q = 0$. JK change to 10, clock pulse, JK change to 01, clock pulse, JK change to 11, clock pulse.

   (b) Start with $J = K = $ clock $= P = Q = 0$. Input sequence: $J = 1$, $K = 1$, clock $= 1$, $J = 0$, $K = 0$, clock $= 0$, $K = 1$, clock $= 1$, clock $= 0$.

   (c) Start with $J = K = $ clock $= P = Q = 0$. Input sequence: clock $= 1$, $J = 1$, $K = 1$, clock $= 0$, $J = 0$, $K = 0$, clock $= 1$, $K = 1$, clock $= 0$.

11.10   Convert a clocked D flip-flop to a clocked J-K flip-flop by adding external gates.

11.11   In Section 11.6, the clock input is not included explicitly in the characteristic (next-state) equation for a clocked J-K flip-flop. However, we can derive a next-state equation which includes the clock (C) if we interpret the variables in a special way. Consider a time interval in which it is known that either a clock pulse will occur ($C = 1$) or will not occur ($C = 0$). Let Q represent the state of the flip-flop before the start of the interval, and let Q^+ represent the state of the flip-flop after the interval. Assume that J and K remain constant during the interval. Construct a truth table and derive the equation for Q^+ in terms of J, K, C, and Q.

11.12 A gated latch (G-L flip-flop) behaves as follows: If $G = 0$, the flip-flop does not change state. If $G = 1$, the next state of the flip-flop is equal to the value of L.

(a) Derive the characteristic (next-state) equation for the flip-flop.

(b) Show how an S-R flip-flop can be converted to a G-L flip-flop by adding gate(s) and inverters(s). *Hint:* What values must S and R have so that the flip-flop will be set and reset at the proper time when $G = 1$? How can you prevent the flip-flop from changing state when $G = 0$?

11.13 (a) Complete the following timing diagram for the flip-flop of Fig. 11–20.

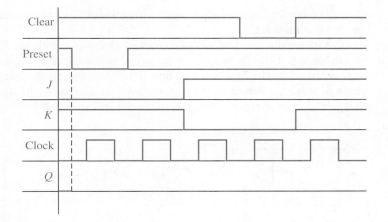

(b) Complete the timing diagram for the following circuit. Note that the CK inputs on the two flip-flops are different.

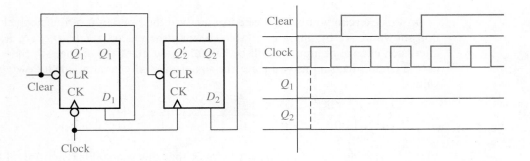

11.14 A reset-dominant flip-flop behaves like an S-R flip-flop, except that the input $S = R = 1$ is allowed, and the flip-flop is reset when $S = R = 1$.

(a) Derive the characteristic equation for a reset-dominant flip-flop.

(b) Show how a reset-dominant flip-flop can be constructed by adding gate(s) to an S-R flip-flop.

11.15   A set-dominant flip-flop is similar to the reset-dominant flip-flop of Problem 11.14 except that the input combination $S = R = 1$ sets the flip-flop. Repeat Problem 11.14 for a set-dominant flip-flop.

11.16   Derive a characteristic equation for the flip-flop of Fig. 11–20, including the preset (P) and clear (C) inputs as well as J and K. Assume that $P = C = 0$ will never occur.

PROGRAMMED EXERCISE 11.17

Cover the bottom part of each page with a sheet of paper and slide it down as you check your answers.

The internal logic diagram of a clocked D flip-flop follows. This flip-flop consists of two basic S-R flip-flops with added gates. When the clock input (CK) is 1, the value of D is stored in the first S-R flip-flop (P). When the clock changes from 1 to 0, the value of P is transferred to the output flip-flop (Q). Thus, the operation is similar to that of the master-slave J-K flip-flop shown in Fig. 11–17(a).

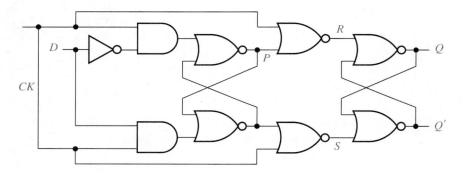

In·this exercise you will be asked to analyze the operation of the clocked D flip-flop shown above by filling in a table showing the values of CK, D, P, S, R, and Q after each change of input. It will be helpful if you mark the changes in these values on the circuit diagram as you trace the signals. Initially, assume the following signal values:

CK	D	P	S	R	Q	
0	0	0	0	1	0	(stable)

Verify by tracing signals through the circuit that this is a stable condition of the circuit; that is, no change will occur in P, S, R, or Q. Now assume that CK is changed to 1:

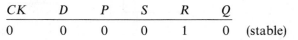

	CK	D	P	S	R	Q	
1.	0	0	0	0	1	0	(stable)
2.	1	0	0	0	1	0	?
3.							

Trace the change in CK through the circuit to see if a change in P, S, or R will occur. If a change does occur, mark row 2 of the above table "unstable" and enter the new values in row 3.

Answer:	2.	1	0	0	0	1	0	(unstable)
	3.	1	0	0	0	0	0	(stable)
	4.	1	1	0	0	0	0	(unstable)
	5.	1	1					?

Verify that row 3 is stable; that is, by tracing signals show that no further change in P, S, R, or Q will occur. Next D is changed to 1 as shown in row 4. Verify that row 4 is unstable, fill in the new values in row 5, and indicate if row 5 is stable or unstable.

		CK	D	P	S	R	Q	
Answer:	5.	1	1	1	0	0	0	(stable)
	6.	0	1	1	0	0	0	?
	7.	0	1					?
	8.	0	1					

Then CK is changed to 0 (row 6). If row 6 is unstable, indicate the new value of S in row 7. If row 7 is unstable, indicate the new value of Q in row 8. Then determine whether row 8 is stable or not.

		CK	D	P	S	R	Q	
Answer:	7.	0	1	1	1	0	0	(unstable)
	8.	0	1	1	1	0	1	(stable)
	9.	0	0					(stable)
	10.	1	0					
	11.	1	0					

Next D is changed back to 0 (row 9). Fill in the values in row 9 and verify that it is stable. CK is changed to 1 in row 10. If row 10 is unstable, fill in row 11 and indicate whether it is stable or not.

Answer:	9.	0	0	1	1	0	1	(stable)
	10.	1	0	1	1	0	1	(unstable)
	11.	1	0	0	0	0	1	(stable)
	12.	0	0					
	13.	0	0					
	14.	0	0					

CK is changed back to 0 in row 12. Complete the rest of the table.

Answer:	12.	0	0	0	0	0	1	(unstable)
	13.	0	0	0	0	1	1	(unstable)
	14.	0	0	0	0	1	0	(stable)

Using the above results, plot *P* and *Q* on the following timing diagram. Verify that your answer is consistent with the description of flip-flop operation given in the first paragraph of this exercise.

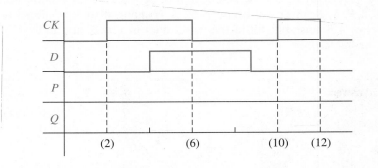

12

Counters and Similar Sequential Networks

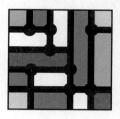

OBJECTIVES

1. Given the present state and desired next state of a flip-flop, determine the required flip-flop inputs.

2. Given the desired counting sequence for a counter, derive the flip-flop input equations.

3. Given the desired behavior of a sequential network whose next state (that is, the state after receiving an input clock pulse) depends only on the present state, design the network.

4. Explain the procedures used for deriving flip-flop input equations.

5. Construct a timing diagram for a counter by tracing signals through the network.

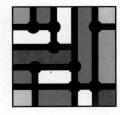

STUDY GUIDE

1. Study Section 12.1, *Design of a Binary Counter*, and Section 12.2, *Counters for Other Sequences*.

   (a) For Fig. 12–2, if $ABC = 101$ and an input pulse occurs, which of the T inputs will be pulsed?

   (b) Complete the following timing diagram for the binary counter of Fig. 12–2.

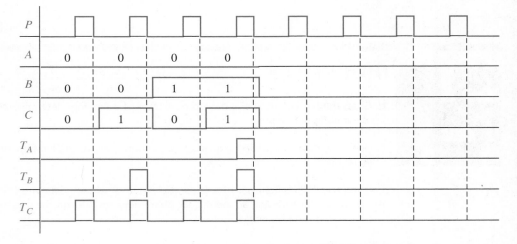

   (c) Using the results of (b), draw a state graph for this binary counter (similar to Fig. 12–3).

(d) Use Table 12–3 to verify that the values of T_A, T_B, and T_C in Table 12–1 are correct.

(e) What happens if the network of Fig. 12–5 is started in one of the don't care states and then an input pulse occurs? In particular, augment the state graph of Fig. 12–7 to indicate the result for starting in states 101 and 110.

2. Study Section 12.3, *Counter Design Using S-R Flip-Flops.*

   (a) Referring to Table 12–4(c):

   If $Q = Q^+ = 0$, explain in words why R is a don't care.

   If $Q = Q^+ = 1$, explain in words why S is a don't care.

   If $Q = 0$ and $Q^+ = 1$, what value should S have and why?

   If $Q = 1$ and $Q^+ = 0$, what value should R have and why?

   (b) For Fig. 12–8, derive the R_B and S_B maps from the B^+ map, and derive the R_C and S_C maps from the C^+ map.

   (c) In Fig. 12–8, where do the gate inputs (A, B, C, etc.) come from?

   (d) For Fig. 12–8(c), which flip-flop inputs will be pulsed if $ABC = 100$ and a P pulse occurs?

   (e) Complete the following state graph by tracing signals in Fig. 12–8(c). Compare your answer with Fig. 12–3. What will happen if the counter is in state 001 and a P pulse occurs?

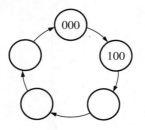

3. Study Section 12.4, *Counter Design Using J-K Flip-Flops,* and Section 12.5, *Short-Cut Method for Deriving J-K Flip-Flop Input Equations.*

(a) Referring to Table 12–6(c).

If $Q = Q^+ = 0$, explain in words why K is a don't care.

If $Q = Q^+ = 1$, explain in words why J is a don't care.

If $Q = 0$ and $Q^+ = 1$, explain why both $JK = 10$ and $JK = 11$ will produce the required state change.

If $Q = 1$ and $Q^+ = 0$, give two sets of values for J and K which will produce the required state change, and explain why your answer is valid.

(b) Verify that the maps of Fig. 12–9(a) can be derived from the maps of Fig. 12–9(b).

(c) Compare the number of logic gates in Figs. 12–8 and 12–9. The J-K realization requires fewer gates than the S-R realization for two reasons:

(1) The J-K maps have more don't cares than the S-R maps.
(2) Clocked J-K flip-flops are used so that it is unnecessary to provide AND gates for the input pulses.

(d) Draw in the implied feedback connections on the network of Fig. 12–9(c).

(e) By tracing signals through the network, verify that the state sequence for Fig. 12–9(c) is correct.

(f) Find a minimum expression for F_1 and for F_2. (*Hint:* No variables are required.)

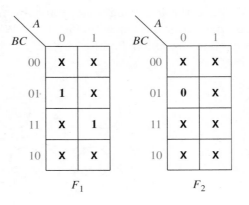

F_1 F_2

(g) By applying the steps of the short-cut method given on p. 312 determine J_B and K_B from the following map:

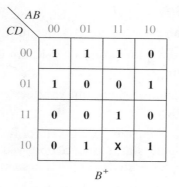

$$B^+$$

Steps (4) and (5) of the short-cut method are easy to remember since a change from $Q = 0$ to $Q^+ = 1$ requires $J = 1$, and a change from $Q = 1$ to $Q^+ = 0$ requires $K = 1$.

4. Study Section 12.6, *Counter Design Using D Flip-Flops,* Section 12.7, *Design of a Code Converter,* and Section 12.8, *Shift Registers.*

   (a) Verify the J-K flip-flop input equations, which are derived in Fig. 12–12.

   (b) Sketch the network for a 4-bit cyclic left-shift register using clocked J-K flip-flops. For such a shift register, why is it possible to shift information into one flip-flop at the same time information is shifted out to the next flip-flop without causing a timing problem?

5. Study Section 12.9, *Derivation of Flip-Flop Input Equations—Summary.*

   (a) Make sure that you know how to derive input equations for the different types of flip-flops. It is important that you understand the procedures for deriving the equations; merely memorizing the rules is not sufficient.

   (b) Table 12–9 is provided mainly for reference. It is not intended that you memorize this table; instead you should understand the reasons for the entries in the table. If you understand the reasons why a given map entry is 0, 1, or X, you should be able to derive the flip-flop input maps without reference to a table.

6. Work Problem 12.1, 12.2, 12.3, or 12.4 as assigned. Use both the standard method and the short-cut method for part (c). Work Problems 12.5, 12.13, 12.15, 12.16, and 12.18.

7. *Lab Problem* (required). This lab exercise introduces the use of J-K flip-flops in lab in preparation for a sequential network design problem (Unit 16).

   (a) Study the information on J-K flip-flops in the Laboratory Information handout.

   (b) Go to lab and check out your design for Problem 12.1(c), 12.2(c), 12.3(c), or 12.4(c).

   (c) Draw a complete state graph (of the form of Fig. 12–7) for your counter showing the state sequence observed in lab, including what happens when you start in each one of the states not in the prescribed counting sequence.

8. Bring your solution to Lab Problem 7 with you when you come to take the readiness test.

Counters and Similar Sequential Networks

Counters are one of the simplest types of sequential networks. A counter is usually constructed from two or more flip-flops which change state in a prescribed sequence when input pulses are received. In this unit, you will learn procedures for deriving flip-flop input equations for counters. These procedures will be applied to more general types of sequential networks in later units.

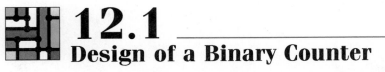

12.1
Design of a Binary Counter

The counters discussed in this chapter are all synchronous counters. This means the operation of the flip-flops is synchronized by the common input pulse (P) so that when several flip-flops must change state, the state changes occur simultaneously. Ripple counters, in which the state change of one flip-flop triggers the next flip-flop in line, are discussed in Chapter 18.

We will first construct a binary counter using three T flip-flops to count pulses (Fig. 12–1). We will assume that all the flip-flops change state immediately following the falling edge of the input pulse. The *state* of the counter is determined by the states of the individual flip-flops; for example, if flip-flop A is in state 0, B in state 1, and C in state 1, the state of the counter is 011. Initially, all flip-flops will be set to the 0 state. When a pulse is received, the counter will change to state 001; when a second pulse is received, the state will change to 010; etc. The

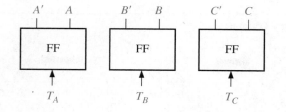

Figure 12–1
Flip-Flops for Binary Counter

sequence of flip-flop states is $ABC = 000, 001, 010, 011, 100, 101, 110, 111, 000, \ldots$
Note that when the counter reaches state 111, the next pulse resets it to the 000
state and then the sequence repeats.

First we will design the counter by inspection of the counting sequence; then
we will use a systematic procedure which can be generalized to other types of
counters. The problem is to determine the flip-flop inputs—T_A, T_B, and T_C. From
the above counting sequence, observe that C changes state every time a pulse is
received. Since pulsing T_C causes C to change state, the pulse source must be connected directly to the T_C input. Next, observe that B changes state when a pulse
is received only if $C = 1$. Therefore, an AND gate is connected to T_B as shown
in Fig. 12–2, so that if $C = 1$ and a pulse is received, B will change state. Similarly,
A changes state when a pulse is received only if B and C are both 1. An AND
gate is connected to T_A so that A will change state if $B = 1$, $C = 1$, and a pulse
is received.

Now we will verify that the network of Fig. 12–2 counts properly by tracing
signals through the network. Initially, $ABC = 000$, so when the first pulse arrives
it gets through only to T_C. The state changes to 001, so when the second pulse
arrives it gets through to T_B and T_C, and the state changes to 010. This process

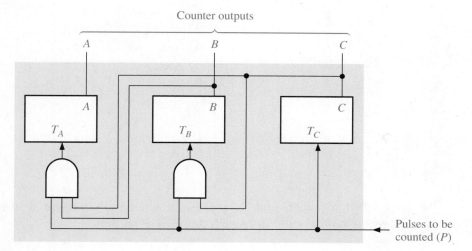

Figure 12–2
Synchronous Binary Counter

Table 12–1

State Table for Binary Counter

Present State			Next State			Flip-Flop Inputs		
A	B	C	A^+	B^+	C^+	T_A	T_B	T_C
0	0	0	0	0	1	0	0	1
0	0	1	0	1	0	0	1	1
0	1	0	0	1	1	0	0	1
0	1	1	1	0	0	1	1	1
1	0	0	1	0	1	0	0	1
1	0	1	1	1	0	0	1	1
1	1	0	1	1	1	0	0	1
1	1	1	0	0	0	1	1	1

continues until finally when state 111 is reached, the next pulse gets through to T_A, T_B, and T_C, and all flip-flops return to the zero state.

Next we will redesign the binary counter by using a state table (Table 12–1). This table shows the present state of flip-flops A, B, and C (before a pulse is received) and the corresponding next state (after the pulse is received). Although the pulse is not explicit in the table, it is understood to be the input. For example, if the flip-flops are in state $ABC = 011$ and a pulse is received, the next states will be $A^+B^+C^+ = 100$. A third column in the table is used to derive the inputs for T_A, T_B, and T_C. Whenever the entries in the C and C^+ columns differ, flip-flop C must change state and T_C must be 1. Similarly, if B and B^+ differ, B must change state so T_B must be 1. For example, if $ABC = 011$, $A^+B^+C^+ = 100$ and all three flip-flops must change state, so $T_AT_BT_C = 111$.

T_A, T_B, and T_C are now derived from the table as functions of A, B, and C. By inspection, $T_C = 1$. Karnaugh maps are plotted for T_A and T_B,

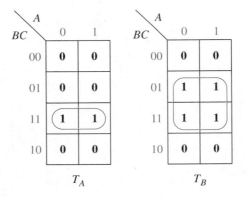

$$T_A \qquad\qquad T_B$$

from which $T_A = BC$ and $T_B = C$. Since a pulse (P) is required to initiate each change of state, we multiply each input by P so that

$$T_A = BCP \qquad T_B = CP \qquad T_C = P$$

These equations yield the same network derived previously.

12.2
Counters for Other Sequences

In some applications, the sequence of states of a counter is not in straight binary order. Figure 12–3 shows the *state graph*[1] for such a counter. The arrows indicate the state sequence. If this counter is started in state 000, the first pulse will take it to state 100, the next pulse to 111, etc. The count pulse is implicitly understood to be the input to the network.

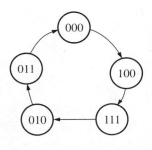

Figure 12–3
State Graph for Counter

The corresponding state table for the counter is Table 12–2. Note that the next state is unspecified for present states 001, 101, and 110.

Table 12–2
State Table for Fig. 12–3

A B C	A^+ B^+ C^+
0 0 0	1 0 0
0 0 1	– – –
0 1 0	0 1 1
0 1 1	0 0 0
1 0 0	1 1 1
1 0 1	– – –
1 1 0	– – –
1 1 1	0 1 0

We will design the counter specified by Table 12–2 using clocked T flip-flops. We could derive T_A, T_B, and T_C directly from this table as in the preceding example. However, it is often more convenient to plot "*next-state maps*" showing A^+, B^+, and C^+ as functions of A, B, and C, and then derive T_A, T_B, and T_C from these maps. The next state maps in Fig. 12–4(a) are easily plotted from inspection of Table 12–2. From the first row of the table, the $ABC = 000$ squares on the A^+, B^+, and C^+ maps are filled in with 1, 0, and 0, respectively. From

---

[1] Also called a state diagram.

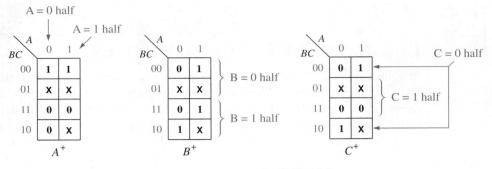

(a) Next state maps for Table 12-2

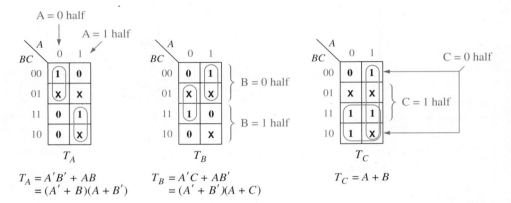

$$T_A = A'B' + AB$$
$$= (A' + B)(A + B')$$

$$T_B = A'C + AB'$$
$$= (A' + B')(A + C)$$

$$T_C = A + B$$

(b) Derivation of T inputs

Figure 12–4

the second row, the $ABC = 001$ squares on all three maps are filled in with don't cares. From the third row, the $ABC = 010$ squares on the A^+, B^+, and C^+ maps are filled in with 0, 1, and 1, respectively. The next-state maps can be quickly completed by continuing in this manner.

Next, we will derive the maps for the T inputs from the next-state maps. In the following discussion, the general symbol Q represents the present state of the flip-flop (A, B, or C) under consideration and Q^+ represents the next state (A^+, B^+, or C^+) of the same flip-flop. Given the present state of a T flip-flop (Q) and the desired next state (Q^+), the T input must be 1 whenever a change of state is required. Thus, $T = 1$ whenever $Q^+ \neq Q$ as shown in Table 12–3.

Table 12–3

Input for T Flip-Flop

Q	Q^+	T
0	0	0
0	1	1
1	0	1
1	1	0

$$T = Q^+ \oplus Q$$

In general, the next-state map for flip-flop Q gives Q^+ as a function of Q and several other variables. The value written in each square of the map gives the value of Q^+, while the value of Q is determined from the row or column headings. Given the map for Q^+, we can then form the map for T_Q by simply putting a 1 in each square of the T_Q map for which Q^+ is different from Q. Thus, to form the T_A map in Fig. 12–4(b) from the A^+ map in Fig. 12–4(a), we place a 1 in the $ABC = 000$ square of T_A because $A = 0$ and $A^+ = 1$ for this square. We also place a 1 in the 111 square of T_A because $A = 1$ and $A^+ = 0$ for this square.

If we don't care what the next state of a flip-flop is for some combination of variables, we don't care what the flip-flop input is for that combination of variables. Therefore, if the Q^+ map has a don't care in some square, the T_Q map will have a don't care in the corresponding square. Thus, the T_A map has don't cares for $ABC = 001$, 101, and 110 since A^+ has don't cares in the corresponding squares.

Instead of transforming the Q^+ map into the T_Q map one square at a time, we can divide the Q^+ map into two halves corresponding to $Q = 0$ and $Q = 1$, and transform each half of the map. From Table 12–3, whenever $Q = 0$, $T = Q^+$, and whenever $Q = 1$, $T = (Q^+)'$. Therefore, to transform the Q^+ map into a T map, we copy the half for which $Q = 0$ and complement the half for which $Q = 1$, leaving the don't cares unchanged.

We will apply this method to transform the A^+, B^+, and C^+ maps for our counter shown in Fig. 12–4(a) into T maps. For the first map, A corresponds to Q (and A^+ to Q^+), so to get the T_A map from the A^+ map we complement the second column (where $A = 1$) and leave the rest of the map unchanged. Similarly, to get T_B from B^+ we complement the bottom half of the B map, and to get T_C from C^+ we complement the middle two rows. This yields the maps and equations of Fig. 12–4(b) and the network shown in Fig. 12–5. The input pulse (P) is

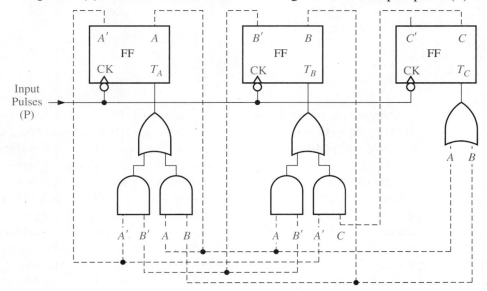

Figure 12–5
Counter Using T Flip-Flops

connected to the clock (CK) input of each flip-flop so that the flip-flops can change state only in response to an input pulse. The gate inputs connect directly to the corresponding flip-flop outputs as indicated by the dashed lines. To facilitate reading similar circuit diagrams, such connecting wires will be omitted in the remainder of the book.

The timing diagram of Fig. 12–6, derived by tracing signals through the network, verifies that the counter functions according to the state diagram of Fig. 12–3. For example, starting with $ABC = 000$, $T_A = 1$ and $T_B = T_C = 0$. Therefore, when the pulse comes along, only flip-flop A changes state, and the new state is 100. Then $T_A = 0$ and $T_B = T_C = 1$, so flip-flops B and C change state when the next pulse occurs, etc. Note that the flip-flops change state immediately following the input clock pulse.

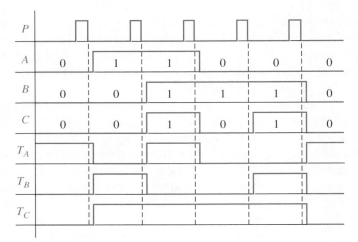

Figure 12–6
Timing Diagram for Fig. 12–5

Although the original state table for the counter (Table 12–2) is not completely specified, the next states of states 001, 101, and 110 have been specified in the process of completing the network design. For example, if the flip-flops are initially set to $A = 0$, $B = 0$, and $C = 1$ and a pulse is applied, tracing signals through the network shows that $T_A = T_B = 1$ so that the state will change to 111. This behavior is indicated by the dashed line in Fig. 12–7. Once state 111 is reached, successive pulses will cause the counter to continue in the original counting sequence as indicated on the state graph. When the power in a network is first turned on, the initial states of the flip-flops may be unpredictable. For this reason, all of the don't care states in a counter should be checked to make sure that they eventually lead into the main counting sequence unless a power-up reset is provided.

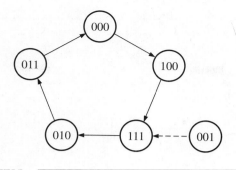

Figure 12–7
State Graph for Counter

In summary, the following procedure can be used to design a counter using T flip-flops:

1. Form a state table which gives the next flip-flop states for each combination of present flip-flop states.
2. Plot the next state maps from the table.
3. Plot a T input map for each flip-flop. When filling in the T_Q map, T_Q must be 1 whenever $Q^+ \neq Q$. This means that the T_Q map can be formed from the Q^+ map by complementing the $Q = 1$ half of the map and leaving the $Q = 0$ half unchanged.
4. Find the T input equations from the maps and realize the network.

12.3
Counter Design Using S-R Flip-Flops

The procedures used to design a counter with S-R flip-flops are similar to the procedures discussed in Sections 12.1 and 12.2. However, instead of deriving an input equation for each T flip-flop, S and R input equations must be derived. We will now develop methods for deriving these S and R flip-flop input equations.

Table 12–4(a) describes the behavior of the S-R flip-flop. Given S, R, and Q, we can determine Q^+ from this table. However, the problem we must solve is to determine S and R given the present state Q and the desired next state Q^+. If the present state of the flip-flop is $Q = 0$, and the desired next state is $Q^+ = 1$, a 1 must be applied to the S input to set the flip-flop to 1. If the present state is 1, and the desired next state is 0, a 1 must be applied to the R input to reset the flip-flop to 0. Restrictions on the flip-flop inputs require that $S = 0$ if $R = 1$, and $R = 0$ if $S = 1$. Thus when forming Table 12–4(b), the rows corresponding to $QQ^+ = 01$ and 10 are filled in with $SR = 10$ and 01, respectively. If the present state and next state are both 0, S must be 0 to prevent setting the flip-flop to 1. However, R may be either 0 or 1 since when $Q = 0$, $R = 1$ has no effect on the flip-flop state. Similarly, if the present state and next state are both 1, R must be

Table 12–4

S-R Flip-Flop Inputs

(a)				(b)				(c)			

S R Q	Q^+
0 0 0	0
0 0 1	1
0 1 0	0
0 1 1	0
1 0 0	1
1 0 1	1
1 1 0	$-$ } inputs not
1 1 1	$-$ } allowed

Q Q^+	S R
0 0	{ 0 0
	{ 0 1
0 1	1 0
1 0	0 1
1 1	{ 0 0
	{ 1 0

Q Q^+	S R
0 0	0 X
0 1	1 0
1 0	0 1
1 1	X 0

$$Q^+ = S + R'Q \qquad (SR = 0)$$

Table 12–5

A B C	A^+ B^+ C^+	S_A	R_A	S_B	R_B	S_C	R_C
0 0 0	1 0 0	1	0	0	X	0	X
0 0 1	– – –	X	X	X	X	X	X
0 1 0	0 1 1	0	X	X	0	1	0
0 1 1	0 0 0	0	X	0	1	0	1
1 0 0	1 1 1	X	0	1	0	1	0
1 0 1	– – –	X	X	X	X	X	X
1 1 0	– – –	X	X	X	X	X	X
1 1 1	0 1 0	0	1	X	0	0	1

0 to prevent resetting the flip-flop, but S may be either 0 or 1. The required S and R inputs are summarized in Table 12–4(b). Table 12–4(c) is the same as 12–4(b), except the alternative choices for R and S have been indicated by don't cares.

Next we will redesign the counter of Fig. 12–3 using S-R flip-flops. Table 12–2 is repeated in Table 12–5 with columns added for the S and R flip-flop inputs. These columns can be filled in using Table 12–4(c). For $ABC = 000$, $A = 0$ and $A^+ = 1$, so $S_A = 1$, $R_A = 0$. For $ABC = 010$ and 011, $A = 0$ and $A^+ = 0$, so $S_A = 0$ and $R_A = X$. For $ABC = 100$, $A = 1$ and $A^+ = 1$, so $S_A = X$ and $R_A = 0$. For row 111, $A = 1$ and $A^+ = 0$, so $S_A = 0$ and $R_A = 1$. For $ABC = 001$, 101, and 110, $A^+ = X$, so $S_A = R_A = X$. Similarly, the values of S_B and R_B are derived from the values of B and B^+, and S_C and R_C are derived from C and C^+. The resulting flip-flop input functions are mapped in Fig. 12–8(a).

It is generally faster and easier to derive the S-R flip-flop input maps directly from the next-state maps than to derive them from the state table as was done above. For each flip-flop, we will derive the S and R input maps from the next state (Q^+) map using Table 12–4(c) to determine the values for S and R. Just as we did for the T flip-flop, we will use the next-state maps for A^+, B^+, and C^+ in Fig. 12–4(a) as a starting point for deriving the S-R flip-flop input equations. For

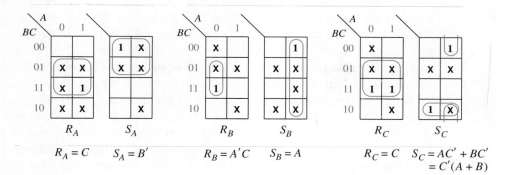

$$R_A = C \qquad S_A = B'$$

$$R_B = A'C \qquad S_B = A$$

$$R_C = C \qquad S_C = AC' + BC'$$
$$= C'(A + B)$$

(a) S-R flip-flop equations

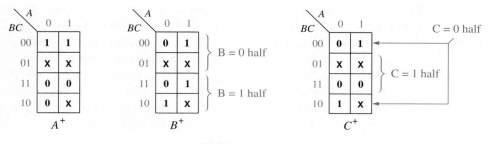

(b) Next state maps

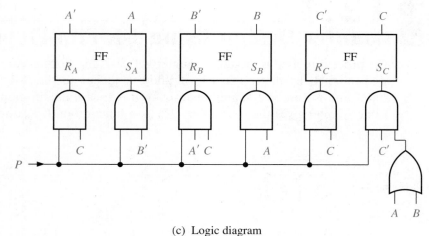

(c) Logic diagram

Figure 12–8
Counter of Fig. 12–3 Using S-R Flip-Flops

convenience, these maps are repeated in Fig. 12–8(b). We will consider one half
of each next state map at a time when deriving the input maps. We will start
with flip-flop A ($Q = A$ and $Q^+ = A^+$) and consider the $A = 0$ column of the
map. From Table 12–4(c), if $A = 0$ and $A^+ = 1$, then $S = 1$ and $R = 0$. Therefore,
for every square in the $A = 0$ column where $A^+ = 1$, we plot $S_A = 1$ and $R_A = 0$
(or blank) in the corresponding squares of the input maps. Similarly, for every
square in the $A = 0$ column where $A^+ = 0$, we plot $S_A = 0$ and $R_A = $X on the
input maps. For the $A = 1$ column, if $A^+ = 0$, we plot $S_A = 0$ and $R_A = 1$; if
$A^+ = 1$, we plot $S_A = $X and $R_A = 0$. Don't cares on the A^+ map remain don't
cares on the S_A and R_A maps, since if we don't care what the next state is, we
don't care what the input is. In a similar manner, we can derive the S_B and R_B
maps from the B^+ map by working with the $B = 0$ (top) half of the map and the
$B = 1$ (bottom) half of the map. As before, 1's are placed on the S or R map when
the flip-flop must be set or reset. S is a don't care if $Q = 1$ and no state change
is required, and $R = $X if $Q = 0$ and no state change is required. Finally, S_C and
R_C are derived from the C^+ map. Figure 12–8(c) shows the resulting network.
Note that the connecting wires between the flip-flop outputs and the gate inputs
have been omitted to facilitate reading the diagram. The input pulse (P) is ANDed
with each flip-flop input so that a change of state only occurs when a pulse is
received. This design assumes that the pulses are of the proper width so that the
state of the counter will change only once for each pulse.

12.4
Counter Design Using J-K Flip-Flops

The procedure used to design a counter with J-K flip-flops is very similar to that
used for S-R flip-flops. The J-K flip-flop is similar to the S-R flip-flop except
that J and K can be 1 simultaneously, in which case the flip-flop changes state.
Table 12–6(a) gives the next state (Q^+) as a function of J, K, and Q. Using this

Table 12–6
J-K Flip-Flop Inputs

(a)			(b)		(c)		
$J\ K\ Q$	Q^+		$Q\ Q^+$	$J\ K$	$Q\ Q^+$	$J\ K$	
0 0 0	0		0 0	0 0 / 0 1	0 0	0 X	
0 0 1	1				0 1	1 X	
0 1 0	0		0 1	1 0 / 1 1	1 0	X 1	
0 1 1	0				1 1	X 0	
1 0 0	1		1 0	0 1 / 1 1			
1 0 1	1				$Q^+ = JQ' + K'Q$		
1 1 0	1		1 1	0 0 / 1 0			
1 1 1	0						

table, we can derive the required input conditions for J and K when Q and Q^+ are given. Thus if a change from $Q = 0$ to $Q^+ = 1$ is required, either the flip-flop can be set to 1 by using $J = 1$ (and $K = 0$) or the state can be changed by using $J = K = 1$. In other words, J must be 1, but K is a don't care. Similarly, a state change from 1 to 0 can be accomplished by resetting the flip-flop with $K = 1$ (and $J = 0$) or by changing the flip-flop state with $J = K = 1$. When no state change is required, the inputs are the same as the corresponding inputs for the S-R flip-flops. The J-K input requirements are summarized in Tables 12–6(b) and 12–6(c).

Table 12–7

A B C	A^+ B^+ C^+	J_A	K_A	J_B	K_B	J_C	K_C
0 0 0	1 0 0	1	X	0	X	0	X
0 0 1	– – –	X	X	X	X	X	X
0 1 0	0 1 1	0	X	X	0	1	X
0 1 1	0 0 0	0	X	X	1	X	1
1 0 0	1 1 1	X	0	1	X	1	X
1 0 1	– – –	X	X	X	X	X	X
1 1 0	– – –	X	X	X	X	X	X
1 1 1	0 1 0	X	1	X	0	X	1

We will now redesign the counter of Fig. 12–3 using J-K flip-flops. Table 12–2 is repeated in Table 12–7 with columns added for the J and K flip-flop inputs. We will fill in these columns using Table 12–6(c). For $ABC = 000$, $A = 0$ and $A^+ = 1$, so $J_A = 1$ and $K_A = X$. For $ABC = 010$ and 011, $A = 0$ and $A^+ = 0$, so $J_A = 0$ and $K_A = X$. The remaining table entries are filled in similarly. The resulting J-K flip-flop input functions are plotted in Fig. 12–9(a).

The J-K flip-flop input maps can also be derived directly from the next state maps. From Table 12–6(c), when $Q = 0$, $J = Q^+$ and $K = X$; and when $Q = 1$, $J = X$ and $K = (Q^+)'$. Thus the $Q = 0$ half of the J map is the same as Q^+ and the $Q = 1$ half is all X's. The $Q = 0$ half of the K map is all X's and the $Q = 1$ half is the complement of Q^+. The next-state maps of Fig. 12–4(a) are repeated in Fig. 12–9(b). We will derive the J-K maps of Fig. 12–9(a) directly from these next-state maps using the method described above. The $A = 0$ half of the J_A map is the same as the corresponding half of the A^+ map, and the $A = 1$ half of the J_A map is all don't cares. The $A = 1$ half of the K_A map is the complement of the A^+ map, and the $A = 0$ half of the K_A map is all don't cares. We can derive the J_B and K_B maps from the B^+ map in a similar manner, and also derive J_C and K_C from the C^+ map. After deriving the flip-flop input equations from the J-K maps, we can draw the logic diagram of Fig. 12–9(c). Since clocked J-K flip-flops have been used, the input pulses go directly to the clock (CK) inputs on the flip-flops rather than into AND gates as in Fig. 12–8(c).

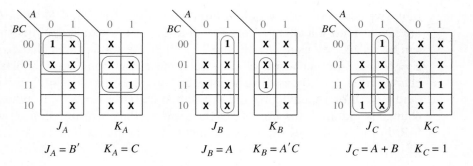

$$J_A = B' \quad K_A = C \qquad J_B = A \quad K_B = A'C \qquad J_C = A + B \quad K_C = 1$$

(a) J-K flip-flop input equations

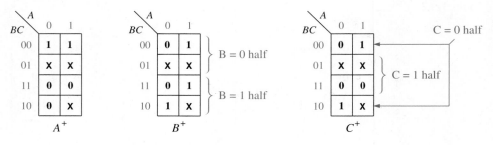

(b) Next state maps

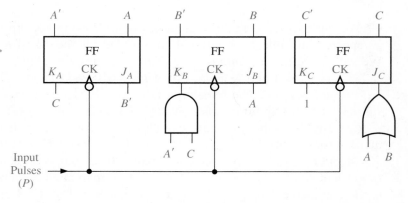

(c) Logic diagram (omitting the feedback lines)

Figure 12–9
Counter of Fig. 12–3 Using J-K Flip-Flops

12.5
Short-Cut Method for Deriving J-K Flip-Flop Input Equations

We will now show a method for reading the J-K input equations directly off the next-state maps without the necessity of plotting separate J and K maps. From Fig. 12–9, note that the functions J_A and K_A do not contain the variable A. Similarly, J_B and K_B are independent of B, and J_C and K_C are independent of C. It is true in general that the minimized J and K input equations for flip-flop Q will not depend on Q. This occurs because the $Q = 1$ half of the J map is all don't cares. Therefore, any 1 on the $Q = 0$ half of the J map can be combined with a don't care on the $Q = 1$ half to eliminate the variable Q. A similar situation holds for K since the $Q = 0$ half of the K map is all don't cares.

From Table 12–6(c), when $Q = 0$, $J = Q^+$. Therefore, since J is independent of Q, we can read J directly from the $Q = 0$ half of the Q^+ map. This is illustrated in Fig. 12–10. The next-state maps of Fig. 12–4(a) have been replotted with each 3-variable map divided into two 2-variable maps. For the A^+ map, the first column ($A = 0$) constitutes a map giving J_A as a function of B and C. Similarly, the top ($B = 0$) half of the B^+ map gives J_B as a function of A and C, and the top and bottom rows of the third map constitute a map for J_C. On each map, since J is independent of the variable Q, the values of Q ($Q = A$, B, or C) have been crossed out to facilitate reading the expression for J. The J functions read from these maps are the same as those read from the maps in Fig. 12–9(b).

From Table 12–6(c), when $Q = 1$, $K = (Q^+)'$ or $K' = Q^+$. Therefore, since K (and hence K') is independent of Q, the $Q = 1$ half of the Q^+ map serves as a map for K'. We can read K directly from this K' map by reading the 0's instead of the 1's. For example, the $A = 1$ column of the A^+ map in Fig. 12–10 constitutes a map for K'_A. By combining the 0 on this map with a don't care, we get $K_A = C$.

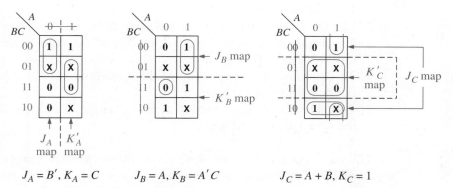

$$J_A = B', K_A = C \qquad J_B = A, K_B = A'C \qquad J_C = A + B, K_C = 1$$

Figure 12–10
Short-cut Method for Deriving J-K Equations

Similarly, we get K_B by reading the 0's on the bottom half of the B^+ map, and we get K_C from the middle two rows of the C^+ map. The K functions read from these maps are the same as those derived in Fig. 12–9.

We can prove the general validity of the short-cut method by starting with the characteristic equation for the J-K flip-flop:

$$Q^+ = JQ' + K'Q \tag{12–1}$$

If we assume that Q^+ is a function of Q and n other variables, then

$$Q^+ = F(Q, X_1, X_2, \ldots, X_n) \tag{12–2}$$

Therefore,

$$Q^+ = JQ' + K'Q = F(Q, X_1, X_2, \ldots, X_n) \tag{12–3}$$

Letting $Q = 0$ yields

$$Q^+|_{Q=0} = J = F(0, X_1, X_2, \ldots, X_n) \tag{12–4}$$

Letting $Q = 1$ yields

$$Q^+|_{Q=1} = K' = F(1, X_1, X_2, \ldots, X_n) \tag{12–5}$$

and

$$K = (Q^+|_{Q=1})' = F'(1, X_1, X_2, \ldots, X_n) \tag{12–6}$$

Given an $n + 1$ variable map for Q^+ which corresponds to (12–2), setting $Q = 0$ is equivalent to choosing the $Q = 0$ half of the map and eliminating Q. Equation (12–4) indicates that the resulting n-variable map is a map for J. Similarly, setting $Q = 1$ in (12–2) is equivalent to choosing the $Q = 1$ half of the Q^+ map and eliminating Q. The result is an n-variable map for K' as indicated by (12–5). Reading the 0's on the K' map then gives an expression for K.

In summary, the steps for determining the J and K inputs for flip-flop Q by the short-cut method are:

1. Plot the next-state (Q^+) map.
2. Identify the $Q = 0$ and $Q = 1$ halves of the map.
3. Cross out the values of Q on the edge of the map (since J and K are independent of Q).
4. To determine J as a function of the remaining variables, loop the *1's* on the $Q = 0$ half of the map.
5. To determine K as a function of the remaining variables, loop the *0's* on the $Q = 1$ half of the map.

The short-cut method described above offers two advantages over the standard method: (1) Plotting separate maps for J and K is unnecessary. (2) The number of variables to be worked with is reduced by 1 (since the J_Q and K_Q submaps are independent of Q).

12.6
Counter Design Using D Flip-Flops

For a D flip-flop, $Q^+ = D$, so the D input map is identical with the next-state map. Therefore, the equation for D can be read directly from the Q^+ map. For the counter of Fig. 12–3, the following equations can be read from the next-state maps shown in Fig. 12–4(a):

$$D_A = A^+ = B' \qquad D_B = B^+ = A + BC'$$
$$D_C = C^+ = AC' + BC' = C'(A + B)$$

This leads to the network shown in Fig. 12–11 using clocked D flip-flops.

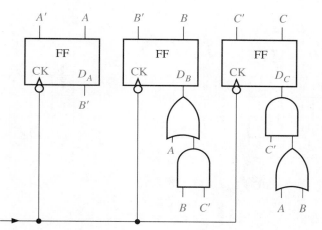

Figure 12–11
Counter of Fig. 12–3 Using D Flip-Flops

12.7
Design of a Code Converter

The same design technique used for counters can be applied to any sequential network which has a single pulse input to initiate state changes and no other external inputs. For example, consider the design of an 8-4-2-1 BCD to excess-3 code converter using four flip-flops. Initially, one of the BCD digits 0 through 9 is stored in the flip-flops. After a pulse is applied to the network, the corresponding excess-3 coded digit should appear in the flip-flops. The state table for the converter is given by Table 12–8. Figure 12–12 gives the next-state maps, the J-K input equations, and the resulting network. The short-cut method was used to derive the J-K equations. The circuitry for initially loading the BCD digit into the flip-flops has been omitted from the diagram.

Table 12–8
State Table for Code Converter

A B C D	A⁺ B⁺ C⁺ D⁺
0 0 0 0	0 0 1 1
0 0 0 1	0 1 0 0
0 0 1 0	0 1 0 1
0 0 1 1	0 1 1 0
0 1 0 0	0 1 1 1
0 1 0 1	1 0 0 0
0 1 1 0	1 0 0 1
0 1 1 1	1 0 1 0
1 0 0 0	1 0 1 1
1 0 0 1	1 1 0 0

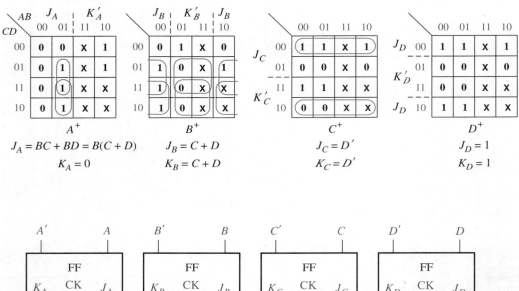

$$J_A = BC + BD = B(C + D) \qquad J_B = C + D \qquad J_C = D' \qquad J_D = 1$$
$$K_A = 0 \qquad\qquad K_B = C + D \qquad K_C = D' \qquad K_D = 1$$

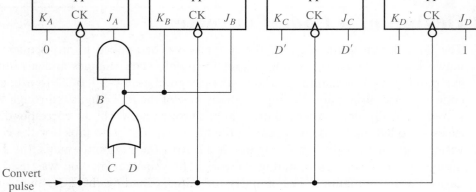

Figure 12–12
BCD to Excess-3 Code Converter

12.8
Shift Registers

A shift register is a group of flip-flops in which a binary number can be stored. This number can be shifted to the left or right when a shift pulse is applied. Bits shifted out one end of the register may be lost, or if the shift register is of cyclic type, bits shifted out one end are shifted back in the other end. Figure 12–13(a) illustrates a 4-bit cyclic right-shift register constructed from S-R flip-flops. If the initial contents of the register is 0111, after one pulse the contents is 1011. After a second pulse, the state is 1101, then 1110, and the fourth pulse returns the register to the initial 0111 state. Note that the outputs of flip-flop A are fed into the inputs of flip-flop B through AND gates. If $A = 1$, flip-flop B is set to 1 by the shift pulse; if $A = 0$, flip-flop B is reset to 0 by the shift pulse. The other flip-flops are connected in a similar manner. The AND gates can be eliminated if clocked flip-flops are used as in Fig. 12–13(b).

To assure proper operation of the shift register of Fig. 12–13(a), the change of state of the flip-flops must be delayed until the shift pulse is completed; otherwise, several shifts could occur for one pulse. The necessary delay can be built into the flip-flop, in which case the shift pulse width must be less than the flip-flop delay. Alternately, the flip-flop can be designed to respond to the trailing edge

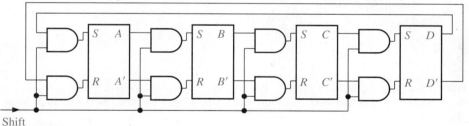

Shift
pulses   (a)

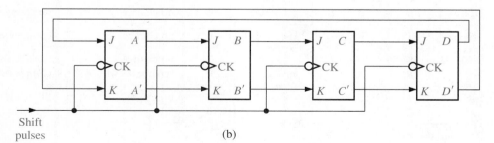

Shift
pulses   (b)

Figure 12–13
Cyclic Right-Shift Registers

of the pulse, in which case the pulse width is not important. In any case, the operation of the flip-flops in the shift register is synchronized by the common shift pulse so that the flip-flops change state simultaneously after the pulse is over.

12.9
Derivation of Flip-Flop Input Equations—Summary

The input equation for the flip-flops in a sequential network may be derived from the next-state equations by using truth tables or by using Karnaugh maps. For networks with three to five variables it is convenient to first plot maps for the next-state equations and then transform these maps into maps for the flip-flop inputs.

Given the present state of a flip-flop (Q) and the desired next state (Q^+), Table 12–9 gives the required inputs for various types of flip-flops. For the D flip-flop, the input is the same as the next state. For the T flip-flop, the input is 1 whenever a state change is required. For the S-R flip-flop, S is 1 whenever the flip-flop must be set to 1 and R is 1 when it must be reset to 0. We don't care what S is if the flip-flop state is 1 and must remain 1; we don't care what R is if the flip-flop state is 0 and must remain 0. For a J-K flip-flop, the J and K inputs are the same as S and R, respectively, except that when one input is 1 the other input is X. This difference arises because $S = R = 1$ is not allowed, but $J = K = 1$ causes a change of state.

Table 12–9

Determination of Flip-Flop Input Equations from Next-State Equations Using Karnaugh Maps

Type of Flip-Flop	Input	$Q = 0$		$Q = 1$		Rules for Forming Input Map From Next State Map*	
		$Q^+ = 0$	$Q^+ = 1$	$Q^+ = 0$	$Q^+ = 1$	$Q = 0$ Half of Map	$Q = 1$ Half of Map
Delay	D	0	1	0	1	no change	no change
Trigger	T	0	1	1	0	no change	complement
Set-Reset	S	0	1	0	X	no change	replace 1's with X's**
	R	X	0	1	0	replace 0's with X's**	complement
J-K	J	0	1	X	X	no change	fill in with X's
	K	X	X	1	0	fill in with X's	complement

Q^+ means the next state of Q
X is a don't care
* Always copy X's from the next state map onto the input maps first.
** Fill in the remaining squares with 0's.

EXAMPLE (illustrating the use of Table 12–9):

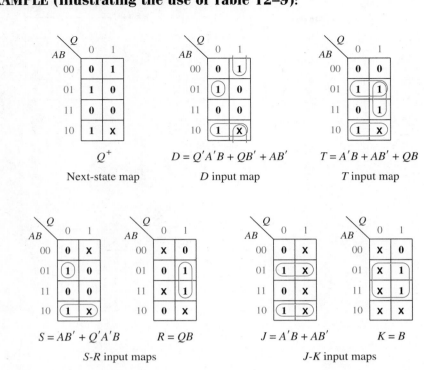

Next-state map

$$Q^+$$

$$D = Q'A'B + QB' + AB'$$

D input map

$$T = A'B + AB' + QB$$

T input map

$$S = AB' + Q'A'B \qquad R = QB$$

S-R input maps

$$J = A'B + AB' \qquad K = B$$

J-K input maps

Table 12–9 summarizes the rules for transforming next-state maps into flip-flop input maps. Before applying these rules, we must copy any don't cares from the next state maps onto the input maps. Then we must work with the $Q = 0$ and $Q = 1$ halves of each next-state map separately. The rules given in Table 12–9 are easily derived by comparing the values of Q^+ with the corresponding input values. For example, in the $Q = 0$ column of the table, we see that J is the same as Q^+, so the $Q = 0$ half of the J map is the same as the Q^+ map. In the $Q = 1$ column, $J = \mathsf{X}$ (independent of Q^+), so we fill in the $Q = 1$ half of the J map with X's.

For the S-R flip-flop, note that when $Q = 0$, $R = \mathsf{X}$ if $Q^+ = 0$; and when $Q = 1$, $R = 1$ if $Q^+ = 0$. Therefore, to form the R map from the Q^+ map, replace 0's with X's on the $Q = 0$ half of the map and replace 0's with 1's on the $Q = 1$ half (and fill in 0's for the remaining entries). Similarly, to form the S map from the Q^+ map, copy the 1's on the $Q = 0$ half of the map, and replace the 1's with X's on the $Q = 1$ half.

Examples of deriving 4-variable input maps are given in Fig. 12–14. In each case, Q_i represents the flip-flop for which input equations are being derived and A, B, and C represent other variables on which the next state depends. As shown in Fig. 12–14(a), a 1 is placed on the T_1 map whenever Q_1 must change state. In

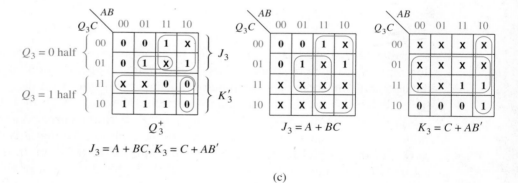

Figure 12–14
Derivation of Flip-Flop Input Equations Using
4-Variable Maps

Fig. 12–14(b), 1's are placed on the $Q_2 = 0$ half of the S_2 map whenever Q_2 must be set to 1, and 1's are placed on the $Q_2 = 1$ half of the R_2 map whenever Q_2 must be reset. Figure 12–14(c) illustrates derivation of J_3 and K_3 both by using separate J and K maps and by using the short-cut method. In the latter case, plotting separate J and K maps is not necessary because J_3 is read directly from the $Q_3 = 0$ half of the Q_3^+ map, and K_3 is read directly from the 0's of the $Q_3 = 1$ half. As will be seen in Unit 14, the methods used to derive flip-flop input equations for counters are easily extended to general sequential networks.

The procedures for deriving flip-flop input equations discussed in this unit can be extended to other types of flip-flops. If we want to derive input equations for a different type of flip-flop, the first step is to construct a table which gives the next state (Q^+) as a function of the present state (Q) and the flip-flop inputs. From this table, we can construct another table which gives the required flip-flop input combinations for each of the four possible pairs of values of Q and Q^+. Then using this table, we can plot a Karnaugh map for each input function and derive minimum expressions from the maps.

PROBLEMS

12.1 Design a counter which counts in the following sequence:
0000, 1000, 1100, 1010, 1110, 0001, 1001, 1101, 1011, 1111, 0000, . . .
(a) Use clocked T flip-flops, AND gates, and OR gates.
(b) Use S-R flip-flops, AND gates, and OR gates.
(c) Use clocked J-K flip-flops and NAND gates.
(d) Use clocked D flip-flops and NOR gates.

12.2 Work Problem 12.1 using the sequence:
0000, 0010, 0100, 0110, 1000, 0001, 0011, 0101, 0111, 1101, 0000, . . .

12.3 Work Problem 12.1 using the sequence:
0000, 1111, 1011, 1101, 1001, 0001, 1110, 1010, 1100, 1000, 0000, . . .

12.4 Work Problem 12.1 using the sequence:
0000, 1101, 0111, 0101, 0011, 0001, 1000, 0110, 0100, 0010, 0000, . . .

12.5 By tracing signals through the network, draw a timing diagram for the counter of Fig. 12–11 showing P, A, B, C, D_A, D_B, and D_C.

12.6 Design a decade counter which counts in the sequence:
0000, 0001, 0010, 0011, 0100, 0101, 0110, 0111, 1000, 1001, 0000, . . .
(a) Use clocked J-K flip-flops.
(b) Use S-R flip-flops.
(c) Use clocked T flip-flops.
(d) Draw a complete state diagram for the counter of (a) showing what happens when the counter is started in each of the "unused" states.

12.7 Repeat Problem 12.6 for the sequence:
0000, 1001, 1000, 0111, 0110, 0101, 0100, 0011, 0010, 0001, 0000, . . .

12.8 Redesign the network of Fig. 12–12 using
(a) unclocked T flip-flops   (b) clocked D flip-flops

12.9   Design a 3-bit counter which counts in the sequence:
001, 011, 010, 110, 111, 101, 100, 001, . . .
(a) Use clocked D flip-flops.
(b) Use clocked J-K flip-flops.
(c) Use clocked T flip-flops.
(d) Use S-R flip-flops.
(e) What will happen if the counter of (a) is started in state 000?

12.10   Repeat Problem 12.9 for the sequence:
001, 100, 101, 111, 110, 010, 011, 001, . . .

12.11   Design a decade counter which counts in the 6-3-1-1 code sequence (see Table 1–1).
(a) Use clocked D flip-flops.
(b) Use clocked T flip-flops.
(c) Use clocked J-K flip-flops.
(d) What will happen if the counter of (c) is started in state 1101?

12.12   Repeat Problem 12.11 for a Gray-code counter.

12.13   An M-N flip-flop works as follows:
If $MN = 00$, the next state of the flip-flop is 0.
If $MN = 01$, the next state of the flip-flop is the same as the present state.
If $MN = 10$, the next state of the flip-flop is the complement of the present state.
If $MN = 11$, the next state of the flip-flop is 1.
(a) Complete the following table (use don't cares when possible):

Present State Q	Next State Q^+	M	N
0	0		
0	1		
1	0		
1	1		

(b) Using the above table and Karnaugh maps, derive and minimize the input equations for a counter composed of 3 M-N flip-flops which counts in the following sequence:

$$ABC = 000, 001, 011, 111, 101, 100, 000, . . .$$

12.14   An L-M flip-flop works as follows:
If $LM = 00$, the next state of the flip-flop is 1.
If $LM = 01$, the next state of the flip-flop is the same as the present state.
If $LM = 10$, the next state of the flip-flop is the complement of the present state.
If $LM = 11$, the next state of the flip-flop is 0.
(a) Complete a table similar to the one in Problem 12.13(a).
(b) Work Problem 12.13(b) using 3 L-M flip-flops and the counting sequence

$$ABC = 000, 100, 101, 111, 011, 001, 000, . . .$$

12.15 A network diagram for a K-G flip-flop follows.

Q Q^+	K	G
0 0		
0 1		
1 0		
1 1		

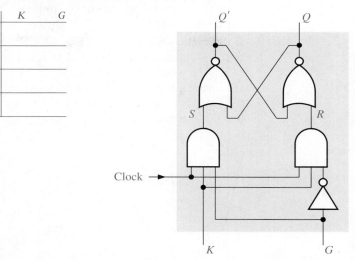

(a) Find an equation which gives the next state of the flip-flop (that is, the state after the clock pulse has occurred) in terms of the present state (Q) and the inputs (K and G).

(b) Complete the table, giving all possible pairs of values for K and G in each case (don't use don't cares).

(c) A logic network contains several K-G flip-flops. The desired next state of one of the K-G flip-flops is given by $Q^+ = XY + Q$, where X and Y are outputs of other flip-flops in the network. Find K and G in terms of X, Y, and Q. (Several different solutions are possible for K and G. Find at least two different solutions.)

12.16 A sequential network contains a register of four flip-flops. Initially a binary number N ($0000 \leqslant N \leqslant 1001$) is stored in the flip-flops. After a single input pulse is applied to the network, the register should contain $N + 0101$. In other words, the function of the sequential network is to add 5 to the contents of a 4-bit register. Design the network using J-K flip-flops.

12.17 Repeat Problem 12.16 for a network that adds 3 to the contents of the register (initially $0000 \leqslant N \leqslant 1100$).

12.18 A sequential network has two registers. Each register is composed of four clocked (master-slave) J-K flip-flops. The flip-flops in the first register are labeled A, B, C, and D; the flip-flops in the second register are labeled E, F, G, and H.

(a) Show how to interconnect the flip-flops so that a single pulse (P) will interchange the contents of the two registers; that is, after the pulse the new value of A should be the value of E before the pulse and the new value of E should be the value of A before the pulse, and similarly for B and F, C and G, and D and H.

(b) Show the required connections if S-R flip-flops and AND gates are used instead of clocked J-K flip flops. What problem will arise if flip-flops of the type shown in Fig. 11–6(a) are used with no added delay? If S-R flip-flops with added delay as seen in Fig. 11–12(b) are used, what restrictions must be placed on the pulse width to assure proper operation of the network?

12.19 If the cyclic shift register of Fig. 12–13(b) is changed so that D is connected to the K input of flip-flop A and D' is connected to J, determine the sequence of register states.

(a) Draw a complete state graph showing all states.

(b) Derive a complete state table showing all states.

(c) What is the sequence of states starting with $ABCD = 0000$?

13

Analysis of Clocked Sequential Networks

OBJECTIVES

1. Analyze a sequential network by signal tracing.

2. Given a sequential network, write the next-state equations for the flip-flops and derive the state graph or state table. Using the state graph, determine the state sequence and output sequence for a given input sequence.

3. Explain the difference between a Mealy machine and a Moore machine.

4. Given a state table, construct the corresponding state graph, and conversely.

5. Given a sequential network or a state table and an input sequence, draw a timing chart for the network. Determine the output sequence from the timing chart, neglecting any "false" outputs.

6. Draw a general model for a clocked Mealy or Moore sequential network. Explain the operation of the network in terms of these models. Explain why a clock pulse is needed to ensure proper operation of the network.

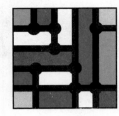

STUDY GUIDE

1. Study Section 13.1, *A Sequential Parity Checker*.

   (a) Explain how parity can be used for error detection.

   (b) Verify that the parity checker (Fig. 13–4) will produce the output waveform given in Fig. 13–2 when the input waveform is as shown.

2. Study Section 13.2, *Analysis by Signal Tracing and Timing Charts*.

   (a) What is the difference between a Mealy machine and a Moore machine?

   (b) For normal operation of clocked sequential networks of the types discussed in this section, when should the inputs be changed?

   When do the flip-flops change state?

   At what times can the output change for a Moore network?

   At what times can the output change for a Mealy network?

   (c) At what time (with respect to the clock) should the output of a Mealy network be read?

(d) Why can false outputs appear in a Mealy network and not in a Moore network?

What can be done to eliminate the false outputs?

If the output of a Mealy network is used as an input to another Mealy network synchronized by the same clock pulse, will the false outputs cause any problem? Explain.

(e) Examine the timing diagram of Fig. 13–8. Note there are two types of false outputs. A false 0 output occurs if Z is 1 during two successive clock pulses and Z goes to 0 between the clock pulses. A false 1 output occurs if Z is 0 during two successive clock pulses and Z goes to 1 between the clock pulses. When the output is different during two successive clock pulses, the output may be temporarily incorrect immediately following the clock pulse but before the input has changed to its next value. In this case, we will not say that a false output has occurred since the sequence of outputs is still correct.

3. Study Section 13.3, *State Tables and Graphs*.

   (a) In Equations (13–1) through (13–4), at what time (with respect to the clock pulse) is the right-hand side evaluated?

   What does Q^+ mean?

   (b) Derive the timing chart of Fig. 13–6 using Table 13–2(a).

   (c) What is the difference between the state graphs for Mealy and Moore machines?

(d) For a state table, Table 13–3(b) for example, what do the terms "*present state*", "*next* state", and "*present* output" mean with respect to the clock pulse?

(e) Why does a Moore state table have only one output column?

4. The following timing chart was derived from the network of Fig. 13–7.

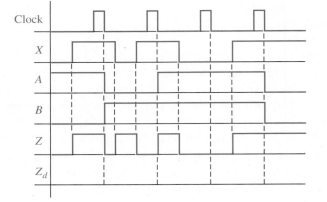

(a) Noting that extra input changes which occur between clock pulses cannot affect the state of the network, what is the effective input sequence seen by the flip-flops in the network?

(b) Using Table 13–3, verify the waveforms given for *A*, *B*, and *Z*.

(c) Indicate any false outputs. What is the "correct" output sequence from the network?

(d) Using the effective input sequence from (a), determine the output sequence from the state graph (Fig. 13–11). This output sequence should be the same as your answer to (c). Why can't false outputs be determined from the state graph?

(e) The output Z is fed into a clocked D flip-flop using the same clock (CK) as the network. Sketch the waveform for Z_d. Does Z_d have any false outputs?

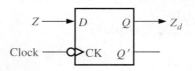

(f) Starting with Fig. 13–11, construct the corresponding state table. Verify that your answer is the same as Table 13–3(b). Note that the output label on a given arrow of the graph is associated with the state from which the arrow originates.

(g) Assume that the flip-flops in Fig. 13–7 are changed to flip-flops which trigger on the rising edge of the clock; that is, the inversion circles are removed from the clock inputs. Also, the clock waveform in Fig. 13–8 is replaced with

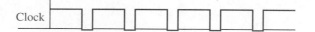

The input waveform is left unchanged. What changes, if any, would occur in the remainder of the timing diagram? Explain.

5. Consider the following state tables:

P.S.	Mealy N.S. X = 0	1	Z X = 0	1
S_0	S_1	S_0	0	0
S_1	S_0	S_2	1	0
S_2	S_0	S_0	1	0

P.S.	Moore N.S. X = 0	1	Z
S_0	S_1	S_0	0
S_1	S_3	S_2	0
S_2	S_3	S_0	0
S_3	S_3	S_0	1

(a) Draw the corresponding state graphs.

(b) Show that the same output sequence is obtained from both state graphs when the input sequence is 010 (ignore the initial output for the Moore network).

(c) Using the state tables, complete the following timing diagrams for the two networks. Note that the Mealy network has a false output, but the Moore does not. Also note that the output from the Moore network is delayed with respect to the Mealy.

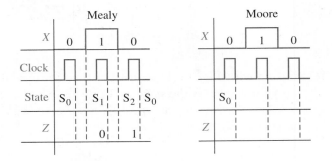

6. Study Section 13.4, *General Models for Sequential Networks*.

(a) A Mealy sequential network has the form shown below. The combinational network realizes the following equations:

$$Q_1^+ = X_1'Q_1 + X_1Q_1'Q_2' \qquad Z_1 = X_1Q_1$$
$$Q_2^+ = X_1Q_2' + X_2'Q_1 \qquad Z_2 = X_1'Q_1 + X_2Q_2'$$

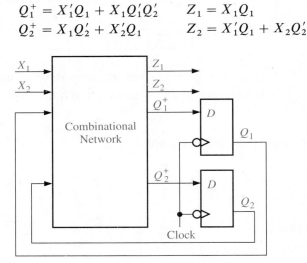

Initially, $X_1 = X_2 = 1$ and $Q_1 = Q_2 = 0$ as shown.

(1) Before the clock occurs, show the values of the four combinational network outputs on the above diagram and on the timing chart given below.

(2) Show the signal values on the network and timing chart immediately after the clock pulse.

(3) Show any further changes in signal values which will occur after the new values of Q_1 and Q_2 have propagated through the network.

(4) Next change X_1 to 0 and repeat steps (1), (2), and (3). Show values for each step on the network and on the timing chart.

(5) Next change the inputs to $X_1 = 1$ and $X_2 = 0$ and repeat steps (1), (2), and (3).

(6) Change X_2 to 1 and repeat.

(b) Draw a block diagram for a general model of a Mealy network using J-K flip-flops as memory elements. If the network has n output variables and k flip-flops, how many outputs will the combinational subnetwork have?

(c) Why does use of a clock pulse prevent timing problems?

(d) In Equations (13–5) and (13–6), what do the symbols δ and λ mean?

Equation (13–6) is for a Mealy network. What is the corresponding equation for a Moore network?

(e) For Table 13–5,

$\delta(S_3, 1) =$ _____ $\lambda(S_3, 1) =$ _____

$\delta(S_1, 2) =$ _____ $\lambda(S_1, 2) =$ _____

7. Work Programmed Exercise 13.1.

8. Work Problems 13.2 through 13.5.

9. When you are satisfied that you can meet the objectives, take the readiness test.

Analysis of Clocked Sequential Networks

The sequential networks which we have considered up to this point have had no inputs other than an input pulse or clock pulse which causes the network to change state. We will now consider sequential networks which have additional inputs. In general, the sequence of outputs and the sequence of flip-flop states for such networks will depend on the input sequence which is applied to the network. Given a sequential network and an input sequence, we can analyze the network to determine the flip-flop state sequence and the output sequence by tracing the 0 and 1 signals through the network. Although signal tracing may be adequate for small networks, for larger networks it is better to construct a state graph or state table which represents the behavior of the network. Then we can determine the output and state sequences from the graph or table. Such graphs and tables are also useful for the design of sequential networks.

In this chapter we will also study the timing relationships between the inputs, clock pulse, and outputs for sequential networks by constructing timing diagrams. These timing relationships are very important when a sequential network is used as part of a larger digital system. After analyzing several specific sequential networks, we will discuss a general model for a sequential network which consists of a combinational network together with flip-flops which serve as "memory".

13.1
A Sequential Parity Checker

When binary data is transmitted or stored, an extra bit (called a parity bit) is frequently added for purposes of error detection. For example, if data is being transmitted in groups of 7 bits, an eighth bit can be added to each group of 7 bits such that the total number of ones in each block of 8 bits is odd. When the total number of 1 bits in the block is odd, we say that the parity is odd. (Alternately, the parity bit could be chosen such that the total number of 1's in the block is even, in which case we would have even parity.) Some examples of 8-bit words with odd parity are:

seven data bits	parity bit
0000000	1
0000001	0
0110110	1
1010101	1
0111000	0

If any single bit in the 8-bit word is changed from 0 to 1 or from 1 to 0, the parity is no longer odd. Thus, if any single bit error occurs in transmission of a word with odd parity, the presence of this error can be detected because the number of 1 bits in the word has been changed from odd to even.

As a simple example of a sequential network which has one input in addition to the clock, we will design a parity checker for serial data. (Serial implies that the data enters the network sequentially, one bit at a time.) This network has the form shown in Fig. 13–1.

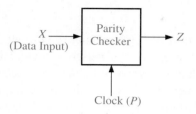

Figure 13–1
Block Diagram for Parity Checker

When a sequence of 0's and 1's is applied to the X input, the output of the network should be $Z = 1$ if the total number of 1 inputs received is odd; that is, the output should be 1 if the input parity is odd. Thus, if data which originally had odd parity is transmitted to the network, a final output of $Z = 0$ indicates that an error in transmission has occurred.

We will assume that the X input is synchronized with the clock and changes only between clock pulses. The value of X is determined at the time the clock is high. The clock input is necessary in order to distinguish consecutive 0's or consecutive 1's on the X input. Typical input and output waveforms are shown in Fig. 13–2.

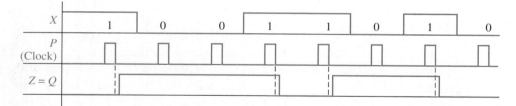

Figure 13–2
Waveforms for Parity Checker

We will start the design by constructing a state graph (Fig. 13–3). The sequential network must "remember" whether the total number of 1 inputs received is even or odd; therefore, only two states are required. We will designate these states as S_0 and S_1, corresponding respectively to an even number of 1's received and an odd number of 1's received. We will start the network in state S_0 since initially zero 1's have been received and zero is an even number. As

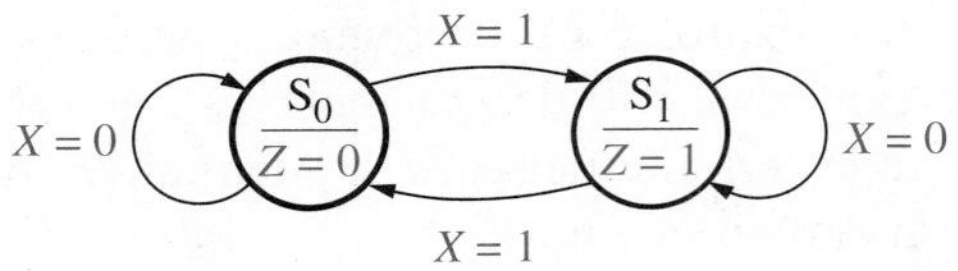

$$X = 0 \quad \overbrace{\boxed{\frac{S_0}{Z=0}}}^{X=1} \quad \underbrace{\boxed{\frac{S_1}{Z=1}}}_{X=1} \quad X=0$$

Figure 13–3
State Graph for Parity Checker

indicated in Fig. 13–3, if the network is in state S_0 (even number of 1's received) and $X = 0$ is received, the network must stay in S_0 since the number of 1's received is still even. However, if $X = 1$ is received, the network goes to state S_1 since the number of 1's received is then odd. Similarly, if the network is in state S_1 (odd number of 1's received) a 0 input causes no state change, but a 1 causes a change to S_0 since the number of 1's received is then even. The output Z should be 1 whenever the network is in state S_1 (odd number of 1's received). The output is listed below the state on the state graph.

Table 13–1(a) gives the same information as the state graph in tabular form. For example, the table shows that if the present state is S_0, the output is $Z = 0$, and if the input is $X = 1$, the next state will be S_1.

Table 13–1
State Table for Parity Checker

(a)

Present State	Next State $X=0$	$X=1$	Present Output
S_0	S_0	S_1	0
S_1	S_1	S_0	1

(b)

Q	Q^+ $X=0$	$X=1$	T $X=0$	$X=1$	Z
0	0	1	0	1	0
1	1	0	0	1	1

Since only two states are required, a single flip-flop (Q) will suffice. We will let $Q = 0$ correspond to state S_0 and $Q = 1$ correspond to S_1. We can then set up a table which shows the next state of flip-flop Q as a function of the present state and X. If we use a T flip-flop, T must be 1 whenever Q and Q^+ differ. From Table 13–1(b), the T input must be 1 whenever $X = 1$. Figure 13–4 shows the resulting network.

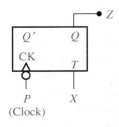

Figure 13–4

(Clock)

Figure 13–2 shows the output waveform for the network. When $X = 1$, the flip-flop changes state after the falling edge of the clock pulse. Note that the final value of Z is 0 since an even number of 1's was received. If the number of 1's received had been odd, the final value of Z would be 1. In this case, it would be necessary to reset the flip-flop to the proper initial state ($Q = 0$) before checking the parity of another input sequence.

13.2
Analysis by Signal Tracing and Timing Charts

In this section we will analyze clocked sequential networks to find the output sequence resulting from a given input sequence by tracing 0 and 1 signals through the network. The basic procedure is as follows:

1. Assume an initial state of the flip-flops (all flip-flops reset to 0 unless otherwise specified).
2. For the first input in the given sequence, determine the network output(s) and flip-flop inputs.
3. Apply the clock pulse to the flip-flops and determine the new set of flip-flop states.
4. Determine the output(s) which corresponds to the new states.
5. Repeat 2, 3, and 4 for each input in the given sequence.

As we carry out the analysis, we will construct a timing chart which shows the relationship between the input signal, clock pulse, flip-flop states, and network output. We have already seen how to construct timing charts for flip-flops (Unit 11) and counters (Unit 12).

Unless otherwise specified, we will use one of the following two types of flip-flops in this unit:

1. Flip-flops that change state on the falling edge of the clock pulse.
2. Flip-flops that change state in response to a pulse of a specified width. In this case we assume that the response time of the flip-flop is greater than the clock pulse width.

In either case, the sequential network will change state shortly after the clock pulse is over, that is, after the clock goes from high to low. The network inputs will normally be changed between clock pulses when the clock pulse is low. The output may change at the time the flip-flops change state or at the time the input changes depending on the type of network.

If we use flip-flops which change state on the rising edge of the clock pulse instead of the falling edge, operation of the sequential network will be similar except that the state change occurs after the clock pulse goes from low to high. In this case, the inputs will normally be changed when the clock pulse is high.

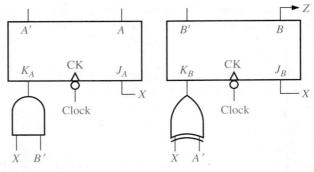

Figure 13–5
Moore Sequential Network to be Analyzed

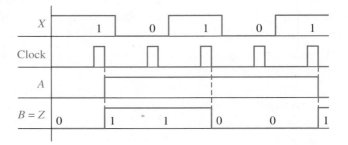

Figure 13–6
Timing Chart for Fig. 13–5

Two types of clocked sequential networks will be considered—those in which the output depends only on the present state of the flip-flops and those in which the output depends on both the present state of the flip-flops and on the value of the network inputs. If the output of a sequential network is a function of the present state only (as in Figs. 13–4 and 13–5), the network is often referred to as a *Moore machine*. The state graph for a Moore machine has the output associated with the state (as in Figs. 13–3 and 13–9). If the output is a function of both the present state and the input (as in Figs. 13–7 and 13–8), the network is referred to as a *Mealy machine*. The state graph for a Mealy machine has the output associated with the arrow going between states (as in Fig. 13–11).

As an example of a Moore network, we will analyze Fig. 13–5 using an input sequence $X = 10101$. The input is assumed to change between clock pulses and the initial state is $A = B = 0$ as shown in Fig. 13–6. Since Z is a function only of the present state (in this case, $Z = B$), the output will only change when the state changes. If $X = 1$, $J_A = K_A = J_B = 1$, and the state will change to $A = B = 1$ after the first clock pulse.[1] Then X is changed to 0, and no change

---

[1] Actually, there will be a short propagation delay between the falling edge of the clock pulse and the time the flip-flops change state. Such small delays have been omitted from Fig. 13–6 and other timing diagrams in this and subsequent units.

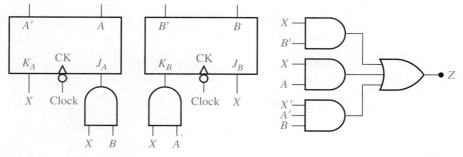

Figure 13–7
Mealy Sequential Network to be Analyzed

of state or output will occur with the second clock pulse since all flip-flop inputs are 0. Then X is changed to 1, and $J_A = J_B = K_B = 1$, so the next clock pulse causes B to become 0. When the fourth clock pulse occurs, $X = 0$ and no change of state or output takes place. Then, with $X = 1$, $J_A = K_A = K_B = J_B = 1$, and the fifth clock pulse causes both flip-flops to change state so that the final state is $A = 0$, $B = 1$. The input, state, and output sequences are plotted on the timing chart of Fig. 13–6 and are also listed below:

$$X = 1 \ 0 \ 1 \ 0 \ 1$$
$$A = 0 \ 1 \ 1 \ 1 \ 1 \ 0$$
$$B = 0 \ 1 \ 1 \ 0 \ 0 \ 1$$
$$Z = (0) \ 1 \ 1 \ 0 \ 0 \ 1$$

If the initial 0 output is ignored the output sequence is $Z = 11001$. Note that for the *Moore* network, the output which results from application of a given input does not appear until after the clock pulse; therefore, the output sequence is displaced in time with respect to the input sequence.

As an example of a Mealy network, we will analyze Fig. 13–7 and construct a timing chart using the input sequence $X = 10101$. The input is assumed to change between clock pulses as shown in Fig. 13–8. In this example, the output depends on both the input (X) and the flip-flop states (A and B), so Z may change either when the input changes or when the flip-flops change state. Initially, assume that the flip-flop states are $A = 0$, $B = 0$. If $X = 1$, the output is $Z = 1$ and $J_B = K_A = 1$. After the falling edge of the first clock pulse, B changes to 1 so Z changes to 0. If the input is changed to $X = 0$, Z will change back to 1. All flip-flop inputs are then 0, so no state change occurs with the second clock pulse. When X is changed to 1, Z becomes 0 and $J_A = K_A = J_B = 1$. A changes to 1 on the falling edge of the third clock pulse, at which time Z changes to 1. Next, X is changed to 0 so Z becomes 0 and no state change occurs with the fourth clock pulse. Then X is changed to 1 and Z becomes 1. Since $J_A = K_A = J_B = K_B = 1$, the fifth clock pulse resets the network to the initial state. The input, state, and output sequences are plotted on the timing chart of Fig. 13–8 and are also listed

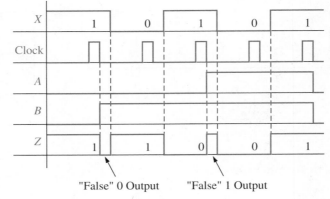

Figure 13–8
Timing Chart for Network of Fig. 13–7

below:

$$X = 1 \quad 0 \quad 1 \quad 0 \quad 1$$
$$A = 0 \quad 0 \quad 0 \quad 1 \quad 1 \quad 0$$
$$B = 0 \quad 1 \quad 1 \quad 1 \quad 1 \quad 0$$
$$Z = 1(0)1 \quad 0(1)0 \quad 1 \qquad \text{("false" outputs are indicated in parentheses)}$$

Careful interpretation of the output waveform (Z) of the Mealy network is necessary. For a clocked sequential network of this type, the value of the input during (and immediately preceding) the clock pulse determines the next state of the flip-flops. Extra input changes which might occur between clock pulses cannot affect the state of the flip-flops. In a similar manner, the output is only of interest during (and immediately preceding) the clock pulse, and extra output changes which might occur between clock pulses should be ignored. After the network has changed state and before the input is changed, the output may assume a "false" value as indicated on the timing chart. This "false" value arises because the network has assumed a new state but the old input associated with the previous state is still present.

Two types of "false" outputs can occur as indicated in Fig. 13–8. In one case the output Z momentarily goes to 0 when it is expected to remain 1; in the other case the output Z momentarily goes to 1 when it is expected to remain 0. These "false" outputs are often referred to as "glitches" and "spikes". In both cases, two changes of output occur when no change is expected. Ignoring the "false" outputs, by reading the output only during the clock pulse, the output sequence for the network is $Z = 11001$. The false outputs could be eliminated if the input X was allowed to change only at the same time as the falling edge of the clock pulse. If the output of the network is fed into a second sequential network which uses the same clock, the "false" outputs will not cause any problem because the inputs to the second network can cause a change of state only when a clock pulse occurs. Since the output of a Moore network can change state only when the flip-flops change state and not when the input changes, no false outputs can appear in a Moore network.

For the *Mealy* network, the output which corresponds to a given input appears immediately following application of that input. Since the correct output appears before the clock pulse, the output sequence is *not* displaced in time with respect to the input sequence as was the case for the Moore network.

13.3
State Tables and Graphs

In the previous section we analyzed clocked sequential networks by signal tracing and construction of timing charts. Although this is satisfactory for small networks and short input sequences, construction of state tables and graphs provides a more systematic approach which is useful for analysis of larger networks and which leads to a general synthesis procedure for sequential networks.

The state table specifies the next state and output of a sequential network in terms of its present state and input. The following method can be used to construct the state table:

1. Determine the flip-flop input equations and the output equations from the network.
2. Derive the next-state equation for each flip-flop from its input equations using one of the following relations:

$$D \text{ flip-flop} \qquad Q^+ = D \qquad\qquad (13\text{--}1)$$
$$T \text{ flip-flop} \qquad Q^+ = T \oplus Q \qquad\qquad (13\text{--}2)$$
$$S\text{-}R \text{ flip-flop} \qquad Q^+ = S + R'Q \qquad\qquad (13\text{--}3)$$
$$J\text{-}K \text{ flip-flop} \qquad Q^+ = JQ' + K'Q \qquad\qquad (13\text{--}4)$$

3. Plot a next-state map for each flip-flop.
4. Combine these maps to form the state table. Such a state table, which gives the next state of the flip-flops as a function of their present state and the network inputs, is frequently referred to as a transition table.

As an example of the above procedure, we will derive the state table for the network of Fig. 13–5:

1. The flip-flop input equations and output equation are

$$J_A = X \qquad K_A = XB' \qquad\qquad Z = B$$
$$J_B = X \qquad K_B = X \oplus A'$$

2. The next-state equations for the flip-flops are

$$A^+ = J_A A' + K_A' A = XA' + (X' + B)A$$
$$B^+ = J_B B' + K_B' B = XB' + (X \oplus A')'B = XB' + (XA' + X'A)B$$

3. The corresponding maps are

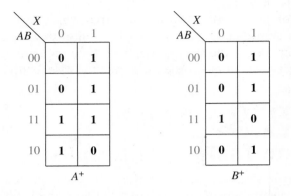

4. Combining these maps yields the transition table in Table 13–2(a), which gives the next state of both flip-flops (A^+B^+) as a function of the present state and input. The output function is then added to the table. In this example, the output depends only on the present state of the flip-flops and not on the input, so only a single output column is required.

Using Table 13–2(a), we can construct the timing chart of Fig. 13–6 or any other timing chart for some given input sequence and specified initial state. Initially $AB = 00$ and $X = 1$, so $Z = 0$ and $A^+B^+ = 11$. This means that *after* the clock pulse, the flip-flop state will be $AB = 11$. Then with $AB = 11$, the output is $Z = 1$. The next input is $X = 0$, so $A^+B^+ = 11$ and the clock pulse produces no state change. Continuing in this manner, we can complete the timing chart.

Table 13–2

Moore State Tables for Fig. 13–5

(a)

AB	A^+B^+ $X=0$	$X=1$	Z
00	00	11	0
01	00	11	1
11	11	10	1
10	10	01	0

(b)

Present State	Next State $X=0$	$X=1$	Present Output (Z)
S_0	S_0	S_2	0
S_1	S_0	S_2	1
S_2	S_2	S_3	1
S_3	S_3	S_1	0

If we are not interested in the individual flip-flop states, we can replace each combination of flip-flop states with a single symbol which represents the state of the network. Replacing 00 with S_0, 01 with S_1, 11 with S_2, and 10 with S_3 in Table 13–2(a) yields Table 13–2(b). The Z column is labeled "Present Output" because it is the output associated with the "Present State." The state graph of Fig. 13–9 represents Table 13–2(b). Each node of the graph represents a state of the network, and the corresponding output is placed in the circle below the state symbol. The arrow joining two nodes is labeled with the value of X which

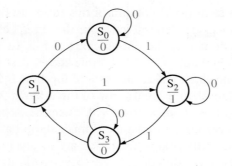

Figure 13–9
Moore State Graph for Fig. 13–5

will cause a state change between these nodes. Thus if the network is in state S_0 and $X = 1$, a clock pulse will cause a transition to state S_2.

Next we will construct the state table and graph for the Mealy machine of Fig. 13–7. The next-state and output equations are

$$A^+ = J_A A' + K_A' A = XBA' + X'A$$
$$B^+ = J_B B' + K_B' B = XB' + (AX)'B = XB' + X'B + A'B$$
$$Z = X'A'B + XB' + XA$$

The next-state and output maps (Fig. 13–10) combine to form the transition table in Table 13–3(a). Given values for A, B, and X, the current value of the output is

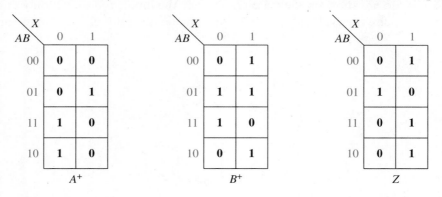

Figure 13–10

Table 13–3

Mealy State Tables for Fig. 13–7

(a)

| | A^+B^+ | | Z | |
AB	$X = 0$	1	$X = 0$	1
00	00	01	0	1
01	01	11	1	0
11	11	00	0	1
10	10	01	0	1

(b)

| Present State | Next State | | Present Output | |
	$X = 0$	1	$X = 0$	1
S_0	S_0	S_1	0	1
S_1	S_1	S_2	1	0
S_2	S_2	S_0	0	1
S_3	S_3	S_1	0	1

determined from the Z column of this table, and the states of the flip-flops after the clock pulse are determined from the A^+B^+ columns.

We can construct the timing chart of Fig. 13–8 using Table 13–3(a). Initially with $A = B = 0$ and $X = 1$, the table shows that $Z = 1$ and $A^+B^+ = 01$. Therefore, after the clock pulse, the state of flip-flop B will change to 1 as indicated in Fig. 13–8. Now, from the 01 row of the table, if X is still 1, the output will be 0 until the input is changed to $X = 0$. Then the output is $Z = 1$, and the next clock pulse produces no state change. Finish stepping through the state table in this manner and verify that A, B, and Z are as given in Fig. 13–8.

If we let $AB = 00$ correspond to network state S_0, 01 to S_1, 11 to S_2, and 10 to S_3, we can construct the state table in Table 13–3(b) and the state graph of Fig. 13–11. In Table 13–3(b), the "Present Output" column gives the output associated with the present state and present input. Thus, if the present state is S_0 and the input changes from 0 to 1, the output will immediately change from 0 to 1. However, the state will not change to the next state (S_1) until after the clock pulse. For Fig. 13–11, the labels on the arrows between states are of the form X/Z, where the symbol before the slash is the input and the symbol after the slash is the corresponding output. Thus, in state S_0 an input of 0 gives an output of 0, and an input of 1 gives an output of 1. For any given input sequence, we can easily trace out the state and output sequences on the state graph. For the input sequence $X = 10101$, verify that the corresponding output sequence is 11001. This agrees with Fig. 13–8 if the false outputs are ignored. Note that the false outputs do *not* show on the state graph since the inputs are shown only during the clock pulse interval and no provision is made for input changes between clock pulses.

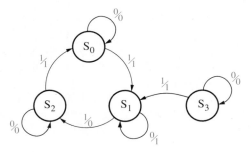

Figure 13–11
Mealy State Graph for Fig. 13–7

Table 13–4 shows a state table for a Mealy sequential network with two inputs and two outputs. Figure 13–12 shows the corresponding state graph. The notation 00, 01/00 means if $X_1 = X_2 = 0$ or $X_1 = 0$ and $X_2 = 1$, then $Z_1 = 0$ and $Z_2 = 0$.

The synthesis procedure for sequential networks, discussed in detail in Units 14 through 16, is just the opposite of the procedure used for analysis. Starting with the specifications for the sequential network to be synthesized, a state graph

Table 13–4
A State Table with Multiple Inputs and Outputs

Present State	Next State				Present Output ($Z_1 Z_2$)			
	$X_1 X_2 = 00$	01	10	11	$X_1 X_2 = 00$	01	10	11
S_0	S_3	S_2	S_1	S_0	00	10	11	01
S_1	S_0	S_1	S_2	S_3	10	10	11	11
S_2	S_3	S_0	S_1	S_1	00	10	11	01
S_3	S_2	S_2	S_1	S_0	00	00	01	01

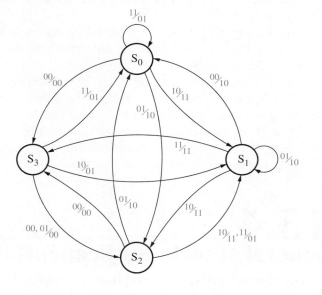

Figure 13–12
State Graph for Table 13–4

is constructed. This graph is then translated to a state table, and codes are assigned for each state. Flip-flop input equations are then derived, and finally the logic diagram for the network is drawn. For example, to synthesize the network in Fig. 13–7, we would start with the state graph of Fig. 13–11. Then we would derive Table 13–3(b), Table 13–3(a), the next-state and output equations, and finally Fig. 13–7.

Several important points concerning the construction and interpretation of timing charts are summarized below:

1. When constructing timing charts, note that a state change will normally occur after the falling (or rising) edge of the clock pulse, depending on the type of flip-flop used.
2. The input will normally be changed in between clock pulses.
3. For a Moore network, the output can change only when the state changes, but for a Mealy network the output can change when the input changes as well as when the state changes. A "false" output may occur between the

time the state changes and the time the input is changed to its new value. (In other words, if the state has changed to its next value, but the old input is still present, the output may be temporarily incorrect.)

4. False outputs are difficult to determine from the state graph, so use either signal tracing through the network or use the state table when constructing timing charts for Mealy networks.

5. When using a Mealy state table for constructing timing charts, the procedure is as follows:

(a) For the first input, read the present output and plot it.

(b) Read the next state and plot it (following the appropriate edge of the clock pulse).

(c) Go to the row in the table which corresponds to the next state and read the output under the old input column and plot it. (This may be a "false" output.)

(d) Change to the next input and repeat steps (a), (b), and (c).
   (*Note:*   If you are just trying to read the correct output sequence from the table, step (c) is naturally omitted.)

6. For Mealy networks that change state on the falling edge of the clock, the best time to read the output is during the clock pulse, since the output will always be correct during that time.

13.4
General Models for Sequential Networks

A sequential network can be divided conveniently into two parts—the flip-flops which serve as memory for the network and the combinational logic which realizes the input functions for the flip-flops and the output functions. Figure 13–13 illustrates the general model for a clocked Mealy sequential network with m inputs, n outputs, and k clocked D flip-flops used as memory. Drawing the model in this form emphasizes the presence of feedback in the sequential network since the flip-flop outputs are fed back as inputs to the combinational subnetwork. The combinational subnetwork realizes the n output functions and the k next state functions, which serve as inputs to the D flip-flops:

$$
\left.
\begin{aligned}
Z_1 &= f_1(X_1, X_2, \ldots, X_m, Q_1, Q_2, \ldots, Q_k)\\
Z_2 &= f_2(X_1, X_2, \ldots, X_m, Q_1, Q_2, \ldots, Q_k)\\
&\vdots\\
Z_n &= f_n(X_1, X_2, \ldots, X_m, Q_1, Q_2, \ldots, Q_k)
\end{aligned}
\right\} n \text{ output functions}
$$

$$
\left.
\begin{aligned}
Q_1^+ &= D_1 = g_1(X_1, X_2, \ldots, X_m, Q_1, Q_2, \ldots, Q_k)\\
Q_2^+ &= D_2 = g_2(X_1, X_2, \ldots, X_m, Q_1, Q_2, \ldots, Q_k)\\
&\vdots\\
Q_k^+ &= D_k = g_k(X_1, X_2, \ldots, X_m, Q_1, Q_2, \ldots, Q_k)
\end{aligned}
\right\}
\begin{aligned}
&k \text{ next-state}\\
&\text{functions}
\end{aligned}
$$

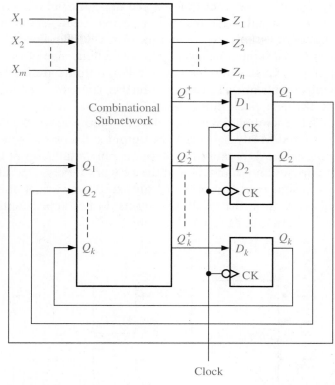

Figure 13–13
General Model for Mealy Network Using Clocked
D Flip-Flops

When a set of inputs is applied to the network, the combinational subnetwork generates the outputs $(Z_1, Z_2, \ldots, Z_n)$ and the flip-flop inputs $(D_1, D_2, \ldots, D_k)$. Then a clock pulse is applied and the flip-flops change to the proper next state. This process is repeated for each set of inputs. Note that at a given point in time, the outputs of the flip-flops represent the present state of the network $(Q_1, Q_2, \ldots, Q_k)$. These Q_i's feed back into the combinational network, which generates the flip-flop inputs using the Q_i's and the X inputs. When D flip-flops are used, $D_i = Q_i^+$; therefore, the combinational network outputs are labeled Q_1^+, Q_2^+, etc. Although the above model uses D flip-flops, a similar model may be used for other types of clocked flip-flops, in which case the combinational network must generate the appropriate flip-flop inputs instead of the next state functions.

The clock pulse synchronizes the operation of the flip-flops and prevents timing problems. The gates in the combinational subnetwork have finite propagation delays, so when the inputs to the network are changed a finite time is required before the flip-flop inputs reach their final values. Because the gate delays are not all the same, the flip-flop input signals may contain transients and they may change at different times. Since the clock pulse is not applied until all flip-flop input signals have reached their final steady-state values, the unequal gate delays do not cause any timing problems. All flip-flops which must change state do so at the same time, usually on the falling edge of the clock pulse. When the flip-flops change state, the new flip-flop outputs are fed back into the combinational subnetwork. However, no further change in the flip-flop states can occur until the next clock pulse.

The general model for the clocked Moore network (Fig. 13–14) is similar to the clocked Mealy network. The output subnetwork is drawn separately for the Moore network because the output is only a function of the present state of the flip-flops and not a function of the network inputs. Operation of the Moore network is similar to that of the Mealy except when a set of inputs is applied to the Moore network, the resulting outputs do not appear until after the clock pulse causes the flip-flops to change state.

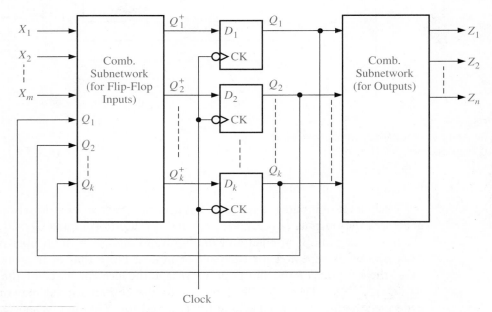

Figure 13–14
General Model for Moore Network Using
Clocked D Flip-Flops

To facilitate the study of sequential networks with multiple inputs and outputs, assignment of symbols to represent each combination of input values and each combination of output values is convenient. For example, we can replace Table 13–4 with Table 13–5 if we let $X = 0$ represent the input combination

Table 13–5
State Table with Multiple Inputs and Outputs

Present State	Next State				Present Output (Z)			
	$X = 0$	1	2	3	$X = 0$	1	2	3
S_0	S_3	S_2	S_1	S_0	0	2	3	1
S_1	S_0	S_1	S_2	S_3	2	2	3	3
S_2	S_3	S_0	S_1	S_1	0	2	3	1
S_3	S_2	S_2	S_1	S_0	0	0	1	1

$X_1 X_2 = 00$, $X = 1$ represent $X_1 X_2 = 01$, etc., and similarly let $Z = 0$ represent the output combination $Z_1 Z_2 = 00$, $Z = 1$ represent $Z_1 Z_2 = 01$, etc. In this way we can specify the behavior of any sequential network in terms of a single input variable X and a single output variable Z.

Table 13–5 specifies two functions, the next-state function and the output function. The next-state function, designated δ, gives the next state of the network (i.e., the state after the clock pulse) in terms of the present state (S) and the present input (X):

$$S^+ = \delta(S, X) \tag{13–5}$$

The output function, designated λ, gives the output of the network (Z) in terms of the present state (S) and input (X):

$$Z = \lambda(S, X) \tag{13–6}$$

Values of S^+ and Z can be determined from the state table. From Table 13–5, we have

$$\delta(S_0, 1) = S_2 \qquad \delta(S_2, 3) = S_1$$
$$\lambda(S_0, 1) = 2 \qquad \lambda(S_2, 3) = 1$$

We will use the λ and δ notation introduced above when we discuss equivalent sequential networks in Unit 15.

PROGRAMMED EXERCISE 13.1

Cover the bottom of each page with a sheet of paper and slide it down as you check your answers.

13.1a In this exercise you will analyze the following sequential network using a state table and a timing chart.

Derive the next state and output equations.

$A^+ =$ _____

$B^+ =$ _____

$Z =$ _____

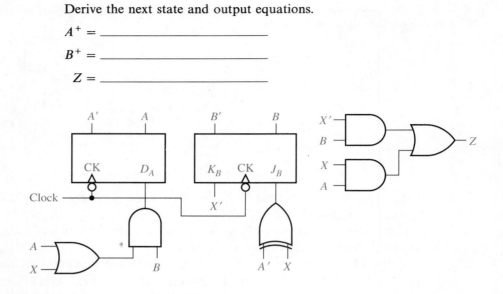

Answer: $Z = XA + X'B$, $B^+ = (A' \oplus X)B' + XB = A'B'X' + AB'X + XB$
$A^+ = B(A + X)$

13.1b Plot these equations on maps and complete the transition table:

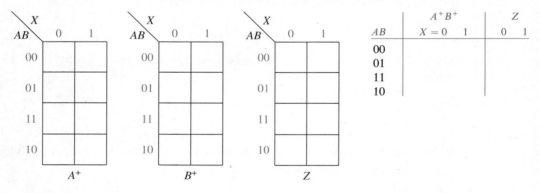

Answer to 13.1b:

	AB	A^+B^+		Z	
		$X = 0$	1	0	1
S_0	00	01	00	0	0
S_1	01	00	11	1	0
S_2	11	10	11	1	1
S_3	10	00	01	0	1

13.1c Convert your transition table to a state table using the given state numbering.

	Next State		Output	
	$X = 0$	1	0	1
S_0				
S_1				
S_2				
S_3				

Answer to 13.1c:

	$X = 0$	1	0	1
S_0	S_1	S_0	0	0
S_1	S_0	S_2	1	0
S_2	S_3	S_2	1	1
S_3	S_0	S_1	0	1

13.1d Complete the corresponding state graph.

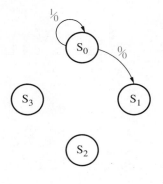

Answer to 13.1d:

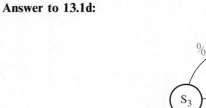

13.1e   Using this graph, determine the state sequence and output sequence if the initial state is S_0 and the input sequence is $X = 0, 1, 0, 1$.

(1) The initial output with $X = 0$ in state S_0 is $Z = $ _____ and the next state is _____.

(2) The output in this state when the next input ($X = 1$) is applied is $Z = $ _____ and the next state is _____.

(3) When the third input ($X = 0$) is applied, the output is $Z = $ _____ and the next state is _____.

(4) When the last input is applied, $Z = $ _____ and the final state is _____.

In summary, the state sequence is $S_0,$ ___, ___, ___, ___. The output sequence is $Z = $ _____.

Answer to 13.1e: S_0, S_1, S_2, S_3, S_1 $Z = 0011$

13.1f   The above sequence for Z is the "correct" output sequence. Next we will determine the timing chart including any false outputs for Z. Assuming that X changes midway between clock pulses, draw the waveform for X ($X = 0, 1, 0, 1$).

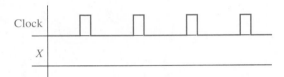

Answer:

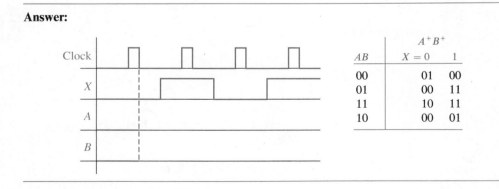

AB	A^+B^+	
	$X = 0$	1
00	01	00
01	00	11
11	10	11
10	00	01

13.1g   Referring to the transition table, sketch the waveforms for A and B assuming that initially $A = B = 0$. The state sequence is

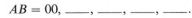

$$AB = 00, \text{\_\_\_}, \text{\_\_\_}, \text{\_\_\_}, \text{\_\_\_}.$$

Answer: (Note that A and B change immediately after the clock pulse.)

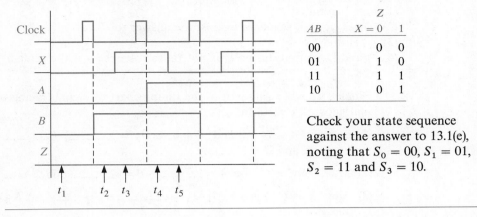

AB	Z X = 0	1
00	0	0
01	1	0
11	1	1
10	0	1

Check your state sequence against the answer to 13.1(e), noting that $S_0 = 00$, $S_1 = 01$, $S_2 = 11$ and $S_3 = 10$.

13.1h Using the output table, sketch the waveform for Z. At time t_1, $X = A = B = 0$, so $Z =$ _____. At time t_2, $X =$ _____ and $AB =$ _____, so $Z =$ _____. At time t_3, $X =$ _____ and $AB =$ _____, so $Z =$ _____. Complete the waveform for Z, showing the output at t_4, t_5, etc.

Answer: (Note that Z can change immediately following the change in X or immediately following the clock pulse.)

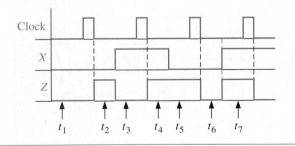

13.1i (1) Since this is a Mealy network, the correct times to read the output are during intervals t_1, _____, _____ and _____.

(2) The correct output sequence is therefore $Z =$ _____.

(3) False outputs may occur during intervals _____, _____ and _____.

(4) In two of these intervals, false outputs actually occur. These intervals are _____ and _____.

Answer:

    (1) t_1, t_3, t_5 and t_7

    (2) Check your Z sequence against the answer to 13.1e.

    (3) t_2, t_4 and t_6

    (4) t_2 and t_6 (output during t_4 is not "false" because it is the same as t_5).

13.1j   Finally, we will verify part of the timing chart by signal tracing on the original network (see 13.1a).

    (1) Initially, $A = B = 0$ and $X = 0$ so $D_A =$ _____, $J_B =$ _____, $K_B =$ _____ and $Z =$ _____.

    (2) After the clock pulse $A =$ _____, $B =$ _____ and $Z =$ _____.

    (3) After X is changed to 1, $D_A =$ _____, $J_B =$ _____, $K_B =$ _____ and $Z =$ _____.

    (4) After the clock pulse $A =$ _____, $B =$ _____ and $Z =$ _____.

    Check your answers against the timing chart. Answer to (1) corresponds to t_1, (2) to t_2, (3) to t_3 and (4) to t_4.

PROBLEMS

13.2   Construct a state graph for the shift register shown below. (X is the input and Z is the output.)

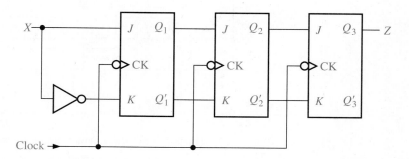

13.3   (a) For the following sequential network, find the next-state equation or map for each flip-flop. Using these next-state equations or maps, construct a (Moore) state table and graph for the network.

        (b) What is the output sequence when the input sequence is $X = 01100$?

        (c) Draw a timing diagram for the input sequence in (b). Show P_c, X, A, B, and Z. Assume that the input changes between clock pulses.

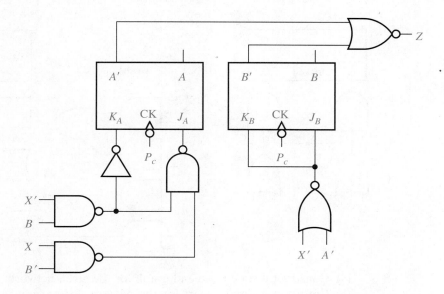

13.4   Draw a timing chart for the following network starting with an initial state $ABC = 000$ and using an input sequence $X = 01010$. Assume that the input changes occur midway between clock pulses. Pay particular attention to the times at which the flip-flops change state and the times at which Z changes. Indicate false outputs, if any. Verify that your answer is correct by using the state table for the network.

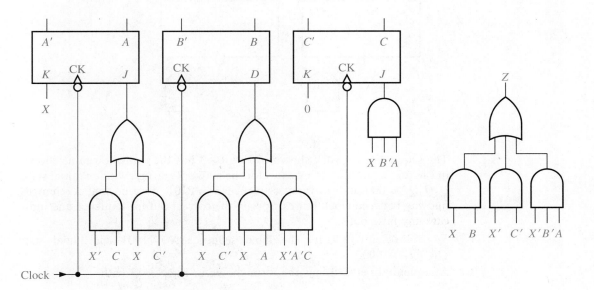

13.5   (a) For the following sequential network, write the next-state equations for flip-flops A and B.
   (b) Using these equations, find the state table and draw the state graph.

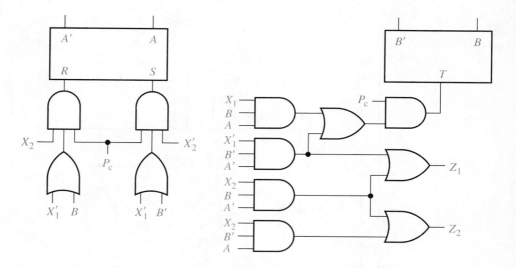

13.6 (a) Construct a state table and graph for the given network.
   (b) Construct a timing chart for the network for an input sequence $X =$ 10011. Indicate at what times Z has the correct value and specify the correct output sequence. (Assume that X changes midway between clock pulses.) Initially, $Q_1 = Q_2 = 0$.

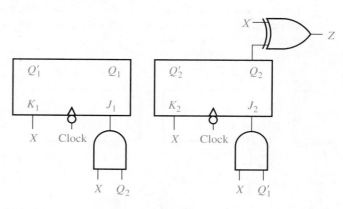

13.7 The sequential network shown in Fig. 16–3 has the transition table shown in Fig. 16–2. Draw a timing chart for the network starting with an initial state $Q_1Q_2Q_3 = 000$ and an input sequence $X = 0101$. Assume that X changes midway between clock pulses. Specify the correct output sequence and indicate any false outputs.

13.8 Work Problem 13.7 for the input sequence $X = 1001$ and initial state $Q_1Q_2Q_3 = 000$.

13.9 A sequential network has the form shown in Fig. 13–13 with

$$D_1 = Q_2Q_3' \qquad D_3 = Q_2' + X$$
$$D_2 = Q_3 \qquad Z = XQ_2' + X'Q_2$$

(a) Construct a state table and state graph for the network.

    (b) Draw a timing diagram for the network showing X, clock, Q_1, Q_2, Q_3, and Z. Use the input sequence $X = 01011$ and assume that X changes midway between clock pulses. Indicate any "false" outputs on the diagram.

    (c) Compare the output sequence obtained from the timing diagram with that from the state graph.

    (d) At what time with respect to the clock should the input be changed in order to eliminate the false output(s)?

13.10 Repeat Problem 13.9 for the equations below and the input sequence $X = 01100$.

$$D_1 = Q_3'X' \qquad\qquad D_3 = Q_1'X + Q_1Q_2$$
$$D_2 = Q_3'Q_1 + XQ_2' \qquad Z = XQ_3 + X'Q_3'$$

13.11 A Mealy sequential network has 1 input, 1 output, and 2 flip-flops. A timing chart for the network follows. Construct a state table and state graph for the network.

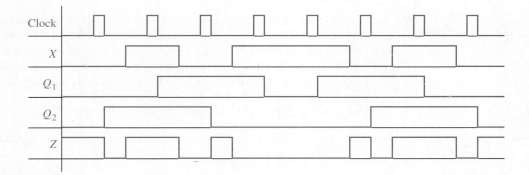

13.12 Repeat Problem 13.11 for the following timing chart.

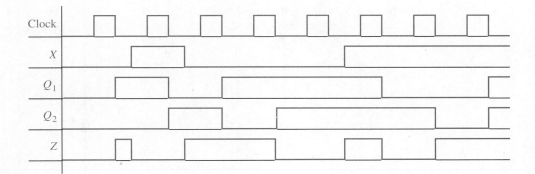

13.13   Given the following timing chart for a sequential network, construct as much of the state table as possible.

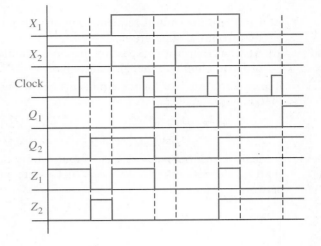

13.14   A sequential network of the form shown in Fig. 13–13 is constructed using a ROM and two D flip-flops. The contents of the ROM is given in the table.
(a) Draw a timing diagram for the network for the input sequence $X_1X_2 =$ 10, 01, 11, 10. Assume that input changes occur midway between clock pulses. Indicate any false outputs on the diagram, and specify the correct output sequence for Z_1 and Z_2.
(b) Construct a state table and state graph for the network.

Q_1	Q_2	X_1	X_2	D_1	D_2	Z_1	Z_2
0	0	0	0	0	0	1	0
0	0	0	1	0	0	1	0
0	0	1	0	0	1	1	0
0	0	1	1	0	1	1	0
0	1	0	0	1	1	0	0
0	1	0	1	1	1	1	0
0	1	1	0	1	0	0	1
0	1	1	1	1	0	1	1
1	0	0	0	1	1	0	0
1	0	0	1	0	0	0	0
1	0	1	0	1	1	0	1
1	0	1	1	0	0	0	1
1	1	0	0	1	0	0	0
1	1	0	1	0	1	0	0
1	1	1	0	1	0	0	0
1	1	1	1	0	1	0	0

UNIT

14

Derivation of State Graphs and Tables

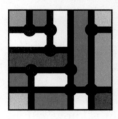

OBJECTIVES

1. Given a problem statement for the design of a Mealy or Moore sequential network, find the corresponding state graph and table.

2. Explain the significance of each state in your graph or table in terms of the input sequences required to reach that state.

3. Check your state graph using appropriate input sequences.

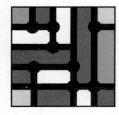

STUDY GUIDE

1. Study Section 14.1, *Design of a Sequence Detector.*

   (a) Verify that the state graph in Fig. 14–4 will produce the correct output sequence for Z when the input sequence for X is as given in Equation (14–1).

   (b) Using the equations from the Karnaugh maps on p. 361, construct the next-state table for the network and verify that it is the same as given in Table 14–2, except that the new table will have four states because the don't cares were assigned in the process of designing the network.

   (c) Complete the design of the Moore sequential network whose transition table is given by Table 14–4. Use clocked J-K flip-flops for A and B.

   (d) Verify that the state graph of Fig. 14–6 gives the correct output sequence when the input sequence (14–1) is applied. (Ignore the initial output for the Moore graph.)

2. Study Section 14.2, *More Complex Design Problems.*

3. Study Section 14.3, *Guidelines for Construction of State Graphs.* Study the examples carefully and observe how some of the guidelines were applied.

4. Work through Programmed Exercises 14.1 and 14.2.

5. A very important part of deriving state tables or state graphs is knowing how to tell when your answer is right (or wrong!). One way to do this is to make up a suitable list of test sequences, apply them to the state graph, and check the resulting output sequences.

6. To gain proficiency in construction of state tables or graphs requires a fair amount of practice. Work Problems 14.3, 14.5, 14.7, 14.9, and 14.11. The problems on the readiness tests will be about the same order of difficulty as these problems, so make sure that you can work them in a reasonable time.

   Note: Don't look at the answers to these problems in the back of the book until you have tried the problems and checked your answers using the following test sequences:

14.3 $X = 0\ 1\ 1\ 1\ 0\ 1\ 0\ 1$
      $Z = (0)\ 0\ 0\ 0\ 0\ 1\ 1\ 1\ 1$

(Solution should have 5 self-loops[1])

14.5 $X = 1\ 1\ 0\ 0\ 1\ 0\ 1$ $X = 0\ 0\ 1\ 1\ 1\ 0\ 0\ 1\ 0\ 1\ 1$
      $Z_1 = 0\ 0\ 0\ 0\ 0\ 0\ 1$ $Z_1 = 0\ 0\ 0\ 0\ 0\ 0\ 0\ 0\ 0\ 0\ 0$
      $Z_2 = 0\ 0\ 0\ 0\ 0\ 0\ 0$ $Z_2 = 0\ 0\ 0\ 1\ 0\ 0\ 0\ 0\ 0\ 0\ 1$

(Solution should have 4 self-loops)

14.7 $X_1 = \quad 0\ 0\ 1\ 1\ 0\ 1\ 0\ 1\ 1\ 0\ 1\ 0\ 0$
      $X_2 = \quad 0\ 1\ 0\ 1\ 0\ 0\ 0\ 1\ 0\ 1\ 1\ 1\ 0$
      $Z = (0)\ 0\ 0\ 0\ 1\ 1\ 1\ 0\ 0\ 0\ 1\ 1\ 1$

(Solution should have at least 4 self-loops)

14.9 (a) $X = 0\ 0\ 1\ 1\ 0\ 1\ 0\ 1\ 0\ 1\ 1$
           $Z = 1\ 1\ 0\ 0\ 0\ 1\ 1\ 0\ 0\ 0\ 1$

(Solution should have 3 self-loops)

      (b) $X = 1\ 1\ 1\ 0\ 0\ 1\ 0\ 1\ 0\ 1$
           $Z = 0\ 0\ 0\ 0\ 1\ 0\ 0\ 0\ 0\ 1$

14.11 (a) $X_1 = 0\ 0\ 1\ 1\ 1\ 1\ 0\ 0\ 1\ 0\ 0$
            $X_2 = 0\ 1\ 0\ 1\ 1\ 0\ 1\ 0\ 0\ 1\ 1$
            $Z_1 = 0\ 1\ 1\ 1\ 0\ 0\ 0\ 0\ 1\ 0\ 0$
            $Z_2 = 0\ 0\ 0\ 0\ 0\ 1\ 1\ 1\ 0\ 1\ 0$

       (b) Should get same sequences as above after initial output of $Z_1Z_2 = 00$

7. If you have the *LogicAid* program available, use it to check your state tables. This has several advantages over looking at the answers in the back of the book. First, *LogicAid* will determine whether or not your solution is correct even if your states are numbered differently from those in the solution, or even if the number of states is different. Second, if your solution is wrong, *LogicAid* will find the shortest input sequence for which your state table fails, and you can use this sequence to help locate the error in your solution. If you are having trouble learning to derive state graphs, *LogicAid* has a state graph tutor mode which can be used to check partial state graphs. By using the partial graph checker, you can check your graph after adding each state and then correct any errors before proceeding to the next state.

8. Read Section 14.4, *Serial Data Code Conversion*.

---

[1] A self-loop is an arrow which starts at one state and goes back to the same state.

(a) Complete the following timing diagram showing waveforms for the NRZ, NRZI, RZ, and Manchester coding schemes:

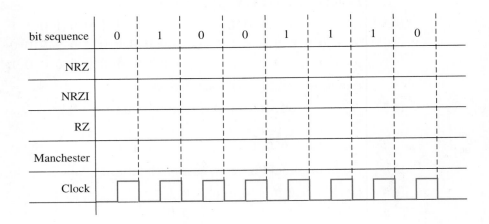

(b) The timing chart of Fig. 14–18(b) shows several glitches. By referring to the state table, explain why the second glitch is present.

(c) Consider Fig. 14–18. If an error in data transmission occurs, the input sequence $X = 01$ or 10 could occur. Add an ERROR state to the state diagram. The network should go to this error state if such an error occurs.

(d) Work Problem 14.26.

9. When you are satisfied that you can meet all of the objectives, take the readiness test.

Derivation of State Tables

In Unit 13 we analyzed sequential networks using timing charts and state graphs. Now we will consider the design of sequential networks starting from a problem statement which specifies the desired relationship between the input and output sequences. The first step in the design is to construct a state table or graph which specifies the desired behavior of the network. Flip-flop input equations and output equations can then be derived from this table. Construction of the state table or graph, one of the most important and challenging parts of sequential network design, is discussed in detail in this unit.

14.1
Design of a Sequence Detector

To illustrate the design of a clocked Mealy sequential network, we will design a sequence detector. The network has the form shown in Fig. 14–1.

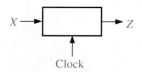

Figure 14–1
Sequence Detector to be Designed

The network will examine a string of 0's and 1's applied to the X input and generate an output $Z = 1$ only when a prescribed input sequence occurs. It will be assumed that the input X can only change between clock pulses. Specifically, we will design the network so that any input sequence ending in 101 will produce an output $Z = 1$ coincident with the last 1. The network does not reset when a 1 output occurs. A typical input sequence and the corresponding output sequence are

$$
\begin{array}{lcccccccccccccccc}
X = & 0 & 0 & 1 & 1 & 0 & 1 & 1 & 0 & 0 & 1 & 0 & 1 & 0 & 1 & 0 & 0 \\
Z = & 0 & 0 & 0 & 0 & 0 & 1 & 0 & 0 & 0 & 0 & 0 & 1 & 0 & 1 & 0 & 0 \\
\text{(time:} & 0 & 1 & 2 & 3 & 4 & 5 & 6 & 7 & 8 & 9 & 10 & 11 & 12 & 13 & 14 & 15)
\end{array}
\qquad (14\text{–}1)
$$

Initially, we do not know how many flip-flops will be required, so we will designate the network states as S_0, S_1, etc., and later assign flip-flop states to correspond to the network states. We will construct a state graph to show the sequence of states and outputs which occur in response to different inputs. Initially, we will start the network in a reset state designated S_0. If a 0 input is received, the network can stay in S_0 since the input sequence we are looking for does not start with 0. However, if a 1 is received we must go to a new state (S_1) to "remember" that the first input in the desired sequence has been received (Fig. 14–2). The labels on the graph are of the form X/Z, where the symbol before the slash is the input and the symbol after the slash is the corresponding output.

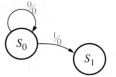

Figure 14–2

When in state S_1, if we receive a 0 the network must change to a new state (S_2) to remember that the first two inputs of the desired sequence (10) have been received. If a 1 is received in state S_2, the desired input sequence (101) is complete and the output should be 1. The question arises whether the network should then go to a new state or back to S_0 or S_1. Since the network is not supposed to reset when an output occurs, we cannot go back to S_0. However, since the last 1 in a sequence can also be the first 1 in a new sequence, we can return to S_1 as indicated in Fig. 14–3.

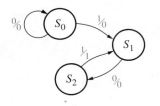

Figure 14–3

The graph of Fig. 14–3 is still incomplete. If a 1 input occurs when in state S_1, we can stay in S_1 since the sequence is simply restarted. If a 0 input occurs in state S_2 we have received two 0's in a row and must reset the network to state S_0 since 00 is not part of the desired input sequence, and going to one of the other states could lead to an incorrect output. The final state graph is given in Fig. 14–4. Note that for a single input variable each state must have two exit lines (one for each value of the input variable) but may have any number of entry lines depending on the network specifications.

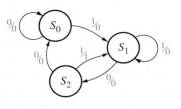

Figure 14–4
Mealy State Graph for Sequence Detector

State S_0 is the starting state, state S_1 indicates that a sequence ending in 1 has been received, and state S_2 indicates that a sequence ending in 10 has been received. An alternative way to start the solution would be to first define states in this manner and then construct the state graph. Converting the state graph to a state table yields Table 14–1. For example, the arc between S_2 and S_1 is labeled 1/1. This means that when the present state is S_2 and $X = 1$ the present output is 1. This 1 output is present as soon as X becomes 1, that is *before* the state change occurs. Therefore, the 1 is placed in the S_2 row of the table.

At this point, we are ready to design a network which has the behavior described by the state table. Since one flip-flop can have only two states, two

Table 14–1

Present State	Next State		Present Output	
	$X = 0$	$X = 1$	$X = 0$	$X = 1$
S_0	S_0	S_1	0	0
S_1	S_2	S_1	0	0
S_2	S_0	S_1	0	1

flip-flops are needed to represent the three states. Designate the two flip-flops as A and B. Let flip-flop states $A = 0$, $B = 0$ correspond to network state S_0; $A = 0$, $B = 1$ correspond to S_1; and $A = 1$, $B = 0$ correspond to network state S_2. Each network state is then represented by a unique combination of flip-flop states. Substituting the flip-flop states for S_0, S_1 and S_2 in the state table yields the transition table (Table 14–2).

Table 14–2

AB	A^+B^+		Z	
	$X = 0$	$X = 1$	$X = 0$	$X = 1$
00	00	01	0	0
01	10	01	0	0
10	00	01	0	1

From this table, we can plot the next state maps for the flip-flops and the map for the output function Z:

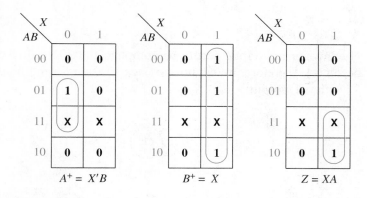

$$A^+ = X'B \qquad B^+ = X \qquad Z = XA$$

The flip-flop inputs are then derived from the next state maps using the same method that was used for counters (Section 12.9). If D flip-flops are used, $D_A = A^+ = X'B$ and $D_B = B^+ = X$, which leads to the network shown in Fig. 14–5. Initially, we will reset both flip-flops to the zero state. By tracing signals through the network, you can verify that an output $Z = 1$ will occur when an input sequence ending in 101 occurs. To avoid reading false outputs, always read the value of Z after the input has changed and before the clock pulse.

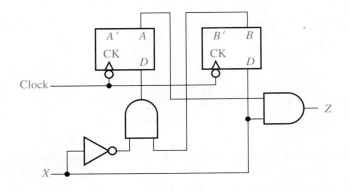

Figure 14–5

The procedure for finding the state graph for a Moore machine is similar to that used for a Mealy machine except that the output is written with the state instead of with the transition between states. We will rework the previous example as a Moore machine to illustrate the procedure. The network should produce an output of 1 only if an input sequence ending in 101 has occurred. The design is similar to that for the Mealy machine up through the point where the input sequence 10 has occurred, except that 0 output is associated with states S_0, S_1 and S_2:

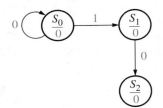

Now, when a 1 input occurs to complete the 101 sequence, the output must become 1; therefore, we cannot go back to state S_1 and must create a new state S_3 with a 1 output:

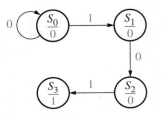

We now complete the graph as shown in Fig. 14–6. Note the sequence 100 resets the network to S_0. A sequence 1010 takes the network back to S_2 since another 1 input should cause Z to become 1 again.

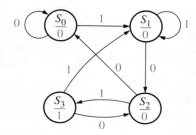

Figure 14–6
Moore State Graph for Sequence Detector

The state table corresponding to the network is given by Table 14–3. Note that there is a single column for the output since the output is determined by the present state and does not depend on X. Note that in this example the Moore machine requires one more state than the Mealy machine which detects the same input sequence.

Table 14–3

Present State	Next State $X = 0$	$X = 1$	Present Output (Z)
S_0	S_0	S_1	0
S_1	S_2	S_1	0
S_2	S_0	S_3	0
S_3	S_2	S_1	1

Since there are four states, two flip-flops are required to realize the network. Using the state assignment $AB = 00$ for S_0, $AB = 01$ for S_1, $AB = 11$ for S_2, and $AB = 10$ for S_3, the following transition table for the flip-flops results (Table 14–4):

Table 14–4

AB	A^+B^+ $X = 0$	$X = 1$	Z
00	00	01	0
01	11	01	0
11	00	10	0
10	11	01	1

The output function is $Z = AB'$. Note that Z depends only on the flip-flop states and is independent of X, while for the corresponding Mealy machine, Z was a function of X. Derivation of the flip-flop input equations is straightforward and will not be given here.

14.2
More Complex Design Problems

In this section we will derive a state graph for a sequential network of somewhat greater complexity than the previous examples. The network to be designed again has the form shown in Fig. 14–1. The output Z should be 1 if the input sequence ends in either 010 *or* 1001, and Z should be 0 otherwise. Before attempting to draw the state graph, we will work out some typical input-output sequences to make sure that we have a clear understanding of the problem statement. We will determine the desired output sequence for the following input sequence:

$$X = 0\ 0\ 1\ 0\ 1\ 0\ 0\ 1\ 0\ 0\ 0\ 1\ 0\ 0\ 1\ 1\ 0$$

$$\qquad\qquad a\qquad b\quad c\ d\qquad\quad e\qquad f$$

$$Z = 0\ 0\ 0\ 1\ 0\ 1\ 0\ 1\ 1\ 0\ 0\ 0\ 1\ 0\ 1\ 0\ 0$$

At point a, the input sequence ends in 010, one of the sequences we are looking for, so the output is $Z = 1$. At point b, the input again ends in 010 so $Z = 1$. Note that overlapping sequences are allowed since the problem statement does not say anything about resetting the network when a 1 output occurs. At point c, the input sequence ends in 1001, so Z is again 1. Why do we have a 1 output at points d, e, and f?

We will start construction of the state graph by working with the two sequences which lead to a 1 output. Then we will later add additional arrows and states as required to make sure that the output is correct for other cases. We start off with a reset state S_0 which corresponds to having received no inputs. Whenever an input is received which corresponds to part of one of the sequences we are looking for, the network should go to a new state to "remember" having received this input. Figure 14–7 shows a partial state graph which gives a 1 output for the sequence 010. In this graph S_1 corresponds to having received a sequence ending in 0, S_2 to a sequence ending in 01, and S_3 to a sequence ending in 010. Now, if a 1 input is received in state S_3, we again have a sequence ending in 01, which is part of the input sequence we are looking for. Therefore we can go back to state S_2 (arrow a) since S_2 corresponds to having received a sequence ending in 01. Then if we get another 0 in state S_2, we go to S_3 with a 1 output. This is correct since the sequence again ends in 010.

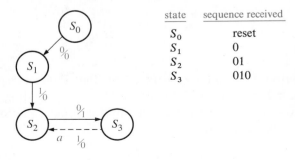

state	sequence received
S_0	reset
S_1	0
S_2	01
S_3	010

Figure 14–7

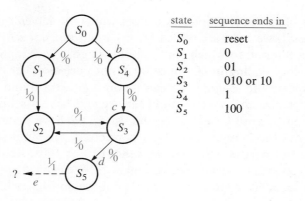

state	sequence ends in
S_0	reset
S_1	0
S_2	01
S_3	010 or 10
S_4	1
S_5	100

Figure 14–8

Next we will construct the part of the graph corresponding to the sequence 1001. Again we start in the reset state S_0, and when we receive a 1 input, we go to S_4 (Fig. 14–8, arrow b) to remember that we have received the first 1 in the sequence 1001. The next input in the sequence is 0, and when this 0 is received we should ask the question: Should we create a new state to correspond to a sequence ending in 10, or can we go to one of the previous states on the state graph? Since S_3 corresponds to a sequence ending in 10, we can go to S_3 (arrow c). The fact that we didn't have an initial 0 this time does not matter since 10 starts off the sequence we are looking for. If we get a 0 input when in S_3, the input sequence received will end in 100 regardless of the path we took to get to S_3. Since there is no state so far corresponding to the sequence 100, we create a new state S_5 to indicate having received a sequence ending in 100.

If we get a 1 input when in state S_5, this completes the sequence 1001 and gives a 1 output as indicated by arrow e. Again we ask the question, can we go back to one of the previous states, or do we have to create a new state. Since the end of the sequence 1001 is 01, and S_2 corresponds to a sequence ending in 01, we can go back to S_2 (Fig. 14–9). If we get another 001, we have again completed the sequence 1001 and get another 1 output.

We have now taken care of putting out a 1 when either the sequence 010 or 1001 is completed. Next, we will go back and complete the state graph to take

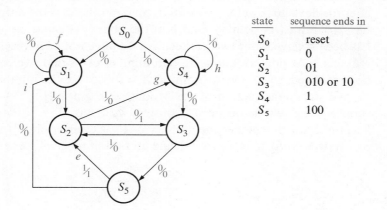

state	sequence ends in
S_0	reset
S_1	0
S_2	01
S_3	010 or 10
S_4	1
S_5	100

Figure 14–9

care of the other input sequences which we haven't already accounted for. In state S_1, we have accounted for a 1 input but not a 0 input. If we are in S_1 and get a 0 input, to which state should we go? If a 0 input occurs in S_1, we have a sequence ending in 00. Since 00 is not part of either of the input sequences for which we are looking, we can ignore the extra 0 and stay in S_1 (arrow f). No matter how many extra 0's occur, we still have a sequence ending in 0, and we stay in S_1 until a 1 input occurs. In S_2, we have taken care of the 0 input case, but not the 1 input case. If a 1 is received, the input sequence ends in 11. Since 11 is not part of either the sequence 010 or 1001, we do not need a state which corresponds to a sequence ending in 11. We can't stay in S_2 since S_2 corresponds to a sequence ending in 01. Therefore, we go to S_4 which corresponds to having received a sequence ending in 1 (arrow g). S_3 already has arrows corresponding to 0 and 1 inputs, so we examine S_4 next. If a 1 is received in S_4, the input sequence ends in 11. We can stay in S_4 and ignore the extra 1 (arrow h) since 11 is not part of either sequence for which we are looking. In S_5, if we get a 0 input, the sequence ends in 000. Since 000 is not contained in either 010 or 1001, we can go back to S_1 since S_1 corresponds to having received a sequence ending in one (or more) 0's. This completes the state graph since every state has arrows leaving it which correspond to both 0 and 1 inputs. We should now go back and check the state graph against the original input sequences to make sure that a 1 output is always obtained for a sequence ending in 010 or 1001 and that a 1 output does not occur for any other sequence.

Next we will derive the state graph for a Moore sequential network with one input X and one output Z. The output Z is to be 1 if the total number of 1's received is odd and at least two consecutive 0's have been received. A typical input and output sequence is

$$X = \begin{matrix} 1 & 0 & 1 & 1 & 0 & 0 & 1 & 1 \\ \uparrow & & & \uparrow & & \uparrow & \uparrow & \uparrow \\ a & & & b & & c & d & e \end{matrix}$$

$$Z = (0)\ 0\ 0\ 0\ 0\ 0\ 1\ 0\ 1$$

We have shifted the Z sequence to the right to emphasize that for a Moore network an input change does not affect Z immediately, but Z can change only after the next clock pulse. The initial 0 in parentheses is the output associated with the reset state. At points a and b in the above sequence, an odd number of 1's has been received, but two consecutive 0's have not been received, so the output remains 0. At points c and e, an odd number of 1's and two consecutive 0's have been received, so $Z = 1$. At point d, $Z = 0$ because the number of 1's is even.

We start construction of the Moore state graph (Fig. 14–10) with the reset state S_0, and we associate a 0 output with this state. First, we will consider keeping track of whether the number of 1's is even or odd. If we get a 1 input in S_0, we will go to state S_1 to indicate an odd number of 1's received. The output

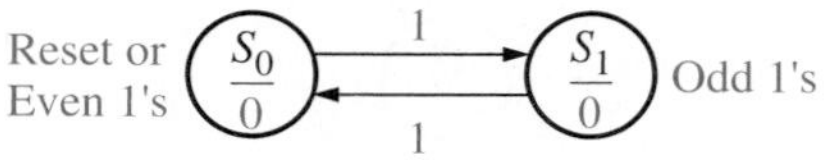

Figure 14–10

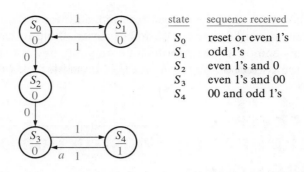

Figure 14-11

for S_1 is 0 since two consecutive 0's have not been received. When a second 1 is received, should we go to a new state or go back to S_0? For this problem, it is unnecessary to distinguish between an even number of 1's and no 1's received, so we can go back to S_0. A third 1 then takes us to S_1 (odd number of 1's), a fourth 1 to S_0 (even 1's), and so forth.

If a 0 is received in S_0, this starts a sequence of two consecutive 0's, so we go to S_2 (0 output) in Fig. 14-11. Another 0 then takes us to S_3 to indicate two consecutive 0's received. The output is still 0 in S_3 since the number of 1's received is even. Now if we get a 1 input, we have received an odd number of 1's and go to S_4. (Why can't we go to S_1?) In S_4 we have received two consecutive 0's and an odd number of 1's, so the output is 1.

If we receive a 1 in S_4, we have an even number of 1's and two consecutive 0's, so we can return to S_3 (arrow a). The output in S_3 is 0, and when we get another 1 input, the number of 1's is odd, so we again go to S_4 with a 1 output. Now suppose that we are in S_1 (odd number of 1's received) and we get a 0. We cannot go to S_2 (why?) so we go to a new state S_5 (Fig. 14-12, arrow b) which corresponds to an odd number of 1's followed by a 0. Another 0 results in two consecutive 0's and we can go to S_4 (arrow c) which gives us a 1 output.

Now we must go back and complete the state graph by making sure that there are two arrows leaving each state. In S_2, a 1 input means that we have received an odd number of 1's. Since we have not received two consecutive 0's, we must return to S_1 (arrow d) and start counting 0's over again. Similarly, if we receive a 1 in S_5, we return to S_0 (why?). Now, what should happen if we receive a 0 in S_3? Referring to the original problem statement, we see that once

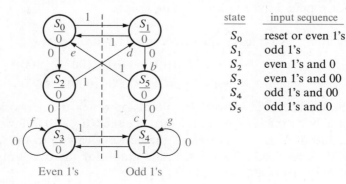

Figure 14-12   Even 1's   Odd 1's

two consecutive 0's have been received, additional 0's can be ignored. Therefore, we can stay in S_3 (arrow f). Similarly, extra 0 inputs can be ignored in S_4 (arrow g). This completes the Moore state diagram, and we should go back and verify that the correct output sequence is obtained for various input sequences.

14.3
Guidelines for Construction of State Graphs

Although there is no one specific procedure which can be used to derive state graphs or tables for every problem, the following guidelines should prove helpful:

1. First construct some sample input and output sequences to make sure that you understand the problem statement.
2. Determine under what conditions, if any, the network should reset to its initial state.
3. If only one or two sequences lead to a nonzero output, a good way to start is to construct a partial state graph for those sequences.
4. Another way to get started is to determine what sequences or groups of sequences must be "remembered" by the network and set up states accordingly.
5. Each time you add an arrow to the state graph, determine whether it can go to one of the previously defined states or whether a new state must be added.
6. Check your graph to make sure there is one and only one path leaving each state for each combination of values of the input variables.
7. When your graph is complete, test it by applying the input sequences formulated in part 1 and making sure the output sequences are correct.

Several examples of deriving state graphs or tables follow.

EXAMPLE 1   A sequential network has one input (X) and one output (Z). The network examines groups of four consecutive inputs and produces an output $Z = 1$ if the input sequence 0101 or 1001 occurs. The network resets after every four inputs. Find the Mealy state graph.

Solution: A typical sequence of inputs and outputs is

$$X = 0101 \mid 0010 \mid 1001 \mid 0100$$
$$Z = 0001 \mid 0000 \mid 0001 \mid 0000$$

The vertical bars indicate the points at which the network resets to the initial state. Note that an input sequence of either 01 or 10 followed by 01 will produce an output of $Z = 1$. Therefore, the network can go to the same state if either 01 or 10 is received. The partial state graph for the two sequences leading to a 1 output is shown in Fig. 14–13.

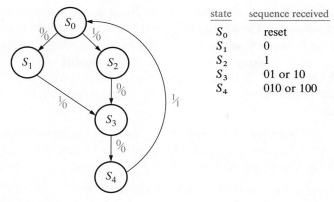

state	sequence received
S_0	reset
S_1	0
S_2	1
S_3	01 or 10
S_4	010 or 100

Figure 14–13
Partial State Graph for Example 1

Note that the network resets to S_0 when the fourth input is received. Next we add arrows and labels to the graph to take care of sequences which do not give a 1 output as shown in Fig. 14–14.

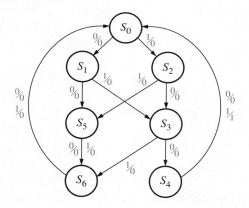

Figure 14–14

Addition of states S_5 and S_6 was necessary so that the network would not reset to S_0 before four inputs were received. Note that once a 00 or 11 input sequence has been received (state S_5), no output of 1 is possible until the network is reset.

EXAMPLE 2 Find the Mealy state graph for a sequential network which generates the output sequence 0101 <u>110</u> <u>110</u> <u>110</u> . . .

Solution:

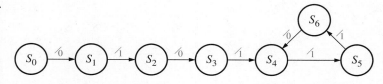

(A blank space above the slash indicates that the network has no input other than the clock.)

In general, a sequence can be divided into a nonperiodic part followed by a periodic part. Therefore, the general form for a sequence generator will be a linear string of states leading into a loop as in the above example.

EXAMPLE 3   A sequential network has two inputs (X_1, X_2) and one output (Z). The output remains a constant value unless one of the following input sequences occurs:

(a) The input sequence $X_1X_2 = 01, 11$[2] causes the output to become 0.
(b) The input sequence $X_1X_2 = 10, 11$ causes the output to become 1.
(c) The input sequence $X_1X_2 = 10, 01$ causes the output to change value.

Derive a Moore state graph for the network.

Solution: The only sequences of input pairs which affect the output are of length two. Therefore, the previous and present inputs will determine the output, and the network must "remember" only the previous input pair. At first it appears that three states are required, corresponding to the last input received being $X_1X_2 = 01, 10$ and (00 or 11). Note that it is unnecessary to use a separate state for 00 and 11 since neither input starts a sequence which leads to an output change. However, for each of these states the output could be either 0 or 1, so we will initially define six states as follows:

Previous Input (X_1X_2)	Output (Z)	State Designation
00 or 11	0	S_0
00 or 11	1	S_1
01	0	S_2
01	1	S_3
10	0	S_4
10	1	S_5

Using this state designation we can then set up a state table[3] (Table 14–5).

Table 14–5

Present State	Z	Next State $X_1X_2 = 00$	01	11	10
S_0	0	S_0	S_2	S_0	S_4
S_1	1	S_1	S_3	S_1	S_5
S_2	0	S_0	S_2	S_0	S_4
S_3	1	S_1	S_3	S_0	S_5
S_4	0	S_0	S_3	S_1	S_4
S_5	1	S_1	S_2	S_1	S_5

---

[2] This notation means $X_1 = 0$, $X_2 = 1$ followed by $X_1 = 1$, $X_2 = 1$.
[3] The 6-row table given here can be reduced to 5 rows using the methods given in Unit 15.

The S_4 row of this table was derived as follows. If 00 is received, the input sequence has been 10, 00 so the output does not change and we go to S_0 to remember that the last input received was 00. If 01 is received, the input sequence has been 10, 01 so the output must change to 1 and we go to S_3 to remember that the last input received was 01. If 11 is received, the input sequence has been 10, 11 so the output should become 1 and we go to S_1. If 10 is received, the input sequence has been 10, 10 so the output does not change and we remain in S_4. Verify for yourself that the other rows in the table are correct. The state graph is shown in Fig. 14–15.

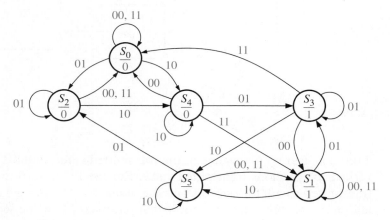

Figure 14–15
State Graph for Example 3

14.4
Serial Data Code Conversion

As a final example of state graph construction, we will design a converter for serial data. Binary data is frequently transmitted between computers as a serial stream of bits. As shown in Fig. 14–16(a), a clock signal is often transmitted along with the data so the receiver can read the data at the proper time. Alternatively (Fig. 14–16(b)), only the serial data is transmitted and a clock recovery circuit (called a digital phase-locked loop) is used to regenerate the clock signal at the receiver.

Figure 14–17 shows four different coding schemes for serial data together with the clock used to synchronize the data transmission. The example shows transmission of the bit sequence 0, 1, 1, 1, 0, 0, 1, 0. With the NRZ (non-return-to-zero) code, each bit is transmitted for one bit time without any change. With the NRZI (non-return-to-zero-inverted) code, data is encoded by the presence or absence of transitions in the output signal. For each 0 in the original sequence, the bit transmitted is the same as the previous bit transmitted. For each 1 in the original sequence, the bit transmitted is the complement of the previous bit transmitted. Thus, the above sequence is encoded as 0, 1, 0, 1, 1, 1, 0, 0. In other words,

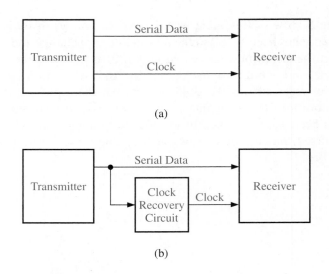

(a)

(b)

Figure 14–16
Serial Data Transmission

a 0 is encoded by no change in the transmitted value, and a 1 is encoded by inverting the previous transmitted value. For the RZ (return-to-zero) code, a 0 is transmitted as a 0 for one full bit time, but a 1 is transmitted as a 1 for the first half of the bit time and then the signal returns to 0 for the second half. For the Manchester code, a 0 is transmitted as 0 for the first half of the bit time and 1 for the second half, but a 1 is transmitted as 1 for the first half and 0 for the second half. Thus, the encoded bit always changes in the middle of the bit time.

We will design a sequential network which converts an NRZ-coded bit stream to a Manchester-coded bit stream (Fig. 14–18(a)). In order to do this, we will use

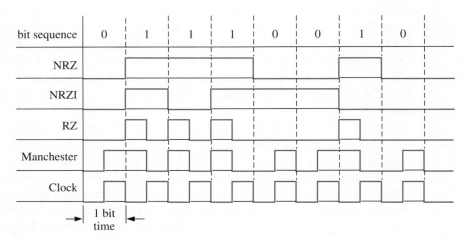

Figure 14–17
Coding Schemes for Serial Data Transmission

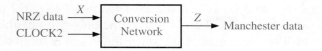

(a) Conversion network

NRZ (X)	0	0	1	1	1	1	1	1	0	0	0	0	1	1	0	0
Manchester (ideal)	0	1	1	0	1	0	1	0	0	1	0	1	1	0	0	1
CLOCK2																
State	S_0	S_1	S_0	S_2	S_0	S_2	S_0	S_2	S_0	S_1	S_0	S_1	S_0	S_2	S_0	S_1
Z (actual)																

→| |←1 Clock Period

(b) Timing chart

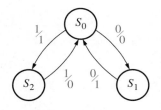

(c) State graph

| Present | Next State | | Output (Z) | |
State	$X = 0$	$X = 1$	$X = 0$	$X = 1$
S_0	S_1	S_2	0	1
S_1	S_0	–	1	–
S_2	–	S_0	–	0

(d) State table

Figure 14–18
Mealy Network for NRZ to
Manchester Conversion

a clock (CLOCK2) that is twice the frequency of the basic clock (Fig. 14–18(b)).
In this way, all output changes will occur on the same edge of CLOCK2, and
we can use the standard synchronous design techniques which we have been
using in this unit. First we will design a Mealy network to do the code conversion.
Note that if the NRZ bit is 0, it will be 0 for two CLOCK2 periods. Similarly,

if the NRZ bit is 1, it will be 1 for two CLOCK2 periods. Thus, starting in the reset state (S_0 in Fig. 14–18(c)), the only two possible input sequences are 00 and 11. For the sequence 00, when the first 0 is received, the output is 0. At the end of the first CLOCK2 period, the network goes to S_1. The input is still 0, so the output becomes 1 and remains 1 for one CLOCK2 period, and then the network resets to S_0. For the sequence 11, when the first 1 is received, the output is 1 for one clock period and then the network goes to S_2. Then the output is 0 for one clock period and the network resets to S_0.

When we convert the Mealy graph to a state table (Fig. 14–18(d)), the next state of S_1 with an input of 1 is not specified and is represented by a dash. Similarly, the next state of S_2 with a 0 input is not specified. The dashes are like

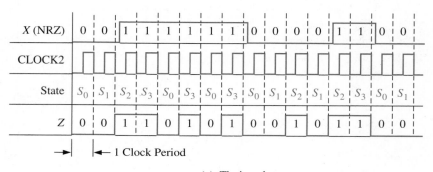

(a) Timing chart

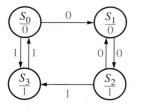

(b) State graph

Present State	Next State X = 0	Next State X = 1	Present Output (Z)
S_0	S_1	S_3	0
S_1	S_2	–	0
S_2	S_1	S_3	1
S_3	–	S_0	1

(c) State table

Figure 14–19
Moore Network for NRZ to
Manchester Conversion

don't cares, in that we don't care what the next state will be since the corresponding input sequence never occurs. A careful timing analysis for the Mealy network shows some possible "glitches" (false outputs) in the output waveform (Fig. 14–18(b)). The input waveform may not be exactly synchronized with the clock, and we have exaggerated this condition in the figure by shifting the input waveform to the right so that the input changes do not line up with the clock edges. For this situation, we will use the state table to analyze the occurrence of glitches in the Z output. The first glitch shown in the timing chart occurs when the network is in state S_1 with an input $X = 0$. The state table shows that the output is $Z = 1$, and when the clock goes low, the state changes to S_0. At this time, the input is still $X = 0$, so Z becomes 0. Then X changes to 1, Z becomes 1 again, so a glitch has occurred in the output during the time interval between the clock change and the input change. The next glitch occurs in S_2 with $X = 1$ and $Z = 0$. When the clock goes low, the output momentarily becomes 1 until X is changed to 0.

To overcome the possible glitch problem with the Mealy network, we will redesign the network in Moore form (Fig. 14–19). Since the output of a Moore network cannot change until after the active edge of the clock, the output will be delayed by one clock period. Starting in S_0, the input sequence 00 takes us to state S_1 with a 0 output and then to S_2 with a 1 output. Starting in S_0, 11 takes us to S_3 with a 1 output, and the second 1 can take us back to S_0, which has a 0 output. To complete the graph, we add the two arrows starting in S_2. Note that a 1 input cannot occur in S_1, and a 0 output cannot occur in S_3, so the corresponding state table has two don't cares.

PROGRAMMED EXERCISE 14.1

Cover the lower part of each page with a sheet of paper and slide it down as you check your answers. *Write* your answer in the space provided before looking at the correct answers.

Problem: A clocked Mealy sequential network with one input (X) and one output (Z) is to be designed. The output is to be 0, unless the input is 0 following a sequence of *exactly* two 0 inputs followed by a 1 input.

To make sure you understand the problem statement, specify the output sequence for each of the following input sequences:

(a) $X = 0\ 0\ 1\ 0$

   $Z = $ _____

(b) $X = \dots 1\ 0\ 0\ 1\ 0$ (... means any input sequence not ending in 00)

   $Z = \dots$ _____

(c) $X = \dots 0\ 0\ 0\ 1\ 0$

   $Z = \dots$ _____

(d) $X = 0\ 0\ 1\ 0\ 0\ 1\ 0\ 0\ 0\ 1\ 0$

$Z = $ _____

(e) Does the network reset after a 1 output occurs? _____

Answers:

(a) $Z = 0001$ (b) $Z = \ldots 00001$ (c) $Z = \ldots 00000$

(d) $Z = 00010010000$ (e) No

Note that no 1 output occurs in answer (c) because there are 3 input 0's in a row.

Add arrows to the following graph so that the sequence $X = 0010$ gives the correct output (don't add another state).

Answer:

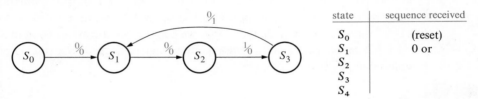

state	sequence received
S_0	(reset)
S_1	0 or
S_2	
S_3	
S_4	

Note that the arrow from S_3 returns to S_1 so that an additional input of 010 will produce another 1 output.

Add a state to the above graph which corresponds to "3 or more consecutive 0's received". Also complete the above table to indicate the sequence received which corresponds to each state.

Answer:

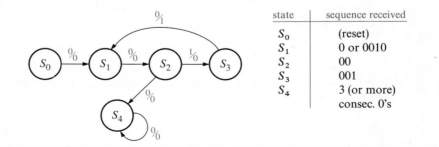

state	sequence received
S_0	(reset)
S_1	0 or 0010
S_2	00
S_3	001
S_4	3 (or more) consec. 0's

The above state graph is not complete since there is only one arrow leaving most states. Complete the graph by adding the necessary arrows. Return to one of the previously used states when possible.

Answer:

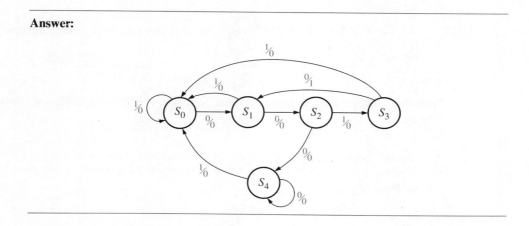

Verify that this state graph gives the proper output sequences for the input sequences listed at the start of this exercise. Write down the Mealy state table which corresponds to the above graph.

Answer:

Present State	Next State 0	Next State 1	Output 0	Output 1
S_0	S_1	S_0	0	0
S_1	S_2	S_0	0	0
S_2	S_4	S_3	0	0
S_3	S_1	S_0	1	0
S_4	S_4	S_0	0	0

PROGRAMMED EXERCISE 14.2

Problem: A clocked Moore sequential network should have an output of $Z = 1$ if the total number of 0's received is an even number greater than zero, provided that two consecutive 1's have never been received.

To make sure that you understand the problem statement, specify the output sequence for the following input sequence:

$$X = \quad 0\ 0\ 0\ 0\ 1\ 0\ 1\ 0\ 1\ 1\ 0\ 0\ 0\ 0$$

$$Z = (0) \underline{\hspace{7cm}}$$

↑
└── this 0 is the initial output before any inputs have been received

Answer: $Z = (0)\ 0\ 1\ 0\ 1\ 1\ 0\ 0\ 1\ 1\ 0\ 0\ 0\ 0\ 0$

Note that once two consecutive 1's have been received, the output can never become 1 again.

To start the state graph, consider only 0 inputs and construct a Moore state graph which gives an output of 1 if the total number of 0's received is an even number greater than zero.

Answer:

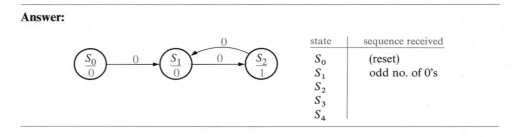

state	sequence received
S_0	(reset)
S_1	odd no. of 0's
S_2	
S_3	
S_4	

Now add states to the above graph so that starting in S_0, if two consecutive 1's are received followed by any other sequence, the output will remain 0. Also complete the above table to indicate the sequence received that corresponds to each state.

Answer:

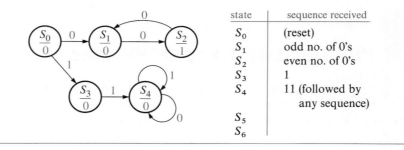

state	sequence received
S_0	(reset)
S_1	odd no. of 0's
S_2	even no. of 0's
S_3	1
S_4	11 (followed by any sequence)
S_5	
S_6	

Now complete the graph so that each state has both a 0 and 1 arrow leading away from it. Add as few extra states to the graph as possible. Also complete the above table.

Answer:

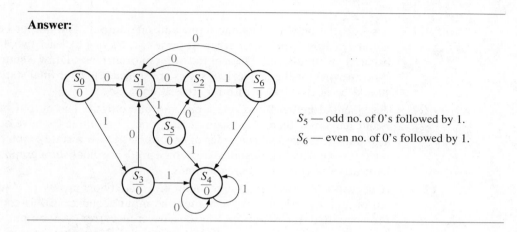

S_5 — odd no. of 0's followed by 1.

S_6 — even no. of 0's followed by 1.

Verify that this state graph gives the proper output sequence for each input sequence at the start of this exercise. Write down the Moore state table which corresponds to the above graph. (Note that a Moore table has only one output column.)

Answer:

Present State	Next State 0	Next State 1	Output
S_0	S_1	S_3	0
S_1	S_2	S_5	0
S_2	S_1	S_6	1
S_3	S_1	S_4	0
S_4	S_4	S_4	0
S_5	S_2	S_4	0
S_6	S_1	S_4	1

PROBLEMS

14.3 A sequential network has one input and one output. The output becomes 1 and remains 1 thereafter when at least two 0's *and* at least two 1's have occurred as inputs, regardless of the order of occurrence. Draw a state graph (Moore type) for the network (9 states are sufficient). Your final state graph should be neatly drawn with no crossed lines.

14.4 A sequential network has one input and one output. The output becomes 1 and remains 1 thereafter when at least one 1 and three 0's have occurred as inputs, regardless of the order of occurrence. Draw a state graph (Moore type) for the network (8 states are sufficient). Your final state graph should be neatly drawn with no crossed lines.

14.5 A sequential network has one input (X) and two outputs (Z_1 and Z_2). An output $Z_1 = 1$ occurs every time the input sequence 101 is completed provided that the sequence 011 has never occurred. An output $Z_2 = 1$ occurs every time the input 011 is completed. Note that once a $Z_2 = 1$ output has occurred, $Z_1 = 1$ can never occur, but *not* vice versa. Find a Mealy state graph and state table (minimum number of states is 8).

14.6 A sequential network has one input (X) and two outputs (Z_1 and Z_2). An output $Z_1 = 1$ occurs every time the input sequence 010 is completed provided that the sequence 100 has never occurred. An output $Z_2 = 1$ occurs every time the input 100 is completed. Note that once a $Z_2 = 1$ output has occurred, $Z_1 = 1$ can never occur, but *not* vice versa. Find a Mealy state graph and state table (minimum number of states is 8).

14.7 A sequential network has two inputs (X_1, X_2) and one output (Z). The output remains a constant value unless one of the following input sequences occurs:
(a) The input sequence $X_1X_2 = 00$, 11 causes the output to become 0.
(b) The input sequence $X_1X_2 = 01$, 11 causes the output to become 1.
(c) The input sequence $X_1X_2 = 10$, 11 causes the output to toggle.
Derive a Moore state table and state graph.

14.8 A sequential network has two inputs (X_1, X_2) and one output (Z). The output remains a constant value unless one of the following input sequences occurs:
(a) The input sequence $X_1X_2 = 01$, 00 causes the output to become 0.
(b) The input sequence $X_1X_2 = 11$, 00 causes the output to become 1.
(c) The input sequence $X_1X_2 = 10$, 00 causes the output to toggle.
Derive a Moore state table and state graph.

14.9 A sequential network has one input (X) and one output (Z). Draw a Mealy state graph for each of the following cases:
(a) The output is $Z = 1$ iff the total number of 1's received is divisible by 3. (*Note:* 0, 3, 6, 9, . . . are divisible by 3).
(b) The output is $Z = 1$ iff the total number of 1's received is divisible by 3 *and* the total number of 0's received is an even number greater than zero (9 states are sufficient).

14.10   A sequential network has one input (X) and one output (Z). Draw a Mealy state graph for each of the following cases:
(a) The output is $Z = 1$ iff the total number of 1's received is divisible by 4. (*Note:* 0, 4, 8, 12, ... are divisible by 4).
(b) The output is $Z = 1$ iff the total number of 1's received is divisible by 4 *and* the total number of 0's received is an odd number (8 states are sufficient).

14.11   A sequential network has two outputs. The inputs $(X_1 X_2)$ represent a 2-bit binary number, N. If the present value of N is greater than the previous value, then Z_1 is 1. If the present value of N is less than the previous value, then Z_2 is 1. Otherwise, Z_1 and Z_2 are 0. When the first pair of inputs is received, there is no previous value of N, so we cannot determine whether the present N is greater than or less than the previous value, therefore, the "otherwise" category applies.
(a) Find a Mealy state table or graph for the network (minimum number of states, including starting state, is 5).
(b) Find a Moore state table for the network (minimum number of states is 11).

14.12   A sequential network has two inputs and two outputs. The inputs (X_1, X_2) represent a 2-bit binary number, N. If the present value of N plus the previous value of N is greater than 2, then the Z_1 is 1. If the present value of N times the previous value of N is greater than 2, then Z_2 is 1. Otherwise, Z_1 and Z_2 are 0. When the first pair of inputs is received, use 0 as the previous value of N.
(a) Find a Mealy state table or graph for the network (minimum number of states is 4).
(b) Find a Moore state table for the network (minimum number of states is 10, but any correct answer with 16 or fewer states is acceptable).

14.13   A Moore sequential network has one input and one output. When the input sequence 011 occurs, the output becomes 1 and remains 1 until the sequence 011 occurs again in which case the output returns to 0. The output then remains 0 until 011 occurs a third time, etc. For example, the input sequence

$$X = 0\ 1\ 0\ 1\ 1\ 0\ 1\ 0\ 1\ 1\ 0\ 1\ 0\ 0\ 1\ 1\ 1$$

has the output

$$Z = 0\ 0\ 0\ 0\ 1\ 1\ 1\ 1\ 0\ 0\ 0\ 0\ 0\ 0\ 1\ 1$$

Derive the state graph (6 states minimum).

14.14   Work Problem 14.13 if the input sequence 101 causes the output to change state. For example, the input sequence

$$X = 0\ 1\ 0\ 1\ 0\ 1\ 0\ 0\ 1\ 0\ 1\ 0\ 1\ 1\ 0\ 1\ 0$$

has the output

$$Z = 0\ 0\ 0\ 1\ 1\ 0\ 0\ 0\ 0\ 0\ 1\ 1\ 0\ 0\ 0\ 1\ 1$$

(6 states minimum)

14.15   The input to a sequential network consists of groups of 5 bits. Each group of 5 bits represents a 2-out-of-5 binary-coded decimal digit (see Table 1–1). After receiving 5 bits, the network should output a 1 and reset if the bit pattern represents a valid 2-out-of-5 BCD digit; otherwise the network should output a 0 and reset. Derive a Mealy state graph (13 states minimum).

14.16   A Mealy sequential network has two inputs and one output. If the total number of 0's received is ≥ 4 and at least 3 pairs of inputs have occurred, then the output should be 1 coincident with the last input pair in the sequence. Whenever a 1 output occurs, the network resets. Derive a state graph and state table. Specify the meaning of each state. For example, S_0 means reset, S_1 means 1 pair of inputs received but no 0's received, etc.

EXAMPLE:

Input sequence: $X_1 = 1\ 1\ 1\ 0\ 0\ 0\ 1\ 1\ 1\ 0\ 0\ 0\ 1\ 1\ 0\ 0\ 0\ 1\ 0$

$X_2 = 1\ 0\ 0\ 0\ 0\ 0\ 1\ 1\ 1\ 1\ 1\ 0\ 1\ 0\ 0\ 0\ 1\ 0$

Output sequence: $Z\ = 0\ 0\ 0\ 1\ 0\ 0\ 1\ 0\ 0\ 0\ 0\ 1\ 0\ 0\ 1\ 0\ 0\ 1$

14.17   A Moore sequential network has one input and one output. The output should be 1 if the total number of 1's received is odd and the total number of 0's received is an even number greater than 0. Derive the state graph and table (6 states).

14.18   A sequential network has an input X and an output Z. The output is the same as the input was two clock periods previously. For example,

$$X = 0\ 1\ 0\ 1\ 1\ 0\ 1\ 0\ 1\ 1\ 0\ 1\ 0\ 0\ 0\ 1$$
$$Z = 0\ 0\ 0\ 1\ 0\ 1\ 1\ 0\ 1\ 0\ 1\ 1\ 0\ 1\ 0\ 0$$

The first two values of Z are 0. Find a Mealy state graph and table for the network.

14.19   A sequential network has an input X and an output Z. The output is the same as the input was three clock periods previously. For example,

$$X = 0\ 1\ 0\ 1\ 1\ 0\ 1\ 0\ 1\ 1\ 0\ 1\ 0\ 0\ 0\ 1$$
$$Z = 0\ 0\ 0\ 0\ 1\ 0\ 1\ 1\ 0\ 1\ 0\ 1\ 1\ 0\ 1\ 0$$

The first three values of Z are 0. Find a Mealy state graph and table for the network.

14.20   A sequential network has an input X and two outputs, S and V. X represents a 4-bit binary number N which is input least significant bit first. S represents a 4-bit binary number equal to $N + 2$, which is output least significant bit first. At the time the fourth input occurs, $V = 1$ if $N + 2$ is too large to be represented by four bits; otherwise, $V = 0$. The network always resets after the fourth bit of X is received. Find a Mealy state graph and table for the network.

EXAMPLE:

$X = 0111$ (binary 14 with the least significant bit first)

$S = 0000$ (since $14 + 2 = 16$, and 16 requires 5 bits)

$V = 0001$

14.21   A sequential network has an input X and two outputs, D and B. X represents a 4-bit binary number N which is input least significant bit first. D represents a 4-bit binary number equal to $N - 2$, which is output least significant bit first. At the time the fourth input occurs, $B = 1$ if $N - 2$ is less than 0; otherwise $B = 0$. The network always resets after the fourth bit of X is received. Find a Mealy state graph and table for the network.

EXAMPLE:

$$X = 0001 \quad 1000 \quad 1100$$
$$D = 0110 \quad 1111 \quad 1000$$
$$B = 0000 \quad 0001 \quad 0000$$

14.22 A sequential network has an input X and outputs Y and Z. YZ represents a 2-bit binary number equal to the number of 1's that have been received as inputs. The network resets when the total number of 1's received is 3, or when the total number of 0's received is 3. Find a Moore state graph and table for the network.

14.23 A sequential network has an input X and outputs Y and Z. YZ represents a 2-bit binary number equal to the number of pairs of adjacent 1's that have been received as inputs. For example, the input sequence 0110 contains one pair, the sequence 01110 two pairs, and the sequence 0110111 contains three pairs of adjacent 1's. The network *resets* when the total number of pairs of 1's received reaches 4. Find a Moore state graph and table for the network.

EXAMPLES:

Input sequence: $X = 0\,1\,0\,1\,1\,0\,1\,1\,1\,0\,0\,1\,0\,1\,0\,1\,0\,1\,1\,1\,0\,1\,1\,0\,1\,1\,0\,0\,1\,0$

Output sequences: $Y = 0\,0\,0\,0\,0\,0\,0\,1\,1\,1\,1\,1\,1\,1\,1\,1\,1\,0\,0\,0\,0\,0\,0\,0\,1\,1\,1\,1\,1$

$Z = 0\,0\,0\,0\,1\,1\,1\,0\,1\,1\,1\,1\,1\,1\,1\,1\,1\,0\,0\,0\,0\,1\,1\,1\,0\,0\,0\,0\,0\,0$

Input sequence: $X = 1\ 1\ 1\ 1\ 1\ 1\ 1\ 1$

Output sequences: $Y = 0\ 0\ 1\ 1\ 0\ 0\ 0\ 1$

$Z = 0\ 1\ 0\ 1\ 0\ 0\ 1\ 0$

Hint: Be sure that the network resets as shown in the examples.

14.24 A sequential network with one input and one output is used to stretch the first two bits of a 4-bit sequence as follows:

Input	Output
00XX	0000
01XX	0011
10XX	1100
11XX	1111

After every four bits, the network resets. Find a Mealy state graph and table for the network. The third and fourth bits of the input sequence can be either 1 or 0, so make sure that the network will work for all possible combinations.

14.25 A sequential network is to be used to control the operation of a vending machine which dispenses a $0.25 product. The network has three inputs, N, D, and Q, and two outputs, R and C. The coin detector mechanism in the vending machine is synchronized with the same clock as the sequential network you are to design. The coin detector outputs a single 1 to the N, D, or Q input for every nickel, dime, or quarter, respectively, that the customer inserts. Only one input will be 1 at a time. When the customer has inserted at least $0.25 in any combination of nickels, dimes, and quarters, the vending machine must give change and dispense the product. The coin return mechanism gives change by returning nickels to the customer. For every 1 output on C, the coin return mechanism will return one nickel to the customer. The product is dispensed when the network outputs a single 1 on output R. The network should reset after dispensing the product.

EXAMPLE: The customer inserts a nickel, a dime, and a quarter. The network inputs and outputs could look like this:

INPUTS: $N = 0\ 0\ 0\ 1\ 0\ 0\ 0\ 0\ 0\ 0\ 0\ 0\ 0\ 0\ 0\ 0\ 0$

$D = 0\ 0\ 0\ 0\ 0\ 0\ 0\ 1\ 0\ 0\ 0\ 0\ 0\ 0\ 0\ 0\ 0$

$Q = 0\ 0\ 0\ 0\ 0\ 0\ 0\ 0\ 0\ 0\ 1\ 0\ 0\ 0\ 0\ 0\ 0$

OUTPUTS: $R = 0\ 0\ 0\ 0\ 0\ 0\ 0\ 0\ 0\ 0\ 0\ 0\ 0\ 0\ 1\ 0\ 0$

$C = 0\ 0\ 0\ 0\ 0\ 0\ 0\ 0\ 0\ 0\ 0\ 1\ 1\ 1\ 0\ 0\ 0$

Note that any number of zeros can occur between 1 inputs.

Derive a Moore state table for the sequential network, and for each state indicate how much money the customer has inserted or how much change is due.

14.26 (a) Derive the state graph and table for a Mealy sequential network which converts a serial stream of bits from NRZ code to NRZI code. Assume that the clock period is the same as the bit time as in Fig. 14–17.
(b) Repeat (a) for a Moore sequential network.
(c) Draw a timing diagram for your answer to (a), using the NRZ waveform in Fig. 14–17 as the input waveform to your network. If the input changes occur slightly after the clock edge, indicate places in the output waveform where "glitches" (false outputs) can occur.
(d) Draw the timing diagram for your answer to (b), using the same input waveform as in (c).

14.27 (a) Derive the state graph and table for a Mealy sequential network which converts a serial stream of bits from Manchester code to NRZ code. Assume that a double frequency clock (CLOCK 2) is available.
(b) Repeat (a) for a Moore sequential network.
(c) Draw a timing diagram similar to Fig. 14–18(b) for your answer to (a), using the Manchester waveform in Fig. 14–18(b) as the input waveform to your network. If the input changes occur slightly after the clock edge, indicate places in the output waveform where "glitches" (false outputs) can occur. If possible, assign the don't cares in the output part of your state table to eliminate some of the glitches.
(d) Draw the timing diagram for your answer to (b), using the same input waveform as in (c).

15

Reduction of State Tables State Assignment

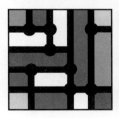

OBJECTIVES

1. Define equivalent states, state several ways of testing for state equivalence, and determine if two states are equivalent.

2. Define equivalent sequential networks and determine if two networks are equivalent.

3. Reduce a state table to a minimum number of rows.

4. Specify a suitable set of state assignments for a state table, eliminating those assignments which are equivalent with respect to cost of realizing the network.

5. State three guidelines which are useful in making state assignments, and apply these to making a good state assignment for a given state table.

6. Given a state table and assignment, form the transition table, and derive flip-flop input equations.

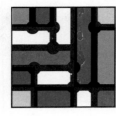

STUDY GUIDE

1. Study Section 15.1, *Elimination of Redundant States*.
2. Study Section 15.2, *Equivalent States*.

   (a) State in words the meaning of $\lambda_1(p, \underline{X}) = \lambda_2(q, \underline{X})$.

   (b) Assuming that N_1 and N_2 are identical networks with the following state graph, use Definition 15.1 to show that p is *not* equivalent to q. (Calculate $\lambda(p, \underline{X})$ and $\lambda(q, \underline{X})$ for $\underline{X} = 0$, $\underline{X} = 1$, $\underline{X} = 00$, $\underline{X} = 01$, etc.)

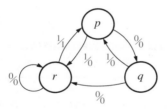

   (c) Suppose you were given two sequential networks (N_1 and N_2) in black boxes with only input and output terminals available. Each box has a reset button. The button on N_1 resets it to state p and the button on N_2 resets it to state q. Could you experimentally determine if $p \equiv q$ using Definition 15.1? Explain.

   (d) Apply Theorem 15.1 to show that in Table 15–6, $S_2 \not\equiv S_3$.

   (e) Note the difference between the *definition* of state equivalence (Definition 15.1) and the state equivalence *theorem* (Theorem 15.1). The definition requires examination of output sequences but not next states, while the theorem requires looking at *both the output and next state* for each single input. Make sure that you know both the definition and the theorem.

   Write out the definition of equivalent states:

Write out the state equivalence theorem:

When you check your answers, note that the theorem requires equal outputs and *equivalent* next states. This distinction between equal and equivalent is very important.

3. Study Section 15.3, *Determination of State Equivalence Using an Implication Table.*

   (a) Fill in the implication chart below to correspond to the given table (first pass only).

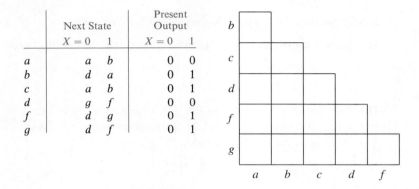

	Next State		Present Output	
	X = 0	1	X = 0	1
a	a	b	0	0
b	d	a	0	1
c	a	b	0	1
d	g	f	0	0
f	d	g	0	1
g	d	f	0	1

   Your answer should have 8 squares with X's, 2 squares with 1 implied pair, and 4 squares with 2 implied pairs. There should be a check in square *f*-*g* since the only nontrivial implication of *f*-*g* is *f*-*g* itself.

   (b) Now go through your chart and eliminate all nonequivalent pairs (several passes may be required). What is the only equivalent state pair?

   (c) Find all of the equivalent states in the following table using an implication table:

	Next State		Present Output	
	X = 0	1	X = 0	1
a	b	c	0	1
b	d	b	0	0
c	e	a	0	1
d	d	e	0	0
e	e	e	0	0

   (You should have found 4 pairs of equivalent states. If you found only 2 pairs, reread Section 15.3).

   Reduce the table to 2 rows.

4. Study Section 15.4, *Equivalent Sequential Networks*. Define equivalent sequential networks. (Make sure you know the difference between equivalent *states* and equivalent *networks*.)

5. Work Problems 15.1, 15.3, and 15.5 using the methods of Sections 15.3 and 15.4. When forming the implication charts for state equivalence, follow the convention used in the text. That is, label the bottom of the chart starting with the first state and ending with the next-to-last state. Then label the left side of the chart starting with the second state at the top and ending with the last state at the bottom.

6. Study Section 15.5, *Incompletely Specified State Tables*.

   (a) State two reasons why a state table might be incompletely specified.

   (b) For Table 15–5(a), fill in the don't care outputs in the $X = 0$ column as 1 and 0 (instead of 0 and 1). Show that with this choice of outputs, the minimum number of states is 3.

7. Read Section 15.6, *Derivation of Flip-Flop Input Equations*.

   (a) Review the short-cut method for deriving J-K flip-flop input equations (Section 12.5). The J and K input equations for flip-flop Q_i are independent of which variable?

   (b) Plot the map for the output function (Z) from the transition table of Table 15–6(b) and derive the minimum equation for Z.

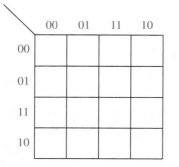

(c) Use the short-cut method to derive the J-K input equations for flip-flops A and B from the next-state maps of Fig. 15–10. Your answers should be

$$J_A = X_2 B, \qquad\qquad K_A = X_2' B',$$
$$J_B = X_1 A' + X_1 X_2, \qquad K_B = X_1' X_2 + X_1' A$$

8. Study Section 15.7, *Equivalent State Assignments.*

(a) Fill in the missing assignments (numbered 8 through 18) in Table 15–8. First list the remaining assignments with 01 in the first row and then the assignments with 10 in the first row.

(b) Why is it unnecessary to try all possible state assignments to be assured of finding a minimum cost network?

(c) For symmetrical flip-flops, why is it always possible to assign all 0's to the starting state and still obtain a minimum network?

(d) Complete the transition table given below for Table 15–9 using assignment "a". Then complete the next-state maps and derive $J_1, K_1, J_2, K_2, D_1,$ and D_2.

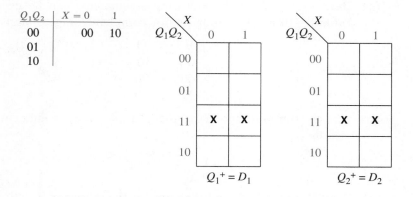

$Q_1 Q_2$	$X = 0$	1
00	00	10
01		
10		

$Q_1^+ = D_1$ $Q_2^+ = D_2$

Starting with the equations for assignment "a", replace all of the 1's with 2's and all 2's with 1's. Verify that the resulting equations are the same as those for assignment "b".

Starting with the J and K equations for assignment "a", replace each Q with Q' and vice versa. Then replace the equations for J with the corresponding K equations and vice versa. (This corresponds to the transformation given in Fig. 15–12.) Verify that the resulting equations are the same as for assignment "c".

Complement the right-hand side of the D equations for assignment "a", and then replace each Q with Q' and vice versa. (This corresponds to the transformation given in Fig. 15–13.) Verify that the resulting equations are the same as for assignment "c".

(e) Show that each of the assignments in Table 15–8 is equivalent to one of the assignments in Table 15–10.

(f) Why are the following two state assignments equivalent in cost?

A	000	011
B	001	111
C	011	101
D	101	110
E	100	010
F	010	001
G	110	000

(g) Show that each of the following assignments can be generated from Table 15–10 by permuting and/or complementing columns:

10	11	01
01	01	11
00	00	00
11	10	10

(h) Why is the trial-and-error method of state assignment of limited usefulness?

(i) Read Problem 15.6, and then answer the following questions regarding state assignments before you work the problem:

(1) Why should a column *not* be assigned all 0's or all 1's?

(2) Why should two columns *not* be given the same assignment?

(3) Does interchanging two columns affect the cost of realizing the network?

(4) Does interchanging two rows affect the cost?

(5) Why is an assignment which has two identical rows invalid?

(6) Consider the following 2 assignments: (1) (3) (5)   (3) (1) (5)
(The number at the top of each   0 0 0   0 0 0
column is the decimal equivalent   0 0 1• 0 0 1
of the binary number in the   0 1 0   1 0 0
column.)   1 1 1   1 1 1

If we try the column assignment (1) (3) (5), why is it unnecessary to try (3) (1) (5)?

Why is it desirable to assign the column values in increasing numerical order?

9. Study Section 15.8, *Guidelines for State Assignment.*

(a) Why do the guidelines for making state assignments help in making an economical assignment?

(b) What should be done if all the adjacencies specified by the guidelines cannot be satisfied?

(c) The state assignment guidelines for Fig. 15–14(a) indicate that the following sets of states should be given adjacent assignments:

    (1) (S_0, S_1, S_3, S_5) (S_3, S_5) (S_4, S_6) (S_0, S_2, S_4, S_6)
    (2) (S_1, S_2) (S_2, S_3) (S_1, S_4) $(S_2, S_5)2X$ $(S_1, S_6)2X$

Since the adjacencies from guideline 1 are generally most important, we will start by placing one of the largest groups from guideline 1 in four adjacent squares:

S_0	
S_1	
S_3	
S_5	

Note that (S_3, S_5) is also satisfied by this grouping. Place S_2, S_4, and S_6 in the remaining squares to satisfy as many of the remaining guidelines as possible. Keeping in mind that groups labeled $2X$ should be given preference over groups which are not repeated. Compare your answer with Fig. 15–14(b).

(d) Complete the transition table for the state table of Fig. 15–16(a) using the assignment of Fig. 15–16(b).

	Q_1 Q_2 Q_3	$Q_1^+ Q_2^+ Q_3^+$			
		$X = 0$	1	0	1
a	0 0 0	000	100	0	0
b	1 1 1	011	110	0	1
c	1 0 0	100	000	0	0

(e) Complete the next state and output maps, and verify that the cost of realizing the corresponding equations with an AND-OR gate network is 13 gates and 35 gate inputs.

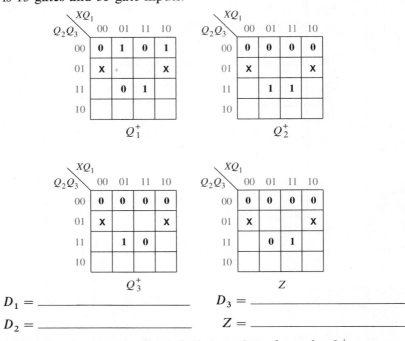

$$D_1 = \underline{\hspace{4cm}} \qquad D_3 = \underline{\hspace{4cm}}$$

$$D_2 = \underline{\hspace{4cm}} \qquad Z = \underline{\hspace{4cm}}$$

(f) Using the short-cut method, find J_1 and K_1 from the Q_1^+ map.

$$J_1 = \underline{\hspace{4cm}}$$

$$K_1 = \underline{\hspace{4cm}}$$

10. Work Problems 15.7, 15.9, and 15.11.

11. When you are satisfied that you can meet all of the objectives, take the readiness test.

Reduction of State Tables
State Assignment

Given a description of the desired input-output behavior of a sequential network, the first step in designing the network is to derive a state table using methods similar to the ones discussed in the previous unit. Before we realize this state table using flip-flops and logic gates, reduction of the state table to a minimum number of states is desirable. In general, reducing the number of states in a table will reduce the amount of logic required, and the number of flip-flops may also be reduced. For example, if a table with 9 states is reduced to 8 states, the number of flip-flops required is reduced from 4 to 3, with a possible corresponding reduction in the amount of input logic for the flip-flops. If the table is further reduced to 6 states, 3 flip-flops are still required, but the presence of more don't cares in the flip-flop input equations will probably further reduce the required logic.

Given the reduced state table, the next step in synthesizing the network is to assign binary flip-flop states to correspond to the network states. The way in which this assignment is made will determine the amount of logic required for the network. The problem of finding a good state assignment which leads to an economical network is a difficult one, but some guidelines for achieving this are discussed in Sections 15.7–15.8.

15.1
Elimination of Redundant States

In Unit 14, we were careful to avoid introducing unnecessary states when setting up a state graph or table. We will now approach the problem of deriving the state graph somewhat differently. Initially, when first setting up the state table we will not be overly concerned with inclusion of extra states, but when the table is complete we will eliminate any redundant states. In previous units, we have used the notation $S_0, S_1, S_2, \ldots$ to represent states in a sequential network. In this unit, we will frequently use $A, B, C, \ldots$ (or $a, b, c, \ldots$) to represent these states.

We will rework Example 1 in Section 14.3. Initially, we will set up enough states to remember the first three bits of every possible input sequence. Then when the fourth bit comes in, we can determine the correct output and reset the network to the initial state. As indicated in Table 15–1, we will designate state A as the reset state. If we receive a 0, we go to state B; if we receive a 1, we go to state C. Similarly, starting in state B, a 0 takes us to state D to indicate that the sequence 00 has been received, and a 1 takes us to state E to indicate that 01 has been received. The remaining states are defined in a similar manner. When

Table 15–1
State Table for Sequence Detector

Input Sequence	Present State	Next State		Present Output	
		$X = 0$	$X = 1$	$X = 0$	$X = 1$
reset	A	B	C	0	0
0	B	D	E	0	0
1	C	F	G	0	0
00	D	H	I	0	0
01	E	J	K	0	0
10	F	L	M	0	0
11	G	N	P	0	0
000	H	A	A	0	0
001	I	A	A	0	0
010	J	A	A	0	1
011	K	A	A	0	0
100	L	A	A	0	1
101	M	A	A	0	0
110	N	A	A	0	0
111	P	A	A	0	0

the fourth input bit is received, we return to the reset state. The output is 0 unless we are in state J or L and receive a 1, which corresponds to having received 0101 or 1001.

Next we will attempt to eliminate redundant states from the table. The input sequence information was only used in setting up the table and will now be disregarded. Looking at the table, we see that there is no way of telling states H and I apart. That is, if we start in state H the next state is A and the output is 0; similarly, if we start in state I the next state is A and the output is 0. Hence, there is no way of telling states H and I apart and we can replace I with H where it appears in the next state portion of the table. Having done this, there is no way to reach state I, so row I can be removed from the table. We say that H is *equivalent* to I ($H \equiv I$). Similarly, rows K, M, N, and P have the same next state and output as H, so K, M, N, and P can be replaced by H and these rows can be deleted. Also, the next states and outputs are the same for rows J and L, so $J \equiv L$. Thus, L can be replaced with J and eliminated from the table. The result is shown in Table 15–2.

Having made these changes in the table, rows D and G are identical and so are rows E and F. Therefore, $D \equiv G$, and $E \equiv F$, so states F and G can be eliminated. Figure 15–1 shows a state diagram for the final reduced table. Note that this is identical to the state graph of Fig. 14–14 except for the designations for the states. The procedure used to find equivalent states in this example is

Table 15-2

State Table for Sequence Detector

Present State	Next State X = 0	X = 1	Present Output X = 0	X = 1
A	B	C	0	0
B	D	E	0	0
C	F E	G D	0	0
D	H	I H	0	0
E	J	K H	0	0
F	L J	M H	0	0
G	N H	P H	0	0
H	A	A	0	0
I	A	A	0	0
J	A	A	0	1
K	A	A	0	0
L	A	A	0	1
M	A	A	0	0
N	A	A	0	0
P	A	A	0	0

known as *row matching*. In general, row matching is *not* sufficient to find all equivalent states, except in the special case where the network resets to the starting state after receiving a fixed number of inputs.

Present State	Next State X = 0	X = 1	Output X = 0	X = 1
A	B	C	0	0
B	D	E	0	0
C	E	D	0	0
D	H	H	0	0
E	J	H	0	0
H	A	A	0	0
J	A	A	0	1

(a)

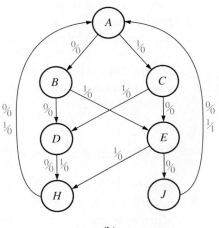

(b)

Figure 15-1
Reduced State Table and Graph for
Sequence Detector

15.2
Equivalent States

As we have seen in the previous example, state tables can be reduced by eliminating equivalent states. A state table with fewer rows often requires fewer flip-flops and logic gates to realize; therefore, determination of equivalent states is important to obtaining economical realizations of sequential networks.

Let us now consider the general problem of state equivalence. Basically, two states are equivalent if there is no way of telling them apart from observation of the network inputs and outputs. Consider two sequential networks (these may be different networks or two copies of the same network), one which is started in state p and one which is started in state q (Fig. 15–2):

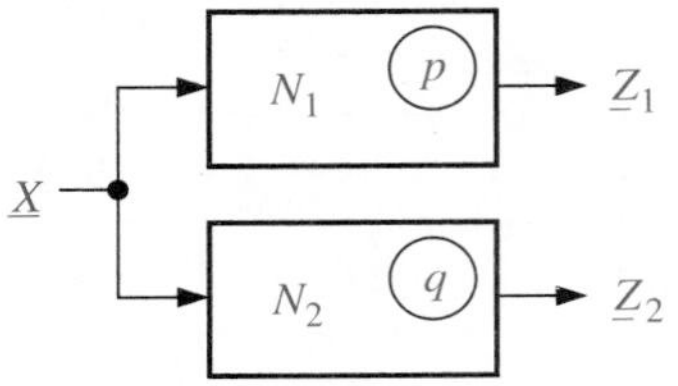

Figure 15–2

Let $\underline{X}$ represent a sequence of inputs $X_1, X_2, \ldots, X_n$. Feed the same input sequence $\underline{X}$ into both networks and observe the output sequences $\underline{Z}_1$ and $\underline{Z}_2$. If these output sequences are the same, so far so good. Then reset the networks to the states p and q and try a different input sequence for $\underline{X}$ and again compare output sequences. If for every possible input sequence $\underline{X}$ these output sequences are the same, then there is no way of telling states p and q apart by observing the terminal behavior of the networks, and we say p is equivalent to q ($p \equiv q$). On the other hand, if for some input sequence $\underline{X}$ the output sequences $\underline{Z}_1$ and $\underline{Z}_2$ are different, then we can distinguish between states p and q, and they are not equivalent. Since the output sequence is a function of the initial state and the input sequence, we will write

$$\underline{Z}_1 = \lambda_1(p, \underline{X}) \qquad \underline{Z}_2 = \lambda_2(q, \underline{X})$$

We can then state formally the definition of state equivalence as follows:

Definition 15.1: Let N_1 and N_2 be sequential networks (not necessarily different). Let $\underline{X}$ represent a sequence of inputs of arbitrary length. Then state p in N_1 is equivalent to state q in N_2 iff $\lambda_1(p, \underline{X}) = \lambda_2(q, \underline{X})$ for every possible input sequence $\underline{X}$.

Definition 15.1 is often difficult to apply directly in practice, since it may require testing the network with an infinite number of input sequences in order to prove that two states are equivalent. A more practical way of testing for state equivalence makes use of the following theorem:

Theorem 15.1[1]   Two states p and q of a sequential network are equivalent iff for every single input X, the outputs are the same and the next states are *equivalent*, that is,

$$\lambda(p, X) = \lambda(q, X) \qquad \text{and} \qquad \delta(p, X) \equiv \delta(q, X)$$

where $\lambda(p, X)$ is the output given the present state p and input X and $\delta(p, X)$ is the next state given the present state p and input X.

The row matching procedure previously discussed is a special case of this theorem where the next states are actually the same instead of just being equivalent.

We will use the above theorem to show that Table 13–4 has no equivalent states. By inspection of the output part of the table, the only possible pair of equivalent states is S_0 and S_2. From the table,

$$S_0 \equiv S_2 \quad \text{iff} \quad S_3 \equiv S_3, \quad S_2 \equiv S_0, \quad S_1 \equiv S_1 \quad \text{and} \quad S_0 \equiv S_1$$

But $S_0 \not\equiv S_1$ (because the outputs differ), so the last condition is not satisfied and $S_0 \not\equiv S_2$.

15.3
Determination of State Equivalence Using an Implication Table

In this section we will discuss a procedure for finding all of the equivalent states in a state table. If the equivalent states found by this procedure are eliminated, then the table can be reduced to a minimum number of states. We will use an implication table (sometimes referred to as a pair chart) to check each pair of states for possible equivalence. Nonequivalent pairs are systematically eliminated until only equivalent pairs remain.

We will use the example of Table 15–3 to illustrate the implication table method. The first step is to construct a chart of the form shown in Fig. 15–3. This chart has a square for every possible pair of states. A square in column i and row j corresponds to state pair i-j. Thus, the squares in the first column correspond to state pairs a-b, a-c, etc. Note that squares above the diagonal are not included in the chart since if $i \equiv j$, $j \equiv i$, and only one of the state pairs i-j and j-i is needed. Also, squares corresponding to pairs a-a, b-b, etc. are omitted. To fill in the first column of the chart, we compare row a of Table 15–3 with each of the other rows. Since the output for row a is different than the output for row c, we place an X in the a-c square of the chart to indicate that $a \not\equiv c$.

---

[1] See Appendix C.2 for proof.

Table 15–3

Present State	Next State X = 0 1	Present Output
a	d c	0
b	f h	0
c	e d	1
d	a e	0
e	c a	1
f	f b	1
g	b h	0
h	c g	1

Similarly, we place X's in squares a-e, a-f and a-h to indicate that $a \not\equiv e$, $a \not\equiv f$, and $a \not\equiv h$ because of output differences. States a and b have the same outputs, and thus by Theorem 15.1,

$$a \equiv b \quad \text{iff} \quad d \equiv f \quad \text{and} \quad c \equiv h$$

To indicate this, we place the "implied pairs", d-f and c-h, in the a-b square. Similarly, since a and d have the same outputs, we place a-d and c-e in the a-d square to indicate that

$$a \equiv d \quad \text{iff} \quad a \equiv d \quad \text{and} \quad c \equiv e$$

The entries b-d and c-h in the a-g square indicate that

$$a \equiv g \quad \text{iff} \quad b \equiv d \quad \text{and} \quad c \equiv h$$

Next, row b of the state table is compared with each of the remaining rows of the table, and column b of the implication chart is filled in. Similarly, the remaining columns in the chart are filled in to complete Fig. 15–3. Self-implied

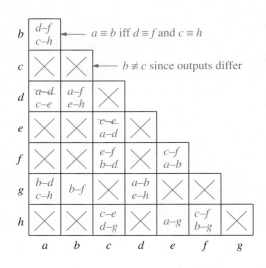

Figure 15–3
Implication Chart for Table 15–3

pairs are redundant, so *a-d* can be eliminated from square *a-d*, and *c-e* from square *c-e*.

At this point, each square in the implication table has either been filled in with an X to indicate that the corresponding state pair is not equivalent or filled in with implied pairs. We now check each implied pair. If one of the implied pairs in square *i-j* is not equivalent, then by Theorem 15.1, $i \not\equiv j$. The *a-b* square of Fig. 15–3 contains two implied pairs (*d-f* and *c-h*). Since $d \not\equiv f$ (*d-f* square has an X in it), $a \not\equiv b$ and we place an X in the *a-b* square as shown in Fig. 15–4. Continuing to check the first column, we note that the *a-d* square contains the implied pair *c-e*. Since square *c-e* does not contain an X, we cannot determine at this point whether or not $a \equiv d$. Similarly, since neither square *b-d* nor *c-h* contains an X, we cannot determine immediately whether $a \equiv g$ or not. Going on to the second column, we place X's in squares *b-d* and *b-g* since we have already shown $a \not\equiv f$ and $b \not\equiv f$. In a similar manner, we check each of the remaining columns and X out squares *c-f*, *d-g*, *e-f* and *f-h*. Figure 15–4 shows the resulting chart.

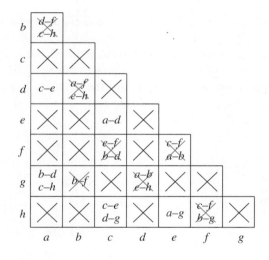

Figure 15–4
Implication Chart After First Pass

In going from Fig. 15–3 to Fig. 15–4, we found several additional non-equivalent state pairs. Therefore, we must go through the chart again to see if the added X's make any other pairs nonequivalent. Rechecking column *a*, we find that we can place an X in square *a-g* since square *b-d* has an X. Checking the remaining columns, we X out squares *c-h* and *e-h* since *d-g* and *a-g* have X's. This completes the second pass through the implication table as shown in Fig. 15–5. Since we added some X's on the second pass, a third pass is required. No new X's are added on the third pass through the table, so all squares which correspond to nonequivalent state pairs have been Xed out. The coordinates of the remaining squares must then correspond to equivalent state pairs. Since square

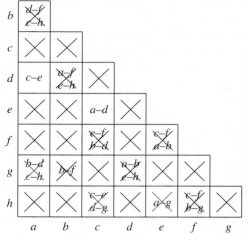

Figure 15–5
Implication Chart After Second Pass

a-d (in column *a*, row *d*) does not contain an X, we conclude that $a \equiv d$. Similarly, square *c-e* does not contain an X, so $c \equiv e$. All other squares contain X's, so there are no other equivalent state pairs. Note that we determined equivalent states from the column-row coordinates of the squares without X's, *not* by reading the implied pairs contained within the squares. If we replace *d* with *a* and *e* with *c* in Table 15–3, we can eliminate rows *d* and *e*, and the table reduces to 6 rows as shown in Table 15–4.

Table 15–4

Present State	Next State $X = 0$	1	Output
a	*a*	*c*	0
b	*f*	*h*	0
c	*c*	*a*	1
f	*f*	*b*	1
g	*b*	*h*	0
h	*c*	*g*	1

The implication table method of determining state equivalence can be summarized as follows:

1. Construct a chart which contains a square for each pair of states.
2. Compare each pair of rows in the state table. If the outputs associated with states *i* and *j* are different, place an X in square *i-j* to indicate that $i \not\equiv j$. If the outputs are the same, place the implied pairs in square *i-j*. (If the next states of *i* and *j* are *m* and *n* for some input *x*, then *m-n* is an

implied pair.) If the outputs and next states are the same (or if i-j only implies itself), place a check ($\checkmark$) in square i-j to indicate that $i \equiv j$.

3. Go through the table square-by-square. If square i-j contains the implied pair m-n, and square m-n contains an X, then $i \not\equiv j$, and an X should be placed in square i-j.
4. If any X's were added in step 3, repeat step 3 until no more X's are added.
5. For each square i-j which does not contain an X, $i \equiv j$.

If desired, row matching can be used to partially reduce the state table before constructing the implication table. Although we have illustrated this procedure for a Moore table, the same procedure applies to a Mealy table.

15.4
Equivalent Sequential Networks

Next, we will consider equivalence between sequential networks. Essentially, two sequential networks are equivalent if they are capable of doing the same "work". Equivalence between sequential networks is defined as follows:

Definition 15.2:   Sequential network N_1 is equivalent to sequential network N_2 if for each state p in N_1 there is a state q in N_2 such that $p \equiv q$, and conversely, for each state s in N_2 there is a state t in N_1 such that $s \equiv t$.

Thus if $N_1 \equiv N_2$, for every starting state p in N_1 we can find a corresponding starting state q such that $\lambda_1(p, \underline{X}) = \lambda_2(q, \underline{X})$ for all input sequences $\underline{X}$ (i.e., the output sequences are the same for the same input sequence). Thus, in a given application N_1 could be replaced with its equivalent network N_2.

If N_1 and N_2 have only a few states, one way to show that $N_1 \equiv N_2$ is to match up pairs of equivalent states by inspection and then show that Theorem 15.1 is satisfied for each pair of equivalent states. If N_1 and N_2 both have a minimum number of states and $N_1 \equiv N_2$, then N_1 and N_2 must have the same number of states. Otherwise, one network would have a state left over which was not equivalent to any state in the other network and Def. 15.2 would not be satisfied.

Figure 15–6 shows two reduced state tables and their corresponding state graphs. By inspection of the state graphs, it appears that if the networks are equivalent we must have A equivalent to either S_2 or S_3 since these are the only states in N_2 with self-loops. Since the outputs of A and S_2 correspond, the only possibility is $A \equiv S_2$. If we assume that $A \equiv S_2$, this implies that we must have $B \equiv S_0$, which in turn implies that we must have $D \equiv S_1$ and $C \equiv S_3$. Using the state tables, we can verify that the above assumptions are correct since for every pair of assumed equivalent states the next states are equivalent and the outputs are equal when $X = 0$ and also when $X = 1$. This verifies that $N_1 \equiv N_2$.

	N_1			
	X = 0	1	X = 0	1
A	B	A	0	0
B	C	D	0	1
C	A	C	0	1
D	C	B	0	0

	N_2			
	X = 0	1	X = 0	1
S_0	S_3	S_1	0	1
S_1	S_3	S_0	0	0
S_2	S_0	S_2	0	0
S_3	S_2	S_3	0	1

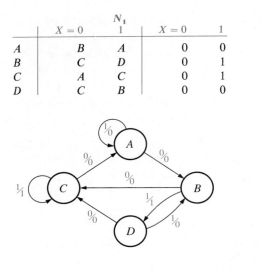

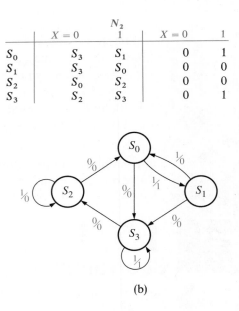

(a)   (b)

Figure 15–6
Tables and Graphs for Equivalent Networks

The implication table can easily be adapted for determining equivalence of sequential networks. Since the states of one network must be checked for equivalence against states of the other network, an implication chart is constructed with rows corresponding to states of one network and columns corresponding to states of the other. For example, for the networks of Fig. 15–6 we can set up the implication table of Fig. 15–7(a). The first column of Fig. 15–7(a) is filled in by comparing row A of the state table in Fig. 15–6(a) with each of the rows in Fig. 15–6(b). Since states A and S_0 have different outputs, an X is placed in the A-S_0 square. Since states A and S_1 have the same outputs, the implied next state pairs (B-S_3 and A-S_0) are placed in the A-S_1 square, etc. The remainder of the

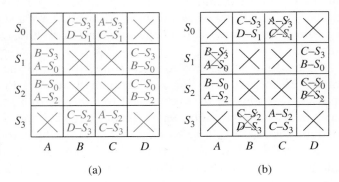

(a)   (b)

Figure 15–7
Implication Tables for Determining
Network Equivalence

table is filled in similarly. In the next step, Fig. 15–7(b), squares corresponding to additional nonequivalent state pairs are crossed out. Thus, square A-S_1 is crossed out because $A \not\equiv S_0$. Similarly, square B-S_3 is crossed out because $C \not\equiv S_2$, square C-S_0 because $A \not\equiv S_3$, and square D-S_2 because $B \not\equiv S_2$. Another pass through the table reveals no additional nonequivalent pairs; therefore, the remaining equivalent state pairs are

$$A \equiv S_2 \qquad B \equiv S_0 \qquad C \equiv S_3 \qquad D \equiv S_1$$

Since each state in N_1 has an equivalent state in N_2 and conversely, $N_1 \equiv N_2$.

15.5
Incompletely Specified State Tables

When a sequential network is used as part of a larger digital system, it frequently happens that certain sequences will never occur as inputs to the sequential network. In other cases, the output of the sequential network is only observed at certain times rather than at every clock time. Such restrictions lead to unspecified next states or outputs in the state table. When such don't cares are present, we say that the state table is incompletely specified. Just as don't cares in a truth table can be used to simplify the resulting combinational network, don't cares in a state table can be used to simplify the sequential network.

The following example illustrates how don't cares arise in a state table. Assume that network A (Fig. 15–8) can only generate two possible output sequences, $X = 100$ and $X = 110$. Thus, the sequential network subsystem (B) has only two possible input sequences. When the third input in the sequence is received, the output of B is to be $Z = 0$ if 100 was received and $Z = 1$ if 110 was received. Assume that network C ignores the value of Z at other times so that we don't care what Z is during the first two inputs in the X sequence. The possible input-output sequences for network B are listed below, where t_0, t_1 and t_2 represent 3 successive clock times:

$$
\begin{array}{ccc|ccc}
t_0 & t_1 & t_2 & t_0 & t_1 & t_2 \\
\hline
X = 1 & 0 & 0 & Z = - & - & 0 \\
1 & 1 & 0 & & - & - & 1 \\
\end{array}
\qquad \text{(– is a don't care output)}
$$

State Table 15–5(a) will produce the required outputs. Note that the next state entry for S_0 with $X = 0$ is a don't care since 0 can never occur as the first input in the sequence. Similarly, the next state entries for S_2 and S_3 with $X = 1$ are don't cares since $X = 1$ cannot occur as the third input in the sequence. If we

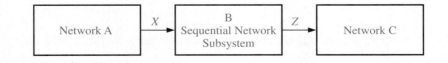

Figure 15–8

Table 15–5

Incompletely Specified State Table

	X = 0	1	0	1			X = 0	1	0	1			X = 0	1	0	1
S_0	–	S_1	–	–		S_0	(S_0)	S_1	(0)	–		S_0	S_0	S_1	0	–
S_1	S_2	S_3	–	–		S_1	S_2 S_0	S_3	(1)	–		S_1	S_0	S_1	1	–
S_2	S_0	–	0	–		S_2	S_0	(S_1)	0	–						
S_3	S_0	–	1	–		S_3	S_0	(S_3)	1	–						

(a)	(b)	(c)

$$S_0 \equiv S_2, S_1 \equiv S_3$$

fill in the don't cares in the state table as indicated in Table 15–5(b), we can use row matching to reduce the table to two states as shown in Table 15–5(c).

As illustrated in the above example, one method of reducing incompletely specified state tables is to fill in the don't cares in an appropriate manner and then reduce the table using one of the methods which apply to completely specified state tables. This procedure may be applied to small tables or to tables with only a few don't cares, but in general it does not lead to a minimum-row reduced table. Determining the best way to fill in the don't cares may require considerable trial and error, and even if the best way of filling in the don't cares is found, the resulting table cannot always be reduced to a minimum-row table. General procedures are known which will reduce an incompletely specified state table to a minimum number of rows,[2] but discussion of such procedures is beyond the scope of this text.

15.6
Derivation of Flip-Flop Input Equations

After the number of states in a state table has been reduced, the following procedure can be used to derive the flip-flop input equations:

1. Assign flip-flop state values to correspond to states in the reduced table.
2. Construct a transition table which gives the next states of the flip-flops as a function of the present states and inputs.
3. Derive next state maps from the transition table.
4. Find flip-flop input maps from the next state maps using the techniques developed in Unit 12, and find the flip-flop input equations from the maps.

As an example, we will design a sequential network to realize Table 15–6(a). Since there are 7 states, we will need 3 flip-flops. We will designate the flip-flop

---

[2] See, for example, Hill and Peterson, *Introduction to Switching Theory and Logical Design*, 3d edition, Chapter 13.

Table 15–6

	(a) state table				(b) transition table				
						$A^+B^+C^+$		Z	
	$x = 0$	1	0	1	ABC	$X = 0$	1	0	1
S_0	S_1	S_2	0	0	000	110	001	0	0
S_1	S_3	S_2	0	0	110	111	001	0	0
S_2	S_1	S_4	0	0	001	110	011	0	0
S_3	S_5	S_2	0	0	111	101	001	0	0
S_4	S_1	S_6	0	0	011	110	010	0	0
S_5	S_5	S_2	1	0	101	101	001	1	0
S_6	S_1	S_6	0	1	010	110	010	0	1

outputs as A, B, and C. We could make a straight binary state assignment for which S_0 is represented by flip-flop states $ABC = 000$, S_1 by $ABC = 001$, S_2 by $ABC = 010$, etc. However, using a different assignment may lead to simpler flip-flop input equations. As an example, we will use the following assignment for the states of flip-flops A, B and C:

$$S_0 = 000, \quad S_1 = 110, \quad S_2 = 001, \quad S_3 = 111, \quad S_4 = 011, \quad S_5 = 101, \quad S_6 = 010$$

$$(15–1)$$

This state assignment is derived in Section 15.8 and the reasons why it leads to an economical solution are given in that section. Starting with Table 15–6(a), we substitute 000 for S_0, 110 for S_1, 001 for S_2, etc. Table 15–6(b) shows the resulting transition table. This table gives the next states of flip-flops A, B, and C in terms of the present states and the input X. We can fill in the next-state maps, Fig. 15–9(a), directly from this table. For $XABC = 0000$ the next state entry is 110, so we fill in $A^+ = 1$, $B^+ = 1$ and $C^+ = 0$; for $XABC = 1000$ the next state entry is 001, so we fill in $A^+ = 0$, $B^+ = 0$ and $C^+ = 1$; etc. Since the state assignment $ABC = 100$ is not used, the map squares corresponding to $XABC = 0100$ and 1100 are filled with don't cares.

Once the next-state maps have been plotted from the transition table, the flip-flop input equations can be derived using the techniques developed in Unit 12. As shown in Fig. 15–9(a), the D flip-flop input equations can be derived directly from the next-state maps since $D_A = A^+$, $D_B = B^+$, and $D_C = C^+$. If J-K flip-flops are used, the J and K input equations can be derived from the next state maps using the short-cut method as illustrated in Fig. 15–9(b). As was shown in Section 12.5, the $A = 0$ half of the A^+ map is a map for J_A and the $A = 1$ half is a map for K'_A. Therefore, we can determine J_A by looping 1's on the $A = 0$ half of the map, and we can determine K_A by looping 0's on the $A = 1$ half. We have crossed out the values of A at the top of the A^+ map since J_A and K_A do not depend on A. We can derive J_B, K_B, J_C, and K_C from the B^+ and C^+ maps in a manner similar to J_A and K_A.

Table 15–7(a) represents a sequential network with two inputs (X_1, X_2) and two outputs (Z_1, Z_2). Since it has four states, two flip-flops (A, B) are required to

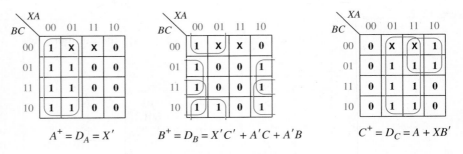

$$A^+ = D_A = X'$$

$$B^+ = D_B = X'C' + A'C + A'B$$

$$C^+ = D_C = A + XB'$$

(a) Derivation of D flip-flop input equations

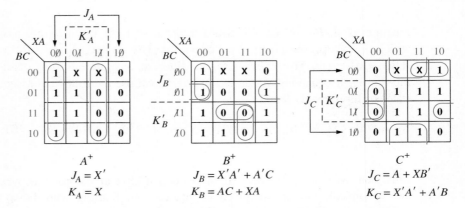

$$A^+$$
$$J_A = X'$$
$$K_A = X$$

$$B^+$$
$$J_B = X'A' + A'C$$
$$K_B = AC + XA$$

$$C^+$$
$$J_C = A + XB'$$
$$K_C = X'A' + A'B$$

(b) Derivation of J-K flip-flop input equations

Figure 15–9
Next-State Maps for Table 15–6

realize the table. We will use the state assignment $AB = 00$ for S_0, $AB = 01$ for S_1, $AB = 11$ for S_2, and $AB = 10$ for S_3. By substituting the corresponding values of AB for the state names, we obtain the transition table, Table 15–7(b). We can then fill in the next-state and output maps (Fig. 15–10) from the transition table. For example, when $X_1X_2AB = 0011$, $A^+B^+ = 10$ and $Z_1Z_2 = 11$; therefore, we fill in the 0011 squares of the A^+, B^+, Z_1 and Z_2 maps with 1, 0, 1, and 1, respectively. We can read the D flip-flop input equations directly from the next-state maps.

Table 15–7

	(a) state table									(b) transition table								
	Next State				Outputs (Z_1Z_2)						A^+B^+				Outputs (Z_1Z_2)			
	$X_1X_2 =$				$X_1X_2 =$						$X_1X_2 =$				$X_1X_2 =$			
P.S.	00	01	11	10	00	01	11	10		AB	00	01	11	10	00	01	11	10
S_0	S_0	S_0	S_1	S_1	00	00	01	01		00	00	00	01	01	00	00	01	01
S_1	S_1	S_3	S_2	S_1	00	10	10	00		01	01	10	11	01	00	10	10	00
S_2	S_3	S_3	S_2	S_2	11	11	00	00		11	10	10	11	11	11	11	00	00
S_3	S_0	S_3	S_2	S_0	00	00	00	00		10	00	10	11	00	00	00	00	00

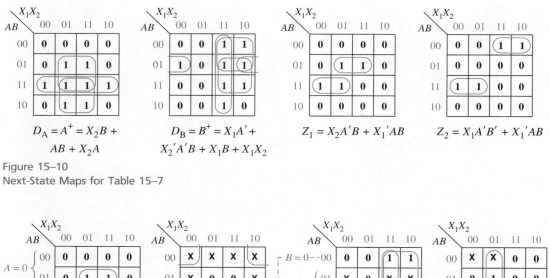

$$D_A = A^+ = X_2 B + AB + X_2 A$$

$$D_B = B^+ = X_1 A' + X_2' A' B + X_1 B + X_1 X_2$$

$$Z_1 = X_2 A' B + X_1' AB$$

$$Z_2 = X_1 A' B' + X_1' AB$$

Figure 15–10
Next-State Maps for Table 15–7

$$S_A = X_2 B$$

$$R_A = X_2' B'$$

$$S_B = X_1 X_2 + X_1 A'$$

$$R_B = X_1' X_2 + X_1' A$$

Figure 15–11
Derivation of S-R Equations for Table 15–7

If J-K flip-flops are used, the J and K equations can be read from the next state maps using the short-cut method. If T or S-R flip-flops are used, the flip-flop input maps can be derived from the next state maps using the techniques given in Section 12.9. As an example, the S-R equations for Table 15–7 are derived in Fig. 15–11. The S_A and R_A maps are derived from the A^+ map by applying Table 12–4(c) to the $A = 0$ and $A = 1$ halves of the map. S_B and R_B are derived in a similar manner.

15.7
Equivalent State Assignments

After the number of states in a state table has been reduced, the next step in realizing the table is to assign flip-flop states to correspond to the states in the table. The cost of the logic required to realize a sequential network is strongly dependent on the way this state assignment is made. Several methods for choosing state assignments to obtain economical realizations are discussed in this chapter. The trial and error method described below is useful only for a small number of states. The guideline method discussed in Section 15.8 produces good solutions for some problems, but it is not entirely satisfactory in other cases. The SHR

Table 15–8
State Assignments for 3-Row Tables

	1	2	3	4	5	6	7		19	20	21	22	23	24
S_0	00	00	00	00	00	00	01	...	11	11	11	11	11	11
S_1	01	01	10	10	11	11	00		00	00	01	01	10	10
S_2	10	11	01	11	01	10	10		01	10	00	10	00	01

technique[3] produces optimum solutions for J-K flip-flops with a reasonable amount of computation and is usually the best method to use if an optimum solution is required.

If the number of states is small, it may be feasible to try all possible state assignments, evaluate the cost of the realization for each assignment, and choose the assignment with the lowest cost. Consider a state table with three states (S_0, S_1, and S_2) as in Table 14–1. Two flip-flops (A and B) are required to realize this table. The four possible assignments for state S_0 are $AB = 00$, $AB = 01$, $AB = 10$ and $AB = 11$. Choosing one of these assignments leaves three possible assignments for state S_1 because each state must have a unique assignment. Then, after state S_1 is assigned, we have two possible assignments for state S_2. Thus, there are $4 \times 3 \times 2 = 24$ possible state assignments for the three states, as shown in Table 15–8. As an example, for assignment 7, the entry 01 in the S_0 row means that flip-flops A and B are assigned values 0 and 1, respectively.

Trying all 24 of these assignments is not really necessary. If we interchange two columns in one of the given assignments, the cost of realization will be unchanged because interchanging columns is equivalent to relabeling the flip-flop variables. For example, consider assignment 1 in Table 15–8. The first column of this assignment shows that flip-flop A is assigned the values 0, 0 and 1 for states S_0, S_1 and S_2, respectively. Similarly, the second column shows that B is assigned the values 0, 1 and 0. If we interchange the two columns, we get assignment 3, for which A has the values 0, 1, and 0 and B has the values 0, 0, and 1. We could have achieved the same result by using assignment 1 and labeling the flip-flop variables BA instead of AB. If we interchange the columns of assignment 2, we get assignment 4, so assignments 2 and 4 have the same cost. Similarly, assignments 5 and 6 have the same cost. Interchanging rows, however, will generally change the cost of realization. Thus, assignments 4 and 6 will have a different cost for most state tables.

If symmetrical flip-flops such as T, J-K, or S-R are used, complementing one or more columns of the state assignment will have no effect on the cost of realization. Consider a J-K flip-flop imbedded in a network, Fig. 15–12(a). Leave the network unchanged and interchange the J and K leads and the Q_k and Q_k' leads, Fig. 15–12(b). If network A is started with $Q_k = p$ and network B with $Q_k = p'$, the behavior of the two networks will be identical except the value of Q_k will always be complemented in the second network because whenever J is 1 in the

[3] James R. Story, Harold J. Harrison, and Erwin A. Reinhard, "Optimum State Assignment for Synchronous Sequential Circuits," *IEEE Transactions on Computers,* Vol. C-21, Dec. 1972, pp. 1365–1373.

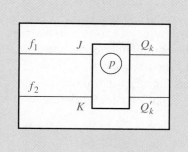

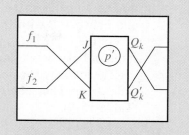

(a) Network A

(b) Network B
(identical to A except leads to flip-flop
Q_k are crossed)

Figure 15–12
Equivalent Networks Obtained by
Complementing Q_k

first network K will be 1 in the second and conversely. The state table for the second network is therefore the same as for the first except the value of Q_k is complemented for the second network. This implies that complementing one or more columns in the state assignment will not affect the cost of the realization when J-K flip-flops are used. Similar reasoning applies to T and S-R flip-flops. Thus in Table 15–8, assignments 2 and 7 have the same cost, and so do assignments 6 and 19.

If unsymmetrical flip-flops are used such as a D flip-flop, it is still true that permuting (i.e., rearranging the order of) columns in the state assignment will not affect the cost; however, complementing a column may require adding an inverter to the network as shown in Fig. 15–13. If different types of gates are available, the

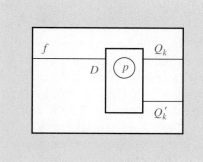

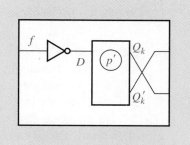

(a) Network A

(b) Network B
(identical to A except for connections to
flip-flop Q_k)

Figure 15–13
Equivalent Networks Obtained by
Complementing Q_k

network can generally be redesigned to eliminate the inverter and use the same number of gates as the original. If network A in Fig. 15–13 is started with $Q_k = p$ and network B with $Q_k = p'$, the behavior of the two networks will be identical, except the value of Q_k will always be complemented in network B because f is the same in both networks and $D = f'$ for network B.

The following example illustrates the effect of interchanging or complementing state assignment columns on the equations for realizing a specific state table (Table 15–9).

Table 15–9

Assignments			Present State	Next State		Output	
"a"	"b"	"c"		$X = 0$	1	0	1
00	00	11	S_1	S_1	S_3	0	0
01	10	10	S_2	S_2	S_1	0	1
10	01	01	S_3	S_2	S_3	1	0

The J-K and D flip-flop input equations for the three assignments can be derived using Karnaugh maps as explained in Unit 12 and Section 15.6. The resulting J-K input equations are:

Assignment "a"	Assignment "b"	Assignment "c"
$J_1 = XQ_2'$	$J_2 = XQ_1'$	$K_1 = XQ_2$
$K_1 = X'$	$K_2 = X'$	$J_1 = X'$
$J_2 = X'Q_1$	$J_1 = X'Q_2$	$K_2 = X'Q_1'$
$K_2 = X$	$K_1 = X$	$J_2 = X$
$Z = X'Q_1 + XQ_2$	$Z = X'Q_2 + XQ_1$	$Z = X'Q_1' + XQ_2'$
$D_1 = XQ_2'$	$D_2 = XQ_1'$	$D_1 = X' + Q_2'$
$D_2 = X'(Q_1 + Q_2)$	$D_1 = X'(Q_2 + Q_1)$	$D_2 = X + Q_1Q_2$

Note that assignment "b" in Table 15–9 was obtained by interchanging the columns of "a". The corresponding equations for assignment "b" are the same as for "a" except that subscripts 1 and 2 are interchanged. Assignment "c" was obtained by complementing the columns of "a". The Z equation for "c" is the same as for "a" except that Q_1 and Q_2 are complemented. The K and J equations for "c" are the same, respectively, as the J and K equations for "a" with the Q's complemented. The D equations for "c" can be obtained by complementing those for "a" and then complementing the Q's. Thus, the cost of realizing Table 15–9 using J-K flip-flops and any kind of logic gates will be exactly the same for all three assignments. If both AND and OR (or NAND and NOR) gates are available, the cost of realizing the three sets of D equations will be the same. If only NOR gates are available, for example, then realizing D_1 and D_2 for assignment "c" would require two additional inverters compared with "a" and "b".

By complementing one or more columns, any state assignment can be converted to one in which the first state is assigned all 0's. If we eliminate assignments which can be obtained by permuting or complementing columns, Table 15–8 reduces to three assignments (Table 15–10). Thus, when realizing a 3-state sequential network with symmetrical flip-flops, it is only necessary to try three different state assignments to be assured of a minimum cost realization. Similarly, only three different assignments must be tried for four states.

Table 15–10

Nonequivalent Assignments for 3 and 4 States

	3-State Assignments			4-State Assignments		
States	1	2	3	1	2	3
a	00	00	00	00	00	00
b	01	01	11	01	01	11
c	10	11	01	10	11	01
d	––	––	––	11	10	10

We will say that two state assignments are *equivalent* if one can be derived from the other by permuting and complementing columns. Two state assignments which are not equivalent are said to be *distinct*. Thus a four-row table has three distinct state assignments and any other assignment is equivalent to one of these three. Unfortunately, the number of distinct assignments increases very rapidly with the number of states as shown in Table 15–11. Hand solution is feasible for 2, 3, or 4 states; computer solution is feasible for 5 through 8 states; but for 9 or more states it is not practical to try all assignments even if a high-speed computer is used.

Table 15–11

Number of Distinct (Nonequivalent) State Assignments

No. of States	Minimum No. of State Variables	No. of Distinct Assignments
2	1	1
3	2	3
4	2	3
5	3	140
6	3	420
7	3	840
8	3	840
9	4	10,810,800
⋮	⋮	⋮
16	4	$\approx 5.5 \times 10^{10}$

15.8
Guidelines for State Assignment

Since trying all nonequivalent state assignments is not practical in most cases, other methods of state assignment are needed. The next method to be discussed involves trying to choose an assignment which will place the 1's on the flip-flop input maps in adjacent squares so that the corresponding terms can be combined. This method does not apply to all problems, and even when applicable does not guarantee a minimum solution.

Assignments for two states are said to be adjacent if they differ in only one variable. Thus, 010, and 011 are adjacent, but 010 and 001 are not. The following *guidelines* are useful in making assignments which will place 1's together (or 0's together) on the next-state maps:

1. States which have the same next state for a given input should be given adjacent assignments.
2. States which are the next states of the same state should be given adjacent assignments.

A third guideline is used for simplification of the output function:

3. States which have the same output for a given input should be given adjacent assignments.

Application of Guideline 3 will place 1's together on the output maps.

When using the state assignment guidelines, the first step is to write down all of the sets of states which should be given adjacent assignments according to the guidelines. Then, using a Karnaugh map, try to satisfy as many of these adjacencies as possible. A fair amount of trial and error may be required to fill in the map such that the maximum number of desired state adjacencies are obtained. When filling in the map, keep in mind the following:

(a) Assign the starting state (reset state) to the "0" square on the map. Nothing is to be gained by trying to put the starting state in different squares on the map since the same number of adjacencies can be found no matter where you put the starting state. Usually, assigning "0" to the starting state simplifies initialization of the network.
(b) Adjacency conditions from Guideline 1 and adjacency conditions which are required two or more times should be satisfied first.
(c) When guidelines require that 3 or 4 states be adjacent, these states should be placed within a group of 4 adjacent squares on the assignment map.
(d) If the output table is to be considered, then Guideline 3 should also be applied. The priority given to adjacency conditions from Guideline 3 should generally be less than that given to Guidelines 1 and 2 if a single output function is being derived. If there are 2 or more output functions, a higher priority for Guideline 3 may be appropriate.

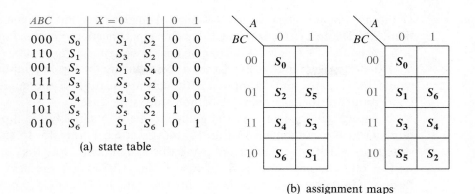

ABC		$X = 0$	1	0	1
000	S_0	S_1	S_2	0	0
110	S_1	S_3	S_2	0	0
001	S_2	S_1	S_4	0	0
111	S_3	S_5	S_2	0	0
011	S_4	S_1	S_6	0	0
101	S_5	S_5	S_2	1	0
010	S_6	S_1	S_6	0	1

(a) state table

(b) assignment maps

Figure 15–14

The following example should clarify the application of Guidelines 1 and 2. The state table from Table 15–6 is repeated in Fig. 15–14(a) so that we can illustrate derivation of the state assignment. According to Guideline 1, S_0, S_2, S_4 and S_6 should be given adjacent assignments because they all have S_1 as a next state (with input 0). Similarly, S_0, S_1, S_3, and S_5 should have adjacent assignments because they have S_2 as a next state (with input 1); also S_3 and S_5 should have adjacent assignments, and so should S_4 and S_6. Application of Guideline 2 indicates that S_1 and S_2 should be given adjacent assignments since they are both next states of S_0. Similarly, S_2 and S_3 should have adjacent assignments since they are both next states of S_1. Further application of Guideline 2 indicates that S_1 and S_4, S_2 and S_5 (two times), and S_1 and S_6 (two times) should be given adjacent assignments. In summary, the sets of adjacent states specified by Guidelines 1 and 2 are

1. (S_0, S_1, S_3, S_5) (S_3, S_5) (S_4, S_6) (S_0, S_2, S_4, S_6)
2. (S_1, S_2) (S_2, S_3) (S_1, S_4) $(S_2, S_5)2x$ $(S_1, S_6)2x$

We will attempt to fulfill as many of these adjacency conditions as possible. A Karnaugh map will be used to make the assignments so that states with adjacent assignments will appear in adjacent squares on the map. If the guidelines require that 3 or 4 states be adjacent, these states should be placed within a group of 4 adjacent squares on the assignment map. Two possible ways of filling in the assignment maps are shown in Fig. 15–14(b). These maps were filled in by trial and error, attempting to fulfill as many of the above adjacency conditions as possible. Conditions from Guideline 1 are given preference to conditions from Guideline 2. Conditions which are required two times (such as S_2 adjacent to S_5, and S_1 adjacent to S_6) are given preference over conditions which are required only once (such as S_1 adjacent to S_2, and S_2 adjacent to S_3).

The left assignment map in Fig. 15–14(b) implies an assignment for the states of flip-flops A, B, and C which is listed to the left of the state table in Fig. 15–14(a). This assignment is the same as the one given in Equations (15–1). We derived the

D flip-flop input equations and J-K input equations for this assignment in Section 15.6. The cost of realizing the D flip-flop input equations given in Fig. 15 — 9(a) is 6 gates and 13 inputs. If a straight binary assignment ($S_0 = 000$, $S_1 = 001$, $S_2 = 010$, etc.) were used instead, the cost of realizing the flip-flop input equations would be 10 gates and 39 inputs. Although application of the guidelines gives good results in this example, this is not always the case.

Next, we will explain why the guidelines help to simplify the flip-flop equations when the assignment of Fig. 15–14(a) is used. Figure 15–15 shows a next state map which was constructed using this assignment. Note that if $X = 0$ and $ABC = 000$, the next state is S_1; if $X = 1$ and $ABC = 000$, the next state is S_2. Because Guideline 1 was used in making the state assignment, S_1 appears in four adjacent squares on the next-state map, S_5 appears in two adjacent squares, etc.

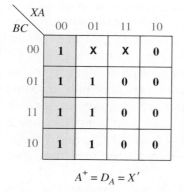

(a) Next state maps for Fig. 15-14

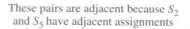

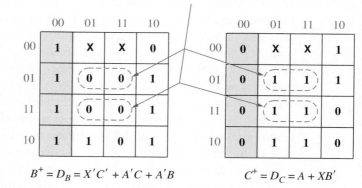

$$A^+ = D_A = X'$$

$$B^+ = D_B = X'C' + A'C + A'B$$

$$C^+ = D_C = A + XB'$$

(b) Next state maps for Fig. 15-14 (cont.)

Figure 15–15
Next-State Maps for Fig. 15–14

The next state maps for the individual flip-flops, Fig. 15–15(b), can be derived in the usual manner from a transition table, or they can be derived directly from Fig. 15–15(a). Using the latter approach, wherever S_1 appears in Fig. 15–15(a), it is replaced with 110 so that 1, 1 and 0 are plotted on the corresponding squares of the A^+, B^+, and C^+ maps, respectively. The other squares on the next-state maps are filled in similarly.

Since four S_1's are adjacent in Fig. 15–15(a), the corresponding squares on the A^+, B^+ and C^+ maps have four adjacent 1's or four adjacent 0's as indicated by the blue shading. This illustrates why Guideline 1 helps to simplify the flip-flop equations. Each time Guideline 2 is applied, two out of the three next-state maps will have an additional pair of adjacent 1's or adjacent 0's. This occurs because two of the three state variables are the same for adjacent assignments.

Next, we will apply the state assignment guidelines to Fig. 15–16(a). First, we list the sets of adjacent states specified by each Guideline:

1. (b, d) (c, f) (b, e)
2. $(a, c)2x$ (d, f) (b, d) (b, f) (c, e)
3. (a, c) (b, d) (e, f)

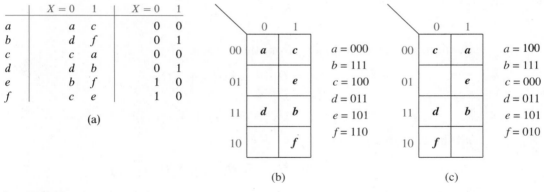

	$X = 0$	1	$X = 0$	1
a	a	c	0	0
b	d	f	0	1
c	c	a	0	0
d	d	b	0	1
e	b	f	1	0
f	c	e	1	0

(a)

(b) $a = 000$ (c)
$b = 111$
$c = 100$
$d = 011$
$e = 101$
$f = 110$

$a = 100$
$b = 111$
$c = 000$
$d = 011$
$e = 101$
$f = 010$

Figure 15–16
State Table and Assignments

Next, we try to arrange the states on a map so as to satisfy as many of the above pairs as possible, but giving preference to the duplicated pairs (b, d) and (a, c). Two such arrangements and the corresponding assignments are given in Figs. 15–16(b) and (c). For (c), all adjacencies are satisfied except (b, f), (c, e) and (e, f). We will derive D flip-flop input equations for this assignment. First, we construct the transition table (Table 15–12) from the state table (Fig. 15–16(a)) by replacing a with 100, b with 111, c with 000, etc. Then we plot the next-state and output maps (Fig. 15–17) from the transition table. The D flip-flop input

Table 15–12

Transition table for Fig. 15–16(a)

	$Q_1^+ Q_2^+ Q_3^+$			
$Q_1 Q_2 Q_3$	$X = 0$	1	$X = 0$	1
1 0 0	100	000	0	0
1 1 1	011	010	0	1
0 0 0	000	100	0	0
0 1 1	011	111	0	1
1 0 1	111	010	1	0
0 1 0	000	101	1	0

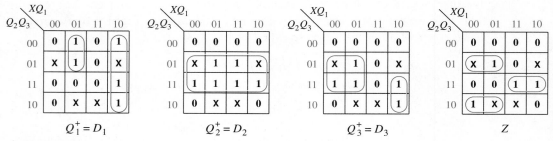

$$Q_1^+ = D_1 \qquad Q_2^+ = D_2 \qquad Q_3^+ = D_3 \qquad Z$$

Figure 15–17
Next-State and Output Maps for Table 15–12

equations can be read directly from these maps:

$$D_1 = Q_1^+ = X'Q_1 Q_2' + XQ_1'$$
$$D_2 = Q_2^+ = Q_3$$
$$D_3 = Q_3^+ = XQ_1'Q_2 + X'Q_3$$

and the output equation is

$$Z = XQ_2 Q_3 + X'Q_2'Q_3 + X'Q_2 Q_3'$$

The cost of realizing these equations is 10 gates and 26 gate inputs.

The assignment of Fig. 15–16(b) satisfies all of the guidelines except (d, f) and (e, f). Using this assignment, the cost of realizing the state table with D flip-flops is 13 gates and 35 gate inputs. We would expect that this assignment would produce better results than Fig. 15–16(c) since it satisfies one more of the adjacencies given by the guidelines, but just the opposite is true. As illustrated by this example, the assignment which satisfies the most guidelines is not necessarily the best assignment. In general, it is a good idea to try several assignments which satisfy most of the guidelines and choose the one which gives the lowest cost solution.

The guidelines work best for D flip-flops and J-K flip-flops. They do not work as well for T and S-R flip-flops. In general, the best assignment for one type of flip-flop is not the best for another type.

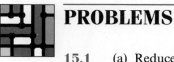

PROBLEMS

15.1   (a) Reduce the following state table to a minimum number of states.

Present State	Next State X = 0	1	Present Output X = 0	1
a	c	f	0	0
b	d	e	0	0
c	h	g	0	0
d	b	g	0	0
e	e	b	0	1
f	f	a	0	1
g	c	g	0	1
h	c	f	0	0

   (b) You are given two identical sequential networks which realize the above state table. One network is initially in state "*a*" and the other network is initially in state "*c*". Specify an input sequence of length three which could be used to distinguish between the two networks, and give the corresponding output sequence from each network.

15.2   (a) Reduce the following state table to a minimum number of states.

Present State	Next State X = 0	1	Present Output X = 0	1
a	h	c	1	0
b	c	d	0	1
c	h	b	0	0
d	f	h	0	0
e	c	f	0	1
f	f	g	0	0
g	g	c	1	0
h	a	c	1	0

   (b) Answer (b) of Problem 15.1 for this state table with initial states "*d*" and "*c*".

15.3   Reduce the following state table to a minimum number of states.

Present State	Next State X = 0	1	Present Output (Z)
a	f	d	0
b	d	a	1
c	h	b	0
d	b	c	1
e	g	b	0
f	a	h	0
g	e	c	0
h	c	f	0

15.4   Reduce the following state table to a minimum number of states.

Present State	Next State X = 0	1	Present Output (Z)
a	e	e	1
b	c	e	1
c	i	h	0
d	h	a	1
e	i	f	0
f	e	g	0
g	h	b	1
h	c	d	0
i	f	b	1

15.5   Digital engineer B. I. Nary has just completed the design of a sequential network which has the following state table:

Present State	Next State x = 0	1	Output 0	1
S_0	S_5	S_1	0	0
S_1	S_5	S_6	0	0
S_2	S_2	S_6	0	0
S_3	S_0	S_1	1	0
S_4	S_4	S_3	0	0
S_5	S_0	S_1	0	0
S_6	S_5	S_1	1	0

His assistant, F. L. Ipflop, who has just completed this course, claims that his design can be used to replace Mr. Nary's network. Mr. Ipflop's design has the following state table:

	Next State x = 0	1	Output 0	1
a	a	b	0	0
b	a	c	0	0
c	a	b	1	0

(a) Is Mr. Ipflop correct? (Prove your answer.)
(b) If Mr. Nary's network is always started in state S_0, is Mr. Ipflop correct? (Prove your answer by showing equivalent states, etc.)

15.6   It is sometimes possible to save logic by using more than the minimum number of flip-flops. (This rarely results in overall savings since flip-flops are usually considerably more expensive than gates.) For both (a) and (b), fill in each state assignment by columns and then check for duplicate rows instead of filling in the assignments by rows and checking for permuted columns. If the columns are assigned in ascending numerical order and the first row is all 0's, then equivalent assignments will not be generated. Do not list degenerate assignments for which two columns are identical or complements of each other, or assignments where one column is all 0's or all 1's.

(a) Consider a state table with three states to be realized using three J-K flip-flops. To be sure of getting the minimum amount of logic, how many different state assignments must be tried? Enumerate these assignments.

(b) For four states and three flip-flops, 29 assignments must be tried. Enumerate 10 of these, always assigning 000 to the first state.

15.7 A sequential network with one input and one output has the following state table:

Present State	Next State $X = 0$	$X = 1$	Present Output
S_1	S_5	S_4	0
S_2	S_1	S_6	1
S_3	S_7	S_8	1
S_4	S_7	S_1	0
S_5	S_2	S_3	1
S_6	S_4	S_2	0
S_7	S_6	S_8	0
S_8	S_5	S_3	1

(a) For this part of the problem, do not consider the flip-flop input equations (this means that you can ignore the next state part of the table). Make a state assignment which will minimize the output equation, and derive the minimum output equation for your assignment.

(b) Forget about your solution to (a). Apply Guidelines 1 and 2 to make a state assignment, assigning 000 to S_1. Derive input equations for D flip-flops using this assignment.

15.8 A sequential network with one input and one output has the following state table:

Present State	Next State $X = 0$	$X = 1$	Present Output
A	D	G	1
B	E	H	0
C	B	F	1
D	F	G	0
E	C	A	1
F	H	C	0
G	E	A	1
H	D	B	0

(a) For this part of the problem, do not consider the flip-flop input equations (this means that you can ignore the next state part of the table). Make a state assignment which will minimize the output equation, and derive the minimum output equation for your assignment.

(b) Forget about your solution to (a). Apply Guidelines 1 and 2 to make a state assignment, assigning 000 to A. Derive input equations for D flip-flops using this assignment.

15.9   The following table is to be realized using J-K flip-flops.
(a) Find a good state assignment using the three guidelines (do not reduce the table first.) Try to satisfy as many of the adjacency conditions as possible.
(b) Using this assignment, derive the J-K flip-flop input equations and the output equations. Use the short-cut method.

	$X = 0$	1	$X = 0$	1
			Z	
A	A	E	0	0
B	C	B	0	1
C	A	F	0	0
D	C	B	0	1
E	F	E	0	0
F	A	F	0	0

15.10   Work Problem 15.9 for the following table:

	$X = 0$	1	$X = 0$	1
			Z	
A	F	D	0	0
B	D	B	0	0
C	A	C	0	1
D	F	D	0	0
E	A	C	0	1
F	F	B	0	0

15.11   (a) For the following state table, use the 3 guidelines to determine which of the 3 possible nonequivalent state assignments should give the best solution.

	$X_1X_2 = 00$	01	11	10	$X_1X_2 = 00$	01	11	10
					Z_1Z_2			
A	A	C	B	D	00	00	00	00
B	B	B	D	D	00	00	10	10
C	C	A	C	A	01	01	01	01
D	B	B	C	A	01	01	10	10

(b) Using your answer to (a), derive T flip-flop input equations and the output equations.

15.12   (a) For the following state table, use the 3 guidelines to determine which of the 3 possible nonequivalent state assignments should give the best solution.

	$X_1X_2 = 00$	01	11	10	$X_1X_2 = 00$	01	11	10
					Z_1Z_2			
A	A	A	C	C	01	01	01	01
B	B	D	B	D	11	11	11	11
C	A	A	B	D	11	11	00	00
D	D	B	A	C	01	01	01	01

(b) Using your answer to (a), derive J-K flip-flop input equations and the output equations.

15.13 (a) Reduce the following state table to a minimum number of states using an implication chart.

(b) Use the guideline method to determine a suitable state assignment for the reduced table.

(c) Realize the table using D flip-flops.

(d) Realize the table using J-K flip-flops.

	$X = 0$	1	Z
A	A	B	1
B	C	E	0
C	F	G	1
D	C	A	0
E	I	G	1
F	H	I	1
G	C	F	0
H	F	B	1
I	C	E	0

15.14 Repeat Problem 15.13 for the following table:

	$X = 0$	1	Z
A	I	C	1
B	B	I	1
C	C	G	1
D	I	C	0
E	D	E	0
F	I	C	0
G	E	F	0
H	H	A	1
I	A	C	1

15.15 Make a suitable state assignment and realize the state graph of Fig. 14–9 using:

(a) D flip-flops   (b) S-R flip-flops

15.16 Make a suitable state assignment and realize the state graph of Fig. 14–12 using:

(a) J-K flip-flops   (b) T flip-flops

15.17 Reduce each of the following state tables to a minimum number of states:

(a)

	$XY = 00$	01	11	10	Z
a	a	c	e	d	0
b	d	e	e	a	0
c	e	a	f	b	1
d	b	c	c	b	0
e	c	d	f	a	1
f	f	b	a	d	1

(b)

	$X = 0$	1	0	1
a	b	c	1	0
b	e	d	1	0
c	g	d	1	1
d	e	b	1	0
e	f	g	1	0
f	h	b	1	1
g	h	i	0	1
h	g	i	0	1
i	a	a	0	1

15.18   Reduce each of the following tables to a minimum number of states:

(a)

	$XY = 00$	01	11	10	Z
a	b	i	c	g	0
b	b	c	f	g	0
c	h	d	d	f	1
d	h	c	e	g	1
e	b	c	i	g	0
f	f	i	i	k	0
g	j	k	g	h	0
h	e	f	c	g	0
i	i	i	i	d	0
j	b	f	c	g	0
k	a	c	e	g	1

(b)

	$XY = 00$	01	11	10	$XY = 00$	01	11	10
						Z		
a	a	a	g	k	1	0	0	0
b	c	f	g	d	0	0	0	0
c	g	c	a	i	1	0	0	0
d	a	d	g	i	1	0	0	0
e	f	h	g	a	0	0	0	0
f	g	c	d	k	1	0	0	0
g	c	j	g	e	0	1	0	0
h	g	h	d	k	1	0	0	0
i	h	h	g	d	0	0	0	0
j	j	j	g	k	1	0	0	0
k	c	c	g	d	0	0	0	0

15.19   Networks N and M have the state tables that follow.
(a) Without first reducing the tables, determine whether networks N and M are equivalent.
(b) Reduce each table to a minimum number of states, and then show that N is equivalent to M by inspection of the reduced tables.

M

	$X = 0$	1	
S_0	S_3	S_1	0
S_1	S_0	S_1	0
S_2	S_0	S_2	1
S_3	S_0	S_3	1

N

	$X = 0$	1	
A	E	A	1
B	F	B	1
C	E	D	0
D	E	C	0
E	B	D	0
F	B	C	0

15.20   Make a suitable state assignment and realize the state table of Problem 14.5 using J-K flip-flops and NAND gates.

15.21   Make a suitable state assignment and realize the state table of Problem 14.6 using J-K flip-flops and NAND gates.

15.22   Reduce the state table of Problem 14.7 to a minimum number of rows. Then make a suitable state assignment and realize the state table using D flip-flops.

15.23 Reduce the state table of Problem 14.8 to a minimum number of rows. Then make a suitable state assignment and realize the state table using D flip-flops.

15.24 Realize the following state table using a minimum number of AND and OR gates together with
(a) a clocked J-K flip-flop (use the short-cut method)
(b) a clocked D flip-flop
(c) a T flip-flop
(d) an S-R flip-flop
(e) For (d), what would happen if $X_1 = 0$, $X_2 = 1$, $X_3 = 1$ and the clock pulse is too long?

	$X_1 X_2 X_3$								Z
	000	001	010	011	100	101	110	111	
A	A	A	B	B	B	B	A	A	0
B	A	B	B	A	A	B	B	A	1

15.25 A logic designer who had not taken this course designed a sequential network with an input W using 3 T flip-flops. The input equations for these flip-flops are

$$T_A = W'A'B + W'BC' + A'BC' + AB'C + WB'C + WAC$$
$$T_B = W'A'C + W'A'B + A'BC + AB'C' + WB'C' + WAC'$$
$$T_C = W'AC + W'B'C' + WBC + WA'C'$$

and the output equation is $Z = W'A'BC'$.

Find an equivalent sequential network which uses fewer states. Try to minimize the amount of logic required.

16

Sequential Network Design

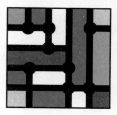

OBJECTIVES

1. Design a sequential network using gates and flip-flops.

2. Test your network by simulating it and by constructing it in lab.

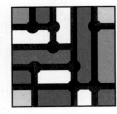

STUDY GUIDE

1. Study Sections 16.1, *Summary of Design Procedure,* and 16.2, *Design Example—Code Converter.*

   (a) Why are the states in the next-state part of Table 16-2 listed in a different order from the states in Table 15–1?

   (b) Consider the design of a sequential network to convert an 8-4-2-1 code to a 6-3-1-1 code (see Table 1–1). If the least significant bit of an 8-4-2-1 coded digit is fed into the network at t_0, can the least significant bit of the 6-3-1-1 coded digit be determined immediately? Explain. Why can't the technique described in this section be used to design the 8-4-2-1 to 6-3-1-1 code converter?

2. Work out your assigned design problem by hand. Then, if you have *Logic-Aid* or a similar program available, check your state table using the state table checker and then verify that your logic equations are correct. Try at least two different state assignments and choose the one which requires the smallest number of logic gates.

3. Check your solution carefully before simulating it. Test it "on paper" by applying a sequence of 0's and 1's and tracing signals to make sure that the outputs are correct.

4. Study Section 16.3, *Simulation and Testing of Sequential Networks.*

   (a) Observe the simulator output of Fig. 16–6(b), and note the times at which the Z output changes. Assuming that each gate and flip-flop in Fig. 16–5 has a 10-ns delay, explain the Z waveform.

   (b) Suppose that you are testing the network of Fig. 16–3, and that when you set $X = 0$ and $Q_1Q_2Q_3 = 011$ and pulse the clock, the network goes to state 101 instead of 100. What would you do to determine the cause of the malfunction?

5. Read Section 16.4, *Overview of Computer-aided Design,* for general information.

   Verify that the NOR-gate equations given in Fig. 16–10(a) are equivalent to the equations given in Fig. 13–7. In Fig. 16–10(b), note that whenever two wires cross, they are on different sides of the PC board. Trace the wiring for several connections to verify that it correctly implements the flip-flop input equations.

6. Answer the following questions before you simulate your network or test it in lab. At which of the following times will the output of your network be correct? (If you are not absolutely sure that your answer is correct, review Section 13.2, paying particular attention to the timing charts for Mealy networks.)

   (a) During the clock pulse

   (b) Immediately following the clock pulse (before the input is changed to the next value)

   (c) After the input has been changed to the next value, but before the next clock pulse occurs

7. **(a)** Explain how it is possible to get false outputs from your network even though the network is correctly designed and working properly.

   (b) If the output of your network was fed into another sequential network using the same clock, would the false outputs cause any problem? Explain.

8. When you get your network working properly, determine the output sequences for the given test sequences. Demonstrate operation of your network to a proctor and have him or her check your output sequences. After successful completion of the project, turn in your design and the test results. (No readiness test is required.)

Sequential Network Design

We have already studied the various steps in sequential network design—derivation of state tables (Unit 14), state table reduction (Unit 15), state assignment (Unit 15), and derivation of flip-flop input equations (Unit 12). This unit contains a summary of the design procedure, a comprehensive design example, and procedures for testing your network in lab.

16.1
Summary of Design Procedure

1. Given the problem statement, determine the required relationship between the input and output sequences, and derive a state table. For many problems, it is easiest to first construct a state graph.
2. Reduce the table to a minimum number of states. First eliminate duplicate rows by row matching, then form an implication table and follow the procedure in Section 15.3.
3. If the reduced table has m states ($2^{n-1} < m \leqslant 2^n$), n flip-flops are required. Assign a unique combination of flip-flop states to correspond to each state in the reduced table. The guidelines given in Section 15.8 may prove helpful in finding an assignment which leads to an economical network. If an optimum assignment is necessary, the SHR procedure may be used.
4. Form the transition table by substituting the assigned flip-flop states for each state in the reduced state table. The resulting transition table specifies the next states of the flip-flops and the output in terms of the present states of the flip-flops and the input.
5. Plot next-state maps and input maps for each flip-flop and derive the flip-flop input equations. (Depending on the type of gates to be used, either determine the sum-of-products form from the 1's on the map or the product-of-sums form from the 0's on the map.) Derive the output functions.
6. Realize the flip-flop input equations and the output equations using the available logic gates.
7. Check your design by signal tracing, laboratory testing, or computer simulation.

16.2
Design Example—Code Converter

We will design a sequential network to convert BCD to excess-3 code. The input and output will be serial with the least significant bit first. A list of allowed input and output sequences is shown in Table 16–1.

Table 16–1 lists the desired inputs and outputs at times t_0, t_1, t_2, and t_3. After receiving four inputs, the network should reset to the initial state, ready to receive another group of four inputs. It is not clear at this point whether a sequential network can actually be realized to produce the output sequences as specified

Table 16–1

X Input (BCD)				Z Output (excess-3)			
t_3	t_2	t_1	t_0	t_3	t_2	t_1	t_0
0	0	0	0	0	0	1	1
0	0	0	1	0	1	0	0
0	0	1	0	0	1	0	1
0	0	1	1	0	1	1	0
0	1	0	0	0	1	1	1
0	1	0	1	1	0	0	0
0	1	1	0	1	0	0	1
0	1	1	1	1	0	1	0
1	0	0	0	1	0	1	1
1	0	0	1	1	1	0	0

above without delaying the output. For example, if at t_0 some sequences required an output $Z = 0$ for $X = 0$ and other sequences required $Z = 1$ for $X = 0$, it would be impossible to design the network without delaying the output. For the following table we see that at t_0 if the input is 0 the output is always 1, and if the input is 1 the output is always 0; therefore, there is no conflict at t_0. At time t_1 the network will have available only the inputs received at t_1 and t_0. There will be no conflict at t_1 if the output at t_1 can be determined only from the inputs received at t_1 and t_0. If 00 has been received at t_1 and t_0, the output should be 1 at t_1 in all 3 cases where 00 occurs in the table. If 01 has been received, the output should be 0 at t_1 in all 3 cases where 01 occurs. For sequences 10 and 11 the outputs at t_1 should be 0 and 1, respectively. Therefore, there is no output conflict at t_1. In a similar manner we can check to see that there is no conflict at t_2, and at t_3 all four inputs are available so there is no problem.

We will now proceed to set up the state table (Table 16-2), using the same procedure as in Section 15.1. The arrangement of next states in the table is different from that in Table 15–1 because in this example the input sequences are received least significant bit first, while for Table 15–1 the first input bit received is listed first in the sequence. Dashes (don't cares) appear in this table because only 10 of the 16 possible 4-bit sequences can occur as inputs to the code converter. The output part of the table is filled in using the reasoning discussed in the above paragraph. For example, if the network is in state B at t_1 and a 1 is received, this means that the sequence 10 has been received and the output should be 0.

Next we will reduce the table using row matching. When matching rows which contain dashes (don't cares), a dash will "match" with any state or with any output value. By matching rows in this manner, we have $H \equiv I \equiv J \equiv K \equiv L$ and $M \equiv N \equiv P$. After eliminating I, J, K, L, N, and P, we find $E \equiv F \equiv G$ and the table reduces to 7 rows (Table 16–3).

Table 16–2

State Table for Code Converter

Time	Input Sequence Received (Least Significant Bit First)	Present State	Next State X = 0	1	Present Output (Z) X = 0	1
t_0	reset	A	B	C	1	0
t_1	0	B	D	F	1	0
	1	C	E	G	0	1
t_2	00	D	H	L	0	1
	01	E	I	M	1	0
	10	F	J	N	1	0
	11	G	K	P	1	0
t_3	000	H	A	A	0	1
	001	I	A	A	0	1
	010	J	A	–	0	–
	011	K	A	–	0	–
	100	L	A	–	0	–
	101	M	A	–	1	–
	110	N	A	–	1	–
	111	P	A	–	1	–

An alternate approach to deriving Table 16–2 is to start with a state graph. The state graph (Fig. 16–1) has the form of a tree. Each path starting at the reset state represents one of the ten possible input sequences. After the paths for the input sequences have been constructed, the outputs can be filled in by working backwards along each path. For example, starting at t_3, the path 0 0 0 0 has outputs 0 0 1 1 and the path 1 0 0 0 has outputs 1 0 1 1. Verify that Table 16–2 corresponds to this state graph.

Table 16–3

Reduced State Table for Code Converter

Time	Present State	Next State X = 0	1	Present Output (Z) X = 0	1
t_0	A	B	C	1	0
t_1	B	D	E	1	0
	C	E	E	0	1
t_2	D	H	H	0	1
	E	H	M	1	0
t_3	H	A	A	0	1
	M	A	–	1	–

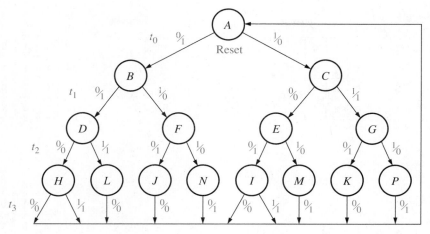

Figure 16–1
State Graph for Code Converter

Three flip-flops are required to realize the reduced table since there are seven states. Each of the states must be assigned a unique combination of flip-flop states. Some assignments will lead to economical networks with only a few gates, while other assignments will require many more gates. Using the guidelines given in Section 15.8, states B and C, D and E, and H and M should be given adjacent assignments in order to simplify the next-state functions. To simplify the output function, states (A, B, E, and M) and (C, D, and H) should be given adjacent assignments. A good assignment for this example is given on the map and table in Fig. 16–2. Flip-flops Q_1 and Q_2 have been assigned according to the four time blocks, and flip-flop Q_3 is used to distinguish between the two states in a given block. Thus flip-flops Q_1 and Q_2 form a counter which counts the number of

Q_3 Q_1Q_2	0	1
00	A	—
01	B	C
11	M	H
10	E	D

Time	Present State	$Q_1Q_2Q_3$	$Q_1^+Q_2^+Q_3^+$ $X=0$	1	Z 0	1
t_0	A	000	010	011	1	0
t_1	B	010	101	100	1	0
	C	011	100	100	0	1
t_2	D	101	111	111	0	1
	E	100	111	110	1	0
t_3	H	111	000	000	0	1
	M	110	000	---	1	–

Figure 16–2
Assignment Map and Transition Table for
Flip-Flops

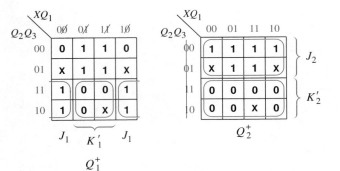

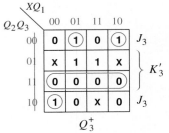

$$J_1 = K_1 = Q_2 \qquad J_3 = X'Q_1'Q_2 + X'Q_1Q_2' + XQ_1'Q_2'$$
$$J_2 = K_2 = 1 \qquad K_3 = Q_2$$

$$Z = X'Q_3' + XQ_3$$

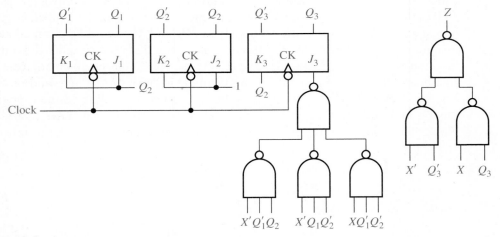

Figure 16–3
Completion of Code Converter Design

inputs received. If two inputs have been received in a sequence, $Q_1Q_2 = 10$, which means the network is in state D or E depending on whether Q_3 is 0 or 1. After the state assignment has been made, the transition table is filled in according to the assignment, and the next-state maps are plotted as shown in Fig. 16–3. The J-K input equations are then read off the Q^+ maps as indicated.

16.3
Simulation and Testing of Sequential Networks

Simulation of a digital system can take place at several levels of detail. At the functional level, system operation is described in terms of a sequence of transfers between registers, adders, memories, and other functional units. Simulation at this level may be used to verify the high-level system design. At the logic level, the system is described in terms of logic elements like gates and flip-flops and their interconnections. Logic level simulation may be used to verify the correctness of the logic design and to analyze the timing. At the circuit level, each gate is described in terms of its circuit components like transistors, resistances, and capacitances. Circuit level simulation gives detailed information about voltage levels and switching speeds. In this text, we will only consider simulation at the logic level.

Simulation of sequential networks is similar to the simulation of combinational networks described in Section 10.3. However, for sequential networks, the propagation delays associated with the individual logic elements must be taken into account, and the presence of feedback may cause complications. The simulator output usually includes timing diagrams which show the times at which different signals in the network change. The delays in the gates and flip-flops may be modeled in several ways. The simplest method is to assume that each element has one unit of delay. Use of this unit delay model is generally sufficient to verify that the design is logically correct. If a more detailed timing analysis is required, each logic element may be assigned a nominal delay value. The nominal or typical delays are usually provided by the device manufacturer on the specification sheets.

In practice, no two gates of a given type will have *exactly* the same delay, and the value of the delay may change depending on temperature and voltage levels. For these reasons, manufacturers often specify a minimum and maximum delay value for each type of logic element. Some simulators can take the minimum and maximum delay values into account. Instead of showing the exact time at which a signal changes, the simulator output indicates a time interval in which the signal may change. Figure 16–4 shows the output from an inverter which has a nominal delay of 10 ns, a minimum delay of 5 ns and a maximum delay of 15 ns. A shaded region indicates that the inverter output may change at any time during the interval. Min-max delay simulators can be used to verify that a digital system will operate correctly as long as the delay in each element is within its specified range.

Testing of sequential networks is generally more difficult than testing combinational networks. If the flip-flop outputs can be observed, then the state table can be verified directly on a row-by-row basis. The state table can be checked out

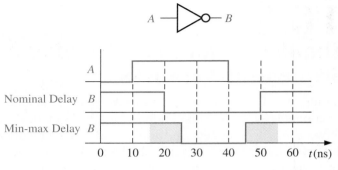

Figure 16–4
Simulator Output for an Inverter

with a simulator or in lab as follows:

1. Using the direct set and clear inputs, set the flip-flop states to correspond to one of the present states in the table.
2. For a Moore machine, check to see that the output is correct. For a Mealy machine, check to see that the output is correct for each input combination.
3. For each input combination, clock the network and check to see that the next state of the flip-flops is correct. (Reset the network to the proper state before each input combination is applied.)
4. Repeat 1, 2, and 3 for each of the present states in the table.

In many cases when a sequential network is implemented as part of an integrated circuit, only the inputs and outputs are available at the IC pins, and observing the state of the internal flip-flops is impossible. In this case, testing must be done by applying input sequences to the network and observing the output sequences. Determining a small set of input sequences which will completely test the network is generally a difficult problem. The set of test sequences must traverse all arcs on the state graph, but this is generally not a sufficient test.

Figure 16–5 shows a simulator screen for testing the Mealy sequential network of Fig. 13–7. In order to step through the network one input at a time, switches are used for the Clock and X inputs. Another switch is used to reset both flip-flops, and two switches are used to set flip-flops A and B. Probes are used to observe the Z output and the state of the flip-flops. After X has been set to the desired value, the clock pulse is simulated by flipping the Clock switch to 1 and back to 0.

If an incorrect Z output is found in the process of verifying the state table, the output network can be checked using the techniques discussed in Section 10.3. If one of the next states is wrong, this may be due to an incorrect flip-flop input. After determining which flip-flop goes to the wrong state, the network should be reset to the proper present state and the flip-flop inputs should be checked *before* applying another clock pulse.

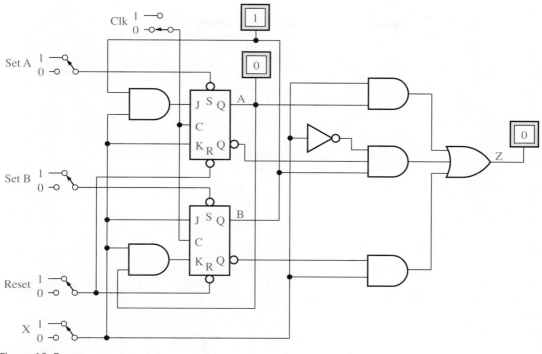

Figure 16–5
Simulation Screen for Fig. 13–7

EXAMPLE: Assume that you have built the network of Fig. 16–3 and you are checking out the state table of Fig. 16–2. Suppose that when you set the flip-flop states to 010, set $X = 1$, and pulse the clock, the network goes to state 101 instead of 100. This indicates that flip-flop Q_3 went to the wrong state. You should then reset the flip-flops to state 010 and observe the inputs to flip-flop Q_3. Since the flip-flop is supposed to remain in state 0, J_3 should be 0. If $J_3 = 1$, this indicates that either J_3 was derived wrong or that the J_3 network has a problem. Check the J_3 map and equation to make sure that $J_3 = 0$ when $X = 1$ and $Q_1Q_2Q_3 = 010$. If the map and equation are correct, then the J_3 network should be checked using the procedure in Section 10.3.

After you have verified that the network works according to your state table, you must then check the network to verify that it works according to the problem statement. To do this, you must apply appropriate input sequences and observe the resulting output sequence. When testing a Mealy network, you must be careful to read the outputs at the proper time to avoid reading false outputs (see Section 13.2). Note from Fig. 13–8, if the output is read immediately following the 1 to 0 change of the clock, a false output may be read.

Instead of manually stepping through the input sequence, simulated input waveforms may be defined for X and Clock. For the example of Fig. 16–5,

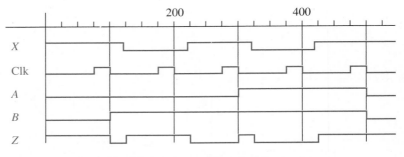

(a) Simulator output with unit delay model

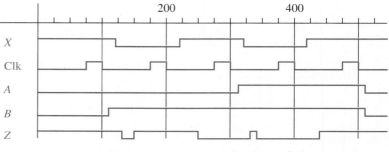

Figure 16–6

(b) Simulator output with nominal delay of 10 ns

Fig. 16–6 shows the simulator input waveform for the test sequence $X = 1\,0\,1\,0\,1$. When the simulator is run, the timing chart for A, B, and Z will be generated as shown. Note that the simulator output is very similar to the timing chart of Fig. 13–8. The simulator output in Fig. 16–6(a) assumes the unit delay model, that is, each gate or flip-flop has one unit of delay. Figure 16–6(b) shows the same simulation using a nominal delay of 10 ns for each gate and flip-flop.

So far in our discussion of sequential networks, we have assumed that the inputs are properly synchronized with the clock; that is, all inputs change in between clock pulses. This is no problem in the laboratory if we use a manual clock, since we can easily change the inputs between clock pulses. However, if we operate our circuits at a high clock rate, then synchronization becomes a problem. We must either generate our input sequences in synchronization with the clock, or we must use a special circuit to synchronize the inputs with the clock. The former can be accomplished by loading the inputs into a shift register and then using the network clock to shift them into the network one at a time as shown in Fig. 16–7.

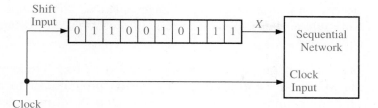

Figure 16–7
Using a Shift Register to Generate Synchronized Inputs

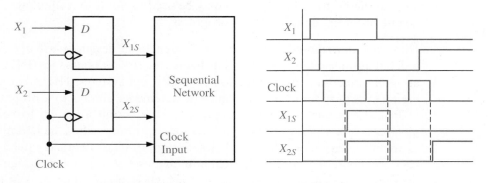

Figure 16–8　　　(a) Synchronizer circuit　　　(b) Synchronizer inputs and outputs

If the input changes are not synchronized with the clock, edge-triggered D flip-flops can be used to synchronize them as shown in Fig. 16–8. In this figure, although X_1 and X_2 change at arbitrary times with respect to the clock, X_{1S} and X_{2S} always change immediately following the clock pulse; therefore, the inputs to the sequential network are properly synchronized.[1]

16.4
Overview of Computer-aided Design

A wide variety of computer-aided design (CAD) software tools are available to assist in the design of digital systems. Some of these CAD programs will run on a personal computer and others require a more powerful workstation for execution. Several functions performed by these CAD tools are discussed below.

---

[1] A simple synchronizer of this type may occasionally fail to operate properly. For a discussion of synchronizer design, see John F. Wakerly, *Digital Design Principles and Practices*, Prentice-Hall, 1990.

Generation and minimization of logic equations. Programs of this type accept truth tables, state tables, or state graphs as input and generate minimized logic equations.

Generation of bit patterns for programming PLDs. These programs generate a file which can be downloaded to a PLD programmer to program PALs and other programmable logic devices. (See Unit 19 for more details.)

Schematic capture. This type of program allows the designer to interactively enter and edit a logic diagram for a digitial design. The program provides libraries of standard logic components which can be selected for inclusion in the diagram. In addition to a plot of the logic diagram, the output from a schematic capture program may include a parts list, a list of interconnections between the ICs, and a circuit description file. This file may be used as input to a simulator, PC board layout program, or other CAD programs.

Hardware description languages. Although logic design is usually done using block diagrams and schematics, hardware description languages (HDLs) provide an alternative way to describe logic circuits and systems. HDLs can describe a digital system in terms of a sequence of statements, similar to a program written in Pascal or other high-level language. HDLs permit a system to be described at several levels of detail. A high-level description specifies the overall behavior of the system, while a low-level description specifies detailed interconnections between components. HDLs facilitate the use of top-down design methods, in which a system is first described at a high level and then broken down into modules and sub-modules. At each design stage, the HDL description can be fed into a simulator for testing and debugging. Two commonly used hardware description languages are VHDL[2] and Verilog HDL. Figure 16–9 shows a VHDL description of the circuit of Fig. 13–7.

Simulation. We have already discussed several types of simulators in Sections 10.3 and 16.3. By using such simulators at various points in the design process, designers can correct many errors and resolve critical timing problems before any hardware is actually built. Use of a simulator is essential when an IC is being designed, because correction of design errors after the IC has been fabricated is very time-consuming and costly.

Test generation. As digital systems become more complex, testing the finished product becomes increasingly difficult. It is not practical to test the system using all possible combinations or sequences of inputs. Automatic test generation programs are available which attempt to generate a relatively small set of input patterns that will adequately test the system in a reasonable length of time.

---

[2] VHDL was originally developed for the Department of Defense for description and documentation of complex application-specific integrated circuits. The language is described in *VHDL: Hardware Description and Design* by Roger Lipsett, Kluwer Academic Publishers, 1989.

```
– – VHDL model of a Mealy sequential network
entity Mealy is
        port (
                X, Clock : in Bit          – – X and Clock are input bits
                Z : out Bit );             – – Z is an output bit
end Mealy;

– – Implementation of the Mealy network
architecture M137 of Mealy is
component JKFF
        port (J, K, CK: in Bit; Q, NQ : out Bit);
end component
signal A, AN, B, BN, JA, KB: Bit;          – – define local signals

begin
        – – create two J-K flip-flops and define the connections
        FlipFlopA: JKFF port map (JA, X, Clock, A, AN);
        FlipFlopB: JKFF port map (X, KB, Clock, B, BN);

        – – define combinational logic for system
        JA  <= X and B;
        KB <= X and A;
        Z   <= (X and BN) or (X and A) or ((not X) and AN and B);
end M137;
```

Figure 16–9
VHDL Description of Network of Fig. 13-7

PC board layout.   Most digital systems are built by mounting the integrated circuit components on a printed circuit board. The wiring on such PC boards is made up of thin metallic strips which interconnect the ICs. In order to make all of the required connections, these boards typically have two, three, or more layers of interconnect wiring. PC board layout programs perform two main functions—they determine the placement of the ICs on the board and they route the connections between the ICs. The output of the layout program includes a set of plots which show the wiring on each layer of the PC board. Figure 16–10 shows a two-layer PC board layout for the circuit of Fig. 13–7. To reduce the number of IC packages required, the AND and OR gates have been converted to NORs. The resulting circuit uses three ICs—a 74LS02 quad NOR gate, a 74LS73 dual J-K flip-flop, and a 74LS27 triple 3-input NOR gate. The PC board wiring for the top layer is shown in blue and for the bottom layer in black. The small circles at the points where blue and black wires meet represent feed-through holes which connect between the top and bottom of the board.

IC design and layout.   A digital integrated circuit is typically composed of inter-connected transistors which are fabricated on a chip of silicon. Such ICs are usually made of several layers of conducting material separated by layers of insulating material with appropriate connections between layers. The patterns for paths on each layer are transferred into the layers during the fabrication process using masks which are similar to photographic negatives. CAD tools for IC

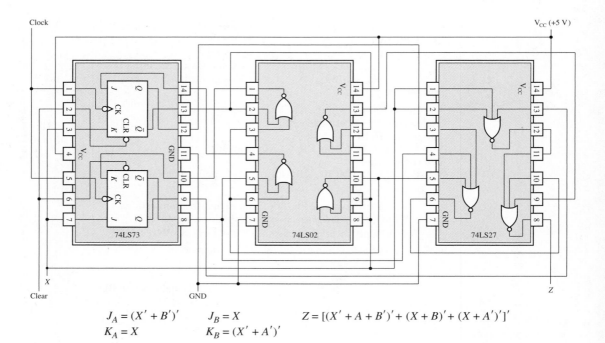

$$J_A = (X' + B')' \qquad J_B = X \qquad Z = [(X' + A + B')' + (X + B)' + (X + A')']'$$
$$K_A = X \qquad K_B = (X' + A')'$$

(a) IC connections

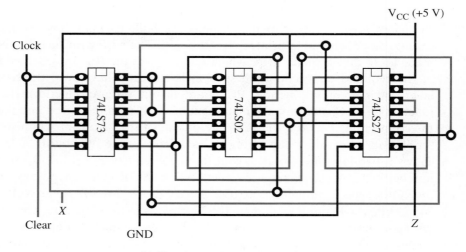

(b) Two-layer PC board layout for (a)

Figure 16–10
Realization of Fig. 13–7 Using ICs Mounted on a
PC Board

design facilitate the process of specifying the geometries of the transistors, placing the transistors on the chip, and routing the interconnections between them. Libraries of standard modules are available for inclusion in the chip designs. Automatic checking of the designs is provided to verify consistency with design rules. The output from the IC design program includes the mask patterns necessary for fabricating the IC.

Many CAD systems integrate several of the above CAD tools into a single package so that you can, for example, input a logic diagram, simulate its operation, and then lay out a PC board or IC. Design of large, complex integrated circuits and digital systems would not be feasible without the use of appropriate CAD tools.

DESIGN PROBLEMS

The following problems require the design of a Mealy sequential network of the form shown in Fig. 16–11. For purposes of testing, the input X will come from a toggle switch, and the clock pulse will be supplied manually from a push button or switch.

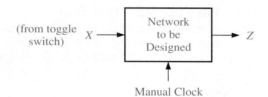

Figure 16–11

16.1   Design a clocked sequential network (Fig. 16–11) which investigates an input sequence X and will produce an output of $Z = 1$ for any input sequence ending in 0010 *or* 100.

EXAMPLE:

$$X = 1\ 1\ 0\ 0\ 1\ 0\ 0\ 1\ 0\ 1\ 0\ 0\ 1\ 0\ 1$$
$$Z = 0\ 0\ 0\ 1\ 0\ 1\ 1\ 0\ 1\ 0\ 0\ 1\ 0\ 1\ 0$$

Notice that the circuit does not reset to the start state when an output of $Z = 1$ occurs. However, your circuit should have a start state and should be provided with a method for manually resetting the flip-flops to the start state. A minimum solution requires 6 states. Design your network using NAND gates, NOR gates, and three J-K flip-flops. Any solution which is minimal for your state assignment and which uses 10 or fewer gates and inverters is acceptable; the best known solution uses 3. (Assign 000 to the start state.)

TEST PROCEDURE: First check out your state table by starting in each state and making sure that the present output and next state are correct for each input. Then, starting in the proper initial state, determine the output sequence for each of the following input sequences:

(1) 0 0 1 1 0 1 0 0 1 0 1 0 1 0 0 0 1 0 0 1 0 0 1 0
(2) 1 1 0 0 1 1 0 0 1 0 1 0 1 0 0 1 0 1 0 1 0 0 1 0

16.2   Design a clocked sequential network (Fig. 16–11) which investigates an input sequence X and will produce an output of $Z = 1$ for any input sequence ending in 1101 or 011.

EXAMPLE:

$$X = 0\ 0\ 1\ 1\ 0\ 1\ 1\ 0\ 1\ 0\ 1\ 1\ 0\ 1\ 0$$
$$Z = 0\ 0\ 0\ 1\ 0\ 1\ 1\ 0\ 1\ 0\ 0\ 1\ 0\ 1\ 0$$

Notice that the circuit does not reset to the start state when an output of $Z = 1$ occurs. However, your circuit should have a start state and should be provided with a method for manually resetting the flip-flops to the start state. A minimum solution requires 6 states. Design your network using NAND gates, NOR gates and three J-K flip-flops. Any solution which is minimal for your state assignment and which uses 10 or fewer gates and inverters is acceptable; the best known solution uses 3. (Assign 000 to the start state).

TEST PROCEDURE: First check out your state table by starting in each state and making sure that the present output and next state are correct for each input. Then, starting in the proper initial state, determine the output sequence for each of the following input sequences:

(1) 1 1 0 0 1 0 1 1 0 1 0 1 0 1 1 1 0 1 1 0 1 1 0 1
(2) 0 0 1 1 0 0 1 1 0 1 0 1 0 1 1 0 1 0 1 0 1 1 0 1

16.3   Design a sequential network (Fig. 16–11) to convert excess-3 code to BCD code. The input and output should be serial with the least significant bit first. The input X represents an excess-3 coded decimal digit, and the output Z represents the corresponding BCD code. Design your network using three J-K flip-flops, NAND gates, and NOR gates. Any solution which is minimal for your state assignment and which uses 12 or fewer gates and inverters is acceptable; the best known solution uses 6. (Assign 000 to the reset state.)

TEST PROCEDURE: First check out your state table by starting in each state and making sure that the present output and next state are correct for each input. Then, starting in the reset state, determine the output sequence for each of the ten possible input sequences and make a table.

16.4   Design a sequential network (Fig. 16–11) which adds six to a binary number in the range 0000 through 1001. The input and output should be serial with the least significant bit first. Find a state table with a minimum number of states. Design the network using NAND gates, NOR gates, and three J-K flip-flops. Any solution which is minimal for your state assignment and which uses 10 or fewer gates and inverters is acceptable; the best known solution uses 6. (Assign 000 to the reset state).

TEST PROCEDURE: First check out your state table by starting in each state and making sure that the present output and next state are correct for each input. Then starting in the reset state, determine the output sequence for each of the ten possible input sequences and make a table.

16.5 Design a clocked sequential network (Fig. 16–11) which investigates an input sequence X and will produce an output of $Z = 1$ for any input sequence ending in 0110 *or* 101.

EXAMPLE:

$$X = 0 \ 1 \ 0 \ 1 \ 1 \ 0 \ 1$$
$$Z = 0 \ 0 \ 0 \ 1 \ 0 \ 1 \ 1$$

Notice that the circuit does not reset to the start state when an output of $Z = 1$ occurs. However, your circuit should have a start state and should be provided with a method for manually resetting the flip-flops to the start state. A minimum solution requires 6 states. Design your network using NAND gates, NOR gates, and three J-K flip-flops. Any solution which is minimal for your state assignment and which uses 12 or fewer gates and inverters is acceptable; the best known solution uses 6. (Assign 000 to the start state.)

TEST PROCEDURE: First check out your state table by starting in each state and making sure that the present output and next state are correct for each input. Then, starting in the proper initial state, determine the output sequence for each of the following input sequences:

(1) 0 0 1 1 0 1 1 1 1 0 0 1 0 1 0 0

(2) 1 0 1 0 0 0 1 1 1 1 0 1 1 0 0 0

16.6 Design a clocked sequential network which investigates an input sequence X and which will produce an output of $Z = 1$ for any input sequence ending in 0101 provided that the sequence 110 has never occurred.

EXAMPLE:

$$X = 0 \ 1 \ 0 \ 1 \ 0 \ 1 \ 1 \ 0 \ 1 \ 0 \ 1$$
$$Z = 0 \ 0 \ 0 \ 1 \ 0 \ 1 \ 0 \ 0 \ 0 \ 0 \ 0$$

Notice that the circuit does not reset to the start state when an output of $Z = 1$ occurs. However, your circuit should have a start state and should be provided with a method for manually resetting the flip-flops to the start state. A minimum solution requires 6 states. Design your network using NAND gates, NOR gates, and three J-K flip-flops. Any solution which is minimal for your state assignment and which uses 9 or fewer gates and inverters is acceptable; the best known solution uses 7. (Assign 000 to the start state.)

TEST PROCEDURE: First check out your state table by starting in each state and making sure that the present output and next state are correct for each input. Then, starting in the proper initial state, determine the output sequence for the following input sequences:

(1) $X = 0\ 1\ 0\ 1\ 0\ 0\ 0\ 1\ 0\ 1\ 1\ 0$

(2) $X = 1\ 0\ 1\ 0\ 1\ 0\ 1\ 1\ 0\ 1\ 0\ 1$

16.7   Design a clocked Mealy sequential network which investigates an input sequence X and which will produce an output of $Z = 1$ if the total number of 1's received is even (consider zero 1's to be an even number of 1's) and the sequence 00 has occurred at least once. *Note:* The *total* number of 1's received includes those received before and after 00.

EXAMPLE:

$$X = 1\ 0\ 1\ 0\ 1\ 0\ 0\ 1\ 1\ 0\ 1$$
$$Z = 0\ 0\ 0\ 0\ 0\ 0\ 1\ 0\ 0\ 1$$

Notice that the circuit does not reset to the start state when an output of $Z = 1$ occurs. However, your circuit should have a start state and should be provided with a method of manually resetting the flip-flops to the start state. A minimum solution requires 6 states. Design your network using NAND gates, NOR gates, and three J-K flip-flops. Any solution which is minimal for your state assignment and which uses 12 or fewer gates and inverters is acceptable; the best known solution uses 7. (Assign 000 to the start state.)

TEST PROCEDURE: First check out your state table by starting in each state and making sure that the present output and next state are correct for each input. Then, starting in the proper initial state, determine the output sequence for each of the following input sequences:

(1) $X = 0\ 1\ 1\ 0\ 0\ 1\ 0\ 1\ 0\ 0$

(2) $X = 1\ 0\ 1\ 1\ 1\ 1\ 0\ 0\ 1\ 1\ 1\ 0$

16.8   Design a Mealy sequential network (Fig. 16–11) which investigates an input sequence X and will produce an output of $Z = 1$ for any input sequence ending in 0011 or 110.

EXAMPLE:

$$X = 1\ 0\ 1\ 0\ 0\ 1\ 1\ 0\ 0\ 1\ 1$$
$$Z = 0\ 0\ 0\ 0\ 0\ 0\ 1\ 1\ 0\ 0\ 1$$

Notice that the circuit does not reset to the start state when an output of $Z = 1$ occurs. However, your circuit should have a start state and should be provided with a method for manually resetting the flip-flops to the start state. Design your network using NAND gates, NOR gates, and three J-K flip-flops. Any solution which is minimal for your state assignment, and which uses 9 or fewer gates and inverters is acceptable; the best known solution uses 6. (Assign 000 to the start state.)

TEST PROCEDURE: First check out your state table by starting in each state and making sure that the present output and next state are correct for each input. Then, starting in the reset state, determine the output sequence for each of the following input sequences:

(1) $X = 0\ 0\ 0\ 1\ 0\ 0\ 0\ 1\ 1\ 0\ 1\ 0$

(2) $X = 1\ 1\ 1\ 0\ 0\ 1\ 0\ 0\ 0\ 1\ 1\ 0$

16.9 Design a Mealy sequential network which investigates an input sequence X and produces an output Z which is determined by two rules. The initial output from the network is $Z = 0$. Thereafter, the output Z will equal the *preceding* value of X (rule 1) until the input sequence 001 occurs. Starting with the next input after 001, the output Z will equal the *complement* of the *present* value of X (rule 2) until the sequence 100 occurs. Starting with the next input after 100, the network output is again determined by rule 1, etc. Note that overlapping 001 and 100 sequences may occur.

EXAMPLE:

$$\text{Rule:}\quad 1\ 1\ 1\ 1\ 2\ 2\ 2\ 2\ 2\ 1\ 1\ 2$$
$$X = 1\ 0\ 0\ 1\ 1\ 0\ 1\ 0\ 0\ 0\ 1\ 1$$
$$Z = 0\ 1\ 0\ 0\ 0\ 1\ 0\ 1\ 1\ 0\ 0\ 0$$

Design your network using NAND gates, NOR gates, and three J-K flip-flops. Your circuit should be provided with a method for manually resetting the flip-flops to the start state. A minimum solution requires 6 states. Any solution which is minimal for your state assignment, and which uses 10 or fewer gates and inverters is acceptable; the best known solution uses 6. (Assign 000 to the start state.)

TEST PROCEDURE: First check out your state table by starting in each state and making sure that the present output and next state are correct for each input. Then, starting in the reset state, determine the output sequence for each of the following input sequences:

(1) $X = 1\ 0\ 0\ 1\ 0\ 0\ 1\ 0\ 0\ 0\ 1\ 1$

(2) $X = 0\ 1\ 1\ 0\ 0\ 0\ 0\ 1\ 1\ 0\ 1\ 1$

16.10 The $8, 4, -2, -1$ BCD code is similar to the 8421 BCD code except that the weights are negative for the two least significant bit positions. For example, 0111 in $8, 4, -2, -1$ code represents

$$8 \times 0 + 4 \times 1 + (-2) \times 1 + (-1) \times 1 = 1$$

Design a Mealy sequential network to convert $8, 4, -2, -1$ code to 8421 code. The input and output should be serial with the least significant bit first. The input X represents an $8, 4, -2, -1$ coded decimal digit and the output Z represents the corresponding 8421 BCD code. After 4 time steps the network should reset to the starting state regardless of the input sequence. Design your network using three J-K flip-flops, NAND gates and NOR gates. Any solution which is minimal for your state assignment and which uses 7 or fewer gates is acceptable. (Assign 000 to the reset state.)

TEST PROCEDURE: First check out your state table by starting in each state and making sure that the present output and next state are correct for each input. Then, starting in the reset state, determine the output sequence for each of the ten possible input sequences and make a table.

16.11   Design a Mealy sequential network (Fig. 16–11) which adds 5 to a binary number in the range 0000 through 1010. The input and output should be serial with the least significant bit first. Find a state table with a minimum number of states. Design the network using NAND gates, NOR gates, and three J-K flip-flops. Any solution which is minimal for your state assignment and which uses 10 or fewer gates and inverters is acceptable; the best known solution uses 7. (Assign 000 to the reset state.)

TEST PROCEDURE: First check out your state table by starting in each state and making sure that the present output and the next state are correct for each input. Then starting in the reset state, determine the output sequence for each of the eleven possible input sequences and make a table.

16.12   Design a Mealy sequential network (Fig. 16–11) to convert a 4-bit binary number in the range 0000 through 1010 to its 10's complement. (The 10's complement of a number N is defined as $10 - N$.) The input and output should be serial with the least significant bit first. The input X represents the 4-bit binary number, and the output Z represents the corresponding 10's complement. After 4 time steps, the network should reset to the starting state regardless of the input sequence. Find a state table with a minimum number of states. Design the network using NAND gates, NOR gates, and three J-K flip-flops. Any solution which is minimal for your state assignment and which uses 10 or fewer gates and inverters is acceptable; the best known solution uses 7. (Assign 000 to the reset state.)

TEST PROCEDURE: First check out your state table by starting in each state and making sure that the present output and the next state are correct for each input. Then starting in the reset state, determine the output sequence for each of the eleven possible input sequences and make a table.

16.13   Design a Mealy sequential network which investigates an input sequence X and which will produce an output of $Z = 1$ for any input sequence ending in 1010, provided that the sequence 001 has occurred at least once.

EXAMPLE:

$$X = 1\ 0\ 1\ 0\ 0\ 1\ 0\ 1\ 0\ 1\ 0$$
$$Z = 0\ 0\ 0\ 0\ 0\ 0\ 0\ 0\ 1\ 0\ 1$$

Notice that the circuit does not reset to the start state when an output of $Z = 1$ occurs. However, your circuit should have a start state and should be provided with a method of manually resetting the flip-flops to the start state. A minimum solution requires 6 states. Design your network using NAND gates, NOR gates, and three J-K flip-flops. Any solution which is minimal for your state assignment and which uses 9 or fewer gates and inverters is acceptable; the best known solution uses 6. (Assign 000 to the start state.)

TEST PROCEDURE: First check out your state table by starting in each state and making sure that the present output and the next state are correct for each input. Then starting in the proper initial state, determine the output sequence for the following input sequences:

(1) $X = 1\ 0\ 0\ 1\ 0\ 0\ 1\ 1\ 0\ 1\ 0\ 1$

(2) $X = 1\ 0\ 1\ 0\ 0\ 0\ 1\ 0\ 1\ 0\ 1\ 0$

16.14 Design a Mealy sequential network which investigates an input sequence X and which will produce an output of $Z = 1$ whenever the total number of 0's in the sequence is odd, provided that the sequence 01 has occurred at least once.

EXAMPLE:

$$X = 1\ 1\ 0\ 0\ 0\ 1\ 1\ 0\ 1\ 0$$
$$Z = 0\ 0\ 0\ 0\ 0\ 1\ 1\ 0\ 0\ 1$$

A minimum solution requires 5 states. Design your network using NAND gates, NOR gates, and three J-K flip-flops. Your circuit should have a start state and should be provided with a method of manually resetting the flip-flops to the start state. Any solution which is minimal for your state assignment and which uses 9 or fewer gates and inverters is acceptable; the best known solution uses 4. (Assign 000 to the start state.)

TEST PROCEDURE: First check out your state table by starting in each state and making sure that the present output and the next state are correct for each input. Then starting in the proper initial state, determine the output sequence for the following input sequences:

(1) $X = 1\ 0\ 0\ 0\ 1\ 1\ 0\ 1\ 0\ 0\ 1$

(2) $X = 0\ 0\ 0\ 0\ 1\ 0\ 1\ 0\ 0\ 0\ 1$

17

Iterative Networks

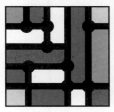

OBJECTIVES

1. Given a problem statement, design a unilateral iterative network.

2. Explain the relationship between iterative and sequential networks, and convert from one to the other.

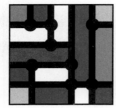

STUDY GUIDE

1. Study Section 17.1 *Design of a Parity Checker*.

   (a) If inputs 10111 are simultaneously applied to the network of Fig. 17–2(b), show the outputs of each gate on the network. If the same 5 inputs (left bit first) are applied sequentially to Fig. 17–3, give the flip-flop output (a_i) after each clock pulse. Compare these outputs with the gate outputs in the iterative network.

   (b) Compare the parity checker of Fig. 17–3 with the one designed in Section 13.1.

2. Study Section 17.2, *Design of a Comparator*.

   (a) Draw a state graph for the comparator of Table 17–2. Compare several pairs of binary numbers using the scheme represented by Table 17–2 and make sure you understand why this method works. Draw a network similar to Fig. 17–4 with 5 cells. Show the values of all the cell inputs and outputs if $X = 10101$ and $Y = 10011$.

   (b) If the state table for a typical cell of an iterative network has n states, what is the minimum number of leads required between each pair of adjacent cells?

   (c) Redesign the sequential comparator of Fig. 17–7 using J-K flip-flops.

3. Study Sections 17.3 and 17.4.

   (a) Why is there a dead-end state in Fig. 17–8?

(b) What are some of the advantages and disadvantages of using iterative networks?

(c) How can an iterative network be converted to a sequential network?

(d) How do you determine the secondary inputs to the first cell of an iterative network (a_1 and b_1)?

4. (a) Review the *Guidelines for Construction of State Graphics* in Section 14.3. These guidelines apply equally well to sequential and iterative networks.

(b) Review the *Summary of Design Procedure* for sequential networks (Section 16.1). Write out a similar procedure for iterative networks.

(c) Review the three *Guidelines for State Assignment* (Section 15.8). Do these guidelines also apply to iterative networks?

5. Work Problems 17.1, 17.2, 17.4, 17.6, and 17.8.

Once you understand the relationship between iterative and sequential networks, this unit *should* present no particular difficulty. The method used to construct the state graph for an iterative network is essentially the same as for a sequential network. However, many students find that going from the word statement of an iterative network problem to the state graph is a little "tricky". For this reason, it is important to work the assigned problems carefully before you attempt the readiness test. Before you look at the answers in the back of the book for each of these problems, check your state graphs using the information given below.

17.1 The Moore state graph has two states. Each state has a self-loop for three out of the four possible input combinations. Check your solution for the following pattern of cell inputs and outputs:

$$i - 6\ 5\ 4\ 3\ 2\ 1\ 0$$
$$X_i - 0\ 0\ 1\ 0\ 1\ 1\ 0$$
$$Y_i - 0\ 1\ 1\ 0\ 0\ 1\ 0$$
$$\text{cell output } (a_{i+1}) - 0\ 0\ 1\ 1\ 1\ 0\ 0$$

17.2   Three of the four states in the Moore state graph should have self-loops. Two of the states should have a "1" output. Check your graph using the sequences given in the problem statement.

17.4   Each of the four states in the Moore state graph should have a self-loop. One of the states should have a "1" output. Check your graph using the following test sequences:

$$X = 01010111 \quad \text{gives a final output of } Z = 1$$
$$X = 00011110 \quad \text{gives a final output of } Z = 0$$

17.6   Three of the six states in the Moore state graph should have self-loops. Two of the states should have a "1" output. Check your graph using the following test sequences:

$$\text{An input } 000101000 \quad \text{gives a final output } Z = 1$$
$$\text{An input } 01010010 \quad \text{gives a final output } Z = 0$$

17.8   Five of the seven states in the Mealy state graph should have self-loops. Check your graph using the test sequence given in the problem statement and some others which you make up.

6. If you have the *LogicAid* program available, use it to check your state tables.

7. When you are satisfied that you can meet all of the objectives, take the readiness test.

Iterative Networks

An iterative network consists of a number of identical cells interconnected in a regular manner. Some operations, like binary addition, naturally lend themselves to realization with an iterative network because the same operation is performed on each pair of input bits. The regular structure of an iterative network makes it easier to fabricate in integrated circuit form than networks with less regular structures.

The simplest form of iterative network consists of a linear array of combinational cells with signals between cells traveling in only one direction (Fig. 17–1). Each cell is a combinational network with one or more primary inputs (x_i) and possibly one or more primary outputs (z_i). In addition, each cell has one or more secondary inputs (a_i) and one or more secondary outputs (a_{i+1}). The a_i leads carry information about the "state" of the previous cell.

The primary inputs to the cells $(x_1, x_2, \ldots, x_n)$ are applied in parallel; that is, they are all applied at the same time. The a_i signals then propagate down the line of cells. Since the network is combinational, the time required for the network to reach a steady state condition is determined only by the delay times of the gates in the cells. As soon as steady state is reached, the outputs may be read.

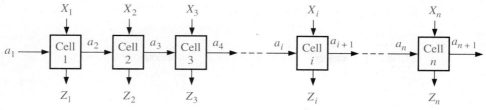

Figure 17–1
Unilateral Iterative Network

Thus the iterative network can function as a parallel-input, parallel-output device, in contrast with the sequential network in which the input and output are serial. One can think of the iterative network as receiving its inputs as a sequence in space in contrast with the sequential network which receives its inputs as a sequence in time.

17.1
Design of a Parity Checker

First we will design a parity-checking network which determines whether the number of ones in an n-bit word is even or odd. We will use a network of the form of Fig. 17–1, except that the z outputs from each cell are not needed. If the number of ones in $x_1 x_2 x_3 \cdots x_n$ is odd, we want the a_{n+1} output from the last cell to be one; otherwise, $a_{n+1} = 0$. Since all of the cells are identical, we only need to design a typical cell (cell i). We will construct a table showing the relation between the secondary input (a_i) for the typical cell and the corresponding output (a_{i+1}). The design procedure is similar to constructing a state table for a sequential network in which a_i corresponds to the present state and a_{i+1} corresponds to the next state. The a_i input must indicate whether the number of ones contained in the x-inputs to the left of cell i is even or odd, and a_{i+1} indicates whether the number of ones up to and including x_i is even or odd. Letting 0 stand for an even number of ones and 1 stand for an odd number, we obtain Table 17–1.

Table 17–1

No. of 1's	a_i	a_{i+1}	
		$x_i = 0$	$x_i = 1$
even	0	0	1
odd	1	1	0

Note that if the number of 1's to the left of cell i is even and x_i is 1, the number of 1's is then odd; however, if x_i is 0 the number of 1's is still even.

From inspection of Table 17–1,

$$a_{i+1} = x_i'a_i + a_i'x_i = a_i \oplus x_i \qquad (17\text{--}1)$$

Thus, a typical cell can consist of a single exclusive-OR gate (Fig. 17–2(a)).

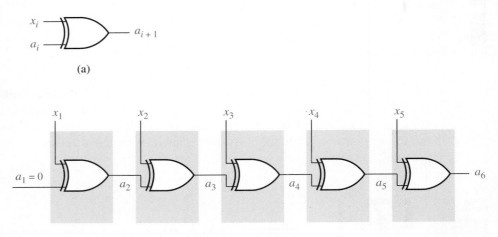

(a)

(b) Iterative parity checker ($n = 5$)

Figure 17–2

The a_1 input to the first cell must be 0 since no ones are received to the left of the first cell and 0 is an even number. The equation for the first cell can then be simplified if desired:

$$a_2 = x_1'a_1 + a_1'x_1 = x_1 \qquad (17\text{--}2)$$

Thus, cell 1 can be replaced with a wire. All of the other cells are identical to cell i. The x inputs are fed into the network in parallel, and as soon as the signals have had time to propagate through the network, the a_{n+1} output from the last cell indicates whether the total number of x's which are 1 is even or odd. Figure 17–2(b) shows the complete iterative network for $n = 5$. The output a_6 will be 1 if an odd number of x inputs are 1.

Table 17–1 could also be interpreted as the state table for a sequential network in which the x_i inputs are received sequentially in time. In this case, a_i represents the present state of the network and a_{i+1} represents the next state. The sequential network is easily constructed using a clocked D flip-flop. The next state equation for the flip-flop is Equation (17–1), so $D = a_i \oplus x_i$ and the

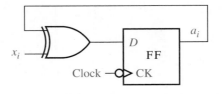

Figure 17–3
Sequential Parity Checker

network is shown in Fig. 17–3. The flip-flop is initially set to the 0 state and after the x inputs have been received, the final state of the flip-flop indicates whether the total number of ones received is even or odd.

17.2 Design of a Comparator

Next, we will design a network which compares two n-bit binary numbers and determines if they are equal or which one is larger if they are not equal. Direct design as a $2n$-input combinational network is not practical for n larger than 3 or 4, so we again use the iterative approach. Designate the two binary numbers to be compared as

$$X = x_1 x_2 \cdots x_n \qquad \text{and} \qquad Y = y_1 y_2 \cdots y_n$$

Figure 17–4 shows the form of the iterative network, although the number of leads between each pair of cells is not yet known. Comparison proceeds from left to right. The first cell compares x_1 and y_1 and passes on the result of the comparison to the next cell, the second cell compares x_2 and y_2, etc. Finally, x_n and y_n are compared by the last cell, and the output network produces signals to indicate if $X = Y$, $X > Y$, or $X < Y$.

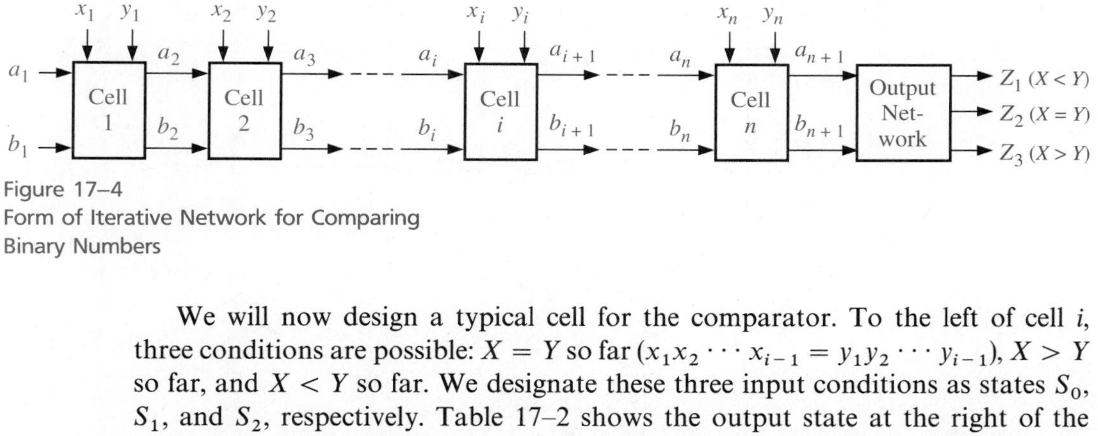

Figure 17–4
Form of Iterative Network for Comparing Binary Numbers

We will now design a typical cell for the comparator. To the left of cell i, three conditions are possible: $X = Y$ so far ($x_1 x_2 \cdots x_{i-1} = y_1 y_2 \cdots y_{i-1}$), $X > Y$ so far, and $X < Y$ so far. We designate these three input conditions as states S_0, S_1, and S_2, respectively. Table 17–2 shows the output state at the right of the cell (S_{i+1}) in terms of the $x_i y_i$ inputs and the input state at the left of the cell (S_i). If the numbers are equal to the left of cell i and $x_i = y_i$, the numbers are still

Table 17–2
State Table for Comparator

	S_i	S_{i+1}: $x_i y_i = 00$	01	11	10	$Z_1 Z_2 Z_3$
$X = Y$	S_0	S_0	S_2	S_0	S_1	0 1 0
$X > Y$	S_1	S_1	S_1	S_1	S_1	0 0 1
$X < Y$	S_2	S_2	S_2	S_2	S_2	1 0 0

Table 17–3

Transition Table for Comparator

a_ib_i	$x_iy_i = 00$	$a_{i+1}b_{i+1}$ 01	11	10	$Z_1Z_2Z_3$
0 0	00	10	00	01	0 1 0
0 1	01	01	01	01	0 0 1
1 0	10	10	10	10	1 0 0

equal including cell i, so $S_{i+1} = S_0$. However, if $S_i = S_0$ and $x_iy_i = 10$, then $x_1x_2 \cdots x_i > y_1y_2 \cdots y_i$ and $S_{i+1} = S_1$. If $X > Y$ to the left of cell i, then regardless of the values of x_i and y_i, $x_1x_2 \cdots x_i > y_1y_2 \cdots y_i$, so $S_{i+1} = S_1$. Similarly, if $X < Y$ to the left of cell i, then $X < Y$ including the inputs to cell i, and $S_{i+1} = S_2$.

The logic for a typical cell is easily derived from the state table. Since there are three states, two intercell leads are required. Using the guidelines from Section 15.8 leads to the state assignment $a_ib_i = 00$ for S_0, 01 for S_1, and 10 for S_2. Substituting this assignment into the state table yields Table 17–3. Figure 17–5

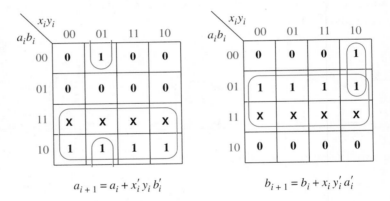

$$a_{i+1} = a_i + x_i' y_i b_i' \qquad b_{i+1} = b_i + x_i y_i' a_i'$$

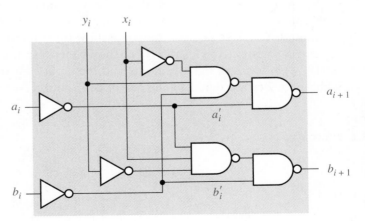

Figure 17–5

Typical Cell for Comparator

shows the Karnaugh maps, next-state equations, and realization of a typical cell using NAND gates. Inverters must be included in the cell since only a_i and b_i and not their complements are transmitted between cells.

The $a_1 b_1$ inputs to the left end cell must be 00 since we must assume that the numbers are equal (all zero) to the left of the most significant bit. The equations for the first cell can then be simplified if desired:

$$a_2 = a_1 + x_1' y_1 b_1' = x_1' y_1$$
$$b_2 = b_1 + x_1 y_1' a_1' = x_1 y_1' \qquad (17\text{-}3)$$

For the output circuit, let $Z_1 = 1$ if $X < Y$, $Z_2 = 1$ if $X = Y$, $Z_3 = 1$ if $X > Y$. Figure 17–6 shows the output maps, equations, and circuit.

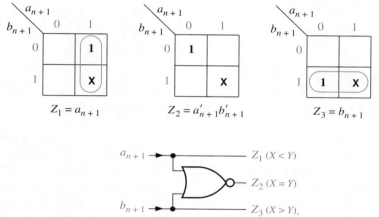

$$Z_1 = a_{n+1} \qquad Z_2 = a_{n+1}' b_{n+1}' \qquad Z_3 = b_{n+1}$$

Figure 17–6
Output Network for Comparator

Conversion to a sequential network is again straightforward. If x_i and y_i inputs are received serially instead of in parallel, Table 17–2 is interpreted as a state table for a sequential network, and the next state equations are the same as in Fig. 17–5. If D flip-flops are used, the typical cell of Fig. 17–5 can be used as the combinational part of the sequential network, and Fig. 17–7 shows the

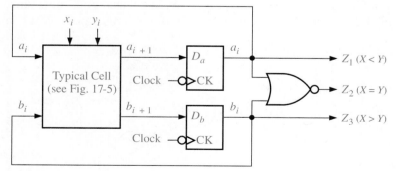

Figure 17–7
Sequential Comparator for Binary Numbers

resulting network. After all of the inputs have been read in, the output is determined from the state of the two flip-flops.

The above two examples indicate that the design of a unilateral iterative network is very similar to the design of a sequential network. The principal difference is that for the iterative network the inputs are received in parallel as a sequence in space, while for the sequential network the inputs are received serially as a sequence in time. For the iterative network, the state table specifies the output state of a typical cell in terms of its input state and primary inputs, while for the corresponding sequential network, the same table specifies the next state (in time) in terms of the present state and inputs. If D flip-flops are used, the typical cell for the iterative network can serve as the combinational logic for the corresponding sequential network. If other flip-flop types are used, the input equations can be derived in the usual manner.

17.3
Design of a Pattern Detector

A third example illustrates the design of an iterative network to detect a given input pattern. The problem is to design an iterative network which has an output of 1 from the last cell only if the input sequence contains exactly one group of one or more consecutive ones. For example, the input sequence 000111000 will produce a 1 output from the last cell, but 001100100 will not. The network will have the same form as Fig. 17–4, except there will be only one Z output.

We will solve this problem by first constructing a state graph (Fig. 17–8). Starting in state S_0, the network will remain in S_0 as long as 0's are received. When a 1 is received, the network goes to state S_1 and remains there as long as additional 1's are received. When a 0 is received, this terminates the first group of 1's, so a change to a new state is necessary. If additional 0's are received, the network remains in S_2, but if another 1 is received, the state changes to S_3 to indicate that a second group of 1's has been started. Once this occurs, a 1 output is no longer possible since the sequence contains two groups of 1's. Therefore a 0 output is associated with S_3. S_3 is a "dead-end" state since once two groups of 1's have occurred, a 1 output is no longer possible no matter what input

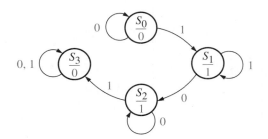

Figure 17–8

Table 17–4

	(a) state table for typical cell				(b) transition table		

S_i	$x_i = 0$	$x_i = 1$	Z
S_0	S_0	S_1	0
S_1	S_2	S_1	1
S_2	S_2	S_3	1
S_3	S_3	S_3	0

S_{i+1} spans the $x_i=0$ and $x_i=1$ columns above.

$a_i b_i$	$x_i = 0$	$x_i = 1$	Z
00	00	01	0
01	11	01	1
11	11	10	1
10	10	10	0

$a_{i+1} b_{i+1}$ spans the $x_i=0$ and $x_i=1$ columns above.

sequence follows. A 1 output is associated with both states S_1 and S_2, since in both cases exactly 1 consecutive group of 1's has occurred.

Table 17–4(a) gives the corresponding state table for a typical cell. The states in this table have the following significance:

S_0—starting state or all 0's received
S_1—first 1 or group of 1's received
S_2—first group of 1's followed by one or more 0's
S_3—two or more groups of 1's (no 1 output possible)

The output is listed with the understanding that an output network is only required following the last cell.

Since there are four states, two intercell leads are required to carry the state information between cells. Since the next-state equations for an iterative network are the same as for a corresponding sequential network, we can apply the state assignment procedures of Section 15.8. The assignment guidelines suggest the following adjacencies:

1. (S_1, S_2) (S_0, S_1) (S_2, S_3)
2. (S_0, S_1) (S_1, S_2) (S_2, S_3)
3. (S_1, S_2) (S_0, S_3)

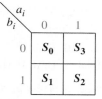

All the adjacencies are satisfied by the assignment

$$S_0 = 00, \qquad S_1 = 01, \qquad S_2 = 11, \qquad S_3 = 10$$

Using this assignment, Table 17–4(b) gives the transition table for a_i and b_i from which the typical cell (Fig. 17–9) is easily synthesized. The output from the last cell is

$$Z = a'_{n+1} b_{n+1} + a_{n+1} b_{n+1} = b_{n+1}$$

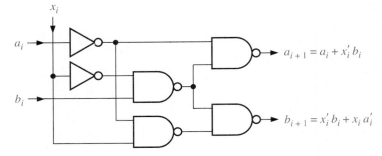

Figure 17–9
Typical Cell for Table 17–4(b)

17.4
Iterative Networks with Outputs from Each Cell

In the three examples of iterative networks given in this unit, the output was taken from the last cell only. It was convenient to assume that the output was only a function of the state of the last cell, so a Moore type state table was used. In this section, we will design an iterative network which has an output from each cell (as in Fig. 17–1). If the output of cell i depends only on the inputs of the preceding cells and not on x_i, then z_i is only a function of the secondary input state of the cell, and a Moore table should be used. On the other hand, if z_i also depends on x_i, a Mealy table is required.

The following example illustrates the design of a Mealy iterative network. The output of cell i (z_i) should be 1 iff the input to cell i (x_i) is 0 and the inputs to the cells immediately to the left of cell i consist of a group of an even number of consecutive 1's. In other words, the output of a cell is 1 if its input is a 0 which terminates a group of an even number of consecutive 1's. First, we construct a typical input-output sequence:

$$x_i = 0\ 1\ 1\ 0\ 0\ 1\ 1\ 1\ 0\ 1\ 1\ 1\ 1\ 0\ 0\ 0\ 0\ 1\ 0\ 0$$
$$z_i = 0\ 0\ 0\ 1\ 0\ 0\ 0\ 0\ 0\ 0\ 0\ 0\ 0\ 1\ 0\ 0\ 0\ 0\ 0\ 0$$

We then define 3 states: S_0 (reset), S_1 (odd number of consecutive 1's), and S_2 (even number of consecutive 1's). Figure 17–10 shows the resulting state graph.

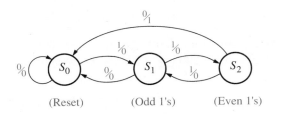

Figure 17–10

	$a_i b_i$	$a_{i+1} b_{i+1}$		z_i	
		$x_i = 0$	1	$x_i = 0$	1
S_0	00	00	01	0	0
S_1	01	00	10	0	0
S_2	10	00	01	1	0

(a) transition table

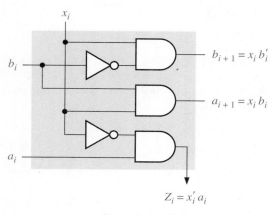

(b) typical cell

Figure 17–11

Note that the network resets whenever a 0 input is received, and that the output is 1 only when a 0 is received following an even number of 1's.

Figure 17–11 shows the transition table and resulting typical cell. Since the initial state is S_0, $a_1 = b_1 = 0$, and the equations for the first cell can be simplified to

$$b_2 = x_1, \qquad a_2 = 0, \qquad z_1 = 0$$

As is shown in this unit, the procedure used to design iterative networks is very similar to that used to design sequential networks with D flip-flops. A Moore iterative network which has an output network following the last cell is analogous to a Moore sequential network in which the output is observed after the entire input sequence has been applied. A Mealy iterative network which has an output from each cell is analogous to a Mealy sequential network in which the output is observed after applying each input.

For problems where an iterative network can be used, it offers several advantages over an ordinary combinational network:

1. It is easier to design an economical network.
2. It is cheaper to build a large number of identical cells than to fabricate one large complex network.
3. The iterative network is easily expanded to accommodate more inputs simply by adding more cells.

The principal disadvantage of the iterative network is that the signal must propagate through a large number of cells, so the response time will be longer than a combinational network with fewer levels.

PROBLEMS

17.1 Two binary numbers, $X = x_n \cdots x_3 x_2 x_1 x_0$ and $Y = y_n \cdots y_3 y_2 y_1 y_0$, are to be compared by an iterative network. The comparator should compare the least significant bits first so that the intercell signals will propagate from right to left:

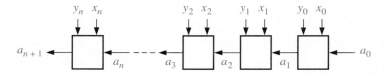

Only one lead should be used between each pair of cells. The output from the left end cell should be $a_{n+1} = 1$ if $X > Y$ and $a_{n+1} = 0$ if $X \leq Y$. Design a typical cell using NAND gates.

17.2 An iterative network has a form similar to Fig. 17–4. The output Z is to be 1 iff at least one of the inputs x_i is 1 and no group of 2 or more consecutive 1 inputs occurs.

For example,

$$0\ 0\ 1\ 0\ 1\ 0\ 0\ 0\ 1\ 0\ 0 \quad \text{gives an output } Z = 1$$
$$0\ 0\ 1\ 0\ 1\ 1\ 0\ 0\ 0\ 0\ 0 \quad \text{gives an output } Z = 0$$

Derive the equations and a NOR-gate network for a typical cell and for the output network.

17.3 An iterative network has a form similar to Fig. 17–4. The output Z is to be 1 iff no group of three or more consecutive 1 inputs occurs.

For example,

$$0\ 0\ 1\ 0\ 1\ 0\ 0\ 1\ 1\ 1\ 0\ 1\ 0 \quad \text{gives an output } Z = 0$$
$$0\ 0\ 1\ 0\ 1\ 0\ 1\ 1\ 0\ 0\ 0\ 1\ 0 \quad \text{gives an output } Z = 1$$

Derive the equations and a NOR-gate network for a typical cell and for the output network.

17.4 An iterative network has a form similar to Fig. 17–4. The output Z is to be 1 iff the total number of x-inputs which are 1 is an odd number greater than 2. Derive the equations and a NAND-gate network for a typical cell and the output network. Specify a_1 and b_1 and simplify the first cell.

17.5 An iterative network has a form similar to Fig. 17–4. The output Z is to be 1 iff the total number of x-inputs which are 1 is exactly 2. Derive the equations and a NAND–gate network for a typical cell and the output network. Specify a_1 and b_1 and simplify the first cell.

17.6 An iterative network has an output $Z = 1$ from the last cell iff the sequence of cell inputs contains one appearance of one of the following patterns and no other 1's:

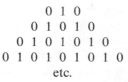

etc.

Note that the pattern may be preceded and followed by any number of 0's. Draw a Moore state graph for the typical cell, and derive the equations for a typical cell.

17.7 An iterative network has an output $Z = 1$ from the last cell iff the sequence of cell inputs contains one appearance of the following patterns and no other 1's:

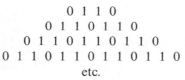

etc.

Note that the pattern may be preceded and followed by any number of 0's. Draw a Moore state graph for the typical cell, and derive the equations for a typical cell.

17.8 Each cell of an iterative network has two inputs (x_i and y_i) and one output (z_i). The output for cell i is defined as follows:

If any three consecutive cells to the left of cell $i + 1$ have the inputs $xy = 11, 00, 10$ (in that order), the output from cell i will be 1 unless the sequence $xy = 11, 00, 10$ has occurred a second time to the left of cell $i + 1$.

EXAMPLE:

i	1	2	3	4	5	6	7	8	9	10	11	12	13	14	15
$x_i y_i$	01	11	00	10	00	10	11	00	11	00	10	11	10	11	10
z_i	0	0	0	1	1	1	1	1	1	1	0	0	0	0	0

Draw a Mealy state graph (with a minimum number of states) for the typical cell.

17.9 Each cell of an iterative network has one primary input (X_i). The output from the last cell is $Z = 1$ iff the total number of X_i inputs which are 1 is ≥ 4.
(a) Find a Moore state graph with a minimum number of states.
(b) Derive the logic equations for a typical cell and for the output.
(c) Design the first three cells of the network making simplifications where possible.

17.10 Repeat Problem 17.9 if the output from the last cell is $Z = 1$ iff the total number of X_i inputs which are 0 is ≥ 3.

17.11   Each cell of an iterative network has inputs X_i and Y_i. The network has two outputs, Z_1 and Z_2. $Z_1 = 1$ if $X_i = Y_i$ in every cell. $Z_2 = 1$ if X_i and Y_i are complements in every cell.

(a) Draw a block diagram for the network.

(b) Find a Moore state graph with a minimum number of states.

(c) Design a typical cell using only NAND gates. Assign 00 to the initial state.

(d) Design the output network.

(e) Simplify the first cell if possible.

(f) Draw a diagram that shows how your design could be converted to a sequential network which has 1 output under the same conditions as above, except that the inputs are received serially instead of in parallel.

17.12   The typical cell (shown as follows) for an iterative network has two inputs (x_i and y_i) and one output (z_i).

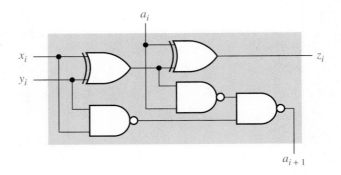

(a) Derive a truth table for the typical cell.

(b) If four of these cells are connected in an iterative network, determine a_i and z_i for the following inputs:

$$x_3x_2x_1x_0 = 0000 \quad 0100 \quad 1000 \quad 1111$$
$$y_3y_2y_1y_0 = 1010 \quad 0010 \quad 0111 \quad 0010$$
$$a_4a_3a_2a_1a_0 = ????? \quad ????? \quad ????? \quad ?????$$
$$z_3z_2z_1z_0 = ???? \quad ???? \quad ???? \quad ????$$

(c) If $x_3x_2x_1x_0$ and $y_3y_2y_1y_0$ are considered to be binary numbers, what number does $z_3z_2z_1z_0$ represent in terms of X and Y?

17.13   An iterative network has an output of 1 from the last cell iff the input pattern 1011 or 1101 has occurred as inputs to any 4 adjacent cells in the network.

(a) Find a Moore state graph or table with a minimum number of states.

(b) Make a suitable state assignment and derive one of the equations for a typical cell.

(c) Derive the output equation.

·U N I T·

18

MSI Integrated Circuits in Sequential Network Design

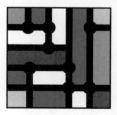

OBJECTIVES

1. Analyze the operation of an integrated circuit shift register, indicate the connections required to perform various shifting functions, and draw a timing diagram.

2. Analyze the operation of an integrated circuit counter, indicate the connections required to perform various counting functions, and draw a timing diagram.

3. Design a sequential network using a counter with clear and load inputs.

4. Explain the operation of 3-state logic and show how 3-state logic can be used to transfer data between registers on a bus.

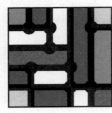

STUDY GUIDE

1. Study Section 18.1, *Integrated Circuit Shift Registers*. Note that the two inverter symbols used in Figs. 18–1(b), 18–3, and 18–7 are equivalent:

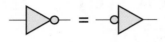

Also, $\bar{Q}$ is often used instead of Q' to indicate the complement.

(a) Compare the block diagrams for the 7491 and 74178 shift registers. Which one changes state on the rising edge of the clock pulse?

The falling edge?

(b) Complete the following timing diagram and table for a 7491 shift register. Assume that $A = 1$.

Clock Pulse Number	State of Shift Register During Clock Pulse $Q_A\ Q_B\ Q_C\ Q_D\ Q_E\ Q_F\ Q_G\ Q_H$
1	0 0 0 0 0 0 0 0
2	
3	
4	
5	
6	
7	
8	
9	
10	
11	
12	
13	
14	
15	
16	

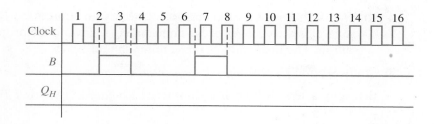

(c) Explain the meaning of Equation (18–2) in words.

(d) Write the next-state equation for flip-flop Q_B of a 74178 shift register.

$Q_B^+ = $ _____

Verify that your equation is consistent with Table 18–1.

(e) Work Problems 18.1 and 18.2(a) and (b).

2. Study Section 18.2, *Integrated Circuit Counters*.

(a) If the ripple counter of Fig. 18–5 is in state 0111, what will be the sequence of transient states after T_A changes from 1 to 0?

(b) Show the required connections so that two 7493A counters will act like a single 8-bit counter.

(c) Note that for the counters described in this unit, Q_A represents the least significant bit, but for the shift registers Q_A represents the most significant bit. This inconsistent notation is used to be compatible with data sheets published by manufacturers of TTL logic.

(d) Note that the 7493A counter changes state on the falling edge of the clock pulse, and the 74S163 changes state on the rising edge of the pulse.

(e) Explain the difference between the asynchronous clear (on the 7493A counter) and the synchronous clear (on the 74S163).

(f) From Fig. 18–7, determine the conditions under which the ripple carry out will be 1.

(g) After the counter of Fig. 18–10 reaches state 1101, the NAND gate output clears the counter. Why is it unnecessary to connect Q_B' to this gate?

(h) Work Problems 18.3(a) and 18.4. Check your solution to 18.3(a) to make sure all state changes occur immediately following the proper clock transition. The final state of the counter should be 15.

3. Study Section 18.3, *Design of Sequential Networks Using Counters.*

(a) Why is the CLEAR function derived before LOAD or *PT*?

(b) Explain the don't cares which appear in the *PT* and *D* columns of Table 18–3.

(c) Work Problems 18.5 and 18.6(a).

4. Study Section 18.4, *Register Transfers and 3-State Logic.*

(a) What are the three possible output "states" of a 3-state buffer?

(b) Referring to Fig. 18–15, how does an inversion symbol (small circle) on the enable input affect the operation of a 3-state buffer?

How does an inversion symbol on the buffer output affect the operation?

(c) Draw a logic circuit which will realize $F = A'B' + AC$, using only 3-state buffers.

(d) Referring to Fig. 18–19, the bus is 8 bits wide; that is, the bus consists of 8 wires. Draw the logic diagram showing the flip-flops and buffers associated with *one* of these bus wires.

(e) Work Problem 18.7.

5. Review the objectives of this unit. If you are satisfied that you can meet these objectives, take the readiness test. You will not need to memorize the type numbers of the TTL shift registers and counters discussed in this unit. However, given data which specifies the operation of these or similar integrated circuits, you should be able to use them or analyze their operation.

MSI Integrated Circuits in Sequential Network Design

This unit introduces the use of MSI integrated circuit shift registers and counters in sequential network design. As examples of integrated circuit shift registers and counters, several typical TTL integrated circuits are described.[1]

18.1
Integrated Circuit Shift Registers

Shift registers with 4, 8, or more flip-flops are available in integrated circuit form. Figure 18–1 illustrates an 8-bit serial-in, serial-out shift register. "Serial in" means that data is shifted into the first flip-flop one bit at a time and the flip-flops cannot be loaded in parallel. "Serial out" means that data can be read only out of the last flip-flop and the outputs from the other flip-flops are not connected to terminals of the integrated circuit. Master-slave S-R flip-flops are used. These flip-flops are similar in operation to the master-slave J-K flip-flops described in Unit 11, except that the input combination $S = R = 1$ is not allowed. The inputs to the first flip-flop are $S = AB$ and $R = (AB)'$. Thus, if $AB = 1$, a 1 is shifted into the register when it is clocked, and if $AB = 0$, a 0 is shifted in. Since the clock input goes through an inverting buffer, the flip-flops change state on the 0-1 transition (leading edge) of the input clock pulse instead of on the 1-0 transition. Figure 18–2 shows a typical timing diagram.

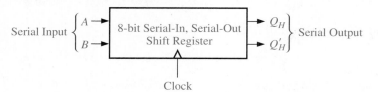

(a) Block diagram

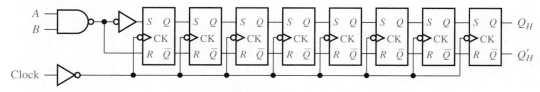

(b) Logic diagram (courtesy of Texas Instruments)

Figure 18–1
7491 TTL Shift Register

---

[1] For further information on TTL logic, see Appendix A.3 of this text and the *TTL Data Book,* published by Texas Instruments.

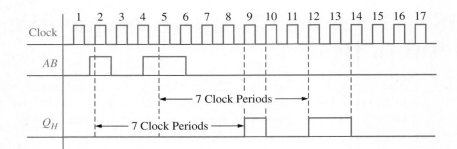

Figure 18–2
Typical Timing Diagram for 7491 TTL Shift
Register

Figure 18–3 shows a 4-bit parallel-in, parallel-out shift register. The shift register has two control inputs, shift enable (SH) and load enable (L). If $SH = 1$ (and $L = 1$ or $L = 0$), clocking the register causes the serial input (SI) to be shifted into the first flip-flop, while the data in flip-flops Q_A, Q_B, and Q_C are shifted right. If $SH = 0$ and $L = 1$, clocking the shift register will cause the four data inputs (D_A, D_B, D_C, D_D) to be loaded in parallel into the flip-flops. If $SH = L = 0$, clocking the register causes no change of state. The input equations for the first flip-flop are

$$S_A = SH \cdot SI + SH' \cdot L \cdot D_A + SH' \cdot L' \cdot Q_A \qquad \text{and} \qquad R_A = S'_A \ (18\text{--}1)$$

The next-state equation is

$$Q_A^+ = SH \cdot SI + SH' \cdot L \cdot D_A + SH' \cdot L' \cdot Q_A \tag{18--2}$$

Table 18–1 summarizes the operation of this shift register. All state changes occur immediately following the trailing edge (1 to 0 transition) of the clock.

Table 18–1

Operation of 74178 Shift Register

Inputs		Next State				
SH (shift)	L (load)	Q_A^+	Q_B^+	Q_C^+	Q_D^+	
0	0	Q_A	Q_B	Q_C	Q_D	(no change)
0	1	D_A	D_B	D_C	D_D	(parallel load)
1	X	SI	Q_A	Q_B	Q_C	(right shift)

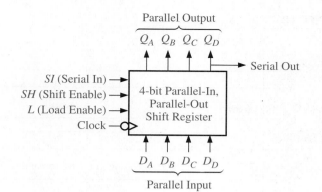

(a) Block diagram

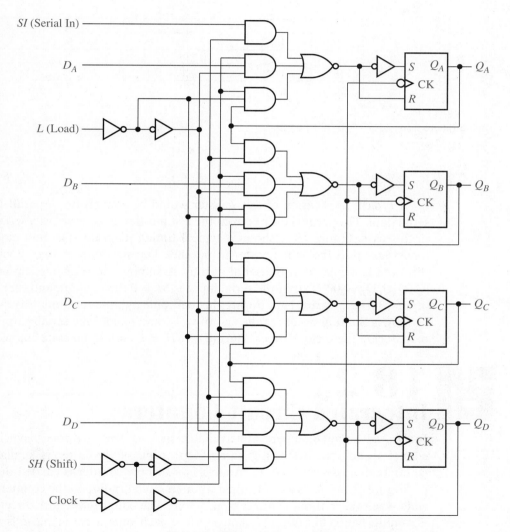

(b) Logic diagram (courtesy of Texas Instruments)

Figure 18–3
74178 TTL Shift Register

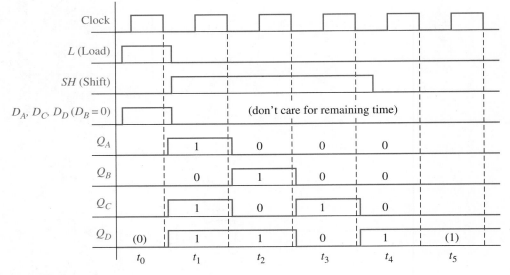

Figure 18–4
Timing Diagram for 74178 TTL Shift Register

A typical application of this register would be conversion of parallel data to serial data. The parallel output from the last flip-flop also serves as a serial output in this case. Figure 18–4 shows a typical timing diagram. The first clock pulse loads data into the shift register in parallel. During the next four clock pulses, this data is available at the serial output. Assuming the register is initially clear ($Q_A Q_B Q_C Q_D = 0000$), that the serial input is $SI = 0$ throughout, and that the data inputs $D_A D_B D_C D_D$ are 1011 during the load time (t_0), the resulting waveforms are as shown. Shifting occurs at the end of t_1, t_2, and t_3, and the serial output can be read during these clock times. During t_4, $SH = L = 0$, so no state change occurs.

18.2
Integrated Circuit Counters

Integrated circuit counters are available in two types—ripple (asynchronous) counters and synchronous counters. Operation of the latter is similar to the counters discussed in Unit 12. Analysis of a ripple counter is carried out below.

Figure 18–5 shows a 4-bit ripple counter. Each flip-flop in the counter changes state when the T input changes from 1 to 0. The count pulse goes directly to the T_A input; hence flip-flop Q_A changes state each time a count pulse is received. Since T_B is connected to Q_A, Q_B will change state each time Q_A changes from 1 to 0. Similarly, Q_C will change each time Q_B changes from 1 to 0, and Q_D changes when Q_C goes from 1 to 0. The state sequence for the counter is given below. Each

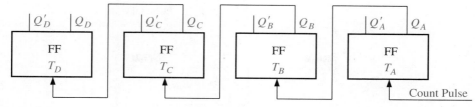

Figure 18–5
4-Bit Ripple Counter

time the T_A input is pulsed, the counter may go through a series of intermediate transient states (enclosed in parentheses) before reaching a final state.

Q_D Q_C Q_B Q_A

| 0 | 0 | 0 | 0 | initial state |

1st count pulse changes Q_A to 1

| 0 | 0 | 0 | 1 |

2nd count pulse changes Q_A to 0

| (0 | 0 | 0 | 0) |

1-0 transition of T_B changes Q_B to 1

| 0 | 0 | 1 | 0 |

3rd count pulse changes Q_A to 1

| 0 | 0 | 1 | 1 |

4th count pulse changes Q_A to 0

| (0 | 0 | 1 | 0) |

1-0 transition of T_B changes Q_B to 0

| (0 | 0 | 0 | 0) |

1-0 transition of T_C changes Q_C to 1

| 0 | 1 | 0 | 0 |

The counter continues to operate in this manner until state 1111 is reached. When a count pulse is applied in state 15 ($Q_D Q_C Q_B Q_A = 1111$), the following sequence of events occurs:

| 1 | 1 | 1 | 1 |

16th count pulse changes Q_A to 0

| (1 | 1 | 1 | 0) |

1-0 transition of T_B changes Q_B to 0

| (1 | 1 | 0 | 0) |

1-0 transition of T_C changes Q_C to 0

| (1 | 0 | 0 | 0) |

1-0 transition of T_D changes Q_D to 0

| 0 | 0 | 0 | 0 | the counter is now reset to state 0 and the state sequence repeats |

Note that in the above analysis, a change of Q_A "ripples" through until all four flip-flops have changed state; hence the name "ripple counter".

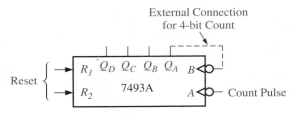

(a) Block diagram

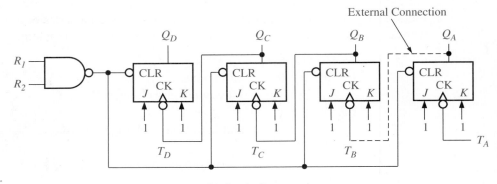

(b) Logic diagram

Figure 18–6
4-Bit Binary Counter

Figure 18–6 shows a 4-bit TTL ripple counter. Since the J and K inputs of the flip-flops are all 1, the CK (clock) input acts as a T input. Since T_B is not connected to Q_A internally, an external connection is required in order to make a 4-bit counter. If both reset inputs (R_1 and R_2) are 1, the clear inputs on the flip-flops are 0, and the counter is reset to the 0000 state. The R_1 and R_2 inputs are often referred to as *asynchronous* (or direct) clear inputs because they clear the counter independently of the clock input.

Figure 18–7 shows a very general type of 4-bit TTL synchronous counter. In addition to performing the counting function, it has provision for clearing the flip-flops and for loading the flip-flops in parallel from the data inputs. All operations are synchronized by the clock, and all state changes take place immediately following the 0-1 transition of the clock input.

This counter has four control inputs—CLEAR, LOAD, P, and T. P and T are used to enable the counting function. Operation of the counter is as follows:

1. If CLEAR $= 0$, all flip-flops are set to 0 immediately following the 0-1 transition of the clock.
2. If CLEAR $= 1$ and LOAD $= 0$, the D inputs are transferred in parallel to the flip-flops immediately following the 0-1 transition of the clock.
3. If CLEAR $=$ LOAD $= 1$ and $P = T = 1$, the count is enabled and the counter state will be incremented by 1 following each 0-1 transition of the clock.

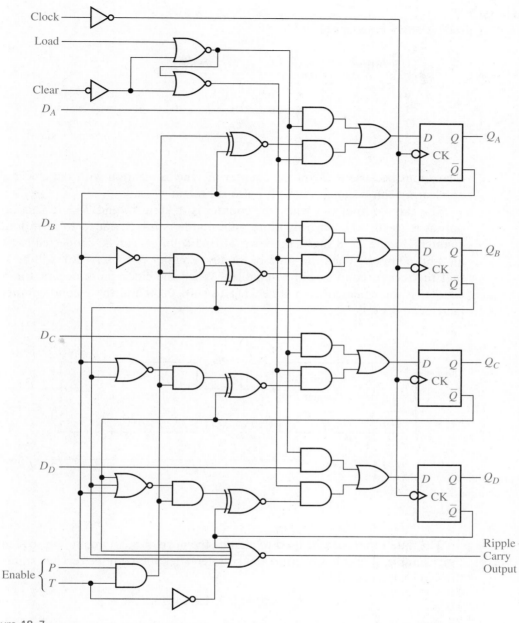

Figure 18–7
74S163 4-Bit Counter Logic Diagram
(Courtesy of Texas Instruments)

Table 18–2 summarizes the operation of the counter. Note that CLEAR overrides the LOAD and count functions in the sense that when CLEAR = 0, clearing occurs regardless of the values of LOAD, P and T. Similarly LOAD overrides the count function. The CLEAR input on the 74S163 is referred to as a *synchronous*

Table 18–2

Operation of 74S163 Synchronous Counter

Control Signals		PT (ENABLE COUNT)	Next State				
CLEAR	LOAD		Q_D^+	Q_C^+	Q_B^+	Q_A^+	
0	X	X	0	0	0	0	(clear)
1	0	X	D_D	D_C	D_B	D_A	(parallel load)
1	1	0	Q_D	Q_C	Q_B	Q_A	(no change)
1	1	1	present state $+1$				(increment count)

clear input because it clears the counter in synchronization with the clock, and no clearing can occur if no clock pulse is present.

The carry output is 1 when the counter is in state 15 and $T = 1$. This carry output is useful when two or more 4-bit counters are cascaded to form longer counters. Figure 18–8 shows how two 74S163 counters can be connected to form an 8-bit counter. When the state of the first counter is 15, CARRY will be 1 so that the second counter will be enabled. When the clock pulse occurs, the first counter is incremented from state 1111 to state 0000 and the second counter is incremented by 1.

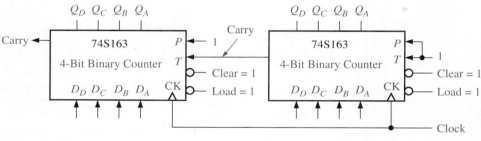

Figure 18–8
8-Bit Counter

The data inputs can be used to change the normal binary counting sequence. For example, if 5 is loaded into the counter after the counter reaches state 15, the state sequence will be

$$5, 6, 7, 8, 9, 10, 11, 12, 13, 14, 15, 5, 6, \ldots$$

The connections required to obtain this counting sequence are shown in Figure 18–9. When the counter reaches state 1111, CARRY = 1, the load is enabled, and the next clock loads 0101 into the flip-flops.

The CLEAR input can also be used to reset the counter to state 0000 when a given state is reached as shown in Figure 18–10. For this example, when the counter reaches state 1101, CLEAR = 0 and the counter is cleared by the next clock pulse. The state sequence will therefore be

$$0, 1, 2, 3, 4, 5, 6, 7, 8, 9, 10, 11, 12, 13, 0, 1, \ldots$$

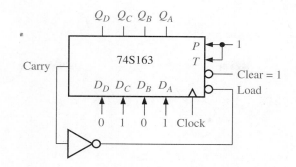

Figure 18–9
11-State Counter

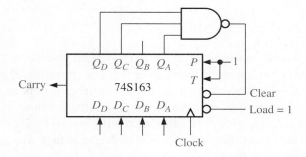

Figure 18–10
14-State Counter

More complicated counting sequences can be obtained by making the CLEAR, LOAD, and data inputs all functions of the counter state.

18.3
Design of Sequential Networks Using Counters

Figure 18–11 shows the state graph for a sequential network with an input X. Note that the form of this graph is a loop of states with a few additional state transitions added. State graphs of this general form can be economically realized using a counter which has load and clear inputs. As an example, we will realize the graph using a 74S163 counter. We will apply the following procedure:

1. Use a straight binary state assignment for the states in the main loop.
2. Use the clear input when transitions to state 0 are required.
3. Activate the counting function when transitions between successive states in the main loop are required.
4. Use the load input when transitions out of the normal counting sequence (except transitions to state 0) are required.

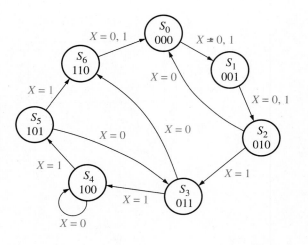

Figure 18–11

The binary state assignment is shown on the state graph, and the CBA and $C^+B^+A^+$ columns of Table 18–3 indicate the required state transitions for $X = 0$ and $X = 1$. We will now derive the counter inputs to realize these state transitions. The inputs are listed in the remaining columns of the table. Since state 111 never occurs, all inputs associated with state 111 are don't cares. Since CLEAR overrides the other inputs, we will derive it first. We must clear the counter for state transitions S_2 to S_0 ($X = 0$) and S_6 to S_0, so CLEAR must be 0 for these transitions. CLEAR must be 1 to avoid clearing the counter for the other transitions. Since LOAD overrides the P and T inputs, we will derive LOAD next. State transitions S_3 to S_6 and S_5 to S_3 are not in the normal counting sequence, so we

Table 18–3
Derivation of Counter Inputs

		C B A	C^+ B^+ A^+	CLEAR	LOAD	D_C D_B D_A	PT
$X=0$	S_0	0 0 0	0 0 1	1	1	X X X	1
	S_1	0 0 1	0 1 0	1	1	X X X	1
	S_2	0 1 0	0 0 0	0	X	X X X	X
	S_3	0 1 1	1 1 0	1	0	1 1 0	X
	S_4	1 0 0	1 0 0	1	1	X X X	0
	S_5	1 0 1	0 1 1	1	0	0 1 1	X
	S_6	1 1 0	0 0 0	0	X	X X X	X
		1 1 1	X X X	X	X	X X X	X
$X=1$	S_0	0 0 0	0 0 1	1	1	X X X	1
	S_1	0 0 1	0 1 0	1	1	X X X	1
	S_2	0 1 0	0 1 1	1	1	X X X	1
	S_3	0 1 1	1 0 0	1	1	X X X	1
	S_4	1 0 0	1 0 1	1	1	X X X	1
	S_5	1 0 1	1 1 0	1	1	X X X	1
	S_6	1 1 0	0 0 0	0	X	X X X	X
		1 1 1	X X X	X	X	X X X	X

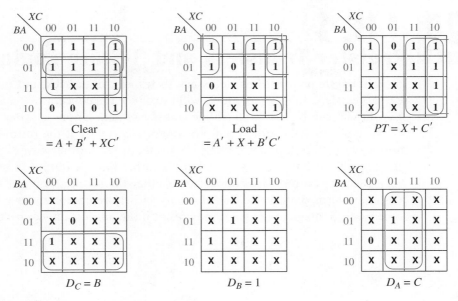

Figure 18–12
Karnaugh Maps for Table 18–3

will use the D inputs to load in the proper next state for these transitions. In state 011 with $X = 0$, we will set LOAD = 0 and $D_C D_B D_A = 110$ so that the next state is S_6. In state 101 with $X = 0$, we will set LOAD = 0 and $D_C D_B D_A = 011$ so that the next state is S_3. When CLEAR is 0, LOAD is a don't care since CLEAR overrides LOAD. For the other transitions, LOAD must be 1 to prevent undesired state changes. When LOAD $\neq$ 0, the D inputs are don't cares since no loading can occur. For state transitions in the main loop, PT must be 1 to enable the counting function. In state S_4 with $X = 0$, PT must be 0 to prevent a change of state. In the remaining rows, PT is a don't care since CLEAR and LOAD override PT.

The required counter input functions can now be derived using the Karnaugh maps in Fig. 18–12. Figure 18–13 shows the final circuit. If the same circuit is realized using J-K flip-flops, 3 flip-flops and 11 gates are required.

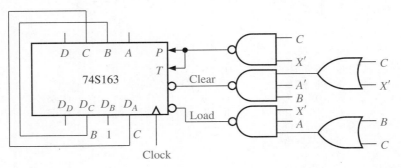

Figure 18–13
Realization of Fig. 18–11

18.4
Register Transfers and 3-State Logic

In digital systems it is often necessary to transfer data back and forth between several registers. In this section we will introduce the concept of 3-state logic and show how it can be used to facilitate transfer of data among a group of registers.

Normally, a logic circuit will not operate correctly if the outputs of two or more gates or flip-flops are directly connected to each other. For example, if one gate has a 0 output (a low voltage) and another has a 1 output (a high voltage), when the gate outputs are connected together the resulting output voltage may be some intermediate value that does not clearly represent either a 0 or a 1. In some cases, damage to the gates may result if the outputs are connected together.

$$A \longrightarrow\!\!\!\!\triangleright\!\!- C \equiv A \longrightarrow\!\!\!\!\triangleright\!\!\!-\!\!\!\circ\!\!\nearrow\!\!\circ\!\!- C$$

Figure 18–14
3-State Buffer

Use of 3-state logic will permit the outputs of two or more gates or flip-flops to be connected together. Figure 18–14 shows a 3-state buffer and its logical equivalent. When the enable input B is 1, the output C equals A; when B is 0, the output C acts like an open circuit. In other words, when B is 0 the output C is effectively disconnected from the buffer output so that no current can flow. This is often referred to as a Hi-Z (high-impedance) state of the output, since the circuit offers a very high resistance or impedance to the flow of current.

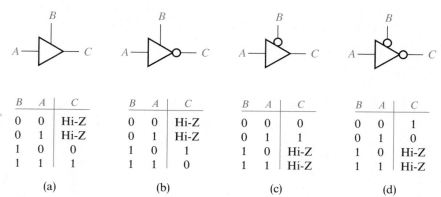

B	A	C
0	0	Hi-Z
0	1	Hi-Z
1	0	0
1	1	1

(a)

B	A	C
0	0	Hi-Z
0	1	Hi-Z
1	0	1
1	1	0

(b)

B	A	C
0	0	0
0	1	1
1	0	Hi-Z
1	1	Hi-Z

(c)

B	A	C
0	0	1
0	1	0
1	0	Hi-Z
1	1	Hi-Z

(d)

Figure 18–15
Four Types of 3-State Buffer

Figure 18–15 shows truth tables for four types of 3-state buffers. In Figs. 18–15(a) and (b) the enable input B is not inverted, so the buffer output is enabled when $B = 1$ and disabled when $B = 0$. That is, the buffer operates normally when $B = 1$, and the buffer output is effectively an open circuit when $B = 0$. In Fig. 18–15(b) the buffer output is inverted—that is, $C = A'$ when the buffer is enabled. The buffers in Figs. 18–15(c) and (d) operate the same as in (a) and (b) except that the enable input is inverted, so the buffer is enabled when $B = 0$.

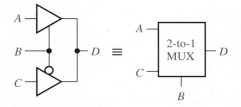

Figure 18–16
Data Selection Using 3-State Buffer

In Fig. 18–16, the outputs of two 3-state buffers are tied together. When $B = 1$, the top buffer is enabled so that $D = A$; when $B = 0$, the lower buffer is enabled so that $D = C$. Therefore, $D = BA + B'C$. This is logically equivalent to using a 2-to-1 multiplexer to select the A input when $B = 1$ and the C input when $B = 0$.

Next we will consider the problem of transferring data from the outputs of two different registers into a third register. Figure 18–17 shows how this can be

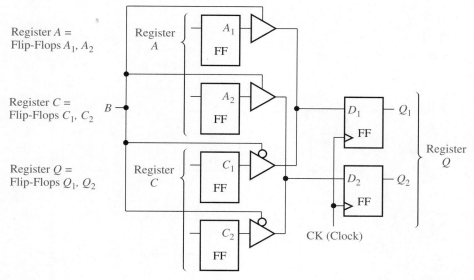

Figure 18–17
Data Transfer Between Registers

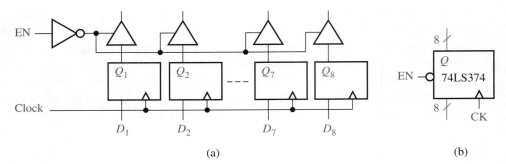

Figure 18–18
Logic Diagram for 74LS374, Octal Register with
3-State Outputs

accomplished using 3-state buffers. If $B = 1$ and a clock is applied to register Q, the data in register A will be stored in Q; if $B = 0$, the data in register C will be stored in Q.

Figure 18–18(a) shows a 74LS374 integrated circuit register which contains 8 D flip-flops with 3-state buffers at the flip-flop outputs. These buffers are enabled when $EN = 0$. A simplified representation for this octal register is shown in Fig. 18–18(b). The notation

$$\diagdown\!\!\frac{8}{}$$

is used to represent 8 wires.

Figure 18–19 shows how data can be transferred from one of four octal registers into a fifth register. The outputs from registers A, B, C, and D are all con-

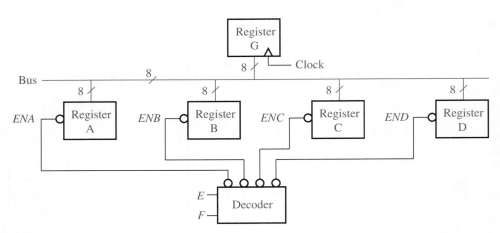

Figure 18–19
Data Transfer Using a 3-State Bus

nected in parallel to a common "bus". The D flip-flop inputs of register G are also connected to the bus. When $ENA = 0$, the 3-state outputs of register A are enabled onto the bus and loaded into register G when the next clock occurs. Similarly, the data in register B, C, or D is transferred to G when ENB, ENC, or END is 0, respectively. The four enable signals may be generated by a decoder. The operation can be summarized as follows:

If $EF = 00$, A is stored in G.
If $EF = 01$, B is stored in G.
If $EF = 10$, C is stored in G.
If $EF = 11$, D is stored in G.

Note that 8 bits of data are transferred in parallel by each clock pulse. As an alternative to using a bus with 3-state logic, eight 4-to-1 multiplexers could be used, but this would lead to a more complex circuit.

PROBLEMS

18.1   The 74178 shift register can be made to shift left by adding external connections between the Q outputs and D inputs. Indicate the appropriate connections on a block diagram of the 74178. Which input line would serve as a serial input in this case? With the connections you have made, what should SH and L be for a left shift? For a right shift?

18.2   (a) Show how to connect a 74178 shift register so that a right *circular* shift is performed.

       (b) Complete the following timing diagram for a 74178 shift register if it is connected as in (a). Assume that $D_A D_B D_C D_D = 1010$.

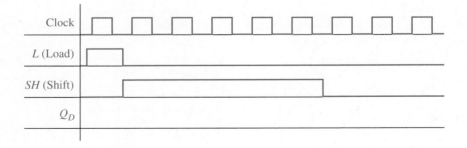

       (c) Repeat (b) for $D_A D_B D_C D_D = 1011$.

18.3 (a) Complete the following timing diagram for a 74S163 counter. Assume that $D_D D_C D_B D_A = 1011$, $T = 1$.

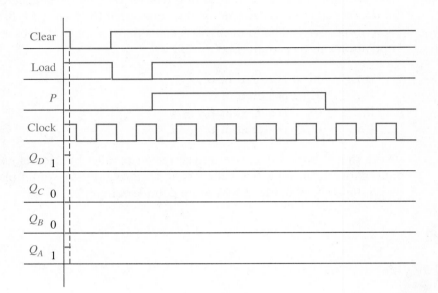

(b) Repeat part a for $D_D D_C D_B D_A = 1100$, $T = 1$.

18.4 Using a 74S163 counter and two NAND gates (plus an inverter if needed), design a counter which counts in the sequence 0, 1, 2, 3, 4, 5, 6, 7, 10, 11, 12, 13, 0, 1,... Note that 10 must be loaded into the counter in state 7 and the counter resets after state 13. Take advantage of the fact that LOAD overrides COUNT, and CLEAR overrides LOAD and COUNT.

18.5 Realize the given state graph using a 74S163 counter with added gates. Note in state 0010, if $X = 1$, then the counter must be loaded with 0101. Take advantage of the fact that LOAD overrides COUNT, and CLEAR overrides LOAD and COUNT.

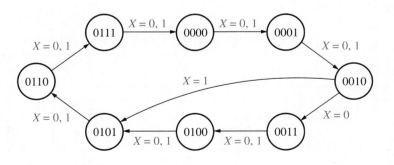

18.6 Realize the given state graphs using a 74S163 counter with added gates. Use the order $Q_D Q_C Q_B Q_A$ for the counter state variables.

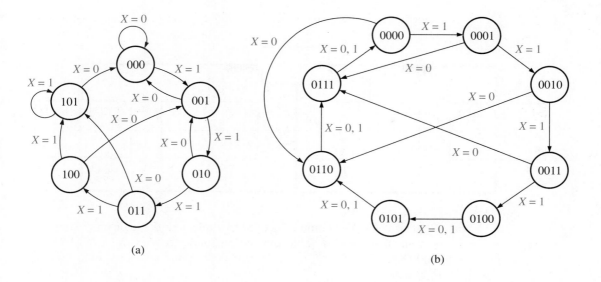

(a)

(b)

18.7 A digital system contains four 74LS374 octal D flip-flop registers. The inputs *and* outputs of all four registers are connected to a common bus so that the contents of any register can be loaded into any other register. A 2-to-4 decoder is used to selectively enable the register outputs, and each register can be clocked separately.

(a) Draw a block diagram of the system.

(b) What should be the decoder inputs and which register(s) should be clocked in order to load the contents of register B into register A? In order to load the contents of register A into both registers C and D?

18.8 A digital system contains four 74LS374 octal D flip-flop registers and a logic unit as shown. The inputs of all four registers are connected to a bus R, which is connected to the output of a logic unit. The outputs from either register A or B can be placed on the X input of the logic unit and the output of either C or D can be placed onto the Y input. The result from the logic unit then appears on the result bus R. After the result appears on the R bus, it can be clocked into any one of the registers. The two control signals, C_1 and C_2, determine the logic operation performed by the logic unit as follows:

C_1C_2	Operation
00	$R_i = X_i$ AND Y_i
01	$R_i = X_i$ OR Y_i
10	$R_i = $ NOT X_i
11	$R_i = $ NOT Y_i

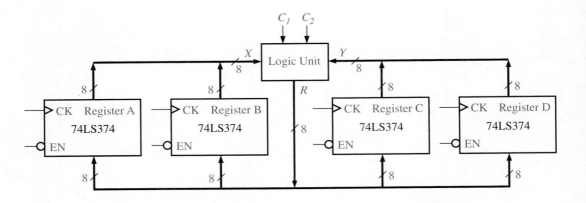

(a) What size of ROM would be needed to implement the logic unit? Show the portion of the ROM table that corresponds to $X_2X_3X_4X_5X_6X_7X_8 = 0000000$ and $Y_2Y_3Y_4Y_5Y_6Y_7Y_8 = 0000000$. (Your answer should contain 16 rows.)

(b) Show how to connect a 2-to-4 decoder so that the rising edge of the next clock pulse will load the result into register A, B, C, or D for control inputs $G_0G_1 = 00$, 01, 10, or 11, respectively.

(c) Show how to connect two control signals, E_0 and E_1, to the registers so that $E_0 = 0$ places the A register contents on the X bus, $E_0 = 1$ places B onto the X bus, $E_1 = 0$ places C onto the Y bus, and $E_1 = 1$ places D onto the Y bus.

18.9 A 74S163 counter is connected as shown in Fig. 18–9, except the D inputs are 1101.

(a) What will be the counting sequence starting in state 0 ($Q_D = Q_C = Q_B = Q_A = 0$)? Assume that CLEAR $= 1$ and $PT = 1$.

(b) Complete the following timing diagram to show Q_D, Q_C, Q_B, Q_A, and CARRY. Assume that initially $Q_DQ_CQ_BQ_A = 1110$.

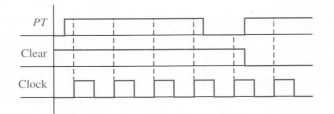

19

Sequential Network Design with Programmable Logic Devices (PLDs)

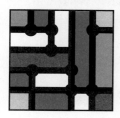

OBJECTIVES

1. Design a sequential network using a ROM (read-only memory) or PLA (programmable logic array) and flip-flops. Analyze such a network.

2. Design a sequential network using a sequential PAL.

3. Explain the operation of a 22V10 or similar PLD; design a sequential network using such a PLD.

4. Explain the operation of a PGA (programmable gate array). Show how combinational and sequential logic can be implemented using a PGA.

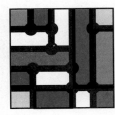

STUDY GUIDE

1. Study Section 19.1 *Design of Sequential Networks Using ROMs and PLAs.*

   (a) Review Section 9.6, *Read-Only Memories*, and Section 9.7, *Programmable Logic Devices.*

   (b) What size ROM would be required to realize a *state* table with 13 states, 2 input variables, and 3 output variables?

   (c) In going from Table 19–1(b) to Table 19–1(c), note that for $X = 0$, $Q_1Q_2Q_3 = 000$, $Z = 1$, and $Q_1^+Q_2^+Q_3^+ = D_1D_2D_3 = 001$; therefore, 1001 is entered in the first row of the truth table. Verify that the other truth table entries are correct.

   (d) Continue the analysis of the PLA realization of the code converter which was started in the last paragraph of Section 19.1. In particular, if $Q_1Q_2Q_3 = 100$ and $X = 1$, what will be the PLA outputs? What will the state be after the clock?

   (e) Work Problems 19.1 and 19.2.

2. Before you study Section 19.2, *Design of Sequential Networks Using PALs*, review the material on PALs in Section 9.7.

   (a) Study the 16R4 PAL shown in Fig. 19–3. Verify that the X's on the diagram implement Equations (19–1).

   (b) Label the pin 2 input Y. Add 1 or more X's to the diagram so that the Z output will only be enabled when $Y = 0$.

   (c) Which buffer must be disabled so that pin 13 can be used as an input rather than an output?

   (d) Work Problem 19.3.

   (e) Derive Equation (19–3(d)) from Table 19–4 by using Karnaugh maps as in Fig. 19–5.

   (f) Using Equations (19–7), verify that the counter will go to the correct next state when the present state is 1000 and $D = 1$; also when the present state is 1011 and $U = 1$.

   (g) Work Problems 19.11 and 19.13.

3. Study Section 19.3, *Other Sequential Programmable Logic Devices* (*PLDs*).

   (a) If the 22V10 is used to realize a Mealy stable table with 24 rows, how many output variables can the table have? If one input variable is used for an asynchronous reset, how many input variables could the table have? Can all tables with this number of inputs be realized with the 22V10? Why or why not?

   (b) For the output macrocell in Fig. 19–7, which fuse(s) should be blown so that the output on the I/O pin equals Q?

   So that it equals D'?

   (c) Work Problem 19.14.

4. Study Section 19.4, *Programmable Gate Arrays* (*PGAs*).

   (a) For Fig. 19–11, list all distinct combinations of variables which can appear at the X and Y outputs.

   If option 2 is chosen in Fig. 19–12, list all of the possible combinations of input variables which can be selected for F (you should find 7).

   (b) If a 2064 LCA has 20 inputs, what is the maximum number of outputs it can have?

   (c) Show how the following function can be realized with 3 logic cells. Give the function realized by each cell.

   $$F = ab'c'd'e' + bcde + a'b'cde'$$

   (d) Work Problems 19.15 and 19.16.

5. When you are satisfied that you can meet all of the objectives, take the readiness test.

Sequential Network Design with Programmable Logic Devices (PLDs)

In this unit the techniques used in Unit 9 for design of combinational networks with read-only memories, programmable logic arrays, and PALs are extended to sequential network design. Then some of the newer programmable logic devices, including programmable gate arrays, are introduced. The use of PLDs simplifies the design of sequential networks and generally leads to lower overall digital system cost.

19.1
Design of Sequential Networks Using ROMs and PLAs

A sequential network can easily be designed using a ROM (read-only memory) and flip-flops. Referring to the general model of a Mealy sequential network given in Fig. 13–13, the combinational part of the sequential network can be realized using a ROM. The ROM can be used to realize the output functions $(Z_1, Z_2, \ldots, Z_n)$ and the next-state functions $(Q_1^+, Q_2^+, \ldots, Q_k^+)$. The state of the network can then be stored in a register of D flip-flops and fed back to the input of the ROM. Thus a Mealy sequential network with m inputs, n outputs, and k state variables can be realized using k D flip-flops and a ROM with $m + k$ inputs (2^{m+k} words) and $n + k$ outputs. The Moore sequential network of Fig. 13–14 can be realized in a similar manner. The next-state and output combinational subnetworks of the Moore network can both be realized with a single ROM or with separate ROMs.

Use of D flip-flops is preferable to J-K flip-flops since use of 2-input flip-flops would require increasing the number of outputs from the ROM. The fact that the D flip-flop input equations would generally require more gates than the J-K equations is of no consequence since the size of the ROM depends only on the number of inputs and outputs and not on the complexity of the equations being realized. For this reason, the state assignment which is used is also of little importance, and generally a state assignment in straight binary order is as good as any.

In Section 16.2, we realized a code converter using gates and J-K flip-flops. We will now realize this converter using a ROM and D flip-flops. The state table for the converter is reproduced in Table 19–1(a). Since there are 7 states, 3 D flip-flops are required. Thus, a ROM with 4 inputs (2^4 words) and 4 outputs is required, as shown in Fig. 19–1. Using a straight binary state assignment, we can construct the transition table, seen in Table 19–1(b), which gives the next state of the flip-flops as a function of the present state and input. Since we are using D flip-flops, $D_1 = Q_1^+$, $D_2 = Q_2^+$, and $D_3 = Q_3^+$. The truth table for the ROM, shown in Table 19–1(c), is easily constructed from the transition table. This gives the ROM outputs (Z, D_1, D_2, D_3) as functions of the ROM inputs (X, Q_1, Q_2, Q_3).

Sequential networks can also be realized using PLAs (programmable logic arrays) and flip-flops in a manner similar to using ROMs and flip-flops. However, in the case of PLAs, the state assignment may be important since use of a good state assignment can reduce the required number of product terms and hence reduce the required size of the PLA.

As an example, we will consider realizing the state table of Table 19–1(a) using a PLA and 3 D flip-flops. The network configuration is the same as Fig. 19–1, except that the ROM is replaced with a PLA of appropriate size. Using a straight binary assignment leads to the truth table given in Table 19–1(c).

Table 19-1

(a) state table

Present State	Next State X = 0	1	Present Output (Z) X = 0	1
A	B	C	1	0
B	D	E	1	0
C	E	E	0	1
D	H	H	0	1
E	H	M	1	0
H	A	A	0	1
M	A	–	1	–

(b) transition table

	$Q_1Q_2Q_3$	$Q_1^+Q_2^+Q_3^+$ X = 0	X = 1	Z X = 0	X = 1
A	000	001	010	1	0
B	001	011	100	1	0
C	010	100	100	0	1
D	011	101	101	0	1
E	100	101	110	1	0
H	101	000	000	0	1
M	110	000	–	1	–

(c) truth table

X	Q_1	Q_2	Q_3	Z	D_1	D_2	D_3
0	0	0	0	1	0	0	1
0	0	0	1	1	0	1	1
0	0	1	0	0	1	0	0
0	0	1	1	0	1	0	1
0	1	0	0	1	1	0	1
0	1	0	1	0	0	0	0
0	1	1	0	1	0	0	0
0	1	1	1	X	X	X	X
1	0	0	0	0	0	1	0
1	0	0	1	0	1	0	0
1	0	1	0	1	1	0	0
1	0	1	1	1	1	0	1
1	1	0	0	0	1	1	0
1	1	0	1	1	0	0	0
1	1	1	0	X	X	X	X
1	1	1	1	X	X	X	X

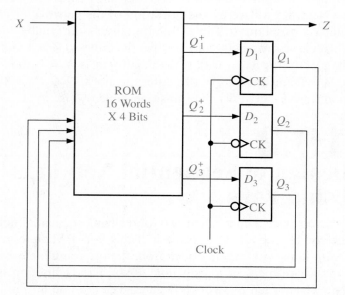

Figure 19-1
Realization of a Sequential Network with a ROM

This table could be stored in a PLA with 4 inputs, 13 product terms, and 4 outputs, but this would offer no advantage over the ROM solution discussed earlier. If the state assignment of Fig. 16–2 is used, the resulting output equation and D flip-flop input equations, derived from the maps in Fig. 16–3, are

$$D_1 = Q_1Q_2' + Q_1'Q_2$$
$$D_2 = Q_2'$$
$$D_3 = Q_2'Q_3 + X'Q_1Q_2' + XQ_1'Q_2' + X'Q_1'Q_2Q_3' \qquad (19\text{--}1)$$
$$Z = X'Q_3' + XQ_3$$

The PLA table which corresponds to these equations is in Table 19–2.

Table 19–2

X	Q_1	Q_2	Q_3	Z	D_1	D_2	D_3
–	1	0	–	0	1	0	0
–	0	1	–	0	1	0	0
–	–	0	–	0	0	1	0
–	–	0	1	0	0	0	1
0	1	0	–	0	0	0	1
1	0	0	–	0	0	0	1
0	0	1	0	0	0	0	1
0	–	–	0	1	0	0	0
1	–	–	1	1	0	0	0

Realization of this table requires a PLA with 4 inputs, 9 product terms, and 4 outputs. When the number of inputs is small, as in this example, the ROM solution is generally more economical than the PLA solution; however, when the number of input variables is large, the PLA solution becomes more attractive.

Next, we will verify the operation of the network of Fig. 19–1 using a PLA which corresponds to Table 19–2. Initially, assume that $X = 0$ and $Q_1Q_2Q_3 = 000$. This selects rows $--0-$ and $0--0$ in the table, so $Z = 1$ and $D_1D_2D_3 = 010$. After the clock, $Q_1Q_2Q_3 = 010$. If the next input is $X = 1$, then row $-01-$ is selected, so $Z = 0$ and $D_1D_2D_3 = 100$. After the clock, $Q_1Q_2Q_3 = 100$. Continuing in this manner, we can verify the transition table of Fig. 16–2.

19.2
Design of Sequential Networks Using PALs

PALs provide a convenient way of realizing sequential networks. In addition to the combinational PALs listed in Table 9–2, PALs are available which contain D flip-flops with inputs driven from the programmable array logic. Figure 19–2 shows a segment of a sequential PAL. The D flip-flop is driven from an OR gate which is fed by two AND gates. The flip-flop output is fed back to the programmable AND array through a buffer. Thus, the AND gate inputs can be con-

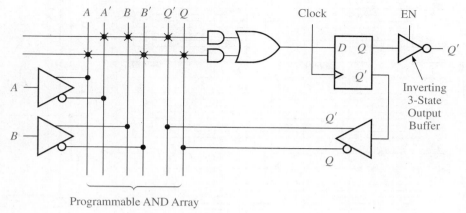

Figure 19–2
Segment of a Sequential PAL

nected to A, A', B, B', Q or Q'. The X's on the diagram show the realization of the next-state equation

$$Q^+ = D = A'BQ' + AB'Q$$

The flip-flop output is connected to an inverting tri-state buffer, which is enabled when EN $= 1$.

Table 19–3 shows the characteristics of some common types of sequential PALs. Each of these PALs contains a register of from 4 to 10 D flip-flops. The first six PALs in the table are similar to the 16R4, which is shown in Fig. 19–3. The 16R4 has an AND gate array with 16 inputs, and it has 4 D flip-flops. Each flip-flop output goes through a tri-state inverting buffer (output pins 14–17). One input (pin 11) is used to enable these buffers. The rising edge of a common clock (pin 1) causes the flip flops to change state. Each D flip-flop input is driven from

Table 19–3
Characteristics of Sequential PALs

Type No.	No. of Inputs (direct + feedback + I/O pins)	No. of Outputs (flip-flops + I/O pins)	No. of AND Gates per OR Gate
16R4	8 + 4 + 4	4 + 4	8
16R6	8 + 6 + 2	6 + 2	8
16R8	8 + 8 + 0	8 + 0	8
20R4	12 + 4 + 4	4 + 4	8
20R6	12 + 6 + 2	6 + 2	8
20R8	12 + 8 + 0	8 + 0	8
20X4	10 + 4 + 6	4 + 6	3/2*
20X8	10 + 8 + 2	8 + 2	3/2
20X10	10 + 10 + 0	10 + 0	–/2

* 3 for combinational outputs, 2 for D flip-flop inputs

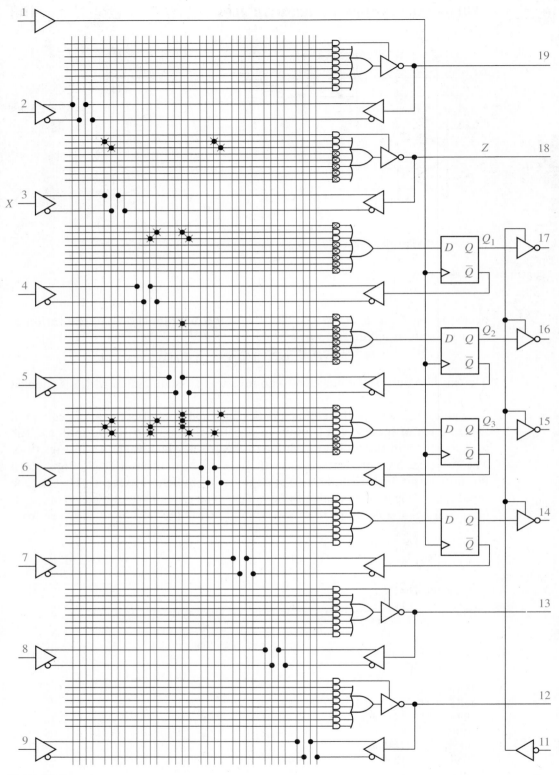

Figure 19–3
Logic Diagram for 16R4 PAL (courtesy of
Monolithic Memories)

an OR gate, and each OR gate is fed from 8 AND gates. The AND gate inputs can come from the external PAL inputs (pins 2–9) or from the flip-flop outputs, which are fed back internally. In addition there are 4 input/output (I/O) terminals (pins 12, 13, 18, and 19) which can be used as either network outputs or as inputs to the AND gates. Thus, each AND gate can have a maximum of 16 inputs (8 external inputs, 4 inputs fed back from the flip-flop outputs, and 4 inputs from the I/O terminals). When used as an output, each I/O terminal is driven from an inverting tri-state buffer. Each of these buffers is fed from an OR gate and each OR gate is fed from 7 AND gates. An eighth AND gate is used to enable the buffer.

When the 16R4 PAL is used to realize a sequential network, the I/O terminals are normally used for the Z outputs. Thus, a single 16R4 with no additional logic could realize a sequential network with up to 8 inputs, 4 outputs, and 16 states. Each next-state equation could contain up to 8 terms, and each output equation could contain up to 7 terms. As an example, we will realize the code converter described by Equations (19–1). Three flip-flops are used to store Q_1, Q_2, and Q_3, and the array logic which drives these flip-flops is programmed to realize D_1, D_2, and D_3 as shown in Fig. 19–3. The X's on the diagram indicate the connections to the AND-gate inputs. The flip-flop outputs are not used externally, so the output buffers are disabled. Since the Z output comes through an inverting buffer, the array logic must realize

$$Z' = (X + Q_3)(X' + Q_3') = XQ_3' + X'Q_3$$

The Z output buffer is permanently enabled in this example, so there are no connections to the AND gate that drives the enable input.

The last three PALs in Table 19–3 are referred to as "XOR PALs". The XOR PALs have an exclusive-OR gate driving each D flip-flop input as shown in Fig. 19–4. In these PALs, each exclusive-OR gate is driven by two OR gates, and

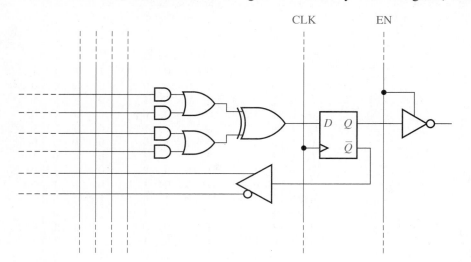

Figure 19–4
Segment of an XOR PAL

each OR gate is driven by two AND gates. The flip-flop outputs can be fed back to AND gate inputs just like in other registered PALs. The general form of the next state equation for each flip-flop in the XOR PAL is

$$Q^+ = D = (P_1 + P_2) \oplus (P_3 + P_4) \tag{19-2}$$

where P_1, P_2, P_3, and P_4 are product terms.

To illustrate the use of XOR PALs, we will design a 4-bit binary up-down counter with three control inputs: U, D, and L. When $U = 1$, the counter is incremented by 1, when $D = 1$, the counter is decremented by 1, and when $L = 1$, the counter is loaded in parallel from its data (D_i) inputs. Table 19–4 shows the next states of the counter for $U = 1$ and for $D = 1$. We will assume that $U = D = 1$ does not occur.

We will first derive the next state equations for the up counter. This counter will be incremented every clock pulse when $U = 1$, and it will remain in the same state when $U = 0$. In every row, $Q_0 \neq Q_0^+$, so flip-flop Q_0 must change state at every clock when $U = 1$. Therefore,

$$Q_0^+ = Q_0 \oplus U \tag{19-3(a)}$$

Observe that Q_1 changes (that is, $Q_1 \neq Q_1^+$) only if $Q_0 = 1$. Therefore,

$$Q_1^+ = Q_1 \oplus UQ_0 \tag{19-3(b)}$$

Q_2 changes only in rows 3 (0011), 7, 11, and 15; only when $Q_1 = Q_0 = 1$. Therefore,

$$Q_2^+ = Q_2 \oplus UQ_1Q_0 \tag{19-3(c)}$$

Finally, Q_3 changes state only in those rows where $Q_2 = Q_1 = Q_0 = 1$; therefore,

$$Q_3^+ = Q_3 \oplus UQ_2Q_1Q_0 \tag{19-3(d)}$$

Table 19–4
Up-Down Counter

Q_3 Q_2 Q_1 Q_0	$U = 1$ Q_3^+ Q_2^+ Q_1^+ Q_0^+	$D = 1$ Q_3^+ Q_2^+ Q_1^+ Q_0^+
0 0 0 0	0 0 0 1	1 1 1 1
0 0 0 1	0 0 1 0	0 0 0 0
0 0 1 0	0 0 1 1	0 0 0 1
0 0 1 1	0 1 0 0	0 0 1 0
0 1 0 0	0 1 0 1	0 0 1 1
0 1 0 1	0 1 1 0	0 1 0 0
0 1 1 0	0 1 1 1	0 1 0 1
0 1 1 1	1 0 0 0	0 1 1 0
1 0 0 0	1 0 0 1	0 1 1 1
1 0 0 1	1 0 1 0	1 0 0 0
1 0 1 0	1 0 1 1	1 0 0 1
1 0 1 1	1 1 0 0	1 0 1 0
1 1 0 0	1 1 0 1	1 0 1 1
1 1 0 1	1 1 1 0	1 1 0 0
1 1 1 0	1 1 1 1	1 1 0 1
1 1 1 1	0 0 0 0	1 1 1 0

Similarly, by inspection of Table 19–4, we can derive the equations for a down counter which is decremented by every clock pulse when $D = 1$:

(a) $Q_0^+ = Q_0 \oplus D$,   (b) $Q_1^+ = Q_1 \oplus DQ_0'$ (19–4)

(c) $Q_2^+ = Q_2 \oplus DQ_0'Q_1'$ (d) $Q_3^+ = Q_3 \oplus DQ_0'Q_1'Q_2'$

Note that Q_1 changes state only when $Q_0 = 0$, Q_2 changes state only when $Q_1 = Q_0 = 0$, etc.

In general, to use an XOR PAL, we must express the next state of Q_i in the form $Q_i^+ = Q_i \oplus F_i$, as in Equations (19–2), (19–3), and (19–4). We can solve for F_i by exclusive-ORing each side of the equation with Q_i:

$$Q_i^+ \oplus Q_i = F_i \oplus Q_i \oplus Q_i = F_i \oplus 0 = F_i \qquad (19–5)$$

We can derive F_i using Karnaugh maps in the same way as we derived T flip-flop input equations in Section 12.2. As an example, we will derive Equation 19–4(c) again, using maps instead of by inspection. First, we plot Q_2^+ from Table 19–4 (see Fig. 19–5). Then, to get the map for F_2, we complement those columns where $Q_2 = 1$. Since we want the counter to change state only when $D = 1$, we will write the next state as

$$Q_2^+ = Q_2 \oplus DF_2 = Q_2 \oplus DQ_1'Q_0'$$

which is the same as Equation 19–4(c).

Now we will continue the design of the up-down counter with control inputs U, D, and L. First consider the case when $U = D = 0$. When $L = 1$, the counter is loaded in parallel from its data (D_i) inputs, and when $L = 0$, the counter state remains unchanged. Thus, the next state equation for each flip-flop is

$$Q_i^+ = LD_i + L'Q_i \quad (i = 0, 1, 2, 3) \qquad (19–6)$$

We will now attempt to combine Equations (19–3), (19–4), and (19–6) to obtain equations for the up-down counter in the same form as Equation (19–2). We will assume that $L = 1$ overrides $U = 1$ or $D = 1$, and $U = D = 1$ never occurs. If

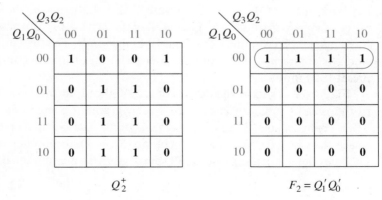

Figure 19–5
Karnaugh Maps for Down Counter

we start with Equation (19–3(a)), replace Q_0 with $(LD_0 + L'Q_0)$, and replace U with $(U + D)$, we get $Q_0^+ = (LD_0 + L'Q_0) \oplus (U + D)$. This equation gives the correct result when L is 0 and U or D is 1. To make sure that $L = 1$ overrides count up or down, we must multiply U and D by L', which gives (19–7(a)). The remaining equations are formed in a similar manner.

$$Q_0^+ = (LD_0 + L'Q_0) \oplus (UL' + DL') \qquad (19\text{–}7\text{(a)})$$
$$Q_1^+ = (LD_1 + L'Q_1) \oplus (UL'Q_0 + DL'Q_0') \qquad (19\text{–}7\text{(b)})$$
$$Q_2^+ = (LD_2 + L'Q_2) \oplus (UL'Q_0Q_1 + DL'Q_0'Q_1') \qquad (19\text{–}7\text{(c)})$$
$$Q_3^+ = (LD_3 + L'Q_3) \oplus (UL'Q_0Q_1Q_2 + DL'Q_0'Q_1'Q_2') \qquad (19\text{–}7\text{(d)})$$

When $L = D = 0$, these equations reduce to (19–3), and when $L = U = 0$, these equations reduce to (19–4). Equations (19–7) are of the proper form to fit into an XOR PAL. We could easily expand the number of bits in the counter by writing equations for Q_4^+, Q_5^+, etc. similar to Equations (19–7). Each equation would require exactly the same number of AND and OR gates regardless of the size of the counter. If we did not use the XOR approach, the number of gates would increase for each successive stage of the counter, and the limits of a conventional PAL would soon be exceeded.

19.3
Other Sequential Programmable Logic Devices (PLDs)

The PALs discussed in Section 19.2 are examples of sequential PLDs. As integrated circuit technology has improved, a wide variety of other PLDs have become available. Some of these are based on extensions of the PAL concept, and others are based on gate arrays (defined in Section 19.4).

The 22V10[1] (Fig. 19–6) is a very versatile PLD which can be used to realize both combinational and sequential networks. It has 12 dedicated input pins and 10 pins which can be programmed as either inputs or outputs. It contains 10 D flip-flops and 10 OR gates. The number of AND gates which feed each OR gate ranges from 8 through 16. Each OR gate drives an "output logic macrocell". Each macrocell contains one of the 10 D flip-flops. The flip-flops have a common clock, a common asynchronous reset (AR) input and a common synchronous preset (SP) input.

Figure 19–7 shows the details of a 22V10 output macrocell. The connections to the output pins are controlled by programming this macrocell. The output MUX control inputs, S_1 and S_0, select one of the data inputs. For example, $S_1S_0 = 10$ selects data input 2. When fuse F_1 is blown ($S_1 = 1$), the flip-flop is by-passed, and the OR gate output is connected to the I/O pin through the multiplexer and output buffer. The

---

[1] 22V10 means a "Versatile" PAL with a total of 22 inputs and outputs, 10 of which are bidirectional I/O (input/output) pins.

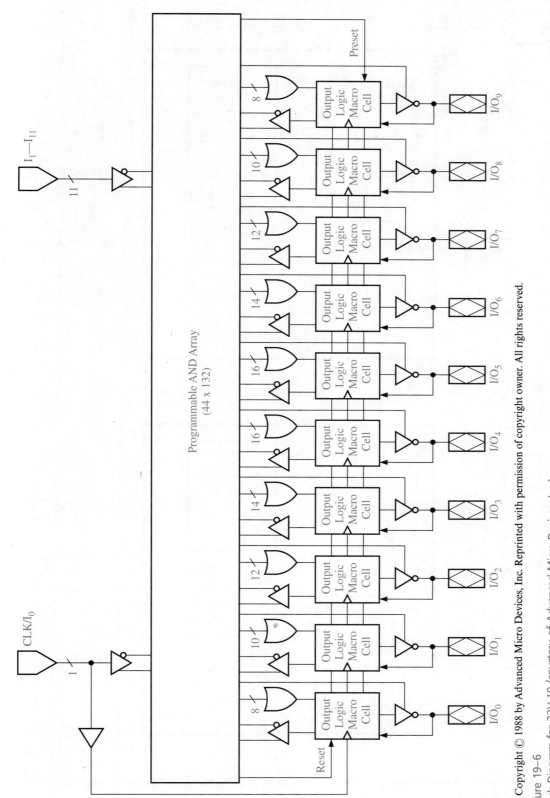

Figure 19–6
Block Diagram for 22V 10 (courtesy of Advanced Micro Devices, Inc.)

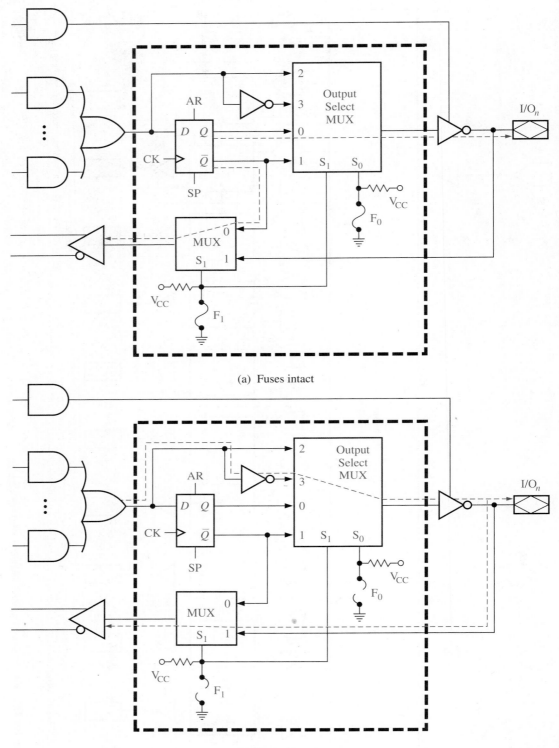

(a) Fuses intact

(b) Fuses blown

Figure 19–7
Output Macrocell

OR gate output is also fed back so that it can be used as input to the AND gate array. If F_1 is intact ($S_1 = 0$), then the flip-flop output is connected to the output pin and it is also fed back so that it can be used for AND gate inputs. When fuse F_0 is blown ($S_0 = 1$), the output is not inverted so that it is active high. When F_0 is intact ($S_0 = 0$), the output is inverted so that it is active low. The output pin is driven by a tri-state inverting buffer. When the buffer output is in the high impedance state, the OR gate and flip-flop are disconnected from the output pin, and the pin can be used as an input. The dashed blue lines on Fig. 19–7(a) show the path through the output macrocell when both fuses are intact, and the dashed blue lines on Fig 19–7(b) show the path with both fuses blown. Note that in the first case, the flip-flop Q output is inverted by the output buffer, and in the second case the OR gate output is inverted twice so there is no net inversion.

As an example of using the 22V10, we will design a sequential traffic light controller for the intersection of "A" street and "B" street. Each street has traffic sensors which detect the presence of vehicles approaching or stopped at the intersection. Sa = 1 means a vehicle is approaching on "A" street, and Sb = 1 means a vehicle is approaching on "B" street. "A" street is a main street and will have a green light until a car approaches on "B". Then the light changes and "B" has a green light. At the end of 50 seconds, the lights will change back unless there is a car on "B" street and none on "A", in which case the "B" cycle is extended 10 more seconds. When "A" is green, it remains green at least 60 seconds, and then the lights change only when a car approaches on "B". Figure 19–8 shows the external connections to the controller. Three of the outputs (Ga, Ya, and Ra) drive the green, yellow, and red lights on "A" street. The other three (Gb, Yb, and Rb) drive the corresponding lights on "B" street.

Figure 19–9 shows a Moore state graph for the controller. For timing purposes, the sequential network is driven by a clock with a 10-second period. Thus, a state change can occur at most once every 10 seconds. To simplify the graph, the following notation is used: GaRb in a state means that Ga = Rb = 1 and all the other output variables are 0. Sa′Sb on an arc implies that Sa = 0 and Sb = 1 will cause a transition along that arc. An arc without a label implies that a state transition will occur when the clock occurs, independent of the input variables.

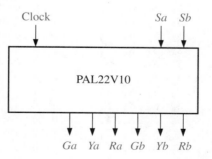

Figure 19–8
Block Diagram of Traffic Light Controller

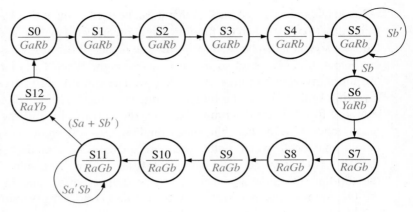

Figure 19–9
State Graph for Traffic Light Controller

Thus, the green "A" light will stay on for 6 clock cycles (60 seconds) and then change to yellow if a car is waiting on street "B".

Table 19–5 shows the state table for the controller. We will implement the table using four D flip-flops with inputs D_1, D_2, D_3, D_4 and outputs Q_1, Q_2, Q_3, Q_4. Using a straight binary state assignment, the following equations were derived from the table with a logic design program:

$$D_1 = Q_1Q_2' + Q_2Q_3Q_4$$
$$D_2 = Q_1'Q_2'Q_3Q_4 + SaQ_1Q_3Q_4 + Sb'Q_1Q_3Q_4 + Q_1'Q_2Q_4' + Q_1'Q_2Q_3'$$
$$D_3 = Q_3Q_4' + SbQ_3'Q_4 + Sa'Q_3'Q_4 + Q_2'Q_3'Q_4 + Sa'SbQ_1Q_4$$
$$D_4 = Sa'SbQ_1Q_3 + Q_2'Q_4' + Q_1'Q_4' + SaSb'Q_2Q_3'Q_4$$

Table 19–5
State Table for Traffic Light Controller

	00	01	10	11	Ga	Ya	Ra	Gb	Yb	Rb	
S_0	S_1	S_1	S_1	S_1	1	0	0	0	0	1	{Green A, Red B}
S_1	S_2	S_2	S_2	S_2	1	0	0	0	0	1	
S_2	S_3	S_3	S_3	S_3	1	0	0	0	0	1	
S_3	S_4	S_4	S_4	S_4	1	0	0	0	0	1	
S_4	S_5	S_5	S_5	S_5	1	0	0	0	0	1	
S_5	S_5	S_6	S_5	S_6	1	0	0	0	0	1	
S_6	S_7	S_7	S_7	S_7	0	1	0	0	0	1	{Ya, Rb}
S_7	S_8	S_8	S_8	S_8	0	0	1	1	0	0	{Ra, Gb}
S_8	S_9	S_9	S_9	S_9	0	0	1	1	0	0	
S_9	S_{10}	S_{10}	S_{10}	S_{10}	0	0	1	1	0	0	
S_{10}	S_{11}	S_{11}	S_{11}	S_{11}	0	0	1	1	0	0	
S_{11}	S_{12}	S_{11}	S_{12}	S_{12}	0	0	1	1	0	0	
S_{12}	S_0	S_0	S_0	S_0	0	0	1	0	1	0	{Ra, Yb}

$$Ga = Q_1'Q_3' + Q_1'Q_2' \qquad Ya = Q_2Q_3Q_4' \qquad Ra = Q_1 + Q_2Q_3Q_4$$
$$Gb = Q_1Q_2' + Q_2Q_3Q_4 \qquad Yb = Q_1Q_2 \qquad Rb = Q_1'Q_2' + Q_1'Q_4' + Q_1'Q_3'$$

Since all of these equations have less than 8 AND terms, they will easily fit in the 22V10. If some equations had so many terms that they would not fit in the 22V10, then it would be necessary to try different state assignments.

If the controller were implemented using J-K flip-flops and gates, 4 flip-flops and 34 gates would be required for the straight binary state assignment. These flip-flops and gates would require about 11 SSI integrated circuits, compared with only one IC for the 22V10 solution. Using the 22V10 leads to a simpler design which avoids the necessity of laying out a circuit board and wiring the ICs. The resulting circuit is smaller, uses less power, and is more reliable.

In this unit we have introduced several different types of PLDs and used them for designing sequential networks. Many other types of PLDs are available[2] together with software packages which facilitate their use. Some of these programs accept input only in the form of logic equations, while others have options for state table, state graph, or logic diagram input. These programs generally produce a data file which is used as input to a PLD programmer to program the PLD for a specific application.

19.4
Programmable Gate Arrays (PGAs)

The PLDs we have discussed so far are capable of implementing a sequential network, but not a complete digital system. Programmable gate arrays (PGAs) are more flexible and more versatile and can be used to implement a small digital system on a single IC chip. A typical PGA is an IC which contains an array of identical logic cells with programmable interconnections. The user can program the functions realized by each logic cell and the connections between the cells.

As an example of a PGA, we will describe the Xilinx XC2064 Logic Cell Array (LCA). Figure 19–10 shows a part of the basic structure, which consists of an interior array of 64 configurable logic blocks (CLBs) surrounded by a ring of 58 input-output interface blocks. The interconnections between these blocks can be programmed by storing data in internal RAM memory cells. Each configurable logic block contains some combinational logic and a D flip-flop, and can be programmed to perform a variety of logic functions.

Figure 19–11 shows a configurable logic block. The trapezoidal blocks on the diagram represent multiplexers which can be programmed to select one of the inputs. For example, the lower input on the combinational logic block can come from either D or Q, and the Y output can come from either F, G, or Q. The

---

[2] See, for example, *Programmable Logic Designer's Guide* by Roger C. Alford, Howard Sams Co., 1989, or *The Programmable Logic Device Handbook* by Von L. Burton, Tab Books, Inc., 1990.

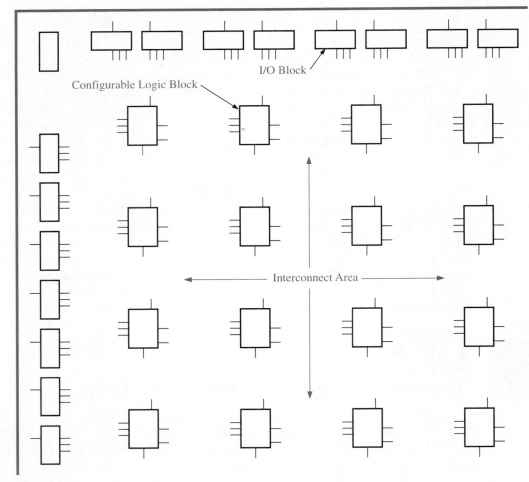

Figure 19–10
Layout of Part of a Programmable Logic Cell
Array (courtesy of Xilinx, Inc.)

combinational logic block contains RAM memory cells and can be programmed to realize any function of 4 variables or any two functions of 3 variables (see Fig. 19–12). For example, it could realize $F = G = f_1(A, B, C, Q)$ *or* $F = f_2(A, B, D)$ and $G = f_3(B, C, Q)$.

The dashed blue lines in Fig. 19–11 show the connections required to configure the logic cell as a J-K flip-flop with preset and clear inputs. The combinational logic has inputs, J, K, and Q and realizes the next state function for the flip-flop, $F = Q^+ = JQ' + K'Q$. It also realizes $G = Q'$ to provide a complemented output for the flip-flop. The preset and clear signals are routed directly to the S (asynchronous set) and R (asynchronous reset) inputs of the D flip-flop.

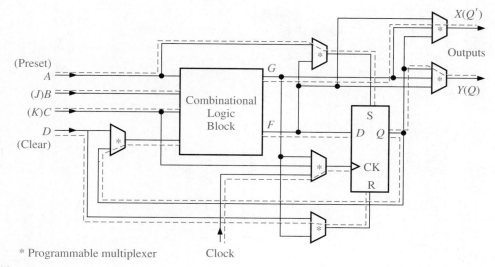

* Programmable multiplexer   Clock

Figure 19–11
Configurable Logic Block for XC2064 LCA
(courtesy of Xilinx, Inc.)

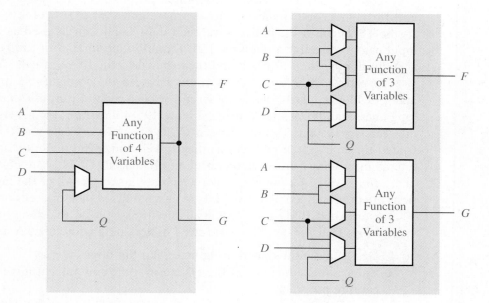

Option 1   Option 2
1 function of 4 variables   2 functions of 3 variables

Figure 19–12
Options for Combinational Logic Block
(courtesy of Xilinx, Inc.)

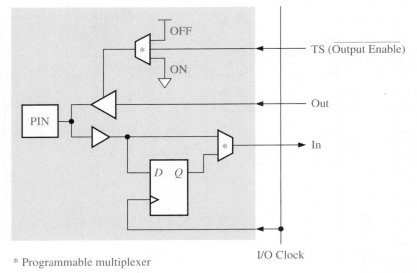

* Programmable multiplexer

Figure 19–13
Input-Output Block for XC2064 LCA
(courtesy of Xilinx, Inc.)

Figure 19–13 shows a configurable input-output block (IOB). The OUT signal goes through a 3-state buffer which can programmed to be OFF, ON, or controlled by the TS signal. If the buffer is off, then the I/O pin can be used as input. The input can go directly through the IOB to the IN terminal, or it can be stored in a D flip-flop by the I/O clock and then routed to the IN terminal.

The programmable interconnections between the configurable logic blocks and I/O blocks can be made in several ways—general purpose interconnects, long lines, and direct interconnects. Figure 19–14 illustrates the general-purpose interconnect system. Signals between CLBs or between CLBs and IOBs can be routed through switch matrices as they travel along the horizontal and vertical interconnect lines. Direct interconnection of adjacent CLBs is possible and long lines are provided to connect CLBs which are far apart. All of the interconnections are programmed by storing bits in internal RAM memory cells on the LCA.

Sophisticated CAD tools are available to assist with the design of systems using Logic Cell Arrays. The basic steps in designing with an LCA are:

1. Design a digital system using gates and flip-flops.
2. Enter a logic diagram of the system into the computer using a schematic capture program.
3. Run an automatic place and route program. This program will break the logic diagram into pieces which will fit into the configurable logic blocks, place the logic blocks in appropriate places in the LCA, and then route the interconnections between the logic blocks.
4. Run a program which will generate the bit pattern necessary to program the LCA.

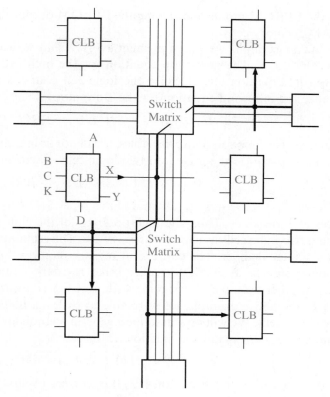

Figure 19–14
LCA General Purpose Interconnect
(courtesy of Xilinx, Inc.)

5. Download the bit pattern into the internal RAM memory cells in the LCA and test the operation of the LCA.

When the final system is built, the bit pattern for programming the LCA is normally stored in an EPROM and automatically loaded into the LCA when the power is turned on. The EPROM is connected to the LCA as shown in Fig. 19–15. The LCA resets itself after the power has been applied. Then it reads the configuration data from the EPROM by supplying a sequence of addresses

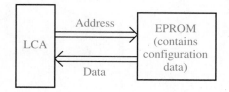

Figure 19–15
EPROM Connections for LCA Initialization

to the EPROM inputs and storing the EPROM output data in the LCA internal RAM memory cells.

As an example, we will implement a 74178 shift register (Fig. 18–3) within an XC2064 LCA. The next-state equation for the high order bit of the register is given in Equation (18–2). Since the logic cell contains a D flip-flop, we must realize the following equation for the D input:

$$D_A = SH\,SI + SH'\,L\,D_A + SH'\,L'\,Q_A \qquad (19\text{–}8)$$

Since D_A is a function of five variables, it will not fit in a single logic cell; therefore, we must partition the logic into two logic cells. Factoring (19–8) yields

$$D_A = SH\,SI + SH'(L\,D_A + L'\,Q_A)$$

If we let $F_1 = L\,D_A + L'\,Q_A$, then we have $D_A = SH\,SI + SH'\,F_1$, which is a function of 3 variables. Thus, the high-order bit of the shift register can be realized using two logic cells as shown in Fig. 19–16. The remaining 3 bits can be realized in a similar manner. The entire shift register requires 8 out of the 64 logic cells leaving 56 cells available to realize other registers, counters, control networks, etc. Another example of designing with an LCA is given in Fig. 20–10.

In the above example, we were able to realize a function of 5 variables with two logic cells. We will now describe a general method for realizing any 5-variable function. First, expand the function as follows:

$$F(a, b, c, d, e) = a'F(0, b, c, d, e) + aF(1, b, c, d, e) \qquad (19\text{–}9)$$

(You can verify that Equation (19–9) is correct by first setting a to 0 on both sides and then setting a to 1 on both sides. Since the equation is true for both $a = 0$ and $a = 1$, it is always true.) Equation (19–9) leads directly to the 3-cell realization shown in Fig. 19–17. Any 6-variable function can be realized in a similar manner with 7 or fewer logic cells. As the number of variables (n) increases,

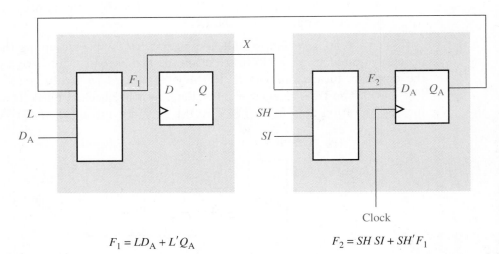

$$F_1 = LD_A + L'Q_A \qquad\qquad F_2 = SH\,SI + SH'F_1$$

Figure 19–16
LCA Realization of One Bit of Shift Register

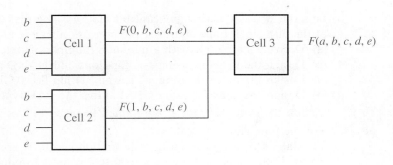

Figure 19–17
General Realization of a 5-Variable Function

the maximum number of logic cells required to realize an *n*-variable function increases rapidly. For this reason, ROMs, PLAs, or PALs may be a better solution than LCAs when *n* is large.

In this section we have used the XC2064 as an example of a programmable gate array. More complex PGAs which are available include the XC3000 series with up to 320 logic cells and 144 I/O blocks, and the XC4000 series with up to 900 logic cells and 240 I/O blocks. The use of such PGAs can greatly reduce the cost of manufacturing a digital system. When a digital system is manufactured in very large volumes, a custom-designed IC (often called an ASIC or application specific integrated circuit) may be the most economical solution.

PROBLEMS

19.1 Draw a block diagram which shows how a ROM and D flip-flops could be connected to realize Table 13–4 (p. 341). Specify the truth table for the ROM using a straight binary state assignment. (Note that a truth table, not a transition table is to be specified.)

19.2 The state table of Fig. 15–14(a) is to be realized using a PLA and D flip-flops.
(a) Draw a block diagram.
(b) Specify the contents of the PLA in tabular form using the state assignment of Fig. 15–14(a). (See Fig. 15–15(b) for the *D* equations.)
(c) If the PLA were replaced with a ROM, what size ROM would be required?

19.3 Realize the state table of Fig. 15–14 using a 16R4 PAL. (See Fig. 15–15(b) for the next state equations.) Mark X's on a copy of the 16R4 diagram to indicate the fuse pattern.

19.4 Work Problem 19.2 using the state table given in Problem 15.9. Derive the *D* equations using the state assignment $A = 000$, $B = 111$, $C = 110$, $D = 101$, $E = 100$, and $F = 010$.

19.5 Design a sequential network to multiply an 8-4-2-1 binary-coded decimal digit by 3 to give a 5-bit binary number. For example, if the input is 0111, the output should be 10101. The input and output to the network should be serial with the least significant bit first. Assume that the input will be 0 at the fifth clock time, and reset the network after the fifth output bit.

(a) Derive a state table with a minimum number of states (3 states).

(b) Design the network using J-K flip-flops and NAND and NOR gates.

(c) Design the network using a PLA and D flip-flops. Give the PLA table.

(d) Design the network using a PAL. Give the PAL type and fuse pattern.

19.6 Realize the state table for Programmed Exercise 14.2 using a 16R4 PAL.

19.7 For the following state table:

(a) Make a binary state assignment and derive the next-state equations for D flip-flops and the outputs (use a computer-aided logic design program).

(b) Can the equations in (a) be implemented in a single 16R4 PAL? If not, find a new state assignment that results in next-state equations with fewer terms. Show the equations needed to realize the state table in a 16R4 PAL.

| | XY | | | | | | | |
	00	01	10	11	00	01	10	11
a	a	b	c	d	0	0	1	0
b	b	c	g	e	1	0	0	1
c	f	i	g	h	1	1	0	0
d	d	d	d	a	0	1	0	1
e	g	c	a	b	1	0	1	1
f	i	f	h	g	1	1	0	1
g	b	g	c	a	0	0	0	0
h	i	h	i	h	0	0	0	1
i	h	i	a	a	1	0	0	0

19.8 An older model Thunderbird car has three left and three right tail lights which flash in unique patterns to indicate left and right turns.

LEFT turn pattern: RIGHT turn pattern:

LC LB LA   RA RB RC   LC LB LA   RA RB RC

Design a Moore sequential network to control these lights. The network has three inputs LEFT, RIGHT, and HAZ. LEFT and RIGHT come from the driver's turn signal switch and cannot be 1 at the same time. As indicated above, when LEFT = 1 the lights flash in a pattern LA on, LA and LB on, LA, LB, and LC on, all off, and then the sequence repeats. When RIGHT = 1, the light sequence is similar. If a switch from LEFT to RIGHT (or vice versa) occurs in the middle of a flashing sequence, the network should immediately go to the IDLE (lights off) state and then start the new sequence. HAZ comes from the hazard switch, and when HAZ = 1, all six lights flash on and off in unison. HAZ takes precedence if LEFT or RIGHT is also on.

Assume that a clock signal is available with a frequency equal to the desired flashing rate.

(a) Draw the state graph (8 states).

(b) Realize the network using six D flip-flops, and make a state assignment such that each flip-flop output drives one of the six lights directly. (Use a CAD program.)

(c) Realize the network using three D flip-flops, using the guidelines to determine a suitable state assignment.

(d) Note the tradeoff between more flip-flops and more gates in (b) and (c). Suggest a suitable PLD for each case.

19.9   The block diagram for an elevator controller for a two-floor elevator follows. The inputs FB_1 and FB_2 are 1 when someone in the elevator presses the first or second floor buttons, respectively. The inputs $CALL_1$ and $CALL_2$ are 1 when someone on the first or second floor presses the elevator call button. The inputs FS_1 and FS_2 are 1 when the elevator is at the first or second floor landing. The output UP turns on the motor to raise the elevator car; $DOWN$ turns on the motor to lower the elevator. If neither UP nor $DOWN$ is 1, then the elevator will not move. R_1 and R_2 reset the latches (described below); and when DO goes to 1, the elevator door opens. After the door opens and remains open for a reasonable length of time (as determined by the door controller mechanism), the door controller mechanism closes the door and sets $DC = 1$. Assume that all input signals are properly synchronized with the system clock.

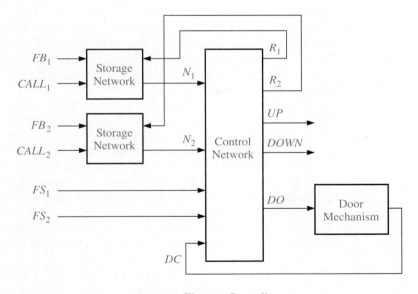

Elevator Controller

(a) If we were to realize a control network that responded to all of the inputs FB_1, FB_2, $CALL_1$, $CALL_2$, FS_1, FS_2, and DC, we would need to implement logic equations with 9 or more variables (7 inputs + at least 2 state variables). However, if we combine the signals FB_i and $CALL_i$ into a signal N_i ($i = 1$ or 2) that indicates that the elevator is needed on the specified floor, we can reduce the number of inputs into the control network. In addition, if the signal N_i is stored so that a single pulse on FB_i or $CALL_i$ will set N_i to 1 until the control network clears it, then the control network will be simplified further. Using a D flip-flop and a minimum number of added gates, design a storage network that will have an output 1 when either input (FB_i or $CALL_i$) becomes 1 and will stay 1 until reset with a signal R_i.

(b) Using the signals N_1 and N_2 that indicate that the elevator is needed on the first or second floor (to deliver a passenger or pick one up or both), derive a state graph for the elevator controller. (Only 4 states are needed.)

(c) Realize the storage networks for N_1 and N_2 and the state graph in a suitable PLD.

19.10   A sequential network will be used for a winner detector circuit for a model car race. Three model cars roll down a track, and at the end of the track there are three detectors, one in each lane. When a car reaches the finish line, the detector in the car's lane will output a 1 to the sequential network (for exactly one clock time). The network has 4 inputs, C_1, C_2, C_3, and R, and six outputs, F_1, F_2, F_3, S_1, S_2, S_3. C_1, C_2, and C_3 are the detector outputs. The car that arrives first should have its F output on, the second car to arrive will have its S output on, and the last car to arrive will have no outputs on. For example, if the cars finish in the order 3, 1, and 2, the outputs F_3 and S_1 will be turned on. R is a reset input that will reset the network to a starting state with all outputs off. Assume that the inputs are synchronized to a clock and that no two cars will arrive at exactly the same time. (This second assumption is reasonable if the clock is fast: If there are one million clock pulses a second, then two cars would have to finish within 1 microsecond of each other to violate the second assumption. After a 30,000,000-microsecond race, two model cars will *very* rarely finish within 1 microsecond!)

(a) Find a Moore state graph for the network (10 states).

(b) Show how the network could be implemented with two ROMs and four D flip-flops (do not make a state assignment or show the ROM table).

(c) If a suitable state assignment is used, the network can be implemented with a single PAL16R4. Recall that the PAL16R4 has four flip-flop outputs and four combinational outputs. If two flip-flop outputs serve as both state variables and network outputs, then a suitable assignment is possible. If the state variables are Q_1, Q_2, Q_3, and Q_4, then let $F_1 = Q_1$ and $F_2 = Q_2$. Find a state assignment using these restrictions, and implement the network with the PAL16R4. (Use a CAD program to derive the equations.)

(d) If the one-in-a-million event occurs and cars 1 and 2 both finish at exactly the same time (F_1 and F_2 both become 1 at the same time), determine what happens to the network designed in (c).

19.11   (a) How would you modify Equations (19–7) so that the counter will always count up if $L = 0$ and $U = D = 1$?

(b) If a 6-bit up-down counter is designed using a 20X8 PAL, write the equations for Q_4^+ and Q_5^+ which correspond to Equations (19–3), (19–4), and (19–7).

19.12 Realize a 4-bit BCD $(0, 1, \ldots, 9)$ up-down counter using a suitable XOR PAL. The counter has control inputs U ($=1$ for up count) and D ($=1$ for down count), but no load inputs. Derive the PAL equations using a method similar to Fig. 19–5, and show the PAL fuse pattern.

19.13 A modulo-11 binary up counter is to be realized using an XOR PAL. The counting sequence is 0, 1, 2, 3, 4, 5, 6, 7, 8, 9, 10, 0, etc. Write the next-state equations in the proper form for use with an XOR PAL.

19.14 An N-bit shift register similar to the 74178 (Fig. 18–3) is to be realized using a 22V10.
  (a) What is the maximum value of N?
     Which fuse(s) should be blown in each output macrocell?
  (b) Write out the logic equations for the D input for the first and last flip-flops.

19.15 On a copy of Fig. 19–11, indicate the inputs and connections needed to realize a clocked T flip-flop with an active-low clear input (CLR), no preset input and no Q' output. Specify F and G. The flip-flop should trigger on the rising edge of the clock.

19.16 Realize the following next-state equation using a 2064 logic cell array. Use a minimum number of cells (3). Draw a diagram which shows the connections to the logic cells and give the functions F and G for each cell. (The equation is already in minimum form.)

$$Q^{+} = UQV'W + U'Q'VX'Y' + UQX'Y + U'Q'V'Y$$
$$+ U'Q'XY + UQVW' + U'Q'V'X$$

19.17 Show how a 74S163 4-bit counter (Fig. 18–7) could be realized using a 2064 LCA. Give the functions realized by each cell and the connections between cells.

20

Networks for Addition and Subtraction

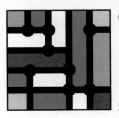

OBJECTIVES

1. Write negative binary numbers in sign and magnitude, 1's complement, and 2's complement forms. Add signed binary numbers using 1's complement and 2's complement arithmetic. Justify the methods used. State when an overflow occurs.

2. Design a full adder and a full subtracter.

3. Analyze, design, and explain the operation of networks for parallel and serial addition or subtraction of binary numbers.

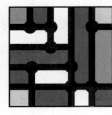

STUDY GUIDE

1. Review Section 1.3 and then study Section 20.1, *Representation of Negative Numbers.*

   (a) In digital systems, why are 1's complement and 2's complement commonly used to represent negative numbers instead of sign and magnitude?

   (b) State two different ways of forming the 1's complement of an n-bit binary number.

   (c) State three different ways of forming the 2's complement of an n-bit binary number.

   (d) If the word length is $n = 4$ bits (including sign), what decimal number does 1000_2 represent in sign and magnitude?

   In 2's complement?   In 1's complement?

   (e) Given a negative number represented in 2's complement, how do you find its magnitude?

   Given a negative number represented in 1's complement, how do you find its magnitude?

   (f) If the word length is 6 bits (including sign), what decimal number does 100000_2 represent in sign and magnitude?

   In 2's complement?   In 1's complement?

(g) What is meant by an overflow? How can you tell that an overflow has occurred when performing 1's or 2's complement addition?

Does a carry out of the last bit position indicate that an overflow has occurred?

(h) Work out some examples of 1's and 2's complement addition for various combinations of positive and negative numbers.

(i) What is the justification for using the end-around carry in 1's complement addition?

(j) The one thing that causes the most trouble with 2's complement numbers is the special case of the negative number which consists of a 1 followed by all 0's (1000 · · · 000). If this number is n bits long, what number does it represent and why? (It is not negative zero.)

(k) How would -5873 be represented in 9's complement?

In 10's complement?

(l) Work Problems 20.1, 20.2, and 20.6.

2. Review Section 12.9 and then work Problem 20.7.

3. Study Section 20.2, *Design of Binary Adders.*

(a) Make sure that you can analyze or design any of the networks given.

(b) For the network of Fig. 20–1, using 1's complement addition, indicate the sum and carry outputs for each cell if $n = 5$, $X = 15$ and $Y = -11$.

(c) Note the difference between the parallel binary adder without accumulator (Fig. 20–1) and the parallel binary adder with accumulator (Fig. 20–5). In the former, the X and Y inputs could come from two different registers; the sum is available at the adder output and does not replace either X or Y. In the latter, the sum replaces the number X, and the original X is no longer available after the add pulse.

(d) In Figs. 20–8 and 20–9, note that T_i is only a function of c_i and y_i even though the next state of the flip-flop (x_i^+) depends on the value of x_i. (Study the maps in Fig. 20–8 if you don't understand why.)

(e) Draw a Mealy state graph for the serial adder.

(f) For the parallel adder of Fig. 20–6, what sequence of control signals is required to add the same number twice to a number which is already in the accumulator?

(g) Give the equations for F and G in Fig. 20–10.

4. Study Section 20.3, *Binary Subtracters*.

(a) Explain how the entries in Table 20–3 were determined and carry out subtraction examples using this table.

(b) Demonstrate that the circuit of Fig. 20–11 works correctly for the following combinations

$$A - B = (-3) - (-6) \qquad\qquad A - B = (+3) - (+6)$$
$$A - B = (-6) - (-3) \qquad\qquad A - B = (+6) - (+6)$$

(c) What modification should be made to the circuit when 1's complement is used for negativ

(d) For the network of Fig. 20–12, indicate the borrow and difference outputs from each cell if $n = 5$, $X = 8$, and $Y = 3$.

(e) Note that the terms "FULL ADDER" and "FULL SUBTRACTER" refer to very specific combinational logic blocks. Each of these blocks has exactly 3 inputs and 2 outputs. Make sure that you know their functions and how to design them.

5. Work Problems 20.9, 20.10, and 20.11.

6. When you are satisfied that you can meet all of the objectives, take the readiness test.

Networks for Addition and Subtraction

This unit applies the techniques for combinational, sequential, and iterative network design to the design of binary adders and subtracters. Before proceeding with this design, the various methods used to represent negative binary numbers will be discussed.

20.1
Representation of Negative Numbers

Several representations of negative binary numbers are possible. In most computers the first bit in a word is used as a sign bit, with 0 used for plus and 1 used for minus. The *sign and magnitude* system is similar to that which people commonly use. For an n-bit word, the first bit is the sign and the remaining $n - 1$ bits represent the magnitude of the number. Thus an n-bit word can represent any one of 2^{n-1} positive integers or 2^{n-1} negative integers. Table 20–1 illustrates this for $n = 4$. Note that 1000 represents minus zero in the sign and magnitude system.

Design of logic networks to do arithmetic with sign and magnitude binary numbers is awkward; therefore, other representations are often used. The 2's complement and 1's complement are commonly used because arithmetic units are easy to design using these systems. For the 2's complement system, a positive number, N, is represented by a 0 followed by the magnitude as in the sign and magnitude system; however, a negative number, $-N$, is represented by its 2's complement, N^*. If the word length is n bits, the *2's complement* of a positive integer N is defined as

$$N^* = 2^n - N \qquad (20\text{-}1)$$

For $n = 4$, $-N$ is represented by $16 - N$ as in Table 20–1. For example, -3 is represented by $16 - 3 = 13 = 1101_2$. As is the case for sign and magnitude numbers, all negative 2's complement numbers have a 1 in the leftmost (sign bit) position.

For the 1's complement system, a negative number, $-N$, is represented by its 1's complement, $\bar{N}$. The *1's complement* of a positive integer N is defined as

$$\bar{N} = (2^n - 1) - N \qquad (20\text{-}2)$$

Table 20–1
Signed Binary Integers (word length $n = 4$)

$+N$	Positive Integers (all systems)	$-N$	Negative Integers		
			Sign and Magnitude	2's Complement N^*	1's Complement $\bar{N}$
+0	0000	−0	1000	----	1111
+1	0001	−1	1001	1111	1110
+2	0010	−2	1010	1110	1101
+3	0011	−3	1011	1101	1100
+4	0100	−4	1100	1100	1011
+5	0101	−5	1101	1011	1010
+6	0110	−6	1110	1010	1001
+7	0111	−7	1111	1001	1000
		−8	----	1000	----

for a word length of n bits. For $n = 4$, $-N$ is represented by $15 - N$ as in Table 20–1. Note that 1111 represents minus zero, and -8 has no representation in a 4-bit system. An alternate way to form the 1's complement is to simply complement N bit-by-bit by replacing 0's with 1's and 1's with 0's. This is equivalent to the definition, Equation (20–2), since $2^n - 1$ consists of all 1's, and subtracting a bit from 1 is the same as complementing the bit. For example, if $n = 6$ and $N = 010101$,

$$2^n - 1 = 111111$$
$$N = 010101$$
$$\bar{N} = \overline{101010}$$

From Equations (20–1) and (20–2).

$$N^* = 2^n - N = (2^n - 1 - N) + 1 = \bar{N} + 1$$

so the 2's complement can be formed by complementing N bit-by-bit and then adding 1. An easier way to form the 2's complement of N is to start at the right and complement all bits to the left of the first 1. For example, if

$$N = 0101100, \text{ then } N^* = 1010100$$

From Equations (20–1) and (20–2),

$$N = 2^n - N^* \qquad \text{and} \qquad N = (2^n - 1) - \bar{N}$$

Therefore, given a negative integer represented by its 2's complement (N^*), we can obtain the magnitude of the integer by taking the 2's complement of N^*. Similarly, to get the magnitude of a negative integer represented by its 1's complement ($\bar{N}$), we can take the 1's complement of $\bar{N}$.

In the 2's complement system the number of negative integers which can be represented is one more than the number of positive integers (not including 0). For example, in Table 20–1, 1000 represents -8, since a sign bit of 1 indicates a negative number, and if $N = 8$, $N^* = 10000 - 1000 = 1000$. In general, in a 2's complement system with a word length of n bits, the number $100 \cdots 000$ (1 followed by $n-1$ 0's) represents a negative number with a magnitude of

$$2^n - 2^{n-1} = 2^{n-1}$$

This special case occurs only for 2's complement. However, -0 has no representation in 2's complement, but -0 is a special case for 1's complement as well as for the sign and magnitude system.

The idea of 2's and 1's complement representation of negative numbers can be extended to number systems with other bases. In general, if the base is R and the word length is n digits, the R's complement of a positive number N is defined as

$$N^* = R^n - N$$

and the $(R - 1)$'s complement is defined as

$$\bar{N} = (R^n - 1) - N$$

For example, for octal numbers ($R = 8$) with $n = 4$, the 8's complement of 0345_8 is $10000_8 - 0345_8 = 7433_8$, and the 7's complement is $(10000 - 1) - 0345 = 7777 - 0345 = 7432_8$. Just as the 1's complement can be formed on a bit-by-bit basis by complementing each bit, the $(R - 1)$'s complement can be formed on a digit-by-digit basis. Thus, for octal numbers the 7's complement can be formed by subtracting each digit from 7.

Addition of 2's Complement Numbers

Addition of n-bit signed binary numbers is straightforward using the 2's complement system. Addition is carried out just as if all the numbers were positive and any carry from the sign position is ignored. This will always give the correct result except when an overflow occurs. When the word length is n bits, we say that an *overflow* has occurred if the correct representation of the sum (including sign) requires more than n bits. The different cases which can occur are illustrated below for $n = 4$.

1. Addition of 2 positive numbers, sum $< 2^{n-1}$.

   $$
   \begin{array}{rl}
   +3 & \quad 0011 \\
   +4 & \quad 0100 \\
   \hline
   +7 & \quad 0111 \quad \text{(correct answer)}
   \end{array}
   $$

2. Addition of 2 positive numbers, sum $\geqslant 2^{n-1}$.

   $$
   \begin{array}{rl}
   +5 & \quad 0101 \\
   +6 & \quad 0110 \\
   \hline
    & \quad 1011 \leftarrow
   \end{array}
   $$
   wrong answer because of overflow ($+11$ requires 5 bits including sign)

3. Addition of positive and negative numbers (negative number has greater magnitude).

   $$
   \begin{array}{rl}
   +5 & \quad 0101 \\
   -6 & \quad 1010 \\
   \hline
   -1 & \quad 1111 \quad \text{(correct answer)}
   \end{array}
   $$

4. Same as case 3 except positive number has greater magnitude.

   $$
   \begin{array}{rl}
   -5 & \quad 1011 \\
   +6 & \quad 0110 \\
   \hline
   +1 \;\;(1) & \quad 0001 \leftarrow
   \end{array}
   $$
   correct answer when carry from sign bit is ignored (this is *not* an overflow)

5. Addition of two negative numbers, $|\text{sum}| \leqslant 2^{n-1}$.

   $$
   \begin{array}{rl}
   -3 & \quad 1101 \\
   -4 & \quad 1100 \\
   \hline
   -7 \;\;(1) & \quad 1001 \leftarrow
   \end{array}
   $$
   correct answer when last carry is ignored (this is *not* an overflow)

6. Addition of two negative numbers, $|\text{ sum }| > 2^{n-1}$.

$$
\begin{array}{rl}
-5 & 1011 \\
-6 & 1010 \\
\hline
(1) & \overline{0101} \leftarrow \text{ wrong answer because of overflow } (-11 \text{ requires 5 bits}
\end{array}
$$
including sign)

Note that an overflow condition (cases 2 and 6) is easy to detect since in case 2 addition of two positive numbers yields a negative result and in case 6 addition of two negative numbers yields a positive answer (for four bits).

Proof that throwing away the carry from the sign bit always gives the correct answer follows for cases 4 and 5:

Case 4. $-A + B$ (where $B > A$)
$$A^* + B = (2^n - A) + B = 2^n + (B - A) > 2^n$$

Throwing away the last carry is equivalent to subtracting 2^n, so the result is $(B - A)$, which is correct.

Case 5. $-A - B$ (where $A + B \leqslant 2^{n-1}$)
$$A^* + B^* = (2^n - A) + (2^n - B) = 2^n + 2^n - (A + B)$$

Discarding the last carry yields $2^n - (A + B) = (A + B)^*$, which is the correct representation of $-(A + B)$.

Addition of 1's Complement Numbers

Addition of 1's complement numbers is similar to 2's complement except that instead of discarding the last carry, it is added to the n-bit sum in the rightmost position. This is referred to as an "end-around" carry. Addition of positive numbers is the same as illustrated for cases 1 and 2 under 2's complement. The remaining cases are illustrated below ($n = 4$).

3. Addition of positive and negative numbers (negative number with greater magnitude).

$$
\begin{array}{rll}
+5 & 0101 & \\
-6 & 1001 & \\
\hline
-1 & 1110 & \text{(correct answer)}
\end{array}
$$

4. Same as case 3 except positive number has greater magnitude.

$$
\begin{array}{rll}
-5 & 1010 & \\
+6 & 0110 & \\
\hline
(1) & \overline{0000} & \\
\quad\;\; \longrightarrow 1 & & \text{(end-around carry)} \\
\hline
& \overline{0001} & \text{(correct answer, \textit{no} overflow)}
\end{array}
$$

5. Addition of two negative numbers, $|\text{sum}| < 2^{n-1}$.

$$\begin{array}{rl}-3 & 1100 \\ -4 & 1011 \\ \hline (1) & 0111 \end{array}$$

    $\longrightarrow 1$ (end-around carry)

    $\overline{1000}$ (correct answer, *no* overflow)

6. Addition of two negative numbers, $|\text{sum}| \geqslant 2^{n-1}$.

$$\begin{array}{rl}-5 & 1010 \\ -6 & 1001 \\ \hline (1) & 0011 \end{array}$$

    $\longrightarrow 1$ (end-around carry)

    $\overline{0100}$ (wrong answer because of overflow)

Again, note that the overflow in case 6 is easy to detect since the addition of two negative numbers yields a positive result.

Proof that the end-round carry method gives the correct result follows for cases 4 and 5:

Case 4. $-A + B$ (where $B > A$)

$$\bar{A} + B = (2^n - 1 - A) + B = 2^n + (B - A) - 1$$

The end-around carry is equivalent to subtracting 2^n and adding 1, so the result is $(B - A)$, which is correct.

Case 5. $-A - B \ (A + B < 2^{n-1})$

$$\bar{A} + \bar{B} = (2^n - 1 - A) + (2^n - 1 - B) = 2^n + [2^n - 1 - (A + B)] - 1$$

After the end-around carry, the result is $2^n - 1 - (A + B) = (\overline{A + B})$, which is the correct representation for $-(A + B)$.

The following examples illustrate addition of 1's and 2's complement numbers for a word length of $n = 8$:

1. Add -11 and -20 in 1's complement.

  $+11 = 00001011$ $+20 = 00010100$

taking the bit-by bit complement,

 -11 is represented by 11110100 and -20 by 11101011

$$\begin{array}{rl}11110100 & (-11) \\ 11101011 & +(-20) \\ \hline (1) \ \ 11011111 \end{array}$$

    $\longrightarrow 1$ (end-around carry)

    $\overline{11100000} = -31$

2. Add -8 and $+19$ in 2's complement

  $+8 = 00001000$

complementing all bits to the left of the first 1, -8, is represented by 11111000

$$
\begin{array}{rl}
11111000 & (-8) \\
00010011 & +19 \\
\hline
(1)00001011 = & +11
\end{array}
$$

└─ (discard last carry)

Note that in both cases, the addition produced a carry out of the left-most bit position, but there is *no overflow* since the answer can be correctly represented with 8 bits (including sign). A general rule for detecting overflow when adding two n-bit signed binary numbers (1's or 2's complement) to get an n-bit sum is:

An overflow occurs if adding two positive numbers gives a negative answer or if adding two negative numbers gives a positive answer.

The principles used for 1's and 2's complement arithmetic can be extended to any base. If we are working with base R numbers, and negative numbers are represented in R's complement, we simply add the numbers and discard the carry from the last digit position. For example, for 4-digit octal numbers,

$$
\begin{array}{rl}
7433 & (-345) \\
+0672 & \\
\hline
10325 & \text{(which is the correct answer when the carry is discarded)}
\end{array}
$$

For $(R-1)$'s complement, an end-around carry is required. If we use 7's complement to represent negative octal numbers, the above example becomes

$$
\begin{array}{rl}
7432 & (-345) \\
+0672 & \\
\hline
10324 & \\
\hookrightarrow +1 & \text{(end-around carry)} \\
\hline
0325 &
\end{array}
$$

20.2
Design of Binary Adders

Parallel Adder

We will start by designing a parallel adder for two n-bit binary numbers,

$$X = x_n x_{n-1} x_{n-2} \cdots x_3 x_2 x_1 \qquad \text{and} \qquad Y = y_n y_{n-1} y_{n-2} \cdots y_3 y_2 y_1$$

We will assume an iterative network of the form shown in Fig. 20–1. The two binary numbers are fed in parallel into the cell inputs. The rightmost cell adds the least significant bits x_1 and y_1 to form a sum digit s_1 and a carry digit c_2. The next cell adds the carry c_2 to bits x_2 and y_2 to form a sum digit s_2 and a carry digit c_3. This process continues as fast as the gates in the cells can operate, and when a steady-state condition is reached the sum $s_n s_{n-1} s_{n-2} \cdots s_3 s_2 s_1$ can be

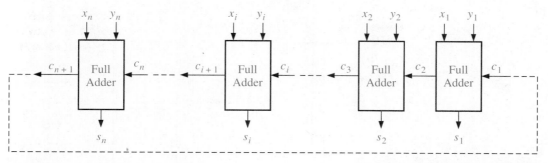

End-around carry for 1's complement

Figure 20–1
Parallel Binary Adder

read out in parallel. This type of adder is also called a ripple-carry adder since the carry "ripples" through from cell to cell until no further carry is generated.

To design the network, we must design a typical cell which adds a carry c_i to bits x_i and y_i to generate a sum digit s_i and a new carry c_{i+1}. Table 20–2 is easily filled in to specify the behavior of this typical cell. For example, for the combination $x_i = 1$, $y_i = 0$, and $c_i = 1$, binary addition yields $1 + 0 + 1 = 10$ which gives a sum digit $s_i = 0$ and a carry $c_{i+1} = 1$. The network which realizes these functions is referred to as a *full adder* and is available in integrated circuit form. The functions for a typical cell are easily determined from Karnaugh maps as shown in Fig. 20–2.

Although designed for positive binary numbers, this adder can also be used with negative numbers expressed in complement form. When 2's complement is used, the last carry (c_{n+1}) is discarded and there is no carry into the first cell. Since $c_1 = 0$, the equations for the first cell may be simplified to

$$s_1 = x_1'y_1 + x_1y_1' \text{ and } c_2 = x_1y_1$$

When 1's complement is used, the end-around carry is accomplished by connecting c_{n+1} to the c_1 input as shown by the dashed line in Fig. 20–1. Even though the network has the form of a closed loop, carries cannot propagate continuously around the loop and a steady-state condition will always be reached. In

Table 20–2

Logic Functions for a Binary Adder

x_i	y_i	c_i	c_{i+1}	s_i
0	0	0	0	0
0	0	1	0	1
0	1	0	0	1
0	1	1	1	0
1	0	0	0	1
1	0	1	1	0
1	1	0	1	0
1	1	1	1	1

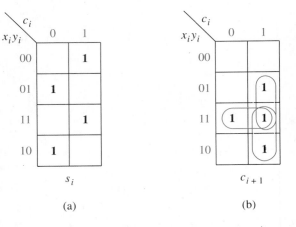

$$s_i = c_i'(x_i'y_i + x_iy_i') + c_i(x_iy_i + x_i'y_i') = c_i'(x_i \oplus y_i) + c_i(x_i \oplus y_i)' = c_i \oplus x_i \oplus y_i$$

$$c_{i+1} = c_i(x_i + y_i) + x_iy_i$$

Figure 20–2
Maps for Typical Cell (full adder)

order to start a carry propagating, we must have a cell with $x_i = 1$ and $y_i = 1$, which generates a carry $c_{i+1} = 1$ (regardless of the value of c_i). Even if this carry propagates around the loop causing c_i to change value, c_{i+1} remains 1 and steady state is reached.

If the number of bits is large, a parallel binary adder of the type shown in Fig 20–1 may be rather slow since the carry generated in the first cell might have to propagate all of the way to the last cell. Other types of adders, such as a carry-lookahead adder[1], may be used to speed up the carry propagation.

Serial Adder

Next we will design a serial adder in which the binary numbers X and Y are fed in serially, one pair of bits at a time. First x_1 and y_1 are fed in; a sum digit s_1 is generated and the carry c_2 is stored. At the next clock time, x_2 and y_2 are fed in and added to c_2 to give the next sum digit s_2 and the new carry c_3, which is stored. This process continues until all bits have been added. Table 20–2 still applies, so we can use the same full adder circuit to generate the sum and carry bits. Adding a delay unit to store the carry gives the serial adder shown in Fig. 20–3(a). It is assumed that the inputs are synchronized with the delay so that the new x and y inputs are present at the same time the previous carry is available at the delay output. In practice, a clocked D flip-flop could be used to achieve this synchronization as seen in Fig. 20–3(b)

---

[1] See, for example, Wakerly, J.F., *Digital Design Principles and Practices*. Englewood Cliffs, NJ: Prentice Hall, 1990.

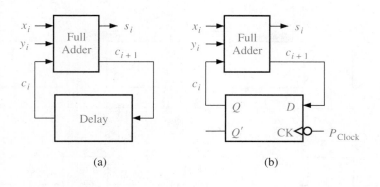

(a)   (b)

Figure 20–3
Serial Adder

We will now modify the serial adder of Fig. 20–3 to use a J-K flip-flop to store the carry instead of the delay. In this case, the c_i column in Table 20–2 can be interpreted as the present state of the carry flip-flop, and the c_{i+1} column as the next state. The next-state map and the derived J-K input maps for the carry flip-flop are shown in Fig. 20–4(a). The resulting serial adder circuit is shown in Fig. 20–4(b).

Parallel Adder with Accumulator

In computer circuits, it is frequently desirable to store one number in a register of flip-flops (called an accumulator) and add a second number to it leaving the result stored in the accumulator. One way to build a parallel adder with an accumulator is to add a flip-flop register to the adder of Fig. 20–1, resulting in the

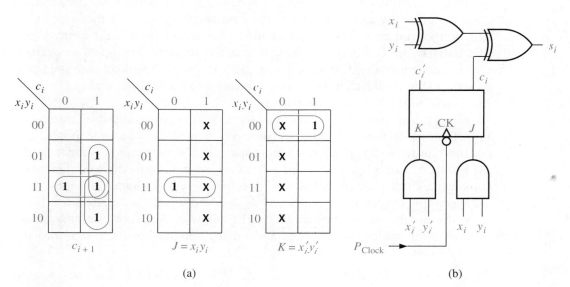

(a)   (b)

Figure 20–4
Serial Adder with Flip-Flop for Carry Storage

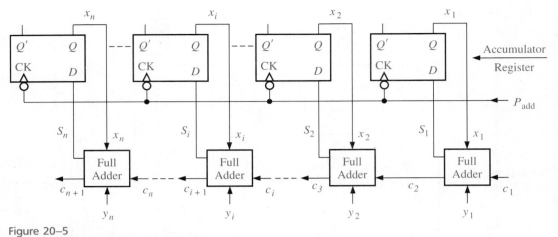

Figure 20–5
Parallel Adder with Accumulator

network of Fig. 20–5. First the number X is entered into the accumulator (by additional gating not shown). The number Y is applied to the full adder inputs, and after the carry has propagated through the adders, the sum appears at the adder outputs. An add pulse (P_{add}) is used to transfer the adder outputs into the accumulator flip-flops. If $s_i = 1$, the next state of flip-flop x_i will be 1. If $s_i = 0$, the next state of flip-flop x_i will be 0. Thus, $x_i^+ = s_i$, and when the add pulse occurs, the number X in the accumulator is replaced with the sum of X and Y.

Before addition can take place, the accumulator must be loaded with X. This can be accomplished in several ways. The easiest way is to first clear the accumulator using the asynchronous clear inputs on the flip-flops, and then put the X data on the y inputs to the adder and add to the accumulator in the normal way. Alternatively, we could add multiplexers at the accumulator inputs so that we could select either the X input data or the adder output to load into the accumulator. This would eliminate the extra step of clearing the accumulator but would add to the hardware complexity.

When the accumulator is part of a larger digital system, an arrangement like Fig. 20–6, which uses a 3-state bus (see Section 18.4), may be appropriate. The addend register is a register of D flip-flops with 3-state outputs (similar to the 74LS374). A 3-state buffer is used to gate input data onto the bus. This data could come from a computer memory or other source. The adder must also have 3-state outputs, since its output must be disabled when the registers are being loaded in order to avoid bus conflicts. The following sequence of events occurs to load the accumulator, load the addend register and load the sum into the accumulator:

1. Put X on the input data lines, set $EN1 = 1$, pulse $C2$ (this puts X onto the bus and loads it into the accumulator).

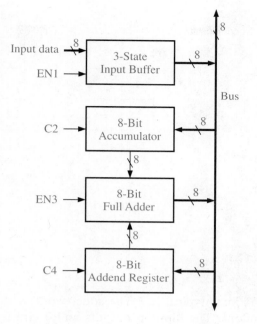

Figure 20–6
Parallel Adder with 3-State Bus

2. Put Y on the input data lines, set $EN1 = 1$, pulse $C4$ (this puts Y onto the bus and loads it into the addend register).
3. Set $EN3 = 1$, pulse $C2$ (this puts the adder output onto the bus and loads it into the accumulator).

An alternate design for Fig. 20–5 is possible by using the accumulator flip-flops to do part of the logic. We will assume an iterative sequential network of the form shown in Fig. 20–7. Here T flip-flops are used, so our problem is to

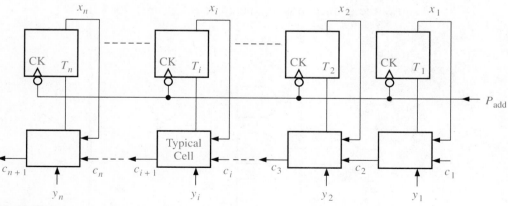

Figure 20–7
Simplified Parallel Adder with Accumulator

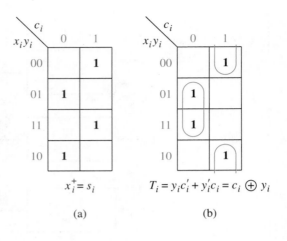

$$x_i^+ = s_i$$

(a)

$$T_i = y_i c_i' + y_i' c_i = c_i \oplus y_i$$

(b)

Figure 20–8

derive T_i for a typical cell. The adder works as follows: First X is entered into the flip-flops. The flip-flop outputs and Y are fed into the typical cells of the adder, and the carry signal is allowed to propagate between cells. Then, after the add line is pulsed, the sum of X and Y appears in the accumulator flip-flops. Table 20–2 still applies, except s_i is now the next state of the accumulator flip-flop, that is, $s_i = x_i^+$. Thus, the next-state map for x_i in Fig. 20–8(a) is the same as Fig. 20–2(a). The corresponding input map for T_i seen in Fig. 20–8(b) is derived from x_i^+ in the usual way. The carry function (c_{i+1}) is the same as for the ordinary parallel adder shown in Fig. 20–2(b), but note that we now generate T_i instead of the more complex function, s_i. Fig. 20–9 shows the resulting typical cell.

One stage of a full adder with accumulator can easily be implemented in one cell of a programmable gate array such as the 2064 LCA (Fig. 19–11). Figure 20–10 shows the connections for one logic cell from a 2064 LCA.

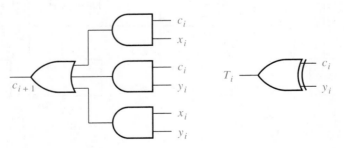

Figure 20–9
Typical Cell for Adder of Fig. 20–7

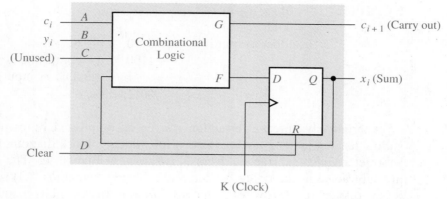

Figure 20–10
Logic Cell Connection for One Bit of Full Adder
with Accumulator

20.3
Binary Subtracters

Subtraction of binary numbers is most easily accomplished by adding the complement of the number to be subtracted. To compute $A - B$, the complement of B is added to A. Either 1's or 2's complement is used depending on the type of adder employed.

The circuit of Fig. 20–11 may be used to form $A - B$ using the 2's complement representation for negative numbers. The 2's complement of B can be formed by first finding the 1's complement and then adding 1. The 1's complement is formed by inverting each bit of B, and the addition of 1 is effectively accomplished by putting a 1 into the carry input of the first full adder.

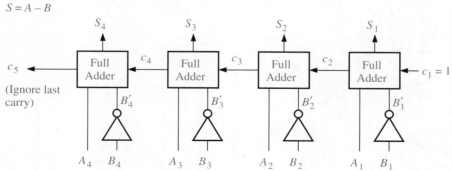

Figure 20–11
Binary Subtracter Using Full Adders

EXAMPLE: $A = 0110$ $(+6)$
$B = 0011$ $(+3)$
The adder output is

$$
\begin{array}{rl}
0110 & (+6) \\
+1100 & (\text{1' complement of 3}) \\
+\quad 1 & (\text{first carry input}) \\
\hline
(1) \quad 0011 &= 3 = 6 - 3
\end{array}
$$

Alternatively, direct subtraction can be accomplished by employing a full subtracter in a manner analogous to a full adder. A block diagram for a parallel subtracter which subtracts Y from X is shown in Fig. 20–12. The first two bits are subtracted in the rightmost cell and a borrow signal ($b_2 = 1$) is generated if it is necessary to borrow from the next column. In cell i, bits b_i and y_i are subtracted from x_i to form the difference d_i, and a borrow signal ($b_{i+1} = 1$) is generated if it is necessary to borrow from the next column.

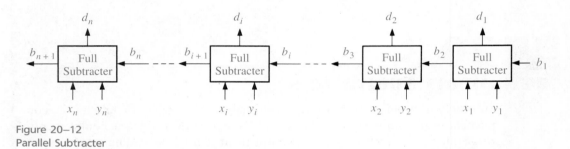

Figure 20–12
Parallel Subtracter

Table 20–3 gives the truth table for a binary full subtracter. Consider the following case, where $x_i = 0$, $y_i = 1$ and $b_i = 1$:

	Column i Before Borrow	Column i After Borrow
x_i	0	10
$-b_i$	-1	-1
$-y_i$	-1	-1
d_i		0 $(b_{i+1} = 1)$

Table 20–3

Truth Table for Binary Full Subtracter

x_i y_i b_i	$b_{i+1}d_i$
0 0 0	0 0
0 0 1	1 1
0 1 0	1 1
0 1 1	1 0
1 0 0	0 1
1 0 1	0 0
1 1 0	0 0
1 1 1	1 1

Note that in column i, we cannot immediately subtract y_i and b_i from x_i. Hence, we must borrow from $i + 1$. Borrowing 1 from column $i + 1$ is equivalent to setting b_{i+1} to 1 and adding 10 (2_{10}) to x_i. We then have $d_i = 10 - 1 - 1 = 0$. Verify that Table 20–3 is correct for the other input combinations and use it to work out several examples of binary subtraction.

PROBLEMS

20.1 By analogy with 1's complement, define the 9's complement of an n-digit decimal number and state a rule for 9's complement addition. Note that a sign digit of 9 indicates a negative number. Add -5367 and $+2489$ using 5-digit numbers. Use 9's complement to represent the negative numbers.

20.2 Add the following numbers in binary using 2's complement to represent negative numbers. Use a word length of 5 bits (including sign) and indicate if an overflow occurs.
    (a) $(-9) + (-11)$ (b) $(-9) + (-7)$ (c) $(-9) + 11$
    (d) $11 + 7$ (e) $(-10) + (-5)$
    Repeat using 1's complement to represent negative numbers.

20.3 Repeat 20.2 for the following numbers:
    (a) $(-10) + (-11)$ (b) $(-10) + (-6)$ (c) $(-8) + (-11)$
    (d) $11 + 9$ (e) $(-11) + (-4)$

20.4 Subtract each of the following pairs of 5-bit binary numbers by adding the complement of the subtrahend to the minuend. Indicate when an overflow occurs. Assume that negative numbers are represented in 1's complement. Then repeat using 2's complement.

01001	10101	10110	00101	11100
−11010	−10000	−01101	−01010	−10101

20.5 Work Problem 20.4 for the following pairs of numbers:

10110	01011	10110	10101
−10100	−11000	−11000	−11010

20.6 A computer has a word length of 8 bits (including sign). If 2's complement is used to represent negative numbers, what range of integers can be stored in the computer? If 1's complement is used? (Express your answers in decimal.)

20.7 Given four flip-flops and four input signals ($X_1, X_2, X_3,$ and X_4), show the required connections so that when a transfer pulse occurs, the values of the inputs will be transferred to the flip-flops. In other words, the next state of the flip-flop Q_i should be $Q_i^+ = X_i$ regardless of the present state of the flip-flop. Solve this problem for clocked J-K flip-flops, S-R flip-flops, and T flip-flops. In each case, add as few gates and inverters as possible.

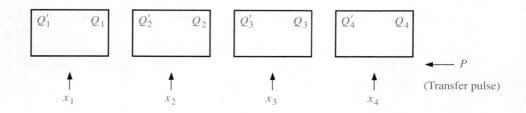

20.8   (a) Design a network which will add three 4-bit numbers to give a 4-bit sum. That is, add $x_3x_2x_1x_0 + y_3y_2y_1y_0 + z_3z_2z_1z_0$ to give a sum $s_3s_2s_1s_0$ and two carries. Use 8 full adders and assume that negative numbers are represented in 2's complement.

  (b) Indicate the changes necessary if negative numbers are represented in 1's complement.

20.9   Design an iterative network for adding three positive binary numbers. These numbers are designated $x_n \cdots x_3x_2x_1$, $y_n \cdots y_3y_2y_1$ and $z_n \cdots z_3z_2z_1$. a typical cell for the adder is of the form:

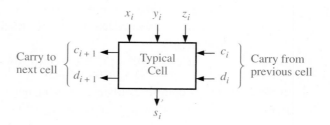

Note that there are two carry signals propagating between cells. Two carry signals are required because when three binary digits are added to the carry coming into the cell, the carry to the next cell may be either 0, 1, or 2 (coded as 00, 01, and 10, respectively).

  (a) Derive a truth table which specifies the operation of a typical cell. (Your table should contain some don't cares.)

  (b) Derive minimum equations for s_i, c_{i+1}, and d_{i+1}.

20.10   Design a parallel subtracter with accumulator using T flip-flops and without using full adders or full subtracters. Your design should be similar to Fig. 20–7, except that the borrow will propagate between cells instead of the carry.

20.11   (a) Assume that the parallel adder of Fig. 20–1 is used to add signed binary numbers (1's or 2's complement). Design an overflow indicator network which has an output of 1 when an overflow occurs.

  (b) Assume that the parallel binary subtracter of Fig. 20–12 is used to subtract signed binary numbers (2's complement). Design an overflow indictor network.

20.12   Design an incrementer circuit that will add 3 to a 4-bit accumulator every time it receives an *INC* pulse. The network should have an output Z that is 1 iff the accumulator is zero.

(a) Design the circuit using logic gates, full adders, and half of a 74LS374 octal D flip-flop.

(b) Design the circuit using half of a 74LS374 octal D flip-flop and a PLA. Specify the size of the PLA and show the PLA table.

20.13   Modify the incrementer ciruit of Problem 20.12 to be an incrementer/decrementer. Add an input UP that controls whether the circuit adds 3 or subtracts 3 from the accumulator . If the input UP is 1, then INC pulse will cause the circuit to add 3 to the accumulator. If the input UP is 0, then the INC pulse will cause the circuit to subtract 3 from the accumulator.

(a) Design the circuit using logic gates, full adders, and half of a 74LS374 octal D flip-flop.

(b) Design the circuit using one half of a 74LS374 octal D flip-flop and a PLA. Specify the size of the PLA and show the PLA table.

20.14   Design a 4-bit binary adder-subtracter with accumulator for signed binary numbers. Use 4 D flip-flops and 4 full adders together with any necessary gates. Use 1's complement to represent negative numbers. The network should have one control input, S. If $S = 1$, the input is subtracted from the accumulator; if $S = 0$, it is added to the accumulator.

(a) Draw the complete logic diagram including provision for overflow detection.

(b) If the accumulator contains 1100, the input is 0010 and $S = 1$, indicate on the diagram the logic values of all of the full adder inputs and outputs at a time just before the answer is clocked into the accumulator.

20.15   The excess-3 code (Table 1–1) is said to be self-complementing because the code for the 9's complement of each decimal digit can be formed by taking the bit-by-bit complement of the corresponding code. For example, the 9's complement of 6 is 3, and the bit-by-bit complement of the code for 6 (1001) is 0110, which is the code for 3. Construct a 2-4-2-1 code that is self-complementing.

20.16   Design a BCD full adder cell. The cell has nine inputs and five outputs. The inputs $X_3 X_2 X_1 X_0$ and $Y_3 Y_2 Y_1 Y_0$ represent two BCD digits and C_{in} is the carry in from the previous cell. The output Z is 4 bits wide ($Z_3 Z_2 Z_1 Z_0$) and there is a carry out bit, C_{out}.

(a) Draw a block diagram showing how to construct a BCD full adder cell from 8 binary full adders and additional logic gates. (*Hint:* If $X + Y < 10$, then the BCD addition of X and Y is the same as binary addition. If $x + y \geqslant 10$, then the BCD addition of $X + Y$ is equal to the 4-bit binary addition of $X + Y + 6$. For example, $8 + 3$ would be $1000 + 0011 = 0001$ with a carry of 1 in BCD. The binary sum of $1000 + 0011 + 0110 = 0001 +$ carry. Use four adders to find $X + Y$ and use another four adders to add a correction factor that is either 0 or 6, depending on the sum $X + Y$.)

(b) What size of PLA would be needed to implement a BCD full adder? What size of ROM would be needed to implement the adder?

(c) Use a computer-aided logic design program such as *LogicAid* to derive the equations for Z_0 and C_{out} directly from the inputs. Assume that invalid BCD digits do not occur. Show the portion of the PLA table that corresponds to Z_0 and C_{out}. (*Note:* In a real application, the method of (a) probably would be used to implement the BCD adder. The equations for Z_3, Z_2, and Z_1 are quite involved and would result in a very complex circuit.)

20.17   Design a BCD comparator cell. The cell has two outputs R_0 and R_1. If the two BCD digits are equal, $R_0 = R_1 = 0$. If X is greater than Y, then $R_0 = 1$, $R_1 = 0$. Otherwise $R_0 = 0$, $R_1 = 1$.

(a) Using a computer-aided logic design program such as *LogicAid*, derive the equations for R_0 and R_1 from the inputs. Assume that invalid BCD digits do not occur.

(b) What size of PLA would be needed to implement a BCD comparator?

(c) Draw a block diagram showing how the BCD comparator could be implemented with four binary comparator cells.

21

Networks for Arithmetic Operations

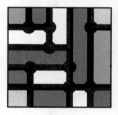

OBJECTIVES

1. Analyze and explain the operation of various networks for adding, subtracting, multiplying, and dividing binary numbers and for similar operations.

2. Draw a block diagram and design the control network for various networks for adding, subtracting, multiplying, and dividing binary numbers and for similar operations.

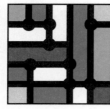

STUDY GUIDE

1. Study Section 21.1, *Serial Adder with Accumulator*.

   (a) Study Fig. 21–2 carefully to make sure you understand the operation of this type of adder. Work out a table similar to Table 21–1 starting with $X = 6$ and $Y = 3$:

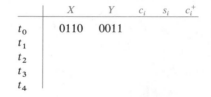

	X	Y	c_i	s_i	c_i^+
t_0	0110	0011			
t_1					
t_2					
t_3					
t_4					

   (b) What changes would be made in the above table if the D input to the addend register (Fig. 21–1) was connected to a logic 0 instead of to y_1?

   (c) Work Problems 21.3 and 21.4.

2. Study Section 21.2, *Design of a Parallel Multiplier*.

   (a) For the binary multiplier of Fig. 21–6, if the initial contents of the accumulator is 000001101 and the multiplicand is 1111, show the sequence of add and shift pulses and the contents of the accumulator at each time step.

   (b) For the state diagram of Fig. 21–7, what is the maximum number of clock pulses required to carry out the multiplication? The minimum number?

   (c) For Fig. 21–6, how many bits would be required for the product register if the multiplier was 6 bits and the multiplicand was 8 bits?

(d) Work Problems 21.5 and 21.6.

(e) Consider the design of a binary multiplier which multiplies 8 bits by 8 bits to give a 16-bit product. What changes would need to be made in Fig. 21–6?

If a multiplier control of the type shown in Fig. 21–7 were used, how many states would be required?

If a control of the type shown in Fig. 21–8 is used, how many bits should the counter have? K should equal 1 in what state of the counter? How many states will the control state graph have?

(f) Work Programmed Exercise 21.1.

3. Study Section 21.3, *Design of a Binary Divider.*

(a) Using the state diagram of Fig. 21–10 to determine when to shift or subtract, work through the division example given at the start of this section.

(b) What changes would have to be made in Fig. 21–11 if the subtraction was done using full adders rather than full subtracters?

(c) For the block diagram of Fig. 21–9, under what conditions will an overflow occur and why?

(d) Work Programmed Exercise 21.2.

(e) Derive the control circuit equations, Equations (21–1).

Hint: Construct the Karnaugh map for Sh by setting $Sh = 1$, $Su = V = 0$ in Table 21–2.

(f) In Fig. 21–11, why is b_4 set equal to 0? Why is one of the inputs to the leftmost full subtracter set to 0?

(g) Work Problems 21.7, 21.8, and 21.9.

4. Optional lab exercises:

(a) Build the serial adder of Fig. 20–4 in lab and test it.

(b) Connect two 4-bit shift registers to the inputs of the adder that you built in (a) to form a serial adder with accumulator (as in Fig. 21–1). Supply the shift pulse manually so that a control circuit is unnecessary. Test your adder using binary numbers in the range 000 to 111.

(c) Build the control circuit of Fig. 21–5, connect it to the network which you built in (b), and test it.

5. When you are satisfied that you can meet all of the objectives, take the readiness test.

Networks for Arithmetic Operations

This unit introduces the concept of using a control network to control a sequence of operations in a digital network. A control network is a sequential network which puts out a sequence of control signals. These signals cause operations like addition or shifting to take place at appropriate times.

The following notation will be used for shift registers in this unit:

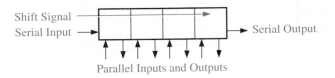

Arrows entering and leaving the ends of the register indicate a serial input and output. Arrows entering and leaving the sides of the register indicate parallel inputs and outputs. A long arrow through the register indicates the shift signal input and the direction of the shift.

21.1
Serial Adder with Accumulator

Figure 21–1 shows a block diagram of a serial adder with an accumulator. Two shift registers are used to hold the numbers to be added, X and Y. The long arrow drawn through the shift register in Fig. 21–1 is the shift pulse input. When this input is pulsed, the contents of the register is shifted right one position and the bit at the D input is entered into x_4 (or y_4). The X-register serves as the accumulator, and after four shift pulses, the number X is replaced with the sum of X and Y. The addend register is connected as a cyclic shift register (similar to the type shown in Fig. 12–13) so that after four shift pulses it is back in its original state and the number Y is not lost. The serial adder in the diagram is identical to the one in Fig. 20–3(b). At each clock time, one pair of bits is added. The shift pulse (P_{shift}) stores the sum bit in the accumulator, stores the carry bit in the carry flip-flop, and causes the addend register to cycle right.

Figure 21–2 illustrates the operation of the serial adder. In this figure, t_0 is the time before the first shift pulse, t_1 is the time after the first shift pulse, t_2 is the time after the second shift pulse, etc. Initially, at time t_0, the accumulator contains X and the addend register contains Y. Since the full adder is a combinational network, x_1, y_1, and c_1 are added immediately to form the sum s_1 and

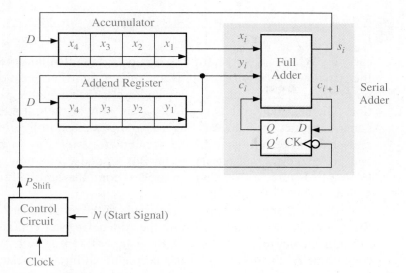

Figure 21–1
Block Diagram for Serial Adder with Accumulator

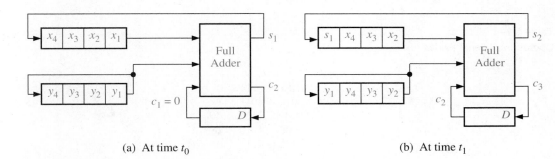

(a) At time t_0

(b) At time t_1

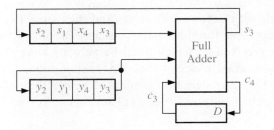

(c) At time t_2

(d) At time t_3

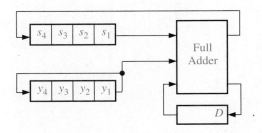

(e) At time t_4

Figure 21–2
Operation of Serial Adder

carry c_2. When the first shift pulse occurs, s_1 is shifted into the accumulator and the remaining accumulator digits are shifted right one position. The same shift pulse stores c_2 in the carry flip-flop and cycles the addend register right one position. The next pair of bits, x_2 and y_2, are now at the full adder input, and the adder generates the sum and carry, s_2 and c_3 as seen in Figure 21–2(b). The second shift pulse shifts s_2 into the accumulator, stores c_3 in the carry flip-flop, and cycles the addend register right. Bits x_3 and y_3 are now at the adder input as seen in Figure 21–2(c), and the process continues until all bit pairs have been added, shown in Figure 21–2(e).

Table 21–1 shows a numerical example of the serial adder operation. Initially, the accumulator contains 0101 and the addend register contains 0111. At t_0, the full adder computes $1 + 1 + 0 = 10$, so $s_i = 0$ and $c_i^+ = 1$. After the first shift pulse (time t_1) the first sum bit has been entered into the accumulator, the carry has been stored in the carry flip-flop, and the addend has been cycled right. After four pulses (time t_4) the sum of X and Y is in the accumulator and the addend register is back to its original state.

Table 21–1

Operation of Serial Adder

	X	Y	c_i	s_i	c_i^+
t_0	0101	0111	0	0	1
t_1	0010	1011	1	0	1
t_2	0001	1101	1	1	1
t_3	1000	1110	1	1	0
t_4	1100	0111	0	(1)	(0)

The control circuit for the adder must now be designed so that after receiving a start signal, the control circuit will put out four shift pulses and then stop. Figure 21–3 shows the state graph and table for the control circuit. The network remains in S_0 until a start signal is received, at which time the network outputs a shift pulse and goes to S_1. Then at successive clock times 3 more shift pulses are outputted. It will be assumed that the start signal is terminated before the network returns to state S_0 so that no further output occurs until another start signal

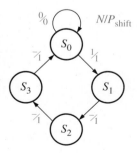

	Next State		P_{shift}	
	$N = 0$	1	0	1
S_0	S_0	S_1	0	1
S_1	S_2	S_2	1	1
S_2	S_3	S_3	1	1
S_3	S_0	S_0	1	1

Figure 21–3
State Graph for Serial Adder Control

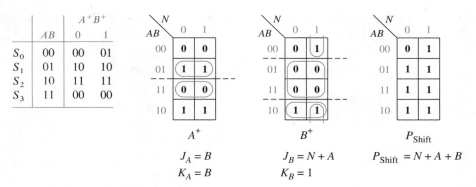

Figure 21–4
Derivation of Control Network Equations

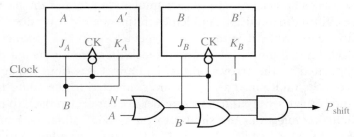

Figure 21–5
Control Circuit for Serial Adder.

is received. Dashes appear on the graph because once S_1 is reached, the network operation continues regardless of the value of N.

When the state graph for a sequential network forms a single loop of states, as in Fig. 21–3, the network has the form of a counter. For this reason, a state assignment which consists of a sequence of consecutive binary numbers usually leads to an economical network. Starting with the state table of Fig. 21–3 and using a straight binary state assignment, the control network equations are derived in Fig. 21–4 using the short-cut method for J and K.

Figure 21–5 shows the resulting network. The clock pulse is ANDed with $(N + A + B)$ since P_{shift} is connected to the clock inputs of the shift registers.

21.2
Design of a Parallel Multiplier

Next we will design a parallel multiplier for positive binary numbers. As illustrated in the example on p. 12, binary multiplication requires only shifting and adding. The same example is reworked below using a slight variation in the procedure. Instead of forming all of the partial products first and then adding, each partial product is added in as soon as it is formed. This eliminates the need for adding more than two binary numbers at a time.

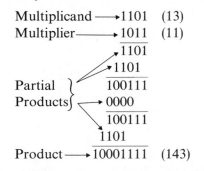

Multiplication of two 4-bit numbers requires a 4-bit multiplicand register, a 4-bit multiplier register, and an 8-bit register for the product. The product register serves as an accumulator to accumulate the sum of the partial products. Instead of shifting the multiplicand left each time before it is added in as was done in the above example, it is more convenient to shift the product register to the right each time. Figure 21–6 shows a block diagram for such a parallel multiplier. As indicated by the arrows on the diagram, 4 bits from the accumulator and 4 bits from the multiplicand register are connected to the adder inputs; the 4 sum bits and the carry output from the adder are connected back to the accumulator. (The actual connections are similar to the parallel adder with accumulator shown in Fig. 20–5.) When an add signal (*Ad*) occurs, the adder outputs are transferred to the accumulator by the next clock pulse, thus causing the multiplicand to be added to the accumulator. An extra bit at the left end of the product register temporarily stores any carry which is generated when the multiplicand is added to the accumulator.

Since the lower four bits of the product register are initially unused, we will store the multiplier in this location instead of in a separate register. As each mul-

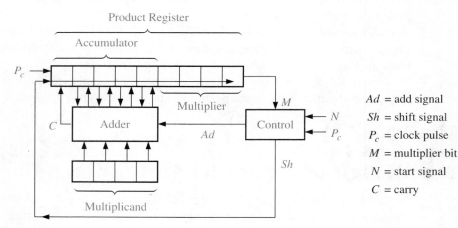

Figure 21–6
Block Diagram for Parallel Binary Multiplier

tiplier bit is used, it is shifted out the right end of the register to make room for additional product bits. A shift signal (*Sh*) causes the contents of the product register (including the multiplier) to be shifted right one place when the next clock pulse occurs. The control circuit puts out the proper sequence of add and shift signals after a start signal ($N = 1$) has been received. If the current multiplier bit (*M*) is 1, the multiplicand is added to the accumulator followed by a right shift; if the multiplier bit is 0, the addition is skipped and only the right shift occurs. The multiplication example (13×11) is reworked below showing the location of the bits in the registers at each clock time.

initial contents of product register	0 0 0 0 0 ¦1 0 1 1	*M* (11)
(add multiplicand since $M = 1$)	1 1 0 1¦	(13)
after addition	0 1 1 0 1 ¦1 0 1 1	
after shift	0 0 1 1 0 1 ¦1 0 1	*M*
(add multiplicand since $M = 1$)	1 1 0 1	
after addition	1 0 0 1 1 1 ¦1 0 1	
after shift	0 1 0 0 1 1 1 ¦1 0	*M*
(skip addition since $M = 0$)		
after shift	0 0 1 0 0 1 1 1 ¦1	*M*
(add multiplicand since $M = 1$)	1 1 0 1	
after addition	1 0 0 0 1 1 1 1 ¦1	
after shift (final answer)	0 1 0 0 0 1 1 1 1¦	(143)

dividing line between product and multiplier—

The control circuit must be designed to output the proper sequence of add and shift signals. Figure 21–7 shows a state graph for the control circuit. The notation

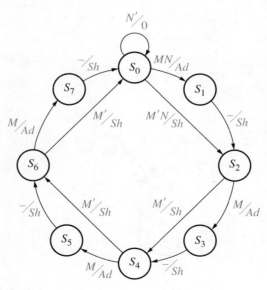

Figure 21–7
State Graph for Multiplier Control

used on this graph is slightly different from that used previously. MN/Ad means if $MN = 1$, then the output Ad is 1 (and the other outputs are 0). M'/Sh means if $M' = 1$ ($M = 0$), then the output Sh is 1 (and the other outputs are 0). In general, we will use the following notation on state diagrams for control networks: X_iX_j/Z_pZ_q means if inputs X_i and X_j are 1 (we don't care what the other input values are), the outputs Z_p and Z_q are 1 (and the other outputs are 0). That is, for a network with four inputs (X_1, X_2, X_3, and X_4) and four outputs (Z_1, Z_2, Z_3, and Z_4), X_1X_4'/Z_2Z_3 is equivalent to $1{-}{-}0/0110$. This type of notation is very useful for large control networks where there are many inputs and outputs.

In Fig. 21–7, S_0 is the reset state, and the network stays in S_0 until a start signal ($N = 1$) is received. Then, if $M = 1$, an add signal is generated, and if $M = 0$, a shift signal is generated. Similarly, in states S_2, S_4, and S_6, M is tested to determine whether to generate an add or shift signal. A shift signal is always generated at the next clock time following an add signal (states S_1, S_3, S_5, and S_7). After four shifts have been generated, the control network returns to the initial state and terminates the multiplication process.

As the state graph indicates, the control performs two functions—generating add or shift signals as needed and counting the number of shifts. If the number of bits is large, it is convenient to divide the control network into a counter and an add-shift control as shown in Fig. 21–8(a). First, we will derive a state graph

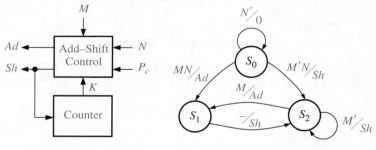

(a) Multiplier control

(b) State graph for add-shift control

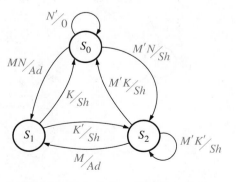

(c) Final state graph for add-shift control

Figure 21–8

for the add-shift control which tests M and N and outputs the proper sequence of add and shift signals (Fig. 21–8(b)). Then we will add a completion signal (K) from the counter which stops the multiplier after the proper number of shifts have been completed. Starting in S_0 in Fig. 21–8(b), when a start signal $(N = 1)$ is received, if $M = 1$, an add signal is generated and the network goes to state S_1, and if $M = 0$, a shift signal is generated and the network goes to S_2. In S_1, a shift signal is generated since a shift always follows an add. In S_2, the next multiplier bit (M) is tested to determine whether to add or shift. The graph of Fig. 21–8(b) will generate the proper sequence of add and shift signals, but it has no provision for stopping the multiplier.

In order to determine when the multiplication is completed, the counter is incremented each time a shift signal is generated. If the multiplier is n bits, a total of n shifts are required. We will design the counter so that a completion signal (K) is generated after $n - 1$ shifts have occurred. When $K = 1$, the network should perform one more addition if necessary, and then do the final shift. The control operation in Fig. 21–8(c) is the same as Fig. 21–8(b) as long as $K = 0$. In state S_2, if $K = 1$, we test M as usual. If $M = 0$, we output the final shift signal and stop; however, if $M = 1$, we add before shifting and go to state S_1. In state S_1, if $K = 1$, we output one more shift signal and then go to S_0. The last shift signal will reset the counter to 0 at the same time the add-shift control returns to the stop state.

As an example, consider the multiplier of Fig. 21–6, but replace the control network with Fig. 21–8(a). Since $n = 4$, a 2-bit counter is needed, and $K = 1$ when the counter is in state 3 (11_2). The following table shows the operation of the multiplier when 1101 is multiplied by 1011. S_0, S_1, and S_2 represent states of the control circuit (Fig. 21–8(c)). The contents of the product register at each step is the same as given on p. 545.

Time	State	Counter	Product Reg.	N	M	K	Ad	Sh
t_0	S_0	00	000001011	0	1	0	0	0
t_1	S_0 .	00	000001011	1	1	0	1	0
t_2	S_1	00	011011011	0	1	0	0	1
t_3	S_2	01	001101101	0	1	0	1	0
t_4	S_1	01	100111101	0	1	0	0	1
t_5	S_2	10	010011110	0	0	0	0	1
t_6	S_2	11	001001111	0	1	1	1	0
t_7	S_1	11	100011111	0	1	1	0	1
t_8	S_0	00	010001111	0	1	0	0	0

At time t_0, the control is reset and waiting for a start signal. At time t_1, the start signal $N = 1$ and $M = 1$, so $Ad = 1$. When the next clock occurs, the output of the adder is loaded into the accumulator and the control goes to S_1. At t_2, $Sh = 1$, so at the next clock shifting occurs and the counter is incremented. At t_3, $M = 1$, so $Ad = 1$ and the adder output is loaded into the accumulator at the next clock. At t_4 and t_5, $Sh = 1$, so shifting and counting occurs. At t_6, three shifts have occurred and the counter state is 11, so $K = 1$. Since $M = 1$, addition occurs and control goes to S_1. At t_7, $Sh = K = 1$, so at the next clock the final shift occurs and the counter is incremented back to state 00.

21.3
Design of a Binary Divider

We will consider the design of a parallel divider for positive binary numbers. As an example, we will design a network to divide a 6-bit dividend by a 3-bit divisor to obtain a 3-bit quotient. The following example illustrates the division process:

$$
\begin{array}{r}
101 \qquad \text{quotient} \\
110\,\overline{)\,100010} \qquad (34 \div 6 = 5 \text{ with a remainder of } 4) \\
110 \qquad \text{dividend} \\
\hline
101 \\
000 \\
\hline
1010 \\
110 \\
\hline
100 \qquad \text{remainder}
\end{array}
$$

Just as binary multiplication can be carried out as a series of add and shift operations, division can be carried out by a series of subtract and shift operations. To construct the divider, we will use a 7-bit dividend register and a 3-bit divisor register as shown in Fig. 21–9. During the division process, instead of shifting the divisor right before each subtraction, we will shift the dividend to the left. Note that an extra bit is required on the left end of the dividend register so that a bit is not lost when the dividend is shifted left. Instead of using a separate register to store the quotient, we will enter the quotient bit-by-bit into the right end of the dividend register as the dividend is shifted left.

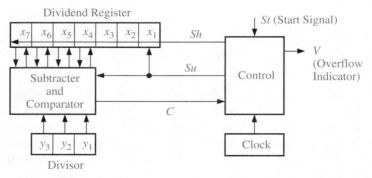

Figure 21–9
Block Diagram for Parallel Binary Divider

The preceding division example (34 ÷ 6) is reworked below showing the location of the bits in the registers at each clock time. Initially, the dividend and divisor are entered as follows:

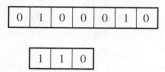

| 0 | 1 | 0 | 0 | 0 | 1 | 0 |

| 1 | 1 | 0 |

Subtraction cannot be carried out without a negative result, so we will shift before we subtract. Instead of shifting the divisor one place to the right, we will shift the dividend one place to the left:

```
1 0 0 0 1 0│0←————————dividing line between dividend and quotient
    1 1 0   │         ↖Note that after the shift, the rightmost
                              position in the dividend register is "empty."[1]
```

Subtraction is now carried out and the first quotient digit of 1 is stored in the unused position of the dividend register:

```
0 0 1 0 1 0│1←————————first quotient digit
```

Next we shift the dividend one place to the left:

```
0 1 0 1 0│1 0
    1 1 0 │
```

Since subtraction would yield a negative result, we shift the dividend to the left again, and the second quotient bit remains zero:

```
1 0 1 0│1 0 0
    1 1 0│
```

A final subtraction is carried out and the third quotient bit is set to 1:

```
0 1 0 0│1 0 1
```
remainder│quotient

The final result agrees with that obtained in the first example.

If as a result of a division operation, the quotient would contain more bits than are available for storing the quotient, we say that an *overflow* has occurred. For the divider of Fig. 21–9, an overflow would occur if the quotient is greater than 7, since only 3 bits are provided to store the quotient. It is not actually necessary to carry out the division to determine if an overflow condition exists, since an initial comparison of the dividend and divisor will tell if the quotient will be too large. For example, if we attempt to divide 34 by 4, the initial contents of the registers would be:

```
        0 1 0 0 0 1 0
            1 0 0
```

---

[1] In effect, the quotient bit is initially set to 0 and if subtraction occurs, it is changed to 1.

Since subtraction can be carried out with a nonnegative result, we should subtract the divisor from the dividend and enter a quotient bit of 1 in the rightmost place in the dividend register. However, we cannot do this because the rightmost place contains the least significant bit of the dividend, and entering a quotient bit here would destroy that dividend bit. Therefore, the quotient would be too large to store in the 3 bits we have allocated for it, and we have detected an overflow condition. In general, for Fig. 21–9, if initially $x_7x_6x_5x_4 \geq y_3y_2y_1$ (i.e., if the left four bits of the dividend register exceed or equal the divisor), the quotient will be greater than 7 and an overflow occurs. Note that if $x_7x_6x_5x_4 \geq y_3y_2y_1$, the quotient is

$$\frac{x_7x_6x_5x_4x_3x_2x_1}{y_3y_2y_1} \geq \frac{x_7x_6x_5x_4000}{y_3y_2y_1} = \frac{x_7x_6x_5x_4 \times 8}{y_3y_2y_1} \geq 8$$

The operation of the divider can be explained in terms of the block diagram of Fig. 21–9. A shift signal (Sh) will shift the dividend one place to the left. A subtract signal (Su) will subtract the divisor from the four leftmost bits in the dividend register and set the quotient bit (the rightmost bit in the dividend register) to 1. If the divisor is greater than the four leftmost dividend bits, the comparator output is $C = 0$; otherwise, $C = 1$. The control circuit generates the required sequence of shift and subtract signals. Whenever $C = 0$, subtraction cannot occur without a negative result, so a shift signal is generated. Whenever $C = 1$, a subtract signal is generated and the quotient bit is set to one.

Figure 21–10 shows the state diagram for the control circuit. Initially, the 6-bit dividend and 3-bit divisor are entered into the appropriate registers. The circuit remains in the stop state (S_0) until a start signal (St) is applied to the control circuit. If the initial value of C is 1, the quotient would require four or more bits. Since space is only provided for a 3-bit quotient, this condition constitutes an overflow, so the divider is stopped and the overflow indicator is set by the V output. Normally, the initial value of C is 0, so a shift will occur first and the control circuit will go to state S_1. Then, if $C = 1$ subtraction occurs. After the subtraction

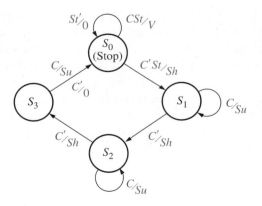

Figure 21–10
State Graph for Control Circuit

Table 21–2

State Table for Fig. 21–10

		$St\ C$							
AB		00	01	11	10	00	01	11	10
00	S_0	S_0	S_0	S_0	S_1	0	0	V	Sh
01	S_1	S_2	S_1	–	–	Sh	Su	–	–
11	S_2	S_3	S_2	–	–	Sh	Su	–	–
10	S_3	S_0	S_0	–	–	0	Su	–	–

is completed, C will always be 0, so the next clock pulse will produce a shift. This process continues until three shifts have occurred and the control is in state S_3. Then a final subtraction occurs if necessary, and the control returns to the stop state. For this example, we will assume that when the start signal (St) occurs, it will be 1 for one clock time, and then it will remain 0 until the control network is back in state S_0. Therefore, St will always be 0 in states S_1, S_2, and S_3.

Table 21–2 gives the state table for the control circuit. Since we assumed that $St = 0$ in states S_1, S_2, and S_3, the next states and outputs are don't cares for these states when $St = 1$. The entries in the output table indicate which outputs are 1. For example, the entry Sh means $Sh = 1$ and the other outputs are 0. Using the state assignment shown in Table 21–2 for J-K flip-flops A and B, the following equations can be derived for the control circuit:

$$J_A = BC', \qquad K_A = B', \qquad J_B = St\ C', \qquad K_B = AC'$$
$$Sh = (St + B)C', \qquad Su = C(B + A), \qquad V = C \cdot St \qquad\qquad (21\text{–}1)$$

Figure 21–11 shows a logic diagram for the subtracter/comparator, dividend register and control network. The subtracter is constructed using four full subtracters. When the numbers are entered into the divisor and dividend registers, the borrow signal will propagate through the full subtracters before the subtracter output is transferred to the dividend register. If the last borrow signal (b_8) is 1, this means that the result would be negative if subtraction were carried out. Hence, if b_8 is 1, the divisor is greater than $x_7x_6x_5x_4$, and $C = 0$. Therefore, $C = b_8'$ and a separate comparator circuit is unnecessary. Gating is added to the flip-flops in the dividend register so that if $Sh = 1$ a left shift will take place when the clock pulse occurs, and if $Su = 1$ the subtracter output will be transferred to the dividend register when the clock pulse occurs. For example,

$$D_4 = Su \cdot d_4 + Sh \cdot x_3 = x_4^+$$

If $Su = 1$ and $Sh = 0$, $x_4^+ = d_4$ and the subtracter output is transferred to the register of flip-flops. If $Su = 0$ and $Sh = 1$, $x_4^+ = x_3$ and a left shift occurs. Since $D_1 = Su$, the quotient bit (x_1) is cleared when shifting occurs ($Su = 0$) and the quotient bit is set to 1 during subtraction ($Su = 1$). Note that the clock pulse is gated so that flip-flops x_7, x_6, x_5, x_4, and x_1 are clocked when Su or Sh is 1, while flip-flops x_3 and x_2 are clocked only when Sh is 1.

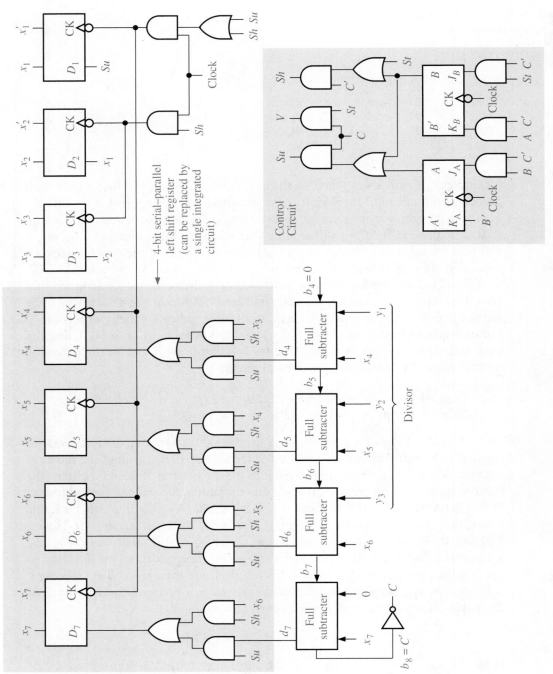

Figure 21–11
Logic Diagram for Binary Divider

PROGRAMMED EXERCISE 21.1

Cover the lower part of each page with a sheet of paper and slide it down as you check your answers. *Write* your answer in the space provided before looking at the correct answers.

This exercise concerns the design of a network which forms the 2's complement of a 16-bit binary number. The network consists of three main components—a 16-bit shift register which initially holds the number to be complemented, a control network, and a counter which counts the number of shifts. The control network processes the number in the shift register one bit at a time and stores the 2's complement back in the shift register. Draw a block diagram of the network. Show the necessary inputs and outputs for the control network including a start signal (N) which is used to initiate the 2's complement operation.

Answer:

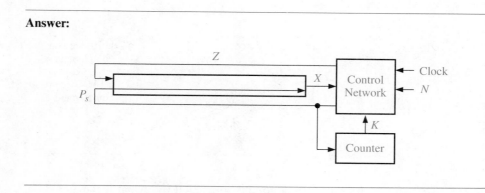

State a rule for forming the 2's complement which is appropriate for use with the above block diagram.

Answer: Starting with the least significant bit, complement all of the bits to the left of the first 1.

Draw a state graph for the control network (3 states) which implements the above rule. The 2's complement operation should be initiated when $N = 1$. (Assume that N will be 1 for only one clock time.) When drawing your graph, do *not* include any provision for stopping the network. (In the next step you will be asked to add the signal K to your state graph so that the network will stop after 16 shifts.) Explain the meaning of each state in your graph.

Answer:

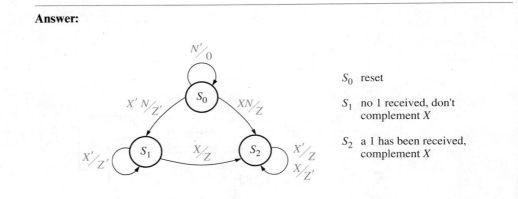

S_0 reset

S_1 no 1 received, don't complement X

S_2 a 1 has been received, complement X

The counter will generate a completion signal (K) when it reaches state 15. Modify your state graph so that when $K = 1$, the network will complete the 2's complement operation and return to the initial state. Also add the P_s output in the appropriate places.

Answer: Check the input labels on all arrows leaving each state of your graph. Make sure that two of the labels on arrows leaving a given state cannot have the value 1 at the same time. Make any necessary corrections to your graph and then check your final answer.

Final Answer:

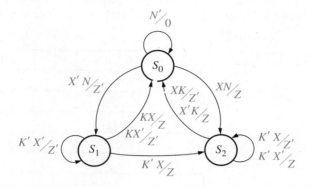

Note: P_s should be added to the graph everywhere Z or Z' appears.

PROGRAMMED EXERCISE 21.2

This exercise concerns the design of a binary divider to divide an 8-bit number by a 4-bit number to find a 4-bit quotient. The right 4 bits of the dividend register should be used to store the quotient. Draw a block diagram for the divider.

Answer:

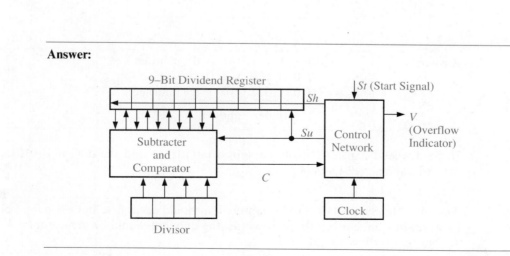

If the contents of the dividend register is initially 10000111 and the divisor is 1101, show the contents of the dividend register after each of the first three clock pulses. Also, indicate whether a shift or subtract should occur next.

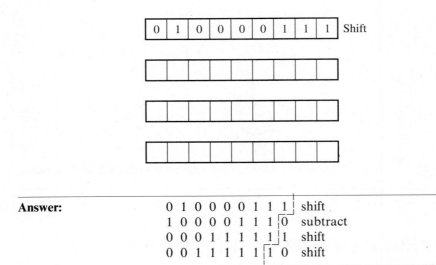

| 0 | 1 | 0 | 0 | 0 | 0 | 1 | 1 | 1 | Shift |

Answer:

```
0 1 0 0 0 0 1 1 1  shift
1 0 0 0 0 1 1 1 0  subtract
0 0 0 1 1 1 1 1 1  shift
0 0 1 1 1 1 1 1 0  shift
```

Now show the remaining steps in the computation, and check your answer by conversion to decimal.

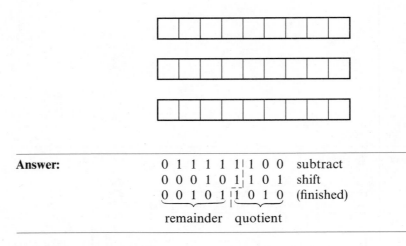

Answer:

```
0 1 1 1 1 1 1 0 0  subtract
0 0 0 1 0 1 1 0 1  shift
0 0 1 0 1 1 0 1 0  (finished)
```

remainder   quotient

If the dividend register initially contained 001101011 and the divisor is 0101, can division take place? Explain.

Answer: No. Since 0110 > 0101, subtraction should occur first, but there is no place to store the quotient bit. In other words, the quotient would be greater than 4 bits so that an overflow would occur.

Draw a state graph for the divider which will produce the necessary sequence of Su and Sh signals. Assume that the comparator output is $C = 1$ if the upper 5 bits of the dividend register is greater than the divisor. Include a stop state in your graph which is different than the reset state. Assume that the start signal (N) will remain 1 until the division is completed. The network should go to the stop state when division is complete or when an overflow is detected. The network should then reset when $N = 0$.

Answer:

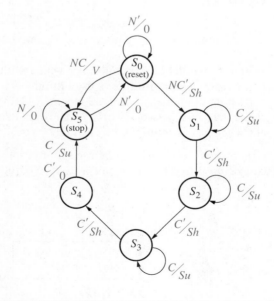

PROBLEMS

21.3 Design a serial subtracter with accumulator for 4-bit binary numbers. Assume that negative numbers are represented by 2's complement. (Use a network of the form of Fig. 21–1 except that the serial adder is replaced with a serial subtracter.) Use clocked J-K flip-flops and any kind of gates.

21.4 A network which adds one to the contents of a shift register has the following form:

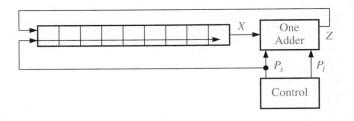

The control circuit outputs a pulse P_i to set ONE ADDER to the proper initial state, followed by the required number of shift pulses (P_S). Design the box labeled "ONE ADDER" using NOR gates and a clocked J-K flip-flop with set and clear inputs.

EXAMPLE:

   Contents of shift register before: 000001000

   Contents of shift register after P_i and 9 shift pulses: 000001001

21.5 Design a parallel binary multiplier which multiplies two 3-bit binary numbers to form a 6-bit product. This multiplier is to be a combinational network consisting of an array of full adders and AND gates (no flip-flops). Demonstrate that your network works by showing all of the signals which are present when 111 is multiplied by 111.

(*Hint:* The AND gates can be used to multiply by 0 or 1 and the full adders can be used to add 2 bits plus a carry. Six full adders are required.)

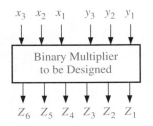

21.6   The binary multiplier of Fig. 21–6 is to be redesigned so that whenever addition occurs the multiplier bit (M) will be set to 0. Thus, if M is 1 at a given clock time and addition takes place, M will be 0 at the next clock time. Thus, we can always add when $M = 1$ and always shift when $M = 0$. This means that the control circuit will not have to change state when $M = 1$, and the number of states can be reduced from 8 to 5. Draw the resulting state graph for the multiplier control.

21.7   In order to allow for a larger number of bits, the control circuit of the binary divider is to be redesigned so that it uses a separate counter and a subtract-shift control which is analogous to Fig. 21–8(a). Draw the state graph for the subtract-shift control.

21.8   This problem concerns the design of a parallel divider to divide two positive binary numbers (8 bits ÷ 4 bits). The design should be similar to the one shown in Fig. 21–11, except that in order to speed up operation of the divider, a shift and subtract operation should take place simultaneously during a single clock pulse. In order to accomplish this, the wires from the dividend register to the full subtracter inputs must be shifted one position with respect to the wires from the full subtracter outputs to the dividend register. In this way the division can be completed in four clock times.

(a) Draw a block diagram for the divider using
   (1) 8 clocked D flip-flops
   (2) 5 full subtracters to perform the necessary subtraction
   (3) a 4-bit register which holds the divisor
   (4) a block labeled "control circuit" which puts out the required four pulses when a start signal is applied
   (5) any other necessary gates and inverters
   Show in detail how the full subtracter inputs and outputs are connected and how the D flip-flops are connected. The difference output from the leftmost subtracter is not used. Note that it will be necessary to gate the subtracter outputs so that when the last borrow bit is $B = 1$, 0 will be subtracted from the dividend register during the shift and subtract operation, and when the borrow bit is 0, the divisor will be subtracted from the leftmost 5 bits of the dividend register during the shift and subtract operation.

(b) If the dividend register initially contains 10010000 and the divisor register contains 1101, show the contents of the dividend register after each clock pulse.

(c) Draw the state graph for the control circuit assuming that once the start signal (N) is set to 1 it will remain 1 for one or more clock times past the completion of the division operation. Then the start signal will be changed to 0 some time between the completion of the division and the start of the next division cycle.

(*Note:* Design of an overflow detector for this type of divider is fairly difficult and is not required for this problem.)

21.9   A serial logic unit has two 8-bit shift registers, X and Y, shown as follows. Inputs K_1 and K_2 determine the operation to be performed on X and Y. When $N = 1$, X and Y are shifted into the logic network one bit at a time and replaced with new values. If $K_1 K_2 = 00$, X is complemented and Y is unchanged. If $K_1K_2 = 01$, X and Y are interchanged. If $K_1K_2 = 10$, Y is set to 0 and each bit of X is replaced with the exclusive-OR of the corresponding bits of X and Y; that is, the new x_i is $x_i \oplus y_i$. If $K_1K_2 = 11$, X is unchanged and Y is set to all 1's.

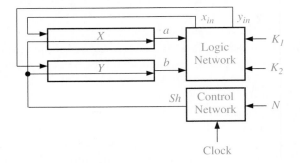

(a) Derive logic equations for x_{in} and y_{in}.

(b) Derive a state graph for the control network. Assume that once N is set to 1 it will remain 1 until all 8 bits have been processed. Then N will be changed back to 0 some time before the start of the next computation cycle.

(c) Realize the logic network using two 4-to-1 multiplexers and a minimum number of added gates.

(d) Realize the control network using a 74S163.

21.10 (a) Draw a block diagram for a parallel multiplier that can multiply two binary numbers, where the multiplier is 3 bits and the multiplicand is 4 bits. Use an 8-bit shift register along with other necessary blocks.

(b) Draw a state graph for the multiplier control.

(c) Illustrate the operation of the multiplier when 11 is multiplied by 5. Specify the sequence of add and shift pulses generated by the control network and specify the contents of the 8-bit register at each clock time.

(d) Draw the logic diagram for the multiplier using two 74178 shift registers, four full adders, three J-K flip-flops, and any necessary gates.

21.11 Work Problem 21.10 if the multiplier is 3 bits and the multiplicand is 5 bits, and show 20 multiplied by 6. Use two 74178 shift registers, five full adders, 4 D flip-flops, and a PLA for (d). Show the PLA table. (*Hint:* Combine the two 74178 shift registers and one D flip-flop to form a 9-bit shift register by storing the carry from the last adder in the D flip-flop.)

21.12 A serial Boolean logic unit has two 16-bit shift registers, A and B. A control signal (C) is used to select the Boolean operation to be performed. If $C = 0$, the contents of A are serially replaced by the bit-by-bit Boolean AND of A and B. If $C = 1$, the contents of A are serially replaced by the bit-by-bit exclusive-OR of A and B. After the numbers have been placed in A and B, and C is set to 0 or 1, a start signal (N) sets the circuit in operation. A counter is used to count the number of shifts. When the counter reaches state 15, it outputs a signal $K = 1$, which causes the control network to stop after one more shift. Assume that N remains 1 and C does not change until the operation is completed. The control then remains in the stop state until N is changed back to 0.

(a) Draw a block diagram of the system, which includes the shift registers, the counter, the control circuit, and a logic network that generates the serial input (SI) to the A register.

(b) Draw a state graph for the control network (3 states).

(c) Design the control network using a PLA and D flip-flops.

(d) Design a logic network that generates SI.

21.13 Design a controller to exchange the contents of registers A and B in Problem 18.8, using register C or D for temporary storage. The controller should be implemented as a sequential network with one input, EXG, that starts the exchange operation. The network has an output $DONE$ that indicates when the exchange operation is complete. In addition, the network has outputs E_0, E_1, G_0, G_1, C_1, and C_2 that control the digital system as described in Problem 18.8. The controller should stay in state 0 until $EXG = 1$. The output $DONE$ should stay zero until the network reaches the end state, at which time $DONE$ becomes 1. The network should stay in the end state until EXG goes to 0.

(a) Draw a Mealy state graph for the network (5 states minimum).

(b) Use a straight binary state assignment and realize the system using a 16R4 PAL (you may use additional inverters if necessary).

21.14 A serial logic unit consists of a 4-bit shift register X and a control unit. The control unit has a start input (ST) and a shift output (SH). In addition, signals C_1 and C_2 are used to select the logic operation performed on the shift register. When $ST = 1$, then

If $C_1 C_2 = 00$, the contents of register X is serially replaced by all zeros.

If $C_1 C_2 = 01$, the contents of register X is serially replaced by all ones.

If $C_1 C_2 = 11$, the contents of register X is serially replaced by its bit-by-bit complement. Assume that $C_1 C_2$ does not change until the selected operation is complete.

(a) Draw a block diagram for the system.

(b) Specify the state graph for the control unit. Assume that ST stays 1 for one clock period.

(c) Design the control unit (not the shift register) using J-K flip-flops and any kind of gates. Also design the logic which generates the serial input to the shift register. *Hint:* The serial input depends only on C_1, C_2, and X.

21.15 Design a binary divider which divides a 7-bit dividend by a 2-bit divisor to give a 5-bit quotient. The system has an input ST that starts the division process.

(a) Draw a block diagram for the subtracter-comparator. You may use full adders or full subtracters.

(b) Draw a block diagram for the rest of the system (do not show the adders or subtracters in the subtracter-comparator block).

(c) Draw the state graph for the control circuit. Assume that the start signal (ST) is present for one clock period.

(d) Give the contents of the dividend register and the value of C at each time step if initially the dividend is 01010011 and the divisor is 11.

21.16 (a) Draw a block diagram for a parallel divider which is capable of dividing a positive 6-bit binary number by a positive 4-bit binary number to give a 2-bit quotient. Use a dividend register, a divisor register, a subtracter-comparator block, and a control block.

(b) Draw a state graph for the control network. Assume that the start signal N remains 1 for one or more clock times after the division is complete, and N must be set to 0 to reset the network.

(c) Show how the subtracter-comparator could be realized using full adders and inverters.

(d) Show the contents of the registers and the value of C after each time step if initially the dividend is 101101 and the divisor is 1101.

21.17 The block diagram for a parallel multiplier for positive binary numbers follows. The counter counts the number of shifts and outputs a signal $K = 1$ after 2 shifts.

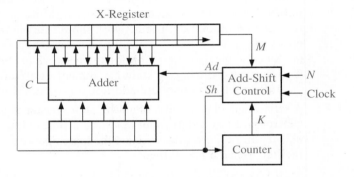

(a) Draw the state graph for the control circuit. Assume that N is 1 for one clock period to start the multiplier.

(b) Complete the following table showing the operation of the network if the multiplicand is 11001 and the multiplier is 111:

State	Counter	X	N	M	K	Ad	Sh
S_0	00	000000111	1	1	0		

21.18 The given multiplier uses only counters to multiply a 4-bit multiplicand by a 4-bit multiplier to obtain an 8-bit product. This "Ultra-Slow Multiplier" is based on the principles that multiplication is repeated addition and that addition is repeated incrementing. The multiplier works as follows: When the ST signal is received, the 8-bit up counter is cleared, N_1 is loaded into 4-bit counter A, and N_2 is loaded into 4-bit counter B. Then the controller decrements A and increments the up counter until A reaches zero. When A reaches zero, B is decremented and A is reloaded with N_1. Then the process is repeated until B reaches zero. When B reaches 0, the 8-bit up counter contains the product.

(a) Draw the state graph for the controller. Assume $ST = 1$ for only one clock time.

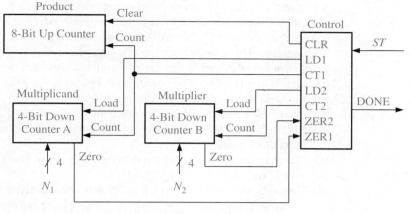

Ultra-Slow Multiplier

(b) Realize the state graph using one or two J-K flip-flops and a minimum number of gates.

(c) Draw a logic diagram for the Ultra Slow Multiplier. Use two 74LS191 up/down counters (described below) for the multiplier and multiplicand counters, and connect two 74S163 counters to form an 8-bit up counter.

(d) If the multiplier is N_1 and the multiplicand is N_2, how many clock periods does it take for the Ultra-Slow Multiplier to calculate the product?

The 74LS191 up/down counter is a 4-bit synchronous counter with an UP/DOWN input. The 74LS191 is similar to the 74S163 counter except for the addition of the UP/DOWN input. When the UP/DOWN input is 1, the counter decrements if counting is enabled. When UP/DOWN is 0, the counter increments if counting is enabled. The CTEN (count enable) input enables counting when 0. When LOAD = 0, the counter state will be set equal to the D inputs.

21.19 The Ultra-Slow Divider, shown in the following block diagram, works on a principle similar to the Ultra-Slow Multiplier in Problem 21.18. When the

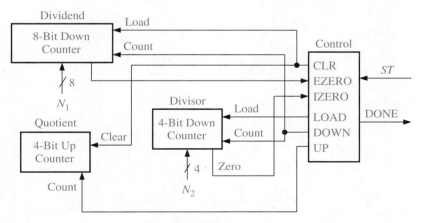

Ultra-Slow Divider

ST signal is received, the 8-bit down counter is loaded with the dividend (N_1), the 4-bit down counter is loaded with the divisor (N_2), and the 4-bit quotient up counter is cleared. The dividend counter and the divisor counter are decremented together, and every time the 4-bit divisor counter reaches zero, it is reloaded with the divisor and the quotient up counter is incremented. When the dividend counter reaches zero, the process terminates and the quotient counter contains the result.

(a) Draw the state graph for the controller.
(b) Realize the state graph using one or two J-K flip-flops and a minimum number of gates.
(c) If the dividend is N_1 and the divisor is N_2, how many clock cycles does it take to calculate the quotient?
(d) How can you tell if an overflow occurs during division?
(e) What will happen in your circuit if the divisor is zero?

22

State Machine Design with SM Charts

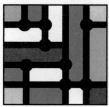

OBJECTIVES

1. Explain the different parts of an SM chart.

2. Given the input sequence to a state machine, determine the output sequence from its SM chart, and construct a timing diagram.

3. Convert a state graph to an SM chart.

4. Construct an SM chart for the control network for a multiplier, divider, or other simple digital system.

5. Determine the next state and output equations for a state machine by tracing link paths on its SM chart.

6. Realize an SM chart using a PLA or ROM and flip-flops.

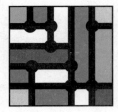

STUDY GUIDE

1. Study Section 22.1, *State Machine Charts*.

   (a) For the example of Fig. 22–2, if $X_1 = 0$ and $X_2 = 1$ when the machine is in state S_1, specify the values of all of the outputs and the exit path number.

   (b) For Figs. 22–6(a) and (b), trace the link paths and determine the outputs when $X_1 = X_3 = 1$.

   (c) Verify that the SM chart and state graph of Fig. 22–7 are equivalent.

   (d) Construct a timing chart for Fig. 22–7(b) when the input sequence is $X = 0, 1, 1, 0$.

   (e) Work Problems 22.1, 22.3, and 22.7.

2. Study Section 22.2, *Derivation of SM Charts*.

   (a) Using the SM chart of Fig. 22–9 to determine when to subtract and when to shift for the binary divider of Fig. 21–9, show the contents of the dividend register at each time step when 28 is divided by 5.

   (b) Compare the SM chart of Fig. 22–10 with the state graph of Fig. 21–8(c) and verify that in each state they will generate the same outputs when the inputs are the same.

   (c) Compare the flowchart for the dice game (Fig. 22–12) with the SM chart. Note that the "Roll Dice" box on the flowchart requires two states to implement on the SM chart. In the first state, the machine waits for the roll button to be pressed; in the second state, it generates a roll signal which lasts until the roll button is released. In state S_1, four variables are tested; if they are all 0, Sp is generated so that the sum will be stored in the point register at the same time the transition from S_1 to S_4 occurs.

   (d) Work Problems 22.9, 22.10, and 22.11.

3. Study Section 22.3, *Realization of SM Charts.*

    (a) For Fig. 22–7(b) find simplified equations for A^+ and B^+.

    (b) Verify Tables 22–1 and 22–2. For Table 22–2, why is $Sp = 1$ only in row 7, and $Win = 1$ in both rows 8 and 9?

    (c) Expand row 17 of Table 22–2 to give the corresponding rows of the ROM table.

    (d) Work Problems 22.13, 22.14, 22.15(a), and 22.16.

State Machine Design with SM Charts

Another name for a sequential network is an algorithmic state machine or simply a state machine. These names are often used when the sequential network is used to control a digital system that carries out a step-by-step procedure or algorithm. The state graphs in Figs. 21–3, 21–7, 21–8, and 21–10 define state machines for controlling adders, multipliers, and dividers. As an alternative to using state graphs, a special type of flowchart, called a state machine flowchart or SM chart, may be used to describe the behavior of a state machine. This unit describes the properties of SM charts and how they are used in the design of state machines.

22.1
State Machine Charts

Just as flowcharts are useful in software design, flowcharts are useful in the hardware design of digital systems. In this section we introduce a special type of flowchart called a state machine flowchart, or SM chart for short. SM charts are also called ASM (algorithmic state machine) charts. We will see that the SM chart offers several advantages. It is often easier to understand the operation of a digital system by inspection of the SM chart instead of the equivalent state graph. A given SM chart can be converted into several equivalent forms, and each form leads directly to a hardware realization.

An SM chart differs from an ordinary flowchart in that certain specific rules must be followed in constructing the SM chart. When these rules are followed, the SM chart is equivalent to a state graph, and it leads directly to a hardware realization. Figure 22–1 shows the three principal components of an SM chart. The state of the system is represented by a *state box*. The state box may contain an *output list*, and a *state code* may be placed outside the box at the top. The *state name* is placed in a circle to the left of the state box. A *decision box* is

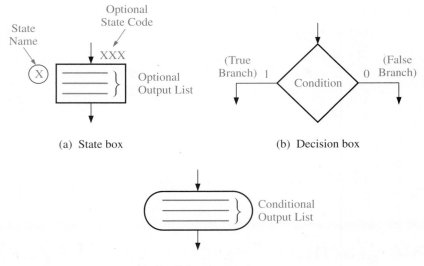

(a) State box   (b) Decision box

(c) Conditional output box

Figure 22–1
Components of an SM Chart

represented by a diamond-shaped symbol with true and false branches. The *condition* placed in the box is a Boolean expression that is evaluated to determine which branch to take. The *conditional output box*, which has curved ends, contains a *conditional output list*. The conditional outputs depend on both the state of the system and the inputs.

An SM chart is constructed from *SM blocks*. Each SM block (Fig. 22–2) contains exactly one state box together with the decision boxes and conditional output boxes associated with that state. An SM block has exactly one *entrance path* and one or more *exit paths*. Each SM block describes the machine operation during the time that the machine is in one state. When a digital system enters the state associated with a given SM block, the outputs on the output list in the state box become true. The conditions in the decision boxes are evaluated to determine which path (or paths) are followed through the SM block. When a conditional output box is encountered along such a path, the corresponding conditional outputs become true. A path through an SM block from entrance to exit is referred to as a *link path*.

For the example of Fig. 22–2, when state S_1 is entered, outputs Z_1 and Z_2 become 1. If inputs X_1 and X_2 are both equal to 0, Z_3 and Z_4 are also 1, and at the end of the state time the machine goes to the next state via exit path 1. On the other hand, if $X_1 = 1$ and $X_3 = 0$, the output Z_5 is 1 and exit to the next state will occur via exit path 3.

A given SM block can generally be drawn in several different forms. Figure 22–3 shows two equivalent SM blocks. In both (a) and (b), the output $Z_2 = 1$ if $X_1 = 0$; the next state is S_2 if $X_2 = 0$ and S_3 if $X_2 = 1$.

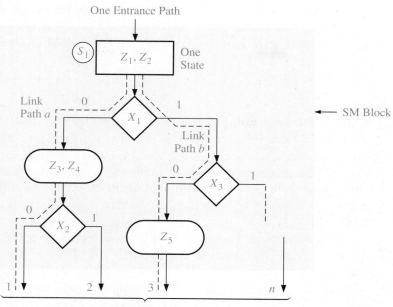

Figure 22–2
Example of an SM Block

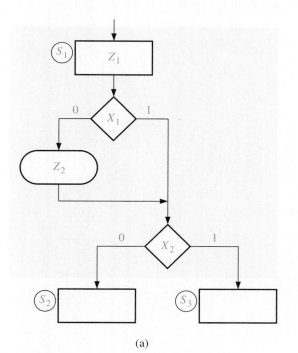

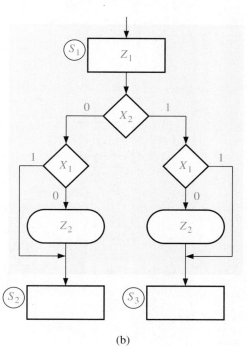

(a)

(b)

Figure 22–3
Equivalent SM Blocks

The SM chart of Fig. 22–4(a) represents a combinational network since there is only one state and no state change occurs. The output is $Z_1 = 1$ if $A + BC = 1$; else $Z_1 = 0$. Figure 22–4(b) shows an equivalent SM chart in which the input variables are tested individually. The output is $Z_1 = 1$ if $A = 1$ or if $A = 0$, $B = 1$ and $C = 1$. Hence,

$$Z_1 = A + A'BC = A + BC$$

which is the same output function realized by the SM chart of Fig. 22–4(a).

Certain rules must be followed when constructing an SM block. First, for every valid combination of input variables, there must be exactly one exit path defined. This is necessary since each allowable input combination must lead to a single next state. Second, no internal feedback within an SM block is allowed. Figure 22–5 shows an incorrect and correct way of drawing an SM block with feedback.

As shown in Fig. 22–6(a), an SM block can have several parallel paths which lead to the same exit path, and more than one of these paths can be "active" at the same time. For example, if $X_1 = X_2 = 1$ and $X_3 = 0$, the link paths marked with dashed lines are active, and the outputs Z_1, Z_2, and Z_3 will be 1. Although Fig. 22–6(a) would not be a valid flowchart for a program for a serial computer, it presents no problems for a state machine implementation. The state machine can have a multiple-output network that generates Z_1, Z_2, and Z_3 at the same time. Figure 22–6(b) shows a serial SM block, which is equivalent to Fig. 22–6(a). In the serial block only one active link path between entrance and exit is possible.

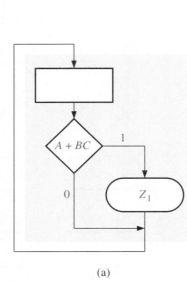

(a)

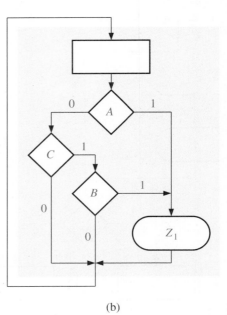

(b)

Figure 22–4
Equivalent SM Charts for a Combinational
Network

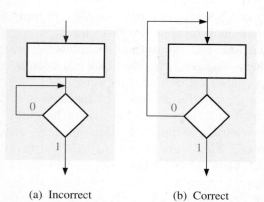

(a) Incorrect   (b) Correct

Figure 22–5
SM Block with Feedback

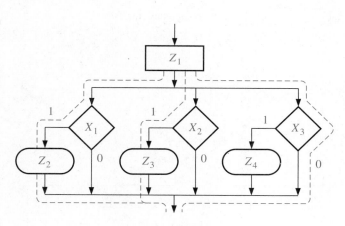

(a) Parallel form

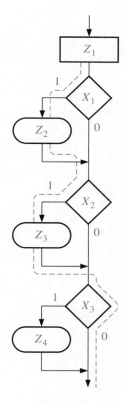

(b) Serial form

Figure 22–6
Equivalent SM Blocks

For any combination of input values the outputs will be the same as in the equivalent parallel form. The link path for $X_1 = X_2 = 1$ and $X_3 = 0$ is shown with a dashed line, and the outputs encountered on this path are Z_1, Z_2, and Z_3. Regardless of whether the SM block is drawn in serial or parallel form, all of the tests take place within one clock time.

A state graph for a sequential machine is easy to convert to an equivalent SM chart. The state graph of Fig. 22–7(a) has both "Moore" and "Mealy" outputs. The equivalent SM chart has three blocks—one for each state. The "Moore" outputs (Z_a, Z_b, Z_c) are placed in the state boxes since they do not depend on the input. The "Mealy" outputs (Z_1, Z_2) appear in conditional output boxes since they depend on both the state and input. In this example, each SM block has only one decision box since only one input variable must be tested. For both the

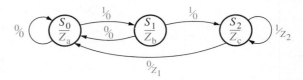

(a) State graph

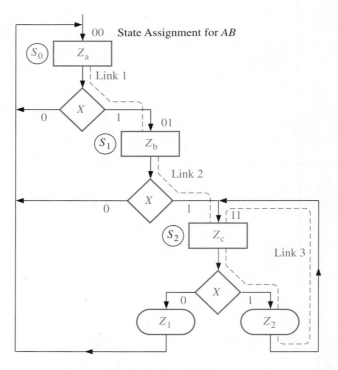

(b) Equivalent SM chart

Figure 22–7
Conversion of a State Graph to an SM Chart

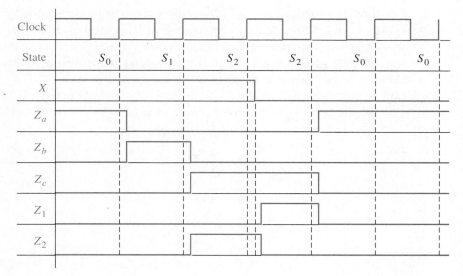

Figure 22–8
Timing Chart for Fig. 22–7

state graph and SM chart, Z_c is always 1 in state S_2. If $X = 0$ in state S_2, $Z_1 = 1$ and the next state is S_0. If $X = 1$, $Z_2 = 1$ and the next state is S_2.

Figure 22–8 shows a timing chart for the SM chart of Fig. 22–7 with an input sequence $X = 1, 1, 1, 0, 0, 0$. In this example, all state changes occur immediately after the rising edge of the clock. Since the Moore outputs (Z_a, Z_b, Z_c) depend on the state, they can only change immediately following a state change. The Mealy outputs (Z_1, Z_2) can change immediately after a state change or an input change. In any case, all outputs will have their correct value during the active edge of the clock.

22.2
Derivation of SM Charts

The method used to derive an SM chart for a sequential control network is similar to that used to derive the state graph. First, we should draw a block diagram of the system we are controlling. Next we should define the required input and output signals to the control network. Then we can construct an SM chart that tests the input signals and generates the proper sequence of output signals.

In this section we will give several examples of SM charts. The first example is an SM chart for control of the parallel binary divider shown in Fig. 21–9. As described in Section 21.3, binary division requires a series of subtract and shift operations. Derivation of an SM chart to generate the proper sequence of subtract and shift signals is very similar to derivation of the state graph of Fig. 21–10.

For the SM chart of Fig. 22–9, S_0 is the starting state. In S_0, the start signal (St) is tested, and if $St = 1$, the compare signal (C) is tested. If $C = 1$, the quotient would be larger than 3 bits, so an overflow signal ($V = 1$) is generated and no state change occurs. If $C = 0$, Sh becomes 1, so at the next clock the dividend is shifted left and the state changes to S_1. C is tested in state S_1. If $C = 1$, subtraction is possible, so Su becomes 1 and no state change occurs. If $C = 0$, $Sh = 1$ and the dividend is shifted as the state changes to S_2. The action in state S_2 is

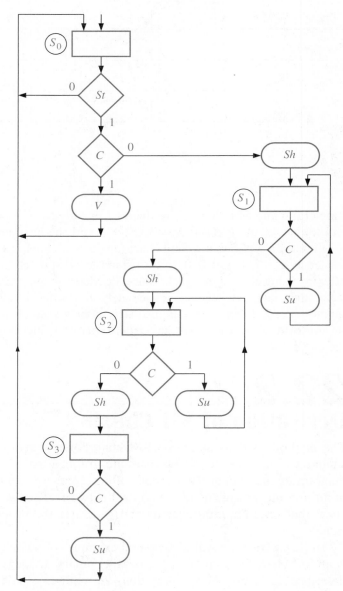

Figure 22–9
SM Chart for Binary Divider

identical to that in state S_1. In state S_3 the next state is always S_0, and $C = 1$ causes subtraction to occur.

Next we will derive the SM chart for the multiplier control of Fig. 21–8(a). This control generates the required sequence of add and shift pulses for a binary multiplier of the type shown in Fig. 21–6. The counter counts the number of shifts and outputs $K = 1$ just before the last shift occurs. The SM chart for the multiplier control (Fig. 22–10) corresponds closely to the state graph of Fig. 21–8(c). In state S_0, when the start signal N is 1, the multiplier bit M is tested to determine whether to add or shift. If $M = 1$, an add signal is generated and the next state is S_1. In S_1 a shift signal is generated since a shift must always follow an add. If $K = 1$, the network returns to S_0 at the time of the last shift; otherwise, the next state is S_2. In S_2, M is tested to determine whether to add or shift. The add is always followed by a shift (state S_1), and after a shift, S_2 is re-entered unless $K = 1$.

As a third example of SM chart construction, we will design an electronic dice game. Figure 22–11 shows the block diagram for the dice game. Two counters are used to simulate the roll of the dice. Each counter counts in the sequence 1, 2, 3, 4, 5, 6, 1, 2, ... Thus, after the "roll" of the dice, the sum of the values

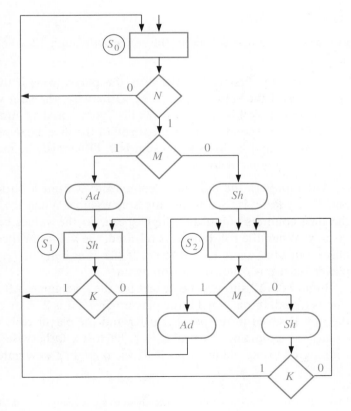

Figure 22–10
SM Chart for Binary Multiplier

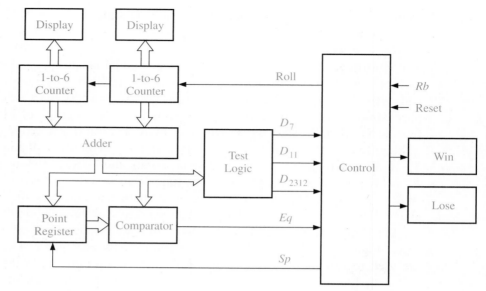

Figure 22–11
Block Diagram for Dice Game

in the two counters will be in the range 2 through 12. The rules of the game are as follows:

1. After the first roll of the dice, the player wins if the sum is 7 or 11. He loses if the sum is 2, 3, or 12. Otherwise, the sum which he obtained on the first roll is referred to as his "point" and he must roll the dice again.
2. On the second or subsequent roll of the dice, he wins if the sum equals his point, and he loses if the sum is 7. Otherwise, he must roll again until he finally wins or loses.

The inputs to the dice game come from two push buttons,[1] Rb (roll button) and *Reset*. *Reset* is used to initiate a new game. When the roll button is pushed, the dice counters count at a high speed, so the values cannot be read on the display. When the roll button is released, the values in the two counters are displayed and the game can proceed. If the *Win* light or *Lose* light is not on, the player must push the roll button again.

Figure 22–12 shows a flowchart for the dice game. After rolling the dice, the sum is tested. If it is 7 or 11, the player wins; if it is 2, 3, or 12, he loses. Otherwise the sum is saved in the point register and the player rolls again. If the new sum equals the point, he wins; if it is 7, he loses. Otherwise, he rolls again. After winning or losing, he must push *Reset* to begin a new game.

---

[1] We will assume at this point that the push buttons are properly debounced and that changes in *Rb* are properly synchronized with the clock. Methods for debouncing and synchronization are discussed in later units.

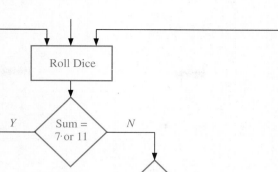

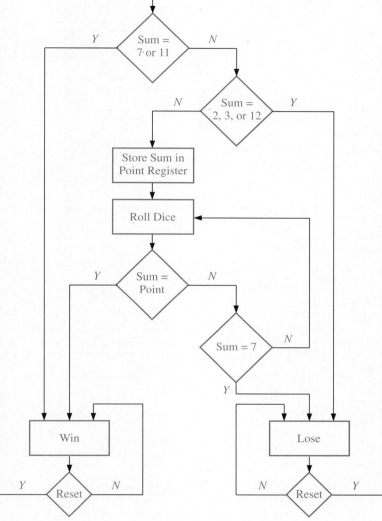

Figure 22–12
Flowchart for Dice Game

The components for the dice game shown in the block diagram (Fig. 22–11) include an adder which adds the two counter outputs, a register to store the "point", test logic to determine conditions for win or lose, and a control network. Input signals to the control network are defined as follows:

$D_7 = 1$ if the sum of the dice is 7
$D_{11} = 1$ if the sum of the dice is 11
$D_{2312} = 1$ if the sum of the dice is 2, 3, or 12

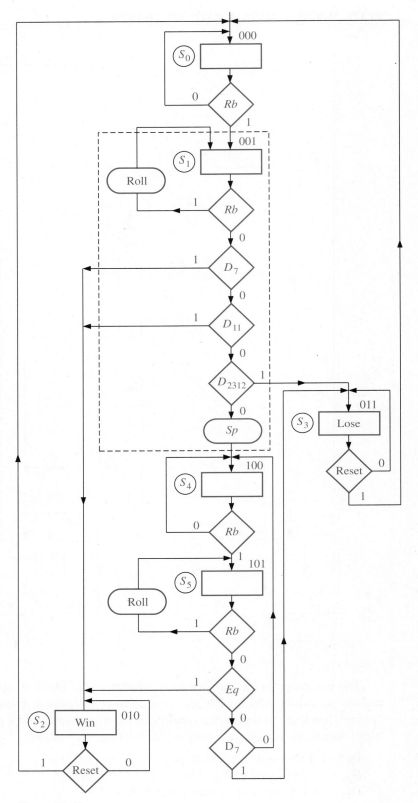

Figure 22–13
SM Chart for Dice Game

$Eq = 1$ if the sum of the dice equals the number stored in the point register
$Rb = 1$ when the roll button is pressed
$Reset = 1$ when the reset button is pressed

Outputs from the control network are defined as follows:

$Roll = 1$ enables the dice counters
$Sp = 1$ causes the sum to be stored in the point register
$Win = 1$ turns on the win light
$Lose = 1$ turns on the lose light

We can now convert the flowchart for the dice game to an SM chart for the control network using the control signals defined above. Figure 22–13 shows the resulting SM chart. The control network waits in state S_0 until the roll button is pressed ($Rb = 1$). Then it goes to state S_1, and the roll counters are enabled as long as $Rb = 1$. As soon as the roll button is released ($Rb = 0$), D_7 and D_{11} are tested. If the sum is 7 or 11, the network goes to state S_2 and turns on the *Win* light; otherwise, D_{2312} is tested. If the sum is 2, 3, or 12, it goes to state S_3 and turns on the *Lose* light; otherwise, the signal Sp becomes 1 and the sum is stored in the point register. It then enters S_4 and waits for the player to "roll the dice" again. In S_5, after the roll button is released, if $Eq = 1$, the sum equals the point and state S_2 is entered to indicate a win. If $D_7 = 1$, the sum is 7 and S_3 is entered to indicate a lose. Otherwise, control returns to S_4 so that the player can roll again. When in S_2 or S_3, the game is reset to S_0 when the *Reset* button is pressed.

22.3
Realization of SM Charts

Methods used to realize SM charts are similar to the methods used to realize state graphs. As with any sequential network, the realization will consist of a combinational subnetwork together with flip-flops for storing the state of the network (see Fig. 13–13). In some cases, it may be possible to identify equivalent states in an SM chart and eliminate redundant states using the same method as was used for reducing state tables. However, an SM chart is usually incompletely specified in the sense that all inputs are not tested in every state, which makes the reduction procedure more difficult. Even if the number of states in an SM chart can be reduced, it is not always desirable to do so since combining states may make the SM chart more difficult to interpret.

Before deriving next-state and output equations from an SM chart, a state assignment must be made. The best way of making the assignment depends on how the SM chart is realized. If gates and flip-flops (or the equivalent PLD realization) are used, the guidelines for state assignment given in Section 15.8 may be useful.

As an example of realizing an SM chart, consider Fig. 22–7(b). We have made the state assignment $AB = 00$ for S_0, $AB = 01$ for S_1 and $AB = 11$ for S_2. After a state assignment has been made, output and next-state equations can be read directly from the SM chart. Since the Moore output Z_a is 1 only in state 00, $Z_a = A'B'$. Similarly, $Z_b = A'B$ and $Z_c = AB$. The conditional output $Z_1 = ABX'$ since the only link path through Z_1 starts with $AB = 11$ and takes the $X = 0$ branch. Similarly, $Z_2 = ABX$. There are three link paths (labeled link 1, link 2, and link 3), which terminate in a state that has $B = 1$. Link 1 starts with a present state $AB = 00$, takes the $X = 1$ branch and terminates on a state in which $B = 1$. Therefore, the next state of B (B^+) equals 1 when $A'B'X = 1$. Link 2 starts in state 01, takes the $X = 1$ branch, and ends in state 11, so B^+ has a term $A'BX$. Similarly, B^+ has a term ABX from link 3. The next-state equation for B thus has 3 terms corresponding to the 3 link paths:

$$B^+ = \underline{A'B'X} + \underline{A'BX} + \underline{ABX}$$

$$\text{link 1} \qquad \text{link 2} \qquad \text{link 3}$$

Similarly, two link paths terminate in a state with $A = 1$, so

$$A^+ = A'BX + ABX$$

The above output and next-state equations can be simplified with a Karnaugh map using the unused state assignment ($AB = 10$) as a don't care condition.

As illustrated above, the next-state equation for a flip-flop Q can be derived from the SM chart as follows:

1. Identify all of the states in which $Q = 1$.
2. For each of these states, find all of the link paths that lead *into* the state.
3. For each of these link paths, find a term that is 1 when the link path is followed. That is, for a link path from S_i to S_j, the term will be 1 if the machine is in state S_i and the conditions for exiting to S_j are satisfied.
4. The expression for Q^+ (the next state of Q) is formed by ORing together the terms found in step 3.

Next, consider the SM chart for the divider control (Fig. 22–9). We can realize this SM chart using gates and flip-flops in the same way we realized the state graph (Fig. 21–10), which leads to the network of Fig. 21–11. As an alternative, we will realize the SM chart with a PLA or ROM and two D flip-flops, using a network of the form shown in Fig. 19–1. As indicated in Table 22–1, the PLA has 4 inputs and 5 outputs. Each row in the table corresponds to one of the link paths in the SM chart. Since S_0 has 3 exit paths, the table has 3 rows for present state S_0. The first row corresponds to the $St = 0$ exit path, so the next state and outputs are 0. In the next row, $St = 1$ and $C = 0$, so the next state is 01 and the other PLA outputs are 100. Since St is not tested in states S_1, S_2, and S_3, St is a don't care in the corresponding rows. The outputs for each row can be filled in by tracing the corresponding link paths on the SM chart. For the last row, the link path from S_3 to S_0 passes through the conditional output Su when $C = 1$, so $Su = 1$ in this row.

If a ROM is used instead of a PLA, each row in the PLA table which has a dash must be replaced with two rows. For example, the first row is replaced with

$$\begin{array}{cccc} 0\ 0\ 0\ 0 & \quad 0\ 0\ 0\ 0\ 0 \\ 0\ 0\ 0\ 1 & \quad 0\ 0\ 0\ 0\ 0 \end{array}$$

Table 22–1
PLA Table for Divider Control

Present State	Q_1	Q_2	St	C	Q_1^+	Q_2^+	Sh	Su	V
S_0	0	0	0	–	0	0	0	0	0
	0	0	1	0	0	1	1	0	0
	0	0	1	1	0	0	0	0	1
S_1	0	1	–	0	1	0	1	0	0
	0	1	–	1	0	1	0	1	0
S_2	1	0	–	0	1	1	1	0	0
	1	0	–	1	1	0	0	1	0
S_3	1	1	–	0	0	0	0	0	0
	1	1	–	1	0	0	0	1	0

since a dash in the C column of the PLA table indicates that the outputs are the same for $C = 0$ and $C = 1$. The final ROM table will have $2^4 = 16$ rows since there are 4 input variables.

Next, we will realize the SM chart for the dice game using a PLA and three D flip-flops as shown in Fig. 22–14. The PLA has 9 inputs and 7 outputs, which are listed at the top of Table 22–2. In state $ABC = 000$, the next state is $A^+B^+C^+ = 000$ or 001 depending on the value of Rb. Since state 001 has five exit paths, the PLA table has five corresponding rows. When Rb is 1, $Roll$ is 1

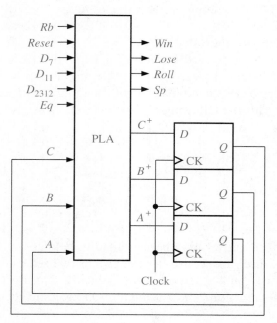

Figure 22–14
PLA Realization of Dice Game Controller

Table 22–2
PLA Table for Dice Game

	ABC	Rb	Reset	D_7	D_{11}	D_{2312}	Eq	A^+	B^+	C^+	Win	Lose	Roll	Sp
1	000	0	–	–	–	–	–	0	0	0	0	0	0	0
2	000	1	–	–	–	–	–	0	0	1	0	0	0	0
3	001	1	–	–	–	–	–	0	0	1	0	0	1	0
4	001	0	–	1	–	–	–	0	1	0	0	0	0	0
5	001	0	–	0	1	–	–	0	1	0	0	0	0	0
6	001	0	–	0	0	1	–	0	1	1	0	0	0	0
7	001	0	–	0	0	0	–	1	0	0	0	0	0	1
8	010	–	0	–	–	–	–	0	1	0	1	0	0	0
9	010	–	1	–	–	–	–	0	0	0	1	0	0	0
10	011	–	0	–	–	–	–	0	1	1	0	1	0	0
11	011	–	1	–	–	–	–	0	0	0	0	1	0	0
12	100	0	–	–	–	–	–	1	0	0	0	0	0	0
13	100	1	–	–	–	–	–	1	0	1	0	0	0	0
14	101	1	–	–	–	–	–	1	0	1	0	0	1	0
15	101	0	–	–	–	–	1	0	1	0	0	0	0	0
16	101	0	–	0	–	–	0	1	0	0	0	0	0	0
17	101	0	–	1	–	–	0	0	1	1	0	0	0	0

and there is no state change. When $Rb = 0$ and D_7 or D_{11} is 1, the next state is 010. When $Rb = 0$ and $D_{2312} = 1$, the next state is 011. For the link path from state 001 to 100, Rb, D_7, D_{11} and D_{2312} are all 0, and Sp is a conditional output. This path corresponds to row 7 of the PLA table, which has $Sp = 1$ and $A^+B^+C^+ = 100$. In state 010, the *Win* signal is always on, and the next state is 010 or 000 depending on the value of *Reset*. Similarly, *Lose* is always on in state 011. In state 101, $A^+B^+C^+ = 010$ if $Eq = 1$; otherwise, $A^+B^+C^+ = 011$ or 100 depending on the value of D_7.

If a ROM is used instead of a PLA, the PLA table must be expanded to $2^9 = 512$ rows. To expand the table, the dashes in each row must be replaced with all possible combinations of 0's and 1's. For example, row 5 would be replaced with the following 8 rows:

001	0	**0**	0	1	**0**	**0**	0	1	0	0	0	0	0
001	0	**0**	0	1	**0**	**1**	0	1	0	0	0	0	0
001	0	**0**	0	1	**1**	**0**	0	1	0	0	0	0	0
001	0	**0**	0	1	**1**	**1**	0	1	0	0	0	0	0
001	0	**1**	0	1	**0**	**0**	0	1	0	0	0	0	0
001	0	**1**	0	1	**0**	**1**	0	1	0	0	0	0	0
001	0	**1**	0	1	**1**	**0**	0	1	0	0	0	0	0
001	0	**1**	0	1	**1**	**1**	0	1	0	0	0	0	0

The added entries have been printed in boldface.

The dice game controller can also be realized using a PAL. The required PAL equations can be derived from Table 22–2 using the method of map-entered variables (Section 7.5) or using a CAD program such as *LogicAid*. Figure 22–15 shows maps for A^+, B^+ and *Win*. Since A^+, B^+, C^+, and Rb have assigned values in most of the rows of the table, these four variables are used on the map edges, and the remaining variables are entered within the map. E_1, E_2, E_3, and E_4 on the maps represent the expressions given below the maps.

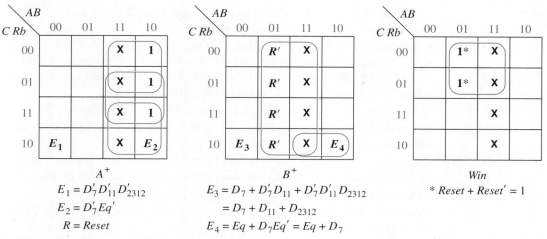

Figure 22–15
Maps Derived from Table 22-2

Below the first map (A^+):
$$E_1 = D_7' D_{11}' D_{2312}'$$
$$E_2 = D_7' Eq'$$
$$R = Reset$$

Below the second map (B^+):
$$E_3 = D_7 + D_7' D_{11} + D_7' D_{11}' D_{2312}$$
$$= D_7 + D_{11} + D_{2312}$$
$$E_4 = Eq + D_7 Eq' = Eq + D_7$$

Below the third map (Win):
$$* \; Reset + Reset' = 1$$

The resulting equations are

$$A^+ = A'B'C\,Rb'\,D_7'\,D_{11}'\,D_{2312}' + A\,C' + A\,Rb + A\,D_7'\,Eq'$$
$$B^+ = A'B'C\,Rb'(D_7 + D_{11} + D_{2312}) + B\,Reset' + A\,C\,Rb'(Eq + D_7)$$
$$C^+ = B'\,Rb + A'B'C\,D_7'\,D_{11}'\,D_{2312} + B\,C\,Reset' + A\,C\,D_7\,Eq'$$
$$Win = B\,C'$$
$$Lose = B\,C$$
$$Roll = B'\,C\,Rb$$
$$Sp = A'B'C\,Rb'\,D_7'\,D_{11}'\,D_{2312}' \tag{22-1}$$

These equations can be implemented using a 16R4 PAL with no external components. Equations (22–1) could also be derived by tracing link paths on the SM chart, then simplifying the resulting equations using the don't care next states. The entire dice game including the control network can be implemented using a 2064 programmable gate array. The total number of logic cells required will be about 33.

This unit has illustrated one way of realizing an SM chart using a PLA or ROM. Alternative procedures are available which make it possible to reduce the size of the PLA or ROM by adding some components to the network. These methods are generally based on transformation of the SM chart to different forms and encoding the inputs or outputs of the network.

PROBLEMS

22.1 Construct an SM block that has 3 input variables (D, E, F), 4 output variables (P, Q, R, S), and 2 exit paths. For this block, output P is always 1, and Q is 1 iff $D = 1$. If D and F are 1 or if D and E are 0, $R = 1$ and exit path

2 is taken. If ($D = 0$ and $E = 1$) or ($D = 1$ and $F = 0$), $S = 1$ and exit path 1 is taken.

22.2 Construct an SM block that has 3 input variables (A, B, C), 4 outputs (W, X, Y, Z), and 2 exit paths. For this block, output Z is always 1, and W is 1 iff A and B are both 1. If $C = 1$ and $A = 0$, $Y = 1$ and exit path 1 is taken. If $C = 0$ or $A = 1$, $X = 1$ and exit path 2 is taken.

22.3 Convert the state graphs of Figs. 13–9 and 13–11 to SM charts.

22.4 Convert the state graphs of Figs. 14–4 and 14–6 to SM charts. Use conditional outputs for Fig. 14–4.

22.5 Convert the state graph of Fig. 13–12 to an SM chart. Test only one variable in each decision box. Try to minimize the number of decision boxes.

22.6 Convert the state graph shown in Fig. 21–7 to an SM chart.

22.7 Complete the following timing diagram for the SM chart of Fig. 22–10. Assume $N = 1$.

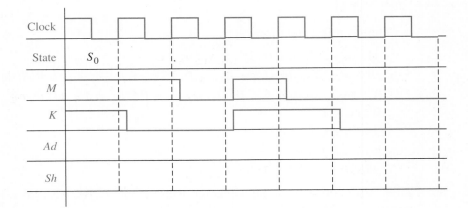

22.8 Complete the following timing diagram for the SM chart of Fig. 22–9.

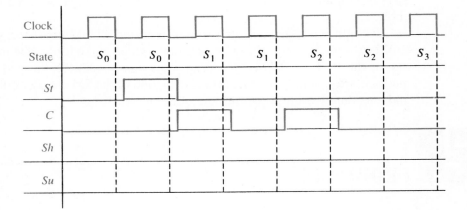

22.9 Solve Problem 21.6 using an SM chart instead of a state graph.

22.10 Work through Programmed Exercise 21.1 using an SM chart instead of a state graph.

22.11 Solve Problem 21.7 using an SM chart instead of a state graph.

22.12 Solve Problem 21.8(c) using an SM chart instead of a state graph.

22.13 (a) For the SM chart of Fig. 22–9, make the following state assignment for the flip-flops A and B:

$$S_0, AB = 00; \ S_1, AB = 01; \ S_2, AB = 11; \ S_3, AB = 10.$$

Derive the next-state and output equations by tracing link paths on the SM chart. Simplify the equations and then draw the network using D flip-flops and NAND gates.

(b) Repeat for the SM chart of Fig. 22–10 using the state assignment:

$$S_0, AB = 00; \ S_1, AB = 01; \ S_2, AB = 10.$$

22.14 (a) Write the next-state and output equations for the dice game by tracing link paths on the SM chart (Fig. 22–13).

(b) Design the block labeled "test logic" on Fig. 22–11.

22.15 (a) Realize the SM chart of Fig. 22–7(b) using a PLA and two D flip-flops. Draw the block diagram and give the PLA table.

(b) Repeat for Fig. 22–10 using the same state assignment as in Problem 22.13(b).

22.16 For the following SM chart:

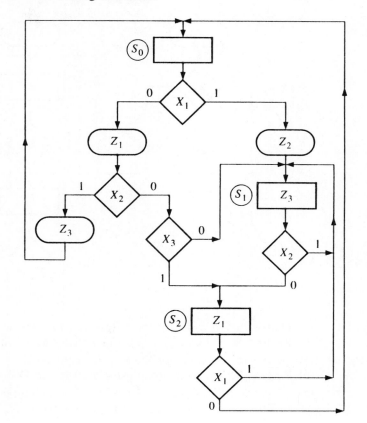

(a) Draw a timing chart that shows the clock, the state (S_0, S_1, or S_2), the inputs X_1 and X_2, and the outputs. Assume that $X_3 = 0$ and the input sequence for $X_1 X_2$ is 01, 00, 10, 11, 01, 10. Assume that all state changes occur on the rising edge of the clock, and the inputs change between clock pulses.

(b) Use the state assignment given in Problem 22.13(b) and derive the next-state and output equations by tracing link paths. Simplify these equations using the don't care state ($AB = 11$) and draw the corresponding network.

(c) Realize the chart using a PLA and D flip-flops. Give the PLA table.

(d) If a ROM is used instead of a PLA, what size ROM is required? Give the first 5 rows of the ROM table.

22.17 Work Problem 22.16 for the following SM chart and the input sequence $X_1 X_2 X_3 = 011, 101, 111, 010, 110, 101, 001$.

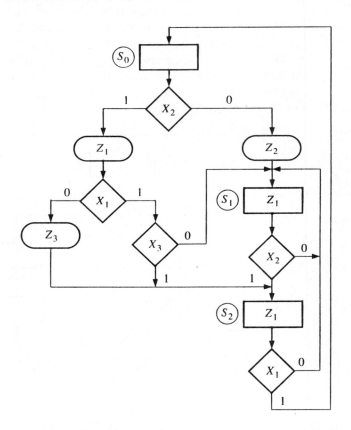

22.18 (a) Derive an SM chart for the Ultra-Slow Divider in Problem 21.19.
(b) Realize the SM chart in (a) using a PLA and D flip-flops.

22.19 (a) Derive an SM chart for the elevator controller in Problem 19.9.
(b) Realize the SM chart in (a) using a PLA and D flip-flops.

22.20 (a) Derive an SM chart for the Thunderbird taillight controller in Problem 19.8.

(b) Realize the SM chart in (a) using a PLA and D flip-flops.

22.21 A sequential logic network will be used to control the motor of a tape player. The logic network, shown as follows, will have five inputs and three outputs. Four of the inputs are the control buttons on the tape player. The input PL is 1 iff the play button is pressed, the input RE is 1 iff the rewind button is pressed, the input FF is 1 iff the fast forward button is pressed, and the input ST is 1 iff the stop button is pressed. The fifth input to the control network is M, which is 1 iff the special "music sensor" detects music at the current tape position. The three outputs of the control network are P, R, and F, which make the tape play, rewind, and fast forward, respectively, when 1. No more than one output should ever be on at a time; all outputs off cause the motor to stop.

The buttons control the tape player as follows: If the play button is pressed, the tape player will start playing the tape (output $P = 1$). If the play button is held down and the rewind button is pressed and released, the tape player will rewind to the beginning of the current song (output $R = 1$ until $M = 0$) and then start playing. If the play button is held down and the fast forward button is pressed and released, the tape player will fast forward to the end of the current song (output $F = 1$ until $M = 0$) and then start playing. If rewind or fast forward is pressed while play is released, the tape player will rewind or fast forward the tape. Pressing the stop button at any time should stop the tape player motor.

(a) Construct an SM chart for the tape player control network.
(b) Realize the control network using a PLA and D flip-flops.
(c) Realize the control network with a suitable PAL (no external gates or flip-flops are permitted).

23

Analysis of Asynchronous Sequential Networks

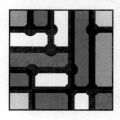

OBJECTIVES

1. Explain the differences between asynchronous and synchronous networks. Define fundamental mode operation.

2. Explain the difference between total state and internal state and between unstable and stable total states.

3. Given an asynchronous sequential network of gates or of gates and *S-R* flip-flops:

   a. Derive the flow table.

   b. Derive the output sequence given the input sequence.

   c. Sketch timing diagrams.

4. Given a flow table, locate critical races, noncritical races, and cycles.

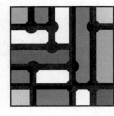

STUDY GUIDE

1. Study Section 23.1, *Introduction*.

   (a) What are the principal differences between synchronous and asynchronous networks?

   (b) Classify each counter in Fig. 23–1 as synchronous or asynchronous and explain your answer.

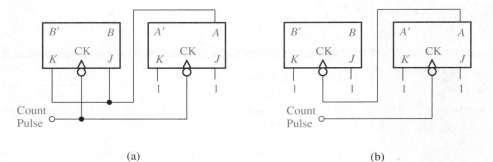

(a)   (b)

Figure 23–1
Counters

2. Study Section 23.2, *Analysis of an Asynchoronous Network with S-R Flip-Flops.*

   (a) Verify the analysis of Table 23–1 by tracing signals through the network.

   (b) Show how Table 23–1 can be derived (except for the flip-flop inputs) using the transition table of Fig. 23–3 and output table of Fig. 23–5.

   (c) If the input to a sequential network is changed only when it is in a stable total state, to what mode of operation does this correspond?

   (d) Given a network diagram and a specified total state, how can you tell if the specified total state is stable or unstable without constructing a flow table?

3. Study Section 23.3, *Analysis of an Asynchronous Gate Network*.

   (a) Verify that the tables in Fig. 23–7 are correct.

   (b) When writing the output sequence for an asynchronous network, use the following convention:

   For each input in the input sequence, specify the resulting output when the network reaches a stable state. If transient outputs occur when the network passes through unstable total states, specify these outputs in parentheses. The output sequence may be condensed by omitting any transient output which is the same as one of the adjacent outputs in the sequence.

   For the flow table and associated output table given below, verify that for the input sequence

   $$X_1 X_2 = 00, \qquad 01, \qquad 11, \qquad 10, \qquad 00$$

   the output sequence is

   $$Z = 0, \qquad (1)\,(0)\,1, \qquad (0) \quad 1, \qquad \cancel{(1)}\,\cancel{(0)}\,0, \qquad (1) \quad 0$$

   Note that the transient outputs have been enclosed in parentheses. The sequence may be condensed by crossing out two of the transient outputs as indicated.

   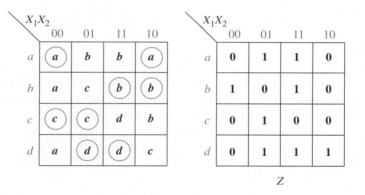

   Z

   (c) For Fig. 23–7, starting in stable total state $X_1 X_2 Q_1 Q_2 = 1100$, determine the complete output sequence (including transient outputs) for the input sequence 11, 10, 00, 01. Then write the sequence in condensed form.

   (d) If we start at some point in a network and can trace through a series of gates (in the direction of signal flow) and get back to the same point, we say that the network contains a *closed loop*. For the network of Fig. 23–9, find three closed loops that pass through point c.

   (e) For Fig. 23–9 indicate two possible choices for sets of 3 state variables other than a, c, and d.

   (f) Can "ripple" occur in a synchronous network? Explain.

4. Study Section 23.4, *Race Conditions and Cycles*.

   (a) Verify that the table given in Fig. 23–11 is correct for the given network.

   (b) Trace signals through the network of Fig. 23–11 for $X = 1$ and verify that a cycle occurs.

   (c) Find any race conditions which exist in the table of Fig. 23–7(b) and tell whether they are critical or noncritical.

   (d) Sketch the resulting timing diagrams for X, Q_1, and Q_2 for the given transition table if the input is changed from 1 to 0 while the network is in internal state 11 and
   (1) Q_1 changes before Q_2.
   (2) Q_2 changes before Q_1.
   (3) Q_1 and Q_2 change state simultaneously.

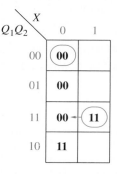

5. Work Problems 23.2, 23.4, 23.6, and 23.8. When drawing timing diagrams for asynchronous networks, exaggerate the time between successive variable changes and use dotted lines if necessary (as in Fig. 23–6) so that the order in which variable changes occur is clearly indicated.

6. When you are satisfied that you can meet the objectives of this unit, take the readiness test.

Analysis of Asynchronous Sequential Networks

23.1 Introduction

The sequential networks we have been studying so far fall in the category of *clocked synchronous networks*. In such networks, a change of state occurs only in response to a clock pulse. When this change of state requires several of the flip-flops to change state, they do so simultaneously because they are synchronized by the common clock pulse. Input changes are assumed to occur between clock pulses, and the output may be read during (or immediately preceding) the clock pulse. Thus the input and output must be in synchronization with the clock pulse. When interpreting the state table for clocked synchronous networks, it is understood that when the input changes, the network does not immediately change state, but rather the network enters the next state *only* upon receiving a subsequent clock pulse.

Although clocked synchronous sequential networks are very useful, there are many applications where they are not suitable. Three situations in which synchronous networks may be unsuitable are:

1. The network has inputs which may change at any time and which cannot be synchronized with a clock.
2. The network is large enough and the response of the logic elements fast enough so that the time taken for the signals to travel down the wires is significant; in this case it may be very difficult to assure that the clock pulse arrives at all flip-flops simultaneously as is necessary to assure proper synchronous operation.
3. We want the network to operate as fast as possible and do not want to have to wait for a clock pulse after the input changes.

In these cases, it may be necessary to use asynchronous sequential networks. As the name implies, the operation of the network is not synchronized by a common clock or other means. When an input change occurs, the state of the network can change almost immediately without waiting for a clock pulse. If several flip-flops must change state, there is no guarantee that they will change at the same time. In fact, we may deliberately design the asynchronous network so that a single input change may produce a sequence of state changes.

The design of asynchronous networks is more difficult than synchronous because of the timing problems involved. In a properly designed synchronous network, timing problems are eliminated because we wait long enough after the external input changes for all flip-flop inputs to reach a steady value before applying the clock pulse. However, for an asynchronous network, special design techniques will be required to eliminate timing problems resulting from unequal delays through various paths in the network. To simplify the analysis and design, we will assume that our asynchronous networks operate in the *fundamental mode*. Fundamental mode operation assumes that the input signals will be changed only when the circuit is in a stable condition, that is, only when no internal signals are changing.

In a fundamental mode network, all of the input signals are considered to be levels. In another type of asynchronous network, called *pulse mode,* the inputs are pulses rather than levels. Operation of pulse-mode networks is similar to that of clocked synchronous networks, except that state changes are triggered by the input pulses rather than by the clock. The following restrictions are usually placed on the input pulses to pulse-mode networks:

1. All input pulses must be of proper duration to trigger a flip-flop.

2. Separation between two successive input pulses (on the same or different input lines) must be sufficient so that the network has time to respond to one pulse before the next one occurs.

When the above restrictions are met, analysis and design of pulse mode networks is straightforward.[1]

23.2
Analysis of an Asynchronous Network with S-R Flip-Flops

In order to gain some insight into the performance of asynchronous sequential networks, we will first analyze the network of Fig. 23–2 by tracing signals using the input sequence $X_1X_2 = 00, 10, 11, 01, 11, 10, 00$.

In this analysis we will assume that the propagation delay in the flip-flops is much greater than the propagation delays in the gates. The timing problems which can result from gate delays will be considered in a later unit. The first column of Table 23–1 lists the present values of the input variables and flip-flop outputs at successive times during the analysis of the network starting with the initial input of $X_1X_2 = 00$ and the assumed starting state of $Q_1Q_2 = 00$. Each combination of values for the circuit inputs and memory outputs (flip-flop outputs in this case) will be called a *total state* of the network. To avoid confusion with the total state, we will often refer to the state of the flip-flops as the *internal state*. For each total state encountered in the analysis of Fig. 23–2, the outputs

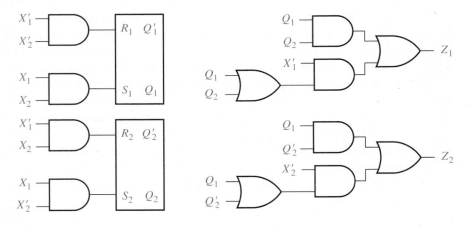

Figure 23–2
Asynchronous Delay Network

---

[1] For a discussion of the design of pulse-mode networks, see Hill and Peterson, *Introduction to Switching Theory and Logical Design,* 3rd ed., Chapter 11.

Table 23–1

Analysis of Fig. 23–2

Present Total State				Flip-Flop Inputs				Outputs		Next Internal State	
X_1	X_2	Q_1	Q_2	R_1	S_1	R_2	S_2	Z_1	Z_2	Q_1^+	Q_2^+
0	0	0	0	1	0	0	0	0	1	0	0
1	0	0	0	0	0	0	1	0	1	0	1
1	0	0	1	0	0	0	1	0	0	0	1
1	1	0	1	0	1	0	0	0	0	1	1
1	1	1	1	0	1	0	0	1	0	1	1
0	1	1	1	0	0	1	0	1	0	1	0
0	1	1	0	0	0	1	0	1	1	1	0
1	1	1	0	0	1	0	0	0	1	1	0
1	0	1	0	0	0	0	1	0	1	1	1
1	0	1	1	0	0	0	1	1	1	1	1
0	0	1	1	1	0	0	0	1	1	0	1
0	0	0	1	1	0	0	0	1	0	0	1

and flip-flop inputs are calculated using the equations

$$R_1 = X_1'X_2' \qquad S_1 = X_1X_2 \qquad R_2 = X_1'X_2 \qquad S_2 = X_1X_2'$$
$$Z_1 = Q_1Q_2 + X_1'(Q_1 + Q_2) \qquad Z_2 = Q_1Q_2' + X_2'(Q_1 + Q_2')$$

and the next internal states are determined from the flip-flop inputs. Thus for total state $X_1X_2Q_1Q_2 = 0000$, the next internal state is $Q_1^+Q_2^+ = 00$. If for a given total state, the next internal state is the same as the present internal state, no change of state will occur and we say that the network is in a *stable total state*. Thus total state $X_1X_2Q_1Q_2 = 0000$ is stable. When we change the input to 10, the network enters total state 1000 which is *unstable* since $Q_1^+Q_2^+ \neq Q_1Q_2$. Subsequently, Q_1Q_2 will change to 01, and the network enters total state 1001, which is stable. The input is then changed to 11 and the network enters total state 1101 which is unstable because $Q_1^+Q_2^+ \neq Q_1Q_2$ and the network will change to stable total state 1111 without any further input change. The analysis is continued in this manner as illustrated in Table 23–1. The stable total states have been underlined. Since we are assuming fundamental mode operation, the input is changed only when the total state is stable, never when it is unstable. The input and output sequences (from Table 23–1) are

$$X_1X_2 = 00, \quad 10, \quad 11, \quad 01, \quad 11, \quad 10, \quad 00$$
$$Z_1Z_2 = 01, \quad 00, \quad 10, \quad 11, \quad 01, \quad 11, \quad 10$$

Except for the initial output, the output for any stable total state is equal to the previous input; thus this network is referred to as an asynchronous delay.

Although the method of analysis illustrated in Table 23–1 is sufficient for analysis of small networks, it is more systematic to analyze the network using a state table. First a *transition* table is constructed which shows the next states of the flip-flops as a function of the present state and inputs. This table can be formed in the same manner as for synchronous networks by mapping the next-state equations for the network. For Fig. 23–2, the next-state equations are

$$Q_1^+ = S_1 + R_1'Q_1 = X_1X_2 + (X_1 + X_2)Q_1$$
$$Q_2^+ = S_2 + R_2'Q_2 = X_1X_2' + (X_1 + X_2')Q_2$$

These equations have been mapped in Fig. 23–3. Each column of this table corresponds to a specific combination of values of the input variables, or to an *input state*. Each row corresponds to a specific assignment of values to the memory variables, or to a present internal state. Each square in the table corresponds to a total state, and the entry in that square is the next internal state for that total state. For example, the square labeled "*a*" in Fig. 23–3 corresponds to a *present* total state $X_1X_2Q_1Q_2 = 1100$, and the corresponding next internal state is $Q_1^+Q_2^+ = 10$. Whenever the next internal state is the same as the present internal state (i.e., $Q_1^+Q_2^+ = Q_1Q_2$), the corresponding total state is stable; if $Q_1^+Q_2^+ \neq Q_1Q_2$, the corresponding total state is unstable. Stable total states are designated on the map by circling the corresponding next internal state entry. For example, in Fig. 23–3 total stable state $X_1X_2Q_1Q_2 = 1001$ has next internal state 01 circled since $Q_1^+Q_2^+ = Q_1Q_2 = 01$.

    A change of input state corresponds to a change between columns of the transition table without any row change. If the new total state is unstable, a row change (internal state change) takes place to the row with the corresponding next internal state. For example, starting in total state 0000 if the input is changed to 10 we change to the 10 column and then to the 01 row as indicated by the arrows on Fig. 23–3.

    The transition table may be converted to a state table in which each internal state or each stable total state is labeled with an arbitrary designation as in Fig. 23–4. The state table of Fig. 23–4(a) is used exactly like the state table for a clocked synchronous network except that for the synchronous case the internal state change does not occur when the input changes but rather when the clock pulse occurs, while for the asynchronous case the internal state change occurs immediately following the input change as fast as the network response will permit. The state table for an asynchronous network is often called a *flow*

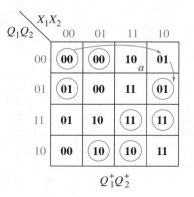

Figure 23–3
Transition Table for Fig. 23–2

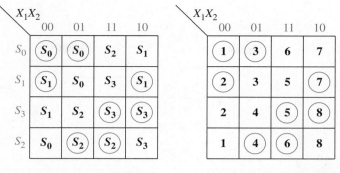

(a) Internal states labeled   (b) Stable total states labeled

Figure 23–4
Flow Tables for Fig. 23–2

table to emphasize this difference. In the flow table of Fig. 23–4(b), the rows are not numbered, but if an input change takes the network to an uncircled total state entry, the state changes to the corresponding circled (stable) total state entry. Figure 23–4(b) can be derived from Fig. 23–4(a) by giving each stable *total* state a distinct number and then filling in each unstable entry with the corresponding next total state.

The flow table, along with the output table, can be used to find the output sequence of the network for any given input sequence. The output table is derived in the usual manner by mapping the output equations. For example, for Fig. 23–2, we will find the output sequence, starting in total state 0000, given the input sequence

$$X_1 X_2 = 00, \quad 10, \quad 11, \quad 01, \quad 11, \quad 10, \quad 00$$

Using one of the flow tables from Fig. 23–4 along with the output table as shown in Fig. 23–5, we get

$$Z_1 Z_2 = 01, \quad 00, \quad 10, \quad 11, \quad 01, \quad 11, \quad 10$$

This sequence, illustrated by the arrows drawn on the flow table in Fig. 23–5, is the same as obtained by the analysis of Table 23–1.

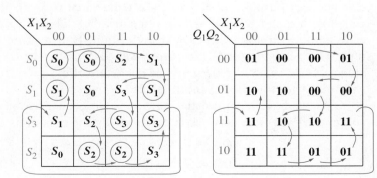

Figure 23–5
Flow Table and Output Table for Fig. 23–2

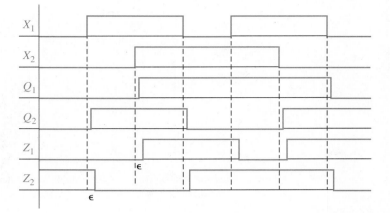

Figure 23–6
Timing Diagram for Fig. 23–2

The above input and output sequences are also illustrated on the timing diagram of Fig. 23–6 where ϵ is the response time for the output to change after the input changes. The value of ϵ may be different for each path through the network or for each state change associated with a given present state and input.

23.3
Analysis of an Asynchronous Gate Network

Construction of asynchronous networks using only gates and without using flip-flops or other explicit memory elements is often possible. Consider, for example, the network of Fig. 23–7 with the "delays" enclosed in dashed boxes not present. Note that there are two feedback paths from the OR gate outputs back to the AND gate inputs. We will associate the state variables Q_1 and Q_2 with these feedback paths. Each gate in the network has some delay associated with it, that is, the output will occur at some nonzero time after the corresponding gate input changes. For purposes of analysis, it is convenient to lump all of the delay associated with each feedback path into a single box labeled "delay". We then associate a state variable with each delay output. If at a given instant of time the input to a delay is 0 (or 1), the output will be 0 (or 1) after the delay time elapses. Hence the delay input represents the next state of the delay output and the delay with the Q_1 output has its input labeled Q_1^+.

Once we have identified the state variables, construction of the flow table is straightforward. The network is described by the equations

$$Q_1^+ = X_1 X_2' + X_1' X_2 Q_2 + X_2 Q_1 Q_2'$$
$$Q_2^+ = X_1' X_2 Q_1' + X_1 Q_2 + X_2 Q_2$$
$$Z = X_1 \oplus Q_1 \oplus Q_2$$

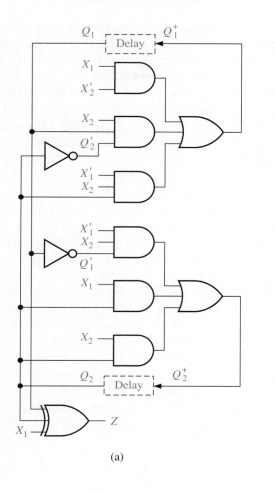

(a)

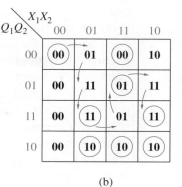

(b)

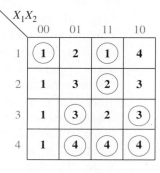

(c)

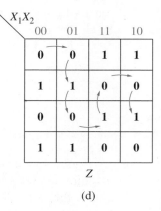

Z

(d)

Figure 23–7
Asynchronous Network Constructed from Gates

These equations are plotted in Figs. 23–7(b) and (d), and the flow table of Fig. 23–7(c) is constructed by replacing each combination of state variables with a state symbol. Circled entries represent stable total states. For any given input sequence, the state and output sequences can be determined from Figs. 23–7(b) or (c), and (d). Starting in total state $X_1X_2Q_1Q_2 = 0000$ if the input is changed to 01, the internal state will change to 01 and then to 11. Note that a single input change produces two internal state changes before a stable total state is reached.[2] If the input is next changed to 11, the network goes to unstable total state 1111 and then to stable state 1101. An input change to 10 will then take the network to unstable total state 1001 followed by stable total state 1011. The output sequence, as indicated on the map of Fig. 23–7(d), is 0 (0) (1) 0 (1) 0 (0) 1, where the outputs in parentheses correspond to unstable total states. Since two successive outputs which are the same cannot be distinguished by an asynchronous network, the output sequence can be condensed to the form 0 (1) 0 (1) 0 1. This sequence has two transient 1 outputs which occur when the network is switching between stable states. Such transient outputs can be eliminated by proper design of the output network as described in Section 25.4.

The best choice of state variables for analysis of an asynchronous network is not always obvious. State variables should be chosen so that if we cut the branch associated with each state variable, all of the closed loops (feedback loops) in the network will be opened. If explicit delays and flip-flops are present, we must associate a state variable with each delay and flip-flop output. If cutting the branches associated with these outputs does not open all closed loops, then additional state variable branches must be chosen. Generally, we wish to choose a minimum set of branches which, when cut, will open all of the remaining closed loops. When such state variable branches have been chosen, a dummy delay element may be placed in each branch (as in Fig. 23–7) in order to define Q^+ and Q. There are often several ways of choosing state variable branches, and a judicious choice will simplify the analysis. As indicated in Fig. 23–8, if a gate output fans out to connect to several gate inputs, the state variable branch should normally be chosen directly at the gate output rather than in one of the fanning branches.

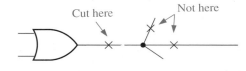

Figure 23–8
Selection of State Variable Branch

Figure 23–9 shows an asynchronous network to be analyzed. If we make cuts at points e and f, it would still be necessary to make two additional cuts (at a and c, for example) in order to open all closed loops. This would then require four state variables. More careful inspection of the circuit shows that making cuts at points a, c, and d will open all closed loops and only three state variables are required. For purposes of analysis, delay elements may be inserted at points a, c, and d in order to define the state variables (Q_1, Q_2, and Q_3). The next states and outputs can then be written as functions of X, Q_1, Q_2, and Q_3.

Figure 23–10 shows a general model for an asynchronous sequential network. The delays may either represent the lumped effect of the gate delays in the

[2] When a single input change produces two or more successive internal state changes, this is sometimes referred to as "ripple" because the effect of the input change ripples through the network to produce a sequence of state changes.

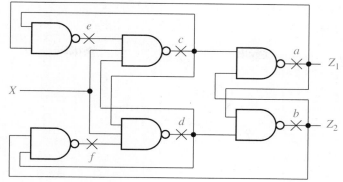

Figure 23–9
Asynchronous Network to be Analyzed

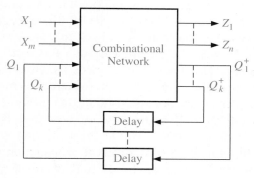

Figure 23–10
General Model for an Asynchronous Sequential
Network

combinational network, or they may represent explicit delays added to the network. This model is similar to the general model for a synchronous network (Section 13.4) except that no method is provided for synchronizing the operation of the delays. Thus a single input change may propagate through the different feedback paths at different times. This may cause timing problems that result in improper operation of the network. Such timing problems are discussed in Section 23.4 and in Unit 26. These timing problems are avoided in a synchronous network by synchronizing the operation of the delays with a clock.

23.4
Race Conditions and Cycles

Consider the network of Fig. 23–11(a) with its corresponding transition table. Note that there is only one stable total state, $XQ_1Q_2 = 000$. If we start in this stable state, then let X change from 0 to 1, we get the condition of Fig. 23–11(c).

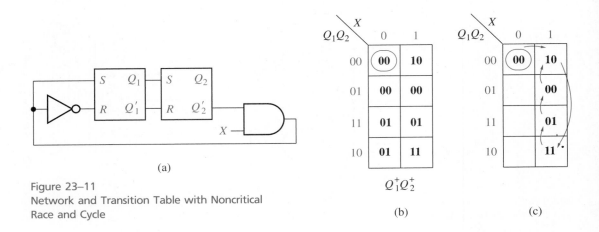

Figure 23–11
Network and Transition Table with Noncritical
Race and Cycle

Immediately after X changes, the present state is 00 and the next state is 10. As soon as the circuit switches to state 10, the next state is 11. From state 11, the network switches to 01 and then back to state 00, all with no further changes in the input. In fact, the circuit will cycle through the unstable states until X is made 0 again. This type of behavior is therefore called a *cycle*.

If X is changed back to 0 when the circuit is in internal state 10, several state change sequences are possible as indicated in Fig. 23–12. When the present internal state is $Q_1Q_2 = 10$ and $X = 0$, the next state should be $Q_1^+ Q_2^+ = 01$. That is, Q_1 should change from 1 to 0 at the same time Q_2 changes from 0 to 1. Since different flip-flops may have different propagation delays, it is possible for Q_2 to change to 1 before Q_1 can change to 0, in which case the circuit is momentarily in the $Q_1Q_2 = 11$ row of the flow table. Then the next state is 01, so the circuit goes to the $Q_1Q_2 = 01$ row, and from there to stable state 00. If the two flip-flops had changed simultaneously, the circuit would have gone directly from state 10 to 01, and then on to 00. If in state 10, Q_1 changes to 0 before Q_2 changes, the network will go directly to state 00.

Whenever two or more flip-flops must change state in response to a single change in input, the result is a *race condition* between the flip-flops. If the resulting

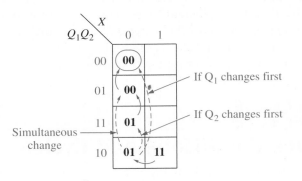

Figure 23–12
Noncritical Race

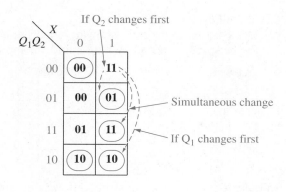

Figure 23–13
Flow Table with Critical Race

stable state is the same no matter in what order the flip-flops change, as in the above example, it is called a *noncritical* race. If it is possible to end up in two or more different stable states depending on the order in which the flip-flops change state, then it is a *critical* race.

The flow table of Fig. 23–13 illustrates a critical race. Starting in total state $XQ_1Q_2 = 000$, if X is changed to 1 both Q_1 and Q_2 are required to change from 0 to 1. However, if Q_2 changes to 1 before Q_1 due to unequal propagation delays, the network will get "stuck" in stable total state 101 and no further state change will occur. On the other hand, if Q_1 changes first the internal state becomes 10 and the network will get stuck in total state 110. Hence the race is critical because the network will go to the proper next state only if both Q_1 and Q_2 change simultaneously.

Several distinct differences between asynchronous and clocked circuits are evident in the networks analyzed in this unit. First, for asynchronous circuits, state changes occur as soon as the input change propagates through the network so that each possible input change must be taken into account when designing asynchronous networks. In a clocked circuit, many input changes may occur between clock pulses, but only the final input value before the clock pulse influences the next state. Also, in asynchronous networks several state changes may occur in response to a single input change. An input sequence like 00, 00, 01, 01, 11 is recognized as a sequence of 5 inputs by a synchronous network; however, since an asynchronous network responds only to input changes, it would treat the above sequence as if it were 00, 01, 11.

PROBLEMS

23.1 For the given flow table,
   (a) find all critical races and tell why they are critical,
   (b) find all noncritical races, and

(c) find all cycles.
(d) Draw a timing diagram showing what happens to Q_1, Q_2, and Z when the network is started in state b and the input is changed from 01 to 00.

	$X_1 X_2$				Z			
$Q_1 Q_2$	00	01	11	10	00	01	11	10
00	ⓐ	c	b	c	0	0	0	0
01	c	ⓑ	ⓑ	d	1	0	1	0
11	d	ⓒ	b	d	0	1	0	0
10	c	ⓓ	b	ⓓ	1	1	0	0

23.2 Initially, $Q_1 = Q_2 = 0$. Construct a flow table for the following network, and use this flow table to determine the shortest input sequence for $X_1 X_2$ which will give an output of $Z = 1$. (A simultaneous change of input variables is not allowed.)

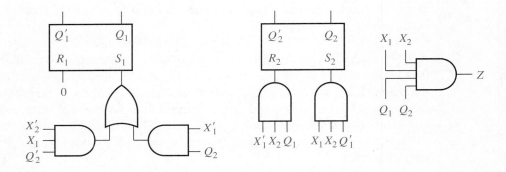

23.3 For the following network, construct a flow table and determine the output sequence. The initial state is 00 and the input sequence is $X_1 X_2 = 00, 01, 11, 10, 00$.

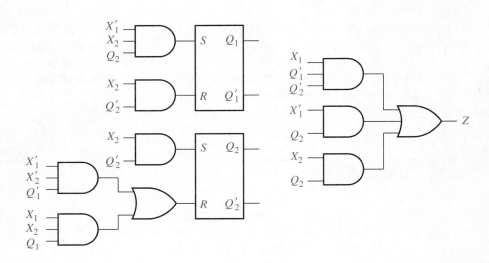

23.4 Construct a flow table for the following network and describe what happens
when X is changed from 0 to 1. If the network is started with $Q_1 = Q_2 = 0$,
how can an output of $Z = 1$ be obtained? Draw a timing diagram showing
$X, Q_1, Q_2,$ and Z indicating the time at which X must change in order to get
an output $Z = 1$.

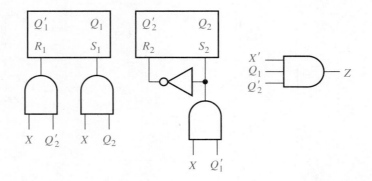

23.5 Repeat Problem 23.4 for the following network.

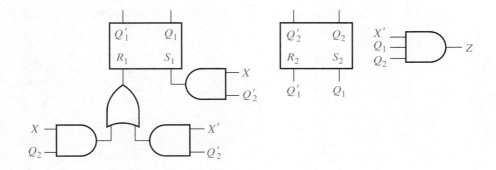

23.6 Analyze the following network using a flow table. What is the output sequence
for the following input sequence: $X_1 X_2 = 00, 10, 11, 01, 11, 10, 00, 01, 00$?
Indicate transients, if any, in parentheses.

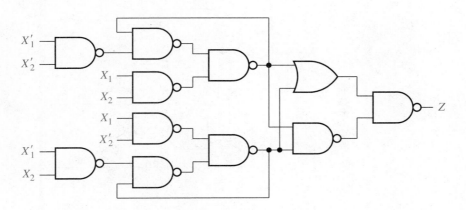

23.7 Analyze the following network using a flow table. What is the output sequence for the following input sequence: $X_1 X_2 = 00, 01, 11, 10, 00, 01, 00, 10$? Indicate transients, if any, in parentheses.

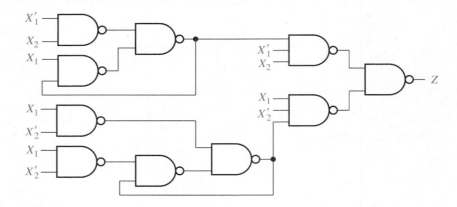

23.8 (a) Analyze the following asynchronous network using a flow table. Starting in the stable total state for which $X = Z = 0$, determine the state and output sequences when the input sequence is $X = 0, 1, 0, 1, 0, 1 \ldots$
(b) Are there any races in the flow table? If so, are they critical races?

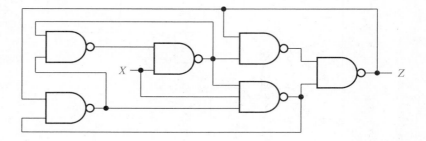

23.9 Work Problem 23.8 for the given asynchronous network.

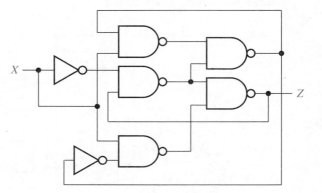

24

Derivation and Reduction of Primitive Flow Tables

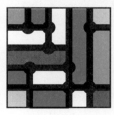

OBJECTIVES

Carry out the following steps in the synthesis of a fundamental mode asynchronous sequential network:

1. Derive a *primitive* flow table from the problem statement.

2. Reduce the flow table to a minimum number of rows.

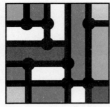

STUDY GUIDE

1. Study Section 24.1, *Derivation of Primitive Flow Tables.*

   (a) Define a *primitive* flow table.

   (b) For a primitive table, why must every allowable input change result in a state change?

   (c) For Table 24–3, why are there two different stable total states with the same output in column 01?

   (d) Why is there exactly one dash in each row of the table?

   (e) Study *Example 2*. Take a sheet of paper and construct the table of Fig. 24–2 row by row making sure you understand the reason for each entry.

   (f) Study *Example 3*. Verify that the output sequences obtained from Table 24–5 are correct for the various input waveforms indicated in Fig. 24–3.

2. Study Section 24.2, *Reduction of Primitive Flow Tables.*

   (a) What is the difference in the definition of equivalent internal states and equivalent stable total states?

   (b) Why is it possible to ignore the outputs when constructing the merger diagram for a reduced primitive flow table?

(c) Consider the following merger diagram. Find four different ways of merging to obtain a minimum-row table (3 rows).

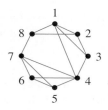

(d) Work Programmed Exercise 24.1.

3. Work Problems 24.3, 24.5, 24.6, 24.7(a), and 24.8.

4. When you are satisfied that you can meet the objectives of this unit, take the readiness test.

Derivation and Reduction of Primitive Flow Tables

The basic design procedure for asynchronous networks is similar to that for synchronous networks. First a state (or flow) table is constructed from the problem statement, then the table is reduced to a minimum number of rows, a state assignment is made, and the table is realized using appropriate logic elements. However, the details of each step are somewhat different for asynchronous networks.

24.1
Derivation of Primitive Flow Tables

The starting point for asynchronous synthesis is usually a *primitive* flow table. The primitive flow table is defined as a flow table which has exactly one stable total state per row. The primitive table can usually be reduced to a table with fewer rows. However, in order to be sure of obtaining a final reduced table with a minimum number of rows, for most problems it is necessary to start with the primitive table rather than trying to construct the reduced table directly.

The following examples illustrate construction of the primitive flow table from the problem statement. To avoid the timing problems which can result when two input variables change simultaneously, we will assume that only one input variable changes at a time and the input changes are spaced so that the network will always reach a stable total state between changes (fundamental mode operation). When constructing a *primitive* flow table, every change in input must result in a state change since only one stable state per row is allowed.

EXAMPLE 1   An asynchronous network has two inputs and one output. The input sequence $X_1X_2 = 00, 01, 11$ causes the output to become 1. The next input change then causes the output to return to 0. No other input sequence will produce a 1 output.

The first row of the flow table (Table 24–1) is constructed as follows. Stable total state ① represents a reset state in which the input is 00. If the input changes to 01, we change to stable total state ② to indicate the sequence 00, 01 has been received, and similarly if the input changes to 10, we change to ③. Note that each time the input changes we go through *one* unstable total state on the way to the corresponding stable total state. The dash in the third column indicates that the double input change, 00 to 11, is not allowed.

We then fill in rows 2 and 3 of the table (Table 24–2). Starting in ②, an input change 01 to 00 causes a return to the reset state (①) since 00 starts the desired sequence over again. From ②, an input change 01 to 11 completes the desired input sequence, so we go to ④ with an output $Z = 1$. Starting in ③, an input change 10 to 00 resets the network to ①. From ③, an input change 10 to 11 does *not* complete the desired sequence so we cannot go to ④ which has a 1 output. Therefore, we introduce a new state in the 11 column (⑤) which has a zero output. The dashes in rows 2 and 3 are present because double input changes 01 to 10 and 10 to 01 are not allowed.

Next we fill in rows 4 and 5, and then add row 6 to complete the primitive table (Table 24–3). Starting in ④ an input change 11 to 01 must change the output to 0, but we cannot go to ② because we should not get another 1 output until the circuit resets. Therefore, in the 01 column we introduce a new state (⑥) with 0 output. From ④, a 11 to 10 change must change the output to 0;

Table 24–1 _____

		00	01	11	10	Z
		\multicolumn{4}{c}{X_1X_2}	
(reset)	1	①	2	–	3	0
(00, 01)	2		②			0
(00, 10)	3				③	0

Table 24–2 _____

		00	01	11	10	Z
(reset)	1	①	2	–	3	0
(00, 01)	2	1	②.	4	–	0
(00, 10)	3	1	–	5	③	0
(00, 01, 11)	4			④		1
(00, 10, 11)	5			⑤		0

Table 24–3
Primitive Flow Table

		X_1X_2				Z
		00	01	11	10	
(reset)	1	①	2	–	3	0
(00, 01)	2	1	②	4	–	0
*	3	1	–	5	③	0
(00, 01, 11)	4	–	6	④	3	1
*	5	–	6	⑤	3	0
*	6	1	⑥	5	–	0

*These states cannot lead to a 1 output without first resetting.

in this case we can go to ③ since ③ cannot lead to a 1 output without resetting first. Starting in ⑤, we cannot get a 1 output without resetting so a change to input 01 or 10 can take us to state 6 or 3, respectively. Starting in ⑥, a change to input 00 resets the circuit and a change to 11 takes us back to state ⑤.

Figure 24–1 shows the state diagram for the primitive flow table (Table 24–3). Note that on the state diagram for a primitive table all arrows leading into a given state must have the same input.

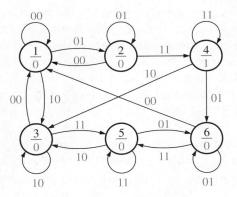

Figure 24–1
State Diagram for Primitive Flow Table

EXAMPLE 2 This example illustrates the design of an edge-triggered clocked T flip-flop shown in Fig. 24–2(a). Although this flip-flop is used as a component in synchronous networks, the internal design of the flip-flop is an asynchronous problem. The flip-flop has two inputs, T and P. The flip-flop will change state if $T = 1$ when the clock (P) changes from 1 to 0. Under all other input conditions, Q should remain constant. We will assume that T and P do not change simultaneously.

Figure 24–2(b) shows the primitive flow table. Because the table is primitive, the state must change each time the input changes. In this example, there is one

			TP				Q
			00	01	11	10	
(TP = 00)	1		①	2	–	3	0
(TP = 01)	2		1	②	4	–	0
(TP = 10)	3		1	–	4	③	0
(TP = 11)	4		–	2	④	5	0
(TP = 10)	5		6	–	7	⑤	1
(TP = 00)	6		⑥	8	–	5	1
(TP = 11)	7		–	8	⑦	3	1
(TP = 01)	8		6	⑧	7	–	1

Figure 24–2   (a) clocked T flip-flop   (b) primitive flow table

stable total state for each combination of values of T, P, and Q. The values of T and P associated with each stable total state have been listed beside the corresponding rows for reference. Note that the output (Q) only changes when the input changes from $TP = 11$ to 10.

EXAMPLE 3   A clock signal (C) is to be gated on and off by another signal (S). The gating network must be such that only complete clock pulses appear at the output (Z) even though S may change in the middle of a clock pulse. Figure 24–3 shows the timing diagram for the network to be designed. Even though a clock is present, this is an asynchronous problem because the input S is allowed to change at any time with respect to the clock. We will assume that S will always be on or off for at least two complete clock pulses.

The flow table can be derived as follows (Table 24–4). Starting in state ① if C goes to 1 and back to 0, we go to state ② and back to ① with no change in output. From state ①, if S goes to 1, we go to state ③ and wait for C to go to 1.

Then when C goes to 1, we go to state ④ with a 1 output. As C goes to 0 we go back to ③, with a 0 output. We then cycle back and forth between ③ and ④ as C turns on and off. This action continues until S goes to 0. If S goes to 0 in state ③, we can immediately reset to state ①. However, if S goes to 0 in state ④ we must wait until the termination of the input clock pulse before Z goes to 0; therefore, we go to ⑤ to maintain the 1 output. From ⑤, the next input change must be C going to 0, in which case we reset to ①. To complete

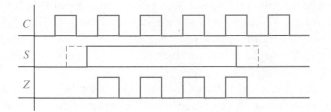

Figure 24–3

Table 24–4

	CS				
	00	01	11	10	Z
1	①	3		2	0
2	1			②	0
3		③	4		0
4		3	④		1

Table 24–5

	CS				
	00	01	11	10	Z
1	①	3	–	2	0
2	1	–	6	②	0
3	1	③	4	–	0
4	–	3	④	5	1
5	1	–	–	⑤	1
6	–	3	⑥	–	0

the flow table (Table 24–5), we must consider the case where S turns on in the middle of a clock pulse. From ② we go to ⑥ and wait for C to go to 0 (we can't go to ④ because we don't want Z to become 1 until the next clock pulse). From ⑥, we then go to ③, so that Z can be cycled on and off as C goes on and off. If we assume that double changes of input cannot occur, the remaining table entries are don't cares. Note that in ⑤, the input change 10 to 11 cannot occur since S is assumed to be off for at least two clock pulses.

24.2
Reduction of Primitive Flow Tables

After formulation of the primitive flow table, the next step in the synthesis of an asynchronous sequential network is reduction of the flow table to a minimum number of rows. This reduction will usually reduce the number of state variables required to realize the table. In general, this will make it easier to complete the design of the network and will reduce the amount of logic required.

Two methods of reducing the primitive flow table are possible. The first method requires two steps—first a minimum-row *primitive* flow table is found, and then this table is further reduced by merging rows. The second method carries out the complete reduction in one step by applying the general reduction method for incompletely specified state tables.[1] The first method is generally less work to carry out and will be discussed here.

---

[1] See Hill and Peterson, *Introduction to Switching Theory and Logical Design*, 3rd ed., Chapters 13 and 14.

A minimum-row *primitive* flow table can be found by eliminating redundant stable total states. To do this, we must find equivalent stable total states. Two stable total states are equivalent iff they have the same inputs and the associated internal states are equivalent. Thus two stable total states are equivalent if (1) their inputs are the same, (2) their outputs are the same, and (3) their next states are equivalent for each possible next input. The following example illustrates determination of equivalent stable total states.

We will reduce Table 24–6 to obtain a minimum-row primitive flow table. From the first column (input 00) states ②, ⑥, and ⑧ have the same outputs. From the second column ⑤ amd ⑫ have the same outputs, from the third column ③ and ⑩ do, and from the last column ④ and ⑪ do. Therefore the sets of potentially equivalent states are

$$(2, 6, 8) \quad (5, 12) \quad (3, 10) \quad (4, 11)$$

Next we examine the next states of the states in each group. With input 01, the next states of ② and ⑥ are 5 and 7. Since $5 \neq 7$, $② \neq ⑥$. Similarly, the next states of ⑥ and ⑧ are 7 and 12. Since $7 \neq 12$, $⑥ \neq ⑧$. However, for ② and ⑧, with input 01 the next states are 5 and 12, and with input 10 both next states are 4. For ⑤ and ⑫, both next states are 6 for input 00, and both are 9 for input 11. For ③ and ⑩, both next states are 7 for input 01, and the next states are 4 and 11 for input 10. Finally for ④ and ⑪ the next states are 2 and 8, and 3 and 10, for inputs 00 and 11, respectively. Since we have found no additional nonequivalent states, the remaining sets of equivalent states are

$$(2, 8) \quad (5, 12) \quad (3, 10) \quad (4, 11)$$

Table 24–6
Primitive Table to be Reduced

	X_1X_2				Z_1Z_2
	00	01	11	10	
1	①	7	–	4	1 1
2	②	5	–	4	0 1
3	–	7	③	11	1 0
4	2	–	3	④	0 0
5	6	⑤	9	–	1 1
6	⑥	7	–	11	0 1
7	1	⑦	14	–	1 0
8	⑧	12	–	4	0 1
9	–	7	⑨	13	0 1
10	–	7	⑩	4	1 0
11	8	–	10	⑪	0 0
12	6	⑫	9	–	1 1
13	8	–	14	⑬	1 1
14	–	12	⑭	11	0 0

Table 24–7
_____

Reduced Primitive Table for Table 24–6

	00	01	11	10	
1	①	7	–	4	11
2	②	5	–	4	01
3	–	7	③	4	10
4	2	–	3	④	00
5	6	⑤	9	–	11
6	⑥	7	–	4	01
7	1	⑦	14	–	10
9	–	7	⑨	13	01
13	2	–	14	⑬	11
14	–	5	⑭	4	00

After eliminating redundant states 8, 10, 11, and 12, the reduced primitive flow table is given by Table 24–7.

Next, we will return to the primitive flow tables derived for Examples 1 and 2 of this unit to determine if these tables can be reduced. For the primitive table of Table 24–3, the only stable total states with the same inputs and outputs are ② and ⑥. The next states of ② and ⑥ for input 11 are 4 and 5. Since 4 ≢ 5, ② ≢ ⑥, and there are no equivalent stable total states. Therefore, this primitive table already has a minimum number of rows.

For the primitive table of Fig. 24–2, since states ① and ⑥ have different outputs, as do states ② and ⑧, ④ and ⑦, and ③ and ⑤, there are no equivalent stable total states.

Each of the minimum-row primitive tables discussed above can be further reduced by merging rows. So far, all of the primitive tables we have worked with have been in Moore form (output a function of the present state only). We can proceed to merge rows in the Moore table, or first convert the Moore table to a Mealy table. The latter procedure is generally preferable since it sometimes leads to a reduced table with fewer rows.

For Table 24–3, the corresponding Mealy form is given in Table 24–8. The Mealy table is formed from the Moore table by associating the output for each row with the corresponding stable total state in that row.[2] Thus for row 2, stable state ② is in the 01 column, so the corresponding output of 0 is placed in the 01 column of the Mealy output table. After all of the outputs associated with stable states have been filled in, the remaining outputs are temporarily left unspecified (as indicted by the dashes in the output table). When the network is in a stable state, the outputs from the Mealy and Moore tables will be identical. After the Mealy table has been reduced and a state assignment has been made,

_____

[2] This type of Moore-Mealy conversion applies only to asynchronous tables. A different conversion procedure is used for synchronous tables because of timing differences.

Table 24–8

Primitive Mealy Flow Table for Table 24–3

	X_1X_2							
	00	01	11	10	00	01	11	10
1	①	2	–	3	0	–	–	–
2	1	②	4	–	–	0	–	–
3	1	–	5	③	–	–	–	0
4	–	6	④	3	–	–	1	–
5	–	6	⑤	3	–	–	0	–
6	1	⑥	5	–	–	0	–	–

the outputs associated with unstable states will be filled in to avoid transients in the output.

After all redundant stable total states have been removed from the primitive table, we will call the resulting table a *reduced primitive flow table*. Two rows of a *reduced* primitive Mealy flow table are compatible and can be merged into a single row iff there are no state conflicts in any column. Thus for Table 24–8 rows 1 and 2 can be merged because column 00 contains ① and 1, column 01 contains 2 and ②, 11 contains – and 4, and 10 contains 3 and –. Merging rows 1 and 2 yields

	00	01	11	10	00	01	11	10
1, 2	①	②	4	3	0	0	–	–

Note that a stable total state and the corresponding unstable state were merged to form a stable total state. Thus, in the (1, 2) row, an input change of 00 to 01 takes us directly from ① to ②, while in the original table the change between stable states ① and ② goes through an intermediate unstable total state 2. Rows 2 and 3 of Table 24–8 cannot be merged because of the state conflict in column 11. (We already know that ④ ≢ ⑤ because all redundant stable total states have been removed from the table.)

To facilitate selection of rows to be merged, we will draw a *merger diagram* (Fig. 24–4). In this diagram, we draw a line between any pair of states which are compatible and can be merged. To form this merger diagram, we first compare

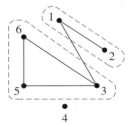

Figure 24–4

Merger Diagram for Table 24–8

row 1 of the reduced primitive table with rows 2 through 6 and find that row 1 is compatible with row 2 and with row 3. Row 2 is then compared with rows 3 through 6, and no further compatible rows are found. Comparing row 3 with rows 4, 5, and 6 shows that 3 and 5 are compatible as are 3 and 6. Row 4 is compatible with neither 5 nor 6, and finally rows 5 and 6 are compatible. The merger diagram indicates that the following row mergers are possible: (1, 2), (1, 3), and (3, 5, 6). Note that 1, 2, and 3 cannot be merged together since 2 and 3 are not compatible. We can form a 3-row table (Table 24–9) by merging rows (1, 2) and (3, 5, 6). To complete the reduced table, the don't cares in the output part of the table must be filled in using the procedure described in Section 25.4.

For a given input sequence, the sequence of stable total states and the output sequence will be the same for the reduced primitive table (Table 24–8) and the final reduced flow table (Table 24–9). The only difference is that in the primitive table every change between stable states goes through an intermediate unstable state, but in the final table some transitions between some stable total states are direct.

When two rows of the reduced primitive Mealy flow table are merged, there will never be any conflicts between outputs. The reason for this is that the outputs are only associated with the *stable* total states. Since we never merge two rows with different *stable* total states in the same column, there are never any output conflicts. Consequently, we can completely ignore the output part of the reduced primitive flow table when merging rows, and then fill in the Mealy output table after the rows have been merged.

Returning to the reduced primitive table of Table 24–7, and comparing each row with all of the following rows, we see that row 1 can merge with 3 and 7, row 2 with 4 and 14, and row 3 with 4 and 6. From the corresponding merger diagram (Fig. 24–5(a)) we can merge rows (1, 7), (2, 4), and (3, 6) to form a 7-row table (Fig. 24–5(b)). Then we form the Mealy output table by entering the output associated with each stable total state. Thus state ① has output 11, ② has output 01, etc.

The minimum-row flow table is generally not unique. Figure 24–6(a) gives the merger diagram for Fig. 24–2. Either of the following mergers will give a 4-row table:

$$(1, 2, 3) \quad (4) \quad (5, 6, 8) \quad (7) \quad \text{or} \quad (1, 3) \quad (2, 4) \quad (5, 6) \quad (7, 8)$$

Using the first merger, the table can be reduced to Fig. 24–6(b).

Table 24–9

Reduced Table for Table 24–8

		00	01	11	10	00	01	11	10
a	(1, 2)	①	②	4	3	0	0	–	–
b	(3, 5, 6)	1	⑥	⑤	③	–	0	0	0
c	4	–	6	④	3	–	–	1	–

		X_1X_2							
		00	01	11	10	00	01	11	10
a	(1, 7)	①	⑦	14	4	11	10	–	–
b	(2, 4)	②	5	3	④	01	–	–	00
c	(3, 6)	⑥	7	③	4	01	–	10	–
d	5	6	⑤	9	–	–	11	–	–
e	9	–	7	⑨	13	–	–	01	–
f	13	2	–	14	⑬	–	–	–	11
g	14	–	5	⑭	4	–	–	00	–

$$Z_1Z_2$$

Figure 24–5   (a) merger diagram   (b) reduced table

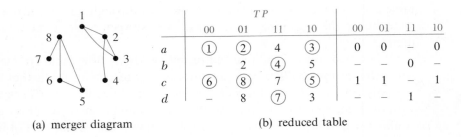

	TP							
	00	01	11	10	00	01	11	10
a	①	②	4	③	0	0	–	0
b	–	2	④	5	–	–	0	–
c	⑥	⑧	7	⑤	1	1	–	1
d	–	8	⑦	3	–	–	1	–

Figure 24–6   (a) merger diagram   (b) reduced table

In summary, a primitive flow table can be reduced to a minimum-row Mealy table using the following procedure:

1. Find a reduced *primitive* flow table by eliminating redundant stable total states:
   (a) Write down the sets of stable total states which have the same input and output. The states in each set are potentially equivalent.
   (b) Let S_i and S_j be a pair of potentially equivalent states found in (a). Determine the next states when the input is changed to column X_k. These next states are $\delta(S_i, X_k)$ and $\delta(S_j, X_k)$. If $\delta(S_i, X_k)$ and $\delta(S_j, X_k)$ are not in the same one of the sets found in (a), then $\delta(S_i, X_k) \neq \delta(S_j, X_k)$ and consequently $S_i \neq S_j$. In this manner check each set of states found in (a) for each possible input change and eliminate the nonequivalent states. Repeat this process until all nonequivalent states have been found and only sets of equivalent states remain.
   (c) Using the sets of equivalent states found in (b), construct a reduced primitive table using only one state from each set.
2. Construct a minimum-row Mealy flow table from the reduced primitive table found in step 1(c):
   (a) Compare each row of the reduced primitive table with all of the succeeding rows and construct a merger diagram. If there are no state conflicts between a pair of rows, these rows are compatible and a line is drawn between the corresponding row numbers on the merger diagram.

(b) Select a minimum set of merged rows from the merger diagram and merge the corresponding rows of the reduced primitive table to form a minimum-row table.

(c) Construct a Mealy output table for the minimum row table by associating the appropriate output with each stable total state.

The procedure outlined above will always reduce a primitive table to a minimum number of rows provided that the only don't cares in the original table arise from forbidden input changes (for example, if only single input variable changes are allowed). If the original table contains don't cares which arise from other conditions, use of the more general procedure for reduction of incompletely specified state tables may be necessary.

In this unit we have specified only the outputs associated with the stable total states in the minimum-row Mealy flow table. After making a state assignment using the methods discussed in Unit 25, we will fill in the unspecified entries so as to avoid unwanted transients in the network output. In some cases, the flow table must be modified in order to make a proper state assignment. For this reason, it is usually desirable to wait to complete the output table until the state assignment has been made.

PROGRAMMED EXERCISE 24.1

Cover the bottom of each page with a sheet of paper and slide it down as you check your answers.

This example illustrates the process of reducing a primitive flow table to a minimum number of rows using the procedure described on page 618.

(a) For the given state table, list the sets of potentially equivalent stable total states. (Total states in each set must have the same inputs and outputs.)

	X_1X_2				Z
	00	01	11	10	
1	①	2	3	4	0
2	8	②	7	9	1
3	1	2	③	9	0
4	1	6	7	④	1
5	⑤	6	7	4	0
6	5	⑥	3	4	1
7	8	2	⑦	9	0
8	⑧	2	3	4	0
9	5	10	3	⑨	1
10	1	⑩	7	9	0
11	5	10	⑪	4	0

Answer to (a):   (1, 5, 8)   (2, 6)   (3, 7, 11)   (4, 9)

(b) For convenience in checking the next states, we will rewrite the state table with the potentially equivalent states grouped together. (This step is not necessary, but for large tables it may be helpful.)

	00	01	11	10
1	①	2	3	4
5	⑤	6	7	4
8	⑧	2	3	4
2	8	②	7	9
6	5	⑥	3	4
3	1	2	③	9
7	8	2	⑦	9
11	5	10	⑪	4
4	1	6	7	④
9	5	10	3	⑨

Are the next states of (1, 5, 8) potentially equivalent for the 01 column?

_____

For the 11 column? _____

For the 10 column? _____

Are the next states of (2, 6) potentially equivalent for all columns?

_____

Are the next states of (3, 7, 11) potentially equivalent for all columns?

_____

At this point, can you conclude that any of the pairs (3, 7), (3, 11), (7, 11) are

not equivalent? _____

What can you say about the equivalence of 4 and 9? _____

Why? _____

List the sets of states which are still potentially equivalent:

Answers to (b): Yes; Yes; Yes; Yes; No; $2 \not\equiv 10$, so $3 \not\equiv 11$ and $7 \not\equiv 11$; $4 \not\equiv 9$ because $6 \not\equiv 10$; (1, 5, 8) (2, 6) (3, 7)

(c) Since we found some nonequivalent states in (b), we must recheck the potentially equivalent states listed above.

At this point, are the next states of (1, 5, 8) potentially equivalent for all

columns? _____

What can you say about the equivalence of states 2 and 6? _____

Why? _____

At this point, are 3 and 7 still potentially equivalent? _____

List the sets of states which are still potentially equivalent:

Answers to (c):   Yes; $2 \not\equiv 6$ because $4 \not\equiv 9$;   Yes;   (1, 5, 8)   (3, 7)

(d) Since we found some nonequivalent states in (c), we are not done yet.

Are any of the pairs (1, 5), (1, 8), (5, 8), (3, 7) not equivalent? _____

Why? _____

At this point we have eliminated all pairs of nonequivalent stable total states.

Which pairs of equivalent stable total states remain?

_____

Answers to (d): $1 \not\equiv 5$ and $5 \not\equiv 8$ because $2 \not\equiv 6$; $1 \equiv 8$ and $3 \equiv 7$

(e) Write out the minimum row primitive flow table by eliminating states 7 and 8 from the original table.

	X_1X_2				
	00	01	11	10	Z
1					
2					
3					
4					
5					
6					
9					
10					
11					

Answer to (e):

	X_1X_2				
	00	01	11	10	
1	①	2	3	4	0
2	1	②	3	9	1
3	1	2	③	9	0
4	1	6	3	④	1
5	⑤	6	3	4	0
6	5	⑥	3	4	1
9	5	10	3	⑨	1
10	1	⑩	3	9	0
11	5	10	⑪	4	0

(f) Although the above table is a minimum-row *primitive* flow table, we can convert it to a nonprimitive Mealy flow table by merging rows. Using a merger diagram, indicate which rows in the above table can be merged.

Merge appropriate rows in the above table and give the merged rows below (including the corresponding rows of the Mealy output table).

Answer to (f):

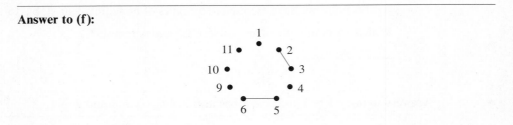

Note that rows 2 and 3 can be merged in spite of the fact that row 2 has a 1 output and row 3 has a 0 output. The merged rows are:

$$1 \quad ② \quad ③ \quad 9 \mid - \quad 1 \quad 0 \quad -$$
$$⑤ \quad ⑥ \quad 3 \quad 4 \mid 0 \quad 1 \quad - \quad -$$

PROBLEMS

24.2   An asynchronous sequential switching network has one input C and one output Z. The input signal is a square wave with a frequency of f. The output of the network should be a square wave with a frequency of $f/3$, as shown in the following timing diagram. Find a minimum-row flow table for this frequency divider network.

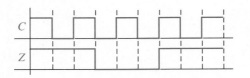

24.3   An asynchronous sequential switching network has two inputs and two outputs. All possible input sequences and the required output sequences are tabulated as follows:

Input sequence:	00, 10, 11, 01, 00
Output sequence:	00, 00, 10, 00, 00
Input sequence:	00, 01, 11, 10, 00
Output sequence:	00, 00, 01, 00, 00
Input sequence:	00, 10, 00, 01, 00
Output sequence:	00, 00, 00, 00, 00
Input sequence:	00, 01, 00, 10, 00
Output sequence:	00, 00, 00, 00, 00

Find a minimum-row flow table.

24.4 An asynchronous sequential network has two inputs X_1 and X_2 and one output Z. When the input $X_1 X_2$ is 11, the output becomes 1 and stays 1 until the input that immediately preceded the $X_1 X_2 = 11$ occurs again, at which time the output becomes 0. When the next 11 is detected, the network performs this operation again. Example:

$$X_1 X_2 = 00 \quad 01 \quad 10 \quad 11 \quad 00 \quad 01 \quad 11 \quad 10 \quad 11 \quad 10 \quad 01 \quad 00$$
$$Z \quad = 0 \quad 0 \quad 0 \quad 1 \quad 1 \quad 1 \quad 1 \quad 0 \quad 1 \quad 0 \quad 0 \quad 0$$

The first input in the sequence is not allowed to be 11. Find a minimum-row flow table.

24.5 Some computers have a step control, which enables the operator to step the computer through a program one cycle at a time. This requires a circuit where a push button can be used to parcel out the clock pulses, one clock pulse each time the push button is pressed. The timing diagram follows. The timing of the push-button signal is random, except that the duration and interval is long compared with the clock duration and interval. Find a minimum-row flow table.

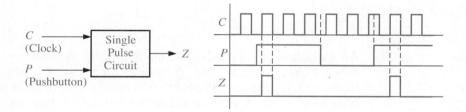

24.6 A sequential network has two inputs $(X_1 X_2)$ and one output (Z). If the input sequence 00, 01, 11 occurs, Z becomes 1 and remains 1 until the input sequence 11, 01, 00 occurs. In this case Z becomes 0 and remains 0 until the first sequence occurs again. (Note that the last input in one sequence may be the first input in the other sequence.) Find a minimum-row flow table.

24.7 For the following primitive flow tables, find the equivalent stable total states and reduce the tables accordingly. Complete the reduction by row merger and then derive a corresponding output table for each table. Are the minimum-row flow tables unique?

(a)

	X_1X_2				
	00	01	11	10	Z_1Z_2
①	11	4	10		01
5	②	–	3		11
5	2	13	③		11
12	–	④	15		00
⑤	–	8	–		10
14	⑥	–	10		11
⑦	6	8	3		01
7	–	⑧	3		00
⑨	11	13	10		01
12	6	13	⑩		11
5	⑪	–	3		11
⑫	2	4	15		01
1	–	⑬	10		00
⑭	–	8	–		10
1	6	4	⑮		11

(b)

	X_1X_2				
	00	01	11	10	Z
①	2	6	3		0
5	②	4	–		0
1	2	6	③		0
–	2	④	7		1
⑤	2	–	7		0
9	8	⑥	12		0
1	–	4	⑦		1
9	⑧	4	–		0
⑨	2	–	10		0
1	–	11	⑩		1
–	8	⑪	10		1
9	–	6	⑫		0

24.8 One type of clocked D flip-flop works as follows:
On the trailing edge of the clock pulse (1 to 0 transition) the output Q assumes the same state which the input D had on the leading edge of the clock pulse (0 to 1 transition). The output does not change at any other time. D may change at any time with respect to the clock. When D changes simultaneously with the leading edge of the clock, the value D had immediately before the change should determine the output after the clock pulse. Find a minimum-row flow table.

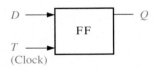

24.9 An unclocked, edge-sensitive J-K flip-flop works as follows:
When J changes from 0 to 1, Q becomes (or remains) 1. When K changes from 0 to 1, Q becomes (or remains) 0. When J and K simultaneously change from 00 to 11, Q changes state. The flip-flop output does not change when J changes from 1 to 0, or K changes from 1 to 0, or JK changes from 11 to 00. Changes of JK from 01 to 10 or 10 to 01 are not permitted. Find a primitive flow table with a minimum number of rows.

24.10 An asynchronous sequential network is designed to capture pulses on an input line X. The network has a single input X, a reset input R and an output Z. If X changes from 0 to 1 or from 1 to 0 while R is 0, then the output Z becomes 1 and remains 1 until the network is reset. Thus, if there is a pulse on the input line when R is 0, the output will become 1 to indicate the occurrence of the pulse. When $R = 1$, $Z = 0$. Find a minimum-row flow table.

25

State Assignment and Realization of Flow Tables

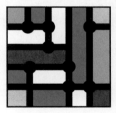

OBJECTIVES

1. Given any flow table, find a state assignment which avoids critical races and construct the expanded flow table.

2. Find a shared row assignment for a given flow table. Know and be able to use standard assignments for 4-, 5-, and 8- row tables.

3. Fill in the output table to avoid transient outputs.

4. Realize a given flow table using gates and S-R flip-flops or gates only.

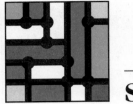

STUDY GUIDE

1. Study Section 25.1, *Introductory Example.*

   (a) What is the most important consideration in making state assignments for asynchronous networks?

   (b) Given a transition table for an asynchronous network, how can you determine if any races are present?

   Verify that Table 25–2 is free of races.

   (c) Review Section 12.3 on derivation of S-R flip-flop input equations, if necessary.

2. Study Section 25.2, *State Assignments for 3- and 4-Row Tables.*

   (a) Verify that Figs. 25–5(b) and 25–6(b) are free of critical races.

   (b) Is the following assignment valid for Fig. 25–4? Justify your answer.

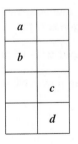

   (c) What are the relative advantages of the assignments of Figs. 25–5(a) and 25–6(a)?

3. Study Section 25.3, *Shared-Row Assignments.*

   (a) Is Fig. 25–7(c) a valid assignment for Table 25–4(a)?

(b) Why isn't the following assignment valid for Table 25–4(a)?

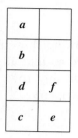

(c) A student has derived the following assignment map for a 6-row table:

In column 10 of the flow table, the following transitions are required:

$$5 \rightarrow 2 \quad \text{and} \quad 3, 4 \rightarrow 1$$

In the student's solution, the transition from state 3 to 1 is direct, and the transition from 4 to 1 is directed through α in order to avoid a critical race. Using the same map, what is a better way of handling the 4 to 1 transition without going through α?

(d) The following transitions are required in a 5-row flow table:

column 00: $d \rightarrow a \quad b, e \rightarrow c$ column 01: $c \rightarrow a \quad e \rightarrow d$

column 11: $b, c \rightarrow d \quad a \rightarrow e$ column 10: $a, d, e \rightarrow b$

Complete the following assignment map so as to avoid critical races. Indicate the transitions for each column by arrows on a copy of the assignment map. Arrange your assignment so that no transitions pass through the shaded square on the map.

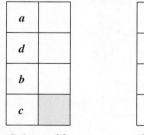

Column 00   Column 01   Column 11   Column 10

(e) What are two possible disadvantages of using the universal assignment of Fig. 25–9?

(f) Given the following flow table and assignment map, modify the flow table as required so that all required transitions between rows are race-free. Do *not* add any rows to the table; however, you may fill in the don't cares if necessary.

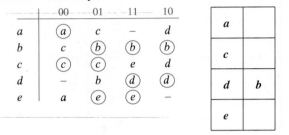

	00	01	11	10
a	(a)	c	–	d
b	c	(b)	(b)	(b)
c	(c)	(c)	e	d
d	–	b	(d)	(d)
e	a	(e)	(e)	–

a	
c	
d	b
e	

4. Study Section 25.4, *Completion of the Output Table.*

(a) The output portion of the following table is to be filled in to avoid transient outputs. Assume that *all* input changes are possible.

Q_1Q_2		00	01	11	10	00	01	11	10
00	1	(1)	2	2	(1)	0	(0) p	q	0
01	2	1	(2)	(2)	3	(0) r	0	1	s
11	3	2	4	(3)	(3)	t	u	1	1
10	4	(4)	(4)	3	1	0	1	(1) v	w

(1) Why was output p assigned 0?

(2) What should output u be?

(3) Why was r assigned 0?

(4) Why can q and t be –'s?

(5) What should s be?

(6) What should w be?

(b) Fill in the output table associated with the following transition table so as to avoid output transients. (Give all possible ways of filling in the first output column.)

	00	01	11	10	00	01	11	10
00	(00)	01	–	10	0		–	
01	00	(01)	(01)	11		1	1	
11	01	–	01	(11)		–		0
10	11	(10)	11	(10)		1		1

(c) Work Programmed Exercise 25.1.

5. Work Problems 25.3, 25.4, 25.5, 25.6(a), and 25.10.

6. Study Section 25.5, *The One-Hot Assignment.*[1]

   (a) A one-hot assignment is made for Table 25–4(a) with $Q_1 = 1$ for row a, $Q_2 = 1$ for row b, etc. The next-state equation for row d is

   $$Q_4^+ = \underbrace{Q_4 Q_2' Q_5'}_{\text{holding term}} + \underbrace{X_1' X_2 (Q_3 + Q_6) + X_1 X_2' (Q_1 + Q_3)}_{\text{transition terms}}$$

   Explain each of the terms in the equation, noting that there are two transitions leaving row d, and 4 transitions entering row d.

   (b) Suppose that Table 25–6 is to be realized using S–R flip-flops using the given one-hot assignment. By inspection of Equations (25–1), write the corresponding S–R equations. *Hint:* Each next-state equation is of the following form:

   $$Q_i^+ = Q_i R' + S$$

   (c) Work Problem 25.9.

7. When you are satisfied that you can meet the objectives, take the readiness test.

State Assignment and Realization of Flow Tables

Once a reduced flow table has been derived for an asynchronous sequential network, the next step in the design is making a state assignment. In choosing a state assignment for *synchronous* networks, the primary objective was simplification of the logic. However, for *asynchronous* networks the primary objective in choosing a state assignment is prevention of critical races, and simplification of the logic becomes a secondary consideration. After a state assignment has been made which is free of critical races, the asynchronous network can be realized using gates and S-R flip-flops or using gates only.

25.1
Introductory Example

We now will complete the design for Example 1 of Unit 24. Table 25–1 gives the reduced flow table of Table 24–9 with the next states labeled in terms of the internal states a, b, and c. The outputs for the unstable total states will be filled

---

[1] This section is optional.

Table 25–1

	X_1X_2							
	00	01	11	10	00	01	11	10
a	⟲ⓐ	ⓐ	c	⟲b	0	0	–	–
b	a	ⓑ	ⓑ	ⓑ	–	0	0	0
c	–	b	ⓒ	b	–	–	1	–

(next state)   (Z)

in after the state assignment has been made. Note that in the 00 column a transition is required from row b to row a, in the 01 column a transition is required from row c to row b, in the 11 column from row a to row c, and in column 10 from a to b and from c to b. The state transition diagram, Fig. 25–1(a), indicates the required transitions. A line drawn between a pair of states indicates a required transition between that pair of states.

Two state variables are required to realize the 3-row flow table. To avoid critical races we must find a state assignment such that only one state variable changes during each state transition. Two attempts to find such an assignment are indicated in Fig. 25–1(b) and (c). In the first case there is a critical race going from state c to state b (10 to 01), and in the second case a critical race going from a to c (00 to 11). In fact, it is impossible to find a race-free assignment in this way. If a single variable changes going from a to b, a single variable changes from b to c, and a single variable changes going from c to a, then there are three single variable changes in all. However, to get back where we started, each variable must change an even number of times. Therefore, we cannot make a race-free assignment for the given 3-row table and we must expand the table to four rows.

If we add an extra row to the table and direct the transition from row c to row b through row d, then we can make the race-free assignment shown in Fig. 25–1(d). Using this assignment, we can construct the transition table of Table 25–2. In column 01, starting in row c, the state variables change from 10 to 11 to 01, thus avoiding a critical race. In column 10, we could also have directed the transition from row c to row b through row d; however, since a transition is already required from row a to row b, we can direct the transition from c to a to b (10 to 00 to 01) as shown in the transition table.

The outputs corresponding to the unstable total states must then be filled in to avoid momentary false outputs during the transitions between stable total states. One way of filling in the output table to do this is indicated in Table 25–2.

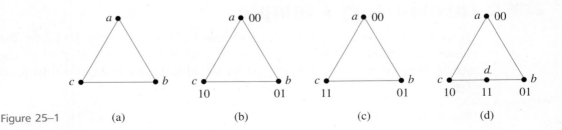

Figure 25–1   (a)   (b)   (c)   (d)

Table 25–2

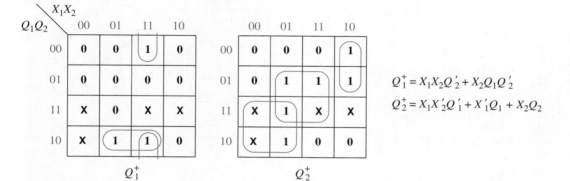

	Q_1Q_2	00	01	11	10	00	01	11	10
a	00	⓪⓪	⓪⓪	10	01	0	0	–	0_v
b	01	00	⓪1	⓪1	⓪1	0_u	0	0	0
d	11	–	01	–	–	–	$-_s$	–	–
c	10	–	11	⑩	00	–	1_t	1	–

$$Q_1^+Q_2^+ \qquad\qquad\qquad Z$$

$\longleftarrow Z = Q_1$

Detailed procedures for completing the output table are discussed in Section 25.4.

Having found a race-free state assignment, we now proceed to realize the network. First we will realize it using gates and delays as shown in Fig. 25–2(a). The next state maps for state variables Q_1 and Q_2 are plotted from the transition

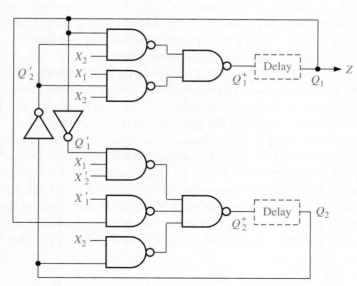

$$Q_1^+ = X_1X_2Q_2' + X_2Q_1Q_2'$$
$$Q_2^+ = X_1X_2'Q_1' + X_1'Q_1 + X_2Q_2$$

Figure 25–2(a)
Gate Realization of Table 25–2

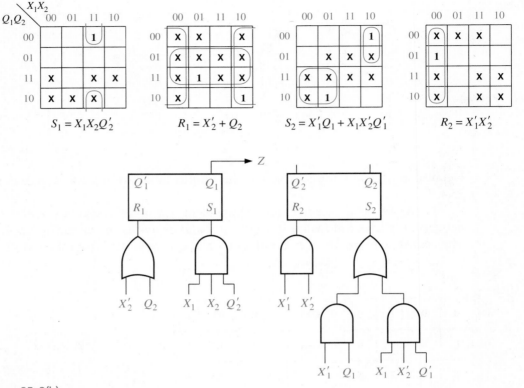

Figure 25–2(b)
S-R Flip-Flop Realization of Table 25–2

table of Table 25–2, and the output function is $Z = Q_1$. The next-state functions, Q_1^+ and Q_2^+ lead directly to the network of Fig. 25–2(a). In most cases, the internal delay in the gates is sufficient to assure proper operation of the network and the delays indicated in the network diagram can be eliminated.

Figure 25–2(b) shows an alternate realization using S-R flip-flops. The flip-flop input functions are derived by converting the next-state maps to S and R maps using the same rules as for synchronous networks. Each S-R flip-flop can be constructed from two cross-coupled NOR gates as discussed in Unit 11.

As an alternative to using S-R flip-flops constructed from cross-coupled NOR gates, flip-flops constructed from cross-coupled NAND gates may be used. Analysis of the NAND-gate flip-flop[2] in Fig. 25–3(a) shows that a 0 applied to the U input will set Q to 1, and a 0 applied to the V input will reset the flip-flop to $Q = 0$. Normally, $U = V = 0$ is not allowed since this would produce 1 outputs from both NAND gates. Figure 25–3(b) shows the inputs required to change the flip-flop state. Comparison with a similar table for the S-R flip-flop, Table 12–4(c),

---

[2] See Problem 11.4.

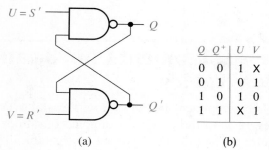

(a)

Q	Q^+	U	V
0	0	1	X
0	1	0	1
1	0	1	0
1	1	X	1

(b)

Figure 25–3
NAND-Gate Flip-Flop and Input Table

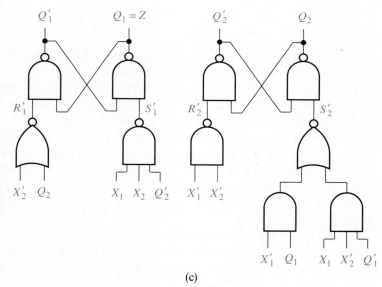

(c)

Figure 25–3(c)
NAND Flip-Flop Realization of Table 25–2

shows that $U = S'$ and $V = R'$. Therefore, the design procedure using NAND gate flip-flops is the same as for S-R flip-flops except that the S and R functions must be complemented. Figure 25–3(c) shows the realization of Table 25–2 using NAND-gate flip-flops. The flip-flop inputs are the complements of the S and R inputs in Fig. 25–2(b).

25.2
State Assignments for 3- and 4- Row Tables

A race-free assignment for any 3-row flow table can be found using two state variables. If, as in the previous example, transitions between all 3 pairs of rows are required, a fourth row is added to the table. Then races can be eliminated by directing the transition between one pair of rows through the added row.

Although a race-free assignment for some 4-row tables requires only two state variables, many 4-row tables require three state variables. In the most general case for a 4-row table, transitions are required between all pairs of rows as illustrated in Fig. 25–4. The transitions for each column are as follows:

column 00: $b \rightarrow a$, $c \rightarrow d$
column 01: $a \rightarrow c$, $b \rightarrow d$
column 11: $a \rightarrow d$, $c \rightarrow b$
column 10: $c \rightarrow a$, $d \rightarrow b$

As can be seen from the state transition diagram, any assignment using two state variables will have critical races. Therefore, at least three state variables are needed. Figure 25–5(a) shows a universal state assignment map which will work for any 4-row table. Since states in adjacent squares differ in only one variable, direct transitions can be made from a to b, b to c, and b to d. On the other hand, the transition from a to d is directed through state e so that only one state variable changes at a time. Similarly, the transition from c to d is directed through g, and c to a goes through f. Using the assignment given by the map, the 4-row table (Fig. 25–4) can be expanded to a 7-row table which is free of races (Fig. 25–5(b)). Note that in every row of this table, the present state and next state differ in at most one state variable.

Figure 25–6(a) shows another universal assignment for 4-row tables. In making this assignment, each state in the original table is replaced by a pair of equivalent states. For example, a is replaced with a_1 and a_2, where $a \equiv a_1 \equiv a_2$.

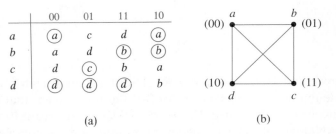

(a)   (b)

Figure 25–4
General 4-Row Table and State Transition Diagram

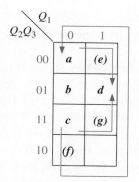

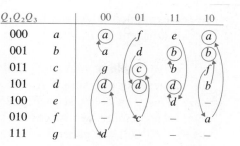

$Q_1Q_2Q_3$		00	01	11	10
000	a	(a)	f	e	(a)
001	b	a	d	(b)	(b)
011	c	g	(c)	b	f
101	d	(d)	(d)	(d)	b
100	e	–	–	d	–
010	f	–	c	–	a
111	g	d	–	–	–

Figure 25–5

(a) Universal state assignment for 4-row tables

(b) Expanded 4-row table

	Q_1	0	1
Q_2Q_3			
00		a_1	b_2
01		d_1	c_2
11		b_1	a_2
10		c_1	d_2

$Q_1Q_2Q_3$		00	01	11	10
000	a_1	(a_1)	c_1	d_1	(a_1)
111	a_2	(a_2)	c_2	d_2	(a_2)
011	b_1	a_2	d_1	(b_1)	(b_1)
100	b_2	a_1	d_2	(b_2)	(b_2)
010	c_1	d_2	(c_1)	b_1	a_1
101	c_2	d_1	(c_2)	b_2	a_2
001	d_1	(d_1)	(d_1)	(d_1)	b_1
110	d_2	(d_2)	(d_2)	(d_2)	b_2

Figure 25–6

(a) Universal assignment for 4-row tables

(b) Expanded 4-row table

Note that a_1 is adjacent to b_2, c_1, and d_1; b_1 is adjacent to a_2, c_1, and d_1; and each state is adjacent to three states of different types. Thus it is always possible to change from a state of a given type to one of the other types by changing a single state variable.

Figure 25–6(b) shows the table of Fig. 25–4 in expanded form using the state assignment of Fig. 25–6(a). The expanded table is formed as follows. First, each row in the original table is replaced with two rows, and the stable total states in each row are filled in. For example, row a is replaced by rows a_1 and a_2, and the stable total states (a_1) and (a_2) are entered in columns 00 and 10. After all stable total states have been entered, the unstable states are filled in by reference to the assignment map. When choosing the next state entry for a given present state, a state which is adjacent to the present state is selected from the map. In the original table, the next states of b are a and d for inputs 00 and 01, respectively.

In the expanded table, the next states for row b_1 are a_2 and d_1 because a_2 and d_1 are adjacent to b_1 on the map; similarly, the next states for b_2 are a_1 and d_2.

For the table of Fig. 25–6(b), if we start in any stable total state and change the input, only one state variable will change in going to the next stable total state. This is in contrast to Fig. 25–5(b) where transitions between some stable total states require two successive state variable changes. Thus, a network based on Fig. 25–6(a) will generally be faster than one based on Fig. 25–5(a); however, more logic is required for the former because there are fewer don't cares in the table. Also, when each of the original stable states is represented by two or more states in the final network, observation of network behavior is more difficult. This may lead to increased system development time and maintenance costs.

When unspecified next state entries (don't cares) are present in the state table, they can often be used in the process of making a race-free state assignment. Consider Table 25–3(a), for example. The transitions needed for each column are:

column 00: $d \to a$
column 01: $a \to b$, $c \to d$
column 11: $b \to c$
column 10: $a \to c$, $b \to d$

Since all possible transitions between pairs of rows are needed, it first appears that adding rows to the table will be necessary in order to achieve a race-free assignment. However, this is not the case because of the don't cares in the table. If we make a 4-row assignment, the transitions in columns 01 and 10 must be satisfied directly since there are no don't cares in these columns. Therefore, we will make a state assignment based on the following transition diagram:

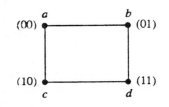

With this assignment, all of the transitions in columns 01 and 10 can be made without races. For column 00, the transition d to a cannot be made directly since this would lead to a critical race; however, since there is a dash in row c, we can make a transition from d to c to a. Similarly, in column 11 the direct transition b to c would lead to a critical race, but by using the – in row a, we can make a transition from b to a to c. Table 25–3(b) shows the resulting flow table with the necessary modifications made to columns 00 and 11 so that all critical races are eliminated.

Table 25–3

	00	01	11	10
a	(a)	b	–	c
b	(b)	(b)	c	d
c	–	d	(c)	(c)
d	a	(d)	(d)	(d)

(a) flow table with don't cares

		00	01	11	10
00	a	(a)	b	c	c
01	b	(b)	(b)	a	d
10	c	a	d	(c)	(c)
11	d	c	(d)	(d)	(d)

(b) flow table with don't cares filled in to eliminate races

25.3
Shared-Row Assignments

This section discusses a general approach to making state assignments in which extra rows are added to the flow table to resolve critical races. An extra row of the flow table may be used in different columns as an intermediate state between different pairs of rows, hence the term *shared row*.

Consider the 6-row table of Table 25–4(a). At least three state variables are required and more may be needed to obtain a race-free assignment. The first step in making a state assignment is to list the required transitions in Table 25–4(b). The notation $e, c \rightarrow a$ means that states e and c must go to state a. There is some flexibility in the way these transitions are carried out. Several possibilities are:

e directly to a and c directly to a

e to c to a

c to e to a

any of the above, but going through an intermediate state (or states) during one (or more) of the transitions

Thus, to avoid critical races, the only requirement is that e, c, and a be placed in a series of adjacent squares on the assignment map, or that they be placed in

Table 25–4

	00	01	11	10
a	(1)	2	5	4
b	(7)	(2)	3	(10)
c	1	8	(3)	4
d	7	(8)	5	(4)
e	1	(9)	(5)	6
f	(11)	8	3	(6)

(a)

Required transitions:

column 00:	$e, c \rightarrow a$	$d \rightarrow b$
column 01:	$a \rightarrow b$	$c, f \rightarrow d$
column 11:	$b, f \rightarrow c$	$a, d \rightarrow e$
column 10:	$a, c \rightarrow d$	$e \rightarrow f$

(b)

a series of adjacent squares with intermediate blank squares. Generally, use of intermediate blank squares should be avoided when possible. If blank squares are not filled in, this will leave more don't cares in the transition table and hence lead to a more economical realization.

The transitions listed in Table 25–4(b) imply that the states in each of the following adjacency sets must be placed in a series of adjacent squares:

column 00: $(a, c, e)(b, d)$
column 01: $(a, b)(c, d, f)$
column 11: $(b, c, f)(a, d, e)$
column 10: $(a, c, d)(e, f)$

We proceed to do this by trial and error, starting with a 3-variable map. State "a" can always be placed in the 000 square with no loss of generality. Then b is placed adjacent to a to satisfy the adjacency set (a, b), and d adjacent to b to satisfy the set (b, d):

a			OR	a	
b	d			b	
				d	

To satisfy the adjacency set (a, d, e), e is placed adjacent to a and d:

a	e		OR	a	
b	d			b	
				d	
				e	

Then f is placed adjacent to e:

a	e		OR	a	
b	d			b	
				d	
	f			e	f

Now we try placing c in different squares so as to satisfy the remaining adjacency sets $[(a, c, e), (c, d, f), (b, c, f), (a, c, d)]$ as shown in Fig. 25–7.

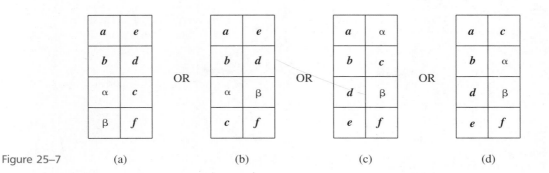

Figure 25–7   (a)   (b)   (c)   (d)

For the map of Fig. 25–7(a), the set (c, d, f) is satisfied directly, set (a, c, e) is satisfied by including α and β in the chain of adjacent squares; that is, e, a, β, α, and c form a string of adjacent squares. Similarly, (b, c, f) is satisfied by including α, and (a, c, d) is satisfied by including α and β. For the map of Fig. 25–7(b), the set (a, c, e) is satisfied directly. Set (c, d, f) is satisfied by including β, (b, c, f) by including α, and (a, c, d) by including α and β. Expanding Table 25–4(a) using the assignment of Fig. 25–7(b) yields Table 25–5.

In column 01 of Table 25–5, the transition from c to d is directed through f and β since c, f, β, and d form a string of adjacent map squares. Similarly, in column 11 the transition from b to c goes through row α since b, α, and c form a string of adjacent squares. In column 10, the transition from a to d goes by way of c, α, and β. In the expanded table, only one state variable changes in each transition between rows; hence there are no races (critical or otherwise). Row α is "shared" between columns 11 and 10 and has a different next state in each of these columns.

When making shared-row assignment, it is often possible to take advantage of don't cares which are present in the flow table. Instead of adding rows to the table, it may be possible to eliminate critical races by directing some of the state transitions through the don't care states as was done in Table 25–3.

Table 25–5
Expanded Table of Table 25–4(a) Using Assignment of Fig. 25–7(b)

		00	01	11	10
000	a	a	b	e	c
001	b	b	b	α	b
010	c	a	f	c	α
101	d	b	d	e	d
100	e	a	e	e	f
110	f	f	β	c	f
011	α	–	–	c	β
111	β	–	d	–	d

α	
β	
γ	δ
	ε

Figure 25–8
Assignment Form for Most 5-Row Tables

Most 5-row tables, including all tables with 14 or fewer columns, can be realized using three state variables with an assignment of the form shown in Fig. 25–8. This is not a universal assignment in the sense of Figs. 25–5(a) and 25–6(a) because the assignment will work only if the proper correspondence is established between α, β, γ, δ, and ε and the five rows of the table. In other words, the states of the table must be arranged on the assignment map in the pattern indicated in Fig. 25–8, and the order of the states on the map must be such that all transitions can be made without races.

Figure 25–9 shows a universal assignment for 8-row tables. For each column of the table the state transitions must be directed through the unused squares on the map in such a way as to avoid races. For example, if the required transitions in a column are a to c, b to h, d to f, and e to g, the transitions would be directed as shown in Fig. 25–9. The 8-row universal assignment will also work for 6- or 7-row tables. However, many 6-, 7-, and 8-row tables can be realized using only 3 state variables, and such an assignment should be attempted before using the universal assignment which requires 4 state variables.

The assignments discussed in this section have the disadvantage that several successive single state variable changes may be required when going from one stable total state to another. The fact that several *successive* changes are needed slows down the operation of the network. Faster operation can be achieved by

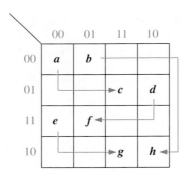

Figure 25–9
Universal Assignment for 8-Row Tables

allowing several state variables to change simultaneously, and making the state assignment such that all races are *noncritical*. In this way it is possible to make all transitions between stable total states without going through any intermediate rows. Such assignments are referred to as STT (single transition time) assignments. In general, STT assignments will require more state variables than shared row assignments. Methods for obtaining STT assignments are discussed by Unger[3] and others and will not be discussed here.

25.4
Completion of the Output Table

After a state assignment has been made which avoids critical races, the next step in designing an asynchronous sequential network is to complete the output table. At this point, the output has been specified for all of the stable total states. The unspecified entries in the Mealy output table must now be filled in so that momentary false outputs do not occur when the network is switching between stable total states. In synchronous networks, a momentary false output will cause no problem if it occurs between clock pulses. However, a momentary false output from an asynchronous network can cause problems if the output is used as an input to another asynchronous network.

A procedure for specifying the outputs for the unstable total states so as to avoid momentary false outputs is described below. Consider the partial flow table of Fig. 25–10 and the four possible output configurations given. In case (a), states ① and ② both have 0 output, so the "–" must be replaced with 0 so that a constant 0 output will be maintained during the transition from ① to ②. Similarly, in case (d), the "–" must be assigned a value 1 to prevent a momentary 0 output during the transition from ① to ②. In cases (b) and (c), the "–" may remain as a don't care since the output changes from 0 to 1 (or 1 to 0) anyway. Thus in case (b) if "–" is assigned a value 0, the output will change only once from 0 to 1 during the transition from state ① to ②; similarly, if "–" is assigned a value 1, the output changes only once during the state transition.

If a given input column can be reached starting in two (or more) different stable total states, then both (all) of the transitions must be considered in filling in the output table. Consider Fig. 25–11 for example. Starting in ①, the output

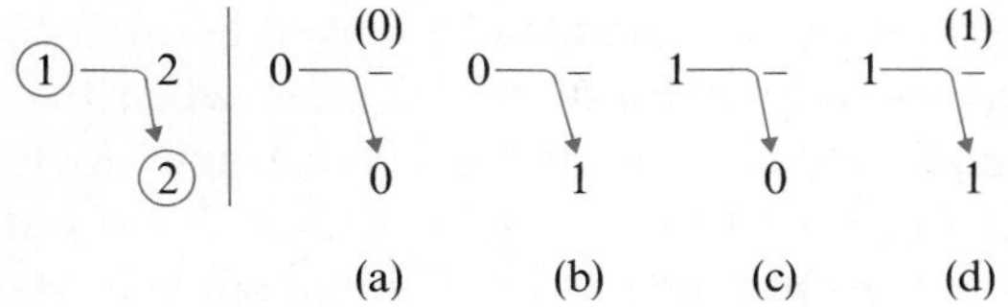

Figure 25–10

(a)   (b)   (c)   (d)

---

[3] S. H. Unger, *Asynchronous Sequential Switching Circuits,* Wiley, 1969, pp. 75–96.

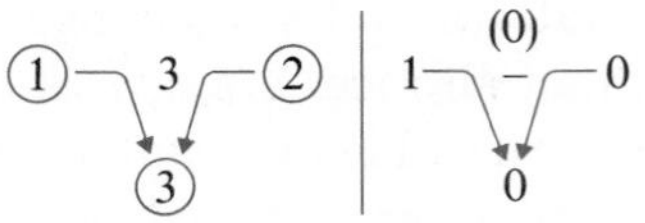

Figure 25–11

changes from 1 to 0 so the "–" could be left as a don't care; however starting in ② , the output must remain a constant 0, so the "–" must be replaced with a 0.

Figure 25–12 shows a partial flow table in which the transition between stable total states ⓐ and ⓒ goes through two intermediate unstable total states and the output changes from 0 to 1. Both of the don't cares in output table (a) cannot be assigned arbitrary values, because this could lead to the output sequence 0 (1) (0) 1, and this sequence contains unwanted transients. If one of the don't cares is assigned a value as in (b) and (c), then the other don't care can be assigned an arbitrary value (0 or 1) without introducing transients. Thus, when filling in the output table we can specify either (b) or (c), but we cannot leave both don't cares in the table as in (a).

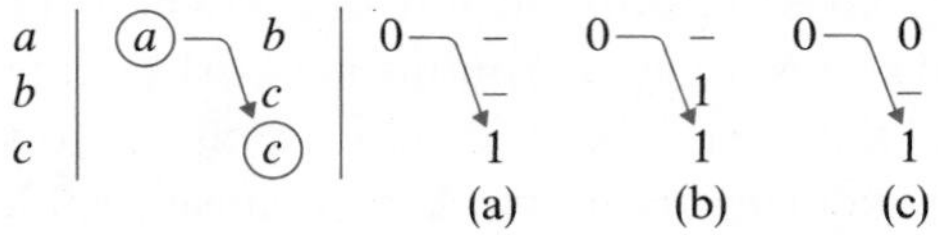

Figure 25–12

In the output table of Table 25–2, the entry labeled u must be 0 as indicated to maintain a constant 0 output when switching between total states $X_1X_2Q_1Q_2 = 0101$ and 0000. Similarly, entry v must be 0 to avoid an output transient when switching between 0000 and 1001. The entries labeled s and t could also be 0 and "–", respectively. However, s and t cannot both be don't cares because this would allow the possibility of a 1010 output sequence during the transition from row c to d to b. The best choice for s and t is "–" and 1 since this simplifies the output function as shown in Table 25–2.

When the output table has two or more output variables, each of the outputs must be considered individually when replacing dashes with 0's or 1's. Figure 25–13 illustrates a case where the output changes from $Z_1Z_2 = 01$ to 11. The intermediate output is filled in as -1 since Z_1 is changing and Z_2 is not.

Figure 25–13

Filling in the output table to eliminate all transients is always possible. If all unstable total states which lead to a stable total state ⓢ are assigned the same output as the output for state ⓢ , then when the input is changed the output will immediately assume its final value and no transient outputs will appear. Consider Fig. 25–14 for example. If the "–'s" in output table (a) are all changed to 1's as in (b), then the output will immediately assume its final value of 1 when the input is changed regardless whether the initial stable total state is ⓐ , ⓑ , ⓒ , or ⓓ . This method of filling in the output has the advantage that the

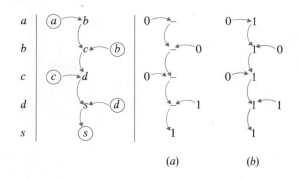

Figure 25–14

response to an input change is fast. It has the disadvantage that the don't cares are eliminated, and this may lead to an uneconomical output network.

After the output table has been completed, the procedure used for realizing the network is similar to that used for synchronous networks. The transition table is formed by substituting the assigned values of the state variables for each state in the flow table. The next-state maps are then plotted from the transition table. If the network is to be realized without using flip-flops, the next-state functions are read from the maps and realized using the available logic gates. If S-R flip-flops are to be used, the S-R flip-flop input maps are derived from the next-state maps in the usual manner. The S and R input functions are then read from the maps and realized using the available logic gates. If the state assignment used is free of critical races and if the output table is filled in correctly, a network realized by the above procedure should, in theory, work correctly. However, timing problems, which cause the network to malfunction, may arise due to gate delays. The detection and correction of such timing problems is the subject of the next unit.

25.5
The One-Hot Assignment

This section describes another method for finding a race-free state assignment. The one-hot assignment uses one state variable for each row of the flow table. The assignment is made such that when the network is in a stable state exactly one of the state variables is 1. In row i of the table, state variable Q_i is 1 and all other state variables are 0. When a transition between row i and row j is required, first state variable Q_j is set to 1 (so that both Q_i and Q_j are 1), and then Q_i is set to 0. Thus each transition between two rows in the flow table goes through one intermediate row and thus requires two state transition times.

The following example illustrates application of the one-hot assignment to Table 25–6. Starting in row a, when $X_1 X_2 = 01$, a transition to row b is required; therefore, row e (with Q_1 and Q_2 both equal to 1) is added to the table and the

Table 25–6
One-Hot Assignment

Q_1	Q_2	Q_3	Q_4		X_1X_2 00	01	11	10	
1	0	0	0	a	ⓐ	b̶ e	c̶ f	ⓐ	⎫
0	1	0	0	b	ⓑ	ⓑ	d̶ g	a̶ e	⎪ original table
0	0	1	0	c	b̶ h	ⓒ	ⓒ	d̶ i	⎬
0	0	0	1	d	a̶ j	e̶ i	ⓓ	ⓓ	⎭
1	1	0	0	e	–	b	–	a	⎫
1	0	1	0	f	–	–	c	–	⎪
0	1	0	1	g	–	–	d	–	⎬ added rows
0	1	1	0	h	b	–	–	–	⎪
0	0	1	1	i	–	c	–	d	⎪
1	0	0	1	j	a	–	–	–	⎭

transition from a to b is directed through row e. Starting in row a, when $X_1X_2 = 11$, a transition to row c is required; therefore row f (with Q_1 and Q_3 both equal to 1) is added to the table, and the transition from a to c is directed through row f. In a similar manner, rows g, h, i, and j are added to the table so that every transition in the original table is directed through one of the added rows.

The next-state equations can be derived from Table 25–6 in the usual manner; however, they can also be derived by inspection of the original table *without* actually writing down the rows added to the table. Considering the original part of Table 25–6 and starting in a stable state in row a ($Q_1 = 1$), if the input is changed to 01, first Q_2 must be set to 1 and then Q_1 must be set to 0. Therefore, the next-state equation for Q_2 must contain a term $X_1'X_2Q_1$ in order to set Q_2 to 1. The next-state equation for Q_1 should contain a term Q_1Q_2', which will keep Q_1 equal to 1 until Q_2 becomes 1. So far we have

$$Q_1^+ = Q_1Q_2' \ldots$$
$$Q_2^+ = X_1'X_2Q_1 + \cdots$$

Since a transition from row a to row c is required when the input is changed to 11, the next-state equation for Q_3 contains a term $X_1X_2Q_1$ in order to set Q_3 to 1. To set Q_1 back to 0 when Q_3 becomes 1, we multiply the Q_1Q_2' term by Q_3', which gives

$$Q_1^+ = Q_1Q_2'Q_3' + \cdots$$
$$Q_2^+ = X_1'X_2Q_1 + \cdots$$
$$Q_3^+ = X_1X_2Q_1 + \cdots$$

Transitions from row b to rows d and a are required for inputs 11 and 10, respectively. Therefore we introduce a term $X_1X_2Q_2$ in the Q_4^+ equation and add

$X_1X_2'Q_2$ to the Q_1^+ equation. To keep Q_2 equal to 1 until Q_4 or Q_1 becomes 1, we add $Q_2Q_1'Q_4'$ to the Q_2^+ equation. At this point we have

$$Q_1^+ = Q_1Q_2'Q_3' + X_1X_2'Q_2 + \cdots$$
$$Q_2^+ = Q_2Q_1'Q_4' + X_1'X_2Q_1 + \cdots$$
$$Q_3^+ = X_1X_2Q_1 + \cdots$$
$$Q_4^+ = X_1X_2Q_2 + \cdots$$

After adding in terms which correspond to the transitions from rows c and d, the final equations are

$$Q_1^+ = Q_1Q_2'Q_3' + X_1X_2'Q_2 + X_1'X_2'Q_4$$
$$Q_2^+ = Q_2Q_1'Q_4' + X_1'X_2Q_1 + X_1'X_2'Q_3$$
$$Q_3^+ = Q_3Q_2'Q_4' + X_1X_2Q_1 + X_1'X_2Q_4$$
$$Q_4^+ = \underbrace{Q_4Q_1'Q_3'}_{\substack{\text{holding} \\ \text{term}}} + \underbrace{X_1X_2Q_2 + X_1X_2'Q_3}_{\substack{\text{transition} \\ \text{terms}}} \qquad (25\text{--}1)$$

Each of these equations has a "holding term" which holds the given state variable in the 1 state until another state variable becomes 1. In addition, each equation contains one or more "transition terms" which cause the state variable to become 1 when the network is in an appropriate state and the appropriate input is applied.

In general, if transitions are required from row i to rows $j, k, \ldots$, the holding term for the Q_i^+ equation is of the form

$$Q_iQ_j'Q_k' \cdots$$

If a transition is required from row i to row j when input X is 1, then the Q_j^+ equation will contain a term of the form Q_iX.

As can be seen from the discussion, the logic equations for the one-hot assignment are relatively simple and easy to derive. Transitions from one row of the original table to another row are always carried out in two steps changing one state variable at a time, so the solution is free of races. The main disadvantage of the one-hot solution is the large number of state variables required.

PROGRAMMED EXERCISE 25.1

Cover the bottom of each page with a sheet of paper and slide it down as you check your answers.

We will make a state assignment and complete the output table for the example of Fig. 24–5(b). This figure is reproduced below with the next-state part of the table converted to internal state notation.

	00	01	11	10	00	01	11	10
a	(a)	(a)	g	b	11	10	--	--
b	(b)	d	c	(b)	01	--	--	00
c	(c)	a	(c)	b	01	--	10	--
d	c	(d)	e	–	--	11	--	--
e	–	a	(e)	f	--	--	01	--
f	b	–	g	(f)	--	--	--	11
g	–	d	(g)	b	--	--	00	--

$$Z_1 Z_2$$

List the state transitions which are required for each column:

$$00 \qquad\qquad 01 \qquad\qquad 11 \qquad\qquad 10$$

List the corresponding sets of adjacent states required for each column:

Answers:

00:	$d \to c$	01:	$g, b \to d$	11:	$a, f \to g$	10:	$a, c, g \to b$
	$f \to b$		$c, e \to a$		$b \to c; d \to e$		$e \to f$
	$(c, d)(b, f)$		$(b, d, g)(a, c, e)$		$(a, f, g)(b, c)(d, e)$		$(a, b, c, g)(e, f)$

We will attempt to satisfy the required *pairs* of adjacent states first. Try to arrange the states b, c, d, e, and f on a map so that as many of the pairs (c, d), (b, f), (b, c), (d, e), and (e, f) as possible are in adjacent squares.

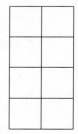

Answer: Four of the five pairs can be made adjacent. Many different solutions are possible. We will work with the one shown below.

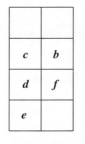

Add a to the map so that (a, c, e) forms a string of adjacent squares. Also add g so that (a, b, c, g) forms a string of adjacent squares. After these additions, which sets of adjacent squares are not directly satisfied?

c	b
d	f
e	

Answer: The map shown below directly satisfies all adjacency sets except:

$$(b, d, g)\ (a, f, g)\ (e, f)$$

a	g
c	b
d	f
e	

Which of these sets can be satisfied by adding an extra row to the table?

Answer: $(a, f, g)\ (e, f)$ can be satisfied by using row α.

a	g
c	b
d	f
e	α

At first it appears that (b, d, g) cannot be satisfied by this assignment and we will have to start over again. However, note that (b, d, g) is required for the 01 column and row f has a – in the 01 column. Therefore, the transition can be made from row

g to row b to row d by way of row f. Using the above assignment complete the expanded flow table below so that no races are present.

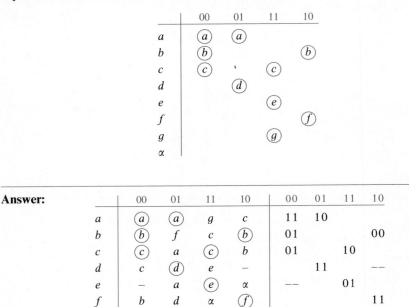

	00	01	11	10
a	(a)	(a)		
b	(b)			(b)
c	(c)		(c)	
d		(d)		
e			(e)	
f				(f)
g			(g)	
α				

Answer:

	00	01	11	10	00	01	11	10
a	(a)	(a)	g	c	11	10		
b	(b)	f	c	(b)	01			00
c	(c)	a	(c)	b	01		10	
d	c	(d)	e	--		11		--
e	--	a	(e)	α	--		01	
f	b	d	α	(f)				11
g	--	b	(g)	b	--		00	
α	--	--	g	f	--	--		

Next we will fill in the blanks in the above output table so that no momentary false outputs will occur. We will use don't cares whenever possible. Double input changes were prohibited for the original primitive table from which this table was derived; therefore, we will consider only single changes of input when filling in the output table. The last column of the output table will be filled in as follows:

Row c: Possible transitions are indicated below. Why must "??" be replaced with 00?

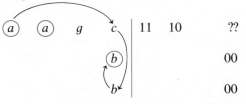

Row a: Why should "??" be replaced with --?

Row e: Why must t and v be replaced with 1's?
Why should s and u be replaced with "–" and 1 or 0 and "–", respectively?

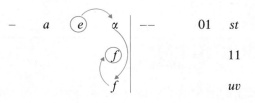

Answer: Check for yourself to verify that when the outputs are filled in as indicated, no momentary false outputs will occur.

When a single input change produces only a single change of internal state variable, filling in the corresponding output entries is straightforward. Identify several such cases in the above flow table and fill in the corresponding output entries.

Answer: (new entries in the table are underlined)

	00	01	11	10	00	01	11	10
a	ⓐ	ⓐ	g	c	11	10	<u>0</u>	--
b	ⓑ	f	c	ⓑ	01		<u>0</u>	00
c	ⓒ	a	ⓒ	b	01	<u>10</u>	10	00
d	c	ⓓ	e	--	<u>1</u>	11	-1	--
e	-	a	ⓔ	α	--	<u>--</u>	01	-1
f	b	d	α	ⓕ	<u>1</u>			11
g	-	b	ⓖ	b	--		00	<u>00</u>
α	-	-	g	f	--	--		11

Now fill in the remaining entries in the 11 column.

Answer: Two of the possibilities are   --   11
                                                 and
                                        00   --

If you feel that you need more practice, fill in the remaining entries in the 01 column.

Answer: Two of the possibilities are   01   -1
                                          -1   and   11
                                          0-   0-

PROBLEMS

25.2   Make a proper assignment of internal state variables for each of the following flow tables. In each case, 3 internal state variables are sufficient. Specify the final state tables in terms of the internal states.

(a)

	00	01	11	10
1	①	①	4	5
2	1	②	②	5
3	③	1	2	③
4	3	2	④	5
5	3	⑤	2	⑤

(b)

	00	01	11	10
a	①	⑤	8	10
b	2	5	⑥	9
c	③	5	6	⑩
d	②	4	⑧	10
e	3	④	7	9
f	1	4	⑦	⑨

25.3   Work Problem 25.2 for the following flow tables.

	$X_1 X_2$			
	00	01	11	10
a	①	4	⑦	10
b	1	⑤	⑧	11
c	2	⑥	8	⑩
d	②	④	9	⑪
e	3	6	⑨	10
f	③	5	7	⑫

	$X_1 X_2$			
	00	01	11	10
a	①	4	⑦	11
b	②	6	⑧	10
c	③	6	7	⑩
d	2	④	9	10
e	1	⑤	9	10
f	3	⑥	7	11
g	2	6	⑨	11
h	1	5	7	⑪

25.4   Using the following assignment for Fig. 25–4, find the expanded flow table. Note that although a direct transition from a_1 to d_1 or d_2 is not possible, a transition from a_1 to a_2 to d_2 is possible since a_1 and a_2 are equivalent states.

a_1	a_2
b_1	b_2
c_1	d_1
c_2	d_2

25.5   Realize Fig. 24–6(b) using: (a) two S-R flip-flops and gates, (b) gates only.

25.6   Make a proper state assignment for each of the following tables using the assignment form of Fig. 25–8, and give the expanded table for each.

(a)

	X_1X_2			
	00	01	11	10
a	①	7	②	10
b	5	③	9	④
c	⑤	⑥	8	10
d	1	⑦	⑧	4
e	1	3	⑨	⑩

(b)

	X_1X_2			
	00	01	11	10
a	①	5	6	⑨
b	②	4	6	⑩
c	3	④	⑥	9
d	1	⑤	⑦	10
e	③	5	⑧	10

25.7 Make a proper state assignment for Problem 24.6.
(a) Realize the flow table with S-R flip-flops and gates.
(b) Realize the flow table with gates only (do not connect gates to form flip-flops).

25.8 Make a proper state assignment for Problem 24.7(a) and fill in the blank entries in the output table to prevent momentary false outputs. Derive the next-state equations with a computer-aided logic design program such as *LogicAid*.
(a) Realize the flow table with S-R flip-flops and gates.
(b) Realize the flow table with gates only (do not connect gates to form flip-flops).

25.9 Make a one-hot assignment for the table of Problem 25.6(a) and derive the next-state equations.

25.10 Make a state assignment for Problem 24.8 such that the Q output equals one of the state variables. Realize the network using S-R flip-flops and any necessary gates.

25.11 Make a proper state assignment for Problem 24.7(b) and fill in the blank entries in the output table to prevent momentary false outputs. Derive the next-state equations with a computer-aided logic design program such as *LogicAid*.
(a) Realize the flow table with S-R flip-flops and gates.
(b) Realize the flow table with gates only (do not connect gates to form flip-flops).

26

Hazards

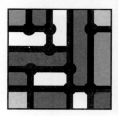

OBJECTIVES

1. Define static 0- and 1-hazards and dynamic hazards and give examples of networks containing such hazards. Explain why hazards in the combinational part of a sequential network can cause the network to go to the wrong state.

2. Given a combinational network, find all of the static 0- and 1-hazards. For each hazard, specify the order in which the gates must switch in order for the hazard to actually produce a false output.

3. Given a switching function, realize it using a two-level network which is free of static and dynamic hazards (for single input variable changes). Be able to transform this network to a higher level network which is also hazard free.

4. Find all of the essential hazards in an asynchronous network by using a flow table. For any given essential hazard, specify the order in which the network elements must switch in order for the network to go to the wrong state. Eliminate essential hazards by adding delays in appropriate places in the network.

5. Find a hazard-free realization of a flow table using S-R flip-flops or cross-coupled NAND gates.

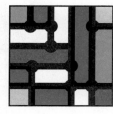

STUDY GUIDE

1. Study Section 26.1, *Hazards in Combinational Networks.*

   (a) Review the discussion of gate delays in Section 11.1. Even though all of the gates in a network are of the same type, each individual gate may have a different propagation delay. For example, for one type of TTL NAND gate the manufacturer specifies a minimum propagation delay of 5 nanoseconds (ns) and a maximum delay of 30 ns. Sketch the gate outputs for the following network when the x input changes from 1 to 0, assuming the following gate delays:

   gate $1 - 5$ ns,   gate $2 - 20$ ns,   gate $3 - 10$ ns.

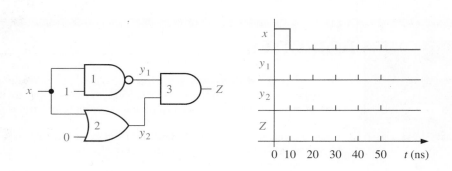

   (b) Consider the network of Fig. 26–1 for the case where $x_1 = y = 1$ and x_2 changes from 0 to 1. For this case, in what order must the gate outputs change in order for the hazard to show up at the network output?

   (c) Define static 0-hazard, static 1-hazard, and dynamic hazard.

2. Study Section 26.2, *Detection of Static 0- and 1-Hazards.*

   (a) When computing the transient output function, F^t, why must each variable and its complement be treated like separate variables?

   (b) Using a Karnaugh map, explain why $F = a'b + ac$ has a 1-hazard for the input change $abc = 011$ to 111, but not for 011 to 010. Then explain it without using the map.

   (c) Explain why $F = (a' + b')(b + c)$ has a 0-hazard for the input change $abc = 100$ to 110, but not for 100 to 000.

3. Study Section 26.3, *Dynamic Hazards.*

   For $a = b = 1$, note that Z^t reduces to $Z^t = c' + cc' = (c + c')c'$.

   If c changes from 0 to 1, in what order must the c's in these expressions change in order for the dynamic hazard to show up?

4. Study Section 26.4, *Design of Hazard-Free Combinational Networks.*

   (a) State two conditions which are sufficient to assure that a sum-of-products expression for F^t represents a hazard-free two-level AND-OR network.

   (b) State two conditions which are sufficient to assure that a product-of-sums expression for F^t represents a hazard-free two-level OR-AND network.

   (c) Why does transforming a network of AND and OR gates to NAND or NOR gates introduce no hazards?

5. Study Section 26.5, *Essential Hazards.*

   (a) How can essential hazards be determined from the flow table?

   (b) For Table 26–1, find two more essential hazards in addition to those mentioned in the text.

   (c) How can essential hazards be eliminated from a network?

(d) If the network of Fig. 26–10 is started in stable total state ⓒ and the input is changed from 0 to 1, specify the sequence of events which must occur in order for the network to go to an incorrect stable total state. At what *one* point in the network should a delay be added to eliminate this essential hazard?

6. Study Section 26.6, *Hazard-Free Realizations Using S-R Flip-Flops.*

   (a) Why is it permissible to have 1-hazards, but not 0-hazards, in the input networks for an S-R flip-flop?

   (b) How can a network be designed which is free of 0-hazards?

   (c) Why is it permissible to have 0-hazards, but not 1-hazards, in the input networks for a NAND-gate flip-flop?

   (d) The following network is part of the realization of a flow table which contains essential hazards. Assume that initially $x_1 = 1$, $x_2 = 0$, $y_1 = 0$ and $y_2 = 1$. If X_2 changing to 1 causes y_2 to go to 0, what sequence of events would cause y_1 to go to the wrong state?

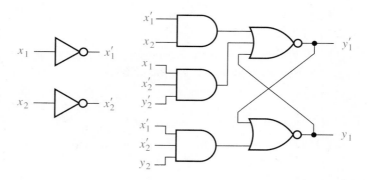

   (e) Assuming that the network delays are concentrated mainly in the gate outputs, how should the above gate structure be changed to eliminate any essential hazards?

(f) The following gate is one of the input gates to a NAND flip-flop as in Fig. 26–15(b). Assuming that the network delays are concentrated mainly in the gate outputs, how should the gate be changed to eliminate any essential hazards?

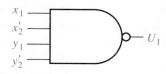

7. Work Problems 26.3(a), 26.4, 26.6(a), and 26.7.

8. When you are satisfied that you can meet the objectives, take the readiness test.

Hazards

Even though an asynchronous sequential network is designed with a race-free state assignment using the procedures described in Unit 25, the network still may malfunction due to timing problems. Such timing problems, which arise due to gate and wiring delays, are referred to as hazards. This unit describes how to detect and eliminate these hazards so that the asynchronous network will function properly.

26.1
Hazards in Combinational Networks

When the input to a combinational network changes, unwanted switching transients may appear at the network output. These transients occur because different paths through the network from input to output may have different propagation delays. For example, consider the network of Fig. 26–1.

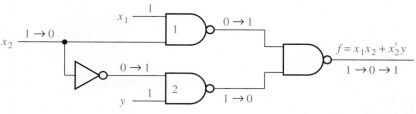

Figure 26–1
Network with 1-Hazard

Consider the case where $x_1 = y = 1$ and x_2 changes from 1 to 0. The network output should remain a constant 1; however, the network output may momentarily go to 0 if the gate outputs switch in the following sequence: gate 1 output goes to 1, then f goes to 0, then the inverter output goes to 1, then gate 2 output goes to 0, and finally f goes back to 1.

If, in response to an input change and for some combination of propagation delays, a network output may momentarily go to 0 when it should remain a constant 1, we say that the network has a *static 1-hazard*. Similarly, if the output may momentarily go to 1 when it should remain a constant 0, we say that the network has a *static 0-hazard*. If, when the output is supposed to change from 0 to 1 (or 1 to 0), the output may change three or more times, we say that the network has a *dynamic hazard*. Figure 26–2 illustrates possible outputs from a network with hazards. In each case the steady-state output of the network is correct, but a switching transient appears at the network output when the input is changed.

In the example of Fig. 26–1, note that although in the steady state x_2 and x_2' are complements, under transient conditions they are not. Thus in the analysis of a network for hazards, we must treat a variable and its complement as if they were two independent variables. The hazard in Fig. 26–1 can be eliminated by adding a redundant gate as shown in Fig. 26–3. During the time when x_2 is switching and $x_2 = x_2' = 0$, the term $x_1 y$ remains 1; hence f remains 1, and no false 0 appears at the network output. In Sections 26.2 and 26.4 we will study a general method for eliminating hazards from combinational networks.

Hazards in the combinational part of a sequential network can cause the sequential network to malfunction. Hazards in the output network can cause momentary false outputs, which may be a serious problem if the output serves as the input to another asynchronous network. As illustrated by the following

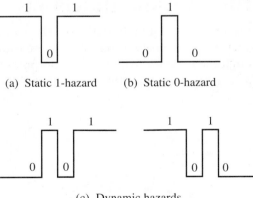

(a) Static 1-hazard   (b) Static 0-hazard

(c) Dynamic hazards

Figure 26–2
Types of Hazards

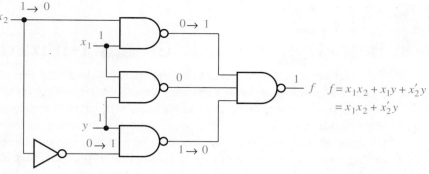

Figure 26–3
Network of Fig. 26–1 with Hazard Removed

example (Fig. 26–4) hazards in the next-state part of the network may cause the network to go to the wrong stable total state. If the network is in stable total state ④ ($x_1 = x_2 = y = 1$) and the x_2 input is changed to 0, the next stable total state should be ⑤. However, if because of the 1-hazard in the network, y momentarily goes to 0, and this feeds back before the x_2' signal goes to 1, the output of gate 2 will remain 1 and the network will end up in state ②. This malfunction can be eliminated by adding an extra gate as in Fig. 26–3.

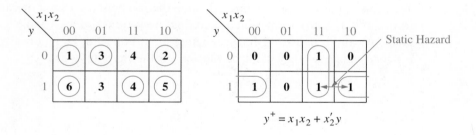

$$y^+ = x_1 x_2 + x_2' y$$

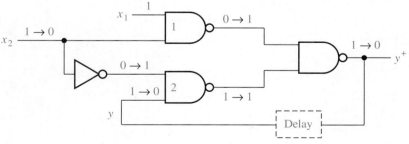

Figure 26–4
Sequential Network with Hazard

26.2
Detection of Static 0- and 1-Hazards

This section presents a systematic approach for detecting the presence of static hazards in a combinational network. We will only consider hazards which occur when a single input variable changes. Analysis begins by determining the *transient output function, F^t*, which represents the behavior of the network under transient conditions. The transient output function for a network is determined in the same way as the ordinary (steady-state) output function except a variable x_i and its complement x_i' are treated as independent variables. This must be done since during transient conditions x_i and x_i' may both momentarily assume the same values. This means that the following theorems of Boolean algebra *cannot* be used when manipulating F^t:

$$XX' = 0, \; X + X' = 1, \; X + X'Y = X + Y, \; XY + X'Z + YZ = XY + X'Z, \text{ etc.}$$

The associative, distributive, and DeMorgan's laws as well as $XX = X$, $X + XY = X$, etc., *can* be used.

The following example illustrates how F^t is used to detect hazards. For Fig. 26–5(a), the transient output function is

$$F^t = abc + (a + d)(a' + c') = abc + aa' + ac' + a'd + c'd \qquad (26\text{--}1)$$

To check for static 1-hazards, the 1-terms of F^t are plotted on a Karnaugh map as in Fig. 26–5(b). (If F is in sum-of-products form, each product term is called a 1-term of F.) The term aa' can momentarily go to 1 when a is changing; however, this cannot cause a 1-hazard since the momentary 1 cannot cause F to go to 0. Similarly, any term which contains the product of a variable and its complement cannot cause a 1-hazard. Thus, such terms can be ignored when checking for 1-hazards (they can't be plotted on the map anyway).

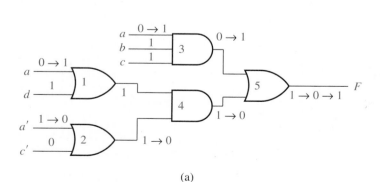

(a)

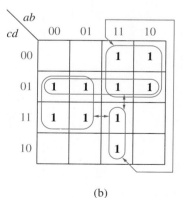

(b)

Figure 26–5
Detection of Static 1-Hazards

If two 1's in adjacent squares on the map of F^t are covered by the same 1-term, changing the input to the network between the corresponding two input states cannot cause a hazard. For example, in Fig. 26–5(b), changing the input from $abcd = 1100$ to 1000 cannot cause a hazard because the corresponding 1's on the map are both covered by the term ac'. This means that when b is changing, the ac' term remains a constant 1; hence F^t remains a constant 1, and there is no 1-hazard. However, if two 1's in adjacent squares on the map are not covered by a single 1-term, a hazard is present. For example, an input change from 0111 to 1111 causes a hazard because the corresponding 1's are not covered by a single 1-term. For this input change, the term $a'd$ must change from 1 to 0 while the term abc changes from 0 to 1. Since all of the other 1-terms are 0 during this transition, F^t can go to 0 if the $a'd$ term goes to 0 before the abc term goes to 1; therefore, a 1-hazard is present. This hazard will actually show up at the network output, as indicated in Fig. 26–5(a), if the gate outputs change in the order: 2, 4, 5, 3, 5. The other two input changes which cause 1-hazards are indicated by arrows on the map.

In Equation (26–1), the term aa' indicates a possible 0-hazard since this term can momentarily go to 1 when it is supposed to remain 0. This 0-hazard is actually present only if the other terms of F^t are 0 while a is changing. If we set $d = 0$, $c' = 0$ ($c = 1$), and $b = 0$, F^t reduces to aa'. Therefore if $b = 0$, $c = 1$, $d = 0$, and a changes, F^t can momentarily go to 1, which indicates the presence of a 0-hazard. Although 0-hazards can be detected by careful inspection of the sum-of-products form of F^t, a more systematic approach uses the product-of-sums form. Factoring F^t by using the second distributive law, $X + YZ = (X + Y)(X + Z)$, gives

$$F^t = (abc + a + d)(abc + a' + c')$$
$$= (a + d)(a + a' + c')(b + a' + c')(c + a' + c')$$

Terms like $a + a' + c'$ and $c + a' + c'$ either remain a constant 1 or momentarily go to 0 and cannot cause a 0-hazard. The remaining 0-terms[1] of F^t are plotted on the map of Fig. 26–6(b). Note that the 0's on this map are in the same location as the implied 0's on the map of Fig. 26–5(b); however, we cannot determine how the 0's are grouped from Fig. 26–5(b).

An alternate procedure for mapping the 0-terms of F^t uses the fact that the 1-terms of $(F^t)'$ are the 0-terms of F^t. From Equation (26–1),

$$(F^t)' = (a' + b' + c')(a'd' + ac)$$
$$= a'd' + a'ac + \cancel{a'b'd'} + ab'c + \cancel{a'c'd'} + acc'$$

Note that two terms were eliminated using $X + XY = X$. When the terms $a'd'$ and $ab'c$ are plotted on the map using 0's instead of 1's, we obtain the same plot of 0-terms of F^t as in Fig. 26–6(b).

---

[1] If F is in product-of-sums form, each sum term is called a 0-term of F.

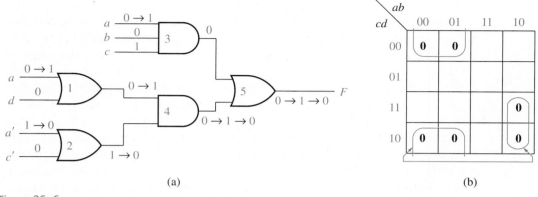

Figure 26–6
Detection of Static 0-Hazards

To detect 0-hazards, we examine pairs of adjacent 0's on the map of Fig. 26–6(b). Two adjacent 0's covered by the same 0-term cannot lead to a 0-hazard. For example, when $abcd$ is changed from 0000 to 0100, no 0-hazard is present because the term $a + d$ remains a constant 0 during this transition and F^t cannot change. If two adjacent 0's are not covered by the same 0-term, a 0-hazard is present. For example, if $abcd$ changes from 0010 to 1010, $a + d$ must change 0 to 1 while $a' + b + c'$ changes 1 to 0; therefore, both terms can momentarily be equal to 1, which indicates a 0-hazard. This 0-hazard will show up at the network output as indicated in Fig. 26–6(a) if the gates switch in the order: 1, 4, 5, 2, 4, 5.

In summary, the following procedure can be used to find all of the static 1- and 0-hazards in a network due to single input variable changes:

1. Determine the transient output function of the network F^t, and reduce F^t to sum-of-products form treating each variable and its complement as separate variables.
2. Examine each pair of adjacent input states for which F^t is 1. If there is no 1-term which includes both input states of the pair, a 1-hazard is present. (This is conveniently accomplished by plotting the 1-terms of F^t on a Karnaugh map and checking each pair of adjacent 1's on the map.)
3. If the sum of products for F^t *does not* contain the product of a variable and its complement, no 0-hazards are present. If the sum of products for F^t *does* contain the product of a variable and its complement, a 0-hazard *may* be present. To detect all 0-hazards,
   (a) Obtain the product-of-sums for F^t by factoring or other means (still treating x_i and x_i' as separate variables).
   (b) Examine each pair of adjacent input states for which F^t is 0. If there is no 0-term which includes both input states of the pair, a 0-hazard is present. (This is conveniently done by plotting the 0-terms of F^t on a Karnaugh map and checking each pair of adjacent 0's on the map.)

Static 1- and 0-hazards can be eliminated by adding additional gates to the network to produce the missing 1-terms and 0-terms. A procedure for designing hazard-free networks is given in Section 26.4.

26.3
Dynamic Hazards

Dynamic hazards due to a change in an input variable x_i can only occur if there are three or more paths between the x_i (and/or x_i') input and the network output. This is necessary since a dynamic hazard involves a triple change in output, so the effect of the input change must reach the output at three different times. A network may have a dynamic hazard even if it is free of static hazards as illustrated by the example of Fig. 26–7. For this network, the transient output func-

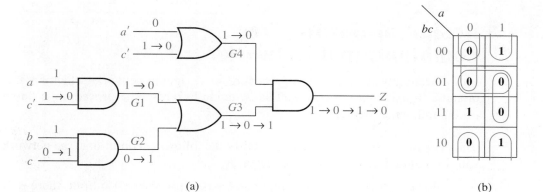

(a)

(b)

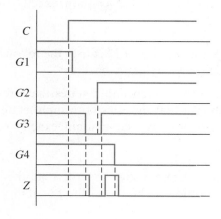

(c)

Figure 26–7
Network with a Dynamic Hazard

tion is

$$Z^t = (ac' + bc)(a' + c') = a'ac' + \underline{a'bc} + \underline{ac'} + bcc'$$
$$= (ac' + b)(ac' + c)(a' + c') = (a + b)(\underline{b + c'})(a + c)(c + c')(a' + c')$$

Plotting the 1-terms and 0-terms of Z^t on the map of Fig. 26–7(b) reveals that there are no 1-hazards or 0-hazards. Inspection of the network shows that the only input variable which could cause a dynamic hazard when it changes is c (since c is the only variable with three paths to the output). If we choose $a = b = 1$, the effect of a change in c can propagate to the output along all three paths. If the gate outputs change in the order shown in Fig. 26–7(c), the $G3$ output undergoes a 1-0-1 change before the $G4$ output changes 1 to 0, and the dynamic hazard shows up at the output.

The procedure used to detect static hazards can be extended to allow the detection of all dynamic hazards; however, this is beyond the scope of this text.[2]

26.4
Design of Hazard-Free Combinational Networks

In this section we will discuss a procedure for designing networks which are free of static 0- and 1-hazards as well as dynamic hazards. The procedure is based on the following theorems:

Theorem 26.1:   If the 1-terms of F^t satisfy the following conditions, the network will not contain static or dynamic hazards:

1. For each pair of adjacent input states that produce a 1 output, there is at least one 1-term that includes both input states of the pair.
2. There are no 1-terms that contain exactly one pair of complementary literals.

Theorem 26.2:   If the 0-terms of F^t satisfy the following conditions, the network will not contain static or dynamic hazards:

1. For each pair of adjacent input states that produce a 0 output, there is at least one 0-term that includes both input states of the pair.
2. There are no 0-terms that contain exactly one pair of complementary literals.

Condition 1 of Theorem 26.1 assures that the network does not contain 1-hazards, and condition 2 eliminates the possibility of 0-hazards and dynamic

---

[2] See McCluskey, E. J., *Introduction to the Theory of Switching Circuits,* for a description of the procedure used to find dynamic hazards.

hazards. Alternatively, condition 1 of Theorem 26.2 assures that the network does not contain 0-hazards, and condition 2 eliminates the possibility of 1-hazards and dynamic hazards. Thus we can use either Theorem 26.1 or 26.2 to design a hazard-free network.

Based on Theorem 26.1, a design procedure for hazard-free networks is:

1. Find a sum-of-products expression (F^t) for the output in which every pair of adjacent 1's is covered by a 1-term. (The sum of all prime implicants will always satisfy this condition.)
2. Manipulate F^t to the desired form (by factoring,[3] DeMorgan's laws, etc.) treating each x_i and x_i' as independent variables so as to prevent introduction of hazards.

An alternative procedure, based on Theorem 26.2 is

1. Find a product-of-sums expression (F^t) for the output in which every pair of adjacent 0's is covered by a 0-term.
2. Manipulate F^t to the desired form without introducing hazards.

The following example illustrates the design of a network which is free of static and dynamic hazards. We will realize

$$f(a, b, c, d) = \sum m(1, 5, 7, 14, 15)$$

first using NAND gates and then using NOR gates. When f is read from the map (Fig. 26–8), a redundant term is included so that all pairs of adjacent 1's are covered and f is free from 1-hazards. Since no terms containing products of literals like xx' are included, f is automatically free of 0-hazards and dynamic hazards. Since simple factoring and application of DeMorgan's laws do not introduce any hazards, f can be realized using NAND gates as shown.

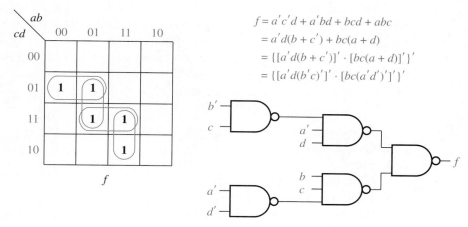

Figure 26–8

---

[3] Simple factoring using the ordinary distributive law does not introduce hazards; however, factoring using $XY + X'Z = (X + Z)(X' + Y)$ can introduce hazards.

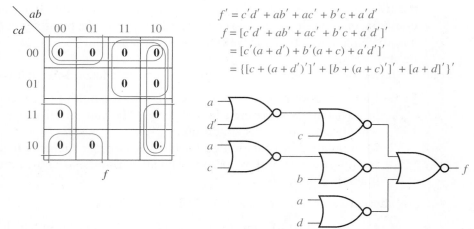

Figure 26–9

To realize f using NOR gates, we start by reading the 0's from the map (Fig. 26–9). Redundant terms are included so that all adjacent 0's are covered, so f is free of 0-hazards. Since no terms containing sums like $x + x'$ are included, f is automatically free of 1-hazards and dynamic hazards. Since factoring and applying DeMorgan's laws do not introduce any hazards, f can be realized using NOR gates as shown.

26.5
Essential Hazards

Even though an asynchronous sequential network is free of critical races and the combinational part of the network is free of static and dynamic hazards, timing problems due to propagation delays may still cause the network to malfunction and go to the wrong state. Consider, for example, the network of Fig. 26–10. Clearly, there are no hazards in the combinational part of the network, and inspection of the flow table shows that there are no critical races. If we start in state $\textcircled{a}$ and change x to 1, the network should go to state $\textcircled{d}$. However, consider the following possible sequence of events:

1. x changes 0 to 1.
2. Gate 2 output changes 0 to 1.
3. Flip-flop y_1 output changes 0 to 1.
4. Gate 4 output changes 0 to 1.
5. Flip-flop y_2 output changes 0 to 1.
6. Inverter output x' changes 1 to 0.
7. Gate 1 output changes 0 to 1, gate 2 output changes back to 0, and gate 4 output changes back to 0.
8. Flip-flop output y_1 changes back to 0.

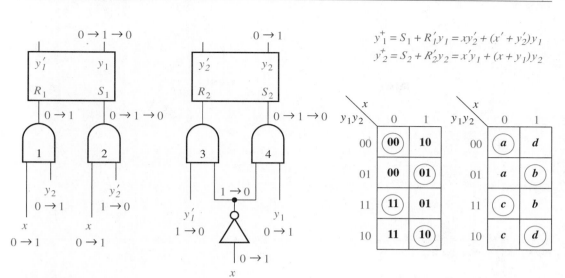

Figure 26–10
Figure 26–10
Network with Essential Hazards

Note that the final state of the network is $\textcircled{b}$ instead of $\textcircled{d}$. This came about because the delay in the inverter was longer than the other delays in the network, so that in effect part of the network saw the value $x = 1$ while the other part of the network saw the value $x = 0$. The net result was that the network acted as if the input x had changed three times instead of once so that the network went through the sequence of states $y_1y_2 = 00, 10, 11, 01$.

The malfunction illustrated in the previous example is referred to as an essential hazard. Essential hazards can be located by inspection of the flow table. We will define an essential hazard as follows:

> A flow table has an *essential hazard* starting in stable total state $\textcircled{s}$ for input variable x_i iff the stable total state reached after one change in x_i is different from the stable total state reached after three changes in x_i.

If an essential hazard exists in the flow table for stable total state $\textcircled{s}$ and input x_i, then when the network is realized there will be some combination of propagation delays which will cause the network to go to the wrong state when x_i is changed starting in $\textcircled{s}$. This occurs because the change in x_i reaches different parts of the network at different times. Figure 26–11 illustrates portions of several flow tables. Essential hazards exist for state $\textcircled{a}$ in cases (d) and (e).

In order to test a flow table for essential hazards, it is necessary to test each stable total state for each possible input change using the definition given above. For example, the flow table in Table 26–1 has essential hazards starting in $\textcircled{1}$ and changing x_1, starting in $\textcircled{5}$ and changing x_1, and starting in $\textcircled{4}$ and changing x_2.

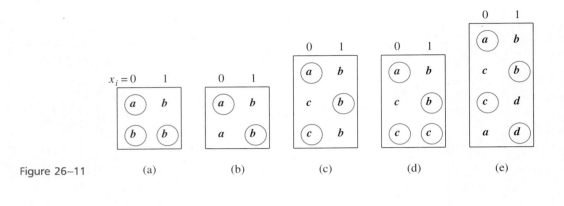

Figure 26–11   (a)   (b)   (c)   (d)   (e)

Table 26–1

Flow Table with Essential Hazards

$y_1 y_2$	$x_1 x_2$ 00	01	11	10
00	①	2	–	5
01	3	②	6	⑤
11	③	2	⑥	7
10	1	④	6	⑦

     Essential hazards can be eliminated by adding delays to the network. For the example of Fig. 26–10, if we add a sufficiently large delay to the output of flip-flop y_1, then the change in x will propagate to all of the gates before the change in y_1 does and the essential hazard is eliminated. For Table 26–1, to eliminate the essential hazard starting in ①, it is necessary to delay the change in y_2 until the change in x_1 has had a chance to propagate through the network.

     In summary, in order to design an asynchronous network which is free of timing problems, we must:

1. Make a state assignment which is free of critical races
2. Design the combinational part of the network so that it is free of hazards (this may require adding redundant gates)
3. Add delays in the feedback paths for the state variables as required to eliminate essential hazards

26.6
Hazard-Free Realizations Using S-R Flip-Flops

Use of S-R flip-flops simplifies the design of hazard-free asynchronous networks. A momentary 1 applied to the S or R input can set or reset the flip-flop; however, a momentary 0 applied to S or R will have no effect on the flip-flop state. There-

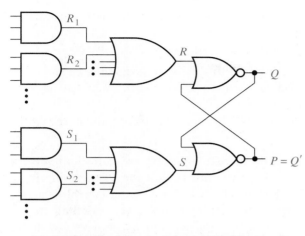
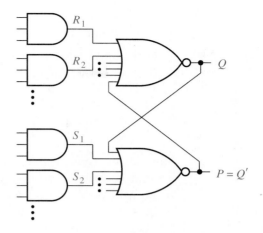
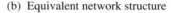

(a) *S-R* flip-flop driven by 2-level AND-OR networks   (b) Equivalent network structure

Figure 26–12
Gate Structures for S-R Flip-Flop Realization of
Flow Table

fore, the networks realizing S and R must be free of 0-hazards (since a 0-hazard can produce a momentary false 1), but the S and R networks may contain 1-hazards. A minimum two-level sum-of-products expression may contain 1-hazards, but it is inherently free of 0-hazards. For this reason, the minimum sum of products can be used as a starting point for realizing the S or R flip-flop input equations. In the process of realizing S and R, simple factoring or other transformations which do not introduce 0-hazards can, of course, be applied to the minimum sum-of-products expressions.

Figure 26–12(a) shows a typical network structure with the S-R flip-flop constructed from cross-coupled NOR gates. If multiple-input NOR gates are available, the OR gates can be eliminated as shown in Fig. 26–12(b). The two structures are equivalent since in both cases

$$Q = (P + R_1 + R_2 + \cdots)' \quad \text{and} \quad P = (Q + S_1 + S_2 + \cdots)'$$

Even if an asynchronous network is realized using S-R flip-flops, and the S and R networks are free of 0-hazards, essential hazards may still be present. Such essential hazards may be eliminated as discussed in Section 26.5 by adding delays in the feedback paths for the state variables. An alternative method for eliminating essential hazards[4] involves changing the gate structure of the network. This alternative method can be applied only if the wiring delays in the network are small compared with the gate delays and if we can assume that all of the gate delays are concentrated at the gate outputs.

---

[4] Armstrong, Friedman, and Menon, "Realization of Asynchronous Sequential Circuits Without Inserted Delay Elements," *IEEE Transactions on Computers,* Vol. C-17, pp. 129–134, February 1968.

As illustrated in Section 26.5, the following sequence of events is required for an essential hazard to cause a network to malfunction:

1. An input variable changes.
2. A state variable changes in response to the input variable change.
3. The effect of the state variable change propagates through the network and initiates another state variable change before
4. the original input variable change has propagated through the entire network.

Thus, in an asynchronous network with S-R flip-flops, we can eliminate the essential hazards by arranging the gate structure so that the effect of any input change will propagate to all flip-flop inputs before any state variable changes can propagate back to the flip-flop inputs. For example, we can eliminate the essential hazard in Fig. 26–10 by replacing the R_2 and S_2 networks with the network of Fig. 26–13. Assuming that wiring delays are negligible and that the gate delay is concentrated at the gate output, any change in x will propagate to R_2 and S_2 before flip-flop y_1 can change state and this change in y_1 can propagate to R_2 and S_2. This eliminates the essential hazard.

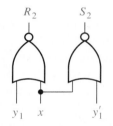

Figure 26–13

Next, we will consider a more general case in which the network is of the form of Fig. 26–12(b). Each AND gate can have inputs of the form shown in Fig. 26–14(a), where the x's are external inputs to the network and the y's are fed back from flip-flop outputs. If there are essential hazards in the flow table, then the network could malfunction due to the inverter delays. If we replace the AND gate with the NOR-AND network of Fig. 26–14(b), the inverters on the x variables are eliminated. In the revised circuit, a change in any x will propagate to the S_i (or R_i) terminal before a flip-flop can change state and the corresponding y signal can propagate to S_i or R_i. Therefore, if we replace all of the AND gates in Fig. 26–12 with NOR-AND combinations as indicated in Fig. 26–14, all of the essential hazards will be eliminated. (We are still assuming that the network delays are largely concentrated at the gate outputs. Given a sufficiently long propagation delay in one of the x wires, an essential hazard could still cause a malfunction.)

Figure 26–15 shows two of the possible gate configurations when NAND flip-flops are used to realize a state variable in an asynchronous network. If minimum sum-of-products expressions are derived for S and R, then the complements of these expressions will be minimum product-of-sums expressions for S' and R'. If S and R are free of 0-hazards, S' and R' will be free of 1-hazards.

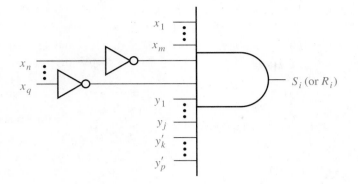

(a) AND gate with general inputs

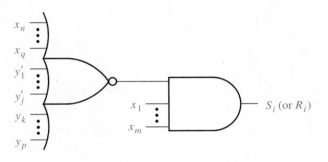

(b) Replacement for (a)

Figure 26–14
A Gate Transformation for Elimination of
Essential Hazards

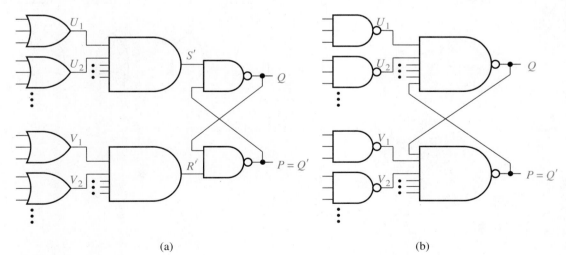

(a)   (b)

Figure 26–15
Gate Structure for NAND Flip-Flop Realization
of Flow Table

Y_1Y_2		X_1X_2 00	01	11	10
0 0	a	$\textcircled{a}$	b	d	$\textcircled{a}$
0 1	b	c	$\textcircled{b}$	$\textcircled{b}$	a
1 1	c	$\textcircled{c}$	d	b	$\textcircled{c}$
1 0	d	a	$\textcircled{d}$	$\textcircled{d}$	c

(a) Flow table

Y_1Y_2	X_1X_2 00	01	11	10
0 0	00	01	10	00
0 1	11	01	01	00
1 1	11	10	01	11
1 0	00	10	10	11

(b) Transition table

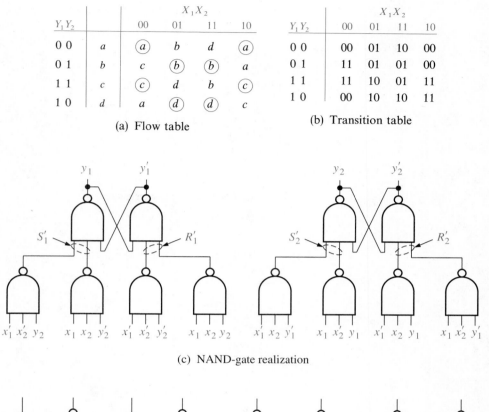

(c) NAND-gate realization

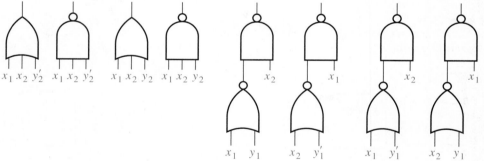

Figure 26–16   (d) Gate transformation to eliminate essential hazards

This is exactly what is needed for the NAND flip-flops since a 0 applied to S' or R' can change the flip-flop state but a 1 cannot. If multiple-input NAND gates are available, Fig. 26–15(a) can be transformed to Fig. 26–15(b) by eliminating the AND gates and replacing the OR gates by NAND gates with complemented inputs. Note that for both networks

$$Q = (P \cdot U_1 \cdot U_2 \ldots)' \quad \text{and} \quad P = (Q \cdot V_1 \cdot V_2 \ldots)'$$

If a network constructed using the configuration of Fig. 26–15(b) contains essential hazards, they can be eliminated by replacing each NAND gate (except the flip-flop) with a NOR-NAND configuration or equivalent, using a transformation similar to Fig. 26–14.

The example of Fig. 26–16 illustrates realization of a flow table using the gate structure of Fig. 26–15(b). First, the transition table is formed from the flow table using the given race-free state assignment. The flip-flop input equations, derived from the transition table in the usual manner, are

$$S_1' = (X_1'X_2'Y_2)'(X_1X_2Y_2')' \qquad R_1' = (X_1'X_2'Y_2')'(X_1X_2Y_2)'$$
$$S_2' = (X_1'X_2Y_1')'(X_1X_2'Y_1)' \qquad R_2' = (X_1'X_2Y_1)'(X_1X_2'Y_1')'$$

Figure 16–16(c) shows the resulting network. Assuming that the gate delays are largely concentrated at the gate outputs, the essential hazards can be eliminated by making the transformation shown in Fig. 26–16(d).

PROBLEMS

26.1 Find all of the essential hazards in the following flow table. For each hazard, specify the initial value of $X_1X_2Q_1Q_2$ and which input variable is changing. How can the essential hazard which occurs starting in b be eliminated?

		X_1X_2			
	Q_1Q_2	00	01	11	10
a	00	(a)	b	(a)	d
b	01	a	(b)	c	–
c	11	–	d	(c)	d
d	10	a	(d)	a	(d)

26.2 For the following flow table, find all of the essential hazards. For each hazard, specify the initial stable state and which input variable is changing. Explain how one of the essential hazards can be eliminated.

	x_1x_2			
y_1y_2	00	01	11	10
00	(1)	2	–	3
01	1	(2)	4	(3)
11	–	5	(4)	3
10	1	(5)	(6)	3

26.3 Find all of the static hazards in the following networks. For each hazard, specify the values of the variables which are constant and the variable which is changing. Indicate how all of these hazards could be eliminated by adding gates to the existing networks. (This means that you can add gates or gate inputs to a network as it stands, but you cannot change any of the connections in the given networks.)

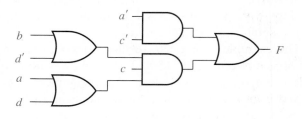

(a)

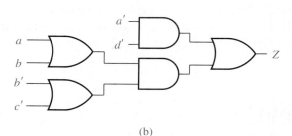

(b)

26.4 (a) Find all of the static hazards in the following network. For each hazard, specify the values of the input variables and which variable is changing when the hazard occurs. Also specify the order in which the gate outputs must change.

   (b) There is a dynamic hazard which occurs when the output of the network changes from 0 to 1. Specify the values of the input variables before and after. In which order must the gate outputs switch in order for this hazard to occur?

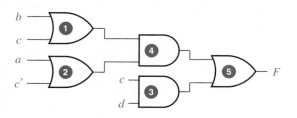

26.5 Repeat Problem 26.4 for the following network.

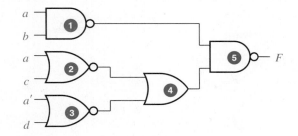

26.6 Find a hazard-free realization for each of the following functions using only 3-input NOR gates.
(a) $f(a, b, c, d) = \sum m(0, 2, 6, 7, 8, 10, 13)$
(b) $f(a, b, c, d) = \sum m(2, 3, 6, 7, 8, 10, 13)$

26.7 Find all of the essential hazards in the flow table of Fig. 24–6(b). Make any necessary changes so that your solution to Problem 25.5 is free of all hazards.

27

Asynchronous Sequential Network Design

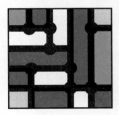

OBJECTIVES

1. Use the short-cut method to derive S-R flip-flop input equations for an asynchronous network.

2. Design, construct, and test an asynchronous sequential network.

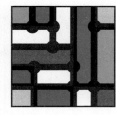

STUDY GUIDE

1. Study Section 27.1, *Summary of Design Procedure.*

2. Study Section 27.2, *Short-Cut Method for Deriving S-R Flip-Flop Input Equations.*

   (a) Under what conditions can the short-cut method be applied for deriving S-R input equations?

   (b) If you are interested in a proof of the method, read Appendix C.3.

   (c) Given the next-state map for flip-flop Q_i, how do you read S_i from the map when using the short-cut method? How do you read R_i?

3. Read Section 27.3, *Design Example.*

   (a) Verify that the flow table of Table 27–1 meets the problem specifications.

   (b) Verify that the designs of Figs. 27–8 and 27–9 are correct and free of hazards.

4. Read Section 27.4, *Testing Asynchronous Sequential Networks.* When a toggle switch is used as an input to an asynchronous network, why is a switch filter necessary?

5. Work out the solution to your assigned design problem, and check to see that your solution meets all of the design specifications. If you use a CAD program like *LogicAid* to derive the minimum logic equations from the state table, you will need to modify these equations to obtain a hazard-free solution. If you express each next-state function as a sum of all its prime implicants, the resulting expression will be hazard-free.

6. Carry out the simulation or lab testing as specified for your problem. If you have difficulty getting your circuit to work, try starting in each stable total state and verify that the output is correct and that the circuit goes to the proper next state when the input is changed.

7. When you get your network working properly, demonstrate its operation to a proctor. After successful completion of the project, turn in your design and test results. (No readiness test is required.)

Asynchronous Sequential Network Design

We have already studied the various steps in the design of asynchronous sequential networks—derivation and reduction of flow tables (Unit 24), state assignment to avoid critical races (Unit 25), and derivation of hazard-free realizations (Unit 26). This unit contains a summary of the design procedure and a comprehensive design example.

27.1
Summary of Design Procedure

1. Given the problem statement, determine the required relationship between the input and output. Derive a primitive flow table which has one stable total state per row, and specify the output associated with each stable total state.
2. Reduce the primitive flow table to a minimum number of rows. This may conveniently be done in two steps. First, determine equivalent stable total states and find a minimum-row *primitive* flow table. Then merge rows in this table to find the final reduced table. A merger diagram may be helpful in selecting rows to be merged.
3. Find a state assignment which eliminates all critical races between state variables. In this process it may be necessary to expand the flow table by adding rows.
4. Form the transition table by substituting the assigned values of the state variables for each state in the expanded flow table. If a Mealy output table is used, fill in unspecified entries as required to avoid transients in the output. Plot the next-state maps and output maps from the transition table.
5. If flip-flops are not used, find a hazard-free realization for each next-state function using available logic gates.
6. If S-R flip-flops are used, plot the flip-flop input maps and find a realization which is free of 0-hazards for each S and R. (If NAND-gate flip-flops are used, the flip-flop inputs are the complements of S and R and must be free of 1-hazards.)
7. Find a hazard-free realization of the output functions.
8. If essential hazards are present in the flow table, add delays in the feedback paths or modify the gate structure as required to eliminate the essential hazards.
9. Check your design by laboratory testing or computer simulation.

27.2
Short-Cut Method for Deriving S-R Flip-Flop Input Equations

Most asynchronous networks are designed so that no cycles are present in the flow table. When the state assignment procedures discussed in Unit 25 are used, the resulting transition table will generally be free of all races (both critical and noncritical). This section introduces a fast method for deriving S-R flip-flop input equations which can be applied to any cycle-free asynchronous flow table provided that a race-free state assignment is used. This method is based on the following theorem:

> If a cycle-free asynchronous flow table is realized with S-R flip-flops using a race-free state assignment, then for each flip-flop Q_i, there exist S and R equations which are independent of Q_i.

Note, for example, that in Fig. 25-2(b), the S-R equations for flip-flop Q_1 depend on Q_2, but not on Q_1. Similarly, the S-R equations for flip-flop Q_2 depend on Q_1, but not on Q_2. (A general proof of the above theorem is given in Appendix C.3.)

From the following table, observe that when $Q_i = 0$, $S_i = Q_i^+$; similarly, when $Q_i = 1$, $R_i = (Q_i^+)'$.

Q_i	Q_i^+	S_i	R_i
0	0	0	X
0	1	1	0
1	0	0	1
1	1	X	0

Thus, since S_i is independent of Q_i, we can read S_i directly from the $Q_i = 0$ half of the Q_i^+ map. Similarly, we can read R_i directly from the 0's of the $Q_i = 1$ half of the Q_i^+ map. Note that this is exactly the same procedure as for the short-cut

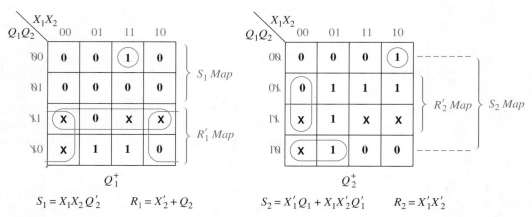

$$S_1 = X_1 X_2 Q_2' \qquad R_1 = X_2' + Q_2 \qquad\qquad S_2 = X_1' Q_1 + X_1 X_2' Q_1' \qquad R_2 = X_1' X_2'$$

Figure 27-1
Derivation of S-R Equations by Short-Cut Method

method for deriving J-K flip-flop input equations (Section 12.5) except that J is replaced with S and K with R. The S-R equations will be exactly the same as the J-K equations, and the short-cut method for deriving J-K equations can be applied. In general, the short-cut method for deriving S-R equations does *not* apply to *synchronous* networks because state assignments for synchronous networks permit two or more state variables to change simultaneously.

The next-state maps from Fig. 25–2(a) are reproduced in Fig. 27–1 to illustrate the short-cut method. Note that the resulting S-R equations are the same as those derived from the S-R maps in Fig. 25–2(b).

27.3
Design Example

Figure 27–2 shows a system of pipes with flowmeters to measure the fluid flowing through pipes A and B. The flowmeter in pipe A puts out a series of pulses with a pulse rate proportional to the flow in pipe A, and similarly the pulse rate from the other flowmeter is proportional to the rate of flow in pipe B. A "digital pulse subtracter" is to be designed to determine the rate of flow in pipe C. Thus the output pulse rate from the subtracter should be equal to the difference of the pulse rates from flowmeters A and B.

Figure 27–3(b) shows a typical timing diagram for the pulse subtracter. Input lines A and B each receive a series of pulses of varying frequency and pulse width. Under normal operation, the pulse frequency on line A is greater than that on line B and the number of pulses on the output line is the difference of the number of pulses received on lines A and B. Should the pulse frequency on line B exceed that of A, the extra B pulses are ignored and no pulses are output on line Z. The output pulses should have the same width as the A pulses.

We will design the network so that when an A pulse occurs, an output pulse will occur. However, if a B pulse starts before (or during) an A pulse, we cancel the effect of the next A pulse so that it does not produce an output pulse. The output will never be turned on or off in the middle of an A pulse. In constructing the primitive flow table, we will assume that only one input variable changes at a time. (In actual practice, A and B might occasionally change simultaneously, but this will occur so infrequently that the error produced by ignoring simultaneous changes will be negligible compared with the error in the flowmeters.)

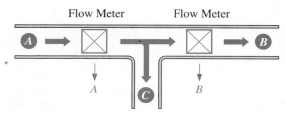

Figure 27–2
System of Pipes with Flowmeters

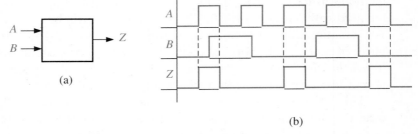

(a)

(b)

Figure 27–3
Digital Pulse Subtracter

Sketching the various waveforms which can occur (Fig. 27–4) is helpful in constructing the primitive flow table. The circled numbers under each waveform indicate the corresponding stable total states which are reached in the primitive flow table (Table 27–1).

1. If no B pulse occurs, $Z = A$:

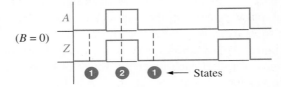

2. If a B pulse is started before an A pulse, the A pulse is canceled:

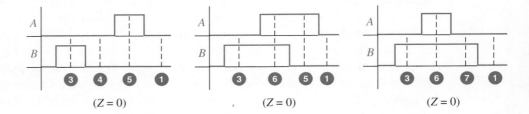

3. If several A pulses occur during a B pulse, only the first one is canceled:

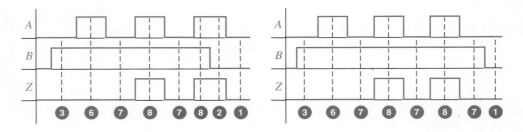

4. If a B pulse starts in the middle of an A pulse, the next A pulse is canceled:

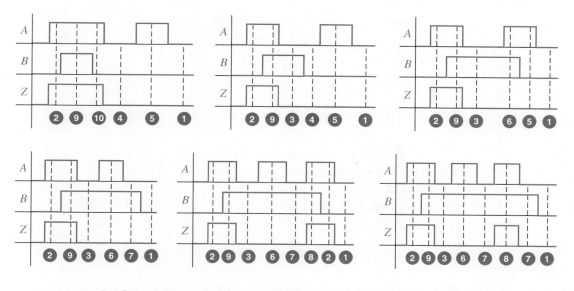

5. If the B pulse frequency is higher than A, the extra B pulses are ignored:

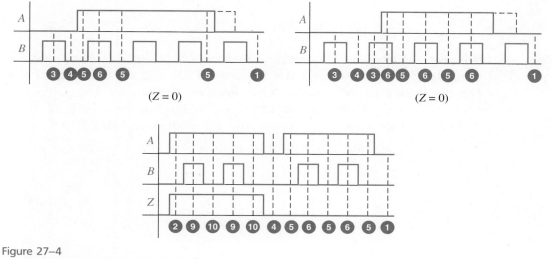

Figure 27–4
Timing Diagrams for Pulse Subtracter

Table 27–1 shows the resulting primitive flow table together with the significance of each stable total state.

Table 27–1

Primitive Flow Table for Pulse Subtracter

		AB				Z
		00	01	11	10	
reset	1	①	3	–	2	0
A on, Z on	2	1	–	9	②	1
B on, cancel next A	3	4	③	6	–	0
cancel next A	4	④	3	–	5	0
A on (canceled)	5	1	–	6	⑤	0
A on (canceled), B on	6	–	7	⑥	5	0
B on (don't cancel next A)	7	1	⑦	8	–	0
A on, B on, Z on (don't cancel next A)	8	–	7	⑧	2	1
A on, B on, Z on, cancel next A	9	–	3	⑨	10	1
A on, Z on, cancel next A	10	4	–	9	⑩	1

For the primitive table (Table 27–1), the sets of stable total states which have the same inputs and outputs are

$$(1, 4) \quad (3, 7) \quad (8, 9) \quad \text{and} \quad (2, 10)$$

However, $1 \not\equiv 4$ because the next states in column 10 (2 and 5) are not equivalent. Similarly, $3 \not\equiv 7$ because $6 \not\equiv 8$, $8 \not\equiv 9$ because $3 \not\equiv 7$, and $2 \not\equiv 10$ because $1 \not\equiv 4$. Therefore, this primitive table has a minimum number of rows. The merger diagram of Fig. 27–5 shows the table can be reduced to five rows (Table 27–2). The following transitions between rows are required in Table 27–2:

$$e \to b \quad c, d \to a; \quad a, e \to b \quad c \to d; \quad b \to c \quad a \to e; \quad b \to c \quad d \to a$$

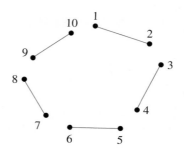

Figure 27–5
Merger Diagram for Table 27–1

Table 27–2
Reduced Table

	00	01	11	10
a	①	3	9	②
b	④	③	6	5
c	1	7	⑥	⑤
d	1	⑦	⑧	2
e	4	3	⑨	⑩

AB (column group label)

To avoid critical races, we must construct a state assignment which has the following adjacency sets:

$$(b, e) \quad (a, c, d); \quad (a, b, e) \quad (c, d); \quad (b, c) \quad (a, e); \quad (b, c) \quad (a, d)$$

The map of Fig. 27–6 satisfies all of these adjacencies directly except (b, c), and (b, c) is satisfied by adding row f. Table 27–3 is the expanded flow table based on this assignment.

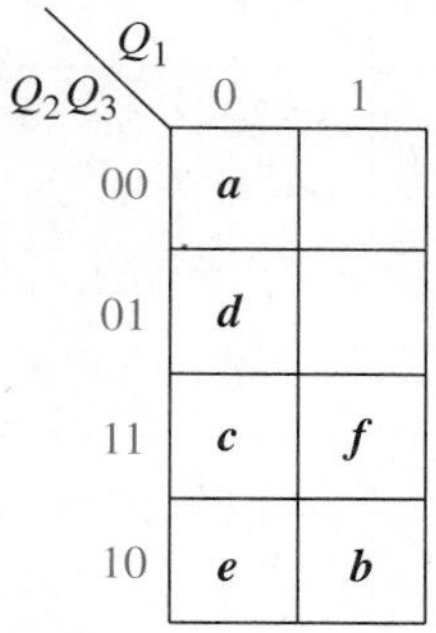

Q_2Q_3 \ Q_1	0	1
00	a	
01	d	
11	c	f
10	e	b

Figure 27–6
State Assignment for Table 27–2

Table 27–3
Expanded Flow Table

		00	01	11	10	00	01	11	10
000	a	ⓐ	e	e	ⓐ	0	0	1	1
110	b	ⓑ	ⓑ	f	f	0	0	0	0
011	c	d	d	ⓒ	ⓒ	0	0	0	0
001	d	a	ⓓ	ⓓ	a	0	0	1	1
010	e	b	b	ⓔ	ⓔ	–	0	1	1
111	f	–	–	c	c	–	–	0	0

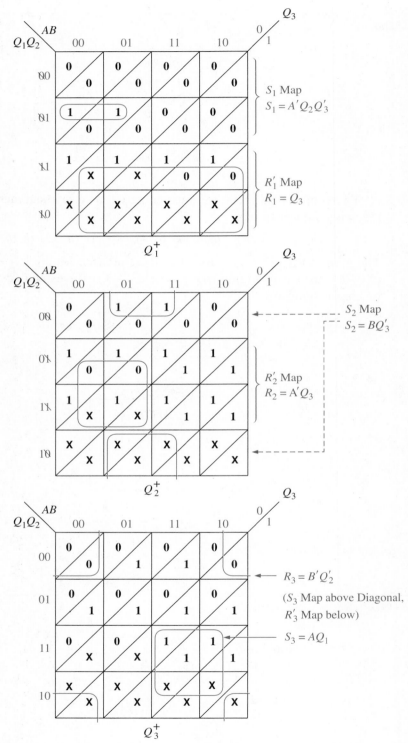

Figure 27–7
Derivation of S-R Equations by Short-Cut Method

Table 27–4

Transition Table

$Q_1Q_2Q_3$	AB 00	01	11	10	00	01	11	10
0 0 0	000	010	010	000	0	0	1	1
0 0 1	000	001	001	000	0	0	1	1
0 1 0	110	110	010	010	–	0	1	1
0 1 1	001	001	011	011	0	0	0	0
1 1 0	110	110	111	111	0	0	0	0
1 1 1	–	–	011	011	–	–	0	0

$$Q_1^+Q_2^+Q_3^+ \qquad\qquad Z$$

Table 27–4 is the transition table. The S-R flip-flop equations are derived from the transition table using Karnaugh maps as shown in Fig. 27–7. The output equation, also derived from a Karnaugh map, is

$$Z = AQ_1'Q_3' + AQ_2'$$

Figure 27–8 shows the resulting network. The S-R input functions are hazard-free since each requires only one gate, and the Z function is also free of hazards. However, inspection of Table 27–3 shows that there are essential hazards starting in the following total states:

$$b{-}01, d{-}01, d{-}11, e{-}11, e{-}10$$

Therefore, it may be necessary to add delays to the flip-flop outputs in order to assure proper operation of the network.

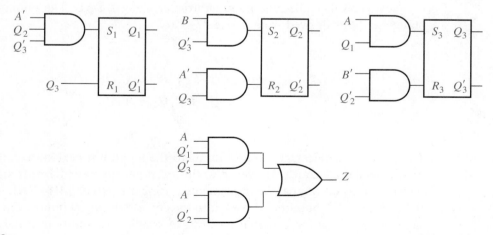

Figure 27–8

Realization of Pulse Subtracter using S-R Flip-Flops

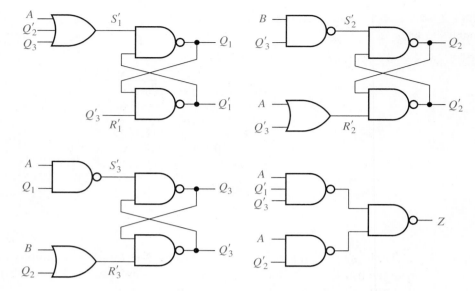

Figure 27–9
Realization of Pulse Subtracter with NAND Flip-Flops

Figure 27–9 shows an alternate realization using NAND flip-flops. The flip-flop inputs are the complements of those in Fig. 27–8. The gate structure has been chosen so as to eliminate the essential hazards, assuming that the network delays are largely concentrated at the gate outputs. Note that A and B require no inverters, and that they appear as inputs to the same gates as the Q's which feed back from the flip-flop outputs.

Next we will realize the pulse subtracter using a PAL. The minimum next-state equations derived from Table 27–3 are

$$Q_1^+ = X_1'Q_2Q_3' + Q_1Q_3'$$
$$Q_2^+ = Q_2Q_3' + X_1Q_2 + X_2Q_3'$$
$$Q_3^+ = X_2Q_3 + Q_2Q_3 + X_1Q_1$$
$$Z = X_1Q_1'Q_3' + X_1Q_2'$$

In general, it is necessary to add terms to the minimum next-state equations to eliminate static hazards. However, in this example, no static hazards are present. The above equations can be implemented using a 12H6 or 14H4 PAL (see Table 9–2) with the Q^+ outputs fed back into the corresponding Q inputs. The resulting network may contain essential hazards, in which case addition of delays in the feedback loop may be necessary.

27.4
Testing Asynchronous Sequential Networks

The following problems each require the design and testing of a fundamental mode asynchronous sequential network. For purposes of lab testing, the inputs will normally come from toggle switches. When a mechanical switch is operated, the switch contact will vibrate or bounce several times before coming to rest. This means that when a switch is closed, its output will contain a series of noise pulses instead of simply changing from 0 to 1. The spurious 1 or 0 output pulses can cause an asynchronous network to malfunction. For this reason, it is important that the toggle switch outputs be filtered to eliminate the effects of contact bounce. If the switches available in lab are not filtered, a simple filter can be built using a NAND-gate flip-flop (Fig. 27–10). A single-pole double-throw switch is connected to the flip-flop inputs. When the switch is moved to the upper position, a 0 is applied to the S' input and X becomes 1. Even if the switch bounces and makes intermittent contact in the upper position, the flip-flop cannot change state and its output will remain 1 until the switch is moved to the lower position. When the switch is moved to the lower position, a 0 is applied to R' and X becomes 0. Again, the flip-flop state will be unaffected by contact bounce. Thus, the X and X' outputs from the flip-flop will not contain spurious noise pulses and can be used as inputs to an asynchronous network.

When a network contains hazards, these hazards may or may not cause the network to malfunction depending on the distribution of gate and wiring delays in the network. For this reason, it may be necessary to insert added delay into the network in order to actually observe the presence of hazards. Also, it may be necessary to insert delay in the feedback paths of some networks to eliminate essential hazards. Normally, 2, 4, or 6 inverters in series will provide sufficient delay for these purposes. If necessary, a resistor-capacitor network can be placed between two of the inverters to increase the delay, or a special delay module may be used.

If your asynchronous network does not function properly when you build it in laboratory, determining the cause of the malfunction will generally be more

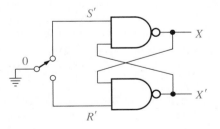

Figure 27–10
Contact Bounce Filter

Open all feedback
loops and insert switches

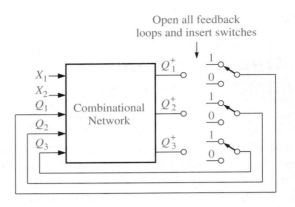

Figure 27–11
Troubleshooting an Asynchronous Network

difficult than for a clocked synchronous network. If you find that your network goes to the wrong state in response to some input change, the following procedure is suggested for tracking down the error:

1. Open all feedback loops and connect the state variables to switches as indicated in Fig. 27–11.
2. Set the switches to correspond to a given present state. Read the corresponding next state from the Q^+ outputs. If the next state is not correct, track down the error in the combinational network in the usual way.
3. If the network always generates the correct next state with the feedback loops open, but it goes to the wrong state when the switches are removed and the feedback loops are closed, this indicates that a race or hazard is present.

DESIGN PROBLEMS

27.1   Figure 27–12(a) illustrates a small room with a display set up. The room will hold only two people at a time. Visitors can enter or exit only through the turnstiles as shown. Each turnstile puts out a 1 signal whenever someone is in it. Whenever there are two people in the room, the entrance turnstile is locked to prevent additional entries and is not unlocked until one of the two people in the room starts to leave. It is unlocked at all other times. The room light is to be on whenever someone is entering, in, or leaving the room. Design an asynchronous circuit for Fig. 27–12(b) to furnish the signals indicated.

$X_1 = 1$ if the entrance turnstile is in use, and $X_2 = 1$ if the exit turnstile is in use.

$Z_1 = 1$ should turn on the light, and $Z_2 = 1$ should lock the entrance turnstile.

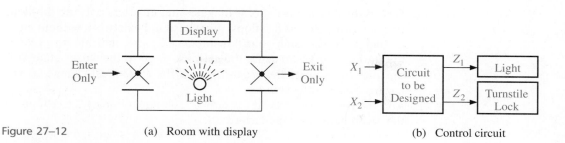

Figure 27–12   (a)   Room with display   (b)   Control circuit

Assume both inputs will not change simultaneously, although both inputs may be 1 simultaneously.

1. Derive a minimum-row flow table (6 rows).
2. Design the network using NAND gates and inverters only (no flip-flops or gates connected as flip-flops). Make sure your realization is free of combinational logic hazards.
3. Find all of the essential hazards. For one of the essential hazards indicate the order in which the gate outputs must change in order for the hazard to cause the network to go to the wrong state. Indicate where a delay element should be added to the network in order to eliminate this hazard.
4. Determine a suitable input sequence to test the network.

TESTING

5. Simulate or construct and test the network designed in part 2 using the sequence determined in part 4.
6. If no essential hazards show up, add delay to the appropriate gate output so that the essential hazard analyzed in part 3 will show up. Then add delay in the appropriate place(s) to eliminate the essential hazard(s) which were observed, and demonstrate that the network functions properly.

27.2   An "inhibited-toggle" flip-flop (Fig. 27–13) has a trigger input, T, and inhibit inputs, I_0 and I_1. The flip-flop output (Q) will change state if $I_0 = 1$ when T changes from 0 to 1, or if $I_1 = 1$ when T changes from 1 to 0. The flip-flop will not change state under any other conditions. You may assume that I_0 and I_1 will always be constant when T is changing.

1. Find a minimum-row flow table for the flip-flop (4 rows). (List the input variables in the order TI_0I_1.)

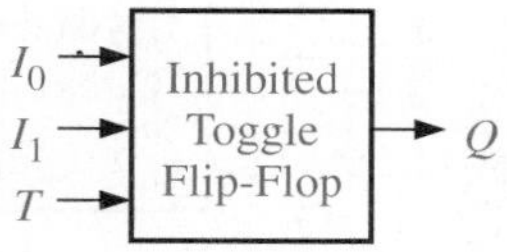

Figure 27–13

2. Design the flip-flop using NAND gates and inverters only (no flip-flops or gates connected as flip-flops). First design the network without eliminating hazards. Using your flow table and maps, indicate how one of the static hazards can cause the network to go to the wrong state. For this hazard, indicate the order in which the gates must change for the hazard to actually show up.

3. Add the necessary gates to the network designed in part 2 to eliminate the combinational logic hazards.

TESTING

4. Simulate or construct and test the network designed in part 3. If any essential hazards show up, add delays to eliminate them.

5. Remove the gates which were added to eliminate the combinational hazards so that you can test the design of part 2. Demonstrate that the static hazard which you analyzed in part 2 will actually cause the network to malfunction. You will probably have to add some delay to one of the gate outputs in order to make the hazard show up.

6. Reconnect the gates which were removed leaving any added delay in place and demonstrate that the network again functions properly.

27.3   A push-button combination lock (Fig. 27–14) for a door operates as follows:

When locked, the following input sequence will unlock the door: $X_1 X_2 =$ 00, 01, 11, 10, 00.

After the door is unlocked, (1) each time X_1 is depressed, the electric door opener will operate, and (2) depressing and releasing X_2 will relock the door.

Any sequence other than those given above will ring the alarm. For example, if the door is locked, the sequence 00, 01, 00 will ring the alarm; if the door is unlocked, the sequence 10, 11 will ring the alarm. Once the alarm starts ringing, it will keep ringing until the power is shut off.

You may assume that simultaneous input changes do not occur.

1. Derive a minimum-row flow table (7 rows).

2. Design the network using NAND gates and inverters only (no flip-flops or gates connected as flip-flops). Make sure your realization is free of combinational logic hazards.

3. Find all of the essential hazards. For one of the essential hazards indicate the order in which the gate outputs must change in order for the hazard to cause the network to go to the wrong state. Indicate where a delay element should be added to the network in order to eliminate each of the essential hazards.

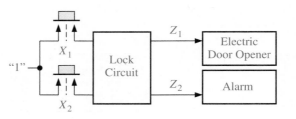

Figure 27–14

TESTING

4. Simulate or construct and test the network designed in part 2.
5. If no essential hazards show up, add delay to the appropriate gate output so that the essential hazard analyzed in part 3 will show up. Then add delay in the appropriate place(s) to eliminate the essential hazard(s) which were observed, and demonstrate that the network functions properly.

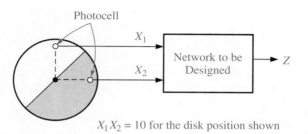

Figure 27–15

$X_1 X_2 = 10$ for the disk position shown

27.4 This problem concerns the design of an asynchronous sequential switching network (Fig. 27–15) to detect the direction of rotation of a shaft. A disk mounted on the shaft is half transparent and half opaque. Two photocells mounted in front of the disk detect light coming through the disk. Each photocell outputs a logic 1 when the transparent part of the disk is behind it; otherwise, it outputs a 0. The single output of the circuit is to be 1 when the shaft is rotating clockwise and 0 when the shaft is rotating counterclockwise. If the direction of rotation changes, the output should change as soon as possible.

1. Synthesize the network using only NAND and NOR gates (no flip-flops or gates connected as flip-flops). Design two different output networks, one which is minimum and one which is free of hazards.
2. Synthesize the network using two NAND-gate flip-flops and NAND and NOR gates. The output network should be the same as in part 1.

TESTING

3. Test the design of part 1 using the minimum output network.
4. Test the design of part 2 using each of the output networks. Check the output for transients by connecting Z to the T (clock) input of a J-K flip-flop. If the hazard doesn't show up when using the minimum output network, add some delay in the appropriate place so that the hazard will become apparent. Then make sure that your output is transient-free when the hazard-free output network is used.

27.5 Same as Problem 27.1 except:

2. Design the network using NAND gates connected as flip-flops. Use the gate configuration of Fig. 26–15(b).

In parts 3 and 6, do not use delays to eliminate the essential hazards. Instead, change the gate structure to eliminate the essential hazards using the technique described in Section 26.6.

27.6   Same as Problem 27.3 except:

    2. Design the network using NAND gates connected as flip-flops. Use the gate configuration of Fig. 26–15(b).

    In parts 3 and 5, do not use delays to eliminate the essential hazards. Instead, change the gate structure to eliminate the essential hazards using the technique described in Section 26.6.

27.7   A coin sorter uses three photocells to distinguish dimes, nickels, and quarters as shown in Fig. 27–16. As the coins roll down a chute past the photocells, 1, 2, or 3 photocells may be covered in sequence depending on the coin. The coin sorter uses an asynchronous network to determine which coin has passed by the photocells. The network has inputs $P1$, $P2$, and $P3$ from the photocells and outputs D, N, and Q. When the first photocell is covered, $P1 = 1$, etc. After a dime has rolled past the photocells, the network output D becomes 1 and remains 1 until the next coin comes along. Similarly, after a nickel, N becomes 1 and remains 1 until the next coin. And after a quarter, Q becomes 1 and remains 1 until the next coin. Design and test a network to meet the above specifications, following the steps given in Problem 27.3. Be sure to take advantage of the many don't cares in the flow table when you make your state assignment. Minimum number of rows in the flow table is six.

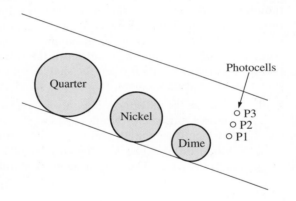

Figure 27–16

27.8   Work Problem 27.1, 27.2, 27.3, 27.4 or 27.7 using a suitable combinational PAL or other PLD. If internal feedback is used within the PLD, it will be impossible to eliminate any essential hazards since there is no way to add delays to the feedback paths. If you wish to demonstrate the presence and removal of essential hazards, you will need to use external feedback.

A

Discrete and Integrated Circuit Logic Gates

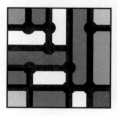

OBJECTIVES

1. Given the circuit diagram for a network of diode AND and OR gates, determine the function realized for positive and negative logic.

2. Explain the operation of a simple transistor logic circuit, assuming that the transistors act like ideal switches.

3. Be familiar with the operation of TTL logic gates.

4. Explain the operation of a MOS and CMOS logic circuit, assuming that the MOSFETs act like ideal switches.

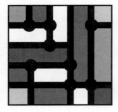

STUDY GUIDE

1. Study Section A.1, *Diode AND and OR Gates.*

   (a) Review Section 3.5, *Positive and Negative Logic.*

   (b) For Fig. A–2, if $e_1 = 2$, $e_2 = 5$, $e_3 = 1$, $E = +8$ volts, which diodes will be conducting and what will e_o be?

   (c) For Fig. A–3, if $e_1 = 2$, $e_2 = 5$, $e_3 = 1$, $E = -2$ volts, which diodes will be conducting and what will e_o be?

   (d) The bias voltage for a diode gate should always be chosen so that it forces current through the diodes and one of the diodes will always be conducting (or on the verge of conduction with zero voltage across the diode and zero current through the diode). When choosing values for the bias voltage (E), note the following:

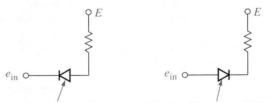

   Diode will conduct if $E > e_{in}$ Diode will conduct if $E < e_{in}$

   For the following gates, what range must E be so that one of the diodes always conducts if the input voltages can be -3 or $+3$?

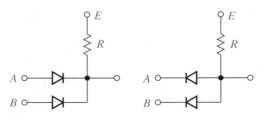

(e) Work Problems A.1 and A.2.

(f) Diodes can be connected in a regular pattern to form a memory array for a read-only memory (ROM) or a programmed logic array (PLA). If the switching elements in the memory array of Fig. 9–23 are diodes (connected to point in the same direction as the arrows on the switching elements), verify that these diodes form a set of OR gates which realize the functions given in Equations (9–9). If the switching elements in Fig. 9–27 are replaced with diodes, verify that resulting diode array is equivalent to the AND and OR gate array shown in Fig. 9–28.

2. Study Section A.2, *Transistor Logic Circuits.*

(a) Complete the following table for the network of Fig. A–6(a) and verify that the network realizes the NOR function for positive logic.

A	B	C	F
0	0	0	
0	0	$+V$	
0	$+V$	0	
0	$+V$	$+V$	
$+V$	0	0	
$+V$	0	$+V$	
$+V$	$+V$	0	
$+V$	$+V$	$+V$	

(b) Complete the following table for the network of Fig. A–7(a) and verify that the network realizes the NAND function for positive logic.

A	B	C	F
0	0	0	
0	0	$+V$	
0	$+V$	0	
0	$+V$	$+V$	
$+V$	0	0	
$+V$	0	$+V$	
$+V$	$+V$	0	
$+V$	$+V$	$+V$	

(c) For the networks of Figs. A–6(a) and A–7(a), if all transistors are replaced by PNP and the supply voltage is changed to $-V$, what functions would be realized if $-V$ is a logic 1 and 0 volts is a logic 0?

(d) For the networks of Figs. A–6(a) and A–7(a), if no changes are made in the network but 0 volts is a logic 1 and $+V$ is a logic 0, what functions would be realized? (*Hint:* negative logic theorem).

(e) Work Problem A.3.

3. Study Section A.3, *TTL Integrated Circuit Logic.*

   (a) Referring to Table A–3, if standard TTL integrated circuit packages are used what type and how many IC's would you use to implement Fig. 8–16(b)?

   (b) Referring to Table A–4, what TTL family would you select to obtain the lowest power consumption if speed of operation was not important?

   _____

   What TTL family would you select if fast operation was the most important consideration? _____

   (c) Referring to Fig. A–10, an input of 0.3 volts will act like a logic _____, an input of 4.2 volts will act like a logic _____, and an input of 1.5 volts _____. If the input is a logic 0, the output voltage will be in the range _____ and if the input is a logic 1, the output voltage will be in the range _____.

4. Study Section A.4, *MOS and CMOS Logic.*

   (a) For the following MOS logic network, draw a switch analog and determine the function realized by the network.

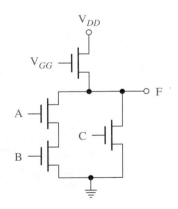

   (b) Work Problems A.4 and A.5.

A.1
Diode AND and OR Gates

AND and OR gates can be realized with a variety of circuits. This section describes how such gates can be constructed using diodes. The logic function realized by a given diode circuit configuration depends on whether we interpret the input and output voltage levels according to positive or negative logic.[1]

Figure A–1(a) shows the symbol used for a diode. The arrow in the diode symbol indicates the normal direction of current flow. The diode characteristic in Fig. A–1(b) shows the diode current (i) as a function of the voltage drop across the diode ($v = v_a - v_b$). When the diode is conducting in the forward direction (i positive), the voltage drop across the diode is very small; when a negative voltage is applied across the diode, the current flowing in the reverse direction is very small. Thus, the diode can act as a two-state switching device. In the conducting state, $v \approx 0$: in the nonconducting state $i \approx 0$. For purposes of analysis, we will assume that the forward voltage drop and reverse current are both negligible so that the diode has an ideal characteristic as shown in Fig. A–1(c). Thus we will treat the diode as a switch which closes if $v_a > v_b$ and opens if $v_a < v_b$.

Consider the diode gate circuit shown in Fig. A–2. The sources e_1, e_2, and e_3 represent external signals applied to the gate. The voltage source labeled "E" is sometimes referred to as the *bias* voltage. E is chosen so that

$$e_1 \leqslant E, \qquad e_2 \leqslant E, \qquad e_3 \leqslant E$$

With this restriction at least one of the diodes will be conducting or at its break-point ($i = 0$, $v = 0$). It is easy to verify that the output voltage e_o will be the *minimum* of the three input voltages e_1, e_2, and e_3. For example if $e_1 < e_2$ and $e_1 < e_3$, then diode D_1 will conduct. Since the forward drop across D_1 is negligible, the output voltage will be $e_o = e_1$. Since e_o is then less than e_2 and e_3, diodes D_2 and D_3 will have a negative voltage applied and will not conduct.

When this gate is used to perform logic functions, the input voltages are restricted to a pair of values. For example, if we choose voltages 0 and $+V$ as

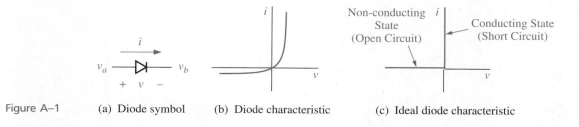

Figure A–1   (a) Diode symbol   (b) Diode characteristic   (c) Ideal diode characteristic

---

[1] See Section 3.5 for a definition of positive and negative logic.

Figure A–2
Diode Gate with External Inputs

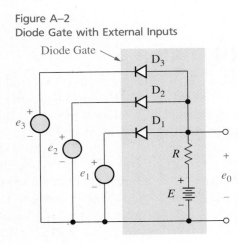

Table A–1

e_1	e_2	e_3	e_o
0	0	0	0
0	0	$+V$	0
0	$+V$	0	0
0	$+V$	$+V$	0
$+V$	0	0	0
$+V$	0	$+V$	0
$+V$	$+V$	0	0
$+V$	$+V$	$+V$	$+V$

input signals, we can complete a table of voltages (Table A–1) using the relation

$$e_o = \text{minimum }(e_1, e_2, e_3)$$

Table A–1 is identical to Fig. 3–1(b). If we translate this table according to positive logic (0 volts is a logic 0 and $+V$ volts is a logic 1), we see that e_o is 1 if e_1, e_2 and e_3 are all 1, so the gate of Fig. A–2 performs the AND function for positive logic. If we translate the table according to negative logic (0 volts is a logic 1 and $+V$ volts is a logic 0), we see that e_o is 1 if e_1 or e_2 or e_3 is 1, so the gate performs the OR function for negative logic.

Consider the diode gate circuit shown in Fig. A–3. The voltage E is chosen so that $E \leqslant e_1$, $E \leqslant e_2$, $E \leqslant e_3$. With this restriction at least one of the diodes will be conducting or at its breakpoint, and the output voltage e_o will be the *maximum* of the three input voltages e_1, e_2, and e_3. To verify this, consider the case where $e_1 > e_2$ and $e_1 > e_3$. Then diode D_1 will conduct, so the output voltage will be $e_o = e_1$. Since e_o is then greater than e_2 and e_3, diodes D_2 and D_3 will

Figure A–3
Diode Gate with External Inputs

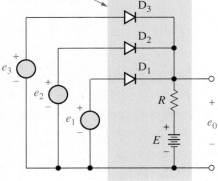

Table A–2

e_1	e_2	e_3	e_o
0	0	0	0
0	0	$+V$	$+V$
0	$+V$	0	$+V$
0	$+V$	$+V$	$+V$
$+V$	0	0	$+V$
$+V$	0	$+V$	$+V$
$+V$	$+V$	0	$+V$
$+V$	$+V$	$+V$	$+V$

have a negative voltage applied and will not conduct. If we choose voltages 0 and $+V$ as input signals, we can complete Table A–2 using the relation

$$e_o = \text{maximum } (e_1, e_2, e_3)$$

Table A–2 is identical to Table 3–1(a). If we translate this table according to positive logic, we see that e_o is 1 if e_1 or e_2 or e_3 is 1, so the gate performs the OR function for positive logic. If we translate the table according to negative logic, we see that e_o is 1 if e_1, e_2 and e_3 are all 1, so the gate of Fig. A–3 performs the AND function for negative logic. Unless otherwise specified, we will use positive logic so that Fig. A–2 is an AND gate and Fig. A–3 is an OR gate.

Practical circuit design considerations limit the number of diode gates which can be cascaded in series to two or three. The number of diode gate inputs which a given diode gate output can drive is also sharply limited. If these limits are exceeded, the voltage levels at the gate outputs may change appreciably from their nominal values so that it is no longer possible to reliably distinguish between a logic 0 and a logic 1. For this reason, diode gates are often used in conjunction with transistor amplifiers so that proper voltage levels can be maintained.

A.2
Transistor Logic Circuits

Transistor logic circuits offer several advantages over diode gate circuits. Transistor gates can realize inversion, they are capable of driving more gate inputs, and they generally operate faster than diode gates.

We will first analyze an inverter which uses an NPN transistor shown in Fig. A–4(a). The current which flows from the collector (C) to the emitter (E) in the transistor is controlled by the input voltage (e_i) applied to the base (B) circuit. In this discussion we will treat transistors like ideal switches. We will assume that when a transistor is cut off, the leakage current flowing from collector to emitter is so small that we can treat the transistor like an open circuit. When the input is 0 volts, the transistor is cut off, no current flows in the collector resistor (R_c), and the output voltage (e_o) is equal to the supply voltage ($+V$). When a transistor is saturated, we will assume that the voltage drop from collector to emitter is so small that we can treat the transistor like a short circuit. The base resistor (R_b) is chosen so that when the input (e_i) is $+V$, the base current will be large enough to cause saturation and the output voltage will be approximately 0. Thus, the operation of the transistor is analogous to a switch in Fig. A–4(b) which is open when e_i is 0 and closed when e_i is $+V$. Figure A–4(c) summarizes the relation between the input and output voltages for the networks of Fig. A–4(a) and A–4(b).

The transistor inverter of Fig. A–4(a) can also be analyzed by drawing a load line on the transistor characteristics as shown in Fig. A–5. The current flowing into the base is

$$i_B \approx e_i/R_b$$

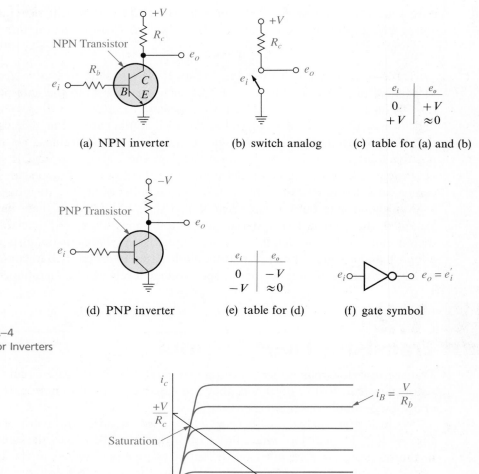

Figure A–4
Transistor Inverters

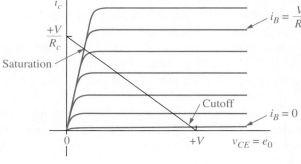

Figure A–5
Load-line Analysis of Figure A–4

When e_i is 0, i_B is 0, and the transistor operates at the cutoff point on the load line with $e_o = +V$. When e_i is $+V$, $i_B \approx V/R_b$, and the transistor operates at the saturation point on the load line with $e_o \approx 0$.

The operation of the PNP inverter in Fig. A–4(d) is similar to the NPN case except that the signs of all the voltages are reversed. The inverter symbol seen in Fig. A–4(f) can represent either type of inverter.

For convenience, we will use positive logic ($+V$ for a logic 1, 0 volts for a logic 0) for NPN transistors and negative logic ($-V$ for a logic 1, 0 volts for a logic 0) for PNP transistors. Then in either case a logic 1 used as a base input will turn on (i.e., saturate) the transistor, and a logic 0 will turn off the transistor.

With this convention, an NPN transistor logic circuit and the corresponding circuit with PNP transistors (and the signs of all voltages reversed) will perform the same logic function. The remainder of this discussion will consider only NPN transistors and positive logic, but all of the results apply equally well to PNP transistors and negative logic.

For the parallel-transistor circuit of Fig. A–6(a), if input A or input B or input C is a logic 1, the corresponding transistor is "on" (saturated) and the output (F) is 0. Hence $F' = A + B + C$, and $F = (A + B + C)' = A'B'C'$. This network performs the OR function followed by inversion and is called an OR-NOT gate, or more commonly, a NOR gate. Symbolically it is represented by an OR gate with an inversion symbol (circle) at the output as in Fig. A–6(b). Fig. A–6(c) shows the switch network analog. If A or B or C is 1, the corresponding switch is closed, there is a path to ground ($\perp$) and F is 0. If A, B, and C are all 0, all the switches are open and F is $+V$ (logic 1).

For the series-transistor network of Fig. A–7(a), if input A and input B and input C are all "1", then all the transistors are on, and the output is 0. Therefore, $F' = ABC$ and $F = (ABC)' = A' + B' + C'$. This network performs the AND function followed by inversion. It is called an AND-NOT gate, or more commonly, a NAND gate. Symbolically, it is represented by an AND gate with an inversion symbol at the output in Fig. A–7(c). Figure A–8 shows an alternative way to construct a NAND gate using a diode AND gate followed by a transistor inverter.

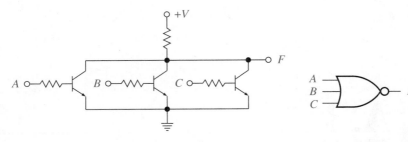

(a) Network   (b) Gate symbol

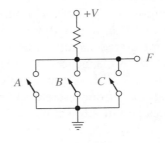

(c) Switch analog

Figure A–6
NPN NOR Gate

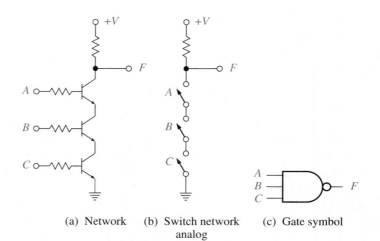

(a) Network   (b) Switch network   (c) Gate symbol
analog

Figure A–7
NPN NAND Gate

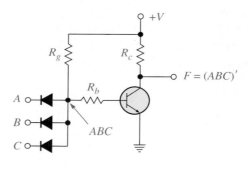

Figure A–8
Diode-Transistor NAND Gate

 # A.3
TTL Integrated Circuit Logic

Logic gates are commonly built in integrated circuit form rather than using discrete components. All of the diodes, transistors and resistors which form a gate are fabricated on a tiny (typically less than 0.1 inch square) "chip" of silicon. Several integrated circuit gates are usually sealed in a small plastic package (typically 0.3 by 0.8 inches). In addition to small size, integrated circuit gates have the advantages of low power consumption and greater reliability as compared with gates built from discrete components. Medium- and large-scale integration techniques permit fabrication of a complete functional unit (like a shift register, counter, memory, or microprocessor) on a single semiconductor chip.

Several types of integrated circuit gates are available including TTL (transistor-transistor logic), ECL (emitter-coupled logic), MOS (metal-oxide-semiconductor) logic, and CMOS (complementary MOS). TTL logic is one of the most commonly

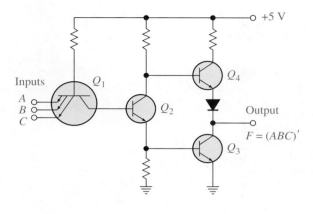

Figure A–9
TTL NAND Gate

used forms of integrated circuit logic and will be discussed in more detail in this section. MOS and CMOS logic is described in Section A.4.

Figure A–9 shows a TTL NAND gate. The input transistor (Q_1), which has multiple emitters, effectively takes the place of the AND gate in Figure A–8. If one or more of the inputs (A, B, C) is low, transistor Q_1 is turned on, and the input to Q_2 is low. Transistor Q_2 is off, so the input to Q_4 is high and the input to Q_3 is low. Therefore, Q_4 is on, Q_3 is off, and the gate output voltage is high. On the other hand, if all of the inputs to Q_1 are high, Q_4 is off, Q_3 is on, and the gate output is low. Since the output is a logic 0 iff $ABC = 1$, the output function is $F = (ABC)'$, and the gate performs the NAND function for positive logic.

Table A–3 lists some commonly available TTL gates. A typical TTL integrated circuit package contains six inverters, four 2-input gates, three 3-input gates or two 4-input gates. The reader should refer to a TTL data book for detailed specifications on these and other types of TTL integrated circuits.

Table A–3
Common TTL Gates

Type Number	Type of Gate	No. of Inputs per Gate	No. of Gates per IC Package
7404	INVERTER	1	6
7400	NAND	2	4
7410	NAND	3	3
7420	NAND	4	2
7430	NAND	8	1
7402	NOR	2	4
7427	NOR	3	3
7408	AND	2	4
7411	AND	3	3
7421	AND	4	2
7432	OR	2	4
7486	EXCLUSIVE-OR	2	4

Table A–4
_____

TTL Integrated Circuit Families

TTL Family	Example Type Number	Typical Power Dissipation per Gate (milliwatts)	Propagation Delay (nanoseconds)	
			Typical	Maximum
standard	7400	10	7	22
Schottky	74S00	19	3	5
low-power Schottky	74LS00	2	9	15
advanced Schottky	74AS00	14	3	4.5
advanced low-power Schottky	74ALS00	2	7	11

In addition to standard TTL, several other families of TTL integrated circuits are available. These families differ in amount of propagation delay and power dissipation as indicated in Table A–4. All of the example type numbers represent a TTL integrated circuit with four 2-input NAND gates. The letters S, LS, AS, or ALS are added to the type number to indicate the family.

The output of a TTL logic gate typically can drive 10 gate inputs of the same family. Figure A–10 shows the transfer characteristic (output voltage vs. input voltage) of a TTL inverter with a 5.0 volt supply voltage and 10 gate inputs connected to its output. Manufacturers specifications guarantee that any input voltage in the range 0 to 0.8 volts will act like a logic 0 and any input voltage in the range 2 volts to 5 volts will act like a logic 1. The output voltage is typically 3.6 volts for a logic 1 and 0.2 volts for a logic 0. The specifications guarantee that under all normal operating conditions a logic 1 output voltage will always be greater than 2.4 volts and a logic 0 output less than 0.4 volts.

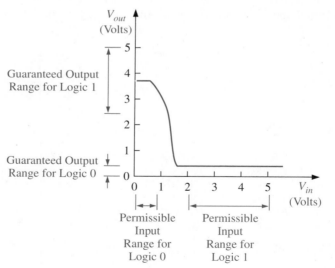

Figure A–10
Typical TTL Inverter Transfer Characteristic

A.4
MOS and CMOS Logic

MOS logic is based on the use of MOSFETs (metal-oxide-semiconductor field-effect transistors) as switching elements. Figure A–11 shows symbols used to represent MOSFETs. The substrate (or body) is a thin slice of silicon. The gate is a thin metallic layer deposited on the substrate and insulated from it by a thin layer of silicon dioxide. A voltage applied to the gate is used to control the flow of current between the drain and source.

In normal operation of an *n*-channel MOSFET shown in Fig. A–11(a), a positive voltage (V_{DS}) is applied between the drain and source. If the gate voltage (V_{GS}) is 0, there is no channel between the drain and source and no current flows. When V_{GS} is positive and exceeds a certain threshold, an *n*-type channel is formed between the drain and source, which allows current to flow from *D* to *S*. Operation of a *p*-channel MOSFET is similar, except V_{DS} and V_{GS} are negative. When V_{GS} assumes a negative value less than the threshold, a *p*-type channel is formed between drain and source, which allows current to flow from *S* to *D*.

The symbol in Fig. A–11(c) may be used to represent either a *p*- or *n*-channel MOSFET. When this symbol is used, it is generally understood that the substrate is connected to the most positive circuit voltage for *p*-channel MOSFETs (or the most negative for *n*-channel). We will use positive logic for *n*-channel MOS circuits and negative logic for *p*-channel MOS circuits. Using this convention, a logic 1 applied to the gate will switch the MOSFET to the "ON" state (low resistance between drain and source) and a logic 0 will switch it to the "OFF" state (high resistance between drain and source).

Figure A–12(a) shows a MOS inverter. When a logic 0 is applied to the gate, the MOSFET is in a high-resistance or OFF state, and the output voltage is

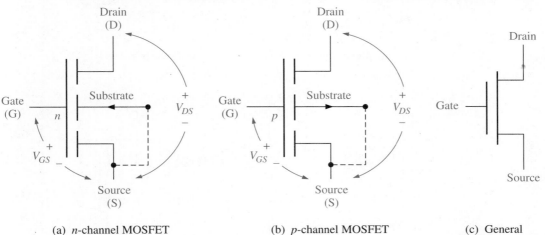

(a) *n*-channel MOSFET   (b) *p*-channel MOSFET   (c) General
                                                                     MOSFET symbol

Figure A–11
MOSFET Symbols

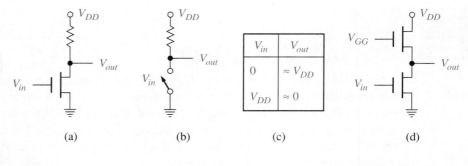

Figure A–12
MOS Inverter

approximately V_{DD}. When a logic 1 is applied to the gate, the MOSFET switches to a low-resistance or ON state, and the output voltage is approximately 0. Thus, operation of the MOSFET is analogous to the operation of a switch in Fig. A–12(b) which is open when V_{in} is a logic 0 and closed when V_{in} is a logic 1. In Fig. A–12(d), a second MOSFET serves as a load resistor. The geometry of this MOSFET and the gate voltage V_{GG} are chosen so that its resistance is high compared with the ON resistance of the lower MOSFET, so that the switching operation of Fig. A–12(d) is essentially the same as Fig. A–12(a).

As shown in Fig. A–13, MOSFETs can be connected in parallel or series to form NOR or NAND gates. Operation is similar to that of the bipolar transistor

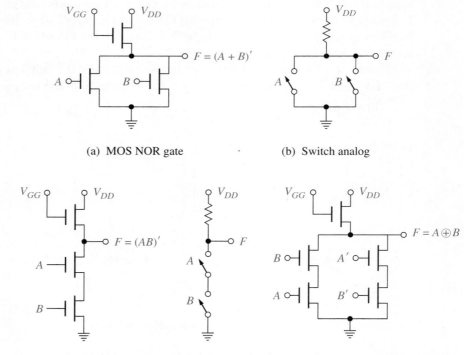

(a) MOS NOR gate   (b) Switch analog

(c) MOS NAND gate   (d) Switch analog   (e) MOS exclusive-OR gate

Figure A–13
MOS Gates

NOR and NAND gates shown in Figs. A–6 and A–7. In Fig. A–13(a), a logic 1 applied to A or B turns on the corresponding MOSFET and F becomes 0. Thus $F' = A + B$ and $F = (A + B)'$. In Fig. A–13(c), a logic 1 applied to the A and B inputs turns on both MOSFETs and F becomes 0. In this case $F' = AB$ and $F = (AB)'$. More complex functions can be realized by using series-parallel combinations of MOSFETs. For example, the network of Fig. A–13(e) performs the exclusive-OR function. The output of this network has a conducting path to ground and $F = 0$ if A and B are both 1 or if A' and B' are both 1. Thus, $F' = AB + A'B'$ and $F = A'B + AB' = A \oplus B$.

CMOS (complementary MOS) logic performs logic functions using a combination of p-channel and n-channel MOSFETs. Compared with TTL, CMOS has the advantage of much lower power dissipation. Figure A–14 shows a CMOS inverter. When 0 volts (logic 0) is applied to the gate inputs, the p-channel MOSFET (Q_1) is ON and the n-channel MOSFET (Q_2) is OFF, so the output is $+V$ (logic 1). When $+V$ (logic 1) is applied to the gate inputs, Q_1 is OFF and Q_2 is ON, so the output is 0 volts (logic 0).

Figure A–15 shows a CMOS NAND gate. If A or B is 0 volts, then Q_1 or Q_2 is ON and the output is $+V$. If A and B are both $+V$, then Q_3 and Q_4 are both ON and the output is 0 volts. This gate therefore performs the NAND function for positive logic as indicated in Fig. A–15(b).

Table A–5 lists some common families of CMOS logic. The original CMOS CD4000 series has been replaced with high speed and advanced CMOS families, both of which have shorter propagation delays. In many applications, the newer

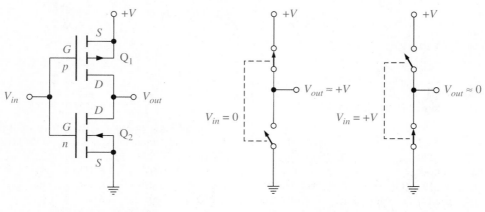

(a) Circuit diagram   (b) Switch analog

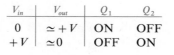

V_{in}	V_{out}	Q_1	Q_2
0	$\simeq +V$	ON	OFF
$+V$	$\simeq 0$	OFF	ON

(c) Truth table

Figure A–14
MOS Inverter

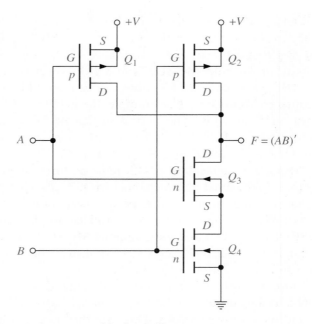

(a) circuit diagram

A	B	F	Q_1	Q_2	Q_3	Q_4
0	0	$+V$	ON	ON	OFF	OFF
0	$+V$	$+V$	ON	OFF	OFF	ON
$+V$	0	$+V$	OFF	ON	ON	OFF
$+V$	$+V$	0	OFF	OFF	ON	ON

(b) truth table

Figure A–15
CMOS NAND Gate

Table A–5 _____
CMOS Integrated Circuit Families

CMOS Family	Example Type Number	Typical Power Dissipation per Gate* (milliwatts)			Typical Propagation Delay* (nanoseconds)	
		Static	1MHz	10MHz	Typical	Maximum
CD 4000 series	CD4011A		0.60	6.0	50	100
high-speed CMOS	74HC00	0.0025	0.60	6.0	18	23
high-speed, TTL compatible	74HCT00	0.0025	0.60	6.0	18	24
advanced CMOS	74AC00	0.005	0.75	7.5	4.3	6.6
advanced, TTL compatible	74ACT00	0.005	0.75	7.5	7.7	12

* 5 volt supply

CMOS logic is being used in place of TTL logic. When no inputs are changing, the static power dissipation is very low. When the CMOS gates are switching, the power dissipation is proportional to the switching frequency. Thus, the power dissipation at a switching frequency of 10MHz is ten times that at 1MHz.

PROBLEMS

A.1 (a) If 0 volts corresponds to a logic 0, and -3 volts to a logic 1, what logic function does the following circuit realize?

(b) If 0 volts corresponds to a logic 1, and -3 volts corresponds to a logic 0, what logic function does the following circuit realize?

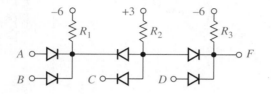

A.2 (a) Assuming that -5 volts is a logic 0, and $+5$ volts is a logic 1, what function is realized by the following diode gate network?

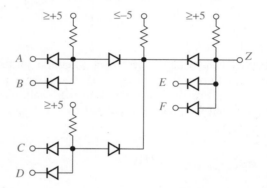

(b) What changes would have to be made in the network to realize the same function if $+5$ volts is a logic 0 and -5 volts is a logic 1?

A.3 Determine the function F realized by the following diode-transistor network:

$$(+V = \text{logic } 1, \ 0 \text{ volts} = \text{logic } 0)$$

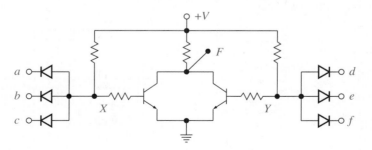

What would F be if $+V = \text{logic } 0$ and $0 \text{ volts} = \text{logic } 1$?

A.4   For the following CMOS network, make a table similar to Fig. A–15(b). What type of CMOS gate is this?

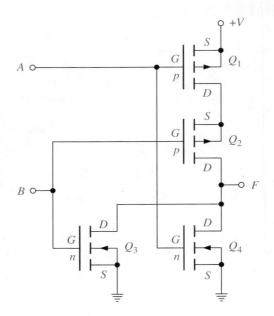

A.5   MOSFETs can be connected in a regular pattern to form the memory array for a read-only memory (see Fig. 9–22) or a programmable logic array (see Fig. 9–26). For the 4 word × 4 bit read-only memory shown below, determine the four output functions realized by the MOS array.

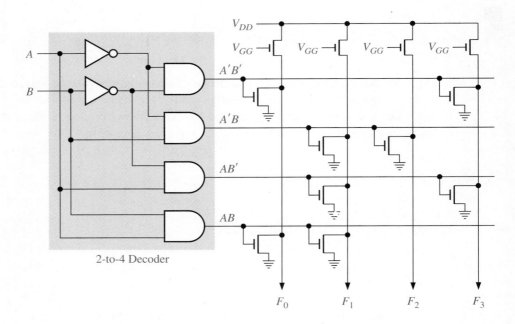

2-to-4 Decoder

B

IEEE Standard Logic Symbols

B.1
Alternative Symbols for Gates and Flip-flops

The Institute of Electrical and Electronics Engineers has published a new standard[1] for logic symbols. This standard presents a general notation for logic diagrams that is consistent with international standards. It provides for representation of devices ranging from simple gates to complex integrated circuits. Although traditional symbols for AND and OR gates are permitted, the standard emphasizes the use of rectangular symbols throughout. Figure B–1 shows some get symbols that are consistent with the new standard. The ≥ 1 symbol used in the OR gate implies that the output is 1 if one or more of the inputs are 1.

The Standard provides for two types of inversion symbols as illustrated in Fig. 8–21. As discussed in Section 8.7, the half-arrow symbol is used for direct polarity indication, in which case external signals are defined in terms of high (H) and low (L). The small circle (bubble) is used when external signals are defined in terms of 0 and 1. Figure B–2 shows four possible inverter symbols. In Fig. B–2(a)

---

[1] *IEEE Standard Graphic Symbols for Logic Functions* (ANSI/IEEE Std 91–1984), Institute of Electrical and Electronics Engineers, 1984.

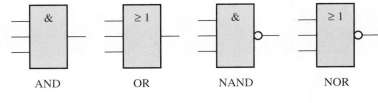

Figure B–1
Rectangular Gate Symbols

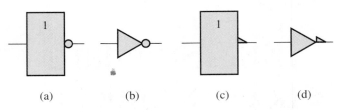

(a) (b) (c) (d)

Figure B–2
Four Symbols for an Inverter

and (b), an internal logic 1 will be inverted to give an external logic 0 output. In Fig. B–2(c) and (d), an internal logic 1 produces an external L output since the output is active low. Logic 0's and 1's are always used internal to a device.

The following example will further clarify the difference between the two types of inversion symbols. Figure B–3(a) represents a physical device described externally in terms of H and L levels. As is evident from the truth table, it performs an OR function for positive logic and an AND function for negative logic. Figure B–3(b) represents a logical device described externally in terms of logic 0's and 1's. It performs the same OR function regardless of whether all external signals are defined in terms of positive or negative logic, but its physical realization would be different in the two cases. The two symbols are equivalent when positive logic is used, but the symbols have different meanings for negative logic.

An edge-triggered J-K flip-flop with preset and clear, such as shown in Fig. 11–20, can be represented by Fig. B–4(a). The preset and clear inputs are labeled S and R internally. The inversion half-arrow indicates that these inputs are activated when the corresponding preset and clear signals are low (logic 0 for positive logic). The general symbol for a control input is C, so the clock input is labeled C1 to indicate control input 1. The internal arrow indicates that this is a dynamic (edge-triggered) input, and the inversion half-arrow indicates that it responds to a H to L transition (falling edge) of the clock signal. The 1 in front

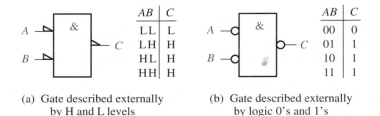

Figure B–3

(a) Gate described externally by H and L levels

(b) Gate described externally by logic 0's and 1's

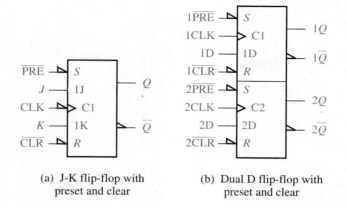

Figure B–4

(a) J-K flip-flop with
preset and clear

(b) Dual D flip-flop with
preset and clear

of J and K in the labels 1J and 1K indicates that these inputs are activated by control input C1.

Figure B–4(b) shows a dual edge-triggered D flip-flop with preset and clear. As in the J-K flip-flop example, S and R designate the active-low preset and clear inputs. C1 and C2 designate the two clock inputs that respond to an L-to-H transition (rising edge) of the clock; 1D and 2D are D inputs that are activated by C1 and C2, respectively.

B.2
Representation of MSI Functions

This section gives examples of how several MSI functions can be represented by the IEEE standard notation. Figure B–5 shows the standard symbol for the 7442 4-line to 10-line decoder of Fig. 9–18. The notation BCD/DEC identifies

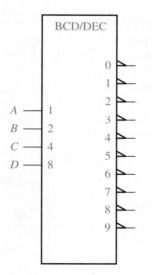

Figure B–5
4-to-10 Line Decoder

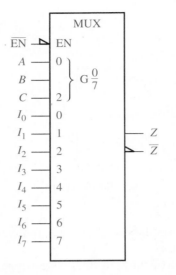

Figure B–6
8-to-1 Multiplexer

this as a decoder which accepts a BCD (binary-coded decimal) input and outputs the corresponding decimal digit. The output inversion symbols indicate that the decimal outputs are active-low, that is the output for the selected decimal digit is L (logic 0 for positive logic).

Figure B–6 represents a 74151 8-to-1 multiplexer similar to the one shown in Figs. 9–10 and 9–11, except that it has an additional enable input ($\overline{EN}$) and an inverted output as well as a noninverted output. The outputs are activated only when $\overline{EN}$ is L. The three control inputs to the multiplexer are identified by

$$\left.\right\} G \frac{0}{7}$$

A common control block may be used when a circuit has one or more inputs which are common to more than one element in the circuit. The common control block has a distinctive shape as shown in Fig. B–7. This figure represents a

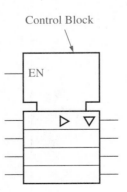

Figure B–7
Quad Tri-State Buffer with Common Control Input

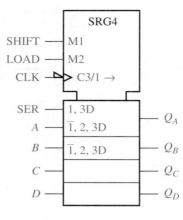

Figure B–8
74178 Shift Register

quadruple tri-state buffer with a common enable. The first triangle in the symbol indicates that the outputs are buffered, that is, they have a higher than normal driving capability. The second triangle indicates that the outputs are tri-state. These outputs are enabled when EN is high.

The symbol for the 74178 4-bit parallel-in, parallel-out shift register (Fig. 18–3) is shown in Fig. B–8. The notation SRG4 identifies this as a 4-bit shift register. C3 identifies the clock input that is activated by an H-to-L transition (falling edge) of CLK. The notation $\overline{1}$, 2, 3D indicates that the corresponding D flip-flop input is active when M1 = 0, M2 = 1, and the active edge of C3 occurs; /1→ means that shifting occurs in response to the clock when M1 = 1.

The 74S163 4-bit synchronous binary counter of Figs. 18–7 and 18–8 is represented by Fig. B–9. CTRDIV16 indicates a divide by 16 counter. C5 is the

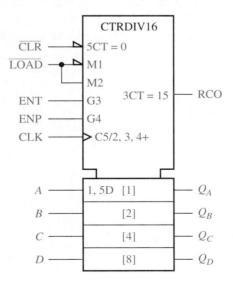

Figure B–9
74S163 Counter

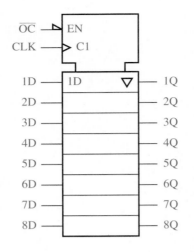

Figure B–10
74374 Octal D Flip-Flop

clock input which is activated by an L-to-H transition (rising edge) of CLK. C5 is followed by $/2, 3, 4+$, which means that the clock increments the counter when $M2 = G3 = G4 = 1$. The notation $5CT = 0$ by the clear input indicates that the counter is set to 0 when the clock (C5) is active and $\overline{CLR}$ is L. The ripple carry output (RCO) is H when G3 is 1 and the count is 15, as indicated by $3CT = 15$. The condition for parallel loading the D flip-flops is indicated by 1, 5D, which means that the D input is active when $M1 = 1$ ($\overline{LOAD}$ is L) and the clock (C5) is active.

Figure B–10 gives the symbol for the octal D flip-flop register of Fig. 18–18. The small triangle near the flip-flop output indicates that the outputs are tri-state. The EN and C1 inputs to the control block are common to all of the flip-flops. When $\overline{OC}$ is L (EN = 1) all outputs are enabled, and an L-to-H transition on CLK (0 to 1 transition on C1) clocks all of the D inputs into the flip-flops.

C

Proofs of Theorems

C.1
Essential Prime Implicants

Section 6.4 presents a method for finding all of the essential prime implicants which is based on finding adjacent 1's on a Karnaugh map. The validity of the method is based on the following theorem:

> If a given minterm m_j of F and all of its adjacent minterms are covered by a single term p_j, then p_j is an essential prime implicant of F.

Proof:

1. Assume p_j is *not* a *prime* implicant. Then it can be combined with another term p_k to eliminate some variable x_i and form another term which does not contain x_i. Therefore, $x_i = 0$ in p_j and $x_i = 1$ in p_k, or vice versa. Then p_k covers a minterm m_k which differs from m_j only in the variable x_i. This means that m_k is adjacent to m_j, but m_k is not covered by p_j. This contradicts the original assumption that all minterms adjacent to m_j are covered by p_j; therefore, p_j is a prime implicant.
2. Assume p_j is *not essential*. Then there is another prime implicant p_h which covers m_j. Since p_h is not contained in p_j, p_h must contain at least one minterm m_h which is adjacent to m_j and not covered by p_j. This is a contradiction, so p_j must be essential.

C.2
State Equivalence Theorem

The methods for determining state equivalence presented in Unit 15 are based on Theorem 15.1:

Two states p and q of a sequential network are equivalent if and only if for every single input x, the outputs are the same and the next states are equivalent.

Proof: We must prove both part 1, the "if" part of the theorem, and part 2, the "only if" part.

1. Assume that $\lambda(p, x) = \lambda(q, x)$ and $\delta(p, x) \equiv \delta(q, x)$ for every input x. Then from Definition 15.1, for every input sequence $\underline{X}$,

$$\lambda[\delta(p, x), \underline{X}] = \lambda[\delta(q, x), \underline{X}]$$

For the input sequence $\underline{Y} = x$ followed by $\underline{X}$, we have

$$\lambda(p, \underline{Y}) = \lambda(p, x) \text{ followed by } \lambda[\delta(p, x), \underline{X}]$$
$$\lambda(q, \underline{Y}) = \lambda(q, x) \text{ followed by } \lambda[\delta(q, x), \underline{X}]$$

Hence $\lambda(p, \underline{Y}) = \lambda(q, \underline{Y})$ for every input sequence $\underline{Y}$, and $p \equiv q$ by Definition 15.1.

2. Assume that $p \equiv q$. Then by Definition 15.1, $\lambda(p, \underline{Y}) = \lambda(q, \underline{Y})$ for every input sequence $\underline{Y}$. Let $\underline{Y} = x$ followed by $\underline{X}$. Then

$$\lambda(p, x) = \lambda(q, x) \text{ and } \lambda[\delta(p, x), \underline{X}] = \lambda[\delta(q, x), \underline{X}]$$

for every sequence $\underline{X}$. Hence from Definition 15.1, $\delta(p, x) \equiv \delta(q, x)$.

C.3
Justification of Short-Cut Method for Deriving S-R Input Equations

The short-cut method for deriving S-R input equations is based on the following theorem:

If a cycle-free asynchronous flow table is realized with S-R flip-flops using a race-free state assignment, then for each flip-flop Q_i, there exist S and R equations which are independent of Q_i.

Proof: Consider two present states S_j and S_k whose state assignment differs only in the state variable Q_i. Let the state assignments be $0t$ and $1t$, respectively, where 0 and 1 are the values of Q_i, and t represents the values of the other state variables.

Since the assignment is race-free, only one state variable can change at a time. For a given input column, the possible next states for S_j *are* $0u$ and $1t$, and for S_k are $1v$ and $0t$, where u and v differ in at most one state variable from t. There are four cases to be considered:

		Present State	Next State	S_i	R_i	
case 1	S_j	$0t$	$0u$	0	X ⎫	choose X = 0, then S_i and R_i
	S_k	$1t$	$1v$	X	0 ⎭	do not depend on Q_i
case 2	S_j	$0t$	$0u$	0	X ⎫	choose X = 1, then S_i and R_i
	S_k	$1t$	$0t$	0	1 ⎭	do not depend on Q_i
case 3	S_j	$0t$	$1t$	1	0 ⎫	choose X = 1, then S_i and R_i
	S_k	$1t$	$1v$	X	0 ⎭	do not depend on Q_i
case 4	S_j	$0t$	$1t$	1	0 ⎫	S_i and R_i depend on Q_i,
	S_k	$1t$	$0t$	0	1 ⎭	but there is a cycle
		↑	↑			
		Q_i	Q_i^+			

The above analysis applies to every pair of present states S_j and S_k whose assignments differ only in Q_i and to every input column. Thus, the don't cares can always be chosen so that S_i and R_i are independent of Q_i unless a cycle or race is present.

References

The following list of basic textbooks in switching theory and logic design is provided for those students who wish to do additional reading concerning the topics covered in this text and their application to digital system design.

References 2, 3, 13, 22, 23, and 29 are particularly applicable to Units 1, 20, and 21 (number systems and arithmetic operations).

References 2, 4, 6, 7, 12, 14, 15, 16, 21, 24, 25, 26, 27, 29, 32, 33, and 34 are particularly applicable to Units 2 through 10 (Boolean algebra and combinational networks).

References 2, 4, 7, 11, 12, 14, 15, 16, 21, 24, 32, 33, 34, and 38 are particularly applicable to Units 11 through 19 (synchronous sequential networks).

References 1, 5, 9, 38, and 39 are particularly applicable to programmable logic devices (Units 9 and 19).

References 10, 11, 24, 30, and 31 are particularly applicable to Unit 22 (SM charts).

References 12, 16, 21, 25, 26, 27, and 37 are particularly applicable to Units 23 through 27 (asynchronous sequential networks).

References 2, 17, 35, 36, and 38 discuss the circuit aspects of digital devices and are particularly applicable to Appendix A.

References 18, 19, 20, and 27 apply particularly to the IEEE standard logic symbols (Unit 8 and Appendix B).

References 8 and 28 provide additional information about simulation of digital systems.

References 2, 3, 4, 10, 13, 14, 22, 23, 30, and 31 extend the material in the text and apply it to digital systems and computer design.

1. Advanced Micro Devices. *PAL Device Data Book*. Sunnyvale, Calif., 1990.

2. Barna, Arpad, and Porat, Dan I. *Integrated Circuits in Digital Electronics,* 2d ed. New York: John Wiley, 1987.

3. Bartee, Thomas C. *Digital Computer Fundamentals,* 6th ed. New York: McGraw-Hill, 1985.

4. Blakeslee, Thomas R. *Digital Design with Standard MSI and LSI,* 2d ed. New York: John Wiley, 1979.

5. Bolton, Martin. *Digital Systems Design with Programmable Logic*. Reading, Mass.: Addison-Wesley, 1990.

6. Brayton, Robert, *et al. Logic Minimization Algorithms for VLSI Synthesis*. Hingham, Mass.: Kluwer Academic Publishers, 1984.

7. Breeding, Kenneth J. *Digital Design Fundamentals*. Englewood Cliffs, N.J.: Prentice-Hall, 1989.

8. Breuer, Melvin, and Friedman, Arthur. *Diagnosis & Reliable Design of Digital Systems*. Rockville, Md.: Computer Science Press, 1976.

9. Burton, Von L. *The Programmable Logic Device Handbook*. Blue Ridge Summit, Pa.: TAB Professional and Reference Books, 1990.

10. Clare, Christopher R. *Designing Logic Systems Using State Machines*. New York: McGraw-Hill, 1973.

11. Comer, David J. *Digital Logic and State Machine Design,* 2d ed. New York: Holt, Rinehart and Winston, 1989.

12. Dietmeyer, D. L. *Logic Design of Digital Systems,* 3d ed. Boston: Allyn and Bacon, 1988.

13. Ercegovac, Milos D., and Lang, Tomás. *Digital Systems and Hardware/Firmware Algorithms*. New York: John Wiley, 1985.

14. Fletcher, William. *An Engineering Approach to Digital Design*. Englewood Cliffs, N.J.: Prentice-Hall, 1980.

15. Friedman, Arthur D. *Logical Design of Digital Systems*. Woodland Hills, Calif.: Computer Science Press, 1975.

16. Hill, F. J., and Peterson, G. R. *Introduction to Switching Theory and Logical Design,* 3d ed. New York: John Wiley, 1981.

17. Holt, Charles A. *Electronic Circuits, Digital and Analog*. New York: John Wiley, 1978.

18. Institute of Electrical and Electronics Engineers. *IEEE Standard Graphic Symbols for Logic Functions* (ANSI/IEEE Std 91-1984). New York: *IEEE*, 1984.

19. Institute of Electrical and Electronics Engineers. *Logic Symbols and Diagrams* (ANSI/IEEE Stds 91-1984 & 991-1986). New York: IEEE, 1987.

20. Kampel, Ian. *A Practical Introduction to the New Logic Symbols,* 2d ed. London: Butterworths, 1986.

21. Kohavi, Z. *Switching and Finite Automata Theory,* 2d ed. New York: McGraw-Hill, 1978.

22. Kostopoulos, George K. *Digital Engineering.* New York: John Wiley, 1975.

23. Mano, M. Morris. *Computer System Architecture.* Englewood Cliffs, N.J.: Prentice-Hall, 1982.

24. Mano, M. Morris. *Digital Design.* Englewood Cliffs, N.J.: Prentice-Hall, 1984.

25. Marcus, Mitchell P. *Switching Circuits for Engineers,* 3d ed. Englewood Cliffs, N.J.: Prentice-Hall, 1975.

26. McCluskey, Edward J. *Introduction to the Theory of Switching Circuits.* New York: McGraw-Hill, 1965.

27. McCluskey, Edward J. *Logic Design Principles.* Englewood Cliffs, N.J.: Prentice-Hall, 1986.

28. Miczo, Alexander. *Digital Logic Testing and Simulation.* New York: Harper & Row, 1986.

29. Mowle, Frederic J. *A Systematic Approach to Digital Logic Design.* Reading, Mass.: Addison-Wesley, 1976.

30. Peatman, John B. *Digital Hardware Design.* New York: McGraw-Hill, 1980.

31. Prosser, Franklin P., and Winkel, David E. *The Art of Digital Design: An Introduction to Top-Down Design,* 2d ed. Englewood Cliffs, N.J.: Prentice-Hall, 1987.

32. Rhyne, V. Thomas. *Fundamentals of Digital Systems Design.* Englewood Cliffs, N.J.: Prentice-Hall, 1973.

33. Sandige, Richard S. *Modern Digital Design.* New York: McGraw-Hill, 1990.

34. Shiva, Sajjan G. *Introduction to Logic Design.* Glenview, Ill.: Scott. Foresman and Company, 1988.

35. Taub, Herbert, and Schilling, Donald. *Digital Integrated Electronics.* New York: McGraw-Hill, 1977.

36. Texas Instruments Engineering Staff. *The TTL Data Book.* Dallas: Texas Instruments, 1988. Also *ALS/AS Logic Data Book,* 1988.

37. Unger, Stephen H. *Asynchronous Sequential Switching Circuits.* New York: Wiley-Interscience, 1969.

38. Wakerly, John F. *Digital Design Principles and Practices.* Englewood Cliffs, N.J.: Prentice Hall, 1990.

39. Xilinx, Inc. *The Programmable Gate Array Design Handbook.* San Jose, Calif.: Xilinx, Inc., 1991.

Answers to Selected Study Guide Questions and Problems

This section contains answers to some of the more difficult study guide questions and answers to all of the problems which are referenced in the study guides. Answers to the remaining problems are not included here, but they are available in the instructor's manual.

Unit 1   Study Guide Answers

2 (e) Two of the rows are:

$$\begin{array}{cc|ccc} 1110 & & 16 & 14 & E \\ 1111 & & 17 & 15 & F \end{array}$$

3 (b)
$$1100_2 - 101_2 = [1 \times 2^3 + 1 \times 2^2 + 0 \times 2^1 + 0 \times 2^0]$$
$$- [1 \times 2^2 + 0 \times 2^1 + 1 \times 2^0]$$

—————— note borrow from column 1

$$= [1 \times 2^3 + 1 \times 2^2 + (0 - 1) \times 2^1 + (10 + 0) \times 2^0]$$
$$- [1 \times 2^2 + 0 \times 2^1 + 1 \times 2^0]$$

—————— note borrow from column 2

$$= [1 \times 2^3 + (1 - 1) \times 2^2 + (10 - 1) \times 2^1 + 10 \times 2^0]$$
$$- [1 \times 2^2 + 0 \times 2^1 + 1 \times 2^0]$$

—————— note borrow from column 3

$$= [(1 - 1) \times 2^3 + (10 - 0) \times 2^2 + 1 \times 2^1 + 10 \times 2^0]$$
$$- [1 \times 2^2 + 0 \times 2^1 + 1 \times 2^0]$$
$$= [0 \times 2^3 + 1 \times 2^2 + 1 \times 2^1 + 1 \times 2^0] = 111_2$$

5 (a)

BCD:	0001	1000	0111
excess-3:	0100	1011	1010
6-3-1-1:	0001	1011	1001
2-out-of-5:	00101	10100	10010

Unit 1   Answers to Problems

1.1 (a) 1365.2_8, 1011110101.010_2 (b) 173.127_8, 1111011.001010111_2

1.2 (a) 273.4_8, 187.5_{10} (b) 155.3_8, 109.375_{10}

1.4 (a) 341.12_5 (96.2857_{10})

1.6 (a)   2   E   B . A 4_{16}
         02 32 23   22 10_4

   (b)
Hex:	0	1	2	3	4	5	6	7	8	9	A	B	C	D	E	F
Base 4:	00	01	02	03	10	11	12	13	20	21	22	23	30	31	32	33

   (c) 2782.6875_{10}

1.9
	Add	Subtract	Multiply
(a)	11010	100	10100101
(b)	10000011	1111	1000010001010

1.11 (a)   11 11
          11011011
        − 1101101
        ─────────
           1101110

   (b)   11   111
          10001100
        − 1100101
        ─────────
           0100111

1.15
	5	3	2	1
0	0	0	0	0
1	0	0	0	1
2	0	0	1	0
3	0	0	1	1
4	0	1	0	1
5	0	1	1	0
6	0	1	1	1
7	1	0	1	0
8	1	0	1	1
9	1	1	0	1

1101 0011 1010 0001
  9   3   7   1

Unit 2   Study Guide Answers

2 (d) 1; 0; 1; 1   (e) 1, 1; 0, 0; 0; 1

3 (a) 4 variables, 10 literals   (d) $F = (A'B)'$ (e) $F = (A + B')C$
  (f) Network should have 2 OR gates, 3 AND gates, and 3 inverters.

4 (b) $A, 0, 0, A; A, 1, A, 1$ 6 (c) $Z = ABC$

7 (a) Sum of products
      Neither
      Product of sums (Here A and B' are each considered to be separate terms in the product.)
      Neither
  (b) Fewer terms are generated.
  (c) $D[A + B'(C + E)] = D(A + B')(A + C + E)$

8 (a) $AE + B'C' + C'D$ (b) $C'DE + AB'CD'E$

Unit 2   Answers to Problems

2.1 (a) $X(X' + Y) = XX' + XY = 0 + XY = XY$
  (b) $(X + Y)(X + Z) = XX + XZ + YX + YZ = X + XZ + YX + YZ$
      $= X(1 + Z + Y) + YZ = X(1) + YZ = X + YZ$
  (c) $XY + XY' = X(Y + Y') = X(1) = X$
  (d) $(A + B)(A + B') = AA + AB' + AB + BB' = A + AB' + AB + BB'$
      $= A(1 + B + B') + 0 = A(1) = A$

2.2 (a)   (c)

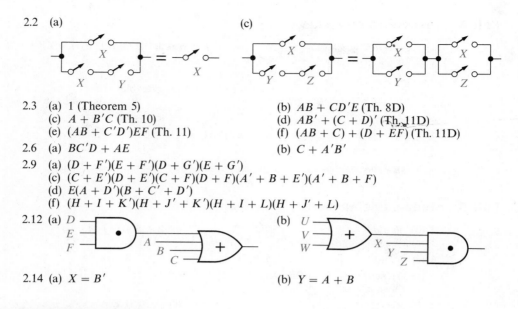

2.3 (a) 1 (Theorem 5)   (b) $AB + CD'E$ (Th. 8D)
    (c) $A + B'C$ (Th. 10)   (d) $AB' + (C + D)'$ (Th. 11D)
    (e) $(AB + C'D')EF$ (Th. 11)   (f) $(AB + C) + (D + EF)$ (Th. 11D)

2.6 (a) $BC'D + AE$ (b) $C + A'B'$

2.9 (a) $(D + F')(E + F')(D + G')(E + G')$
    (c) $(C + E')(D + E')(C + F)(D + F)(A' + B + E')(A' + B + F)$
    (d) $E(A + D')(B + C' + D')$
    (f) $(H + I + K')(H + J' + K')(H + I + L)(H + J' + L)$

2.12 (a)   (b)

2.14 (a) $X = B'$ (b) $Y = A + B$

Unit 3   Study Guide Answers

2 (a) $a' + b + c$ (b) $ab'c'd$ (c) $a(b' + c')$
  (d) $(a + b)(c' + d')$ (e) $a' + b(c + d)$

8 (b) $(b' + d)(b + a)(b + c)$ $(a + d)(b + d)(a' + b' + c)$
  (c) $w'y' + x'y'z' + xy + wyz$

11 (e) $x \oplus y$

12 (a) $+$ $-$ no   (b) $Z^D = (AB' + C' + D)(A' + B + D') + E'F$
  (c) Dual of X' is X'

Unit 3   Answers to Problems

3.3 (a) $[(w' + x') + (y + z')(y' + z)][(w + x) + yz' + y'z]$
    (b) $[(a' + b')c + (d + e') \cdot 0][g' + h \cdot 1][w']$
    (c) $(a' + b)[d' + (e + f)(g + h')] + a[b' + c' + d' + e(f + g')]$

3.5 (a) $[(w + x) + (y' + z)(y + z')][(w' + x') + y'z + yz']$
    (b) $[(a + b)c' + (d' + e) \cdot 0][g + h' \cdot 1][w]$
    (c) $(a + b')[d + (e' + f')(g' + h)] + a'[b + c + d + e'(f' + g)]$

3.9 (a) $ABC' + ABD' + A'B'C + A'CD$
    (b) $B'C + AB'D + BC' + A'BD$ <u>or</u> $B'C + AC'D + BC' + A'CD'$

3.11 (a) $(A + B' + D')(A + C' + D')(A' + B + D)(A' + C' + D)$
    (b) $(A + B' + C)(A + B + D)(A' + C + D')(A' + C' + D)$

3.15 (a) $F = A'B$ (b) $G = T'$

3.18 $F = A'B'C' + A'BCD + ACD' + \{B'CD'$ or $A'B'D'\}$

3.19 (a) No   (b) $[(x \equiv y) \equiv z] = [x \equiv (y \equiv z)]$

3.23 (a) $e_0 = (e_1 \equiv e_2)$ (b) $e_0 = e_1 \oplus e_2$

3.25 (a) $e_0 = e_1 + e_2 + e_3$ (b) $e_0 = e_1 e_2 e_3$

Unit 4   Study Guide Answers

1 (b) $A'B'C + BC'D' + AB'D' + BCD$ (c) Add BCD; eliminate $A'BD$, ABC.

Unit 4   Answers to Problems

4.4 (a) $ABC' + AB'D + A'BD'$ (b) $W'Y' + WX'Y + WXZ$
    (c) $(A + B + C)(A' + C + D)(B' + C' + D')$

4.7 (a) y (b) $xz + y'z$ (c) 1
    (d) $bc + b'c' + a'bd' + a'b'd$ (other solutions possible)   (e) $x'y' + yz + w'z'$
    (f) $A'BD + B'EF + CDE'G$ (g) $abd + b'd' + c'd$

4.11 $(X + Y')(X' + Z)(Y + Z')$ or $(X' + Y)(X + Z')(Y' + Z)$

4.12 $(A + D)(A + E)(C + D' + B' + E) = AC + AD' + AB' + DE$

4.14 $XY' + WX' + W'Y + YZ'$

4.18 (a) Valid   (b) Not valid   (c) Valid

Unit 5   Study Guide Answers

2 (d) $ab'c'd$ (e) $a + b + c' + d'$
    (g) $(a + b' + c)(a' + b + c')(a' + b' + c)(a' + b' + c')$

3 (c) $\sum m(0, 1, 3, 4)$ $\prod M(2, 5, 6, 7)$
    (h) (1) neither   (3) maxterm   (5) minterm
        (2) maxterm   (4) neither   (6) minterm

4 (b) m_{19} (c) $A'BCD'E$
    (e) M_{19} (f) $(A + B' + C' + D + E')$

5 (a) 65536
    (d) $(a_0m_0 + a_1m_1 + a_2m_2 + a_3m_3)(b_0m_0 + b_1m_1 + b_2m_2 + b_3m_3) = \cdots$
        $= a_0b_0m_0 + a_1b_1m_1 + a_2b_2m_2 + a_3b_3m_3$
    (f) $\prod M(2, 5, 6)$ $\sum m(2, 5, 6)$ $\prod M(0, 1, 3, 4, 7)$

6 (b) $\sum m(0, 5) + \sum d(1, 3, 4)$

Unit 5   Answers to Problems

5.1 Answers should be of the form:
    (a) $F = ABC'$ (b) $F = XY + X'Y'$ (c) $G = AB'(CD + EF)$

5.5 (a) $Z = (A'B'C'D'E' + ABCDE)'$ (b) $Y = A'B'CD'E$

5.7 (a) $a = \sum m(0, 1, 2, 4) = x'y'z' + x'y'z + x'yz' + xy'z'$
        $b = \sum m(0, 3, 5, 6) = x'y'z' + x'yz + xy'z + xyz'$
    (b) $a = \prod M(3, 5, 6, 7) = (x + y' + z')(x' + y + z')(x' + y' + z)(x' + y' + z')$
        $b = \prod M(1, 2, 4, 7) = (x + y + z')(x + y' + z)(x' + y + z)(x' + y' + z')$

5.8 (a) $F = \sum m(0, 1, 2, 3, 4, 5, 6, 8, 9, 12) = A'B'C'D' + A'B'C'D + A'B'CD' + A'B'CD$
        $+ A'BC'D' + A'BC'D + A'BCD' + AB'C'D' + AB'C'D + ABC'D'$
    (b) $F = \prod M(7, 10, 11, 13, 14, 15)$
        $= (A + B' + C' + D')(A' + B + C' + D)(A' + B + C' + D')$
        $\cdot (A' + B' + C + D')(A' + B' + C' + D)(A' + B' + C' + D')$

5.9 (a) $\sum m(1, 2, 3, 6, 7)$ (b) $\prod M(0, 4, 5)$
    (c) $\sum m(0, 4, 5)$ (d) $\prod M(1, 2, 3, 6, 7)$

5.10 (a) $\sum m(3,4,6,8,9,12,13)$ (b) $\prod M(0,1,2,5,7,10,11,14,15)$
    (c) $\sum m(0,1,2,5,7,10,11,14,15)$ (d) $\prod M(3,4,6,8,9,12,13)$

5.15 (a) $F = \sum m(5, 6, 7, 10, 11, 13, 14, 15)$ (b) $F = \prod M(0, 1, 2, 3, 4, 8, 9, 12)$

5.16 General rule: product of all maxterms in F_1 or F_2.

5.17 (a) 16
    (b) $F(x, y) = 0$; $x'y'$; $x'y$; x'; xy'; y'; $x'y + xy'$; $x' + y'$; xy;
        $x'y' + xy$; y; $x' + y$; x; $x + y'$; $x + y$; 1

5.21

ABC	DEF
000	0XX
001	XXX
010	X11
011	0XX
100	110
101	XXX
110	0XX
111	101

5.23 (a) With $d(2) = 1$, $d(5) = 0$:
$$F = A'B'C + A'BC' + A'BC$$
$$+ ABC'$$
$$= A'C(B + B') + BC'(A + A')$$
$$= A'C + BC'$$

Unit 6 Study Guide Answers

2 (d)

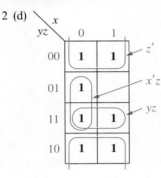

(e) 0, 3, 6

(j) $G = bc + a'c' + ab'$
or $b'c' + ac + a'b$

3 (d) 6, 10, 12, 15; 0, 12, 9, 10
  (g) $f_1 = a'b + bc' + a'cd + ac'd$ $f_2 = b'c + cd + a'bd + ab'd'$
4 (a) $a'b'd'$, $b'c'd'$, $ac'd'$, $ac'd$, $a'b'cd$, etc. (b) $AB'C'$ and $AC'D$ are prime implicants
5 (c) No (f) Yes (i) $A'D'$ because of m_4,
                         $B'D'$ because of m_{10}

6 (b) $A'D'$ is not essential because all of its minterms are covered by other prime implicants.
    BC' is essential because of m_{13}. $B'CD$ is essential because of m_{11}. Minimum sum =
    $B'CD + BC' + BD' + A'B'$.
  (d) $A'C' + ACD + (AB$ or $BC')$
8 (a) $F = AB'D' + B'D'E' + A'BDE$ (b) 8, 16, 25, 26, 28
  (d) $P_1 + P_2 + P_3 + P_4 + BCDE + AC'E$
  (g) $AC'E' + A'DE + ACE + B'CE + (AB'C$ or ADE' or ACD or $AB'E')$

Unit 6 Answers to Problems

6.3 (b) $Z = \sum m(3, 7, 11, 13, 15) = CD + ABD$
  (c) $Z = \prod M(0, 1, 2, 4, 5, 6, 8, 9, 10, 12, 14) = D(A + C)(B + C)$
  (e)

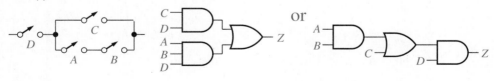

6.5 (a) $f_1 = a'c + ac'$ (b) $f_2 = e'f + de' + df$
  (c) $f_3 = r + t'$ (d) $f_4 = z' + xy' + x'y$

6.8 (b) $F = B' + A'D + ACD'$
(c) $F = (A + B' + D)(A' + B' + D')[(B' + C + D) \text{ or } (A' + B' + C)]$

6.9 (a) $f = b'c' + a'd' + abd + (bcd \text{ or } a'bc)$ [1 other min. solution]
(b) $f = bc + bd + a'cd + b'c'd' + ad'$
(c) $f = ac'd' + a'c'd + abc + (a'b'c' \text{ or } b'c'd')$ [5 other min. solutions]

6.13 (a)

$C_1C_2X_1X_2$	Z
0 0 0 0	0
0 0 0 1	0
0 0 1 0	0
0 0 1 1	1
0 1 0 0	0
0 1 0 1	1
0 1 1 0	1
0 1 1 1	1
1 0 0 0	1
1 0 0 1	0
1 0 1 0	0
1 0 1 1	1
1 1 0 0	0
1 1 0 1	1
1 1 1 0	1
1 1 1 1	0

(b) $Z = C_1C_2'X_1'X_2' + C_2X_1'X_2$
$\quad\quad + C_2X_1X_2' + C_2'X_1X_2$
$\quad\quad + \{C_1'X_1X_2 \text{ or } C_1'C_2X_2$
$\quad\quad \text{ or } C_1'C_2X_1\}$

6.14 (a) $f_1 = a'b' + abd + ac$ (b) $f_2 = (a + b' + c)(a + c' + d)(a' + b)$

6.15 $\underline{w'x} + \underline{wx'z} + \underline{xz'} + \{y'z + w'y' \text{ or } w'y' + xy' \text{ or } y'z + w'z'\}$

6.16 (a) $F = \prod M(0, 1, 9, 12, 13, 14)$
$\quad = (A + B + C + D)(A + B + C + D')(A' + B' + C + D)$
$\quad\quad \cdot (A' + B' + C + D')(A' + B' + C' + D)(A' + B + C + D')$
(b) $F' = A'B'C' + ABD' + AC'D$
(c) $F = (A + B + C)(A' + B' + D)(A' + C + D')$
(d) $F^D = ABC + A'B'D + A'CD'$

6.17 (a) Minterms 0, 1, 2, 3, 4, 5, 7, 8, 10, 11.

6.25 (a) $c'd'e'$ (m_{16}, m_{24})
      $a'ce'$ (m_{14})
      ace (m_{31})
      $a'b'de$ (m_3)

(b) $a'b'de, a'd'e', cd'e, a'ce', a'b'c,$
     $ace, b'ce, c'd'e', a'cd'$

6.27 $F = \underline{BCDE'} + \underline{A'B'CD} + \underline{AB'C'D} + \underline{B'C'E'} + \underline{A'BC'} + BCD'E + A'E'$

6.29 $F = \underline{AC'D'E'} + \underline{A'B'C'E'} + \underline{BDE} + \underline{A'BC} + AB'C'E + A'B'D'$

Unit 7   Study Guide Answers

2 (f) (2, 6)

3 (a) $m_0 - a'b'c'$ $(m_0, m_1) - a'b'$
      $m_1 - a'b'c$ $(m_1, m_5) - b'c$ } prime
      $m_5 - ab'c$ $(m_5, m_7) - ac$
      $m_7 - abc$

(d) $A'B'C'$ and ABC are not prime implicants.

4 (b) $a'c'd', bc', ab'c$

5 (b) $F = bd + a'b, F = bd + bc', F = bc' + a'b, F = a'b + c'd$

Unit 7 Answers to Problems

7.2 (a) $a'c'd$ (1, 5)   (b) $a'b'c'$ (0, 1)
       $b'c'd$ (1, 9) $b'c'd'$ (0, 8)
       $a'b\ d$ (5, 7) $a\ b'd'$ (8, 10)
       $a\ b'd$ (9, 11) $a\ c\ d'$ (10, 14)
       $a\ b\ d'$ (12, 14) $a'd$ (1, 3, 5, 7)
       $b\ c\ d$ (7, 15) $b\ c$ (6, 7, 14, 15)
       $a\ c\ d$ (11, 15)
       $a\ b\ c$ (14, 15)

7.3 (a) $f = a'c'd + ab'd + abd' + bcd$ <u>or</u> $f = b'c'd + a'bd + abd' + acd$

$$
(b)\ f = a'd + bc + \begin{Bmatrix} a'b'c' + ab'd' \\ \text{or} \\ b'c'd' + acd' \\ \text{or} \\ b'c'd' + ab'd' \end{Bmatrix}
$$

7.4 (a) $f = b'cd' + bc' + a'd + (a'b\ \text{OR}\ a'c)$ [1 other solution]
    (b) $f = bc'd' + b'c + cd + ab + (ad\ \text{OR}\ b'd)$ [1 other solution]

7.13 (a) $F = A'B + A'C'D' + AB'D + A'C'E + BCDE$
     (b) $Z = A'B' + ABD + EB'C' + EA'C + FAB + GBD$ [several other solutions]

Unit 8 Study Guide Answers

1 (b) 6 gates, 13 inputs; 5 gates, 11 inputs
2 (a) 0; 1; 1, 1; 0, 0; 1, 1, 1; 0, 0, 0; 0, 0; 1, 1
  (c) $F = de + abd + bcd + acd + abe + bce + ace$
7 (d) $C(A + B) + DE$

Unit 8 Answers to Problems

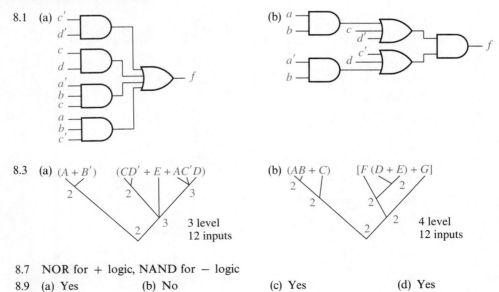

8.1 (a)

(b)

8.3 (a) $(A + B')$ $(CD' + E + AC'D)$

         2   2   3

              2   3   3 level
                           12 inputs

    (b) $(AB + C)$ $[F (D + E) + G]$

         2   2
           2   2

              2   2   4 level
                        12 inputs

8.7 NOR for + logic, NAND for − logic
8.9 (a) Yes   (b) No   (c) Yes   (d) Yes

8.11 (a)

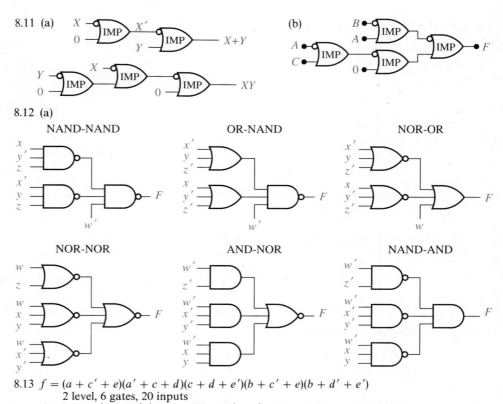

(b)

8.12 (a)

NAND-NAND   OR-NAND   NOR-OR

NOR-NOR   AND-NOR   NAND-AND

8.13 $f = (a + c' + e)(a' + c + d)(c + d + e')(b + c' + e)(b + d' + e')$
     2 level, 6 gates, 20 inputs
     $f = (ab + c' + e)(a'e' + c + d)(b + d' + e')$ 3 level, 6 gates, 16 inputs

8.15 (a) $f = (a + b)(a' + d' + b'c')$

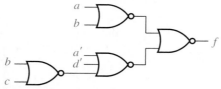

8.16 (a) $F = A'[B' + (D' + E)(C' + D)]^*$ *or* $A'B' + A'(C'D' + DE)$

8.17 (a) $F = B'(A'D' + C'D')$

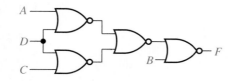

8.24 (a)

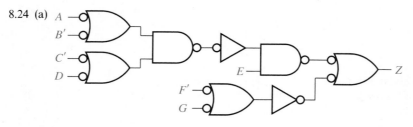

---

* This solution requires a NAND gate connected as an inverter at the network output.

(b)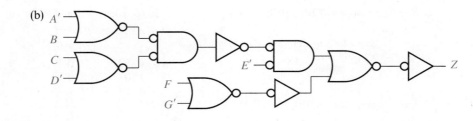

8.25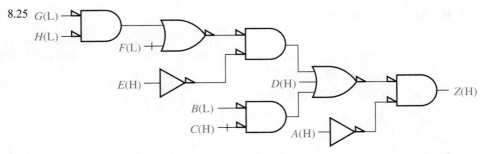

8.26 (a)

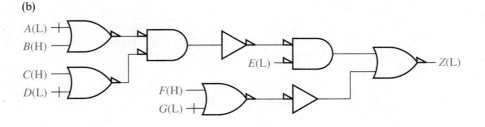

(b)

Unit 9   Study Guide Answers

2 (a) (1) No   (2) Yes   (3) No
   (c) 5 gates, 10 inputs; using common gate: 4 gates, 9 inputs
   (d) $F_1 = \underline{a'cd} + \underline{acd} + ab'c'$ $F_2 = \underline{a'cd} + \underline{bcd} + a'bc' + acd'$
   $F_3 = \underline{bcd} + \underline{acd} + a'c'd$

4 (a) $Z = a'I_0 + aI_1$
   (b) $Z = A'C'I_0 + A'CI_1 + AC'I_2 + ACI_3$ $I_0 = B'$ $I_1 = B'$ $I_2 = 0$ $I_3 = 1$
   (c) $I_0 = 1$ $I_1 = A'$ $I_2 = 0$ $I_3 = 1$ $I_4 = A$ $I_5 = 0$ $I_6 = 1$ $I_7 = A'$
   (d) $I_0 = B'$ $I_1 = B + D$ $I_2 = D'$ $I_3 = B \oplus D$
   (e) $I_0 = A'$ $I_1 = 0$ $I_2 = A$ $I_8 = 1$

5 (a) Inputs BCD; $A = 0$

6 (b) 32 words × 4 bits; 1024 × 8

7 (a) 4 inputs

7 terms ($m_3, m_7, m_{11}, m_{12}, m_{13}, m_{14}, m_{15}$)

3 outputs

(c) 16 words × 5 bits; 16 × 10

(c)

$ABCD$	$F_1F_2F_3$
11--	1 0 1
1-11	1 1 0
110-	0 1 0
0-11	0 1 1

(f) When $ABC = 010$, $F_0F_1F_2F_3 = 0111$.

Unit 9   Answers to Problems

9.1 (a) $\left.\begin{array}{l} f_1 = a'c'd' + ab'c + a'c \\ f_2 = a'c'd' + ab'c + ac' \end{array}\right\}$ 6 gates,   compared to original f_1 and f_2
   16 inputs   which require 8 gates, 18 inputs

$f_1 = A'BC' + BC'D' + AB'C$

9.2 (a) $f_2 = B'C'D' + B'CD + A'C'D' + \left\{\begin{array}{l} A'B'D \\ A'B'C' \end{array}\right\}$ $\left.\begin{array}{l} \\ \\ \end{array}\right\}$ 11 gates,
   34 inputs

$f_3 = A'C'D' + BC'D' + ACD'$

9.3 $\left.\begin{array}{l} f_1 = b'd' + ac'd \\ f_2 = a'd + ac'd \\ f_3 = b'c + ac'd + ab' \end{array}\right\}$ 8 gates,
   18 inputs

9.6 xs-3 = abcd $W = ab + acd = a(b + cd)$ $\left.\begin{array}{l} \\ \\ \\ \end{array}\right\}$

   BCD = WXYZ $X = b'(c' + d') + bcd$ 9 gates,
      $Y = (c' + d')(c + d)$ 19 inputs
      $Z = d'$

9.8 $f_1 = (a + b + c)(b' + d)$ $f_2 = (a + b + c)(b' + c + d)(a' + c)$
   $f_3 = (b' + c + d)(a + c)(b + c')$

9.9 (a) Replace all gates in the AND-OR network which corresponds to Equations 9–2(b) with NAND gates. Invert the c input to the f_2 output gate.

   (b) Replace all gates in answer to 9.8 with NOR.

9.14 (a)

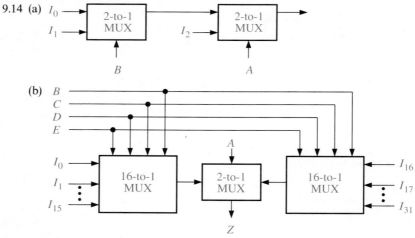

9.15 (a) MUX inputs: $I_0 = I_1 = I_7 = 1$, $I_2 = B'$, $I_3 = B$, $I_4 = I_5 = I_6 = 0$

   (b) $I_0 = 1$, $I_2 = 0$, $I_3 = D$, $I_1 = B'D' + BD = B' \oplus D$ (control inputs A, C)

9.19 Answer similar to Fig. 9–19 with four 5-input NAND-gates:

$W = (m_5'm_6'm_7'm_8'm_9')'$, $X = (m_1'm_2'm_3'm_4'm_9')'$, $Y = (m_0'm_3'm_4'm_7'm_8')'$,
$Z = (m_0'm_2'm_4'm_6'm_8')'$

9.20 $X = A'BD + C'D + AB' + AB'C'D'$
$Y = A'BD + BCD + AB'$
$Z = A'BD + BCD + ABC + AB'C'D'$

ROM table:

$ABCD$	XYZ
0000	000
0001	100
0010	000
0011	000
0100	000
0101	111
⋮	⋮
1111	011

9.22 (a)

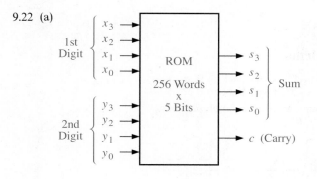

$x_3x_2x_1x_0y_3y_2y_1y_0$	$s_3s_2s_1s_0c$
0 0 0 0 0 0 0 0	0 0 0 0 0
0 0 0 0 0 0 0 1	0 0 0 1 0
. . . .	. . . . .
0 1 0 1 0 0 1 1	xxxxx
0 1 0 1 0 1 0 0	xxxxx
. . . .	. . . . .
1 0 0 1 1 0 0 0	1 0 1 1 1
1 0 0 1 1 0 0 1	0 0 0 0 1
1 0 0 1 1 0 1 0	0 1 1 0 1
1 0 0 1 1 0 1 1	1 1 1 0 1
. . . .	. . . . .

(b) 8 inputs, 100 words, 5 outputs

9.27

$A_4A_3A_2A_1A_0$	$WXYZ$
1 0 0 0 0	0 0 0 0
1 0 0 0 1	0 0 0 1
1 0 0 1 0	0 0 1 0
1 0 0 1 1	0 0 1 1
1 0 1 0 0	0 1 0 0
1 0 1 0 1	0 1 0 1
1 0 1 1 0	0 1 1 0
1 0 1 1 1	0 1 1 1
1 1 0 0 0	1 0 0 0
1 1 0 0 1	1 0 0 1
0 0 0 0 1	1 0 1 0
0 0 0 1 0	1 0 1 1
0 0 0 1 1	1 1 0 0
0 0 1 0 0	1 1 0 1
0 0 1 0 1	1 1 1 0
0 0 1 1 0	1 1 1 1

$W = (A_4A_3')'$ $X = (A_2'A_1' + A_2'A_0' + A_4A_2')'$ $Y = (A_4'A_1A_0 + A_4A_1' + A_1'A_0')'$
$Z = (A_4A_0' + A_4'A_0)'$

Unit 11　Study Guide Answers

1 (a) $Z = 1$　between　$t = 50$　and　$t = 110$

2 (b) $P = Q = 0$　　　　　　　　　　(c) $S = R = 1$　is not allowed

4 (b) Q changes to 1 at time 1 and back to 0 at time 2.

5 (b) $Q^+ = QK' + Q'J$

   (c) Pulse width must be long enough to cause FF to change state, but shorter than the FF delay time, ϵ.

6 (b) Clocked—Q^+ represents the state after a clock pulse.

      Unclocked—Q^+ is the state of the FF at time ϵ (response time) after input pulses on J, K.

7 (b) Q becomes 1 on the trailing edge of the first clock pulse and returns to 0 on the trailing edge of the third clock pulse.

8 (a) clear $= 1$,   preset $= 0$;   clear $= 0$ 9 (b) $S = Q'T$, $R = QT$

Unit 11   Answers to Problems

11.1 V changes to 1 at 15 ns and back to 0 at 25 ns.
      Z changes to 1 at 20 ns and back to 0 at 35 ns.

11.4   (a) R^* and S^* cannot be zero simultaneously.
      (b) $Q^+ = (S^*)' + R^*Q$
      (c)

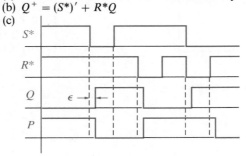

      (d) $S^* = S'$, $R^* = R'$

11.5

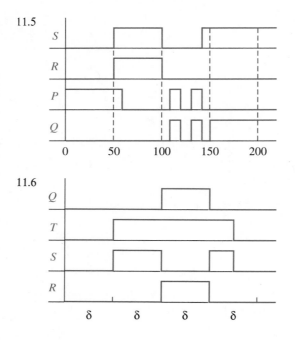

11.6

11.8   (a)

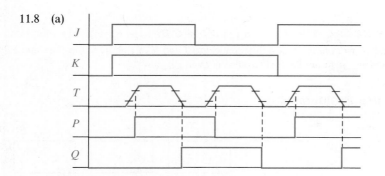

(b) $Q = 1$
(c) $Q = 1$
(d) Inputs must change between clock
      pulses.

11.10 $D = Q^+ = Q'J + QK'$

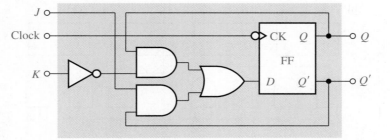

11.11 $Q^+ = C'Q + K'Q + JCQ'$
11.12 (a) $Q^+ = G'Q + GL$ (b) $R = GL'$ $S = GL$
11.13 (a)

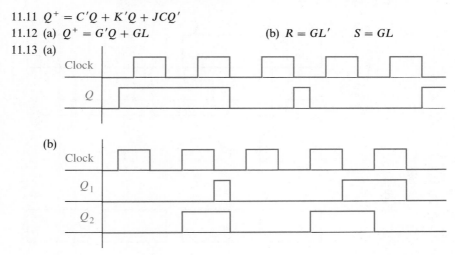

(b)

Unit 12   Study Guide Answers

1 (a) T_C and T_B
   (e) 101 goes to 110 which goes to 011

2 (c) From the flip-flop outputs
   (e) In state 001, $R_A = S_A = 1$, so A^+ is undefined. $B^+ = 0$ and $C^+ = 0$.

3 (f) $F_1 = 1$, $F_2 = 0$

 (g) $J_B = A'C' + C'D + ACD'$, $K_B = A'D + C'D$

4 (b) Q and Q' from leftmost flip-flop connect to J and K of rightmost flip-flop, etc. Flip-flops do not change state until after the pulse is over.

Unit 12   Answers to Problems

12.1 (a)

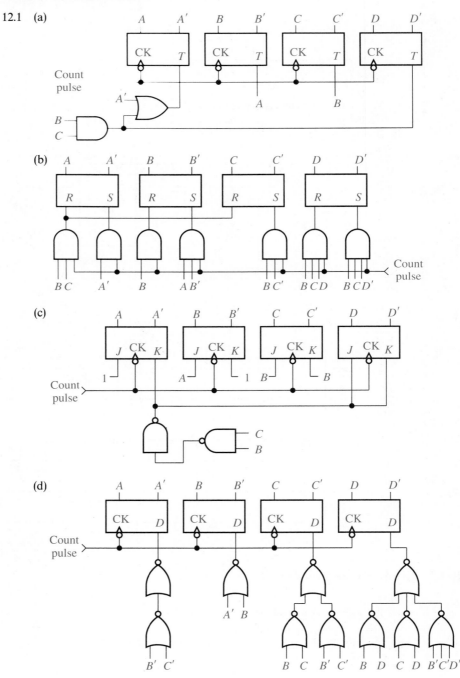

(b)

(c)

(d)

12.2 (a) $T_A = A + BC$ $T_B = AB + B'C + CD'$ $T_C = A'$ $T_D = A$
   (b) $R_A = C'$ or A $R_B = A + BCD'$ $R_C = C$ $R_D = AD$ or AB
       $S_A = BC$ $S_B = B'C$ $S_C = A'C'$ $S_D = AB'$ or AD'
   (c) $J_A = BC$ $J_B = C$ $J_C = A'$ $J_D = A$
       $K_A = 1$ $K_B = A + CD'$ $K_C = 1$ $K_D = A$
   (d) $D_A = BC$ $D_B = B'C + CD + A'BC'$ $D_C = A'C'$
       $D_D = A'D + AD'$ or $A'D + AB'$

12.5 P, A, B, and C should be the same as in Fig. 12–6.

12.13 (a)

Q	Q^+	M	N
0	0	0	X
0	1	1	X
1	0	X	0
1	1	X	1

(b) $M_A = B, N_A = C$;
$M_B = A'C, N_B = A'$;
$M_C = A', N_C = A' + B$

12.15 (a) $Q^+ = KG + QK'$

(b)

Q	Q^+	K	G
		0	0
0	0	0	1
		1	0
0	1	1	1
1	0	1	0
		0	0
1	1	0	1
		1	1

(c) $K = XYQ'$, $G = 1$ or $K = 1$, $G = Q + XY$

12.16

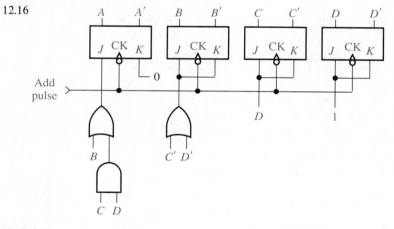

12.18 (a)

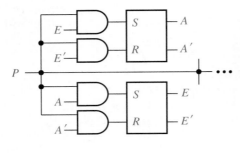

If the S-R flip-flops have no delay, A may switch before E does (or vice versa) and cause loss of information; or one flip-flop may switch twice in the same pulse — as if the new state of E gets back to A before P turns off. If delay is added then P must be shorter than the delay time; then the new state of E cannot affect A, etc.

(b)

Unit 13   Study Guide Answers

2 (a) Mealy: output a function of both input and state
    Moore: output a function of state only
  (b) Change inputs between clock pulses.
    State changes immediately following the clock pulse.
    Moore: output changes only when the flip-flops change state.
    Mealy: output can change when input changes or when state changes.
  (c) During the clock pulse or immediately preceding it
  (d) Mealy: false outputs can appear when the state has changed to its next value but the input has not yet changed
    Moore: no false outputs because output is not a function of input
    Changing the inputs at the same time the state change occurs will eliminate false outputs.

3 (a) Before the clock pulse
    Q^+ means the state of flip-flop Q after the clock (i.e., the next state of flip-flop Q).
  (c) Mealy: output associated with transitions between states
    Moore: output associated with state
  (d) Present: before the clock pulse
    Next: after the clock pulse
  (e) Output depends only on the state and not on the input.

4 (a) 1101   (c) 1001
  (e) No false outputs, but Z_d is delayed by one clock time.

6 (c) Without the clock, flip-flops would change state at different times with respect to each other because of unequal propagation delays through the network. Also, without a clock, as soon as one state change was completed another change could occur without waiting for the next input.
  (d) For a Moore network, $Z = \lambda(S)$.

Unit 13   Answers to Problems

13.2

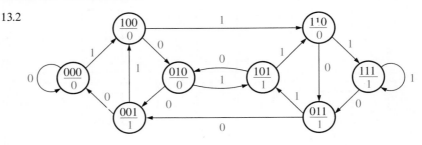

13.3 (a) $A^+ = A(B' + X) + A'(BX' + B'X)$
$B^+ = AB'X + B(A' + X')$
(b) $Z = (0)00101$

Present State	Next State (A^+B^+)		
AB	$x = 0$	$x = 1$	Z
00	00	10	0
01	11	01	0
11	01	10	1
10	10	11	0

(c)

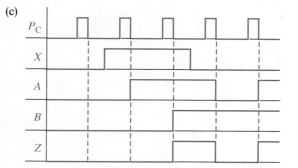

13.4

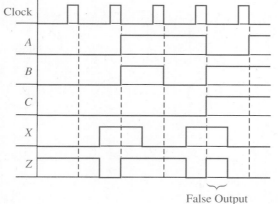

False Output

13.5 (a) $A^+ = AX_2' + AX_1B' + X_2'X_1' + X_2'B'$ $B^+ = BX_1' + BA' + X_1'A'$

(b)

	A^+B^+				Z_1Z_2			
AB	$X_1X_2 = 00$	01	10	11	$X_1X_2 = 00$	01	10	11
00	11	01	10	00	10	10	00	00
01	11	01	01	01	00	11	00	11
10	10	00	10	10	00	01	00	01
11	11	01	10	00	00	00	00	00

Unit 14   Study Guide Answers

1 (b) last row: 11 10 01 0 1
(c) $J_A = BX'$ $K_A = X \oplus B$ $J_B = A + X$ $K_B = A$ $Z = AB'$

Unit 14   Answers to Problems

14.3

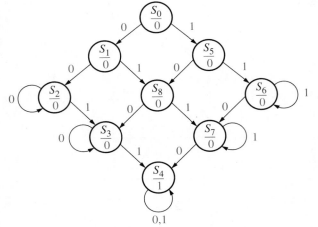

14.5

	$X = 0$	1	$X = 0$	1
S_0	S_4	S_1	00	00
S_1	S_2	S_1	00	00
S_2	S_4	S_3	00	10
S_3	S_2	S_5	00	01
S_4	S_4	S_3	00	00
S_5	S_6	S_5	00	00
S_6	S_6	S_7	00	00
S_7	S_6	S_5	00	01

$$Z_1 Z_2$$

14.7

Previous Input	Output	Present State	Next State $X_1 X_2 = 00$	01	10	11
00	0	S_0	S_0	S_1	S_2	S_3
01	0	S_1	S_0	S_1	S_2	S_7
10	0	S_2	S_0	S_1	S_2	S_7
11	0	S_3	S_0	S_1	S_2	S_3
00	1	S_4	S_4	S_5	S_6	S_3
01	1	S_5	S_4	S_5	S_6	S_7
10	1	S_6	S_4	S_5	S_6	S_3
11	1	S_7	S_4	S_5	S_6	S_7

Note: a 4-state solution is also possible.

14.9 (a)

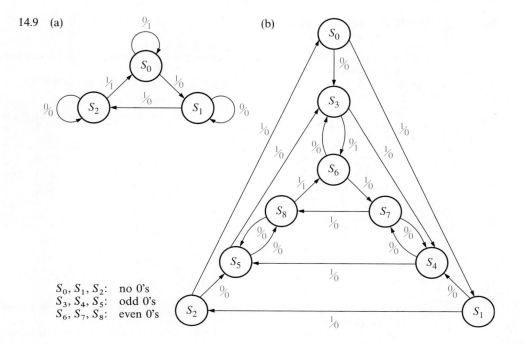

(b)

S_0, S_1, S_2: no 0's
S_3, S_4, S_5: odd 0's
S_6, S_7, S_8: even 0's

14.11 (a)

	$X_1X_2 =$								
	00	01	10	11	00	01	10	11	
S_0	S_1	S_2	S_3	S_4	00	00	00	00	
S_1	S_1	S_2	S_3	S_4	00	10	10	10	
S_2	S_1	S_2	S_3	S_4	01	00	10	10	
S_3	S_1	S_2	S_3	S_4	01	01	00	10	
S_4	S_1	S_2	S_3	S_4	01	01	01	00	

Z_1Z_2

(b)

	$X_1X_2 =$				Z_1Z_2
	00	01	10	11	
S_0	S_1	S_4	S_7	S_{10}	00
S_1	S_1	S_3	S_6	S_9	00
S_2	S_1	S_3	S_6	S_9	01
S_3	S_2	S_4	S_6	S_9	10
S_4	S_2	S_4	S_6	S_9	00
S_5	S_2	S_4	S_6	S_9	01
S_6	S_2	S_5	S_7	S_9	10
S_7	S_2	S_5	S_7	S_9	00
S_8	S_2	S_5	S_7	S_9	01
S_9	S_2	S_5	S_8	S_{10}	10
S_{10}	S_2	S_5	S_8	S_{10}	00

14.26 (a)

	$X = 0$	1	$X = 0$	1
S_0	S_0	S_1	0	1
S_1	S_1	S_0	1	0

(b)

	$X = 0$	1	
S_0	S_0	S_1	0
S_1	S_1	S_0	1

(c, d)

Clock	
NRZ	0 1 1 1 0 0 1 0
NRZI (Mealy)	False output
NRZI (Moore)	

Unit 15   Study Guide Answers

2 (b) $\lambda(p, 01) = 00$ and $\lambda(q, 01) = 01$; therefore, $p \not\equiv q$
   (c) No. You would have to try an infinite number of test sequences to be sure the networks were equivalent.
   (d) $b \equiv c$ iff $a \equiv d$ and $a \equiv b$, but $a \not\equiv b$ because the outputs are different.

3 (a)

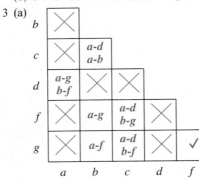

   (b) $f - g$
   (c) $a \equiv c$, $b \equiv d$, $b \equiv e$, $d \equiv e$

		0	1	0	1
a		b	a	0	1
b		b	b	0	0

7 (b) $Z = X'AB' + XA'BC'$

8 (b) Interchanging columns or complementing columns does not affect network cost for symmetric flip-flops.
   (f) Numbering columns from left to right, column 3 is same as column 4, column 2 is column 5 complemented, column 1 is column 6 complemented.

9 (e) $D_1 = XQ_1' + XQ_3 + Q_2Q_3' + X'Q_1Q_2'$ or $D_1 = XQ_1' + XQ_2 + Q_2'Q_3 + X'Q_1Q_3'$
   $D_2 = Q_3, D_3 = X'Q_3 + XQ_2Q_3' + (Q_1'Q_3$ or $Q_1'Q_2)$
   $Z = XQ_2Q_3 + X'Q_2'Q_3 + X'Q_2Q_3'$
   (f) $J_1 = X, K_1 = X'Q_2Q_3 + XQ_2'Q_3'$

Unit 15   Answers to Problems

15.1   (a) *Reduced table:*

	0	1	0	1
a	c	e	0	0
c	a	g	0	0
e	e	a	0	1
g	c	g	0	1

   (b)

state	a	f	f	a	c	g	c	g
input	1	0	1		1	0	1	
output	0	0	1		0	0	0	

   or

	a	f	a	f	c	g	g	g
	1	1	1		1	1	1	
	0	1	0		0	1	1	

15.3   *Reduced table:*

	Next State $X=0$	1	Output
a	f	b	0
b	b	a	1
e	g	b	0
f	a	f	0
g	e	a	0

15.5   (a) No; states S_2 and S_4 have no corresponding states in Mr. Ipflop's design.
   (b) Since there is no way to reach S_2 or S_4 starting from S_0, the networks would perform the same.

15.6 (a) Only *one* assignment—000   001
                            011   OR   010   etc.
                            101   100

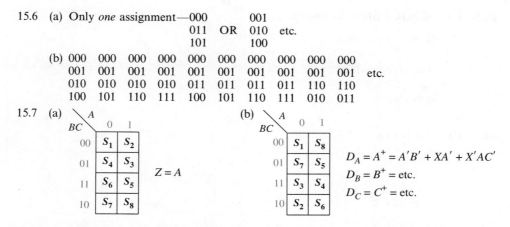

(b) 000 000 000 000 000 000 000 000 000 000
    001 001 001 001 001 001 001 001 001 001 etc.
    010 010 010 010 011 011 011 011 110 110
    100 101 110 111 100 101 110 111 010 011

15.7 (a)

$\begin{array}{c}A\\ BC\end{array}$	0	1
00	S_1	S_2
01	S_4	S_3
11	S_6	S_5
10	S_7	S_8

$Z = A$

(b)

$\begin{array}{c}A\\ BC\end{array}$	0	1
00	S_1	S_8
01	S_7	S_5
11	S_3	S_4
10	S_2	S_6

$D_A = A^+ = A'B' + XA' + X'AC'$
$D_B = B^+ = $ etc.
$D_C = C^+ = $ etc.

15.9 (a) The following assignment satisfies all of the adjacency conditions except (E, F):

$\begin{array}{c}Q_1Q_2\\ Q_3\end{array}$	00	01	11	10
0	A	F	C	E
1			B	D

(b) $J_1 = XQ'_2,$ $K_1 = Q_2Q'_3 + X'Q'_3,$ $J_2 = X'Q_1 + Q_3,$ $K_2 = X'Q'_3,$
    $J_3 = 0,$ $K_3 = X',$ $Z = XQ_3$

15.11 (a) $A = 00,$ $B = 01,$ $C = 10,$ $D = 11$
    (b) $T_1 = X'_1X_2Q'_2 + X'_1Q_1Q_2 + X_1Q'_1Q_2 + X_1X'_2$
        $T_2 = X_1Q'_1Q'_2 + X_1Q_1Q_2,$ $Z_1 = X_1Q_2,$ $Z_2 = X'_1Q_1 + Q_1Q'_2$

Unit 16   Study Guide Answers

1 Because the input sequences are listed in reverse order

4 (b) Reset the state to 010, and check the value of J_3. If $J_3 = 1$ and Q_3 does not change state when the clock is pulsed, the flip-flop may be defective. If $J_3 = 0$, check the network which realizes J_3.

6 (a) Yes
   (b) Not necessarily (see below)

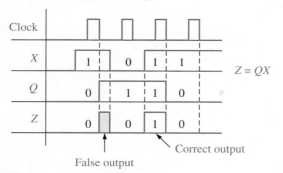

(c) Yes

7 (a) After the state changes (after the clock pulse), and before the input changes, the input and hence the output may temporarily have the wrong value.
   (b) No. The output is correct during the clock pulse.

Unit 17   Study Guide Answers

2 (b) m leads, where $2^{m-1} < n \leqslant 2^m$
  (c) $J_a = x'yb'$ $K_a = 0$ $J_b = xy'a'$ $K_b = 0$

3 (a) Once two groups of 1's have occurred, a 1 output is no longer possible no matter what input sequence follows.

4 (c) Yes

Unit 17   Answers to Problems

17.1

	Input State	a_i	Output State $x_iy_i =$				a_{i+1} $x_iy_i =$			
			00	01	11	10	00	01	11	10
$X > Y$	S_0	1	S_0	S_1	S_0	S_0	1	0	1	1
$X \leqslant Y$	S_1	0	S_1	S_1	S_1	S_0	0	0	0	1

$$a_{i+1} = x_iy_i' + y_i'a_i + x_ia_i$$
$$Z = a_{n+1}$$

17.2

	$x_i = 0$	1	Z
S_0	S_0	S_1	0
S_1	S_2	S_3	1
S_2	S_2	S_1	1
S_3	S_3	S_3	0

a_i	0	1
b_i		
0	S_0	S_2
1	S_3	S_1

$$a_{i+1} = x_i'a_i + x_ib_i'$$
$$= (x_i + a_i)(x_i' + b_i')$$
$$b_{i+1} = x_i + a_i'b_i$$
$$Z = a_{n+1}$$

17.4

	$x_i = 0$	1	Z
S_0	S_0	S_1	0
S_1	S_1	S_2	0
S_2	S_2	S_3	0
S_3	S_3	S_2	1

a_i	0	1
b_i		
0	S_0	S_1
1	S_2	S_3

$$a_{i+1} = x_ia_i' + x_i'a_i$$
$$b_{i+1} = b_i + x_i a_i$$
$$a_0 = 0 \qquad b_0 = 0$$
$$a_1 = x_0 \qquad b_1 = 0$$

17.6

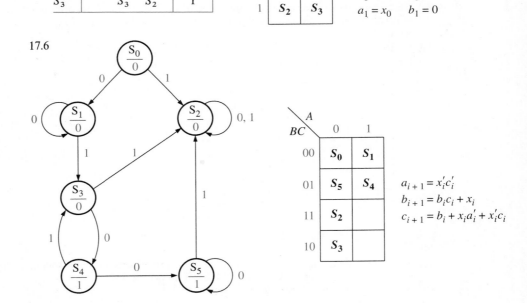

A	0	1
BC		
00	S_0	S_1
01	S_5	S_4
11	S_2	
10	S_3	

$$a_{i+1} = x_i'c_i'$$
$$b_{i+1} = b_ic_i + x_i$$
$$c_{i+1} = b_i + x_ia_i' + x_i'c_i$$

17.8

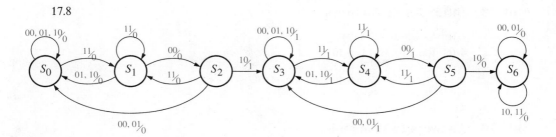

Unit 18   Study Guide Answers

1 (b)

Clock Pulse	$Q_A Q_B Q_C Q_D Q_E Q_F Q_G Q_H$
3	1 0 0 0 0 0 0 0
7	1 0 0 0 1 0 0 0
10	0 0 1 1 0 0 0 1
14	0 0 0 0 0 0 1 1

Q_H is 1 during clock pulses
10, 14, and 15

2 (a) 0111, <u>0110</u>, <u>0100</u>, <u>0000</u>, 1000
  (b) Connect Q_D of right counter to A input of left counter.

Unit 18   Answers to Problems

18.1 Connections: serial input to D_D, Q_D to D_C, Q_C to D_B, Q_B to D_A, serial output from Q_A; for left shift $SH = 0$, $L = 1$; for right shift, $SH = 1$, $L = X$

18.2 (a) Connect Q_D to SI (serial input).
    (b) Q_D starts at 0 and changes value immediately following the trailing edge of clock pulses 2, 3, 4, 5, and 6.

18.3 (a) Q_D, Q_C, Q_B, and Q_A can change value only on the 0–1 transition of the clock. Successive values of Q_D, Q_C, Q_B, Q_A are 1001, 0000, 1011, 1100, 1101, 1110, 1111, 1111, 1111.

18.4 CLEAR $= (Q_D Q_C Q_A)'$ or $(Q_D Q_B' Q_A)'$ LOAD $= (Q_C Q_B Q_A)'$ $PT = 1$
    $D_D = 1$, $D_C = 0$, $D_B = 1$, $D_A = 0$

18.5 CLEAR $= (Q_C Q_B Q_A)'$ LOAD $= (X Q_C' Q_B Q_A')'$ $PT = 1$
    $D_D = 0$, $D_C = 1$, $D_B = 0$, $D_A = 1$

18.6 (a) CLEAR $= (X' B' A)'$ LOAD $= X + B' C'$ $PT = CA' + XC'$
    $D_D = X$, $D_C = A$, $D_B = 0$, $D_A = 1$ or $PT = XA' + XC'$

18.7 (a)

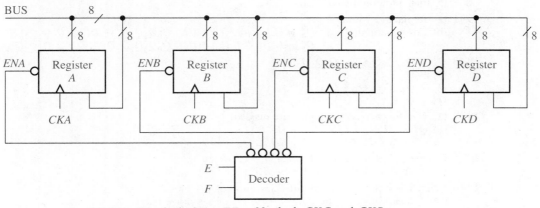

  (b) $EF = 01$, clock CKA; $EF = 00$, clock CKC and CKD

Unit 19   Study Guide Answers

1 (b) 64 words × 7 bits

4 (c) For Fig. 19–11, $F_1(0, b, c, d, e) = bcde + b'cde'$
$$F_2(1, b, c, d, e) = b'c'd'e' + bcde$$
$$F_3(a, b, c, d, e) = aF_1 + a'F_2$$

Unit 19   Answers to Problems

19.1   The block diagram is similar to Fig. 19–1, except it has X_1 and X_2 inputs, Z_1 and Z_2 outputs, and 2 flip-flops.

X_1	X_2	Q_1	Q_2	D_1	D_2	Z_1	Z_2
0	0	0	0	1	1	0	0
0	0	0	1	0	0	1	0
0	0	1	0	1	1	0	0
0	0	1	1	1	0	0	0
0	1	0	0	1	0	1	0
0	1	0	1	0	1	1	0
0	1	1	0	0	0	1	0
0	1	1	1	1	0	0	0
1	0	0	0	0	1	1	1

etc.

19.2   (a) Similar to Fig. 19–1, except change ROM to PLA

(b)

X	A	B	C	Z	D_A	D_B	D_C	
0	–	–	–	0	1	0	0	
0	–	–	0	0	0	1	0	
–	0	–	1	0	0	1	0	
–	0	1	–	0	0	1	0	(0101 may be used
–	1	–	–	0	0	0	1	in place of 010–)
1	–	0	–	0	0	0	1	
0	1	0	–	1	0	0	0	
1	0	1	0	1	0	1	0	

(c) 16 words × 4 bits

19.3   Implement D_A, D_B, and D_C from Fig. 15–15(b); implement $Z' = AB + XB' + X'A' + A'C$ (5 other minimum solutions).

19.11   (a) Replace D with DU'.
(b) For equation (19–7) $Q_4^+ = (LD_4 + L'Q_4) \oplus (UL'Q_0Q_1Q_2Q_3 + DL'Q_0'Q_1'Q_2'Q_3')$
$$Q_5^+ = (LD_5 + L'Q_5) \oplus (UL'Q_0Q_1Q_2Q_3Q_4 + DL'Q_0'Q_1'Q_2'Q_3'Q_4')$$

19.13 $Q_3^+ = Q_3 \oplus (Q_3Q_1 + Q_2Q_1Q_0)$
$Q_2^+ = Q_2 \oplus Q_1Q_0$
$Q_1^+ = Q_1 \oplus (Q_3Q_1 + Q_0)$
$Q_0^+ = Q_0 \oplus (Q_1' + Q_3')$

19.14   (a) $N = 9$ (since $N + 4$ inputs are needed)
(b) $Q_1^+ = SH\,SI + SH'\,LD_1 + SH'\,L'Q_1$
$Q_9^+ = SH\,Q_8 + SH'\,LD_9 + SH'\,L'Q_9$

19.15   Connect CLR to C, G to R, then $G = C'$.
Connect T to B, then $F = B'Q + BQ'$.

19.16   Cell 1 has inputs $vwxy$, output $F_1 = v'w + x'y + vw'$.
Cell 2 has inputs vxy, output $F_2 = vx'y' + v'y + xy + v'x$.
Cell 3 has inputs U, F_1, F_2, output $F_3 = UQF_1 + U'Q'F_2$.

Unit 20   Study Guide Answers

1 (f) sign & mag: -0,   2's comp: -32,   1's comp: -31

  (g) Overflow occurs when adding n-bit numbers and the result requires $n + 1$ bits for proper representation. You can tell that an overflow has occurred when the sum of two positive numbers is negative or the sum of two negative numbers is positive.
A carry out of the last bit position does *not* indicate overflow has occurred.

3 (e)

4 (d) $d_5 = 0, d_4 = 0, d_3 = 1, d_2 = 0, d_1 = 1$
$b_6 = 0, b_5 = 0, b_4 = 1, b_3 = 1, b_2 = 1$

Unit 20   Answers to Problems

20.1   9's comp. of $N = (10^n - 1) - N$
9's comp. of $05367 = 99999 - 05367$ Check: -5367
$\qquad\qquad\qquad = 94632$ $+2489$
$\qquad\qquad\qquad\quad + 02489$ $\overline{-2878}$
$\qquad\qquad\qquad\quad \overline{97121} = -2878$

20.2   2's complement:

  (a) $10111\ (-9)$ (b) $10111\ (-9)$ (c) $10111\ (-9)$
       $\underline{10101\ (-11)}$ $\underline{11001\ (-7)}$ $\underline{01011\ (+11)}$
      $(1)01100$ overflow $(1)10000\ (-16)$ $(1)00010\ (\ +2)$

  (d) $01011\ (+11)$ (e) $10110\ (-10)$
      $\underline{00111\ (\ +7)}$ $\underline{11011\ (\ -5)}$
      10010 overflow $(1)10001\ (-15)$

  1's complement:

  (a) 01011 overflow   (b) 01111 overflow   (c) $00010\ (+2)$
  (d) 10010 overflow   (e) $10000\ (-15)$

20.6   2's complement: -128 to $+127$ 1's complement: -127 to $+127$

20.7   Each J-K flip-flop requires 1 inverter for the K input.
Each S-R flip-flop requires 1 inverter and 2 AND gates.
Each T flip-flop requires 1 EXCLUSIVE-OR gate and 1 AND gate.

20.9   (a)

	$x_i y_i z_i c_i d_i$	$c_{i+1} d_{i+1} s_i$
0	00000	0 0 0
1	00001	0 0 1
2	00010	0 1 0
3	00011	X X X
$\vdots$		$\vdots$
28	11100	0 1 1
29	11101	1 0 0
30	11110	1 0 1
31	11111	X X X

(b) $s_i = x_i y_i' z_i' d_i' + x_i' y_i' z_i d_i' + x_i y_i z_i d_i'$
$\qquad + x_i' y_i z_i' d_i' + x_i' y_i' z_i' d_i + x_i y_i' z_i d_i$
$\qquad + x_i' y_i z_i d_i + x_i y_i z_i' d_i$
$\quad = x_i \oplus y_i \oplus z_i \oplus d_i$
$c_{i+1} = y_i z_i c_i + x_i z_i c_i + x_i y_i c_i + x_i y_i z_i d_i$

$d_{i+1} = x_i' y_i' c_i + x_i' z_i' c_i + y_i' z_i' c_i + x_i y_i' d_i + y_i z_i d_i +$
$\qquad\quad y_i' z_i d_i + x_i z_i c_i' d_i' + x_i' y_i z_i c_i' + x_i y_i c_i' d_i$

20.10   Same as Fig. 20–7 except replace c_i with b_i and replace P_{add} with P_{sub}
Equations for typical cell are $T_i = b_i \oplus y_i$, $b_{i+1} = x_i' y_i + x_i' b_i + y_i b_i$.

20.11   (a) OVERFLOW $= x_n y_n s_n' + x_n' y_n' s_n$ (b) OVERFLOW $= x_n y_n' d_n' + x_n' y_n d_n$

Unit 21   Study Guide Answers

1 (a) t_1 1011 1001 0 0 1
       t_3 0010 0110 1 1 0

2 (a)
```
        0 0 0 0 0 1 1 0 1
add         1 1 1 1
        ─────────────────
        0 1 1 1 1 1 1 0 1
shift 0 0 1 1 1 1 1 1 0
shift 0 0 0 1 1 1 1 1 1
add         1 1 1 1
        ─────────────────
        1 0 0 1 0 1 1 1 1
shift 0 1 0 0 1 0 1 1 1
add         1 1 1 1
        ─────────────────
        1 1 0 0 0.0 1 1 1
shift 0 1 1 0.0 0 0 1 1
```

(b) 8, 4
(c) 15
(e) For Fig. 21–7, 16 states are needed.
For Fig. 21–8, 3-bit counter, control graph unchanged.

3 (b) Change Y to 2's complement by inverting each bit and adding 1 (by setting the carry input to the first full adder to 1). Also change C so that it is equal to the carry out of the last full adder.

(c) Since only 3 bits are available to store the quotient, an overflow will occur if the quotient would be greater than 7 (111). An overflow is easily detected since if initially $x_7x_6x_5x_4 \geqslant y_3y_2y_1$, subtraction is possible but there is no place to store the resulting quotient bit.

Unit 21   Answers to Problems

21.3

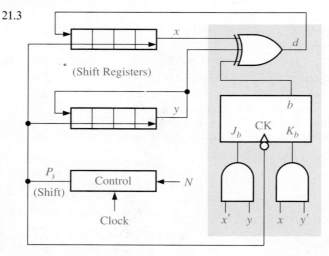

The control circuit is the same as for a serial adder. The logic equations for the control circuit are:

$$J_A = K_A = B$$
$$J_B = N + A, K_B = 1 \text{ or}$$
$$J_B = K_B = N + A + B$$
$$P_s = (N + A + B) \text{ Clock}$$

21.4 The ONE ADDER is similar to a serial adder, except that there is only one input. This means that the carry will be added to X. Thus if the carry flip-flop is initially set to 1, 1 will be added to the input. The P_i pulse can be used to set the carry flip-flop to 1. The P_s pulses then can be used as clock pulses for the adder. Assuming that P_i is used to set the adder network to an initial state of S_1, the state graph is

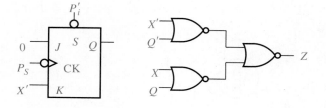

	Q	Q^+		Z	
		$X = 0$	1	0	1
S_0	0	0	0	0	1
S_1	1	0	1	1	0

$$Z = XQ' + X'Q$$
$$= (X' + Q')(X + Q)$$

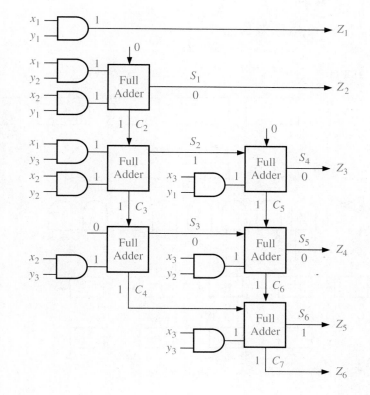

21.5

21.6

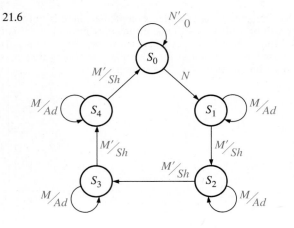

21.7

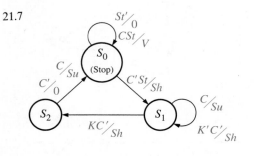

21.8 (a)

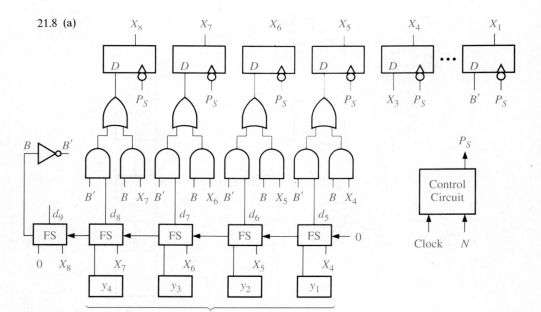

(b) $X = 1\ 0\ 0\ 1\ 0\ 0\ 0\ 0$ (initial)
         $0\ 1\ 0\ 1\ 0\ 0\ 0\ 1$ (after 1 pulse)
         $1\ 0\ 1\ 0\ 0\ 0\ 1\ 0$ (after 2)
         $0\ 1\ 1\ 1\ 0\ 1\ 0\ 1$ (after 3)
         $0\ 0\ 0\ 1\ 1\ 0\ 1\ 1$ (after 4)

              rem.   quotient

(c)

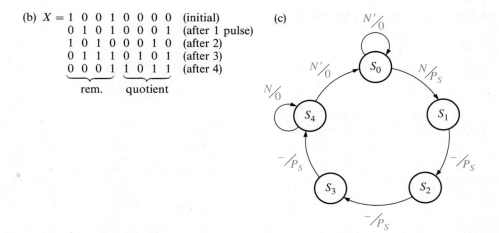

21.9 (a) $X_{in} = K_1' K_2' a' + K_1' K_2 b + K_1 K_2'(a \oplus b) + K_1 K_2 a$
       $Y_{in} = K_1' K_2' b + K_1' K_2 a + K_1 K_2' \cdot 0 + K_1 K_2 \cdot 1$
(b) State graph requires 9 states (wait in last state for $N = 0$).
(d) $Sh = PT = NQ_D'$ CLEAR $= N$ LOAD $= 1$ $D_D = D_C = D_B = D_A = 0$

Unit 22   Study Guide Answers

1 (b) Z_1, Z_2, Z_4 (for both charts)

(d)

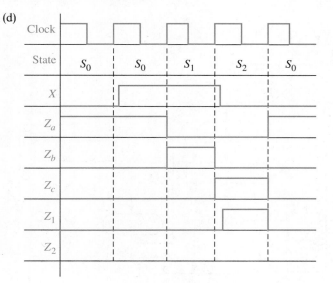

2 (a) $0\ 0\ 1\ 1\ 1\ 0\ 0\ 0$ $C = 0,\ Sh$
    $0\ 1\ 1\ 1\ 0\ 0\ 0\ 0$ $C = 1,\ Su$
    $0\ 0\ 1\ 0\ 0\ 0\ 0\ 1$ $C = 0,\ Sh$
    $0\ 1\ 0\ 0\ 0\ 0\ 1\ 0$ $C = 0,\ Sh$
    $1\ 0\ 0\ 0\ 1\ 0\ 0$ $C = 1,\ Su$
    $0\ 0\ 1\ 1\ 1\ 0\ 1$ (result)

3 (a) $A^+ = BX$
    $B^+ = A'X + BX$

Unit 22   Answers to Problems

22.1

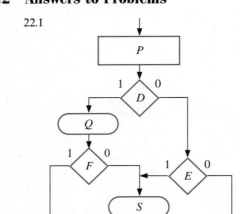

(1)   (2)

22.3 (b)

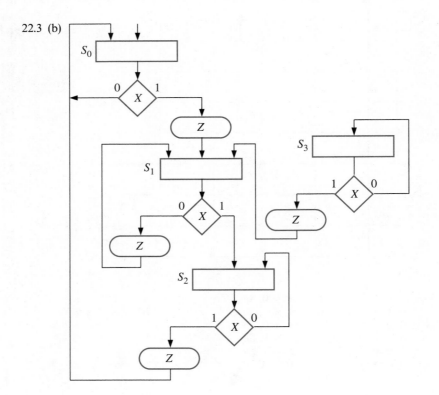

22.7

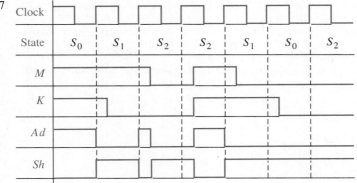

22.9

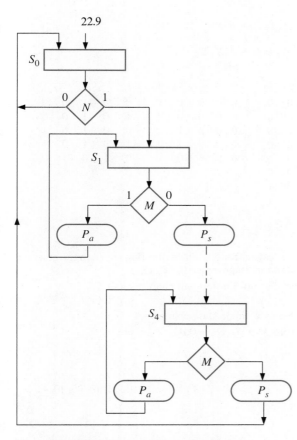

Note: SM blocks for S_2 and S_3 are the same as S_1.

22.11

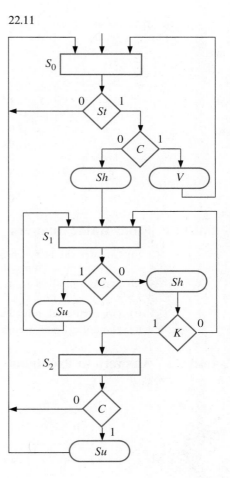

22.13 (a) $A^+ = AB + BC'$ $B^+ = A'B' + A'C'St + BC$
       $V = A'B'C \cdot St$ $Su = AC + BC$ $Sh = A'C'St + BC'$

22.14 (a) $A^+ = A'B'C \cdot Rb'D_7'D_{11}'D_{2312}' + AB'C' + AB' \cdot Rb + AB'Eq'D_7'$
$B^+ = A'B'C \cdot D_7 + A'B'C \cdot D_{11} + A'B \cdot Reset' + AB'C \cdot Rb'Eq'D_7'$
$C^+ = A'B'Rb + A'BC \cdot Reset' + B'C'Rb + AB'C \cdot Rb'Eq'D_7$
$Roll = B'C \cdot Rb$ $Sp = A'B'C \cdot Rb'D_7'D_{11}'D_{2312}'$
$Win = A'BC'$ $Lose = A'BC$
(These equations could be further simplified using don't cares.)

22.15 (a) $A^+ = BX$ $\quad Z_a = A'B'$ $\quad Z_1 = ABX'$
$B^+ = A'X + BX$ $\quad Z_b = A'B$ $\quad Z_2 = ABX$
$\quad\quad\quad\quad\quad\quad Z_c = AB$

X	A	B	A^+	B^+	Z_a	Z_b	Z_c	Z_1	Z_2
1	–	1	1	1	0	0	0	0	0
1	0	–	0	1	0	0	0	0	0
–	0	0	0	0	1	0	0	0	0
–	0	1	0	0	0	1	0	0	0
–	1	1	0	0	0	0	1	0	0
0	1	1	0	0	0	0	0	1	0
1	1	1	0	0	0	0	0	0	1

22.16 (b) $A^+ = A'X_1'X_2'X_3 + BX_2'$ $\quad Z_1 = A + B'X_1'$
$B^+ = A'B'X_1 + BX_2$ $\quad Z_2 = A'B'X_1$
$\quad\quad\quad\quad\quad\quad Z_3 = B + A'X_1'X_2$

(c)

A	B	X_1	X_2	X_3	A^+	B^+	Z_1	Z_2	Z_3
0	–	0	0	1	1	0	0	0	0
–	1	–	0	–	1	0	0	0	0
0	0	1	–	–	0	1	0	1	0
–	1	–	1	–	0	1	0	0	0
1	–	–	–	–	0	0	1	0	0
–	0	0	–	–	0	0	1	0	0
–	1	–	–	–	0	0	0	0	1
0	–	0	1	–	0	0	0	0	1

(d)

A	B	X_1	X_2	X_3	A^+	B^+	Z_1	Z_2	Z_3
0	0	0	0	0	0	0	1	0	0
0	0	0	0	1	1	0	1	0	0
0	0	0	1	0	0	0	1	0	1
0	0	0	1	1	1	0	1	0	1
0	0	1	0	0	0	1	0	1	0

Unit 23   Study Guide Answers

1 (b) Counter (a) is synchronous; (b) is asynchronous since flip-flop B changes state in response to a change in A rather than in response to the clock.

2 (d) Stable if flip-flop excitation is such that no flip-flop will change state

3 (e) b, c, d a, c, f b, d, e etc.
   (f) No; each clock pulse can produce only a single state change.

4 (c) Noncritical race occurs starting from $X_1X_2Q_1Q_2 = 0011$.

Unit 23   Answers to Problems

23.2

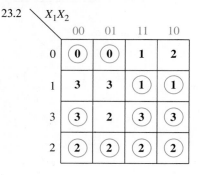

$X_1X_2 = 00, 01, 11, 10, 00, 10, \underline{11}$
$Z = 1$

23.4 When X changes from 0 to 1, the network enters a cycle.
One method to get $Z = 1$:

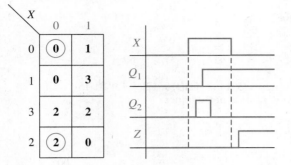

23.6 Output sequence: 1, 0, 1, 0, 0, 1, 0, 1, 1

23.8 (a) State sequence will depend on how state variables are chosen (3 are sufficient). Flow table has 4 stable states.

$$X = 0, 1, 0, 1, \ldots$$
$$Z = 0, 1, 1, 0, \ldots$$

   (b) The network contains critical races (starting in some of the unstable states).

Unit 24   Study Guide Answers

1 (a) A flow table which has exactly one stable total state per row
   (d) Because double input changes are prohibited
2 (a) Equivalent stable total states must also have the same inputs.
   (b) Because the outputs are associated only with stable total states and two rows with stable total states in the same column are never merged
   (c) (4, 5, 6, 7)(1, 2, 8)(3)   or   (4, 5, 6, 7)(1, 2, 3)(8)   or
        (4, 5, 6, 7)(1, 8)(2, 3)   or   (4, 5, 6, 7)(1, 3)(2, 8)

Unit 24   Answers to Problems

24.3 *

	00	01	11	10	00	01	11	10	**
A	Ⓐ	B	Ⓐ	Ⓐ	00		10	00	
B	A	Ⓑ	Ⓑ	A		00	01		

24.5 *

	PC								**
	00	01	11	10	00	01	11	10	
A	Ⓐ	Ⓐ	Ⓐ	B	0	0	0		
B	–	–	C	Ⓑ	–	–		0	
C	–	–	Ⓒ	D	–	–	1		
D	A	A	Ⓓ	Ⓓ			0	0	

Z

---

* The minimum row table for these problems is not unique.
** The blank entries in the output table can be filled in using the technique described in Section 25.4.

24.6

	X_1X_2				Z
	00	01	11	10	
1	①	①	2	3	0
2	1	②	②	4	1
3	1	③	③	③	0
4	④	④	2	④	1

24.7 (a) Equivalent states: (5, 14)(2, 11)(1, 9, 12)(4, 13)(10, 15)
(Minimum row table is not unique).

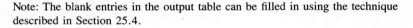

		X_1X_2				00	01	11	10
		00	01	11	10				
a	1, 4	①	2	④	10	01		00	
b	2, 3	5	②	4	③		11		11
c	5, 6	⑤	⑥	8	10	10	11		
d	7, 8	⑦	6	⑧	3	01		00	
e	10	1	6	4	⑩				11

$$Z_1Z_2$$

Note: The blank entries in the output table can be filled in using the technique described in Section 25.4.

24.8

	D Clock				Q
	00	01	11	10	
1	①	①	①	3	0
2	6	②	②	4	0
3	1	2	2	③	0
4	6	④	④	④	1
5	1	⑤	⑤	3	1
6	⑥	5	5	4	1

Unit 25   Study Guide Answers

2 (b) Yes (by adding 4 rows to the table and directing transitions through them, all transitions can be made without races).
(c) Fig. 25–5 may require less logic; Fig. 25–6 may be faster.

3 (a) Yes
(b) There is no way to direct the transitions in column 11 to avoid critical races.
(c) Direct 4 to 1 through 3.
(f) Direct the transitions as follows:
column 00 – b to d to c, column 11 – c to a to e, column 10 – a to e to d

4 (a) (2) 1,   (5) 1,   (6) 0

(b)

00	01	11	10
0	–	–	–
0	1	1	–
0	–	1	0
–	1	1	1

6 (b) $R_1 = Q_2 + Q_3$, $S_1 = X_1X_2'Q_2 + X_1'X_2'Q_4$,   etc.

Unit 25 Answers to Problems

25.3 (a)

a	c
x	y
b	d
f	e

	X_1X_2			
	00	01	11	10
a	(a)	x	(a)	c
b	x	(b)	(b)	d
c	y	(c)	y	(c)
d	(d)	(d)	e	(d)
e	f	c	(e)	c
f	(f)	b	a	(f)
x	a	y	b	–
y	d	d	x	–

(b)

a	d
h	e
f	g
c	b

25.4

	00	01	11	10
a_1	(a_1)	c_2	a_2	(a_1)
a_2	(a_2)	a_1	d_2	(a_2)
b_1	a_1	b_2	(b_1)	(b_1)
b_2	a_2	d_1	(b_2)	(b_2)
c_1	d_1	(c_1)	b_1	c_2
c_2	d_2	(c_2)	c_1	a_1
d_1	(d_1)	(d_1)	(d_1)	b_2
d_2	(d_2)	(d_2)	(d_2)	d_1

25.5 Using the assignment shown yields the following equations:

$Y_1^+ = P'Y_2 + PY_1$ $Y_2^+ = T'Y_1 + TPY_1' + P'Y_2$

$R_1 = P'Y_2'$ $R_2 = T'Y_1' + TPY_1$

$S_1 = P'Y_2$ $S_2 = TPY_1' + T'Y_1$

$Q = Y_1$

y_2 \ y_1	0	1
0	a	d
1	b	c

25.6 (a)

a	d	e	γ
α	β	b	c

25.9 Using the assignment $a = 10000$, $b = 01000$, etc. yields the following next-state equations:

$$Q_1^+ = Q_1Q_4'Q_5' + X_1'X_2'Q_4 + X_1'X_2Q_5$$
$$Q_2^+ = Q_2Q_3'Q_5' + X_1X_2'Q_4 + X_1'X_2Q_5$$
$$Q_3^+ = Q_3Q_4'Q_5' + X_1'X_2'Q_2$$
$$Q_4^+ = Q_4Q_1'Q_2' + X_1'X_2Q_1 + X_1X_2Q_3$$
$$Q_5^+ = Q_5Q_1'Q_2' + X_1X_2'Q_1 + X_1X_2Q_2 + X_1X_2'Q_3$$

25.10

Y_3 \ Y_1Y_2	00	01	11	10
0	1	3	2	
1		5	6	4

$S_1 = CkY_2Y_3'$ $R_1 = CkY_2Y_3$

$S_2 = DCk'Y_1' + D'Ck'Y_1$ $R_2 = DCk'Y_1 + D'Ck'Y_1'$

$S_3 = Ck'Y_1$ $R_3 = Ck'Y_1'$

$Q = Y_3$

Unit 26   Study Guide Answers

1 (a) $Z = 1$ between $t = 25$ and 40 ns.
   (b) First the inverter output, then gate 2, followed by f, followed by gate 1, and finally f again.

3 $Z^+ = (c_1 + c_2')c_3'$ $c_2'(1 \to 0)$, $c_1(0 \to 1)$, $c_3'(1 \to 0)$ to get 1-0-1-0

5 (b) Start in ③ or ⑦ and change X_1.
   (d) 1. X changes 0 to 1.
       2. Gate 1 output changes 0 to 1.
       3. Flip-flop y_1 output changes 1 to 0.
       4. Gate 4 output changes 1 to 0, gate 3 output changes 0 to 1.
       5. Flip-flop y_2 output changes 1 to 0.
       6. Inverter output X' changes 1 to 0.
       7. Gate 1 output changes back to 0, gate 2 output changes to 1.
       8. Flip-flop y_1 output changes back to 1.
       Final state is 10 instead of 01. This essential hazard can be eliminated by delaying the change in y_1' until X' has reached its final value.

6 (d) x_2 changes to 1, y_2' changes to 1, $x_1 x_2' y_2'$ AND gate output changes to 1, y_1' changes to 0 and y_1 changes to 1, and x_2' changes to 0 (too late!).
   (e) Replace lower 2 AND gates with

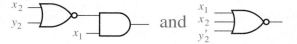

Unit 26   Answers to Problems

26.3 (a) 1-hazard: $a = 0$, $b = 1$, $d = 1$, c changing. To eliminate, add $a'bd$ term to the OR gate at the output.
          0-hazard: $a = 0$, $b = 0$, $c = 1$, d changing. To eliminate, add $(a + b + c')$ to AND gate which realizes $c(b + d')(a + d)$.

26.4 (a) 1-hazard: $a = 0$, $b = 1$, $d = 1$, c changing. Gate outputs—2, 4, 5, 3, 5 (for $c\ 0 \to 1$) or 3, 5, 2, 4, 5 (for $c\ 1 \to 0$)
          0-hazard: $a = 0$, $b = 0$, $d = 0$, c changing. Gate outputs—1, 4, 5, 2, 4, 5 ($c\ 0 \to 1$) or 2, 4, 5, 1, 4, 5 ($c\ 1 \to 0$)
      (b) $abcd = 0001 \to 0011$. Gate outputs—1, 4, 5, 2, 4, 5, 3, 5

26.6 (a) $f = [d' + b(a + c)(a' + c')](a' + b' + cd)(b' + c + ad) - 9$ gates, 22 inputs

26.7 Essential hazards starting in states ③, ④, ⑤ and ⑦ and changing variable P.

$$\left.\begin{array}{l}\text{25.5(a) - add delays to flip-flop outputs}\\ \text{25.5(b) - add delays to } Y_1 \text{ and } Y_2\end{array}\right\} \quad \text{to eliminate essential hazards}$$

To eliminate 1-hazards, add $Y_1 Y_2$ to Y_1^+ and $TY_1'Y_2$ to Y_2^+.

Appendix A   Study Guide Answers

1 (b) $D3$, 1 volt   (c) $D2$, 5 volts   (d) $E < -3$, $E > +3$

2 (c) $F = (A + B + C)'$, $F = (ABC)'$ (d) $F = (ABC)'$, $F = (A + B + C)'$

3 (a) One 7400 and one 7410
   (b) Advanced low-power Schottky; advanced Schottky
   (c) 0, 1, is not permissible, 2.4 to 5, 0 to 0.4

4 (a) $F = (AB + C)'$

Appendix A   Answers to Problems

A.1 (a) $F = (AB + C)D$ (b) $F = (A + B)C + D$

A.2 (a) $Z = (AB + CD)EF$ (b) Reverse the diodes and voltage polarities.

A.3 $F = (a' + b' + c')(d' + e' + f')$

A.4

A	B	F	Q_1	Q_2	Q_3	Q_4	
0	0	$+V$	ON	ON	OFF	OFF	
0	$+V$	0	ON	OFF	ON	OFF	NOR gate
$+V$	0	0	OFF	ON	OFF	ON	
$+V$	$+V$	0	OFF	OFF	ON	ON	

A.5 $F_0 = (A'B' + AB)' = A'B + AB'$, $F_1 = A'B'$, $F_2 = A + B'$, $F_3 = B$

INDEX

12H6, 12L6 239–242
14H4, 14L4 239–240
16R4 493–495
22V10 498–503
7400, 74S00, 74LS00, 74AS00, 74ALS00 706
7473, 74LS73 281
7491 470
7493A 474
74178 470–471, 508, 717
74HC00, 74HCT00, 74AC00, 74ACT00 710
74LS02 439–440
74LS27 439–440
74LS73 439–440
74LS374 482
74S163 474–477

Accumulator
    parallel 527–530
    serial 540–541
Active high 197–198
Active low 197–198
Adder, binary 96–97
    carry-lookahead 526
    parallel 524–526
    parallel with accumulator 527–530
    ripple-carry 524–525

serial 526–527
serial with accumulator 540–543
Addition, binary 10
    1's complement 522–524
    2's complement 521–522
    networks for 524–531, 540–543
Algebraic simplification 33–34, 52–53, 116–117
Algorithmic state machine
    (see State machine)
Alternative gate symbols 194, 713–714
Analog systems 4–5
AND gate 25, 699–701
ASCII code 14, 242
ASIC 509
ASM chart (see SM chart)
Associative law 31–32
Asynchronous sequential network
    (see Sequential network, asynchronous)

Base conversion 7–10
Bias voltage 699
Binary arithmetic 10–12
    (see also Adder, Subtracter, Multiplier, Divider)
Binary coded decimal (BCD) 12–13
Binary numbers 7
    conversion to decimal 7
    signed 519

Boolean algebra 24–36, 47–53
Basic operations 24–26
   basic theorems 29–30
   laws and theorems 40
   simplification theorems 33–34
Boolean expressions 27–29
Borrow 10–11, 532–533
Buffer 480–481
Bus 482–483

Carry 10
   end-around 522–524
   flip-flop 527
CD4000 790–710
Characteristic equation 284–285
Clear input
   asynchronous 474
   synchronous 282–283, 475–476
Clock 277–278, 331, 343–344
Clocked sequential network
   (see Sequential network, synchronous)
CMOS logic 709–710
Code converter
   BCD to excess-3 221–222, 232, 313–314
   sequential 428–432
Codes (BCD, 8-4-2-1, 6-3-1-1,
   excess-3, Gray, 2-out-of-5,
   weighted) 12–13
Combinational network
   definition 5
   design 86–89, 221–222, 252–256
   testing 256–258
Commutative law 31
Comparator 455–458
Complementation 24–25
   (see also Inversion)
Computer-aided design (CAD) 437–441,
   506
Configurable logic block (CLB) 503–506
Consensus theorem 66–67
   dual 67
   illustrated by map 122
Contact bounce 689
Control network
   for divider 550–551
   for multiplier 545–547
   for serial adder 542–543
Counters 298–313
   binary 298–300
   design using D flip-flops 313
   design using J-K flip-flops 308–312
   design using S-R flip-flops 305–308

   design using T flip-flops 298–305
   in sequential network design 477–479
   integrated circuit 472–477, 717–718
   ripple (asynchronous) 472–474
   up-down 496–498
Cycle (in flow table) 602

Data selector (see Multiplexer)
Decimal numbers 7
   binary codes for 12–13
   conversion to binary 8–9
Decoder 227–229, 715–716
Degenerate network forms 191
Delay (D) flip-flop 282
   derivation of input equations 313,
      405–407, 415–416
Delay network, asynchronous 594–595
DeMorgan's laws 47–49
Dice game 575–579
Digital systems 4–5
Diode gates 699–701
Diode-transistor logic 703–704
Distributive law 32
Divider, parallel binary 548–552, 573–575
Division, binary 12, 548
Don't care term 95–96
   in Karnaugh map 125
   in prime implicant chart 163–164
Duality 49, 56–57

ECL 704
EEPROM 233
EPLD 234
EPROM 232–233, 507–508
Equation, proving validity 70–71
Equivalence gate 53
Equivalent sequential networks 401–403
   definition 401
   determination of 401–403
   by implication table 402–403
Equivalent states 396–397
   definition 396–397
   by implication table 397–401
   in SM chart 579
   theorem 397, 720
Espresso-II method 166–167
Essential prime implicant
   definition 128, 159–160
   from Karnaugh map 128–131, 719
   from prime implicant chart 158–160
   multiple output 220–221
Exclusive-OR 51–53

Factoring 35–36, 50–51
False output 336–337
Fan-in 253
    reduction of 253–255
Flip-flop 269–270
    characteristic equation 284–285
    clear, preset inputs 282–283
    clocked T 277–278
    D 282, 715
    edge-triggered 281, 611–612
    J-K 279–281, 714–715
    master-slave 280–281
    S-R 272–276
    T 276–277
    type conversion 285
Flip-flop input equations, derivation
    D 313, 405–407, 415–416
    J-K 308–312, 405–407
    S-R 305–308, 407
        short-cut method for J-K 311–312
        short-cut method for S-R 680–681,
            720–721
        summary 316–319, 404
        T 300–303, 305
Flow chart 567
Flow table 596–597
    primitive 609–610
FPLA 237
Full adder 525
Full subtracter 532–533
Functionally complete 187–189
Fundamental mode 593

Gate delays 181, 270–272
Gate level 180–181
Gate networks 36
    2-level NAND and NOR 189–192
    multi-level 180–185, 192–193
    multiple-output 217–222, 254–255

Hardware description languages (HDLs)
    438–439
Hazard-free design
    of combinational networks 664–666
    using S-R flip-flops 668–673
Hazards
    detection of static 660–663
    dynamic 658, 663–665
    essential 666–668
    static 657–659
    zero and one 658
Hexadecimal number 7, 10
Holding term 645

IEEE standard logic symbols 198–199,
    713–718
Implicant, definition 126, 157
Implication table 397–401
Incompletely specified function 95–96
    simplification 125, 163–164
Incompletely specified sequential
    networks 403–404
Input-output block (IOB) 506
Integrated circuits
    design and layout 439–441
    in combinational network design
        223–243, 256
    in sequential network design 434,
        469–483, 489–503
    MOS, CMOS 707–710
    TTL 469–472, 474–477, 704–706
    SSI, MSI, LSI, VLSI 216–217, 469–483,
        715
Interconnect, general purpose 506–507
Internal state 594
Inversion 47–49
    symbols 198–199, 713–714
Inverter 25, 194, 701–702, 706–708
Iterative networks 452–462
    conversion to sequential 454–455, 457
    definition 452
    design 452–462
    with outputs from each cell 460–462

J-K flip-flop 278–281
    clocked (master-slave) 279–281
    derivation of input equations 308–312
    unclocked 278–279

Karnaugh map 116–137
    3-variable 118–123, 136–137
    4-variable 123–131, 136–137
    5-variable 131–134, 137
    6-variable 133–135
    complementation 122
    multiple-output minimization 217–221

Laboratory testing
    asynchronous networks 689–690
    combinational networks 256–258
    sequential networks 433–437
Latch 274
Link path 568, 580
Literal
    definition 27
    elimination of 69

Logic cell array (LCA) 503–509
LogicAid 113, 153, 357

Majority gate 186
Manchester code 372–374
Map-entered variables 164–166, 582–583
Maxterm, definition 90
Maxterm expansion 90–92
    general 92–94
    simplification of 117
Mealy sequential network 334–337,
    339–343
Merger diagram 616–617
Metal-oxide semiconductor (see MOS)
Microsecond 271
Min-max delay 433–434
Minimum product of sums 117
    from Karnaugh map 125
Minimum sum of products 116–117
    from Karnaugh map 121–123, 126–131
    from prime implicant chart 158–161
Minority gate 186, 188–189
Minterm, definition 89
Minterm expansion 89–92
    general 92–94
    simplification of 117
Mixed logic 197–204
Moore sequential network 334–335, 344
MOS logic 707–709
MOSFET 707
Multi-level gate networks
    design 182–185
    NAND and NOR gates 192–197, 222
Multiple-output gate network
    design 217–222, 254–255
    determination of essential prime
        implicants 220–221
Multiplexer (MUX) 223–227, 716
    data selection 223–224
    function realization 224–227
Multiplication, binary 12, 543–544
Multiplier, parallel binary 543–548, 575
Multiplying out 34–35, 50–51

NAND gate 185, 194, 703–705, 709–710
    2-level networks 189–192
    functionally complete 187
    multi-level networks 192–197
Nanosecond 270
Negative logic
    definition 54
    gates 700–701
    theorem 56–57

Negative number representation 519–521
    sign and magnitude 519
    (see also One's complement, Two's
        complement)
Next state 275–276
    equation 276
    map 301
Nominal delay 433–434, 436
NOR gate 186, 194, 703, 708–709
    2-level networks 189–192
    multi-level networks 192–196
NOT gate (see Inverter)
NRZ, NRZI codes 371–374
Number systems 7

Octal numbers 521
One's (1's) complement
    addition 522–524
    representation of negative number
        519–520
OR gate 26, 700–701
Output table
    asynchronous network 641–643
    synchronous network 339–340
Overflow
    addition 521–524
    division 549–550

PAL 238–243
    in sequential network design 492–498
Parity 330
Parity checker
    iterative 453–455
    sequential 330–333
Pattern detector 458–460
PC board layout 439–440
Petrick's method 161–163
Phase-locked loop 371
PLA 234–238
    in sequential network design 490–492,
        580–582
    table 235–237
Polarity
    indication 198–204
    mismatch 202–204
Positive logic, definition 54
Present state 275
Prime implicant
    chart 158–161
    definition 126, 158
    from Karnaugh map 126
    (see also Essential prime implicant)

Primitive flow table 609–610
  derivation 609–613
  reduced 616
  reduction 613–619
Product of sums 35–36, 90
Programmable array logic (see PAL)
Programmable gate array (PGA) 503–509
Programmable logic array (see PLA)
Programmable logic device (PLD)
    234–243
  bit pattern generation 438
  in sequential network design 498–503
  programmer 243, 438
PROM 232–233
  compared with PLA 237–238
Proofs of theorems 719–721
Propagation delay 270–272
Pulse mode sequential networks 593–594
Pulse subtracter 681–688

Quine-McCluskey method 154–164,
    166–167

R's complement 520–521
Races
  critical 602–603
  non-critical 602–603
Redundant states, elimination of 393–395
Register transfers 480–483
ROM (read-only memory) 229–233
  in sequential network design 490–491,
    580–582
RZ code 372

Schematic capture 438
Schottky TTL logic 706
Sequence detector design 359–368
Sequential network, asynchronous
  analysis 592–598
  comparison with synchronous 592–593,
    603
  completion of output table 641–643
  design 679–688
  general model 600–601
  testing 689–690
  (see also Hazards, Flow table, Races,
    State assignment)
Sequential network, clocked
  (see Sequential network, synchronous)
Sequential network, definition 5
Sequential network, synchronous
  analysis 330–345
  design with flip-flops 428–432

design with PAL 492–498
design with PLA 490–492
design with ROM 490–491
general model 342–344
testing 433–437
timing charts 333–336, 341–342
(see also State graph, State machines,
    State table, Mealy, Moore, State
    assignment)
Serial data
  code conversion 371–375
  transmission of 371–372
Set-Reset (S-R) flip-flop 272–276
  derivation of input equations 305–308,
    407, 680–681
Seven-segment indicator 259
Shift register 315–316
  cyclic 315–316
  integrated circuit 469–472, 717
Short-cut method for
  J-K flip-flop input equations 311–312
  S-R flip-flop input equations 680–681,
    720–721
SHR technique 407–408
Sign and magnitude 519
Signal tracing 333
Simulation
  logic networks 256–258
  sequential networks 433–438
  three-valued 256–257
SM block 568–569
SM chart (State machine chart) 567–573
  derivation 573–579
  realization 579–583
Stable state 272–273, 595
Standard product of sums 90
Standard sum of products 90
State assignment for asynchronous
    network 629–645
  for 3- and 4-row tables 634–637
  one-hot 643–645
  shared-row 637–641
  universal 634–637
State assignment for synchronous
    networks 407–416
  equivalent assignments 407–411
  guidelines 412–416
State graph
  conversion to SM chart 572–573
  derivation 359–371
  for control networks 542–543, 545–547,
    550–551
  for counter 301, 304–305

State graph (*continued*)
for primitive flow table 611
guidelines for construction 368–371
Mealy 334, 340
Moore 334, 338–339
State machine 567
(see also Sequential network,
synchronous)
State table
derivation 359–371
incompletely specified 403–404
Mealy 339–340
Moore 337–338
reduction 393–395
Subtracter, parallel binary 531–533
Subtraction, binary 10–12
by complementation 531–532
networks for 531–532
Sum of products 32, 36, 90
Switches, networks of 26, 29–30
Switching algebra 24
(see Boolean algebra)
Switching network, definition 5
Synchronizer 436–437
Synchronous sequential network
(see Sequential network, synchronous)

Test generation 438
Three-state (tri-state)
buffer 480–482, 506
bus 482–483
logic 480–482
Timing chart (diagram) 270–272
for asynchronous network 598
for counter 304

for flip-flops 274, 274–278, 280–282
for sequential network 333–337,
341–342
for shift register 470, 472
for SM chart 573
Total state 594
Transient output function 660
Transistor, NPN and PNP 701–704
Transistor logic circuits 701–704
Transition table 338, 595–596
Transition term 645
Trigger (T) flip-flop 276–278
derivation of input equations 300–303,
305
Truth table 28–29
construction 96–99
TTL logic 469–472, 474–477, 704–706
Two's (2's) complement
addition 521–522
representation of negative number
519–520

Unstable total state 595

Veitch diagram 136–137
Verilog HDL 438
VHDL 438–439
Voltage level 54

Word problems 86–88, 96–99

XC2064 503–509, 530–531
XC3000 series 509
XC4000 series 509
XOR PAL 493, 495–498